A Plague of Murder

Also by Colin Wilson

NON-FICTION

The Outsider
Religion and the Rebel
The Age of Defeat
Encyclopaedia of Murder (with Patricia Pitman)
Origins of the Sexual Impulse
Beyond the Outsider: The Philosophy of the Future
Voyage to a Beginning (autobiography)
A Casebook of Murder
The Occult
Order of Assassins: The Psychology of Murder
Strange Powers
Mysterious Powers
The Craft of the Novel
The Geller Phenomenon
Science Fiction as Existentialism
The Search for the Real Arthur
Starseekers
The Quest for Wilhelm Reich
Lord of the Underworld: Jung and the Twentieth Century
A Criminal History of Mankind
The Misfits
The Mammoth Book of True Crime
Written in Blood
The Mammoth Book of True Crime 2 (with Damon Wilson)

FICTION

Ritual in the Dark
The World of Violence
Necessary Doubt
The Glass Cage
The Killer
The Schoolgirl Murder Case
The Janus Murder Case
The Mind Parasites
The Space Vampires
Spider World

A Plague of Murder

The Rise and Rise of Serial Killing in the Modern Age

Colin Wilson
and Damon Wilson

Robinson
London

Robinson Publishing Ltd
7, Kensington Church Court
London W8 4SP

First published by Robinson Publishing Ltd 1995

A copy of the British Library Cataloguing in Publication Data for this title is available from the British Library.

ISBN 1-85487-249-4

Printed in the EC

Contents

Introduction

When Jack the Ripper killed five prostitutes in the East End of London in 1888, he became instantly the world's most infamous, and also its best-known murderer. He was not the world's most prolific killer, nor the first to mutilate his victims. France's Gilles de Rais murdered and mutilated more than fifty children. Hungary's Countess Elizabeth Bathory murdered an unknown number of servant girls – the number certainly ran into dozens – to take baths in their blood, and is known to have bitten chunks out of their flesh. But the enduring fascination of the Ripper lay in the mystery of his identity, and in his obvious desire to shock, to spit into the face of society. He was also, as we shall see, one of the first examples of what we now call a sex killer, and therefore, of what is now labelled a serial killer.

A Plague of Murder could be about all those who have killed large numbers of people – in which case, it would have to include the Nazis, and Mafia contract killers, and insane gunmen who go on a rampage and shoot anyone who crosses their path, and terrorists who blow up public buildings. But it is not, because serial killers are different.

The term 'serial killer' was invented in 1978 by FBI agent Robert Ressler to describe obsessive 'repeat killers' like Jack the Ripper. Before that, they were called 'mass murderers', an ambiguous phrase, since it included criminals like the Frenchman Landru 'Bluebeard' who murdered women for their money. Ressler coined the new term because of the increasing number of American multiple sex killers – like Albert DeSalvo,

Ted Bundy, Dean Corll, John Gacy and Henry Lee Lucas – whose crimes had achieved worldwide notoriety. Since then, cases like that of the Milwaukee 'cannibal' Jeffrey Dahmer and the Russian Andrei Chikatilo have made it clear that he was right: there is a fundamental difference between serial killers and other types of murderer.

What drives a man to become a serial killer? One answer – as we shall see in this book is that their self-esteem is often so low that killing is a way of asserting that they exist. In some cases, the killing has no sexual component. Donald Harvey, an American nursing orderly, was sentenced in 1987 for murdering twenty-four people, mostly elderly hospital patients. It emerged later that Harvey had been sexually abused by two adults since he was a child and warned that his mother would be harmed unless he kept silent. Years as a passive object of lust led to the total destruction of his self-esteem; killing hospital patients was his way of asserting that he was a 'doer', a mover, not a nonentity.

In most cases of serial murder there is an element of this kind of self-assertion. Many such killers are naturally 'dominant' – members of what zoologists call 'the dominant 5 per cent' – but find themselves in a situation in which they feel passive and impotent. Psychologically speaking, such killers can differ as radically as the American Henry Lee Lucas, who confessed to 360 murders that were basically motivated by sex, and the British nurse Beverley Allitt, who killed children in hospital out of some strange sense of inadequacy.

The same inadequacy can be seen in the case of Jeffrey Dahmer, who drugged and murdered males he lured back to his Milwaukee apartment, and the Russian Andrei Chikatilo, whose sexual impotence vanished only when he was inflicting multiple stab wounds on his victims.

The desire to inflict pain is an element that links many serial killers. This sadism may or may not have been present early in their lives but could have developed as a result of sexual obsession. Here we encounter one of the strangest and most difficult psychological mysteries connected with the serial killer. Many men, from Casanova and the anonymous Victorian who wrote *My Secret Life* to H. G. Wells and Bertrand Russell, have experienced a desire to sleep with every attractive woman they see; the urge seems to be as uncomplicated as an angler's desire to catch a fish. Yet in others this urge can get out of control and turn into the need to inflict pain and humiliation. One of the most horrific examples of the sadistic rape syndrome was Donald 'Pee Wee' Gaskins. He was imprisoned for murdering nine people, thought to be business acquaintances with whom he had quarrelled. Later it was revealed that he was probably the worst serial killer of this century; he killed consistently and regularly over a number of years, the result of an abnormal and overdeveloped sexual urge. In 1991 he went to the electric chair having confessed to killing over 120 victims.

Gaskins explained that he acted when a boiling rage, like hot lead, welled up from somewhere deep inside. Other serial killers acted only when drunk, or under the influence of drugs. One man, Steve Wilson, killed two prostitutes in a motel in Los Angeles in 1944, cutting them up in the manner of the original Ripper. He told the psychiatrist that he had strong sadistic tendencies which only emerged when he was drunk – his first wife had left him because he liked to creep up on her when she was naked and cut her buttocks with a razor; he would then apologize and kiss the wounds. Wilson was executed in the San Quentin gas chamber in September 1946.

Many other serial killers have committed their murders when drunk – two notable cases being the Briton Dennis Nilsen and Jeffrey Dahmer from Milwaukee. All three – Wilson, Nilsen and Dahmer – have one thing in common: a traumatic childhood. When Steve Wilson was 5, he and his siblings were placed in an orphanage. Dennis Nilsen's father was a violent drunk and Nilsen was farmed out to his grandparents. Jeffery Dahmer's parents quarrelled violently for years before finally separating, and Dahmer complained that his childhood was loveless. The seeds of serial murder are planted in childhood, in a sense of neglect and occasionally of downright abuse. Since this rarely happens in higher-income families, the majority of serial killers are working class, and the few who are not (Dahmer's father was an electrical engineer) are neglected and emotionally deprived.

Can a head injury turn a man into a killer? As we shall see during the course of this book, many serial killers have sustained serious and damaging head injuries early in life, including Joseph Vacher, the nineteenth-century 'Ripper', Earle Nelson, America's 'wandering sex killer', and Albert Fish, who is believed to have killed dozens of children over a lifetime of sexual perversion.

Dr Jonathan Pinckus, a neurologist from Georgetown University in Washington, DC, cites a case of a killer who had been involved in a serious car accident at the age of 16, in which the front of his head came into violent collision with the roof of the car. He was unconscious for several days and spent many weeks in intensive care. His family noted that his behaviour changed after the accident, and that he developed an explosive temper. In due course, he committed a particularly violent double murder, stabbing both victims more than a hundred times. Sentenced to death, he showed no remorse – or any other emotion – about the murder, and no feeling about his impending execution. A brain scan subsequently showed areas of scar tissue in both frontal lobes of the brain; the damage had occurred when his head hit the car roof and his brain had surged forward against the front of the skull.

The brain has the consistency of jelly and is easily damaged. Behind the prefrontal lobes lies an area called the limbic system, which is concerned with feeling, emotion and such responses as aggression. The prefrontal lobes seem to be the part of the brain that inhibits violent responses. But sometimes, when patients have sunk into a state of permanent fear or depression, they can be 'cured' by an operation which severs the connections between the prefrontal lobes and the rest of the brain; it is called lobotomy, a procedure once widespread but now discredited as a treatment for mental illness. The lobotomized patient ceases to experience tension; in fact, he usually turns into a contented cow, incapable of emotion.

Pinckus's diagnosis was that the accident had been the equivalent of a lobotomy operation, destroying the killer's normal feelings and preventing the prefrontal lobes from doing their work of inhibiting violent explosions of emotion.

Other killers perform the equivalent of a lobotomy operation on themselves. Subjected to emotional torment in childhood, they learn the trick of switching off their feelings so that nothing can hurt them. Two obvious examples in this book are Jeffrey Dahmer and Andrei Chikatilo, both apparently gentle and normal people, both incapable of any feeling except for themselves. Such people find that sex restores their ability to feel; in effect, it makes them feel 'more alive'. The other person is unimportant; they have little or no empathy with their fellow human beings. There is a sense in which killers such as Jack the Ripper, Joseph Vacher, Earle Nelson, Albert Fish, Andrei Chikatilo and Jeffrey Dahmer are aliens from another world.

Albert DeSalvo, the Boston Strangler, was one of those possessed of a manic sex drive – his wife testified that he was capable of sex a dozen times a day. DeSalvo estimated that he had raped or sexually attacked about two thousand women; on one occasion he raped four women in one day, then unsuccessfully attacked a fifth. It is hard for a normal human being to understand sexual desire on such a scale. Sexual excitement is like hunger or thirst; it creates physical discomfort until it is satisfied. For most of us, it then goes away and only reappears after a reasonable interval. For DeSalvo the hunger reappeared almost as soon as it was satisfied, creating a permanent state of discomfort like a stone in a shoe.

The purpose of this book is to explore the mind of the serial killer through examples and case histories. They are chronicled from the beginning of the nineteenth century, when the first serial killers emerged, to the mid-1990s, when one policeman declared, 'there may be as many as five thousand of them out there.'

The rise of sex crime in the nineteenth century is linked to the rise of pornography, which first became widely available towards the end of the eighteenth century, with books such as *Fanny Hill* (1747) and the Marquis de Sade's novels, which included *Justine* and *Juliette*. The latter particularly recognized the link between sexual excitement and violence. The marquis himself was twice imprisoned, once for beating prostitutes and again for writing books of such extraordinary violence. In the early years of the twentieth century, killers of the 'bluebeard' type, such as Johann Hoch and Belle Gunness, America's favourite murderess, began to appear and at one period New Orleans was home to a man who killed only Italian shopkeepers. The twenties gave rise to people like Carl Panzram, a cool and calculating, intelligent and articulate 'resentment' killer.

The period following the Second World War saw a decline in the murder rate, but it rose steeply during the fifties. The crime figures always fall during and immediately after wars, but it soon became clear that something strange was happening. An increasing number of murderers seemed to be in the grip of a compulsion to kill, from Christie with his private morgue at 10 Rillington Place to the German Werner Boost who killed courting couples and violated the women. In Britain, the most traumatic crimes of the sixties were the Moors murders, and the most frightening thing about them was that Ian Brady was an articulate and intelligent 'criminal outsider' who shared Sade's obsession with 'the forbidden' and quoted Dostoevsky. Before the end of the decade, Charles Manson would also preach a philosophy that justified murder. But it was the seventies that saw the emergence of serial murder in Robert Ressler's sense, with sex criminals like Dean Corll, John Gacy and Henry Lee Lucas, who killed on an unprecedented scale. And in the eighties and nineties, cases like the Atlanta murders, the Green River killer, the Paris 'phantom', the Night Stalker, the Milwaukee cannibal, the 'Red Ripper' and the Gloucester 'house of horror' revealed that serial murder is a disease that criminologists have not yet even begun to understand.

This book is an attempt to throw some light on the problem by tracing its history and development.

1

Pornography and the Rise of Sex Crime

All this is important to the understanding of the criminal mentality, particularly the serial killer. At the time I am writing these words, a religious cult in Waco, Texas, is under siege by the FBI. A psychologist who has been studying cult members comments that such people are not necessarily unintelligent and easily influenced – that such cults often target highly intelligent people, but concentrate on them when they are in a state of emotional vulnerability, perhaps after the break-up of a love affair, the loss of a job, the failure to pass an exam. Then the potential convert is in a state of low self-esteem, and looks around for something that will give him a sense of exercising his power to choose, his ability to *act* – because action brings relief.

In the Postscript to my history of forensic detection *Written in Blood*, I cite the parallel example of Arthur Koestler, who, after he had lost all his money in a poker game, got drunk at a party, spent the night with a girl he disliked, and discovered that his car radiator had frozen and burst, experienced an intense urge to 'do something desperate' that resulted in the decision to join the Communist Party. In a man with a tendency to physical violence it could just as easily have led to murder.

The case of serial killer Ted Bundy reveals the same pattern. In his early twenties Bundy fell in love with a girl from a wealthy family and they became engaged. He decided to study Chinese because he reasoned that America would enter diplomatic relations with China and need interpreters. But he found the work too hard and dropped out of the course. The girl broke the engagement, which had the effect of totally undermining his self-esteem. Yet it was not this event that caused him to become a serial killer, even though he subsequently developed into a Peeping Tom. He became a law student and worked for the Office of Justice Planning, then became an election worker for the candidate for State governor. His self-confidence increased. Five years after being thrown over, he met his former fiancée persuaded her to marry him, and spent a weekend with her. Then he dumped her as she had dumped him. And it was this act of calculated revenge that turned him from a Peeping Tom into a sex murderer. It gave him the courage – and the contempt for women – to turn his fantasies into reality.

The same psychological mechanism explains the rise in the crime rate during times of economic recession. It is not simply that people steal for money. It is because the psychological trauma of being without a job leads to the feeling of 'anger with fate', and the desire to express it by *abandoning former inhibitions* and 'hitting out'. Graham Greene's favourite quote from Gauguin was: 'Life being what it is, one dreams of revenge.' After one of the Moors murders, Ian Brady – who proclaimed himself an atheist – shook his fist at the sky and shouted: 'Take that, you bastard!' The serial killer Carl Panzram even believed that by killing innocent people – usually children – he was gaining a kind of 'compensatory' revenge on people who had made him suffer.

This element of violent irrationality has always been a basic element in human nature. Shakespeare catches it in *Julius Caesar* when a man being attacked by a mob protests that he is Cinna the poet, not Cinna the conspirator, and his attackers shout: 'Tear him for his bad verses.' But until the nineteenth century, it was rare for this kind of resentment to find expression in sex crime. Crime was largely the result of social deprivation, so the criminal was interested in money and property, not in sex. In overcrowded slums, brothers and sisters often slept in the same bed, and were introduced to incest from an early age. In *The Complete Jack the Ripper*, Donald Rumbelow quotes a friend of Lord Salisbury who was indignantly separating two children having sex on a slum pavement when the boy cried: 'Why do you take hold of me? There are a dozen of them at it down there.' Drunken women would offer their bodies for a few pence, and mothers sell their daughters' virginity for five shillings. Sex was so freely available that there would have been no point in killing for it, or even risking the gallows for rape.

Casanova, who died in 1798, embodies the straightforward physical approach to sex. He is fascinated by the magic of women, and by his own ability to persuade them to yield. His first love affair was with two teenage sisters, who allowed him to spend the night in their room so that he could meet a girl with whom he was in love. When the girl failed to show up, they allowed the young abbé – Casanova was in holy orders – to sleep between them. He instantly broke his promise not to lay a finger on them, and seduced first one, then the other. But he tells this story – like that of his innumerable later conquests – in a language of delicate euphemism: 'Her natural instincts soon working in concert with my own, I reach the goal; and my efforts, crowned with the most complete success, leave me not the shadow of doubt that I have gathered those first fruits to which our predudice makes us attach so great an importance.' He is enough of an eighteenth century rationalist to recognize that there is a certain absurdity in attaching so much importance to taking a girl's virginity. And after he has described a dozen or so similar affairs, we begin to recognize that Casanova's conquests are not the result of an overpowering sexual impulse, but of a desire to think well of himself, to aggrandize his ego. He attaches far more importance to other kinds of conquest – for example, impressing contemporary intellectuals like Voltaire and Rousseau, or holding a dinner table enthralled with his conversation.

In the second half of the eighteenth century, a curious change began to come about. It was at this time that pornography suddenly came into existence: that is, sexual description whose basis was the *forbiddenness* of the sexual act. Earlier works like Aretino's *Dialogues* (1536) and the anonymous *School of Venus* (1655) may seem to contradict that assertion; but they can also be seen as works in the great humanist tradition, arguing against puritanical morality. In the *School of Venus*, Fanchon tells her friend Suzanne: 'Since Robinet fucked me, and I know what is what, I find all my mother's warnings to be but bugbears and good for nothing but frightening children. For my part, I believe we were created for fucking, and when we begin to fuck we begin to live.' Donald Thomas comments: 'Compared with the neurotic and sadistic pornography which has made up so much of the erotic literature of the last two centuries, *The School of Venus* seems almost radiant with innocence.'

The same argument applies to the anticlerical erotica of the eighteenth century, with titles like *Venus in the Cloister* and *The Monastery Gate, or the Story of Dom Bugger*; it was all about priests seducing their penitents or monks impregnating nuns. (In fact, *Venus in the Cloister* was based on a famous scandal in which a Jesuit named Fr Girard seduced one of his penitents.) This type of healthy indecency can trace its ancestry to Boccaccio and Rabelais – the latter writes: 'Even the shadow of a monastery is fruitful.'

The change to genuine eroticism is marked by John Cleland's *Memoirs of a Lady of Pleasure* – usually known as *Fanny Hill* (1747) – which describes how a young servant girl is introduced into a brothel, then into a life of endless sexual adventure. But *Fanny Hill* was preceded by a far more important novel: Samuel Richardson's *Pamela* (1740), the story of a servant girl who resists all her master's attempts at seduction until he capitulates and marries her. Richardson, a printer-turned-author, firmly believed that he was writing a highly moral tale about a virtuous girl. But the public who lingered over scenes in which her master flings her on a bed and throws her skirts over her head were more interested in how soon she would lose her virginity.

Pamela was the first novel in our modern sense of the word: a kind of soap opera about ordinary people rather than strange, distant lands populated by dusky princes and lovelorn shepherds. Within five years, Europe had become a 'nation of readers', and every small town had its lending library. It was then that Cleland introduced a new twist with *Fanny Hill*, in which there was no attempt to pretend that the author's intention was to preach virtue and abstinence.

And yet even *Fanny Hill* is, in a sense, non-pornographic. The sex is Rabelaisian and down-to-earth; when Fanny peers through a crack in the closet-door at the brothel madame about to have sex with her lover, she sees 'her fat brawny thighs hung down; and the whole greasy landscape . . . fairly open to my view: a wide open-mouthed gap, overshaded with a grizzly bush seemed held out like a beggar's wallet . . .' The description could hardly be less erotic.

I have suggested elsewhere that the invention of the novel must be regarded as one of the important steps in mankind's development. The theatre had provided the public with entertainment since the days of the ancient Greeks, but the novel was an invitation to sit alone and use the imagination to conjure up other people's lives. And even though Cleland was sentenced to the pillory, and then persuaded to write no more pornography by the grant of a government pension (which suggests that ministers recognized the danger of free sexual fantasy), others quickly took his place and created a pornography industry.

By far the most important of these figures was the Marquis de Sade, born in the same year that *Pamela* was published. Thrown into jail for atheism, then for kidnapping and whipping a beggar woman, Sade was antiauthoritarian to the point of paranoia. His early fantasies about incest and about the seduction and rape of children can only be understood in the light of his hatred of the Christian church. He was obsessed by 'the forbidden' – it is typical that he seduced and ran away with his wife's younger sister, a canoness (or apprentice nun). Finally, sentenced to prison for a third time for various misdemeanours – including sodomizing prostitutes and almost killing two of them with an aphrodisiac – he poured his sexual frustrations into the works for which he is famous (or infamous), novels like *Philosophy in the Boudoir* and *Justine*. The first is about the debauching of a virgin by an incestuous brother and sister, the second about the endless misfortunes of a pure and virtuous girl. Both might be regarded as blasphemous parodies of Richardson's *Pamela*. His unfinished *120 Days of Sodom* is an attempt at a novel that catalogues every possible sexual perversion.

Freed briefly by the French Revolution, Sade was soon back in prison for writing novels of unparalleled violence and indecency; *Juliette* ends with a scene in which a mother allows her little daughter to be violated and burnt alive while she herself is simultaneously penetrated, vaginally and anally, by two of her lover's henchmen.

In fact, the novels of Sade are even less pornographic than *Fanny Hill*. There is no lingering sensuality, no gloating over sexual fantasy; Sade is more concerned with shouting blasphemies at the top of his voice. He is a man who hates the system so much that his one concern is to defy it. When he describes sexual orgies, it is not to titillate the lecherous, but to upset the guardians of morality.

To understand Sade – and the great majority of serial killers – we only have to recognize that he was an extremely imperious man who loved having his own way. As a born aristocrat, he expected to give orders and have them promptly obeyed. So to be at the mercy of gaolers threw him into a state of sheer outrage. His privileges were always being suspended for losing his temper. In the chronology of his life we read: 'October 10, 1787: Sade berates the prison governor and his aide who come to announce to him suspension of his exercise period.' Thirteen days later it was restored, but in June of the following year we read: 'Sade's exercise period again having been suspended "for impertinence", and he having been informed in writing, the prisoner nonetheless attempts to descend at his regular hour to the yard, and . . . it was only when the officer pointed his gun at him that he retreated, swearing loudly.' Sade was simply incapable of getting used to the idea that he was not an eastern sultan. He never learned to adjust. Frustration of his wishes threw him into a frenzy of rage. And because it was impossible to express that rage by flogging the prison governor and his minions, Sade channelled it into his books. We might say that what fate was trying to teach him was self-discipline; but his imperious temperament made it impossible. And, being highly intelligent, he rationalized his refusal to attempt self-discipline in the only possible way: that is, into a philosophical system in which *everybody* is permitted unlimited violence towards everybody else . . . We shall observe the same syndrome in many of the serial killers of the late twentieth century.

Sade died in the Charenton asylum in December 1814. But his influence was already pervasive. Lord Byron had recently invented a new kind of hero, the world-weary sinner who is also the defiant rebel, and had lived up to his sinister reputation by seducing and impregnating his half-sister, then sodomizing his wife. By the time of Byron's death in exile in 1824, Sade's works already enjoyed a wide underground circulation in England (a country that always seems to have been peculiarly obsessed by sexual morality and immorality), and a new pornography industry was flourishing. And the essence of this new pornography was an obsession with *forbiddenness*. It is full of scenes in which schoolteachers seduce their pupils and butlers seduce the little daughter of the household. In *The Power of Hypnotism*, a youth who has learned hypnosis in Germany uses it to seduce his sister, after which the two of them use it to have sex with their mother and father. Later in the book, the vicar and his two little nieces are hypnotized into joining in an orgy. Nothing could be more unlike the boisterous couplings in Boccaccio or Rabelais, or even in *Fanny Hill*. And Casanova would simply have scratched his head, and wondered why any normal person should want to have sex with his own family members when the world is full of desirable girls. This is sex raised to an unhealthy intensity by the use of a kind of morbid imagination.

Let us try to understand just what has happened.

Sex depends fundamentally upon a certain sexual energy which accumulates in the genitals, like water accumulating in a cistern. Without this energy, neither male nor female can experience sexual excitement. This energy is released by friction – preferably with the genitals of someone of the opposite sex. But when the cistern is full to the top, almost any friction can cause it to brim over – for example, accidentally pressing against a tabletop.

But no matter how full the cistern, it would be difficult to achieve full release without some sense of purpose or direction, which serves as a channel. In animals, this channelling is caused by the smell of the female in season. Human sex has ceased to be seasonal, and the channelling is achieved by a certain sense of 'forbiddenness'. The pleasure of sexuality lies in the male's feeling that the body of any attractive female is 'forbidden territory' until she can be persuaded to give her consent. And no matter how gentle and considerate the male, this desire to enter 'forbidden territory' must be recognized as a form of aggression.

In primitive societies, the forbiddenness is complicated by a social taboo. The male has to approach the parents of the girl he wants to marry and obtain their consent – perhaps even pay them for her. And now, in a sense, she is no longer 'forbidden'. Yet here human imagination comes to the rescue. He continues to want her, even when she is his wife, because it is easy to remember when she was 'forbidden'.

We must recognize another important point that is true of *all* desire. It can be intensified by wanting something badly. You enjoy your dinner more when you are hungry. But you also enjoy it more when you have been looking forward to it. Romantic love is essentially a kind of imaginative build-up, a 'looking forward' to possessing the object of desire. This is a simple but all-important observation: that we can enjoy something twice as much simply by 'taking thought' about it, building up a certain anticipation. Conversely, it is easy to cease to enjoy something by being too casual about it, by taking it for granted.

So 'romantic love' – as expressed by the troubadors, and by Dante and Petrarch and Shakespeare – was an interesting step forward in human history. Human beings were learning to intensify animal sexuality with the use of imagination. But this must be immediately qualified by saying that it was true only for a small number of people. For the 'average man', sex remained as simple and crude as the coupling of two dogs.

With the rise of the novel, more and more inveterate day-dreamers learned to use the imagination and to 'cultivate their sensibilities' – that is, to 'conjure up' other realities, other times and places.

Inevitably – human nature being what it is – an increasing number of these began to use imagination for sexual purposes – that is, for masturbation. There is a very narrow dividing line between a teenage girl imagining being carried off by Byron's Corsair, and allowing herelf to daydream of being ravished by him. And if we look closely at Heathcliff in *Wuthering Heights*, it is easy to see that Emily Brontë daydreamed of a male who was even more brutal and earthy than Byron's swashbuckling heroes. It may seem unnecessarily crude to ask: Did Emily Brontë masturbate as she thought about Heathcliff? But the question is more important than it looks. It makes us aware that imagination was pushing human beings towards the dividing line between the 'permitted' and the 'forbidden'. And – since forbiddenness is another name for criminality – towards the criminal.

In Victorian pornography, this criminal element has become all-important. Now it is a question of seeking out the forbidden for its own sake. Sexual excitement ceases to be associated with naked lovers in bed; instead, the quintessential situation is someone peering through a keyhole or a crack in the lavatory door at something he is 'not supposed to be looking at'. The penis is regarded as a kind of burglar whose task is to get into forbidden places.

What is happening is that this power of the imagination – to increase a pleasure by anticipating it – is being used to create a new kind of sex, what we might call 'superheated sex'.

Normal 'animal' sex can only reach a certain intensity, no matter how much a man wants a woman and vice versa. When they are in bed, close physical contact soon turns into the 'flow experience', in which there is a mutual release of energy. No matter how much they try to control the flow, it soon leads to sexual fulfilment. What the Marquis de Sade discovered was that the initial desire can be made far more intense, far more feverish, by taking advantage of the fact that male sexuality is based on aggression. Moreover, imagination can be used to drag out the whole process to far more than its normal length. 'Animal' intercourse might last from a minute to a quarter of an hour or so. But 'superheated sex' can be kept on the boil for twice or three times that period.

Now in fact, Sade's idea of sex was always far more aggressive than that of the normal male. Even as a young man, he wanted to beat prostitutes and be beaten. He once tried to explain his idea of sex by saying that any kind of blow – even chopping wood with an axe – gives a feeling of satisfaction. Most males are likely to consider this a little peculiar – to feel that Sade is extending sex beyond the idea of the normal sexual impulse. But anyone who reads Sade's works in chronological order can understand how this came about. Sade's first major work is the novel *Justine*, completed in the Bastille in 1787, when he was 47. He had been in prison for eight years. The basic argument of *Justine* is that crime leads to prosperity, while virtue leads to misfortune. Justine is a sweet, timid, modest girl of remarkable beauty; her elder sister Juliette, equally beautiful, is depraved from an early age. Their parents die while they are still in a convent, leaving them destitute, and they are thrown out into the world. The wicked Juliette prospers, while Justine is humiliated, beaten and raped with appalling regularity. Sade obviously felt that he had been badly treated by the world – which on the whole was true – and the novel was intended partly as a Swiftian satire on human selfishness. Sade takes an entirely cynical view of kings, judges and priests; he claims that all indulge their vices to the full, while urging restraint on the rest of society. But, according to Sade, God does not exist, there is no 'moral law', and man was sent into the world solely to enjoy himself. So he is trying to awaken his fellow men to 'the truth' about society, and to overthrow those in authority. Unfortunately, his logic is totally distorted by his hatred of authority and religion, so that he simply refuses to imagine what would happen if everybody set out to satisfy their desires to the full.

In fact, Sade was already writing a novel in which he asks the question: what would happen if a group of human beings was rich and powerful enough to satisfy their desires to the full? The *120 Days of Sodom* is a vast catalogue of the 'forbidden', in which four libertines, who include a bishop and a Lord Chief Justice, spend four months indulging every form of perversion, from the rape of children and virgins to ritual murder. Towards the end, even Sade gets tired of the horrors, and the final scenes are only sketched in outline. He left this work behind in the Bastille when he was released, and it was only found by accident many years later.

So Sade, who has been violently restrained – and rather badly treated – by authority now used his imagination to devise situations that amounted to a continuous scream of defiance. In fact, as an individual, Sade was far from 'sadistic'. He was a genuinely affectionate father, and when he had a chance to sentence his hated mother-in-law to death – as a member of a revolutionary tribunal – he allowed her to go free. But he was crazed with hatred of authority, and his work may be seen as a kind of continuous sex crime of the imagination. A serial killer like Carl Panzram is a kind of Sade who put his daydreams into practise.

Oddly enough, Sade's work is seldom pornographic, in the sense of being sexually stimulating. He never gloats over the lascivious preliminaries and the physical details of sex; when one of his characters commits incest, he merely 'ravishes' his daughter, then teaches her 'all the mysteries of love'. Sade is more interested in expressing his sense of grievance by pouring out indecencies; basically, he is like a schoolboy sticking out his tongue at the headmaster.

What is obvious to the modern reader of Sade is that he is a man who is trying to create a *sexual illusion*, a kind of daydream. If he shows signs of waking up, he redoubles the 'wickedness' to try and stimulate his imagination. When Sade actually seduced his sister-in-law, the apprentice nun, he must have found out that, after the initial thrill, it soon ceased to feel wicked. But Sade's characters never get tired of 'the forbidden'. After Juliette has seduced her clergyman father, she then looks on as he is murdered by her lover. But, as we can see from the *120 Days*, Sade's imagination was unable to sustain the sexual daydream; he kept on inflating the sexual illusion until it burst like a bubble.

Victorian pornography never went this far. It was only concerned with creating an atmosphere of feverish sensuality, with great emphasis on the preliminaries. One well-known piece of Victorian pornography, the anonymous *Raped on the Railway* (1894), clearly reveals the difference between sex in the eighteenth and in the nineteenth centuries. It begins with a prelude on Euston station (to increase our anticipation of what is to come), then a chapter in which a painter named Brandon tries to persuade a veiled lady with whom he is sharing the compartment to 'let me contemplate those heavenly features I so burn to portray'. When he tries to lift her veil, she produces a revolver; but before she can fire it, the train brakes suddenly and flings her into his arms.

There follows a long digression in which the author tells the reader about the painter's earlier life and love affairs; finally he returns us to the carriage, in which the lady – introduced as Mrs Sinclair – is now lying in a 'swoon', The painter unbuttons her dress 'exposing to view two small but beautifully round breasts just showing their little pink nipples above the corset which confined them'. After kissing these, he 'carefully turned back her skirt, and the fine linen petticoats underneath it exposing to view a pair of well-shaped legs encased in black silk stockings, and encircled by very natty-looking garters with red bows'. 'Pulling apart her thighs as gently as though he were touching a sleeping child', he opens the slit of her drawers. 'The charms he sought were, however, hidden from his eyes by a chemise of the finest cambric. Carefully lifting this he saw before his entranced eyes, now gleaming with lust, a forest of golden brown curly hair which extended, in a triangular shape from the line where the thighs join the body, all over the belly. At the apex of this triangle, there peered through a thicker and curlier tuft of hair the pouting red lips of a pretty and very tempting-looking abode of love.'

All this is quite unlike Cleland or Sade. The writer is trying to create in the reader, moment by moment, the actual sensations of a man in the grip of sexual excitement. It is also clear that the writer finds her underwear very nearly as exciting as her body. This is a refinement of sexual desire that Casanova would have found incomprehensible.

As he is about to enter, the lady wakes up. The painter wrestles with her until she is exhausted, then succeeds in penetrating her. She struggles violently until he thrusts into her and 'poured into her vagina the warm flood which she would have been so glad to receive and mingle with her own love fountain, if the tool which was shooting the warm jets into her had come as a friend and not as an enemy'.

After the rape is over, he begs her forgiveness, offering to let her shoot him; she finally agrees to say nothing about the rape if he will promise not to speak to her for the rest of the journey.

But a guard at the next station deduces from her 'tottering walk' and the disarray of her clothes what has happened, and when a man in the next compartment makes a joke about needing a woman, tells him that the lady next door looks as if she has had a 'rare good poking'. As Mrs Sinclair emerges from the toilet, one of the men, described as 'a giant', recognizes her as his sister-in-law. With three companions he gets into her carriage. While they doze, the rapist and his victim are both overpowered and tied up. Then the lady is laid face-downward on the seat, and the men begin 'very carefully and slowly to draw back the panting woman's dress'. 'They then served a stout travelling flannel petticoat in the same way, and also a rose-coloured silk petticoat that she wore next to her drawers.' At this point, the writer pauses to observe that 'the latter article of feminine toilette calls for special remark. There is a great psychological significance in the quality of women's drawers.' And the next part of the undressing is delayed for a page while he discourses on underwear. Finally, the drawers are removed, and for the next six pages or so, the lady's bottom, 'the most wonderful riches that it has ever been the lot of man to gaze upon', is birched until it glows bright red.

Even when she arrives home, Mrs Sinclair's ordeal is not finished. Her brother-in-law – a member of the Society for National Purity – calls on her and makes a determined attempt to rape her; she finally disables him by bending his penis, which causes him such agony that a doctor has to administer morphine.

It is impossible not to recognize the resemblance between *Raped on the Railway* and Sade. The fact that the brother-in-law is a member of the Society of National Purity suggests that all such people are hypocrites – in fact, that they are rapists at heart – while the description of the woman's struggles as her brother-in-law tries to rape her ('her underclothing was in a frightful state, the pink silk petticoat . . . being torn in several places, and her clean white drawers nearly wrenched from the strings that attached them to her waist') is reminiscent of Justine's tribulations.

Yet the difference between *Justine* and *Raped on the Railway* is also enormous. Justine is simply 'violated', and the details are left to the imagination. Mrs Sinclair's breasts, her buttocks, her genitals, her petticoat, her underskirt and her drawers are all described with obsessive precision. Compared to Cleland or Sade, the author of *Raped on the Railway* is in a kind of fever; we an almost hear his heavy breathing as he decribes her underwear. All this is the result of a century and a half of novel-reading.

The main difference between the two books lies in the happy ending of *Raped on the Railway*. In the last chapter, the lady's husband is conveniently killed off in the Boer war; Brandon calls on her, and they end in one another's arms. Yet as the book closes in an atmosphere of reconciliation and morality, we become aware of the paradox involved in the author's attitude to sex. Brandon and Mrs Sinclair will now become husband and wife. But will Brandon's eyes continue to 'gleam with lust' every time his wife takes off her clothes? Obviously not; they will become an ordinary married couple, for whom sex is a pleasure that lasts ten minutes or so, and then is followed by sleep. All this dwelling on rounded breasts, white thighs (and the 'abode of love' between them), pink silk petticoats and fine linen drawers, is a kind of embroidery, a deliberately intensified *illusion*, that has nothing to do with the simple fact of sexual intercourse as described by Cleland. It has been *added* by the Victorian imagination, and is the outcome of a century of romanticism, of regarding women as untouchable goddesses or compassionate angels.

In fact, this feverish romanticism had already begun to manifest in another form. In 1886, a book called *Psychopathia Sexualis* caused such a scandal that the British Medico-Psychological Association debated whether to cancel the author's membership. The author was a German 'alienist' (as psychiatrists were then called), Richard von Krafft-Ebing. And the book begins with an utterly typical case describing how a middle-aged man showed 'increasing perversion of his moral sense', so that he constantly accosted women in the street and asked them to marry him or allow coitus. Placed in an asylum, 'the sexual excitement increased to a veritable satyriasis, which increased until he died.' 'He masturbated continuously, even before others, took delight only in obscene ideas, and thought the men around him were women, and pestered them with obscene proposals.' And this portrait of a man totally obsessed with sex is followed by a gallery of sadists, masochists (Krafft-Ebing invented both words), voyeurs, fetishists, transvestites, vampires and necrophiles.

Among the cases of necrophily is one that throws a great deal of light on the development of 'the sexual illusion'.

> Sergeant Bertrand, a man of delicate physical, constitution and of peculiar character; from childhood silent and inclined to solitude.
>
> The details of the health of his family are not satisfactorily known; but the occurrence of mental diseases in his ancestry is ascertained. It is said that while he was a child he was affected with destructive impulses, which he himself could not explain. He would break whatever was at hand. In early childhood, without teaching, he learned to masturbate. At nine he began to feel inclinations towards persons of the opposite sex. At thirteen the impulse to sexual intercourse became powerfully awakened in him. He now masturbated excessively. When he did this, his fancy always created a room filled with women. He would imagine that he carried out the sexual act with them and then killed them. Immediately thereafter he would think of them as corpses, and of how he defiled them. Occasionally in such situations the thought of carrying out a similar act with

male corpses would come up, but it was always attended with a feeling of disgust.

In time he felt the impulse to carry out such acts with actual corpses. For want of human bodies, he obtained those of animals. He would cut open the abdomen, tear out the entrails, and masturbate during the act. He declares that in this way he experienced inexpressible pleasure. In 1846 these bodies no longer satisfied him. He now killed dogs, and proceeded with them as before. Toward the end of 1846 he first felt the desire to make use of human bodies.

At first he had a horror of it. In 1847, being by accident in a graveyard, he ran across the grave of a newly buried corpse. Then this impulse, with headache and palpitation of the heart, became so powerful that, although there were people near by, and he was in danger of detection, he dug up the body. In the absence of a convenient instrument for cutting it up, he satisfied himself by hacking it with a shovel.

In 1847 and 1848, during two weeks, as reported, the impulse, accompanied by violent headache, to commit brutalities on corpses actuated him. Amidst the greatest dangers and difficulties he satisfied this impulse some fifteen times. He dug up the bodies with his hands, in nowise sensible in his excitement to the injuries he thus inflicted on himself. When he had obtained the body, he cut it up with a sword or pocket-knife, tore out the entrails, and then masturbated. The sex of the bodies is said to have been a matter of indifference to him, though it was ascertained that this modern vampire had dug up more female than male corpses.

During these acts he declares himself to have been in an indescribable state of sexual excitement. After having cut them up, he reinterred the bodies.

In July, 1848, he accidentally came across the body of a girl of sixteen. Then, for the first time, he experienced a desire to carry out coitus on a cadaver.

'I covered it with kisses and pressed it wildly to my heart. All that one could enjoy with a living woman is nothing in comparison with the pleasure I experienced. After I had enjoyed it for about a quarter of an hour, I cut the body up, as usual, and tore out the entrails. Then I buried the cadaver again.' Only after this, as B. declares, had he felt the impulse to use the bodies sexually before cutting them up, and thereafter he had done it in three instances. The actual motive for exhuming the bodies, however, was then, as before, to cut them up; and the enjoyment in so doing was greater than in using the bodies sexually. The latter act had always been nothing more than an episode of the principal one, and had never quieted his desires; for which reason he had later on always mutilated the body.

The medico-legal examiners gave an opinion of 'monomania'. Court-martial sentence to one year's imprisonment.

An account of the case quoted by the sexologist Magnus Hirschfeld includes some important details:

> He denied that he had ever bitten the corpses, as one of the experts asserts.
>
> An interesting feature of the case is that, in addition to and in spite of his necrophile activities, B. entertained relations with girls wherever he was stationed, and completely 'satisfied' them. Several girls wanted to marry him. When the impulse manifested itself, which happened at intervals of about a fortnight, the attack being heralded by a headache, he pursued his necro-sadistic pleasures. And nothing could deter him. Even shots fired at him by sentries, traps laid for him, the most inclement weather, such obstacles as a pond which he had to swim in the middle of winter, the need to lie motionless in wet clothes in icy cold weather – none of these things deterred him. Finally, he was so severely wounded by a trap shot while climbing over the cemetery wall that he could not escape arrest, thereby providing an explanation of the many desecrations of the cemetery that had become known. Under the influence of the surgeon Marchal de Calvi, under whose treatment he was, B. freely admitted everything stating that he was not sure that he would not do such things again. He also declared that the important thing for him was the act of destruction, not the sexual act.
>
> His attitude to women is rather interesting. He said: –
>
> 'I have always loved women to distraction. I have never allowed anyone to offend a woman in my presence. Everywhere I had young and charming mistresses, whom I have been able to satisfy completely and who were devoted to me. This is proved by the fact that some of them, although they came from well-to-do, distinguished families, wanted to follow me. I have never touched a married woman; I always disliked obscene talk. If such talk was started in my presence, I endeavoured to turn the conversation to a different subject. I had a strictly religious education and have always loved and defended religion, though I am not a fanatic.
>
> 'I have always loved destruction. In my childhood my parents would not give me any toys because I smashed everything. In later years I could not keep anything, even a penknife, longer

than a fortnight; by then it was smashed up. It sometimes happens that I buy myself a pipe in the morning, and smash it up in the evening or next morning. In the army I once returned to barracks drunk and smashed everything that I could lay hands on.'

This case is interesting because it allows us such a clear insight into the reason for the rise of sex crime. There had, of course, been sadistic disembowellers before the nineteenth century, like Vlad the Impaler (the original 'Dracula') and the French Marshal Gilles de Rais (who killed children). But these had been members of an upper class who had the leisure to become bored, and to devote themselves to strange pleasures and fantasies. Bertrand was the son of a peasant. The origin of his sadism lay in 'hypersexuality' – sexual desire of almost painful intensity. Fantasies of raping a roomful of women were followed by fantasies of killing them all – a daydream of ultimate power and aggression. (We note that Bertrand is a 'man of delicate physical constitution', and inclined to daydream, so these power fantasies are compensatory.) Since he has no contact with human corpses at this period, he is forced to make do with animal corpses; and since these are unsatisfactory for sexual purposes, his aggression finds expression in disembowelling. From then on, he is 'imprinted' with an association of sex and disembowelling. At 24, Bertrand began to kill and disembowel dogs while he masturbated. So when he came across an open grave with a corpse (a female) the desire to enact his fantasies was overwhelming; he described in his confession the 'insane frenzy' with which he began to beat the corpse with a spade.

The progression, then, is simple: intense sexual desire that finds outlet in daydreams, then in fantasies of rape followed by murder, then in disembowelling animal corpses, then sadistic acts on living dogs, then necrophily on female corpses. (In spite of Krafft-Ebing's assertion, Bertrand said that he felt only disgust when he disinterred a male corpse.) And the medium which causes this progression from fantasy to necrophily is *aggression*. Yet Bertrand continues to feel a powerful inhibition about attacking living women. And so, as far as we can judge, did most of the males suffering from 'hypersexuality'.

In the second half of the nineteenth century, this inhibition finally broke down. Krafft-Ebing also describes one of the first recorded sex crimes in our modern sense of the word:

> Alton, a clerk in England, goes out of town for a walk. He lures a child into a thicket, and returns after a time to his office, where he makes this entry in his notebook: 'Killed today a young girl; it was fine and hot.' The child was missed, searched for, and found cut into pieces. Many parts, among them the genitals, could not be found. A. did not show the slightest trace of emotion, and gave no explanation of the motive of circumstances of the horrible deed. He was a psychopathic individual, and occasionally subject to fits of depression and *taedium vitae*. His father had had an attack of acute mania. A near relative suffered from mania with homicidal impulses. A. was executed.

Krafft-Ebing has it slightly wrong; the clerk was called Frederick Baker, and the town was Alton, Hampshire. It happened in July 1867, and the victim was an 8-year-old girl named Fanny Adams, whom Baker accosted and lured away from her playmates with a promise of sweets, then murdered in a hop garden.

Here, as in the case of Sergeant Bertrand, we can see that the sheer intensity of sexual fantasy leads to dreams of violence and murder. When he finally puts these dreams into action, it is not enough to commit rape: he also has to mutilate the victim and scatter the parts of her body over such a wide area that the phrase 'sweet Fanny Adams' has become a slang term meaning 'nothing'.

Five years later, in 1872, one of the first Jack the Ripper-type killers, Vincent Verzeni, was arrested. The case is again described by Krafft-Ebing:

> Vincenz Verzeni, born in 1849; since 11th January, 1872, in prison; is accused (1) of an attempt to strangle his nurse Marianne, four years ago, while she lay sick in bed; (2) of a similar attempt on a married woman, Arsuffi, aged twenty-seven; (3) of an attempt to strangle a married woman, Gala, by grasping her throat while kneeling on her abdomen; (4) on suspicion of the following murders: –
>
> In December a fourteen-year-old girl, Johanna Motta, set out for a neighbouring village between seven and eight o'clock in the morning. As she did not return, her master set out to find her, and discovered her body near the village, lying by a path in the fields. The corpse was frightfully mutilated with numerous wounds. The intestines and genitals had been torn from the open body, and were found near by. The nakedness of the body and erosions on the thighs made it seem probable that there had

been an attempt at rape; the mouth, filled with earth, pointed to suffocation. In the neighbourhood of the body, under a pile of straw, were found a portion of flesh torn from the right calf, and pieces of, clothing. The perpetrator of the deed remained undiscovered.

On 28th August, 1871, a married woman, Frigeni, aged twenty-eight, set out into the fields early in the morning. As she did not return by eight o'clock, her husband started out to fetch her. He found her a corpse, lying naked in the field, with the mark of a thong around her neck, with which she had been strangled, and with numerous wounds. The abdomen had been slit open, and the intestines were hanging out.

On 29th August, at noon, as Maria Previtali, aged nineteen, went through a field, she was followed by her cousin, Verzeni. He dragged her into a field of grain, threw her to the ground, and began to choke her. As he let go of her for a moment to ascertain whether any one was near, the girl got up and, by her supplicating entreaty, induced Verzeni to let her go, after he had pressed her hands together for some time.

Verzeni was brought before a court. He is twenty-two years old. His cranium is of more than average size, but asymmetrical. The right frontal bone is narrower and lower than the left, the right frontal prominence being less developed, and the right ear smaller than the left (by 1 centimetre in length and 3 centimetres in breadth); both ears are defective in the inferior half of the helix; the right temporal artery is somewhat atheromatous. Bull-necked; enormous development of the *zygomæ* and inferior *maxilla*; penis greatly developed, *frænum* wanting; slight divergent alternating strabismus (insufficiency of the internal rectus muscle, and myopia). *Lombroso* concludes, from these signs of degeneration, that there is a congenital arrest of development of the right frontal lobe. As seemed probable, Verzeni has a bad ancestry – two uncles are cretins; a third, microcephalic, beardless, one testicle wanting, the other atrophic. The father shows traces of pellagrous degeneration, and had an attack of *hypochondria pellagrosa*. A cousin suffered from cerebral hyperæmia; another is a confirmed thief.

Verzeni's family is bigoted and low-minded. He himself has ordinary intelligence; knows how to defend himself well; seeks to prove an *alibi* and cast suspicion on others. There is nothing in his past that points to mental disease, but his character is peculiar. He is silent and inclined to be solitary. In prison he is cynical. He masturbates, and makes every effort to gain sight of women.

Verzeni finally confessed his deeds and their motive. The commission of them gave him an indescribably pleasant (lustful) feeling, which was accompanied by erection and ejaculation. As soon as he has grasped his victim by the neck, sexual sensations were experienced. It was entirely the same to him, with reference to these sensations, whether the women were old, young, ugly, or beautiful. Usually, simply choking them had satisfied him, and he then had allowed his victims to live; in the two cases mentioned, the sexual satisfaction was delayed, and he had continued to choke them until they died. The gratification experienced in this garrotting was greater than in masturbation. The abrasions of the skin on Motta's thighs were produced by his teeth, whilst sucking her blood in most intense lustful pleasure. He had torn out a piece of flesh from her calf and taken it with him to roast at home; but on the way he hid it under the straw-stack, for fear his mother would suspect him. He also carried pieces of the clothing and intestines some distance, because it gave him great pleasure to smell and touch them. The strength which he possessed in these moments of intense lustful pleasure was enormous. He had never been a fool; while committing his deeds he saw nothing around him (apparently as a result of intense sexual excitement, annihilation of perception – instinctive action).

After such acts he was always very happy, enjoying a feeling of great satisfaction. He had never had pangs of conscience. It had never occurred to him to touch the genitals of the martyred women or to violate his victims. It had satisfied him to throttle them and suck their blood. These statements of this modern vampire seem to rest on truth. Normal sexual impulses seem to have remained foreign to him. Two sweethearts that he had, he was satisfied to look at; it was very strange to him that he had no inclination to strangle them or press their hands; but he had not had the same pleasure with them as with his victims. There was no trace of moral sense, remorse and the like.

Verzeni said himself that it would be a good thing if he were to be kept in prison, because with freedom he could not resist his impulses. Verzeni was sentenced to imprisonment for life (*Lombroso*, 'Verzeni e Agnoletti,' Rome, 1873). The confessions which Verzeni made after his sentence are interesting: –

'I had an unspeakable delight in strangling women, experiencing during the act erections and real sexual pleasure. It was even a pleasure only to smell female clothing. The feeling of pleasure while strangling them was much greater than that which I experienced while masturbating. I took great delight in drinking

> Motta's blood. It also gave me the greatest pleasure to pull the hair-pins out of the hair of my victims.
>
> 'I took the clothing and intestines because of the pleasure it gave me to smell and touch them. At last my mother came to suspect me, because she noticed spots of semen on my shirt after each murder or attempt at one. I am not crazy, but in the moment of strangling my victims I saw nothing else. After the commission of the deeds I was satisfied and felt well. It never occurred to me to touch or look at the genitals or such things. It satisfied me to seize the women by the neck and suck their blood. To this very day I am ignorant of how a woman is formed. During the strangling and after it, I pressed myself on the entire body without thinking of one part more than another.'
>
> Verzeni arrived at his perverse acts quite independently, after having noticed, when he was twelve years old, that he experienced a peculiar feeling of pleasure while wringing the necks of chickens. After this he often killed great numbers of them and then said that a weasel had been in the hen-coop.

It is interesting to note that Verzeni found the intestines and the female clothing equally exciting. And this suddenly enables us to understand the emphasis on underwear in *Raped on the Railway*. Mrs Sinclair is at first remote, untouchable, even her face hidden behind a veil. So the artist Brandon sees her as a sexual object, not as a fellow human being – moreover, as a sexual object whose 'forbiddenness' merits aggression. The silk underskirt and the drawers are symbols of her forbiddenness. And the difference between the erotic fantasy of *Fanny Hill* and the pornographic fantasy of *Raped on the Railway* is essentially a difference of aggression. Cleland is interested only in the straightforward pleasures of the 'two backed beast', of the mutual satisfaction men and women can obtain from of their genitals. *Fanny Hill* is a straightforward transference of the pleasures of the bed into fiction, a kind of substitute for an hour in bed with a member of the opposite sex. *Raped on the Railway* is intended as more than a substitute; it is intended to give a higher degree of pleasure by taking its (male) reader on an excursion into the forbidden, in which aggression is expressed first in rape, then in spanking.

The irony of the situation is that it is the development of the human imagination that has led to all this 'superheated sex' with its flavour of criminality. Imagination means that human beings are no longer contented with the narrowness and boredom of their everyday lives; they dream of far horizons and a richer and more satisfying kind of experience. But this enriched imagination is also placed at the service of their sexual fantasy and their will-to-power. The result is a product like *Raped on the Railway*, which takes at least three hours to read, and is therefore far more extended than a normal sexual experience.

Imagination, of course, is not the whole explanation. The social changes brought about by the Industrial Revolution, which packed hundreds of thousands of human beings into a thoroughly artificial environment in the cities, also played their part. Even more important was the frustration induced by Victorian prudery, in which children were brought up to regard any reference to intimate parts of the body as shameful. Even the word 'legs' was unmentionable, and table legs were often covered up with a long tablecloth, or even a kind of stocking, in case they brought a blush to the cheeks of young ladies.

Because we are the heirs of Victorian prudery, we find all this fairly natural, even if rather absurd. But to grasp the real point, imagine what would happen if our society regarded food as shameful and unmentionable, so that only married couples ate together, while single people ate alone, and did their best to give the impression that they had no need of nourishment. A food pornography would develop in which men in a fever of desire would peer through cracks in doors at women eating their dinner, and in which a description of a cherry tart surmounted by a twisted blob of whipped cream would arouse all the illicit thrills of a girl removing her clothes. The sense of wickedness would soon be transferred to food packaging, and fetishists would furtively search through dustbins for empty boxes with erotic pictures of cheesecake and beefburgers. A few dedicated perverts would accumulate drawers full of empty jamjars, opened cans of baked beans, and greaseproof paper in which sausages had been wrapped, while food pedophiles would be attracted only to unripe fruit and baby carrots.

It sounds laughable only because our attitude to food is strictly realistic, like the primitive attitude to sex. We agree that food is one of the great pleasures of life, we sympathize with gourmets who seek out the best restaurants, but we waste no time in daydreaming about ten-course meals. Because food is openly available, and there are no taboos about eating in public, we have not subjected it to the hothouse treatment of the imagination. Yet, biologically speaking, there is a close parallel between our need for food and our need for sex. Both are essential for survival, both can give great pleasure, both can be associated with a will to power (only the rich can afford the finest food). If we make an effort to grasp the underlying reality of sex as we grasp the underlying reality of food, we see that it is based on the man's and woman's mutual need to find a partner, and that the essence of such a relation is that it is based on a sense of *difference*: that obvious yet all-important recognition that men are different from women. The male's sexual pleasure springs from a sense of overcoming this difference. And in a world in which sexual desire was still as 'normal' as our need for food, sexual satisfaction would lead to a simple, monogamous relation, with little or no interest in other partners, and certainly no interest in the kind of *abstract* sexuality – the sexual illusion – that is satisfied by erotic daydreams.

To grasp this is to grasp what has happened to sex since the late eighteen century. Imagination has turned it into a kind of gigantic shadow of itself, like the Spectre of the Brocken, and the straightforward bawdiness of Aretino and *The School of Venus* has been transformed into something far more steamy, criminal and neurotic.

In the first half of the nineteenth century, sex crime became increasingly common, particularly in urban areas – Henry Mayhew even produced a map in the mid-1840s showing where 'carnal' attacks were most common – and the prevalence of sadistic crime slowly increased, although to judge by the cases mentioned by Krafft-Ebing and Hirschfeld it seldom resulted in murder. (The rape of children was not uncommon, because children were more 'forbidden' than adult women.) Even as early as 1790, women in London were terrified by a man who became known as 'the Monster', who slashed at their clothes with a sharp knife, which sometimes caused painful cuts. One girl, Anne Porter, was slashed in the buttocks, and on undressing, found a wound nine inches long and four inches deep. Six months later, she recognized her attacker in the street, and her male companion followed the man home and made a kind of citizen's arrest. The 'monster' proved to be a slightly built man named Renwick Williams, a maker of artificial flowers; although he insisted on his innocence he was sentenced to six years in prison.

Forty years later, in 1829, a man known as 'the Ripper of Bozen' stabbed girls in the lower abdomen, and when caught, admitted that 'he was suffering from a sexual urge amounting to a frenzy', and that he was obsessed by the urge for days on end until he gave way to it, experiencing orgasm as he slashed the girls.

The following case from Krafft-Ebing is again typical:

> C. L., aged forty-two, engineer married, father of two children; from a neuropathic family; father irascible, a drinker; mother hysterical, subject to eclamptic attacks. The patient remembers that in childhood he took particular pleasure in witnessing the slaughtering of domestic animals, especially swine. He thus experienced lustful pleasure and ejaculation. Later he visited slaughter-houses, in order to delight in the sight of flowing blood and the death throes of the animals. When he could find opportunity, he killed the animals himself, which always afforded him a vicarious feeling of sexual pleasure.
>
> At the time of full maturity he first attained to a knowledge of his abnormality. The patient was not exactly opposed in inclination to women, but close contact with them seemed to him repugnant. On the advice of a physician, at twenty-five he married a woman who pleased him, in the hope of freeing himself of his abnormal condition. Although he was very partial to his wife, it was only seldom, and after great trouble and exertion of his imagination, that he could perform coitus with her; nevertheless, he begat two children. In 1866 he was in the war in Bohemia. His letters written at that time to his wife, were composed in an exalted, enthusiastic tone. He was missed after the battle of Königgrätz.

Krafft-Ebing tries to explain such cases by remarking that 'cruelty is natural to primitive man'. But here he seems to be missing the point. What has happened in this case – as in that of Sergeant Bertrand, Vincent Verzeni and Jack the Ripper – is that 'superheated sex', which is based on 'forbiddenness', has become associated with cruelty. The notion that blood and disembowellment can be sexually stimulating will strike most people as incomprehensible; yet all the evidence seems to show that when a person of high sexual drive is subjected continually to the sight and smell of blood, the result is often the development of a sadistic obsession.

One of the most typical of these early cases is described by State Attorney Wulffen and quoted by Hirschfeld:

> Eusebius Pieydagnelle was tried in 1871 for four murders. In the speech he addressed to the jury . . . he begged them to sentence him to death. He said he would have killed himself but for the fact that he believed in a Beyond, and did not want to add a further sin to his score.
>
> Pieydagnelle told the jury that he came from highly respectable parents and had had an excellent education. Unfortunately, opposite their house in Vinuville there was a butcher's shop kept by a M. Cristobal. 'The smell of fresh blood, the appetizing meat, the bloody lumps – all this fascinated me and I began to envy the butcher's assistant, because he could work at the block, with rolled-up sleeves and bloody hands.' Then, in spite of his parents' opposition, he persuaded them to apprentice him to Cristobal. Here he drank blood in secret and wounded the cattle. He derived the greatest excitement when he was permitted to kill an animal himself. 'But the sweetest sensation is when you feel the animal trembling under your knife. The animal's departing life creeps along the blade right up to your hand. The mighty blow that felled the bullocks sounded like sweet music in my ears.' Unfortunately for him, his father took him away from the butcher, and apprenticed him to a notary. But it was too late. He was seized with a terrible depression, a deep melancholia, and since he could no longer kill animals, he began to kill people. Six times he committed murder under the compulsion of the same urge. He tried to isolate himself from the world and lived in a cave in a wood. But it was all in vain; his impulse was stronger than he. His last victim was his first employer, M. Cristobal. The murderer then gave himself up. His first victim was a girl of 15, and he describes his sensation when he killed her as follows: 'As I looked at the lovely creature my first thought was that I should like to kiss her. I bent down . . . But I paused – a stolen kiss is no use. But I could not bring myself to wake her up. I looked at her lovely neck – and at that moment the gleam of the kitchen knife that lay beside the girl struck my eyes. Something drew me irresistibly towards the knife.'

Two years after the publication of *Psychopathia Sexualis*, the Jack the Ripper murders created a sensation that reverberated around the world. For the first time, the general public became aware that something strange and frightening was happening. In an introduction to Donald Rumbelow's *Complete Jack the Ripper*, I tried to explain just why the murders produced such an impact. The Victorians were basically sentimental; they cried at the death of Little Nell and rejoiced at the conversion of Scrooge in *A Christmas Carol*. They gasped with horror in the theatre as William Corder shot Maria Marten in the Red Barn, or the Colleen Bawn was murdered by her spoilt playboy husband. (Both plays were based on real cases.) Victorian society might be divided by class barriers, but where sentiment was concerned, it was one big happy family. The Ripper murders, with their nightmarish mutilations, simply went beyond normal comprehension. It was as if the killer wanted to *shock* the whole community, to fling the murders in its face like a hysterical insult. The crimes seemed to exude the smell of pure evil.

Now, as we have seen, the Ripper murders were a long way from being the first sex crimes; such crimes had been going on intermittently throughout the nineteenth century. But earlier crimes – like those of Vincent Verzeni – were hardly known outside the countries in which they occurred. Reuter had opened a news office in London in 1851; but it was not until Edison invented the 'quadruplex' telegraph in 1874 – in which four messages could be sent along the same wire – that the age of mass communication suddenly began. Jack the Ripper, with his gruesome pseudonym, was the first mass murderer to receive worldwide publicity.

In fact, the Ripper murders merely created a general awareness of something that had been 'in the air' since Sade. They seemed to crystallize the spirit of the *120 Days of Sodom*. And in the year following the murders, Tolstoy was to give expression to a troubled awareness of this change in a short novel called *The Kreutzer Sonata*, about a man named Pozdnichev, who had stabbed his wife in a fit of insane jealousy. Pozdnichev argues passionately that civilization has been poisoned by sexual desire. Simple peasants, he declares, eat and drink a great deal, but they use up the energy in hard physical labour. The leisured classes canalize their excess energies into sex and romance. He tells how, as a teenager, he indulged in masturbation, and finally began making use of prostitutes. This, he argues, is unnatural, a sign of our frenzied and morbid sexuality.

He goes on to describe how his wife and a musician began to take an obvious romantic interest in one another as they played Beethoven's Kreutzer Sonata, and how he became increasingly possessed by jealousy until he caught the two of them alone together, and stabbed his wife. When he begged her forgiveness as she lay on her deathbed, she merely looked at him with 'cold animal hatred', and told him that forgiveness was all rubbish. In fact, Tolstoy is arguing that the intimate relations between man and woman are 'all rubbish', based on illusion. When a lady who is listening suggests that real love is based on spiritual affinity and identity of ideals, Pozdnichev asks sarcastically: 'Do they go to bed together because of identity of ideals?'

The Kreutzer Sonata caused passionate controversy, and even today, few commentators can write about it without taking sides – usually to argue that Pozdnichev is an insane egoist. The truth is that Tolstoy was the one man of genius of his time who saw clearly what had happened to the human sexual urge in the past century: that it had been amplified by the imagination until it had achieved an unhealthy strength. His argument might be paraphrased: 'normal' sexual desire is as straightforward and natural as a fruit punch but human beings have deliberately added raw alcohol to make it more interesting. The result is an erotic cocktail that creates a kind of insanity. Tolstoy must have regarded the Ripper murders as a typical example of this insanity. And in blaming Beethoven, he is not entirely wide of the mark. Beethoven signals the beginning of a new kind of romantic music, a music based on a consciousness of the ego. Tolstoy has simply failed to identify the source of this development as Samuel Richardson and the novelists who followed. How could he recognize it when he himself was perpetuating the 'egoism' in his own novels? Yet the basic theme of his own *Anna Karenina* is the sexual illusion, and how it leads to tragedy.

There is another respect in which Tolstoy is guilty of muddled thinking. In appealing to the Russian peasant as the 'normal' human being, who keeps sex in its proper place, Tolstoy is implying that highly civilized sexuality – the sexual preoccupation displayed by the leisured classes – is somehow abnormal – that it has crossed the line that divides normality from abnormality or perversion. But this fails to recognize that it is totally impossible to draw a clear dividing line between normality and perversion. Perversion depends on a sense of 'forbiddenness', a desire to violate taboos, and *all* sex depends on this sense of forbiddenness. The contact of two bodies has to bring a shock of 'difference', and without this shock, sex would become either mechanical or simply impossible. In animals, the smell of the female on heat triggers 'forbiddenness'. In human beings, this function has been handed over to our minds. *All* sex is based on 'forbiddenness'.

All this raises an interesting question. Tolstoy blames the problem on the leisured class, and there is a sense in which he is obviously correct: earlier 'monsters' like Caligula, Gilles de Rais, Ivan the Terrible, Vlad the Impaler, Countess Bathory,[1] all belonged to the upper classes. So why were the majority of sex killers working-class? Why is it still true that nearly all serial killers are working-class? Conversely, if it was the working classes who were packed like sardines into unhealthy basements during the Industrial Revolution, creating a sexual free-for-all, then why were the leisured classes also infected with the virus?

In *The Misfits* I have suggested that the answer could lie in Rupert Sheldrake's 'hypothesis of formative causation'. Sheldrake points out that heredity cannot be explained entirely in chemical terms: DNA and so on. Something else is needed, and embryologists have concluded that the 'something else' is a factor called 'morphogenetic fields'. The wing of a bird or the tentacle of an octopus is shaped by a kind of electrical 'mould' – just like the moulds into which we pour jellies – which is why many creatures can re-grow a limb that has been cut off. These 'moulds' seem to be magnetic fields, which shape the living molecules just as a magnet can 'shape' iron filings into a pattern. Sheldrake suggests that these 'fields' can be used to explain some rather odd observations made by biologists.

For example, in 1920 the psychologist William McDougal performed an experiment at Harvard to see if baby rats could inherit abilities developed by their parents (the 'inheritance of acquired characteristics' that Darwinists regard as such a fearful heresy). He put white rats into a tank of water from which they could escape up one of two gangplanks. One gangplank had an electric current running through it, and the first generation of rats soon learned to choose the other one. Then McDougal tried the same experiment on their children, and then on

[1] For a fuller account of these see 'A Gallery of Monsters' in my *Second Mammoth Book of True Crime* (Robinson, London, 1990).

their children, and so on. And he found that each generation learned more quickly than its parents – he had proved that the inheritance of acquired characteristics *does* occur.

Now when a scientist performs an experiment on a group of animals, he always keeps an exactly similar group who are *not* subjected to experiments; these are called the 'control group' – the purpose being to have a ready standard of comparison. When a colleague of McDougal's – W. E. Agar of Melbourne – repeated his experiment, he also decided to test the control group at the end of several generations. To his baffled astonishment, these *also* showed the same ability to learn more quickly. And that was impossible, for they had merely been sitting passively in cages. It looked as if the control rats had learned by some kind of telepathy.

Not telepathy, says Sheldrake, but by 'morphic resonance'. The control group of rats 'picked up' the morphogenetic field of the trained rats in the same way that an iron bar can pick up the electrical field of a coil of wire and turn into a magnet. Simple induction.

Incredibly, this seems to work not only with living creatures but with crystals. New chemicals, when synthesized for the first time, are often extremely difficult to crystallize. But as soon as one of them has been crystallized in any laboratory in the world, it becomes easier to crystallize in all the others. At first, it was suspected that scientists travelling from one laboratory to another might be carrying fragments of crystals in their clothes or beards – or even that tiny quantities are carried in the atmosphere. Both explanations seem highly unlikely. The likeliest, Sheldrake suggests, is a process of 'induction' through morphogenetic fields.

A series of experiments has been performed to test the Sheldrake hypothesis and has produced positive results. At Yale, Professor Gary Schwartz found that people who do not know Hebrew were able to distinguish between real words in Hebrew and false words – because Jews all over the world already know the genuine words. Alan Pickering of Hatfield Polytechnic obtained the same result using Persian script. In another experiment, English-speaking people were asked to memorize two rhymes in a foreign language – one a well-known nursery rhyme, one a newly composed rhyme. The result – as the hypothesis of formative causation predicts – is that they learned the nursery rhyme more easily than the newly composed rhyme.

If Sheldrake is correct, then it becomes altogether easier to understand what has been happening since the time of Richardson. The obvious objection to the 'imagination' theory suggested in this book is that the majority of the inhabitants of Europe were illiterate, even in the nineteenth century, so that even the spread of circulating libraries could hardly explain the enormous influence of romanticism and of the 'sexual revolution'. Could a mere change in literary fashion explain why, by the time Krafft-Ebing came to write *Psychopathia Sexualis*, the capital cities of Europe seemed to have an astonishingly high level of sexual perversion? Is it not more likely, for example, that the explanation lies in the increasing stresses of industrial society? (One answer to that objection is that cases of sex crime in the nineteenth century occurred in rural areas as frequently as in cities.) The hypothesis of morphic resonance suggests an altogether more satisfying explanation. If Sheldrake is correct, we would expect the 'imaginative revolution' to spread to every class of society, so that it would affect illiterate working men like Bichel and Pieydagnelle and Verzeni as much as aristocrats like Sade and Byron and Swinburne.

Fortunately – as we shall see in the next chapter – sex crime made a fairly slow start. But by the middle of the 1920s, it was apparent that a new type of human predator was at large, and that in some strange and frightening way, the human race had emerged into a new stage of lost innocence.

2

Mass Murder in the Nineteenth Century

As we have seen, the term 'serial killer' was first used in the late 1970s by FBI agent Robert Ressler, who was a member of the 'psychological profiling' team at the FBI headquarters in Quantico, Virginia. It was meant to describe someone who kills repeatedly and obsessively, usually with a sexual motive. Before that, such criminals were called 'mass murderers'. The disadvantage of this term was that it covered two types of killer: those who killed a number of people at roughly the same time, and those whose murders were spread over a lengthy period of time. Most 'mad gunmen' who run amok and shoot people at random belong to the first category. So does the unknown killer who murdered the whole Evangelista family in Detroit on 2 July 1930, chopping off the heads of all six. It would seem more sensible to describe this type of 'simultaneous' killer as a mass murderer, and reserve the term 'serial killer' for criminals like Jack the Ripper or the Boston Strangler.

Unfortunately, we need a third category for murderers who kill many victims over a long period, but whose motive is financial – like the French 'Bluebeard' Landru, or the 'Brides in the Bath' murderer Joseph Smith. They are certainly serial killers in the sense that their crimes occur 'serially' and not 'simultaneously', yet they lack the obsessive quality that is apparent in the crimes of Jack the Ripper. Perhaps the term 'multiple murderer' might serve to decribe them. But then a further objection arises: in many such cases, there *is* undoubtedly a sexual element present. Landru was as sexually vain as Casanova, and one of his victims was a poor servant girl who became his mistress and from whom he certainly obtained no financial gain. But if this book is not to become impossibly long, such borderline cases must be ignored.

One of the strangest cases of the early nineteenth century is undoubtedly that of the poisoner Anna Zwanziger, and if the sexologist Magnus Hirschfeld is correct when (quoting a State Attorney named Wulffen) he argues that 'the poisoner is actuated by inherent sexual–sadistic motives', then she may be regarded as one of the earliest examples of a serial killer.

The daughter of a Nuremberg innkeeper, Anna Maria Schonleben married a solicitor named Zwanziger who was also an alcoholic, and left her in penury. The constant reading of Goethe's gloomy novel *The Sorrows of Young Werther* led her to attempt suicide on two occasions, and she drifted from place to place, working as a domestic. In Weimar she fled with a diamond ring belonging to her employers, and a public advertisement of the theft came to the attention of her son-in-law, who ordered her out of his home. She found a job as a housekeeper with a judge named Glaser, in Rosendorf, Bavaria. It seems to have struck her that Glaser would make an excellent husband, but there was one impediment: Glaser's wife, from whom he was separated. Anna set about reconciling the two, and was soon able to welcome Frau Glaser back into her home with flowers strewn on the floor. Within a few weeks, Frau Glaser had died in agony. But Judge Glaser showed no sign of wanting to transfer his affection to his housekeeper, who was thin, sallow and 50 years old. Perhaps he was alerted by the stomach ailments suffered by guests after they had eaten meals prepared by Anna; at all events, she decided to move to the house of another judge at Sanspareil, a younger man named Grohmann, who was unmarried but suffered from gout. Regrettably, he had a fiancée, and Anna became increasingly jealous. When the marriage banns were published, Judge Grohmann died suddenly; his doctor attributed the death to natural causes.

Once more Anna found herself a job as a housekeeper to a member of the legal profession, a magistrate named Gebhard. He was also married, and his wife was pregnant; but her health was poor. When she died, accusing the housekeeper of poisoning her, no one took the accusations seriously. But

Gebhard, like the others, showed no sign of wanting to marry Anna. Moreover, as his servants expressed intense dislike of the skinny widow, and told stories of violent colics suffered by those who incurred her displeasure, he finally decided to dismiss her. Half an hour or so after she had left in a carriage for Bayreuth, most people in the household became ill – including the baby, to whom Anna had given a biscuit soaked in milk. It was recalled that Anna had refilled the salt box before she had left, and its contents were submitted for analysis. This was now a simple matter; there were at least three reliable tests for white arsenic. And this is what proved to have been mixed with the salt.

It took the law some time to catch up with her. She lived in Bayreuth a month, then went back to Nuremberg, then tried to persuade her son-in-law in Mainfernheim to take her in. But he was no longer her son-in-law, having divorced the daughter after she had been imprisoned for theft and swindling. Anna went back to Nuremberg, and was arrested on 18 October 1809. In her pockets were found a packet of tartar emetic and a packet of white arsenic.

For six months Anna Zwanziger simply denied everything. But at this point, Frau Glaser's body was exhumed, and the method of Valentine Rose, invented only four years previously, revealed arsenic in the vital organs – arsenic lingers on in the human body (including the hair) for a very long time. When told about this discovery, Zwanziger knew she was trapped; she fell to the floor in convulsions and had to be carried out of court. And a long and detailed confession followed – including the attempted poisoning of fellow servants and guests of her employers, apparently merely for her own entertainment. Sentenced to death, she remarked that it was probably just as well, since it would have been impossible for her to stop poisoning. She was beheaded, by sword, in 1811, more than two years after her arrest.

But such a bare account of her crimes begs the major question: why did she do it? Important clues can be found in Feuerbach's *Remarkable Criminal Trials*. His account of her life throws an entirely new light on the case, and even if we end by feeling no sympathy for the mass murderess, we at least begin to understand why she did it.

Born in Nuremberg in August, 1760, the daughter of an innkeeper, Anna was orphaned by the time she was five. After living for five years with various relatives, she was taken at the age of ten into the house of her guardian, a wealthy merchant, and there received a good education. But when she was fifteen, her guardian decided to marry her to a drunken lawyer named Zwanziger, who was more than twice her age. She objected, but finally had to give way.

Spending most of her days alone, while her husband was out drinking with cronies, she became an avid reader of novels and plays. She was so moved by Goethe's *Sorrows of Young Werther* – which had caused an epidemic of suicide ten years earlier – that she was also tempted to kill herself. She also read Richardson's novel *Pamela*, about a servant girl whose master tries hard to seduce her, but is finally so overcome by her virtue and goodness that he marries her. This also exercised a powerful influence on her. And she was deeply moved by Lessing's tragedy *Emilia Galotti*, about a girl who is pursued by a wicked prince (who has murdered her fiancé) and ends by persuading her father to kill her to prevent rape.

Her husband soon spent her inheritance – he was capable of drinking ten bottles of wine a day, and was soon a hopeless alcoholic. Anna was now forced to become a high-class prostitute to support her husband and two children – although she claimed she only slept with gentlemen. This, at least, was better than starving; she learned to use her physical charms to persuade men to support her. She even thought up a brilliant scheme involving a lottery of watches (we would call it a raffle), which once again made them prosperous; but her husband again spent the money. One lover, a lieutenant, persuaded her to leave her husband, but her husband then persuaded her to return. When she divorced him, he persuaded her to remarry him the next day. Clearly, Anna was not the ruthless bitch Feuerbach represents her as. She admits that she ended by feeling very fond of him.

Finally, Zwanziger died, and after eighteen years, Anna was left on her own. There was no national assistance or social security in Bavaria in 1796. She had to find a way to support herself and her children. She tried to set up a sweetshop in Vienna, but it failed. She became a housekeeper, but had to leave when she had an illegitimate child by a clerk – she put it into a founding's home, where it died.

Anna was now 38, still attractive to men. She found a 'protector' who installed her in lodgings, and tried to supplement her income with doll making. Tired of being a kept woman, she accepted an excellent job as a housekeeper in the home of a minister, but left after a few months – Feuerbach says because of her dirty habits, but more probably because she gave herself 'airs and graces'. For, as Feuerbach remarks perceptively, 'the insupportable thought of having fallen from her station as mistress of a house and family to the condition of a servant, worked so strongly on her feelings as to cause her to behave like a madwoman'. In short, the ups and downs of her life caused her to suffer a mental breakdown. 'She laughed, wept and prayed by turns. She received her mistress's orders with a laugh, and went obediently away, but never executed them.'

Anna was now definitely insane, and in her misery, she retained one basic obsession: to have a man to look after her and protect her. But her physical charms were fast disappearing. Her old 'protector' took her back for a while and got her pregnant again, then left her to chase an actress. She had a miscarriage. After that she attempted suicide by drowning, but was rescued by two fishermen. She was ill with fever for several weeks.

At the age of 44, no longer attractive, Anna was forced to take an ill-paid job as a housemaid; now she was at a kind of rock bottom. She stole a diamond ring and absconded. Her master reacted by placing a notice in the newspapers naming her as a thief, which destroyed any remnants of reputation she still possessed. Her son-in-law, with whom she was staying, threw her out.

In the following year, it looked as if fate had finally smiled on her. Working as a needlework teacher, she attracted an old general and became his mistress. Again she dreamed of security and being in charge of her own household. But he walked out on her, and ignored her letters.

And so, in 1807, after more miserable wandering from place to place, she found herself in Pegnitz, near Bayreuth, where she was offered a job by Judge Glaser. (To explain her preference for judges, we have to remember that her first husband was a lawyer.) At 50, the craving for security had given her the cunning of a madwoman. She poisoned the wife of Judge Glaser, hoping he would marry her – an insane hope, since she was now skinny, sallow and ugly. She moved on to the home of Judge Grohmann, who was unmarried and twelve years her junior. Now, surely, she had found the man who was destined to bring security to her old age . . .? Grohmann suffered from gout, and she enjoyed nursing him. She enjoyed nursing him so much that she began slipping small quantities of arsenic and antimony into his food. Eventually, she overdid it – this seems clear, since she can have had no reason to kill her meal ticket – and he died. Feuerbach says she appeared inconsolable, and this is almost certainly because she was.

This raises an interesting possibility. Was Anna herself an arsenic addict? We know that arsenic was widely used in the nineteenth century as a tonic, and that James Maybrick used it as a drug. If Anna used it herself, then it seems possible that she administered it to Grohmann to help his gout – in which case, she would have been devastated when it killed him.

With her security gone, Anna slipped deeper into madness. She had once been a mistress with servants, an attractive woman whom men had desired; now she was an unwanted nobody. Poisoning brought back once more some sense of self-respect and identity, of being in control of her own destiny – or at least, those of other people. In our own society she would have been confined in an asylum after her trial, and so found some kind of security in her final years. As it was, she knelt at the block, and her head fell into the headsman's basket. Perhaps the woman who had identified with Emilia Galeotti and Pamela felt that it was at least more appropriate than dying in a workhouse.

The year 1811, in which Anna Zwanziger was beheaded, was also the year in which England was shocked by one of the most horrific mass slaughters of the nineteenth century, the Ratcliffe Highway murders. Thomas De Quincey wrote a famous – if not completely reliable – account in the appendix to his essay 'On Murder Considered as one of the Fine Arts'.

Towards midnight on Saturday 7 December, 1811, 18-year-old Margaret Jewell, servant to the young Marr family (Timothy Marr ran a hosier's business in the Ratcliffe Highway), was sent out to purchase oysters for supper; diligent but unlucky in her quest at such a late hour, she returned to the Marr establishment at 1 a.m. to find the door locked and the house silent and dark. De Quincey, in his account, describes masterfully the girl's increasing sensation of horror and foreboding, particularly when recalling the sinister stranger she had seen prowling round the house earlier in the evening, and goes on (doubtless with dramatic licence) to relate how stealthy footsteps were heard from within the building, and how the hysterical servant's screams attracted passers-by and neighbours, so leading, within a few minutes, to the finding of the Marr family (Timothy, wife Cecilia, and young baby) together with their 13-year-old apprentice John Goen, all with their skulls smashed and throats cut; nothing had been taken from the premises. The whole of London, in fact, was appalled by the senseless slaughter, and when another family was murdered, obviously by the same hand, on 19 December, there was panic. Now the victims were an elderly publican Mr Williamson, his wife Catherine, and their maidservant, 50-year-old Bridget Harrington; the killer slipped into the inn, the King's Arms, 81 New Gravel Lane, shortly after closing time on 11 p.m.; Mr Williamson invariably left the front door open to 'oblige' the nocturnal imbiber. The Williamsons' lodger, 26-year-old John Turner, alone in his bedroom, and disturbed by unfamiliar sounds, crept downstairs and, himself unseen, saw a stranger, 'in creaking shoes', bending over one of the corpses; terrified but resolved to remain alive, he returned to his room and effected an escape by knotting his bedclothes together into a 'rope' by which he escaped through the window, dropping on to the local nightwatchman, George Fox, who immediately broke into the public house and found the corpses.

Even greater ferocity had been employed during the second series of murders; Bridget Harrington was almost decapitated, and Mr Williamson (who had evidently put up a struggle for life) savagely hacked in every limb. The couple's grandchild, 14-year-old Kitty Stillwell, had escaped the massacre, the killer apparently having been disturbed by the inquiring watchman. A sailor's maul was discovered by one of the bodies; it bore the initials 'JP' and was found to belong to a Swedish sailor, John Petersen, who, being then on the high seas, had a perfect alibi; he lodged when in London with a Mrs Vermiloe, and it was a fellow-lodger, John Williams, whom the police now suspected. Little is known of his interrogation (at Shadwell Police Office) save that he refused to answer several questions, although admitting that he spent much time at Williamson's tavern. He had been seen walking towards the King's Arms late on the evening of the murders, and had returned to his lodging in the early hours of the morning with a bloodied shirt – the result, Williams explained, of a card-game brawl. Arrested and taken to New Prison at Coldbath Fields, he committed suicide on 28 December by hanging himself from a wall-rail in his cell. He was accorded a suicide's burial, being transported by cart on the morning of 31 December through East End crowds to the cross-roads by Cannon Street and New Road (near present-day Cable Street) where he was buried in quicklime and a stake driven through his heart. (Cross-roads were traditionally selected for suicides so as to confuse their restless souls' sense of direction; one assumed that in Williams' case the stake – reminiscent of Bram Stoker – was an added measure taken by uneasy citizens to ensure his 'staying put'.) De Quincey, in 1854, described Williams as a grotesquely fey, thin, albino-faced creature, but in fact a contemporary print (drawn during the burial procession) shows a stocky, muscular, plebeian labourer-type spreadeagled in death upon a slanting shaft of wood.

The evidence against Williams was circumstantial; the killings terminated, however, upon his death. Popular with women, he had confided to a barmaid friend shortly after the Marr murders: 'I am unhappy, and can't remain easy.' A syphilitic, it has also been suggested that he killed out of a grudge towards humanity.

There is one point upon which De Quincey is obviously reliable: his account of the terror that spread all over the Home Counties as a result of the murders. There was nothing like it again until the crimes of Jack the Ripper. It underlines the point that although murder was common enough, crimes of real atrocity were rare.

Two decades after the crimes of Anna Zwanziger, another German, Gesina Gottfried, was challenging her supremacy as a mass poisoner. Gesina was born in a small town in North Germany. She seems to have had the temperament of Flaubert's Emma Bovary – desire for excitement, wealth, travel. She was attractive and had several suitors. From these, she chose a businessman named Miltenberg. By the age of twenty she had two children. But her husband was a drunkard, and his business was on the verge of bankruptcy. And, like many working-class husbands of the period, he beat his wife. One day, Gesina saw her mother using a white powder to mix bait for mice and rats.

She took some of it, and dropped it into a glass of her husband's beer. He was dead by the next morning. She now pursued a young friend of her husband's called Gottfried, who had displayed signs of being interested in her before Miltenberg's death. But Gottfried was shy and cautious. Her patience soon wore out, and she began to slip small quantities of the white powder, arsenic, into his drink. As he became more ill, he became more reliant on her, and her chances of administering minute doses of poison increased. When her parents got wind of the intimacy with Gottfried, they opposed it. Gesina did not hesitate for a moment; she got herself invited to supper, and dropped arsenic in their beer. Then, carried away with her new-found power, she went on to poison her own two children. Gottfried, now permanently weakened, was persuaded to marry her; a day later, he was dead. His wife succeeded to his property, which had been her central motive all along.

A merchant she met at Gottfried's funeral began to court her. She did not like him, but he had more money than her former lover. She poisoned him with the same patient deliberation that she had already shown in the case of Gottfried. When her brother turned up one day, on leave from the army and drunk, she disposed of him quickly with a glass of poisoned beer – she was not prepared to risk having him around while she poisoned her current lover. The latter was persuaded to make a will in her favour, then he died. It is not known exactly how many more she poisoned. Charles Kingston mentions in *Remarkable Rogues* another lover, a woman to whom she owed five pounds, and an old female acquaintance who tried to borrow money. She moved from place to place during the course of these murders, and ended in Bremen, where she poisoned the wife of her employer, a master wheelwright named Rumf. The wife died shortly after giving birth to a baby, so Gesina was not suspected; it was assumed to be puerperal fever. Rumf's five children died one by one after Gesina took charge of the family. Rumf himself began to feel rather ill after Gesina's meals. One day, when she was away, he tried a meal of pork, and was delighted that it seemed to agree with him. He was so pleased with his pork that he went to look at the joint in the larder when he came home from work the next day. Gesina had sprinkled it with white powder in the meantime, and Rumf knew it had not been there that morning. So he took the leg along to the police, who quickly identified the powder as arsenic. When arrested, Gesina made no attempt to deny her guilt; on the contrary, she confessed to her various crimes with relish. Her execution followed as a matter of course.

A Dutch nurse named van der Linden – of whom, unfortunately, little is known – surpassed Zwanziger and Gottfried by poisoning more than a hundred.

No account of nineteenth-century crime would be complete without at least some reference to the most celebrated of French criminals, Pierre-François Lacenaire. As far as we know, Lacenaire killed only three people, so only just qualifies as a multiple killer. But his attitude of God-defying rebellion, so reminiscent of Sade, and of many serial killers of the late twentieth-century, gives him a psychological significance out of all proportion to his crimes.

In December 1834, a widow named Chardon, and her homosexual son – a begging-letter writer – were stabbed and hatcheted to death in Paris. Chief Inspector Louis Canler found no clues to the killer (or killers).

Two weeks later, a young bank messenger was attacked when he went to call at a flat in rue Montorgueil; someone closed the door behind him and someone stabbed him in the back, while someone else tried to grab his throat. The clerk was strongly built, and managed to struggle free; his assailants ran away. The flat, it turned out, had been rented by a man who called himself 'Mahossier'. Canler searched the registers of dozens of cheap hotels looking for the name – for even if it was an alias, the chances were that the man would use it more than once. He found it at a place called Mother Pageot's. She claimed she was unable to recall Mahossier, but *did* recall his companion, a big, red-headed man. Canler recalled that a big, red-headed man called François was in gaol at the moment, and went to see him. 'Why did you use an alias when you stayed at Mother Pageot's?' he asked, and François replied: 'Because I'd be stupid to use my real name . . .' So François *was* Mahossier's companion.

Mother Pageot now admitted she *did* recall François's companion (the presence of her husband, who hated the police, had made her deny it earlier). He was a courteous man with a high forehead and a silky moustache.

Casual conversation with many criminals finally convinced the detective that this description corresponded to that of a man who also called himself Gaillard. He managed to locate a room in which Gaillard had stayed, and found some republican songs and satirical verses – in Mahossier's handwriting.

Eventually, François broke, and told Canler that a man named Gaillard had murdered the Chardons. Now, for the first time, Canler knew that the murder of the Chardons and the attack on the bank messenger were connected. He also learned that Gaillard had a rich aunt who lived in the rue Bar-du-Bec. This aunt was able to tell Canler that she lived in fear of being murdered by her unsavoury nephew, and that his name was Pierre-François Lacenaire.

Lacenaire was soon arrested for trying to pass a forged bill. And when Lacenaire learned that he had been betrayed, he made a full confession, implicating a crook named Avril in the murder of the Chardons, and François in the attack on the bank messenger.

In jail, awaiting his execution, he wrote his memoirs (which Dostoyevsky later printed in a magazine he edited, to increase circulation). They are a remarkable document, and tell us all we need to know of the man. Lacenaire was born in Lyon, the second child of a well-to-do merchant, in 1800. His elder brother was the favourite son; he developed a sense of injustice that soon expressed itself in thieving. One day his father pointed out the scaffold to him and told him he would end on it if he did not change his ways. Lacenaire was a lone wolf; a description in his memoirs is typical: 'All night I strode along the Quais. I lived ten years in an hour. I wanted to kill myself, and I sat on the parapet by the Pont des Arts, opposite the graves of those stupid heroes of July . . . Henceforth my life was a drawn-out suicide; I belonged no longer to myself, but to cold steel . . . Society will have my blood, but I, in my turn, shall have the blood of society.' He read Rousseau and became a revolutionary. But he had a resentment against life. Failures filled him with a desire to 'spite' life. (He did not believe in God, and so could not spite God.) This in turn was rationalized into a hatred of Society. It would have been useless to point out to him that 'Society' does not exist, and that even if it did, living the life of a criminal would not spite it.

Somewhat more rationally, he hated the complacent rich;

but then, neither of the crimes for which he was hanged was committed against the rich. But he describes in his memoirs how his first murder was of a 'bourgeois' whom he pushed into the river after stealing his watch.

A point came where he decided to be a criminal in the same way that another man might decide to devote his life to poetry. He observed his own lack of 'feeling' about life (like Meursault, the bored hero of Camus' *l'Étranger*), that he had killed two men in duels without the slightest feeling (did Dostoyevsky borrow some of Stavrogin's character from Lacenaire?). He was basically a poet and a metaphysician; he wanted a meaning in life. He surveyed life and found it inscrutable, revealing no sign of an important destiny for himself. And he craved revenge. But he lacked the discipline to carry out his ideal purpose; if he had possessed literary discipline he might have been an earlier Lautreamont or Rimbaud; perhaps even a Swift or Voltaire. He wanted to be a scourge of Society, its sternest critic. In a sense, he was trying to put into effect the gospel of Shaw's Undershaft, the armament manufacturer in *Major Barbara* who said 'Thou shalt starve ere I starve,' and who then used every means in his power to achieve success. (Having achieved it, he became, as he pointed out, a sane and useful member of Society.) But Lacenaire was too much driven by emotion to make a good job of it, and finally brought himself to the guillotine.

The execution was carried out, unannounced, on a cold and foggy January morning. Lacenaire watched Avril's head fall into the basket without flinching; but when he himself knelt under the blade, there was an accident that would have broken another man's nerve; as the blade fell, it stuck half-way, and had to be hauled up again; Lacenaire was looking up at it as it dropped and severed his head.

Here, as in the case of Sade, we encounter the attempt of a man who lacks self-discipline to justify his lack of discipline with a philosophy of revolt. Lacenaire is the first major criminal in whom we encounter the 'philosophy of resentment', which was to become so common in serial killers from Panzram to Manson. We shall encounter it many times in the course of this book.

Oddly enough, one of the first attempts to understand the psychology of the serial killer was made by a novelist – Émile

Zola, who was intrigued by the case of Eusebius Pieydagnelle (which we have already encountered) and by the Jack the Ripper murders. Both cases formed the inspiration for his novel *La Bête Humaine* (1890) – the hero of which is named Jack. Jacques Lantier, 'the human beast', is possessed by an overpowering urge to kill women. At sixteen he is playing with a young relative when she falls down.

> In a flash he had seen her legs revealed to the thigh, and he had flung himself at her. The following year he recalled honing a knife to thrust into another girl's throat. That was a fair-haired little thing whom he saw pass his door every morning. She was very plump-bosomed and very pink, and he had actually selected the spot, a mole directly under her ear. Then came others, and yet others, a succession of nightmares, so many women whose flesh he had touched, to be possessed with that sudden lust for murder . . . One in particular, recently married, who had sat near him at a variety show and laughed loudly. In order not to slit her belly open he had been obliged to run away in the middle of an act . . .

One day he tries to kiss his step-cousin Flora, who lives in the same house – in fact, she finds him very attractive. As he struggles with her, her bodice is torn so her breasts are exposed; then, as she lies there, prepared to yield to him, he seizes a pair of scissors and is about to stab her when he is suddenly overcome with horror, and flees. But later in the novel, he is unable to resist the temptation when he sees his mistress naked, and stabs her to death.

Zola's description of Lantier's torments has remarkable power; no one has ever succeeded in capturing with such realism the urges of a 'sex maniac'. Yet the sheer force of the writing, the insight with which Zola succeeds in describing a man who feels impelled to stab women, again makes us aware of the question: why? And the answer, surely, is that when sexual desire is raised to this morbid intensity, the mere act of copulation seems insufficient. Lovemaking takes place by mutual consent; his step-cousin Flora is willing to yield and allow herself to be possessed. But Lantier's desire is so violent that lovemaking by mutual consent seems an anticlimax. He wants to possess her – as Zola says – to the point of destruction.

This is, in fact, the mechanism of all sexual 'perversion'. Even in someone as apparently 'normal' as D. H. Lawrence, there are hints – in *Women in Love* and *Lady Chatterley's Lover* – that he finds sodomy a more exciting experience than vaginal sex. And anyone who has read *Sons and Lovers* can easily grasp why this is so. For Lawrence, sex is conquest – the triumphant male being permitted to possess the yielding female. His relation with Frieda was so important because she was also a German aristocrat and another man's wife. Possessing her, persuading her to abandon her husband and children, was an enormous stimulus to the working-class Lawrence's self-esteem. The same is true of the gamekeeper Mellors' relationship with Lady Chatterley. So persuading her to permit sodomy – as Mellors does – is an additional proof of conquest. The sexual urge and the urge to self-esteem are inextricably intertwined.

An equally important clue is offered by Krafft-Ebing when he is discussing fetishism. He speaks of a man who could only make love to a woman who was wearing a silk dress, petticoats and a corset, and comments: 'The reason for this phenomenon is apparently to be found in the mental onanism of such individuals. In seeing innumerable clothed forms they have cultivated desires before seeing nudity.'

What is interesting here is that there is obviously something not quite-right about Krafft-Ebing's explanation. It is not because such individuals have cultivated desires before seeing nudity – 99 per cent of young males experience sexual desire before seeing nudity. It is surely because a nude woman is comparatively easy to get used to. *Consciousness is too feeble; it is quickly taken over by habit.* For the same reason, the normal male is not excited by a woman in a bikini, although he *would* be excited by a glimpse up the skirts of the same woman – even if she happened to be wearing a bikini underneath. This is because a sense of 'forbiddenness' is created by the fact that she is clothed, and the excitement is caused by the *contrast* between her skirts and the nakedness underneath. Krafft-Ebing's fetishist needs to make love to a woman in a silk dress, petticoats and a corset (but without knickers) because his first love affair (at fourteen) was with a girl who kept most of her clothes on during lovemaking in case they were interupted. This naturally produced a feeling of alertness, as well as 'wickedness'.

In short, the basic answer is that consciousness is always falling into the sleep of habit, and has to be awakened from this sleep by the contrast produced by 'forbiddenness'. The weaker the individual, the more his consciousness falls asleep, and the more forbiddenness is required to shake it awake.

The habit of novel-reading that was created by *Pamela* meant that gentle, sensitive individuals could compensate for the boredom of everyday life by retreating into a world of daydreams. This was good for the imagination but bad for the ability to cope with the everyday world. 'Escapism' leads to the weakening of the crude vital impulse. This is why so many 'sensitive plants' in the nineteenth century were killed off by their inability to deal with everyday problems. As Tolstoy points out, the healthy peasant avoids these problems – which is why Tolstoy himself decided to become a healthy peasant, and spent more time chopping wood than writing books.

So the steep increase in sexual perversion in the nineteenth century can be directly linked to the development of imagination which was the nineteenth century's most interesting achievement. Does this mean that the development of imagination should be seen as a doubtful blessing? Clearly not; Tolstoy's woodchopping did no harm to his imagination. The problem lies in the tendency of weak individuals to make imagination an excuse for running away from everyday life – in other words, for excusing their own laziness. This is the essence of the 'Outsider' problem.

In short, the rise in sexual perversion and sex crime in the nineteenth century was an unfortunate consequence of its development in the realm of imagination. Krafft-Ebing is correct when he links fetishism with onanism (masturbation). W. B. Yeats admits in his autobiography that the retreat into the fairylands of his early poetry was accompanied by excessive masturbation. And in the original version of *Sons and Lovers*, Lawrence describes becoming sexually excited as he pulls on the stockings of his girlfriend. Once we understand this 'compensatory' mechanism, a great deal about the rise of sex crime suddenly becomes clear.

In the year following the trial of Eusebius Pieydagnelle, 1872, Vincent Verzeni was arrested for sadistic sex crimes, as described above. But it was in the following year that Thomas W. Piper, America's first multiple sex killer, committed his first murder. Piper was the sexton in the Warren Avenue Baptist church in Boston. He was 26 years old, had a large black moustache, and was described as a 'melancholy young man'.

He had apparently been regarded as a quiet and agreeable young man until the 16-year-old daughter of a local minister met him in the vestry one Sunday evening and hurried home to tell her parents that 'she thought he was a very bad man indeed, and was afraid of him'. What Piper proposed to her is unrecorded, but is not difficult to guess.

The Revd. Mr Pentecost, the Baptist minister, later described how he had found Piper reading a novel called *Cord and Creese*; the prosecutor, who read it as a preparation for the trial, commented that its publishers 'ought to be sent to the House of Correction for the rest of their lives'. It also emerged later that Piper kept a bottle with a mixture of whisky and laudanum in a dark corner under his pew.

On the snowy night of 5 December 1873, a man walking along a lonely road near Dorchester heard a thrashing noise in the bushes, and when he went to investigate, was startled when a cloaked figure jumped up and ran away. By the light of his lantern, the man saw the body of a girl lying at his feet in a clearing, the snow around her head covered in blood. The nakedness of the lower part of her body made it clear that he had interrupted a rape. The man gave chase, but the fugitive disappeared over the railway embankment. The girl was later identified as a domestic servant named Bridget Landregan. Nearby was found a 'bat-like' club stained with blood.

A few hours later another unconscious girl was found. This time, it seemed, the rapist had accomplished his purpose. The girl was rushed to hospital, and eventually survived. Her name was Sullivan, but further details were withheld out of respect for her privacy.

In early January 1874, a prostitute named Mary Tynam was found unconscious in her bed; it looked as if she had been battered unconscious with the back of an axe. She also survived the attack, but was too brain-damaged to describe what had happened. She died a year later in an asylum.

The police actually traced the bat-like club to the shop of Thomas Piper, and detained him. But they were unable to find conclusive evidence against him, and he was released.

No more was heard of the sexual crime wave for another year. On the afternoon of 23 May 1875, children began to arrive at the Baptist church for Sunday school. Among them was 5-year-old Mabel Young, accompanied by her aunt, Miss

Augusta Hobbs. When the class was over, Miss Hobbs went to speak to the Revd. Pentecost. When she had finished, she looked around for her niece, and found that she was nowhere to be seen. She and several other women began to search, and to call Mabel's name.

Up in the room below the belfry, Thomas Piper was standing with the unconscious child at his feet. Her head was bleeding from the blow he had struck with the bat-like club, and he threw a piece of newspaper on to the blood. Then he heard a voice downstairs calling 'Mabel'. He opened the door and peeped through; a lady named Mrs Roundy was below. He closed the door and waited. Then, from behind him, he heard the sound of a child crying out. He had been convinced that Mabel was dead – he later admitted that he had heard her 'bones crack' as he hit her twice. In a panic, he picked up the body and carried it under his arm up into the belfry, fumbling frantically with the trapdoor; then he startled the pigeons by throwing Mabel among them.

He went downstairs to the gallery and looked out of the window; it was a drop of about twenty feet to the ground. But he was desperate; he climbed out, hung on to the window ledge, then dropped into the street, landing outside the church door. There he encountered a boy who asked if he could see the pigeons; Piper refused brusquely and went into the church. There, in a state of obvious agitation, he began rearranging the chairs, ignoring the excitement of the people who were looking for Mabel Young.

Someone rushed in from outside. 'We can hear the cries of a child from the tower.' They ran upstairs, but found the tower door locked. Piper claimed that he had lost the key, which he usually kept in a drawer. Some young men forced open the door, and a few moments later, found the battered child. Mabel was carried to a nearby house. The following day she died – like Mary Tynam, without being able to describe what had happened. But by now the police had found the bloodstained 'bat' in the room below the belfry, and Thomas Piper was under arrest.

Before his trial, Piper tried to commit suicide by cutting his wrists with a piece of metal; prompt action saved his life. At his trial in December 1875, the jury was unable to agree. But in a second trial the following January, after evidence about the 'evil literature' he read, Piper was sentenced to death.

On 7 May 1876, Piper sent for his attorney, and told him that he had also been guilty of the previous three sex attacks – on Bridget Landregan, on the girl called Sullivan and on Mary Tynam. He described how, after drinking a mixture of whiskey and laudanum, he had followed Bridget Landregan down the street until she reached the lonely lane through the woods, then knocked her down with the club. The rape had been interrupted, so he ran away. Later the same evening he had attacked the other girl.

According to Piper, the murder of Mary Tynam was not a sex crime. He had already spent the night with her, and after leaving, collected the axe, went back to her room, and battered her unconscious, taking back the money.

He had lured Mabel Young to the belfry by asking her if she wanted to see the pigeons, taking her in by another door in the church so as not to be seen. But, he insisted, he had *not* jumped from the window – the witness who claimed he had seen him land in the street was lying. He concluding his confession by sighing: 'I am a very bad man.'

Piper showed the investigators where he had buried the axe that killed Mary Tynam. Three days later, he was hanged.

Early accounts of the case – with titles like *The Boston Fiend* – are understandably reticent about the sexual motive. Crime historian Jay Robert Nash makes up for this by adding that Piper also confessed to the rape of several children.[1] Richard Dempewolff's chapter in *Famous Old New England Murders* (1942) is also inclined to reticence, but scatters enough clues to clarify the picture. To begin with, Piper admitted that he made the 'bat-like club' three days before attacking Bridget Landregan with the intention of killing someone. This is obviously a euphemism for raping someone. After the interrupted rape, 'being dissatisfied, I made another assault on a girl.'

Asked about the attack on Mabel, Piper said: 'I have not got there yet', then went on to explain that he had a 'strange mania for setting fires', and that just over a week after the rape, he had set fire to the Concord Hall, then, when this was blazing, gone to a nearby shop and tried to start another fire – this second one 'did not burn well'. More than anything else, this

[1] *Bloodletters and Badmen* (M. Evans, Inc., New York, 1973).

makes clear that Piper was a sadistic sex criminal. Pyromania is a well-known form of sexual perversion, and almost without exception, the pyromaniac has an orgasm while watching the fire. Peter Kürten, the Düsseldorf sadist, interspersed murders and violent attacks with setting fire to haystacks and buildings.

The murder of Mary Tynam presents the most interesting puzzle. Piper said he battered her with an axe to get his money back, and this sounds plausible until we look at it more closely. He had spent the night in her room; he crept out in the dawn, and went home for an axe. Would anyone take such a risk – since he was likely to be seen returning and then leaving again – for a few dollars? It sounds far more likely that the same 'mania' that led him to batter two other women and to start fires made him return for the axe. Like Pieydagnelle – and Zola's Jacques Lantier – Piper was driven by a desire to cause injury, to batter women insensible.

The murder of Mabel Young was not a matter of sudden impulse. Several witnesses claimed to have seen the 'cricket bat' leaning against the wall of the vestibule earlier in the day. He approached Mabel before the Sunday school class to ask her if she would like to look at the pigeons afterwards – probably aware of her aunt's habit of engaging the clergyman in conversation. Here, as in the case of Bridget Landregan, he was interrupted before he could complete the rape. So he hid the body, hoping to return later, then dispose of it. But Mabel recovered consciousness and cried out, and Piper's career as a sex attacker came abruptly to an end.

Also in Boston, in April 1874, a 14-year-old boy named Jesse Pomeroy was questioned about the murder of a 4-year-old named Horace Mullen, whose mutilated body had been found in a marsh near Dorchester. Two years earlier, Pomeroy had been sentenced to reform school for enticing seven young boys to lonely places, where they were stripped and beaten, or sadistically injured with a knife. Pomeroy was a tall, gangling boy with a hare lip and a 'white eye'. When he was taken into custody, a knife with bloodstains was found on him; mud on his shoes was similar to that of the marsh where the child's body had been discovered. Plaster casts of footprints were taken, and they proved to be Jesse Pomeroy's.

Pomeroy lived with his mother, a poor dressmaker. She had moved from a house on Broadway Street, south Boston. When the landlord sold the property in July 1874, labourers digging in the cellar found the remains of a girl of about 10. She proved to be a neighbour of the Pomeroys called Patricia Curran, and she had vanished in the previous March. Pomeroy finally confessed to her murder, and to that of Horace Mullen. He admitted that he was driven by an overwhelming desire to inflict pain, and that he chose children because they were easy to overpower.

Pomeroy was sentenced to death, but on appeal this was reduced to a life sentence. He spent most of his imprisonment in solitary confinement, and 'became a highly educated man' through reading. But he made several attempts to escape. The most ambitious involved gaining access to a gas pipe behind a granite block in the wall of his cell, and filling his cell with gas, after which he struck a match. He was hoping that the explosion would blow open the door; it did, but it also blew Jesse Pomeroy out of it. He was badly injured, but recovered. One newspaper report stated that other prisoners were burnt to death in their cells, but this seems unlikely. Pomeroy was finally transferred from the Charleston prison to the Bridgewater State mental hospital. He died there in 1932, after fifty-two years in prison.

In Paris on 15 April 1880, a 4-year-old girl named Louise Dreux vanished from her home in the Grenelle quarter. The following day, neighbours complained of the black smoke pouring from the chimney of a retarded 20-year-old youth named Louis Menesclou, who lived on the top floor of the same building as the Dreux family. When police entered his room they found a child's head and entrails burning in the stove. A forearm was in Menesclou's pocket, and other parts of the body were found in the toilet. In Menesclou's room the police found a poem that contained the lines 'I saw her, I took her.' Menesclou admitted to strangling the child and sleeping with her corpse under his bed. He indignantly denied raping her, but became embarrassed when asked why the child's genitals were missing. Menesclou had been suffering from convulsions from the age of nine months, and came of a family with a history of insanity and alcoholism; his mother had periods of 'mania' when menstruating. He had spent some time in a reformatory, and also in the marines, but proved 'lazy and intractable'. After his execution, his brain was examined, and found to have various 'morbid' abnormalities.

* * *

Twenty years after the execution of Boston bellringer Thomas Piper, an oddly similar case achieved nationwide – in fact worldwide – publicity. Again the central character was a respectable young churchgoer. Theodore Durrant was a medical student, and a Sunday school teacher in the Emanuel Baptist church in San Francisco. He was devoting his romantic attentions to an attractive girl called Blanche Lamont, who had some misgivings about him because he had once made immoral proposals to her during a walk in the park – in fact, she had refused to speak to him for several weeks.

On 3 April 1895, at 4.15 in the afternoon, he met Blanche out of her cookery class, and they were seen to enter the Baptist church together – Durrant had a key. Three-quarters of an hours later, the church organist arrived and found the young man looking pale and shaken – he explained that he had accidentally inhaled some gas. Blanche was nowhere to be seen, and Durrant later insisted he had no idea where she was.

Only a week later, Blanche's friend Minnie Williams accompanied Theodore Durrant into the church. The following morning, women who had come to decorate the church for Easter found Minnie, half naked, in the library, whose walls were covered with blood; half a knife blade was still in her breast. Further search revealed Blanche's naked body in the belfry, perfectly preserved by the cold; she had died from strangulation. Durrant was arrested at a militia training camp and swore his innocence of both murders. But at least fifty witnesses had seen him with both girls immediately before they disappeared.

Durrant's clothes proved to be free of bloodstains. But another young lady to whom Durrant had been attracted was able to suggest an explanation. She described how Durrant had taken her into the church library, excused himself for a while, then reappeared naked. She had fled screaming. He had clearly done the same thing with Blanche and Minnie, then killed them.

Durrant was found guilty and sentenced to death; in January 1898, after a series of appeals, he was finally hanged.

The evidence presented in court allows us an insight not only into Durrant's psychology, but into this whole problem of the rise of sex crime. The fact that he had been seen by so many witnesses indicates that the murders were not carefully planned. The number of young ladies who came forward and revealed that Durrant had proposed that they should enter the library for a 'physical examination' leaves no doubt that he was a highly sexed and intensely frustrated young man who had a strong desire to expose himself. Even so, it requires a considerable effort of imagination to grasp what it must have been like to be a young man of normal sexual impulses in the San Francisco of the late nineteenth century. Police Captain Thomas S. Duke, who describes the case in *Celebrated Criminal Cases of America*, mentions that he has a photograph of Durrant taken at a picnic when he was sixteen, and that 'the position in which he posed proves conclusively that he was a degenerate even as a child'. He presumably means that Durrant had his hand in his pocket in a position that suggested he was holding his penis. It seems incredible that, a mere sixty years later, when San Francisco was at the forefront of the movement for sexual freedom, couples openly had sexual intercourse in the Golden Gate Park.

Suddenly, we can begin to understand the social context of the rise in sex crime in the nineteenth century. As late as the 1860s, men and women bathed naked at respectable seaside resorts. Then sex became taboo; young men were expected to spend years wooing a girl and submitting to long engagements before they were permitted to see her naked. The novelist Robert Musil catches something of the frustration that ensued when he writes of the sex murderer Moosbrugger (in *The Man Without Qualities*): 'Girls were something that he could only look at . . . Now one must just try what that means. Something that one craves for, just as naturally as one craves for bread or water, is only there to be looked at. After a time, one's desire for it becomes unnatural. It walks past, the skirts swaying round its ankles. It climbs over a stile, becoming visible right up to the knees . . .'

'Something that one craves for, just as naturally as for bread or water . . .' If Durrant had dared to assert that his desire for sex was 'natural', he would have been told that, on the contrary, it was sinful. And so, as Musil says, the desire for it became 'unnatural' – inflamed by auto-erotic fantasies – until he began to risk his reputation by openly propositioning young ladies of the church. This is itself reveals how 'unnatural' the desire had become, since the chance of any of them agreeing to a mutual 'examination' was a million to one. But the alternative – picking up a prostitute – almost certainly struck Durrant as unthinkable; his rigid Christian upbringing would probably have made him impotent.

And so eventually, the craving to see a girl naked – and to have her see him naked – becomes so obsessive that he risks everything by inviting her into the library, then takes off his clothes and presents himself to her. Understandably, she screams and runs away – what else did he expect her to do? But now he knows that if he wants to take a girl's virginity – which he imagines as a supreme ecstasy that will sweep away years of frustration like a flash flood – he will have to compel her to stay in the library, and silence her screams.

When it finally happens, it is unplanned. So many girls have declined to accompany him into the library that he expects Blanche to refuse him too. This explains why he meets her openly, travels on a tram car, and is seen entering the church with her. But this time, when he enters the room naked and she screams, he flings himself on her and chokes her into silence. Ten minutes later, with a naked body at his feet, he is suddenly convinced that he will be interrupted at any moment. He grabs her by the hair and drags her up to the belfry (strands of her hair were found caught in the splintered wood of the stairs). When the organist arrives, Durrant is pale and trembling, but Blanche – and her clothes and school books – have been concealed . . .

Convinced that the body will be found at any moment – particularly when he is told that witnesses saw him with Blanche that afternoon – he prepares for arrest. In fact, nothing happens; days go by and he is still free. But he knows that this cannot go on for ever. Sooner or later, the bellringer will notice a smell of decay and will investigate. Now, living in a kind of nightmare, he feels that if he is going to be hanged, he might just as well repeat the pleasure of possessing one of these infinitely desirable young churchgoers who seem to embody the allure of the whole female species . . . And so Blanche's best friend is persuaded to enter the library. This time he is so certain that he will be caught that he makes no attempt at concealment; he stabs her to death, rapes her, then leaves the body on the floor. And the next day, as he goes off to the militia camp, he is aware that he has literally traded his life for just two sexual experiences . . . Does he count 'the world well lost?' Probably not. But then, as Musil suggests, deprivation-needs have turned a natural desire into something that is so morbid and unnatural that it has become an insane compulsion. Theodore Durrant encapsulates the sexual problem of the whole Victorian era.

The rise of sex crime presented the police with a completely new problem. In the average murder case, there is some connection between the killer and the victim, and the task of the detective is to find it. But in sex murders, the victim is chosen at random. So unless the criminal can be caught in the act, or unless he leaves some obvious clue behind, the chances of catching him are a thousand to one. It was the fiasco of the hunt for Jack the Ripper that suddenly made this obvious.

If the Ripper murders produced dismay at Scotland Yard, the police must have been encouraged by their success in arresting two more mentally disturbed killers, both of whom have been suspected of being Jack the Ripper.[1] Dr Thomas Neill Cream, who obtained his medical degree in Canada, was a bald-headed, cross-eyed man, who arrived in London in 1891. He picked up young prostitutes in the Waterloo Road area, and persuaded them to take pills containing strychnine, apparently from motives of pure sadism; four of them died in agony. But Cream was undoubtedly insane: he wrote confused letters accusing well-known public men of the murders, and went to Scotland Yard to complain of being followed by the police. A young constable who had followed him from the house where two prostitutes had been poisoned explained why he suspected the cross-eyed doctor, and Cream's arrest followed swiftly. After his arrest, he wrote to a prostitute to tell her that his name would be cleared by a Member of Parliament, who had over 200 witnesses to prove his innocence. Cream should undoubtedly have been found guilty but insane; he told one prostitute that he lived only for sex, and was probably suffering from tertiary syphilis, with softening of the brain. After his execution in 1892, it was frequently suggested that Cream was

[1] For a comprehensive discussion of the murders and suspects, see *Jack the Ripper: Summing Up and Verdict*; by Colin Wilson and Robin Odell (Transworld, London, 1987).

Jack the Ripper. This seems unlikely for two reasons. No sex murderer has been known to change his *modus operandi* from stabbing to poisoning, and at the time of the Ripper murders, Cream was serving a term in Joliet penitentiary in Chicago for the murder by poison of his mistress's husband. So although Cream's last words on the scaffold were: 'I am Jack the . . .', there can be no doubt that he is the least likely suspect.

George Chapman, a Pole whose real name was Severin Klossowski, *was* in Whitechapel at the time of the Ripper murders, and was suspected at the time by Detective Inspector Frederick Abberline, one of the officers in charge of the investigation. A doctor named Thomas Dutton suggested to Abberline that he should be looking for a Russian or Pole with a smattering of surgical knowledge – it was often asserted, inaccurately, that the mutilations showed medical skill. Chapman, who was 23 in 1888, practised the trade of 'barber-surgeon' – one writer asserts that he rented a shop in the basement of George Yard Buildings, the slum tenement where Martha Turner was stabbed 39 times. But in 1888, Klossowski had no known criminal record. In 1890, he married (bigamously) and went to America. In 1892 he returned to England, met Annie Chapman, a woman with a private income, and allowed her to set him up in a barber's shop in Hastings. But in 1897, she died after a great deal of vomiting; her death was attributed to consumption. In the following year, Klossowski – who was now a publican – married his barmaid Bessie Taylor; she died in 1901 after a long period of vomiting and diarrhoea. He married another barmaid, Maud Marsh, but his mother-in-law became suspicious when her daughter fell ill, and even more suspicious when she herself almost died after drinking a glass of brandy prepared by Chapman (as he now called himself) for his wife. When Maud Marsh died, an autopsy revealed arsenic poisoning, and Chapman was arrested. A second inquest revealed that the poison was antimony, not arsenic; and when the bodies of the previous two women were exhumed, it was discovered that they had also died from antimony poisoning. Although there was no obvious motive for the murders, the evidence against Chapman was overwhelming, and he was sentenced to death.

Abberline had continued to regard Chapman as a prime suspect in the Ripper murders; he had questioned the woman who was his mistress at the time – Lucy Baderski – and she said that Chapman was often out until four in the morning. When Chapman was arrested by Detective Inspector George Godley, Abberline remarked to Godley: 'You've got Jack the Ripper at last.' But although Chapman certainly had the opportunity to commit the Whitechapel murders, the same objection applies to him as to Neill Cream: a sadistic killer who has used a knife is not likely to switch to poison.

So although the police had reason to congratulate themselves on the arrest of two multiple murderers, they must also have recognized that detecting a poisoner is far easier than tracking down a sadistic 'slasher'. It was obvious that the Ripper-type killer was by far the most serious challenge so far to the science of crime detection.

This view was confirmed by a series of murders which began in France in 1894. In May of that year, a 21-year-old mill-girl named Eugénie Delhomme was found behind a hedge near Beaurepaire, south of Lyon; she had been strangled, raped and disembowelled. And during the next three years, the 'French Ripper' went on to commit another ten sex murders of the same type. The next two victims were teenage girls; then a 58-year-old widow was murdered and raped in her home. In September 1895, the killer began killing and sodomizing boys, also castrating them: the first victim was a 16-year-old shepherd, Victor Portalier. Later that month, back near the scene of his first crime, he killed a 16-year-old girl, Aline Alise, and a 14-year-old shepherd boy. Soon after this, he was almost caught when he tried to attack an 11-year-old servant girl, Alphonsine-Marie Derouet, and was driven off by a gamekeeper, who was walking not far behind her. A man was stopped by the police, but allowed to go after producing his papers. He was, in fact, the killer – a 26-year-old ex-soldier (and ex-inmate of an asylum) named Joseph Vacher, whose face was paralysed from a suicide attempt with a revolver.

Imprisonment as a vagrant stopped the murders for six months, but almost as soon as he was released he raped and disembowelled Marie Moussier, the 19-year-old wife of a shepherd; three weeks later, he murdered a shepherdess, Rosine Rodier. In May 1897 he killed a 14-year-old tramp, Claudius Beaupied, in an empty house, and the body was not found for more than six months. The final victim was Pierre Laurent, another 14-year-old shepherd boy, who was sodomized and castrated. On 4 August 1897, he came upon an Amazonian peasant woman named Marie-Eugénie Plantier, who was gathering pine cones in a forest near Tournon, and threw himself on her from behind, clamping a hand over her mouth. She freed herself and screamed; her husband and children, who were nearby, came running, and her husband threw a stone at Vacher, who in turn attacked him with a pair of scissors. Another peasant appeared, Vacher was overcome and dragged off to a nearby inn. There he entertained his captors by playing the accordion while awaiting the police. The 'disemboweller of the south-east' (*l'éventreur du sud-est*) was finally trapped.

There had been a massive manhunt for the disemboweller, and dozens of vagabonds had been arrested on suspicion. An extremely accurate description of Vacher had been circulated, which mentioned his twisted upper lip, the scar across the corner of his mouth, the bloodshot right eye, the black beard and unkempt hair. Yet he committed eleven murders over three years, and if he had not been caught by chance, might well have gone on for another three.

The great pathologist Alexandre Lacassagne spent five months studying Vacher, and concluded that he was only pretending to be insane. Vacher insisted that he had been abnormal since being bitten by a mad dog as a child. Tried for the murder of Victor Portalier, he was sentenced to death in October 1898 and guillotined on 31 December. But there seems to be little doubt that Lacassagne was mistaken; Vacher was undoubtedly insane, and his random mode of operation had enabled him to play hide-and-seek with the combined police forces of south-eastern France.

It was a disturbing lesson for the police and the crime scientists; in the 1890s, the random sex killer constituted a virtually insoluble problem.

Yet new scientific discoveries were beginning to provide the police with some of the techniques they needed. In the year of the Ripper murders, Sir Francis Galton went to Paris to study a new method of criminal identification called 'Bertillonage' (because it was invented by Alphonse Bertillon) which consisted of a record of the criminal's physical statistics – height, colour of eyes, circumference of head, and so on. Galton saw that fingerprinting would be a far simpler method, if only he could devise some method of classifying the prints. He did this over the next three years, and published his results in 1891. Soon after the turn of the century, the new method was being used by Scotland Yard and other police forces in Europe.

So was an equally exciting discovery: the ability to distinguish human from animal bloodstains, developed by a young Viennese doctor named Paul Uhlenhuth. His starting-point was the discovery that blood serum – the colourless liquid that separates out when blood is left to stand – develops 'defensive reactions' against various proteins, including other types of blood. If a chicken's blood is injected into a rabbit, the rabbit's blood will develop defences. If some of the rabbit's blood is then left in a test tube so the serum separates out, and a drop of chicken's blood is added to the serum, it will defend itself by turning cloudy. So if a rabbit is injected with human blood, its serum will turn cloudy when human blood is added. If an unknown bloodstain is dissolved in salt water, and added to the rabbit's serum, it is instantly apparent whether or not it is a human bloodstain.

The first murderer to be trapped by this discovery was a serial sex killer who was driven by the same sadistic impulse as Jack the Ripper.

Around 1 p.m., on 9 September 1898, the mothers of two small girls in the village of Lechtingen, near Osnabrück, became worried when they failed to return home. And when Jadwiga Heidemann and her neighbour Irmgard Langmeier called at the school, they learned that their children had not been to classes that day. The whole village joined in the search, and at dusk, the dismembered body of 7-year-old Hannelore Heidemann was found in nearby woods – some parts had been scattered among the trees. An hour or so later, the remains of 8-year-old Else Langmeier were found hidden in bushes; she had also been mutilated and dismembered.

The police learned that a journeyman carpenter named Ludwig Tessnow had been seen entering Lechtingen from the direction of the woods, and that his clothes seemed to be bloodstained. Tessnow was soon arrested, but insisted that the stains on his clothes were of brown woodstain. A powerful microscope would have revealed that this was a lie, but the Osnabrück police knew nothing of forensic science, and let him go for lack of evidence. But a policeman visited

Tessnow in his workshop, and contrived to knock over a tin of woodstain so that it ran down Tessnow's trousers. In fact, it dried exactly like the other stains. And since Tessnow continued to work in the village, his neighbours concluded that he must be innocent. He remained until January 1899, when he went to work elsewhere.

Two and a half years later, a frighteningly similar crime occurred near the village of Göhren, on the Baltic island of Rügen. On Sunday 1 July 1901, two brothers named Peter and Hermann Stubbe, aged 6 and 8, failed to return home for supper, and parties went into the nearby woods, carrying burning torches and shouting. Shortly after sunrise, the bodies of both children were found in some bushes, their skulls crushed in with a rock and their limbs amputated. Hermann's heart had been removed, and was never found.

The police interviewed a fruit seller who had seen the two boys in the late afternoon; they were talking to a carpenter named Tessnow. Tessnow had recently returned to Rügen, after travelling around Germany, and was regarded as an eccentric recluse. Another neighbour recollected seeing Tessnow returning home in the evening, with dark spots on his Sunday clothes.

Tessnow was arrested and his home searched. Some garments had been thoroughly washed, and were still wet. And a stained pair of boots lay under the stone kitchen sink. Tessnow remained calm under questioning, and seemed to be able to account satisfactorily for his movements on the previous Sunday. Again, he insisted that stains on his clothing were of woodstain.

Three weeks before the murders, seven sheep had been mutilated and disembowelled in a field near Göhren, and their owner had arrived in time to see a man running away; he swore he could recognize him if he saw him again. Brought to the prison yard at Greifswald, the man immediately picked out Tessnow as the butcher of his sheep. Tessnow steadfastly denied it – he was not the sort of man, he said, to kill either sheep or children . . .

The examining magistrate, Johann-Klaus Schmidt, now recalled a case in Osnabrück three years before, and contacted the police there. When they told him that the name of their suspect was Ludwig Tessnow, Schmidt had no doubt that Tessnow was the killer. But how to prove it? At this point, his friend Prosecutor

Ernst Hubschmann of Greifswald recollected reading about a new test for human bloodstains. And at the end of July, Uhlenhuth received two parcels containing Tessnow's Sunday clothes, brown-stained working overalls, and various other items, including a bloodstained rock, probably the murder weapon. It took Uhlenhuth and his assistant four days to examine over a hundred spots and stains, dissolving them in distilled water or salt solution. The overalls were, as Tessnow had claimed, stained with wood dye. But they also found 17 stains of human blood and nine of sheep's blood. It took the Rügen prosecutor a long time to bring Tessnow to trial – German justice was extremely slow-moving – but when he eventually appeared in court, Uhlenhuth was there to give evidence and explain his methods. Ludwig Tessnow was found guilty of murder and sentenced to death.

3

Mass Murder in Europe

In the first decade of the twentieth century, sex crime was still something of a rarity. It seems to have been the triggering mechanism of the First World War that finally released the age of sex crime on Europe. The dubious distinction of being its inaugurator probably goes to the Hungarian Bela Kiss, whose crimes presented an apparently insoluble problem to the police of Budapest.

In 1916, the Hungarian tax authorities noted that it had been a long time since rates had been paid on a house at 17 Rákóczi Street in the village of Cinkota, ten miles north-west of Budapest. It had been empty for two-years, and since it seemed impossible to trace the owner, or the man who rented it, the district court of Pest-Pilis decided to sell it. A blacksmith named Istvan Molnar purchased it for a modest sum, and moved in with his wife and family. When tidying-up the workshop, Molnar came upon a number of sealed oildrums behind a mess of rusty pipes and corrugated iron. They had been solidly welded, and for a few days the blacksmith left them alone. Then his wife asked him what was in the drums – it might, for example, be petrol – and he settled down to removing the top of one of them with various tools. And when Molnar finally raised the lid, he clutched his stomach and rushed to the garden privy. His wife came in to see what had upset him; when she peered into the drum she screamed and fainted. It contained the naked body of a woman, in a crouching position, the practically airless drum had preserved it like canned meat.

Six more drums also proved to contain female corpses. Most of the women were middle-aged; none had ever been beautiful.

And the police soon realized they had no way of identifying them. They did not even know the name of the man who had placed them there. The previous tenant had gone off to the war in 1914; he had spent little time in the house, and had kept himself to himself, so, nobody knew who he was. The police found it difficult even to get a description. They merely had seven unknown victims of an unknown murderer.

Professor Balazs Kenyeres, of the Police Medical Laboratory, was of the opinion that the women had been dead for more than two years. But at least he was able to take fingerprints; by 1916, fingerprinting had percolated even to the highly conservative Austro-Hungarian Empire. However, at this stage, fingerprinting was unhelpful, since it only told them that the women had no criminal records.

Some three weeks after the discovery, Detective Geza Bialokurszky was placed in charge of the investigation; he was one of the foremost investigators of the Budapest police. He was, in fact, Sir Geza (*lovag*), for he was a nobleman whose family had lost their estates. Now he settled down to the task of identifying the female corpses. If Professor Kenyeres was correct about time of death – and he might easily have been wrong, since few pathologists are asked to determine the age of a canned corpse – the women must have vanished in 1913 or thereabouts. The Missing Persons' Bureau provided him with a list of about 400 women who had vanished between 1912 and 1914. Eventually, Bialokurszky narrowed these down to fifteen. But these women seemed to have no traceable relatives. Eventually, Bialokurszky found the last employer of a 36-year-old cook named Anna Novak, who had left her job abruptly in 1911. Her employer was the widow of a Hussar colonel, and she still had Anna's 'servant's book', a kind of identity card that contained a photograph, personal details, and a list of previous employers, as well as, their personal comments. The widow assumed that she had simply found a better job or had got married. She still had the woman's trunk in the attic.

This offered Bialokurszky the clue he needed so urgently: a sheet from a newspaper, *Pesti Hirlap*, with an advertisement marked in red pencil 'Widower urgently seeks acquaintance of mature, warm-hearted spinster or widow to help assuage loneliness mutually. Send photo and details, Poste Restante Central P.O. Box 717. Marriage possible and even desirable.'

Now, at last, fingerprinting came into its own. Back at headquarters, the trunk was examined, and a number of prints were found; these matched those of one of the victims. The Post Office was able to tell Bialokurszky that Box 717 had been rented by a man who had signed for his key in the name of Elemer Nagy, of 14 Kossuth Street, Pestszenterzsebet, a suburb of Budapest. This proved to be an empty plot. Next, the detective and his team studied the agony column of *Pesti Hirlap* for 1912 and 1913. They found more than twenty requests for 'warm-hearted spinsters' which gave the address of Box 717. This was obviously how the unknown killer of Cinkota had contacted his victims. On one occasion he had paid for the advertisement by postal order, and the Post Office was able to trace it. (The Austro-Hungarian Empire at least had a super-efficient bureaucracy.) Elemer Nagy had given an address in Cinkota, where the bodies had been found, but it was not of the house in Rákóczi Street; in fact, it proved to be the address of the undertaker. The killer had a sense of humour.

Bialokurszky gave a press conference, and asked the newspapers to publish the signature of 'Elemer Nagy'. This quickly brought a letter from a domestic servant named Rosa Diosi, who was 27, and admitted that she had been the mistress of the man in question. His real name was Bela Kiss, and she had last heard from him in 1914, when he had written to her from a Serbian prisoner of war camp. Bialokurszky had not divulged that he was looking for the Cinkota mass murderer, and Rosa Diosi was shocked and incredulous when he told her. She had met Kiss in 1914; he had beautiful brown eyes, a silky moustache, and a deep, manly voice. Sexually, he had apparently been insatiable . . .

Other women contacted the police, and they had identical stories to tell: answering the advertisement, meeting the handsome Kiss, and being quickly invited to become his mistress, with promises of marriage. They were also expected to hand over their life savings, and all had been invited to Cinkota. Some had not gone, some had declined to offer their savings – or had none to offer – and a few had disliked being rushed into sex. Kiss had wasted no further time on them, and simply vanished from their lives.

In July 1914, two years before the discovery of the bodies, Kiss had been conscripted into the Second Regiment of the Third Hungarian Infantry Battalion, and had taken part in the long offensive that led to the fall of Valjevo; but before that city had fallen in November, Kiss had been captured by the Serbs. No one was certain what had become of him after that. But the regiment was able to provide a photograph that showed the soldiers being inspected by the Archduke Joseph; Kiss's face was enlarged, and the detectives at last knew what their quarry looked like. They had also heard that his sexual appetite was awe-inspiring, and this led them to show the photograph in the red-light district around Conti and Magyar Street. Many prostitutes recognized him as a regular customer; all spoke warmly of his generosity and mentioned his sexual prowess. But a waiter who had often served Kiss noticed that the lady with whom he was dining usually paid the bill . . .

Now, at last, Bialokurszky was beginning to piece the story together. Pawn tickets found in the Cinkota house revealed that the motive behind the murders was the cash of the victims. But the ultimate motive had been sex, for Kiss promptly spent the cash in the brothels of Budapest and Vienna. The evidence showed that he was, quite literally, a satyr – a man with a raging and boundless appetite for sex. His profession – of plumber and tinsmith – did not enable him to indulge this appetite, so he took to murder. He had received two legacies when he was 23 (about 1903) but soon spent them. After this, he had taken to seducing middle-aged women and 'borrowing' their savings. One of these, a cook named Maria Toth, had become a nuisance, and he killed her. After this he had decided that killing women was the easiest way to make a living as well as indulge his sexual appetites. His favourite reading was true-crime books about con-men and adventurers.

Bialokurszky's investigations suggested that there had been more than seven victims, and just before Christmas 1916, the garden in the house at Cinkota was dug up; it revealed five more bodies, all of middle-aged women, all naked.

But where was Kiss? The War Office thought that he had died of fever in Serbia. He had been in a field hospital, but when Bialokurszky tracked down one of its nurses, she remembered the deceased as a 'nice boy' with fair hair and blue eyes, which seemed to suggest that Kiss had changed identity with another soldier, possibly someone called Mackavee; but the new 'Mackavee' proved untraceable. And although sightings of Kiss were reported from Budapest in 1919 – and even New York as late as 1932 – he was never found.

The first decade of the twentieth century also saw the emergence – and decline – of two female mass murderers: Jeanne Weber and Belle Gunness. Belle – whom we shall consider in the next chapter – seems to have killed purely for profit. Jeanne Weber, on the other hand, was undoubtedly a genuine serial killer – that is, one who kills repeatedly with a sexual motive. As in the case of her German predecessor, Anna Zwanziger (whose crimes took place precisely a century earlier), the sexual motive is less obvious than in the case of male serial killers; but no one who studies the case of the 'ogress of the Goutte D'Or' can fail to be aware of its existence.

In the Goutte d'Or, a slum passageway in Montmartre, lived four brothers named Weber, one of whose wives, Jeanne Weber, had lost two of her three children, and consoled herself with cheap red wine. Just around the corner lived her brother-in-law Pierre and his wife. On 2 March 1905, Mme Pierre asked her sister-in-law if she would baby-sit with her two children, Suzanne and Georgette, while she went to the public *lavoir*, the 1905 equivalent of a launderette. Mme Pierre had been there only a short time when a neighbour rushed in and told her that 18-month-old Georgette was ill – she had heard her choking and gasping as she passed. The mother hurried home, and found her child on the bed, her face blue and with foam around her mouth; her aunt Jeanne was massaging the baby's chest. Mme Pierre took the child on her lap and rubbed her back until her breathing became easier, then went back to the launderette. But when she returned an hour later, with a basket of clean washing, Georgette was dead. The neighbour observed some red marks on the baby's throat, and pointed them out to the father, but he seems to have shrugged it off. Nobody felt any suspicion towards Jeanne Weber, who had behaved admirably and apparently done her best.

Nine days later, when both parents had to be away from home, they again asked Aunt Jeanne to baby-sit. Two-year-old Suzanne was dead when they returned, again with foam around her mouth. The doctor diagnosed the cause of death as convulsions. Aunt Jeanne appeared to be dazed with grief.

Two weeks later, on 25 March, Jeanne Weber went to visit another brother-in-law, Leon Weber, and was left with the seven-month-old daughter Germaine while her mother went shopping. The grandmother, who lived on the floor below, heard sudden cries, and hurried upstairs to find Germaine in 'convulsions', gasping for breath. After a few minutes of rubbing and patting, the baby recovered, and the grandmother returned to her own room. Minutes later, as she talked with a neighbour, she once more heard the child's cries. Again she hurried upstairs and found the baby choking. The neighbour who had accompanied her noticed red marks on the child's throat. When the parents returned, Germaine had recovered.

The following day, Jeanne Weber came to enquire after the baby. And, incredibly, the mother again left her baby-sitting. When she returned, her child was dead. The doctor diagnosed the cause as diphtheria.

Three days later, on the day of Germaine's funeral, Jeanne Weber stayed at home with her own child Marcel; he suffered the same convulsions, and was dead when the others returned.

A week later, on 5 April, Jeanne Weber invited to lunch the wife of Pierre Weber, and the wife of another brother-in-law, Charles. Mme Charles brought her ten-month-old son Maurice, a delicate child. After lunch, Jeanne baby-sat while her in-laws went shopping. When they returned, Maurice was lying on the bed, blue in the face, with foam around his lips, breathing with difficulty. The hysterical mother accused Jeanne of strangling him – there were marks on his throat – and she furiously denied it. So Mme Charles swept up her child in her arms, and hastened to the Hospital Brétonneau. She was sent immediately to the children's ward, where a Dr Saillant examined the marks on Maurice's throat. It certainly looked as if someone had tried to choke him. And when he heard the story of the other four deaths in the past month, Dr Saillant became even more suspicious. So was his colleague Dr Sevestre, and together they informed the police of this unusual case. Jeanne Weber was brought in for questioning, and Inspector Coiret began to look into her background. When he learned that all three of her children had died in convulsions, and that three years earlier, two other children – Lucie Alexandre and Marcel Poyatos – had died in the same mysterious way when in the care of Jeanne Weber, suspicion turned to certainty. The only thing that amazed him was that the Weber family had continued to ask her to baby-sit; they were either singularly fatalistic or criminally negligent. But then, the death of Jeanne's own son Marcel had dispelled any suspicions that might have been forming. When Examining Magistrate Leydet was informed of this, he found himself wondering whether this was precisely why Marcel had died.

The magistrate decided to call in a medical expert, and asked Dr Léon Henri Thoinot, one of Paris's most distinguished 'expert witnesses', second only to Paul Brouardel, the author of a classic book on strangulation and suffocation. Thoinot began by examining Maurice, who had now fully recovered. The child seemed perfectly healthy, and it was hard to see why he should have choked. Thoinot decided it could have been bronchitis. Next, the bodies of three of the dead children – Georgette, Suzanne and Germaine – were exhumed. Thoinot could find no traces of strangulation on their throats. Finally, Thoinot studied the body of Jeanne Weber's son Marcel; again he decided there was no evidence of strangulation – for example, the hyoid bone, which is easily broken by pressure on the throat, was intact.

The accusations of murder had caused a public sensation; Jeanne Weber was the most hated woman in France. The magistrate, Leydet, had no doubt whatsoever of her guilt. Yet at her trial on 29 January 1906, Thoinot once again stated his opinion that there was no evidence that the children had died by violence, while the defence lawyer Henri Robert – an unscrupulous man – intimidated the prosecution witnesses until they contradicted themselves. The 'ogress of the Goutte d'Or' – as public opinion had christened her – was acquitted on all charges. The audience in the courtroom underwent a change of heart and cheered her. And Brouardel and Thoinot collaborated on an article in a medical journal in which they explained once again why Jeanne Weber had been innocent.

The public did not think so. Nor did her husband, who left her. Jeanne Weber decided that she had better move to some place where she was not known. She was a flabby, sallow-faced woman, who had little chance of attracting another male. And at that point, rescue arrived out of the blue. A man named Sylvain Bavouzet wrote to her from a place called Chambon – in the department of Indre – offering her a job as his housekeeper; it seemed he had been touched by her sad tale, and by the injustice that had almost condemned her to death. In the spring of 1907, Jeanne Weber – now calling herself by her unmarried name Moulinet – arrived at the farm of Sylvain Bavouzet, and understood that the offer had not been made entirely out of the goodness of his heart. It was a miserable, poverty-stricken place, and Bavouzet was a widower with three children, the eldest an ugly girl with a hare lip. What he wanted was cheap labour and a female to share his bed. But at least it was a home.

A month later, on 16 April 1907, Bavouzet came home to find that his 9-year-old son Auguste was ill. He had recently eaten a large amount at a local wedding feast, so his discomfort could have been indigestion. The child's sister Louise was sent to the local town Villedieu to ask the doctor to call. But Dr Papazoglou gave her some indigestion mixture and sent her on her way. Hours later, Sylvain Bavouzet arrived, in a state of agitation, and said the boy was worse. When Papazoglou arrived, Auguste was dead, and the new housekeeper was standing by the bedside. The child was wearing a clean shirt, tightly buttoned at the collar, and when this was opened, the doctor saw a red mark around his neck. This led him to refuse a death certificate. The next day, the coroner, Charles Audiat, decided that, in spite of the red mark, Auguste's death was probably due to meningitis.

The dead boy's elder sister Germaine, the girl with the hare lip, hated the new housekeeper. She had overheard what 'Mme Moulinet' had told the doctor, and knew it was mostly lies. Her brother had not vomited just before his death – so requiring a change of shirt. Precisely how Germaine realized that Mme Moulinet was the accused murderess Jeanne Weber is not certain. One account of the case declares that she came upon Jeanne Weber's picture by chance in a magazine given to them by neighbours; another asserts that she searched the housekeeper's bag and found press cuttings about the case. What is certain is that she took her evidence to the police station in Villedieu and accused Mme Moulinet of murdering her brother.

An examining magistrate demanded a new autopsy, and this was performed by Dr Frédéric Bruneau. He concluded that there *was* evidence that Auguste had been strangled, possibly with a tourniquet. (Doctors had found a scarf wrapped around the throat of Maurice Weber, the child who had survived.) Jeanne Weber was arrested. The new accusation caused a sensation in Paris.

Understandably, Henri Robert, the man who had been

responsible for her acquittal, felt that this reflected upon his professional integrity. Thoinot and Brouardel agreed. They decided that the unfortunate woman must once again be saved from public prejudice. Robert agreed to defend her for nothing, while Thoinot demanded another inquest. He carried it out three and a half months after the child's death, by which time decay had made it impossible to determine whether Auguste Bavouzet had been strangled. Predictably, Thoinot decided that Auguste had died of natural causes – intermittent fever. More doctors were called in. They agreed with Thoinot. The latter's prestige was such that Examining Magistrate Belleau decided to drop the charges against Jeanne Weber, although he was personally convinced of her guilt. Henri Robert addressed the Forensic Medicine Society and denounced the ignorance and stupidity of provincial doctors and magistrates. Jeanne Weber was free to kill again.

History repeated itself. A philanthropic doctor named Georges Bonjeau, president of the Society for the Protection of Children, offered her a job in the children's home in Orgeville. There she was caught trying to throttle a child and dismissed. But, like Thoinot and Henri Robert, Bonjeau did not believe in admitting his mistakes and he kept the matter to himself.

She became a tramp, living by prostitution. Arrested for vagrancy, she told M Hamard, chief of the Sûreté, that she had been responsible for the deaths of her nieces. Then she withdrew the statement, and was sent to an asylum in Nanterre, from which she was quickly released as sane. A man named Joly offered her protection, and she lived with him at Lay-Saint-Remy, near Toul, until he grew tired of her and threw her out. Again she became a prostitute, and finally met a lime-burner named Émile Bouchery, who worked in the quarries of Euville, near Commercy. They lived in a room in a cheap inn run by a couple named Poirot. One evening, 'Mme Bouchery' told the Poirots that she was afraid that Bouchery meant to beat her up – as he did periodically when drunk – and asked them if their seven-year-old son Marcel could sleep in her bed. They agreed. At 10 o'clock that evening, a child's screams were heard, and the Poirots broke into Mme Bouchery's room. Marcel was dead, his mouth covered in bloodstained foam. Mme Bouchery was also covered in blood. A hastily summoned doctor realized that the child had been strangled, and had bitten his tongue in his agony. It was the police who discovered a letter from *maître* Henri Robert in Mme Bouchery's pocket, and realized that she was Jeanne Weber.

Once again, the reputations of Thoinot and Robert were at stake (Brouardel having escaped the public outcry by dying in 1906). Incredibly, both declined to admit their error. They agreed that the evidence proved unmistakably that Jeanne Weber had killed Marcel Poirot, but this, they insisted, was her first murder, brought about by the stress of years of persecution. It is unnecessary to say that the French press poured scorn on this view. Yet such was the influence of Thoinot that Jeanne Weber was not brought to trial; instead she was moved out of the public gaze to an asylum on the island of Maré, off New Caledonia in the Pacific. There she died in convulsions two years later, her hands locked around her own throat.

In the year of Jeanne Weber's death, another mass murderer had already embarked on a career that would end under the guillotine. Henri Désiré Landru's motives were strictly commercial; after an unsuccessful career as a swindler, which earned him a number of jail terms, Landru decided that dead victims would have no chance to complain. Between 1914 and 1918 he seduced and murdered ten women (as well as the son of one of his victims) for the sake of their property and savings. He was guillotined in 1922, and his nickname – Bluebeard – has since been applied to all mass killers with purely commercial motives.

England's most celebrated Bluebeard had already gone to the gallows seven years earlier. George Joseph Smith was a petty crook with a cockney accent, and he had served two jail sentences for persuading women to steal for him when he decided that murder was less complicated. His method was to marry a lonely spinster or widow, persuade her to make a will in his favour, then drown her in the bath tub by raising her ankles. His first two victims died in seaside resorts, with minimal publicity. Smith's mistake was to move to Highgate, in London, for his third murder, and the resulting publicity in *The News of the World* drew the attention of relatives of previous victims, who informed the police. Smith was tried only for the death of his last victim, but his fate was sealed when the judge ordered that details of the previous 'accidents' should be revealed to the jury.

The interest of these two mass murderers, in this particular context, is that women who had escaped with their lives testified that both had curiously hypnotic powers, and that a single penetrating glance could deprive them of their will. By contrast, most serial murderers have clearly failed to master the art of seduction – often because they have been physically repulsive.

Yet there is, nevertheless, a basic similarity. Landru, like Casanova, found seduction the most fascinating of sports. The way women yielded and melted as he gazed into their eyes was a kind of drug. He might be a crook and a failure, but when he saw that yielding look in a woman's eyes, he felt like a god. And so, as in the case of the serial killer, the mass murderer kills out of a form of inadequacy.

At the same time as Landru was pursuing his career as a lady-killer in Paris, another mass murderer of women was operating in Berlin. The full details of Georg Karl Grossmann's crimes will never be known, since he committed suicide before he came to trial. But it is clear that, in terms of the number of victims, he is one of the worst mass murderers of the century.

In August 1921 the owner of a top-storey flat in Berlin near the Silesian railway terminus heard sounds of a struggle coming from the kitchen and called the police. They found on Grossmann's kitchen bed (a camp bed) the trussed-up carcass of a recently killed girl, tied as if ready for butchering.

Grossmann had been in the place since the year before the war. He had stipulated for a separate entrance, and had the use of the kitchen, which he never allowed his landlord to enter. He was a big, surly man who kept himself to himself, and lived by peddling. He was not called up during the war (which led the other tenants to assume – rightly – that he had a police record), and lived in self-chosen retirement. He picked up girls with great regularity (in fact, he seldom spent a night alone). He killed many of these sleeping partners and sold the bodies for meat, disposing of the unsaleable parts in the river. (The case became known as *Die Braut auf der Stulle* – 'the bread and butter brides', since a companion for a night is known as a 'bride' in Germany.) At the time of his arrest, evidence was found which indicated that three women had been killed and dismembered in the past three weeks.

Grossmann was a sexual degenerate and sadist who had served three terms of hard labour for offences against children, one of which had ended fatally. He also indulged in bestiality. It is of interest that Grossmann was indirectly involved in the famous 'Anastasia' case – the Grand Duchess Anastasia who was believed by many to be the last surviving member of the Tsar's family. At one point it was announced that 'Anastasia' was really an impostor named Franziska Schamzkovski, a Polish girl from Bütow in Pomerania. Franziska's family were told that their daughter had been murdered by Grossmann on 13 August 1920; an entry in his diary on that date bore the name 'Sasnovski'. Anastasia's enemies insisted that this was not true, that Franziska and Anastasia were the same person.

Grossmann laughed when he heard the death sentence, and afterwards had fits of manic behaviour. He hanged himself in his cell. The number of his victims certainly runs into double figures, since he was 'in business' throughout the war.

The defeat of Germany in 1918 brought soaring inflation, which was soon followed by revolution. In October 1918 the sailors at Kiel mutinied when ordered to go to sea and fight the British. In November an independent socialist republic was proclaimed in Bavaria. On 9 November the Kaiser abdicated and a republic was proclaimed in Berlin. Two days later, the Armistice was signed. In January, there was a communist (Spartacist) revolt, which was crushed by the army; two of its leaders, Rosa Luxemburg and Karl Liebknecht, were killed while under arrest. Magnus Hirschfeld described going to the mortuary with a patient in search of her son, and seeing hundreds of bodies, many mutilated or with their throats slit. He also observed some young girls who kept rejoining the queue who filed past the unidentified bodies, obviously fascinated by the sight of naked male bodies, and unable to remove their eyes from genitals that were swollen with haemorrhages and decay.

In the same paragraph, Hirschfeld also describes standing beside the wife of a State Attorney at an execution, and observing her heaving chest and ecstatic groans as the condemned man was dragged to the executioner's block, followed by a convulsion like a sexual orgasm as the axe fell. These two descriptions – in juxtaposition – suddenly afford us one of those flashes of insight into the rise of sex crime. There is no great gulf between bored working girls, inexperienced and sexually frustrated enough to be fascinated by swollen male genitals, and a State Attorney's wife, so morbidly aroused by the thought of a man's execution that horror turns into sexual excitement. Sade once admitted that his senses were too coarse and blunt, so that it required a strong stimulus to arouse them. But there is a sense in which this is true for all human beings. We are all too mechanical, too prone to sink into a state that is akin to hypnotism. Intense sexual stimulus causes a sudden awakening. A man who catches sight of a woman undressing through a lighted window – as Ted Bundy did – is literally 'galvanized'. This in turn explains why Sade was stimulated by blows; they stirred his jaded senses to sudden attention.

Moreover, having experienced such a sensation once, human beings discover that nature will obligingly reproduce the sexual excitement at the mere thought of the original stimulus – for example, swollen genitals or a man losing his head. The link is created by association of ideas, and persists through habit. And so the straightforward sexual urge – which is, after all, designed simply to ensure the continuation of the species – turns into a kind of monstrous parody of itself.

The mechanism can be seen clearly in the most notorious German sex killer of the post-war period, Fritz Haarmann.

The city of Hanover, in Lower Saxony, was reduced to unparalleled chaos by the poverty and starvation that followed the First World War. It became the centre of crime, black marketeering and prostitution – particularly male prostitution.

In the summer of 1924, the city's inhabitants were disturbed by rumours of a mass murderer. Five skulls were found on the banks of the River Leine within a few weeks, and boys playing in marshland found a sack full of human bones. The skulls were those of boys, one as young as eleven. These skulls had been cleanly removed with a sharp instrument. At first it was suggested that they might have been planted as a joke by medical students, but the fact that fragments of flesh were adhering to some of them made this unlikely. Superstitious servant girls began to talk about a 'werewolf'. Finally, a massive search of the surrounding countryside was organized on Whit Sunday. After more human bones had been found, the river was dammed, and the mud searched by workers. More than five hundred parts of corpses were found. Medical examination revealed that these came from at least twenty-two bodies. And some of the remains were still fresh.

In fact, the police had a suspect – an overweight middle-aged man with a Hitler moustache named Fritz Haarmann, who was known to be homosexual – as the killer obviously was. He was often seen in the company of young men, whom he picked up at the railway station, and witnesses also reported seeing him throw a heavy sack into the river. But the thought that Haarmann might be the 'werewolf' caused some embarrassment, since Haarmann had been working for the police for the past five years – in fact, some people knew him as 'Detective Haarmann'. He mixed freely with the police, and was also a leading member of a patriotic organization called the Black Reichswehr, which was opposed to the French occupation of the Ruhr. He even ran a detective bureau called the Lasso Agency, in partnership with a police official. If Haarmann *was* 'the werewolf' there would be a great many red faces.

The police finally decided to try and trap Haarmann by means of two young policemen from Berlin. But before this could happen, Haarmann fell into their hands by accident. On 23 June 1924, he approached the police and demanded that they arrest a 15-year-old boy called Fromm, who was travelling on forged papers. The boy was taken to the police station at two in the morning. He countered by alleging that he had spent several nights in Haarmann's apartment, and that Haarmann had repeatedly performed homosexual acts on him. He had also held a knife against his throat and asked him if he was afraid to die. The vice squad used this allegation as an excuse to keep Haarmann in custody. The police then hastened to search his room in the Neuerstrasse. There they found many bloodstains, as well as a great deal of clothing that obviously belonged to young men. Confronted with this evidence, Haarmann pointed out that he made a living both as a butcher and an old clothes merchant. And after several days of questioning, the police had to admit that they had no evidence to link Haarmann with the human bones and skulls.

The breakthrough came by chance. A couple named Witzel were the parents of a teenage boy named Robert Witzel, who had disappeared. Robert Witzel's friend had finally admitted to the parents that both he and Robert had been seduced by 'Detective Haarmann.' Some of Witzel's clothes had been found in Haarmann's room, but Haarmann professed to know nothing about them. Now, as Herr Witzel and his wife sat outside the office of Police Commissioner Ratz, a young man walked past them, and Frau Witzel recognized the jacket he was wearing as belonging to her son. When the young man – named Kahlmeyer – was asked where he had obtained the jacket, he acknowledged that he had been given it by Haarmann, who had also given him a pair of trousers in which he had found an identification card belonging to Robert Witzel.

Confronted with this evidence, Fritz Haarmann suddenly broke down, and admitted that he had murdered young men in the act of sexual intercourse; he said that he would suddenly be overcome with an insane desire to bite their throats and strangle them.

Even now, Haarmann refused to make a full confession. When pressed, he burst into tears or violent rages. It took seven days of non-stop interrogation finally to wear him down. Finally, his resistance collapsed, and he took the police to a site where he had hidden the skeleton of a youth of 16 – his last victim, Eric de Vries, killed only a week before his arrest. He now claimed that he had asked the police to take young Fromm into custody because he knew that he would be unable to resist the urge to kill him that night.

There was something oddly childish about Haarmann; it was clear that, in spite of considerable cunning and impudence, he was in some ways mentally retarded. His confession also made it clear that he was – like Zola's *bête humaine* – in the grip of a sadistic obsession that swept him away and made him kill his sex partners.

Haarmann was also known to be intimáte with a young man called Hans Grans, who had not been present at Haarmann's arrest, since he was in prison for stealing a watch. Haarmann's confession soon made it clear that Grans knew about his strange sexual habits, and had often procured murder victims for him. Two weeks after Haarmann's arrest, Grans was also taken into custody.

A psychologist named Theodore Lessing was fascinated by the case. Lessing was also a philosopher – strongly influenced by Schopenhauer and Nietzsche – and a pacifist. He was struck by the parallel between Haarmann's crimes and the carnage of the recent world war. He received permission to interview Haarmann, and got to know him well. This is what he learned.

Friedrich Heinrich Karl Haarmann was born on 25 October 1879, the youngest of six children. His father was a retired railway worker, cantankerous, miserly and inclined to drunkenness. He had married a woman seven years his senior, who brought him a small fortune in property; even so, he remained an indefatigable satyr, even bringing his mistresses into the home. In later life he contracted syphilis.

Haarmann senior seems to have detested the gentle, rather effeminate Fritz, who was pampered by his mother. Fritz, in turn, hated his father. And although he loved to play with dolls, he also had a morbid streak – he liked to tie up his sisters so they looked like bodies, and to tap on windows at night, pretending to be a ghost.

He seems to have suffered from meningitis as a child, and after his death, examination of his skull revealed that the brain touched it in several places, probably as a result of the illness. Again, when he was a 16-year-old recruit in the army, he began to show signs of mental illness and was admitted to hospital. Haarmann blamed a blow on the head which had occurred during bar exercises in the gymnasium, and sunstroke. In fact, both probably reactivated the problems due to the meningitis. Many murderers have changed character after a blow on the head.

This may also explain Haarmann's lifelong record as a child molester. Lessing learned that he had been seduced at school when he was 7 years old – Lessing does not say by whom – and that the offences against children began after a sexual experience with a 'mannish woman', who lured him into her room when he was 16. It seems possible that the experience suddenly convinced Haarmann that he was not heterosexual, and that the attempts to seduce children resulted from a kind of revulsion.

At 17 he was charged with acts of indecency performed with children he had lured into doorways or cellars. He was found to be suffering from 'congenital mental deficiency' (in fact, probably a result of the meningitis) and placed in an asylum at Hildesheim. Because he was regarded as dangerous, he was transferred for a while into a Hanover hospital – presumably with better security – then back to Hildesheim. He developed a kind of terror of mental hospitals, and often said to Lessing: 'Hang me, do whatever you like with me, but don't send me back to the loony bin.' After several escapes, he succeeded in escaping to Switzerland, where he worked in a shipyard near Zurich. By the time he returned to Hanover, his escape seems to have been forgotten.

He quarrelled endlessly with his father, mostly about

Haarmann's refusal to take a regular job – even in his own father's cigar factory. He became engaged to a girl called Erna, who became pregnant by him a few years later. But they were to drift apart.

In 1900, at the age of 21, Haarmann enlisted for his military service, and for a while was an excellent soldier. But on a strenuous route march, he collapsed with dizzy spells – a recurrence of the old trouble with his head. He was dismissed from the army after a diagnosis of mental deficiency, and granted a small pension. This meant that for the rest of his life he was never destitute.

His mother had died while he was in the army. Back in Hanover, Haarmann again quarrelled continously with his father, who tried to have him committed to a mental home. But a doctor who examined him declared that although he was 'morally inferior, of low intelligence, idle, coarse, irritable and totally egotistical, he is not mentally ill as such . . .'

Haarmann had gonorrhoea for a while, which seems to have confirmed his indifference to women. At this point – in his early twenties – he met a 40-year-old homosexual, Adolf Meil, who picked him up at a fair and invited him back to his room. 'He kissed me. I was shy . . . He said: "It's late, stay with me." I did. He did things I'd never imagined . . .' The affair lasted for many years – possibly until Meil's death in 1916.

In 1904 he applied for a job as an invoice clerk in a paint factory, although he had no idea of what this involved. He persuaded an apprentice in the office to do his work, so his own duties were relatively light. He presented invoices to customers in which the price was deliberately low, so they paid in cash, which Haarmann then pocketed. He also became friendly with the factory cleaner, Frau Guhlisch, who had a 10-year old son who was already an accomplished thief. The three of them removed large quantities of paint from the factory, which they sold. They also burgled homes and robbed graveyards, often digging up recently buried corpses . . . Eventually Haarmann was caught and received his first prison sentence – the first of many. Released from jail, he pretended to be an official from the municipal 'disinfection service', calling at homes in which someone had recently died of disease and advising the family to have the place disinfected; he used the opportunity to steal.

He spent the First World War in prison for burglary. Back in Hanover in 1918, he found himself in a Germany suffering from galloping inflation and acute food shortages. It was just the kind of environment in which he was fitted to thrive. He soon discovered that the railway station was the centre of the black market, and it became virtually his headquarters. He also discovered that the police were understaffed and overworked, and were glad of any tip-offs he could offer. Within months, Haarmann was accepted by the police and railway officials as a kind of unofficial policeman. His friendship with crooks, pimps and prostitutes meant that he often got wind of big 'jobs' before they happened; in one case he was instrumental in catching a gang of counterfeiters.

But for a man of Haarmann's sexual tastes, the railway station represented a non-stop temptation. Homeless young men flocked in from the countryside. Haarmann often demanded to see their papers, and even questioned them in the station-master's office. The young men he liked were invited back to his room for food and a bed. They soon learned that the price was to spend the night in bed with Haarmann, engaged in mutual oral sex which often went on for hours before Haarmann reached orgasm. He claimed to be impotent – perhaps as a result of the gonorrhoea – and in any case was not inclined towards sodomy. But he had one disconcerting peculiarity. As he reached sexual ecstasy, he experienced an overpowering desire to bite the windpipe of his sexual partner. If the youth was young or slightly built, he stood no chance against the well-built Haarmann. The result – Haarmann confessed to Lessing – was that his partners often died from lack of air; in some cases, he actually bit through the windpipe.

One of the major shortages in post-war Germany was of meat. Haarmann dealt in the meat of horses and other illegally slaughtered animals. His landlady became accustomed to the sound of chopping and banging from his room, and on one occasion met him coming downstairs with a covered bucket; the cloth slipped aside and she saw that it contained blood. The woman next door received a bag of fresh bones from Haarmann, from which she made brawn. Then she decided that the bones looked too white, and decided not to eat the meat. To Haarmann, the cheerful opportunist, it would probably have seemed sinful to waste the body parts of his victims when they could be sold as meat. Haarmann never actually confessed to this – but then, he made a habit of confessing only to crimes that could actually be proved against him.

Some time in 1919, Haarmann was approached by a 'pretty' youth named Hans Grans. His father was a bookbinder, and Hans was an obsessive reader. But he was less than honest, and already had a varied career of petty crime behind him when he met Haarmann. A friend at the railway station told him that 'that queer over there gave a pretty boy 20 marks the other day.' Grans lost no time in approaching Haarmann and fluttering his eyelashes. Although not specifically homosexual – in fact, he was something of a womanizer – Grans had no objection to selling his body.

What he saw was a plump little man with a full-moon face and a broad and reassuring peasant accent. As he walked he moved his behind in a feminine manner, and his hands were soft and white. The rather high voice quavered like that of an old woman. His teeth were very white, and he had a habit of licking his lips with his fleshy tongue.

Haarmann was fascinated, and lost no time in inviting Hans back to his room and persuading him to undress. But when naked, Hans ceased to be attractive: his body was covered with hair like a monkey. It was not until he shaved it off that Haarmann was able to experience desire.

There was something about Hans that arrested Haarmann's murderous impulses – the mixture of charm, dishonesty and total unscrupulousness. Haarmann became the teacher, Hans the pupil. Haarmann gave him cigarettes and meat to sell, and lent him money which Hans often spent on girls. Hans soon became aware of Haarmann's sexual peculiarities, and often procured boys for him. He discovered what happened to some of the boys when he walked into Haarmann's room one day and found a corpse in the bed. Haarmann told him to go away; the next day, the corpse had gone. It was not difficult for Haarmann to dispose of a body: the river ran past the wall of his lodgings in the Neuestrasse. Provided he dismembered the corpse and carried it down in a bucket, chances of detection were virtually non-existent.

The two of them remained together until Haarmann's arrest – although often separated when one or the other of them was in prison. They sometimes quarrelled violently, on one occasion brandishing knives at one another and shouting 'Murderer!'

More than once, Haarmann ordered Hans to leave – then found himself unable to exist without him, and begged him to return. When Haarmann became angry and violent – as he was prone to – Hans would put his arms round his waist and slip his tongue into his mouth, whereupon Haarmann would melt. Hans always made sure that he held his lover's arms as he did this, knowing that when sexually excited, he would bite the throat. (Later, Haarmann became sentimentally attached to his lawyer, and on one occasion, hugged him enthusiastically; when the lawyer looked anxious, Haarman assured him: 'Don't worry – I won't bite.')

Oddly enough, there was a third member of this partnership, another good-looking boy named Hugo Wittkowski, who was Grans's closest friend. Unlike Grans, Hugo was completely heterosexual, and often brought women to Haarmann's apartment. When Haarmann was in prison for six months, Hugo and Hans allowed young prostitutes to move in, and took a share of their earnings. Haarmann hated Wittkowski, and on one occasion planned to murder the two young men and then commit suicide. Haarmann suffered from the odd delusion that young men found him irresistible, and once shouted at Hugo: 'You've offered yourself to me hundreds of times, but I didn't want you. You weren't good enough for me' – to which Wittkowsky replied simply: 'I only like women.'

Within a few weeks of Haarmann's arrest, the prosecutors had enough evidence to charge him with twenty-seven murders, beginning with a schoolboy called Fritz Rothe in 1918. When asked how many boys he had killed, Haarmann would shrug and say: 'I forget. Perhaps thirty, perhaps forty . . .' Grans was charged as an accessory in at least one murder.

His trial began at the Hanover Assizes on 4 December 1924. It lasted fourteen days and 130 witnesses were called. The public prosecutor was Oberstaatsanwalt Dr Wilde, assisted by Dr Wagenschiefer; the defence was conducted by Justizrat Philipp Benfey and Rechtsanwalt Oz Lotzen. Haarmann was allowed remarkable freedom; he was usually gay and irresponsible, frequently interrupting the proceedings. At one point he demanded indignantly why there were so many women in court; the judge answered apologetically that he had no power to keep them out. When a woman witness was too distraught to give her evidence about her son with clarity, Haarmann got bored and asked to be allowed to smoke a cigar; permission was immediately granted.

He persisted to the end in his explanation of how he had killed his victims – biting them through the throat. Some boys he denied killing – for example, a boy named Hermann Wolf, whose photograph showed an ugly and ill-dressed youth; like Oscar Wilde, Haarmann declared that the boy was far too ugly to interest him.

Haarmann was sentenced to death by decapitation; Grans to twelve years in jail. Haarmann later produced a confession which has much in common with that of Mme de Brinvilliers or Gilles de Rais; it is full of accounts of sexual perversion and the pleasure he took in committing murders that were all inspired by his sexual perversion.

In his account of Haarmann, Theodore Lessing also mentions another case that caused a sensation at the time: that of Karl Denke. On 21 December 1924, a few days after Haarmann had been sentenced to death, a travelling journeyman named Vincenz Oliver called at the home of 54-year-old Denke to beg for food. Denke was known as a recluse – although he was a good churchgoer, and blew the organ in the local church. A retired farmer, he lived in an apartment block which he owned near Munsterberg, in Silesia.

Denke invited the journeyman in and told him to sit down. But instead of bringing him food, he attacked him with a hatchet. Oliver struggled and called out, and the noise was heard by a coachman named Gabriel, who lived in the flat above. Thinking his landlord was in trouble, Gabriel rushed downstairs – to find Oliver almost unconscious. The journeyman was able to gasp out that Denke had tried to kill him. Gabriel called the police and Denke was arrested. A search of the house revealed identity papers belonging to twelve travelling journeymen, as well as clothing. Two tubs proved to contain human meat pickled in brine, and there were also pots of fat and bones. Medical examination revealed that these belonged to thirty victims. A ledger was found in which Denke recorded the dates on which he had pickled the carcases, and the weight. The earliest murder had been in 1921, and the victims were mostly tramps, beggarwomen and journeymen.

Denke never came to trial; he hanged himself with his braces a few days later. It is assumed that he was a cannibal, who had found this ingenious way of overcoming Germany's meat shortage.

German schoolchildren were soon repeating a riddle that went: 'Who is Germany's greatest mass murderer?' The child was instructed to answer: 'Haarmann, ich denke' (Haarmann, I think), which also sounded like a confession of guilt (Haarmann, I, Denke').

They also sang a nursery rhyme that went:

Warte, warte, nur ein weilchen,
Dann kommt Haarmann auch zu dir,
Mit dem kleinen Hackenbeilchen,
Und macht Hackefleisch aus dir.

Wait, wait a little while
Then Haarmann will come to you,
And with his little chopper
Will make mincemeat out of you.

(The English 'mincemeat' misses the sheer gruesomeness of the German *Hackefleish* – hacked flesh.)

Four years after Haarmann's execution, Germany again became the subject of worldwide news coverage as another 'monster' committed a series of sadistic crimes in Düsseldorf. Peter Kürten is Germany's Jack the Ripper, and the book about him, *The Sadist*, by Karl Berg, Professor of Forensic Medicine in the Düsseldorf Academy, is – like Lessing's book on Haarmann – one of the great classics of criminology. Since the English translation (by Olga Illnerr and George Godwin) has been out of print for nearly half a century, I shall allow Berg to introduce the case in his own words:

> In the whole history of crime there is to be found no record comparable in circumstances of frightfulness with the long series of crimes perpetrated in our own time by the Düsseldorf murderer, Peter Kürten.
>
> The epidemic of sexual outrages and murders which took place in the town of Düsseldorf between the months of February and November in the year 1929, caused a wave of horror and indignation to sweep, not only through Düsseldorf, but through all Germany and, it may be said without exaggeration, throughout the whole world.
>
> As one outrage succeeded another and always in circumstances of grim drama; as one type of crime was followed by yet another,

public consternation reached the point of stupefaction.

Kürten, however, has been judged; he now belongs to criminal history.

Kürten's crimes were not merely the subject of exhaustive judicial examination; justice went deeper in his case and sought to probe the soul of this strange and enigmatic man.

In so doing Justice has placed us in a position to understand the nature both of the crimes and of the perpetrator of them. Here, for the medico-jurist, is truly absorbing material for study, for Kürten is a clinical subject who yields, in exchange for a careful analysis, a real enlargement of our knowledge of the abnormal operating in the sphere of crime.

Here is Berg's account of Kürten's first murder of 1929:

> On the 9th of February, 1929, about 9 o'clock in the morning, workmen going to work found in the vicinity of the building upon which they were employed in the Kettwiger-strasse, in the Flingern district, the body of an eight-year-old girl lying under a hedge. The ground at that point sloped slightly towards the hedge, and as the hedge faced a wide open space, it was only by chance that the body was discovered.
>
> The body was completely clothed and clad in a cloak. The clothing, however, was partially burnt and the underclothing still smouldered. The body, which smelled strongly of petroleum, was not in any sort of disorder, for even the openings of the dress and the knickers were not disarranged. A closer examination of the clothing revealed bloodstains from multiple wounds in the breast, wounds made, quite obviously, through the clothing. On the inner part of the knickers near the external genitalia were two small bloodstains. Microscopic examination revealed the presence hereabouts of seminal fluid. In the vagina there was fluid blood which had flowed from a wound 1 cm. in length, at the entrance of the vaginal cavity.
>
> The autopsy showed that the burning had affected practically only the clothing, injuring the skin surface nowhere but on the upper part of the thighs, the neck and chin, over which area the skin was blackened and discoloured, while the hair of the head was a black, charred mass, here and there completely burnt off. On the left breast there was a group of thirteen wounds, the face was bloated and livid. The stabs about the left breast were grouped over an area rather smaller than a hand. Five of the wounds had penetrated the heart, three had pierced the left and right pleuræ; three had penetrated the liver. In the pleural cavities I found 750 cc. of blood. Death must have been swift through internal haemorrhage. The scene of the crime

was without trace of blood. The criminal had attempted to burn the clothing of the body only. There were no traces to suggest that soot had been inhaled, and the burning was without vital reaction. In the tissues of the lumbar region there was some 4 cm. of blood infiltration.

In the stomach was found a mass of chyme, partially digested white cabbage, and remains of meat.

The essential factors to be considered, from the medico-legal standpoint, for a diagnosis of the cause of death and for a theory as to the time of it, as well as for the motive of the murderer, were the characteristic stabs, the congestion of blood which was found in the head, the exact nature of the wounds and the condition of the contents of the stomach, and, last, the injury to the genitalia. So far as the congestion of blood in the head is concerned, one can only suggest that it indicated a forcible strangulation.

The judicial autopsy of the Ohliger child established the time of death, the contents of the stomach assisting to that end.

Death must have occurred very quickly through the heart wounds. There were no visible marks where the strangling grip had been applied, but some manner of strangulation must have initiated the attack though leaving no traces on the skin of the neck. No calls for help were heard in the rather populous neighbourhood where the crime was committed.

The mother deposed that the murdered child had eaten sauerkraut about 2 p.m. and had then set out to visit a friend. At 6 o'clock the friend had advised the child to hurry home before dark. There was a public footpath which she could take and which offered her a short cut.

Bearing in mind the fact that in six hours the stomach could normally complete the work of digestion, then the scarcely digested food found in the stomach indicates that death took place between 6 and 7 o'clock in the evening. The autopsy indicated that the child had been waylaid while on her homeward way.

The condition of the genitals revealed an injury of little consequence on the mucous membrane of the vagina. The hymen was torn about 1 cm. Only slight traces of seminal fluid were found on the child's underclothing. It was clear that an ejaculation could not have taken place into the vagina.

From these considerations I arrived at the conclusion that the criminal's objective had not been coitus, but that he must have inserted a finger smeared with semen under the unopened knickers of the child and thus inserted it, into the vagina. This must have been done with force, for in addition to the scratch at the entrance of the vagina, there was also a trace of bruising of the pelvis.

The stabs in the skin of the breast were all together and parallel. Some of these showed that the knife had been held with the cutting edge of the blade upwardy. I concluded from the position of these wounds that the criminal had done the stabbing in the breast as the child lay unconscious on the ground, delivering the blows in swift succession. Otherwise one would have expected that the stabbings inflicted on a person still conscious would have been placed irregularly. In addition one would expect to find defensive wounds on the hands.

That my conclusions were correct is borne out by the attack which took place on an elderly woman and of which I learned only later. This attack took place five days before the murder of Rosa Ohliger. I attributed it immediately to the same criminal, an assumption which was to be confirmed by later events.

In April 1929 it seemed that the 'monster' had been caught. Following two more attacks on women, an idiot named Stausberg was arrested and confessed to the murders. He had a cleft palate and hare lip. The police were soon convinced that, although he was undoubtedly responsible for the latest attacks, he had not committed the murders. He was sent to a mental home.

For three months, Kürten satisfied himself with affairs with servant girls, whom he attempted to strangle 'playfully'. (All this emerged at the trial.) On 30 July a prostitute named Emma Gross was found strangled in her room, but it seems that Kürten was not responsible for this.

In August, Kürten strangled a girl he referred to as 'Anni', and pushed her body into the river; but the body was not recovered, so it is not certain whether this story was Kürten's invention. Also in late August, a young woman, Frau Mantel, was stabbed in the back as she walked in the western suburb of Lierenfeld, where a fair was being held. Her wound was not serious. In the same month a girl, Anna Goldhausen, and a man, Gustav Kornblum (who was sitting in the park), were stabbed in the back. In neither case were the injuries fatal. Then, on 24 August, a double murder horrified the city. The bodies of two children, 5-year-old Gertrude Hamacher and 14-year-old Louise Lenzen, were found on an allotment near their home. Both had been strangled, and then had their throats cut. Neither had been raped.

The same Sunday afternoon, a servant girl named Gertrude Schulte was on her way to a fair at Neuss, and was spoken to by a man who called himself Fritz Baumgart. In a wood he attempted sexual intercourse, and the girl said, 'I'd rather die.' 'Baumgart' replied, 'Well die then,' and stabbed her several times. But she did not die, and was eventually able to give the police a description of her assailant.

This episode strengthened the police suspicion that there were two maniacs at work, since it seemed unlikely that the same man would kill two children on Saturday, and be out looking for further victims on Sunday.

In September, Kürten attacked three more girls and threw one of them into the river after his attempted strangulation. But these events caused little sensation in comparison with the next murder, which occurred in late September. Another servant girl, Ida Reuter, set out for her Sunday afternoon walk and never returned; the next day she was found in a field near the Rhine meadows. Her head had been battered with a heavy instrument (which turned out to be a hammer), and her handbag and knickers were missing; she was found in a position that indicated sexual assault.

The next case took place a few weeks later, in October. Again the victim was a servant girl, Elizabeth Dorrier. Again she was found (on 12 October) near the River Düssel at Grafenberg. Her death was also due to hammer blows on the head, and her hat and coat were missing.

On 25 October a Frau Meurer was accosted by a man in Flingern, who asked, 'Aren't you afraid to be out alone?' She woke up in hospital, her skin having been broken by a hammer, which had not, however, cracked the skull. Later the same evening, in the centre of the city, a Frau Wanders, who was seeking an escort, was accosted and knocked unconscious with a hammer, which had struck her four blows.

On 7 November a 5-year-old child, Gertrude Albermann, was missing from her home. Two days later her body was found near a factory yard, among nettles and brick rubble; she had been strangled and stabbed thirty-six times.

At this point Kürten imitated the 'Ripper's' tactics by sending a letter to a newspaper, stating where the body could be found, and mentioning the whereabouts of another body. (Kürten had a great admiration for the Ripper, and had studied the case carefully.) A spot in the meadows at Papendelle was mentioned. This letter led to the discovery of the body of Maria Hahn, who had been dead since August. Her body was dug up, after some days of searching, on 14 November, and was found to be completely naked. She had twenty stab wounds. Thousands of spectators streamed out to the spot where her body was found.

Berg comments:

> No other crime is more significant for an understanding of the personality of Kürten than this. Kürten himself has told about it in all its details, and even confessed to the examining magistrate the sexual motive. Here is his statement:
>
> 'On the 8th of August, 1929, I was strolling in the Zoo district. I hadn't any intention of committing any offence on a girl at the time. On the Hansaplatz a girl was sitting on a bench. She accosted me. I sat down beside her and we talked pleasantly together and made a date for an excursion to the Neanderthal the next Sunday. On Sunday, punctually at 1.30 in the afternoon, I found myself in the Hansaplatz where the girl was already waiting. We went to the Neanderthal, visited a beer garden and then on to the Stinter mill. We stayed there for three hours, drank a glass of red wine each. There also I bought her a slab of chocolate. Towards 7 o'clock we went to Erkrath where we had supper with beer. We then strolled past the house of the Morps, and along by the river. Here we decided to have sexual intercourse. After sexual intercourse we left the bank of the river and went into the meadow. Here I decided to kill her. I led Hahn to a big bush near a ditch and there we settled down. It was half-past nine. Suddenly I strangled her until she became unconscious, but she came to herself quickly again. Again I strangled her. After a bit I stabbed her in the throat with the scissors. She lost a lot of blood but regained consciousness, repeatedly asking me in a feeble voice to spare her life. I stabbed her in the breast a blow that probably pierced the heart. I then gave her repeated stabs in the breast and head. The process of dying probably took an hour. I let the body roll into the ditch and threw branches over it. Then I crossed the meadow and came to the road that runs from Morp-Papendell highway. I had taken the handbag of Hahn with me. From it I took the watch of the dead girl. I made a gift of it to somebody later on. The bag with the keys I threw into an oatfield.
>
> 'When I got home my wife was already in bed. Next morning we had a row, because she was suspicious about the night before. She became so excited about it that I made up my mind that I would have to find some way of seeing that the body of Hahn wasn't discovered, otherwise my wife would connect the blood stains on my clothes with it. So I went

again on Monday after finishing work to the scene of the crime and pondered where I could bury the body. I went back to the flat and fetched a shovel, inventing an excuse to give my wife. Near the scene of the crime, in the corner of the wood, I dug a deep hole in a fallow field, and carried the body along the footpath, avoiding the oatfield. By the hole I put the body down. I got into the hole and dragged the body down to me. Here I laid it on its back as one buries a body. A shoe had slipped off when the body was dragged down and I laid it beside it. Then I filled the hole. During the whole of this funeral ceremony a sentimental feeling possessed me. I caressed the hair and the first shovelful of earth I strewed thinly and gently on the body. I stamped the earth down and smoothed the soil as it was before. As my shirt had become bloody in carrying the body I took it off and washed it in the river and put it on again still wet. I hid the shovel near the river, then I went home and arrived there about 6 o'clock. My wife began reproaching me, asked me where I had been wandering all the night. I had cleaned my shoes thoroughly in the grass, using a cleaning rag which I always carried with me. I then drank coffee and went to work in the same clothes. After I had put the body of Hahn in the grave I removed her wrist-watch. Four weeks later I gave the watch to Kaete W . . . W . . . lives in the same house where I live. She often came into my room and we repeatedly had sexual intercourse.'

(The witness W . . . vehemently denied this assertion. I found, as a matter of fact, that she was a virgin with enlarged introitus of the vagina.)

The shovel was in fact found at the place indicated. Frau Kürten confirms the hour at which her husband left her on the 12th of August, namely, about 11 o'clock p.m., when he gave as explanation that he was on night work. Between 5 and 6 o'clock he had come back with dirty shoes and blood on his clothes. Later Kürten admitted that he had not given the wristwatch to the witness W . . . The first assertion that he had done so was an act of vengeance for the trouble she had given him and the part she had taken in bringing about his capture.

The murders were, of course, causing a panic in the Düsseldorf area that can only be compared to that caused by the Ripper in 1888 or by the Ratcliffe Highway murderer in 1811. Inspector Gennat, of the Berlin police, was assigned to the case. He had once had to follow up eight hundred clues to track down a murderer, and was noted for his thoroughness.

The German underworld was also greatly disturbed by the murders (as Fritz Lang showed in his film version of the crimes, *M*), and police raids made the criminals of the Rhine as anxious as the general public to see the murderer taken.

A tailor's dummy, dressed in Dorrier's clothes, was taken around the dance halls of Düsseldorf, in the hope that one of the dancers would recognize the clothes and remember the girl's companion on the day of her death.

But although no one knew it, the murders had come to an end, although the attacks would continue for six months more. There had been eight murders in ten months, and fourteen attacks.

In 1929, there were several attacks on girls walking alone, and Kürten also continued playfully to strangle his girlfriends, some of whom did not seem to object to the treatment. (Evidence of these girls figures largely in the trial.)

Let Berg tell the story of Kürten's capture:

> Suddenly all these uncertainties and perplexities were ended by the capture of the criminal and his confession. This totally unforeseen outcome was not due to the efforts of the police, but to a sheer coincidence, coupled with the criminal's lack of caution.
>
> It was the famous Butlies affair which resulted in the discovery. For that reason I propose to describe it here, and do so in Kürten's own words.
>
> 'On the 14th of May, 1930, I saw a man accost a young girl at the railway station and go off with her. Out of curiosity I followed the couple along the Graf-Adolf-strasse, the Karlstrasse, Klosterstrasse, Kölner Strasse, Stoffeler Strasse to the Volksgarten. When the man wanted to go into the dark park with the girl, she resisted him. I seized the opportunity and approached the couple.
>
> 'I asked him what he meant to do with the girl. He replied that the girl had no lodging and that he proposed to take her to his sister. At this point the girl asked me whether the Achenbachstrasse was in that neighbourhood – it was there the man's sister was supposed to live. When I assured her very convincingly that the street was in an entirely different neighbourhood, she stepped to my side, and the man made off very quickly. We returned. The girl told me that she was out of work and had nowhere to go. She agreed to come with me to my room in the Mettmanner Strasse 71. Round about 11 o'clock we

got to my room which is on the third floor. Then she suddenly said she didn't want any sexual intercourse and asked me whether I couldn't find her some other place to sleep. I agreed. We went by tram to Worringerplatz and on towards the Grafenberger Wald, going along the Wolfschlucht until we came to the last of the houses. Here I seized Butlies with one hand by the neck, pressing her head back very hard and kissing her. I asked her to let me have her. I thought that under the circumstances she would agree, and my opinion was right. Afterwards I asked whether I had hurt her, which she denied. I wanted to take her back to the tram, but I did not accompany her right to it because I was afraid that she might inform the police officer who was standing there. I had no intention of killing Butlies. She had offered no resistance. We had sexual intercourse standing, after I had pulled down her knickers. There was another reason why I could not do anything to her – I had been seen by a friend in the tram. I did not think that Butlies would be able to find her way back again to my apartment in the rather obscure Mettmanner Strasse. So much the more was I surprised when on Wednesday, the 21st of May, I saw Butlies again in my house.'

Butlies supplements this statement thus:

On the 14th of May she had come from Cologne to Düsseldorf. There on the railway station she got into contact with a 'Frau Brückner', and made an appointment with her for 8 o'clock in the evening of that day. She had then waited in vain on the railway station for the woman and in the end had been accosted by a man who wanted to put her up.

Her statement corroborates Kürten's. After her adventure Butlies took the tram from the Grafenberger Wald back to the town. Then she walked the streets of Düsseldorf. At last she went to the *Gertrudishaus*, where she told the Sisters about the attack. On the 17th of May she wrote to her new acquaintance, Frau Brückner, in Düsseldorf – Bilker Allee – a letter in which she hinted that she had fallen into the hands of a murderer. The recipient of the letter, Frau Brügmann, suspected the connection with the Düsseldorf murderer, and took the letter to the criminal police department. The writer of the letter was interrogated and eventually succeeded in finding the house of the unknown man. On her own account she had already made enquiries in different houses in the Mettmanner Strasse for a man of a certain type and, at last, she had heard from the inhabitants of No. 71 that a crying girl had once come in the same way asking for a man of the same description. Her description fitted Peter Kürten, who lodged there. That was on the 21st of May.

Kürten continues his Narrative

'On Wednesday, the 21st of May, I happened to look over the bannisters and saw Butlies and recognized her. She can be recognized easily. She has very fair hair, is slant-eyed and bow-legged. She left the house again. At lunch-time she came back. This time with a police officer. I saw her stand in the entrance door and speak to the landlady. Then in the afternoon she came again to the house, this time coming up to our floor. She entered the flat of the Wimmers and she saw me. She was startled. I think it is likely that she recognized me then. I knew what would happen after that!

'That same evening I fetched my wife from the place where she worked: "I must get out of the flat," I said. I explained the Butlies case to her. But I only mentioned the attempt at sexual intercourse, saying that as it could be called "rape", along with my previous convictions, it was enough to get me fifteen years' penal servitude. Therefore I had to get out. I changed. Throughout the night I walked about. On Thursday, the 22nd of May, I saw my wife in the morning in the flat. I fetched my things away in a bag and rented a room in the Adlerstrasse. I slept quietly until Friday morning.'

The events of this Friday were described to me by Kürten in writing.

'It was at nine in the morning when I went to my flat. Shortly before I reached No. 71 two men came out of it. I found out afterwards they were detectives. I thought right away that they were that. When I went into the flat my wife was still there. When I asked her why she had not gone to work to-day she answered: "I did, but I was taken away from it by two detectives who brought me home." Both these men had searched the place and a few moments before they had gone down the staircase. Then my wife asked me to leave the house saying she did not want me to be arrested there. I did as she asked and later met her – she had gone back to the place where she was employed. I then asked her to come with me for a little while. Two days before I had told her about the Butlies affair. To-day, the 23rd, in the morning, I told my wife that I was also responsible for the Schulte affair, adding my usual remark that it would mean at least ten years' or more separation for us – probably for ever. At that my wife was inconsolable. She spoke of age, unemployment, lack of means and starvation in old age. When the lunch hour approached I had not even then succeeded in calming my wife down. She raved that I should take my life. Then she would do the same, since her future was completely without hope. Then in the late afternoon I told my wife that I could help her. That I could still do something for her. I told her that I was the Düsseldorf murderer. Of course, she didn't think it possible and didn't want to believe it. But then I disclosed everything to her, naming myself the murderer in each case. When she asked me how this could help her, I hinted that a high reward had been offered for the discovery as well as for the capture of the criminal; that she could get hold of that reward, or at least some part of it, if she would report my confession and denounce me to the police. Of course, it wasn't easy for me to convince her that this ought not to be considered as treason, but that, on the contrary, she was doing a good deed to humanity as well as to justice. It was not until late in the evening that she promised me to carry out my request, and also that she would not commit suicide. I then accompanied her almost to the door. It was 11 o'clock when we separated. Back in my lodging I went to bed and fell asleep at once. What happened the next morning, the 24th of May, is known.

'First a bath, then several times around the neighbourhood of the Kortzingens' flat [Kürten had planned a robbery here]. Lunch, a hair-cut, and then, at 3 o'clock I met my wife according to the arrangement and there the arrest took place. As a matter of fact, my wife had carried out my order a bit too quickly for me. I want to point out again that I never collapsed on the 23rd or 24th of May, but kept steadily before me my purpose to the very end.'

Thus Kürten. I now contrast his statement with that of his wife:

'In the morning, after the detectives had brought me from the place where I work, my husband came to the flat. 'You must have done something awful!' I said. 'Yes,' he replied. 'I did it. I did everything.' Then, with that he left the flat. We then met by arrangement at 11.30 in the morning in the Hofgarten. We had dinner in a restaurant in the Duisburger Strasse. I could not eat anything, but he ate up the lot, my portion, too.

'At 2 o'clock we were walking over the Rhine Bridge back and forwards. In the late afternoon I asked him what he meant with his words: 'I have done everything.' 'If you promise solemnly that you won't give me away I'll tell you something,' he said. I promised. 'I have done everything that has happened here in Düsseldorf!' 'What do you mean by that?' I asked. 'Everything – the murders and the attacks.' 'What, those innocent children, too?' I asked. 'Yes,' he said. 'Why did you do that?' I asked him. 'I don't know myself,' he replied, 'it just came over me.'

'Then all the big cases were talked over, including that of

Mülheim. When I got terribly excited about it all, he said, 'I've done something very silly. I ought not to have told you.' That afternoon Kürten was very depressed and in a way I had never seen before. He told me that he had not cried once in his whole life, but yesterday evening, when he was alone, he had cried bitterly. In the afternoon while we spoke only about the fact that the detectives were after him, he was quiet and self-possessed, But towards the evening when I wanted to go home he was as I have never seen him in his life before. He was very cast down. He could not look into my eyes. All the indifference had disappeared. He burst out with it all, telling of the murders and the attacks as if some power forced him to it. I thought he had gone crazy. Nothing had been said about any reward.'

Who could not understand Frau Kürten – who would reproach her that she was not able to carry alone the weight of this ghastly secret – but that she gave it away to the police when pressed by them?

She had a last meeting with her husband near the Rochus Church, for the following day, the 24th.

That, too, the woman, who was quite distraught, reported to the police. The church square was quietly surrounded and Kürten was arrested as he walked towards his wife. He was quite composed. Subsequently, he often told me how he smilingly calmed the detective who advanced excitedly towards him, the revolver levelled at him.

When Kürten was questioned by the police he not only told of the attacks of 1929, but he gave also an account of a long chain of crimes without being questioned. For reasons to which I will return presently he lengthened this chain with some imaginary links, but he soon brought it back again to the facts.

TABLE I

THE SEQUENCE OF THE CRIMES

ACCORDING TO KÜRTEN'S OWN STATEMENT

Born 1883 in Köln-Mülheim. Passed his childhood there. Left for Düsseldorf 1894; 1897 apprenticed as a moulder. In 1899 first convicted for theft.

TABLE OF OFFENCES

Nov. 1899	Attempted strangulation	18-year-old girl unknown
FROM 1900 TO 1904 IN PRISON		
1904	Arson	Barn after harvest

1904	Arson	Hay loft
1904	Arson	Two hay-ricks

1905 TO 1913 IN PRISON

1913	Attempted strangulation	Margarete Schäfer
1913	Murder by strangulation and throat-cutting	Christine Klein, Mülheim
1913	Axe blow	Unknown man
1913	Axe blow	Unknown woman
1913	Axe blow attempt	Hermes, sleeping girl
1913	Strangulation	Gertrud Franken
1913	Arson	Hay-rick and hay wagon

1913 TO 1921 IN PRISON

1921	Strangulation	War widow
1925	Strangulation	Tiede
1925	Strangulation	Mech
1925	Strangulation	Kiefer
1926	Strangulation	Wack
1927	Arson	Three hay-ricks
1927	Arson	Shock of sheaves
1927	Arson	Two barns
1927	Attempted strangulation	Anni Ist
1927	Arson	Two barns
1927	Arson	Plantation
1928	Arson	Barn
1928	Arson	Farmyard
1928	Arson	Shock of sheaves (twice)
1928	Arson	Hay-rick
1928	Arson	Hay wagon
1928	Arson	House
1928	Arson	House
1928	Arson	Shed
1928	Arson	Forest fire
1928	Arson	Haystacks
1928	Arson	Sheds
1929	Arson	Stacks
1929	Arson	Barns, sheds, stacks, (ten cases)

1929

Feb. 3	Attack with scissors	Frau Kühn
Feb. 13	Stabbed and killed	Rudolf Scheer
Mar. 8	Strangled and stabbed after death	Child – Rose Ohliger
March	Attempted strangulation	Edit Boukorn
July	Attempted strangulation	Maria Witt
July	Attempted strangulation	Maria Mass
July	Attempted strangulation	Unknown domestic servant
August	Strangled and stabbed to death	Maria Hahn
August	Strangled and drowned	'Anni', a housemaid
August	Stabbed with dagger	Anna Goldhausen
August	Stabbed with dagger	Frau Mantel
August	Stabbed with dagger	Kornblum
August	Strangled and throat cut	Child – Hamacher
August	Strangled and stabbed	Child – Lenzen
August	Stabbed with dagger	Gertrud Schulte
August	Attempted strangulation and thrown into river	Heer
Sept.	Blow with tool	Rückl
Sept.	Attempted strangulation	Maria Rad
Sept.	Killed by hammer blows	Ida Reuter
October	Killed by hammer blows	Elisabeth Dörrier
October	Attack with hammer	Frau Meurer
October	Attack with hammer	Frau Wanders
November	Strangled and stabbed with scissors	Child – Albermann

1930

February	Attempted strangulation	Hilde
March	Attempted strangulation	Maria del Sant
March	Attempted strangulation	Irma
April	Attempted strangulation	Sibille
April	Attempted strangulation	Unknown girl from Herne
April	Attempted strangulation	Young woman, Hau
April	Attacks	Several girls
April	Attack with hammer	Charlotte Ulrich
May	Attempted strangulation	Maria Butlies
May	Attempted murder	Gertrud Bell

The way in which Kürten enumerated all his offences, tabulated

> here in a sequence chronologically accurate, and the way in which he dictated it with every detail, is quite extraordinary. He was not accused of these crimes one by one, but reeled off on his own account, beginning with No. 1 and ending with No. 79, every single case, dictating them, in fact, to the stenographer and even showing enjoyment at the horrified faces of the many police officers who listened to his recital, day by day.

Kürten was born in Köln-Mulheim in 1883, the son of a moulder, a violent man, boastful and given to drunkenness. The family of thirteen were very poor, and lived for a time in a single room. The environment was heavily charged with sex. According to Kürten, all his sisters were oversexed, and one made sexual advances to him. Kürten was apparently not attracted by her, but he attempted incest with another sister – a sister whom his father attempted to rape, and on whose account the moulder served a term in prison. Kürten senior was in the habit of forcing his wife to have intercourse when he came home drunk, and Kürten frequently witnessed his mother being 'raped'. At the age of 8 he ran away from home for a short time, sleeping in furniture vans. He also admitted to Berg that his taste for sadism had first been awakened by a sadistic dog-catcher who lived in the same house, and who taught Kürten to masturbate the dogs. Kürten often watched him torturing the dogs.

Kürten was the third of thirteen children. His grandfather had served sentences for theft, and cases of delirium tremens, feeble-mindedness and paralysis abound in his family connexions on his father's side. (His mother's side of the family were normal and hard-working people.)

When Kürten was 12, the family moved to Düsseldorf. But according to his own confession, he had already committed his first murder. At the age of 9, he pushed a boy off a raft on the banks of the Rhine, and when another boy dived in to help the first one, he managed to push him under the raft, so that both were drowned.

In his early teens he ran away from home again and lived as a vagabond and robber – attacking mostly girls and women. His adolescent sexuality was abnormal. He attempted intercourse with schoolgirls and with his sister, and masturbated excessively. From his thirteenth year onward he practised bestiality with sheep, pigs and goats. He discovered that he received a powerful sexual sensation when having intercourse with a sheep in the

Düsseldorf meadows and stabbing it simultaneously. He did this many times between his thirteenth and sixteenth years. At 16 he became an apprentice moulder, and received much ill-treatment; finally he stole money and ran away to Coblenz. There he lived with a prostitute who allowed him to ill-treat her. Finally, he was arrested for theft, and received the first of the seventeen sentences that were to take up twenty-seven years of his life. He was then 15. Released from prison two years later in 1899, he discovered that his mother was divorced from his father, and so decided to keep living a vagrant life. He lived with a prostitute of twice his age who enjoyed being maltreated, and this developed his sadistic propensities further.

In November 1899, according to Kürten's own account, he committed what he supposed to be his first adult murder: strangling a girl while having sexual intercourse with her, he thought she had died, and left her in the Grafenberger Wald. But no body was reported in that month, so it seems likely that the girl woke up and went home, saying nothing to anyone.

His first prison period, according to himself, made a real criminal of him; in the cells at the Berger Gate he met hardened criminals, and wanted to rival them. He had himself tattooed.

He served two brief sentences about 1900 for minor fraud, and then attempted to shoot a girl with a rifle, and was given two more years. Together with another sentence for theft, this brought his period in jail up to 1904. During this time, Kürten admitted, he used to dream of revenge, and found that his fantasies of killing excited him sexually. He deliberately committed minor infringements of prison regulations to get solitary confinement, so that he could indulge these fantasies freely. On his release he was called up as a conscript to Metz, but soon deserted. He also committed his first cases of arson, setting fire to barns and hay-ricks. The sight of fire caused him sexual excitement, and he also hoped that tramps might be sleeping in the hay. In 1905 he received seven years in jail for theft (he had been living with another woman who also lived by thieving). He served the term in Münster prison, and had an attack of 'prison psychosis', rolling himself in a bundle of silk and lying under the table, claiming to be a silkworm. He also claimed later that he was able to poison some prisoners in the prison hospital. He nursed fantasies of revenge on society, and dreamed of 'compensatory justice' – that is, that he could get his own back on his tormenters by tormenting someone who was completely innocent. This kind of illogicality is typical of murderers and psychopaths.

As soon as he was released from prison in 1912, he maltreated a servant girl during intercourse, and was soon back in prison for discharging fire arms in a restaurant when he tried to accost a woman and was interrupted by the waiter. For this he received a year in jail.

On 25 May 1913 he committed his first sexual murder. He had become a specialist in robbing business premises. He entered a pub in the Wolfstrasse, Köln-Mulheim, on an evening when the family were out at a fair. In one of the bedrooms he found 13-year-old Christine Klein asleep. He strangled her, cut her throat with a penknife, and penetrated her sexual organs with his fingers. He dropped a handkerchief with his initials on it. But it happened that the child's father was called Peter Klein, and his brother Otto had quarrelled with him on the night of the murder and threatened to do something that Peter 'would remember all his life'. Otto Klein was arrested and tried, but released for lack of evidence. Public opinion was against him, and he was killed in the war, still under the shadow of the murder. Kürten later claimed that it was the memory of his sufferings in jail that prompted the murder. A few weeks after this crime, Kürten was again about to attack a sleeping girl when someone woke up and frightened him off. He also attacked an unknown man and an unknown woman with a hatchet, securing sexual orgasms by knocking them unconscious and seeing their blood. (Since the sadistic dog-catcher, blood had always been Kürten's major sexual stimulant.) He also burned another hay wagon, and attempted to strangle two women. Then, luckily, he spent the next eight years in prison.

In 1921 Kürten returned to Altenberg, declaring that he had been a prisoner of war in Russia. Here he met the woman who became his wife, at the home of his sister. She had had her own misfortunes; she had been engaged to a gardener for eight years and had been his mistress; then he refused to marry her and she shot him. For this she served a five-year jail sentence. When Kürten met her she was a raw-boned, broad-shouldered, prematurely aged woman. It is difficult to know why Kürten was attracted by her; perhaps because she seemed 'solid' and reliable, or perhaps because she had suffered. Until the end of his life, ten years later, she continued to be the only human being for whom he felt normal feelings of affection and attachment. At first, she refused to marry him, but, when Kürten threatened to murder her, she consented. Then, for two years, he lived a fairly respectable life, working as a moulder in Altenberg, and becoming active in trade union circles and in a political club. But his sadistic activities persisted and he was twice charged with maltreating servant girls. In 1925 he returned to Düsseldorf, and was delighted that the sunset was blood-red on the evening of his return. Then began Düsseldorf's 'Reign of Terror'. But it began quietly enough. Like many maniacs of a similar type, Kürten began with a few widely spaced attacks; these became steadily more frequent and more violent, until, in the year 1929, they finally reached a climax. Between 1925 and 1928 Kürten admitted four cases of attempted strangulation of women, and seventeen cases of arson. On two occasions he set houses on fire.

The year 1929 began with six more cases of arson of barns and stacks. Then, on 3 February, a Frau Kuhn was walking home late at night when she was suddenly attacked by a man with a knife. She received twenty-four stab wounds, and was in hospital for many months.

A few days later, on 13 February, a 45-year-old mechanic named Scheer was found dead in the roadway in Flingern; he had been drunk when attacked, and had been stabbed twenty times.

On 9 March workmen discovered the body of 8-year-old Rose Ohliger lying behind a fence on a building site. She had been stabbed thirteen times; there had been some attempt at sexual assault, and an attempt to burn the body with paraffin.

And so began the series of murders that made the 'monster of Düsseldorf' as notorious as Jack the Ripper, and which finally ended with his arrest on 24 May 1930.

It is not surprising that Kürten was not an obvious suspect. Even after his arrest, most of his neighbours and workmates considered that it was a mistake. He was known as a quiet, well-behaved man, a dandy in his dress, intelligent, and a good worker.

Kürten made a full confession of the murders, although he later withdrew it. Gertrude Schulte picked him out of a number of men paraded in front of her. Professor Berg was introduced to Kürten, and remarked that Kürten proved to be an intelligent truthful man, interested in his own case, and anxious to help the psychiatrist to understand the strange urges that had led to his crimes.

Some of the things Kürten revealed to Berg are terrifying. On one occasion when he could not find a victim in the Hofgarten, he seized a sleeping swan, cut off its head, and drank the blood. The swan was found the next morning. On another occasion, he saw a horse involved in a street accident, and had an orgasm. At first he tried to convince Berg that he killed for 'revenge on society', but was later frank in admitting the sexual origin of his crimes. The horror caused by his crimes gave him deep satisfaction. It was for this reason that he had gone back to the body of Rose Ohliger many hours after he had killed her, and poured paraffin on the body. Later still, he had lingered on the edge of the crowd, and had an orgasm provoked by the horror of the spectators.

The following is typical of Kürten's statements about his attacks:

> In March 1930, I went out with my scissors. At the station a girl spoke to me. I took her to have a glass of beer, and we then walked towards the Grafenberg woods. She said her name was Irma. She was about 22. Near the middle of the woods, I seized her by the throat and I held on for a bit. She struggled violently, and screamed. I threw her down the ravine that runs down to the Wolf's Glen and went away.

Many young women gave evidence of similar experiences. One servant girl whom Kürten attempted to strangle complained that he was rough. He told her 'that was what love was'. She met him on several occasions after this! Another believed he was a single man and was going to marry her; one day she inquired at his home and was told he was married; this experience made her particularly bitter against Kürten. On another occasion, Kürten's wife caught him out with a woman and slapped her face. Kürten brushed her cheek with a rose and turned and walked off, leaving the two women together.

Kürten's wife never suspected his perversions; he had sexual intercourse with her periodically, but admitted that he had to imagine sadistic violence in order to go through with the love-making.

With respect to his crimes, Kürten's memory was of astonishing accuracy; seventeen years after the murder of Christine Klein, he was able to describe her bedroom in detail. On other points, his memory was average; it was obvious that he took such intense pleasure in his crimes that every detail remained in his mind. He admitted to dwelling on them afterwards and having sexual orgasms as he recalled their details. He also told Berg that he used to walk through the streets of Düsseldorf and daydream of blowing up the whole city with dynamite. Hitler lost a talented lieutenant in Kürten, one who might have outshone Eichmann or Heydrich in mass murder.

The Hahn case revealed a curious aspect of Kürten's sadism – an element of necrophilia. The naked body had been sexually assaulted, both vaginally and anally; leaves and earthmould were found in the anus. Kürten admitted how, after killing her, he had buried her roughly. Later he decided to alter the location of her grave; he also had an idea that it would be exciting to crucify her body on two trees and leave it to be found. However, the body was too heavy; nevertheless, Kürten changed the location of the grave, and admitted to kissing and fondling the victim when he had dug her up. He returned often to the site of the grave and masturbated on it.

And yet one of Kürten's favourite dream fantasies was of saving Düsseldorf from the 'monster', and having torchlight processions in his honour. He would be nominated police commissioner for his service. (Perhaps Kürten had read the life of Vidocq.)

Kürten's trial opened on 13 April 1931. In accordance with the German custom, it took place in front of three judges. Kürten's counsel was Dr Wehner, a young lawyer; the prosecution was led by the public prosecutor, Dr Jansen. Dr Jansen asked several times that the press and public be excluded – no doubt because he wanted to reveal evidence that would leave no room for any but the death sentence – but his pleas were unsuccessful. Professor Berg gave evidence, describing Kürten as a 'king of sexual perverts'. Professor Sioli gave psychiatric evidence for the prosecution, and Professor Rather for the defence. The defence was of insanity at the time of the murders. The case closed on April 23rd. Kürten's final remarks are of some interest:

> As I now see the crimes committed by me, they are so ghastly that I do not want to attempt any sort of excuse for them. Still, I feel some bitterness when I think of the physician and the lady physician in Stuttgart who have been encouraged by a section of the community to murder and who have stained their hands with

human blood to the extent of fifteen hundred murders.[1] I do not want to accuse, all I want to do is to let you see what passes in my soul. I cannot refrain from reproaching you, Professor Sioli, for saying that the conditions of my home were not the decisive factor. On the contrary, you may well assume that youthful surroundings are decisive for the development of character. With silent longing I have sometimes in my early days glimpsed other families and asked myself why it could not be like that with us.

I contradict the Chief Public Prosecutor when he asserts that it was out of cowardice that I revoked my confession. The very day that I opened up to my wife I well knew the consequences of the confession; I felt liberated in a certain way and I had the firm intention of sticking to my confession so that I could do a last good turn to my wife. But the real reason was that there arrives for every criminal that moment beyond which he cannot go. And I was in due course subject to this psychic collapse. As I have related already, I followed the reports in the newspapers then and, of course, later, very thoroughly. I convinced myself that on the whole the newspaper reports had been moderate. I may say that I used to intoxicate myself with the sensational press, it was the poison which must bear part of the responsibility of my poisoned life. By being moderate now, it has done a great deal to prevent the public from being poisoned. I feel urged to make one more statement: some victims made it rather easy for me to overpower them.

I do not want to forget to mention what I frequently said before – that I detest the crimes and feel deep sorrow for the relatives. I even dare to ask those relatives to forgive me, as far as that may be possible for them. Furthermore, I want to point out emphatically that, contrary to the version of the Chief Public Prosecutor, I never tortured a victim. I do not attempt to excuse my crimes. I have already pointed out that I am prepared to bear the consequences of my misdeeds. I hope that thus I will atone for a large part of what I have done.

Although I can suffer capital punishment only once, you may rest assured that it is one of the many unknown tortures to endure the time before the execution of the sentence, and dozens of times I have lived through the moment of the execution. And when you consider this and recognize my goodwill to atone for all my crimes. I should think that the terrible desire for revenge and hatred against me cannot endure. And I want to ask you to forgive me.

[1] A reference to the case of certain abortionists

The jury was out for an hour and a half, and Kürten was sentenced to death nine times for murder.

For a while there seemed some hope that Kürten might not suffer the death penalty, which had not been carried out since a man named Böttcher had been executed in 1928 for the murder of a woman and a child in a wood near Berlin. It is indicative of the extreme liberalism in Germany in the early 1930s that there was something of a storm at the death penalty on Kürten, and the German Humanitarian League protested. Kürten appealed, but the appeal was rejected. Kürten himself was calm and well-behaved. He was bombarded with letters, love letters and letters describing sadistic punishments arriving in equal quantities. Many people asked for his autograph. (A girl who had been assaulted by Kürten when he was 16 described how he stood one day in front of the waxworks of murderers and burglars and said, 'One day I shall be as famous as they are.')

He was executed at six o'clock on the morning of July 2nd, 1931. He enjoyed his last meal – of Wiener schnitzel, chips, and white wine – so much that he asked for it again. He told Berg that his one hope was that he would hear the sound of his own blood running into the basket, which would give him intense pleasure. (He also admitted to wanting to throttle Berg's stenographer because of her slim, white throat.) He was guillotined, and seemed cheerful and unconcerned at the last.

4

Mass Murder in America, 1890–1920

The most notable American multiple murderer of the nineteenth century was a man named Herman Webster Mudgett, who (understandably) preferred to to call himself Harry Howard Holmes. He belongs to the history of mass murder, but the fact that many of his murders were motivated by sex, and that he was an obsessive seducer, warrants a brief description of his career in this volume. Like so many con-men – Landru, Petiot, Heath, Haigh – Holmes seems to have been one of those born crooks who, from the beginning, looked for a way to do down his fellow human beings. He provides a powerful argument for the belief that certain people are just born bad – in fact, downright rotten. Born in 1860 in Gilmanton, New Hampshire, son of a postmaster, he studied medicine, and was practising his first swindle in his early twenties – involving the faked death of a patient and the theft of a corpse. When he abandoned his wife and child to move to Chicago in 1886, he soon married a girl from a wealthy family and tried forging the signature of a rich uncle. Then he became the assistant of a Mrs Holden, who ran a drugstore; within three years she had vanished, and Holmes was the new owner. He did so well that he built himself a large boarding house opposite the store – which has been christened 'Murder Castle' and 'Nightmare House'. It had chutes leading from most rooms to the basement – where there was a large furnace – and gas pipes so arranged that he could flood any room with gas. It is not known how many 'guests' vanished during the Chicago World Fair of 1893, but it probably ran into double figures. Meanwhile, he had seduced the wife of a jeweller named Conner who rented space in the drugstore; when Conner moved out, both the wife, Julia, and her 18-year-old sister Gertie became his mistresses. Then Gertie became pregnant, and vanished. So did a pretty 16-year-old girl named Emily Van Tassell, who often came into the shop with her mother. If, as seems probable, Holmes killed her in order to possess her, then he certainly qualifies as a sex-killer. When Julia objected to Holmes's new secretary, Emily Cigrand, Julia and her daughter disappeared. Soon after that, so did Emily Cigrand. The following year, so did another mistress – Minnie Williams – and her sister Nannie.

After the World Fair was over, Holmes was hoist with his own petard when he fell in love with a girl called Georgiana Yoke and married her. In jail for fraud, Holmes met a famous train robber called Marion Hedgepeth, and asked his advice on acquiring a crooked lawyer, offering to cut him in on an insurance fraud.

The 'fraud' was actually planned as a mass murder of a family of seven. A fellow crook named Pitezel was supposed to die in a laboratory explosion; Holmes would substitute a corpse bought from a medical school, and would share Pitezel's insurance money with Pitezel's wife. In fact, Pitezel's death was all too real, as was that of three of Pitezel's children who were allowed by their mother to accompany Holmes on a flight around various cities in America and Canada.

Marion Hedgepeth, angered by Holmes's failure to pay him his share of the insurance money, told his story to the insurance company and Holmes was arrested before he could complete the murder plan; a policeman named Geyer followed Holmes's trail around the country and located the remains of the three children – two daughters, aged 11 and 15, and a 9-year-old boy. Holmes was found guilty, and wrote a confession in which he admitted twenty-seven murders; he was hanged in 1895, choking slowly to death on the end of a rope that had been tied by an inefficient hangman.

Was Holmes a serial killer in the modern sense of the word? If we are speaking of obsessive sex killers like Jack the Ripper and the Boston Strangler, the answer is probably no. But if we mean a man who is in the grip of a sexual fever, and who kills repeatedly and obsessively, then the answer must be yes. We are once again confronting the problem of the dividing line between the serial killer – whose motive is rape – and the mass murderer, who kills for gain. There are some cases of mass murder – like Joseph Smith, the 'Brides in the Bath' killer, or Marcel Petiot, the French doctor who offered to help Jewish refugees to escape and then killed them for their money – where there can be no possible doubt that the motive was simply financial gain. But in Holmes, as in Landru, we confront a man in whom the criminal urge and the sexual urge are so closely linked that it is impossible to separate them. Crime itself has become sexualized.

The first decade of the twentieth century was remarkable for the detection of two 'bluebeard' killers, one male, one female.

Johann Hoch – born Schmidt – was a native of Horweiler, Germany; born in 1860, he was destined for the ministry – his father and two brothers were already in the church. In 1887 he abandoned his wife and three children and sailed for America. In Wheeling, West Virginia, he opened a saloon, and married a widow named Caroline Hoch. The minister who performed the ceremony saw Hoch giving his wife some white powder, and hours later she died in agony. Hoch quickly sold the house, claimed on his wife's insurance policy, then faked a suicide by leaving his clothes on a riverbank; after this he disappeared. Later in the same year he married two more women, Martha Steinbucher and Mary Rankin; the first also died in agony, but the second was luckier: Hoch only deserted her.

During the course of the next eight years he married an unknown number of women – ten is a conservative estimate – abandoning some and burying others.

In December 1904, Hoch (as he now called himself) advertised in a Chicago newspaper published in German, claiming to be a wealthy widower in search of a wife. Soon he married a woman named Marie Walcker, who owned a sweet shop. His wife presented him with her entire savings. But she also made the mistake of mentioning that her sister, Mrs Julia Fischer, also had $800 or so deposited in a savings bank. It sealed her fate. A week later she became seriously ill, and the doctor diagnosed the trouble as nephritis. Mrs Fischer was sent for to nurse her sister, and soon Hoch was flirting with her. Mrs Walcker died on 12 January 1905, and Hoch immediately proposed to her sister.

Julia protested that it was too soon to think of such things, but nevertheless married him three days later.

They moved to a flat in Wells Street, but there Hoch was upset to learn that he was being denounced as a murderer and a swindler by one of the tenants – a friend of his late bride, and the woman who had drafted the letter in reply to Hoch's advertisement. While Julia was trying to placate this lady, Hoch vanished, taking $750 he had borrowed from Julia.

Julia notified the Chicago police. The man who was placed in charge of the case, Inspector George Shippy, already had some knowledge of Hoch – in fact, had been instrumental in jailing him six years earlier. Shippy had investigated Hoch on a charge of swindling a furniture dealer by selling furniture that was on hire-purchase, and Hoch had received a twelve-month sentence. The clergyman who had seen Hoch slip a white powder into the food of Caroline Hoch, the Revd. Hermann Haas, learned that Hoch was in jail, and contacted Shippy to tell him of his suspicions. Shippy had Mrs Hoch's body exhumed, but it proved that Hoch had been too clever for him. The vital organs (presumably the stomach and liver) were missing. Shippy investigated Hoch and learned of a trail of abandoned wives from New York to San Francisco. Unfortunately, Hoch had already been released from jail and had vanished.

Shippy immediately requested that the body of Marie Walcker should be exhumed. The post-mortem revealed 7.6 grains of arsenic in the stomach, and 1.25 in the liver. Shippy handed over a picture of Hoch to the press, and requested nationwide publicity.

This quickly produced results. A Mrs Catherine Kimmerle, who ran a boarding house in West Forty-Seventh Street in New York, recognized the photograph as that of a recently arrived boarder named Bartella, who had proposed to her within twenty minutes of entering the house. His ardent manner had frightened her and she had declined.

'Bartella' was quickly arrested, and admitted that he was Hoch. A fountain pen in his possession proved to contain arsenic – which Hoch declared he had bought to commit suicide. The New York police returned him to Chicago.

There Shippy was waiting for him, with a list of a dozen women whom he had married since 1896, five of whom had died soon after the marriage. Five wives whom he had deserted were brought to Chicago to identify him, and the police had difficulty restraining them from attacking the prisoner.

Tried for the murder of Marie Walcker, he was found guilty and sentenced to death. A lady named Cora Wilson, who had never met Hoch, advanced the money for an appeal, declaring that she was convinced of his innocence; this appeal was rejected, and Hoch was hanged on 23 February 1906.

The number of Hoch's victims is a matter for speculation. In the *Encyclopedia of World Crime*, Jay Robert Nash speaks of 'dozens', but the brides who are known to have died soon after marrying him amount only to six. On the other hand Hoch was in America for nine years before he poisoned Caroline Hoch – listed by Thomas S. Duke as the first known victim – so it is highly probable that there were more.

Belle Gunness, America's most notorious murderess, (there was even a Laurel and Hardy film about her) was luckier than Hoch; she escaped before her misdeeds were found out. At least, we think she did.

The end came on the night of 27 April 1908, near the small town of La Porte, Indiana. Earlier that day, Belle Gunness had been to a local lawyer to make her will, leaving her property to her three children, or, if they failed to survive, to the local Norwegian orphanage. She told the lawyer that she was being bothered by her ex-hired man, Ray Lamphere, and that she suspected that he intended to burn down her farm. Just before dawn the next day, the new hired man, Joe Maxson, woke up and smelled burning; when he looked out of the window he saw that flames were bursting out of the windows of the kitchen below. He tried to break into the bedroom in which Belle Gunness should have been asleep with her three children; the door was locked. As Maxson rushed outside, the fire took hold. Neighbours began to arrive, and Maxson harnessed the horse and drove off for the sheriff. By the time the volunteer fire brigade arrived, the farmhouse was little more than a heap of embers. Late that afternoon, investigation of the cellar disclosed the charred corpses of the three children, and the headless corpse of a woman. Ray Lamphere was immediately arrested.

A week later, a man with a Norwegian accent walked into the office of Sheriff Al Smutzer and introduced himself as Asle

Helgelian. He was in search of his younger brother Andrew, who had left his home in Mansfield, South Dakota, to marry a rich widow who signed her letters Bella Gunness. Mrs Gunness had advertised for a husband in a Norwegian newspaper, Andrew had replied, and they had been in regular weekly correspondence for sixteen months before he left for Indiana the previous January. There he had drawn out all his money from the local bank, with Mrs Gunness at his elbow. But when his brother wrote to Mrs Gunness to ask about Andrew, she had answered that Andrew had gone off looking for a friend in Chicago. It was the cashier of the local bank who had sent Asle Helgelian newspaper cuttings about the burning down of the farm. Now he was convinced that his brother was dead – probably buried somewhere on the farm.

Sheriff Smutzer did not seem to take Asle Helgelian seriously. He made sympathetic noises and recommended that he go and stay with a fellow Norwegian who lived close to the Gunness farm. And it was due to Asle Helgelian's urging that Joe Maxson and a neighbour called Daniel Hutson – who had been paid to dig in the ruins – transferred their attention to a 'hog pen' where Mrs Gunness buried rubbish. There all three men began to dig. Soon there was an unpleasant smell like rotten fish, and minutes later they uncovered a dismembered body covered with oilcloth. Asle Helgelian identified it as his brother Andrew. The wrist of the left arm had a defensive cut as if he had been trying to wield off the blow of a hatchet, and the fingers of his right hand were also missing. There was still a tuft of brown curly hair in the hand, presumably torn from the head of his murderer. Medical examination would later reveal strychnine in his stomach.

Four feet down, under rubbish, they uncovered the hacked-up remains of four more victims. The topmost body was that of a blonde girl; this was identified as Belle Gunness's adopted daughter Jennie – who according to Mrs Gunness, had left for school in California eighteen months earlier.

Told about the discovery, Ray Lamphere gasped, and said he had always suspected it. Mrs Gunness had asked him to buy rat poison and chloroform . . .

A few days later they found more graves. One contained the disjoined skeleton of a young man whose head had been split open with an axe. In another grave were the bones of three men. Two days later they found another grave containing a woman's shoes, the remains of a purse, and the skeleton of a youth. That made fourteen bodies so far.

Slowly, most of the bodies were identified. One was Ole Budsberg, who had sold up his home in Iola, Wisconsin, in March 1907, and moved in with Mrs Gunness. Soon after, his sons opened a letter addressed to him; it proved to be from Mrs Gunness, and said that she hoped he was not offended that she had refused him, and hoped he would get settled out west. Other relatives identified the remains of Olaf Lindboe, Henry Gurholt and John Moe (or Moo).

Now it was clear that Belle was a mass murderess, doubts began to arise about the headless body in the cellar. There was evidence that the children had also been poisoned – although a careless mix-up of the stomachs of all four corpses left some doubt about this. The small skulls certainly had holes in them, suggesting that they had been killed by hammer blows. The headless woman's body seemed too small for Belle. Was it not conceivable that she had killed another woman in her place, and removed the head to make sure she was not identified through her teeth?

A number of witnesses soon came forward to state that they had seen Belle on the evening of the fire, driving in a buggy with a dark-haired woman, whom she had apparently fetched from the station . . .

But this theory was also undermined when, after 'sluicing' the ashes as if searching for gold, an ex-miner found Belle's false teeth, and also two of her real teeth, to which the set was anchored. The dentist who made the false teeth had no doubt they were Belle's.

The story was now on every front page in America. Journalists soon ferreted out the life story of Belle Gunness, and it confirmed everyone's worst suspicions.

She had been born Brynhild Poulsdatter Pedersen on 11 November 1859, in the fishing hamlet of Innbygde, on the west coat of Norway. Her father was a poverty-stricken farmer. In 1883, she followed her eldest sister Nellie to Chicago, and in the following year married a watchman named Mads Sorenson. Money was scarce, and Belle supplemented their meagre income by taking in lodgers, and at one point running a candy store. She was living in Chicago during the 1893 World Fair when H. H. Holmes was running a rather more expensive – and successful –

boarding house. But after twelve years of marriage. Mads was still earning only $15 a week. Belle (as she now called herself) hated poverty – her sister Nellie remarked 'My sister was crazy for money.'

She seems to have learned to supplement her income with insurance fraud. In 1896, the candy store she owned was burned down, and in 1898, their home in the suburb of Austin was damaged by fire. Their daughter Caroline died in 1896, and her son Axel in 1898. Both had symptoms of acute colitis, and both were insured. And in July 1900, the day that two insurance policies on her husband happened to overlap, Mads Sorenson died of a similiar illness. The young doctor who was summoned to the deathbed noted the arched body, and suspected strychnine poisoning. But an older colleague told him that he had diagnosed an enlarged heart, and advised him to sign the death certificate. The young doctor later regretted that he had not insisted on a post mortem.

In fact, a post mortem *was* later held, at the request of the dead man's brother, but when it was discovered that the heart *was* enlarged, the coroner did not bother to examine the stomach.

With the $8,500 in insurance money, Belle purchased the farm a mile north of La Porte, a pleasant, small community a dozen miles from Lake Michigan. The farm had been a sporting house, and was a stately-looking building, half brick and half wood, with a large garden, an orchard and numerous outbuildings. It came complete with the brothel's impressive furniture – heavy sideboards, massive chairs and comfortable beds.

Belle now decided to captivate a Wisconsin farmer named Frederickson, but when Frederickson's housekeeper frustrated her plans, married instead the housekeeper's recently widowed son, Peter Gunness. He moved in with Belle in April 1902. Less than a week after their marriage, his baby died suddenly. The doctor who signed the certificate suspected smothering, but he kept his suspicions to himself until many years later.

Eight months later, her husband was the victim of a curious accident. Peter Gunness died on the kitchen floor, scalded with hot brine, and apparently struck down by a heavy meat grinder which, according to his wife, had fallen from the shelf above the stove. His widow explained that she always kept the meat grinder on the shelf, and that Gunness must have dislodged it so it struck the bowl of brine on the stove, then hit him on the head. She did not explain how the meat grinder jumped off the shelf, struck the brine on the stove, then jumped up again to strike the fatal blow. But her 12-year-old adopted daughter Jennie corroborated the main part of the story, and the coroner brought in a reluctant verdict of accidental death.

Six years later, not long before the farm burnt down, her youngest daughter Myrtle told a schoolfriend: 'Mamma killed my papa – she hit him with a meat cleaver.' A more likely weapon was the back of a chopper.

Belle had adopted Jennie when she was a baby, soon after her mother's death. Her father, Anton Olsen, had later invited his daughter for a visit to Chicago, hoping she would want to stay, but Jennie had pined for the farm and gone back. A young hired man named Emile Greening had been in love with her, and had been deeply hurt when Jennie – now sixteen – had departed for California without saying goodbye, just after Christmas 1906. Significantly, Belle had been due to pay Jennie a legacy of $1,800 when she was 18. Emile later identifed Jennie's skull.

When Peter Gunness died, Belle was pregnant again; she called the baby Philip.

Over the next few years Belle had a series of hired men, and most of them seem to have been her lovers. Now in her mid-forties, she was not particularly attractive – a massive woman with high cheekbones and stern eyes – but the few men who slept with her and survived recorded that she had a natural talent for sex that soon made them her slaves. Regrettably, most of them soon began to think of themselves as Belle's husband and the master of the house, and she seems to have disliked this intensely – as far as she was concerned, she was the mistress and they were employees. Many of these hired men left suddenly and unexpectedly – so unexpectedly that Belle was left to finish the ploughing. Relatives later identified some of them in Belle's home-made cemetery.

Belle also introduced a number of suitors to her neighbours – one from Minnesota, one from Wisconsin, one from South Dakota. She later explained that they had changed their minds and left.

In June 1907, Belle approached a young odd-job man named Ray Lamphere and told him she was looking for a man about the house. Ray was a weak-chinned individual with a droopy moustache and eyes like an anxious koala bear. The first evening he spent at the Gunness farm, he experienced the delights of Belle's excellent – if somewhat heavy – Norwegian cuisine, then retired to a comfortable bed in the spare room. Later that night Belle joined him, and proved that she was as skilled in the arts of lovemaking as of cooking. When she left in the early morning, Lamphere could hardly believe his luck. This magnificent woman, with her comfortable home and equally comfortable income, had chosen him as her mate. It seemed too good to be true.

Six months later he learned that it *was* too good to be true. Just before Christmas 1907, a man arrived at the farm, and Belle explained they were engaged. For the next week Ray was in a frenzy of jealousy; then, to his relief, the man disappeared.

But not long after, in early January, another man appeared; this was Andrew Helgelian, who (as his brother later revealed) had spent ten years in jail for post office robbery. Realizing that his mistress was now spending her nights in Helgelian's bed, Ray was again tormented by jealousy.

On the cold, snowy night of 14 January 1908, Belle ordered him to drive to Michigan City to pick up a horse that was being sent by her cousin Mr Moe. But when Lamphere, together with a friend he took along for company, arrived at his destination, there was no horse. The two men went drinking, then to a vaudeville show. Finally, on the way home, the spurned lover announced that he was going to the farm to see what 'the old woman' was up to. The following afternoon, he saw his friend, and told a strange story. He had, he claimed, bored a hole in the floorboards so he could overhear what Belle and Helgelian were talking about. And, he claimed, they were discussing how to poison him . . .

Whatever happened that night, it made Lamphere morose and jumpy. He declined to sleep under Belle's roof, and on 3 February she discharged him, and hired Joe Maxson in his place. And although she was not sexually interested in Joe, or vice versa, Lamphere continued to haunt the farm. He muttered to friends that he had information that would place Belle behind bars. But if he was really trying to blackmail her, she took it remarkably coolly; in fact, she sued him for trespass, and he was fined. She also alleged that he had stolen a silver watch; but Ray insisted that she had given it to him. And since he had displayed it to friends at the time he and Belle were lovers, the sheriff chose to take his word. (The silver watch later proved to be the property of John Moe, one of the vanished suitors.)

And so Ray Lamphere continued to pester his ex-mistress until that afternoon in April when she went to see a solicitor about her will, and told him that she expected Lamphere to burn down her house . . .

This, then, was the situation when Ray Lamphere's trial opened on 9 November 1908, accused of murdering Belle and her children by setting fire to the house. The defence, led by Wirt Worden, based its case on the argument that Belle Gunness was still alive. A witness was produced who claimed to have seen Belle driving to the farm with another woman – and this woman, said Worden, was the headless body found in the ruins. Belle had a long scar on her thigh, and the corpse had no such scar. Moreover, Belle's neighbour Daniel Hutson claimed that he had actually *seen* Belle in her orchard three months after the fire. Worden's case was that Belle had killed her own children, then escaped. Lamphere had told him – Worden – that he had helped Belle to escape on the night of the fire. The implication was that Ray had set fire to the house, believing it to be empty . . .

The prosecution case was that Lamphere had started the fire to revenge himself on his ex-mistress. The body found in the fire *was* that of Belle Gunness, and the head was missing because it had been burnt off. The false teeth – attached to a real tooth from Belle's head – proved it. Lamphére had admitted to getting up at three on the morning of the fire, and leaving the house twenty minutes later. He had admitted passing the farm on his way to work, and telling his new employer that Belle's house was on fire. Lamphere, said the prosecution, had started that fire. A neighbouring boy stated that Lamphere had seen him hiding in the bushes, and had threatened to kill him if he did not go away. Not long after that – just before the first signs of the fire were noticed – he had seen Lamphere running away.

All the same, Worden succeeded in sowing many doubts in the mind of the jury. A doctor stated in court that there was poison in the bodies of the children and the female corpse. The injuries to the skulls were mentioned as proof that the children were murdered. By the end of the trial on Thanksgiving Day (26 November) the jury was confused and divided. But eventually, after many ballots, the foreman announced the verdict. Ray Lamphere *was* guilty of setting fire to the farm.

But Belle, the jury believed, had taken her own life with strychnine . . .

Ray Lamphere was sentenced to from two to twenty-one years' imprisonment. His comment, as he approached the penitentiary, was that he felt he was lucky to be alive when he might have ended up in 'the old woman's' chicken run.

Just over a year later, he died of consumption. Shortly before his death, he told a strange story to a fellow prisoner. Belle, he insisted, was alive; he had taken her away, disguised as a man, in a hired rig, and handed her over to an accomplice. That accomplice, he implied, was the local sheriff, who was in Belle's pay. Then he had returned and set fire to the house. Belle later sent back her false teeth – plus the real ones – for him to place in the ashes after charring them in a fire.

According to Lamphere, he had been Belle's accomplice for the past year or so, and had helped her dispose of several of the bodies. Belle had killed and dissected them, he had buried them. But he had come to suspect that she intended to kill him, and had refused to sleep on the property. They had quarrelled and he left. He was in no position to denounce her because he had been an accomplice. But when she decided it was time to disappear, she offered Ray $500 to help her. She had hired a woman she had seen sitting on a stairway in Chicago, and brought her back to the farm two days before the fire. But the woman had a full set of teeth, and her nose was quite different from Belle's. So her head had to be removed – Ray buried it, together with three other heads, in a rye field. Then he had driven Belle away, handed her to an accomplice, and then set the house on fire early the next morning.

At first sight this sounds by far the likeliest story. But there are strong objections to it. If Lamphere was her accomplice, then presumably he helped her to bury her last victim, Andrew Helgelian. But if he knew that Helgelian was going to die, why was he so frantic with jealousy? And why did he go back to the farm that night to see what the 'old lady' was doing? He should have known what she was doing.

His story of Belle and Helgelian planning to poison him sounds equally unlikely. If Belle wanted to poison Lamphere, she certainly did not need an accomplice. The likeliest explanation is probably that he hung around the farm with a masochistic craving to find out if Belle was in bed with Helgelian. But she had taken care to draw all the curtains and lock all the doors – as a murderess would when she intends to dispose of another victim.

Lillian de la Torre, the author of the best book on the case, *The Truth about Belle Gunness* (1955) has provided a possible solution to the mystery. She is convinced that Lamphere was telling the truth about one thing: that the 'accomplice' in the case was Sheriff Al Smutzer himself, and that he had been in the pay of Belle Gunness from the beginning. He was the man to whom Lamphere handed Belle over after driving her away from the farm that night. But what Belle had not anticipated was Smutzer's treachery. He knew she was carrying a large sum of money (usually estimated at $30,000). There was nothing to prevent him from killing Belle and helping himself. A few weeks later, when it was necessary to prove that it was indeed Belle's body in the ruins, he had returned to the corpse and taken out the dentures, which he planted in the ashes after placing them in a fire to char them.

De la Torre points out that Sheriff Smutzer went to Texas in the course of his investigation – a man there had falsely confessed to being implicated in the case – and that this would be an ideal opportunity to open a bank account and deposit the $30,000. In fact, Smutzer made a habit of going to Texas in the years that followed, and finally stayed there for thirty years, before he returned to Laporte, where he died penniless.

The main objection to this theory is that there is not a scrap of evidence that Mutzer was corrupt. Yet we also have to admit that it is hard to fault Lillian de la Torre's logic. Either it was Belle in the burnt-out farmhouse or it was not. And if it was Belle, then either she killed herself, or she was murdered – probably by Lamphere. But there was not time for Lamphere to walk out to the farm, kill Belle and the children, set fire to the house, and hurry on to his other job, all in the space of an hour. In any case, Lamphere was hardly the type – he was too weak. Besides, there was poison in the bodies – we are not sure which because the stomachs were accidentally put in the same jar – which suggests that Belle administered it the night before.

So if the headless corpse was Belle, she committed suicide. That, it might be argued, is just conceivable. Although she may have poisoned two of her children in Chicago, we may assume that she felt attachment to the children she had brought up in La

Porte, particularly to baby Philip. Maxson spoke of her love of playing games with the children – they were playing just before the last time he saw them – and everyone agreed that she seemed to be a good mother. But now, at last, after at least eight years of murder, her crimes looked as if they were catching up with her. Relatives of the victims were asking questions, and any day might arrive and make trouble. If they did, that fool Lamphere might tell all he knew, and although it was not much, it might be enough to bring the sheriff with a search warrant of her property. She may have felt that the end was close. And for all we know, she was running out of money. It was true that she had collected many sums of a thousand dollars or so over the years, but with a farm to run and children to bring up, she might well be coming close to the end of her resources. (There was only $700 in her account when she died.) And it was too risky to advertise for yet another husband. So Belle may have decided it was time to die, and to take her children with her, as many suicides do. She also may have decided to take Lamphere with her – which is why, after she made her will, she remarked that she expected him to burn down the house.

Against this hypothesis we have to place what we know of Belle's psychology. She was a survivor. She had killed two husbands, and possibly as many as twenty other men (there were twenty watches found in the ruins). She had murdered her own adopted daughter and possibly two of her children. If it meant killing her own family to save her neck, Belle would not have hesitated. The headless body seemed too small for Belle, and the suggestion – made by a doctor at the trial – that it had shrunk by two-thirds in the heat sounds unlikely.

Yet the most convincing evidence that Belle died in the fire – the evidence that convinced the coroner – is the teeth. When a reporter asked the sheriff whether Belle could not simply have removed her teeth before she fled, the sheriff shook his head, and pointed to the real tooth the false teeth were attached to. This tooth had a gold cap, and a dentist in court said that it would have been impossible to pull out the tooth without splitting this cap.

But if Belle was lying dead and buried, then her killer could have removed her teeth by digging them out of her gums. So we are faced with the unavoidable conclusion: either Belle committed suicide, or someone else killed her – the accomplice to whom Lamphere claimed he delivered her. And we know enough of Belle to know that it is highly unlikely that she committed suicide.

Lillian de la Torre suggests that Jennie was killed because she suspected that Peter Gunness had been murdered. That is unlikely. She gave her evidence in Belle's favour at the inquest, and the coroner signed a certificate of accidental death. That was old history. From what we know of Belle's psychology, Jennie was murdered because Belle was due to pay her $1,800 on her eighteenth birthday, and Belle hated to part with money. A secondary motive may have been the fact that having a 16-year-old girl around the house robbed her of the privacy necessary for murdering and dismembering husbands.

There is one other point on which we might take issue with Lillian de la Torre. That accomplice may not, after all, have been Sheriff Smutzer. Clutched in Andrew Helgelian's hand was a bunch of hair torn from the head of his killer. It was not Belle's hair, or Ray Lamphere's. We do not know if it belonged to Sheriff Smutzer, but it seems unlikely – surely someone would have recollected that Smutzer looked as if he had been in a fight four months earlier, with a lock of his hair torn out by the roots? Belle had had a number of lovers over the years, including a hired man named Peter Colson, who was never under suspicion. That lock of hair in Helgelian's hand certainly belonged to *somebody*, and that somebody was not Belle.

One other person seems to have known the truth. Ray Lamphere's best friend, a woman known as Nigger Liz, claimed to know exactly what happened, and told Wirt Worden that she would send for him and reveal it on her death bed. Unfortunately, Worden was out of town when Nigger Liz sent for him, and by the time he got back, she was dead.

How *do* we explain a woman who can murder husbands and children, and dismember lovers? The key undoubtedly lies in Nellie's remark: 'My sister was crazy for money.' Belle went to America to escape the poverty of the Norwegian farm; it was the land of opportunity, and she hoped to become – at the very least – a comfortable, middle-class housewife with a home to be proud of. But marriage to Mads Sorenson proved a mistake; it soon became obvious that he was never going to rise in the world. Then, after twelve years of uphill struggle, the candy store caught fire, and she received the insurance money. It may well be that the fire was accidental. At all events, it taught her that there *were* ways of making large sums of money without slaving like a dirt farmer. Significantly, it was at this point that they moved to the comfortable Chicago suburb of Austin, and at last Belle had the kind of home she wanted. (Nellie quoted her as saying: 'I would never remain with this man if it was not for the nice home he has.') Mads was still earning only $15 a week, but fortunately there were a few more insurance windfalls on fires, and on the death of two children from colic. And finally, on 30 July 1900, Belle made a killing in both senses of the word when Mads died in convulsions on the day two insurance policies overlapped, and she received the huge sum of $8,500.

Now, at last, she was able to buy the home of her dreams. The sporting house that had belonged to Mattie Altic was a kind of mansion. At last, she was living in the surroundings she felt she had always deserved. But more insurance fraud was out of the question – it would have raised too much suspicion. She had to find new ways of increasing her wealth. And she did it with a boldness that in a businessman would have been a guarantee of success. The truth is that Belle shared the sense of enterprise that turned Andrew Carnegie and Cornelius Vanderbilt into millionaires. It is not surprising that Americans feel ambivalent about her.

A quarter of a century after the Jack the Ripper murders, New Orleans had its own spectacular series of apparently unsolved murders; the killer became known as the Mad Axeman. But in this case, they seem to have been inspired by the same deep resentment against Italians that the Ripper felt against prostitutes.

On the morning of 24 May 1918, an Italian cobbler named Jake Maggio was awakened by a groaning sound coming from the next room, where his brother Joe slept with his wife. As he entered the room, he saw a woman lying on the floor, her head almost severed from her body; Joe lay in bed groaning. Nearby lay a bloodstained axe and a cut-thoat razor, which had been used to slash Joe's throat. He died soon after.

By the time the police arrived, Jake and his second brother Andrew had found how the intruder entered – through a panel chiselled out of the back door. Jake and Andrew were arrested as suspects, but soon released.

On the pavement two streets away someone had chalked on the pavement: 'Mrs Maggio is going to sit up tonight, just like Mrs Toney.' It reminded the police that seven years earlier there had been four axe murders of Italian grocers including a Mrs Tony Schiambra. They had been attributed to the criminal organization, 'the Black Hand', which was rife in New Orleans.

Five weeks after the Maggio killings, a bread delivery man found a back door with a panel chiselled out. When he knocked the door was opened by a man covered in blood. He was a Pole named Besumer, and inside lay a woman who was known as his wife. She was still alive, and told of being struck by a big white man wielding a hatchet. She died later, and Besumer was charged with her murder.

But that night the axeman struck again – a young married man, Edward Schneider, returned home to find his pregnant wife lying in bed covered in blood. Rushed to hospital she survived, and gave birth a week later. The attacker seemed to have entered by an open window.

Five days later, a barber named Romano became the next victim. His niece, heard noises in his bedroom, and went in to find him being attacked by a big man wearing a black slouch hat. As she screamed, the man 'vanished as if he had wings'. A panel had been chipped out of the door.

New Orleans was in a panic reminiscent of that which had swept London in the days of Jack the Ripper. There were several false alarms, and one man found an axe and chisel outside his back door . . . On 30 August 1918, a man named Nick Asunto heard a noise, and went to investigate; he saw a heavily built man with an axe, who fled as he shouted. All New Orleans began taking elaborate precautions against the Axeman.

For the time being, the attacks ceased, and the ending of the war in 1918 gave people other things to think about. But in March 1919, a grocer named Jordano heard screams from a house across the street, and found another grocer, Charles Cortimiglia, unconscious on the floor, while his wife – a dead baby in her arms – sat on the floor with blood streaming from her head. She said she had awakened to see a man attacking her husband with an axe, and when she snatched up her baby, he killed the child with a blow, then struck her . . . The door panel had been chiselled out. Yet when Mrs Cortimiglia began to recover, she accused Jordano, the man who had found her, of being the killer, and although her husband (now also recovering) insisted that this was untrue, Jordano and his son were arrested.

Three days after the attack, the local newspaper received a letter signed 'The Axeman', datelined 'From Hell' (as in the case of a Jack the Ripper letter), and declaring that he would be coming to New Orleans next Tuesday at 12.15, but would spare any house playing jazz music. The following Tuesday, the streets of New Orleans rocked with Jazz, and the Axeman failed to appear . . . Someone even wrote a 'Mysterious Axeman Jazz'.

Besumer, who had been in custody since his arrest, was tried and acquitted. But the Jordanos, to everyone's amazement, were found guilty, although Charles Cortimiglia repeated that they were innocent.

And the attacks went on – although there was to be only one further death. On 10 August 1919, a grocer named Steve Boca woke to find a shadowy figure holding an axe beside the bed. When he woke again, he was bleeding from a skull wound. He managed to stagger down to the home of a friend, Frank Genusa, and the frantic police arrested Genusa – then shamefacedly released him.

On 2 September a druggist named Carlson heard scratching noises from the back door, and fired his revolver through the panel. The intruder fled, leaving behind a chisel.

The next day, neighbours found 19-year-old Sarah Lauman unconscious; she had been attacked with an axe and three teeth knocked out. She could remember nothing when she recovered.

The last attack was on a grocer named Mike Pepitone. His wife – in a separate bedroom – heard sounds of a struggle, and entered his room in time to see a man vanishing. Her husband had been killed with an axe blow so violent that it spattered blood up the wall. Again, a chiselled door panel revealed how the axeman had gained entry.

Then the murders ceased. The Jordanos were finally released when Mrs Cortimiglia confessed that she had lied because she hated them. Now, she said, her husband had left her, and she had smallpox – Saint Joseph had appeared to her and told her to confess. The Jordanos were released.

But Mrs Pepitone, widow of the last victim, was to enter the story again. On 7 December 1920, in Los Angeles, she had shot and killed a man named Joseph Mumfre, from New Orleans, in the street. She claimed he was the axeman. She was sentenced to ten years in prison, but released after three.

Was Mumfre the Axeman? He could well have been. He had been released from prison just before the 1911 murders, then sent back for the next seven years. Released again just before the first of the 1918 murders, he had been back in prison during the 'lull' between August 1918 and March 1919, when they began again. He left New Orleans shortly after the murder of Mike Pepitone.

What was his motive? Almost certainly, he was a sadist who wanted to attack women, not men. Joe Maggio was left alive; his wife was killed. Besumer was only knocked unconscious; his attractive wife died of her injuries. Many of the later victims were women, and it seems likely that he attacked the men when in search of women victims.

Why Italian grocers? In fact, many of the victims were not Italians. *But all kept small shops*. And a small shop is a place where an attractive wife can be seen serving behind the counter. Mrs Pepitone never revealed how she tracked down Mumfre, but it seems likely that he was a customer, and she recognized him and followed his trail to Los Angeles.

5

Mass Murder in America, 1920–1940

H. H. Holmes may or may not be classified as a serial killer, depending on our view of whether his crimes were pathological or purely commercial. Johann Hoch and Belle Gunness were undoubtedly mass murderers and not serial killers. Earle Nelson, also known as 'the Dark Strangler' and 'the Gorilla Murderer', was undoubtedly a serial killer in our modern sense of the word.

On 24 February 1926, a man named Richard Newman went to call on his aunt, who advertised rooms to let in San Francisco; he found the naked body of the 60-year-old woman in an upstairs toilet. She had been strangled with her pearl necklace, then repeatedly raped. Clara Newman was the first of twenty-two victims of a man who became known as 'the Gorilla Murderer'. The killer made a habit of calling at houses with a 'Room to Let' notice in the window; if the landlady was alone, he strangled and raped her. His victims included a 14-year-old girl and an 8-month-old baby. And as he travelled around from San Francisco to San Jose, from Portland, Oregon to Council Bluffs, Iowa, from Philadelphia to Buffalo, from Detroit to Chicago, the police found him as elusive as the French police had found Joseph Vacher thirty years earlier. Their problem was simply that the women who could identify 'the Dark Strangler' (as the newspapers had christened him) were dead, and they had no idea of what he looked like. But when the Portland police had the idea of asking newspapers to publish descriptions of jewellery that had been stolen from some of the strangler's victims, three old ladies in a South Portland lodging-house recalled that they had bought a few items of jewellery from a pleasant young man who had stayed with them for a few days. They decided – purely as a precaution – to take it to the police. It proved to belong to a Seattle landlady, Mrs Florence Monks, who had been strangled and raped on 24 November 1926. And the old ladies were able to tell the police that the Dark Strangler was a short, blue-eyed young man with a round face and slightly simian mouth and jaw. He was quietly spoken, and claimed to be deeply religious.

On 8 June 1927, the strangler crossed the Canadian border, and rented a room in Winnipeg from a Mrs Catherine Hill. He stayed for three nights. But on 9 June, a couple named Cowan, who lived in the house, reported that their 14-year-old daughter Lola had vanished. That same evening, a man named William Patterson returned home to find his wife absent. After making supper and putting the children to bed, he rang the police. Then he dropped on his knees beside the bed to pray; as he did so, he saw his wife's hand sticking out. Her naked body lay under the bed.

The Winnipeg police recognized the *modus operandi* of the Gorilla Murderer. A check on boarding-house landladies brought them to Mrs Hill's establishment. She assured them that she had taken in no suspicious characters recently – her last lodger had been a Roger Wilson, who had been carrying a Bible and been highly religious. When she told them that Roger Wilson was short, with piercing blue eyes and a dark complexion, they asked to see the room he had stayed in. They were greeted by the stench of decay. The body of Lola Cowan lay under the bed, mutilated as if by Jack the Ripper. The murderer had slept with it in his room for three days.

From the Patterson household, the strangler had taken some of the husband's clothes, leaving his own behind. But he changed these at a second-hand shop, leaving behind a fountain pen belonging to Patterson, and paying in $10 bills stolen from his house. So the police now had a good description not only of the killer, but of the clothes he was wearing, including corduroy trousers and a plaid shirt.

The next sighting came from Regina, 200 miles west; a landlady heard the screams of a pretty girl who worked for the telephone company, and interrupted the man who had been trying to throttle her; he ran away. The police guessed that he might be heading back towards the American border, which would take him across prairie country with few towns; there was a good chance that a lone hitch-hiker would be noticed. Descriptions of the wanted man were sent out to all police stations and post offices. Five days later, two constables saw a man wearing corduroys and a plaid shirt walking down a road near Killarney, 12 miles from the border. He gave his name as Virgil Wilson and said he was a farm-worker; he seemed quite unperturbed when the police told him they were looking for a mass murderer, and would have to take him in on suspicion. His behaviour was so unalarmed they were convinced he was innocent. But when they telephoned the Winnipeg chief of police, and described Virgil Wilson, he told them that the man was undoubtedly 'Roger Wilson', the Dark Strangler. They hurried back to the jail – to find that their prisoner had picked the lock of his handcuffs and escaped.

Detectives were rushed to the town by aeroplane, and posses spread out over the area. 'Wilson' had slept in a barn close to the jail, and the next morning broke into a house and stole a change of clothing. The first man he spoke to that morning noticed his dishevelled appearance and asked if he had spent the night in the open; the man admitted that he had. When told that police were on their way to Killarney by train to look for the strangler, he ran away towards the railway. At that moment, a police car appeared; after a short chase, the fugitive was captured.

He was identified as Earle Leonard Nelson, born in Philadelphia in 1897; his mother had died of venereal disease contracted from his father. At the age of 10, Nelson was knocked down by a streetcar and was unconscious with concussion for six days. From then on, he experienced violent periodic headaches. He began to make a habit of peering through the keyhole of his cousin Rachel's bedroom when she was getting undressed. At 21, he was arrested after trying to rape a girl in a basement. Sent to a penal farm, he soon escaped, and was recaptured peering in through the window of his cousin as she undressed for bed. A marriage was unsuccessful; when his wife had a nervous breakdown, Nelson visited her in hospital and tried to rape her in bed. Nothing is known of Nelson's whereabouts for the next three years, until the evening in February 1926, when he knocked on the door of Mrs Clara Newman in San Francisco, and asked if he could see the room she had to let . . .

* * *

Like Earle Nelson, Albert Fish had also suffered a blow on the head in childhood. But Fish, unlike Nelson and most other serial killers, was at large for an unusually long time, so that we have no idea of how many murders he committed over the years. The case is certainly one of the strangest in the bizarre history of serial murder.

On 28 May 1928 a mild-looking old man called on the family of a doorman named Albert Budd in a basement in Manhattan. He explained he had come in answer to a job advertisement placed in a New York newspaper by Budd's 18-year-old son Edward. His name, he said, was Frank Howard, and he owned a farm on Long Island. The old man so charmed the Budds that the following day they allowed him to take their 10-year-old daughter Grace to a party; she left in a white confirmation dress, holding Howard's hand. The Budds never saw Grace again; the address at which the party was supposed to be held proved fictitious, and no farmer by the name of Frank Howard could be traced on Long Island. The kidnap received wide publicity, and the police investigated hundreds of tips. Detective Will King of the Missing Persons Bureau became particularly obsessed with the crime and travelled thousands of miles in search of 'Frank Howard'.

Six years later, the Budds received an unsigned letter that was clearly from the kidnapper. He stated that he had taken Grace Budd to an empty house in Westchester, then left her picking flowers while he went inside and stripped off his clothes; then he leaned out of the upstairs window and called her in. Confronted by this skinny naked man, Grace began to cry and tried to run away; he seized her and strangled her. Then he cut her in half, and took the body back home, where he ate parts of it. 'How sweet her little ass was, roasted in the oven. It took me nine days to eat her entire body. I did not fuck her tho I could of had I wished.' (In fact, Fish was to admit to his attorney that this was untrue.) Finally, he took the bones back to the cottage and buried them in the garden.

With a brilliant piece of detective work, Will King traced the writer – the letter had arrived in an envelope with the inked-out logo of a chauffeurs' benevolent association on the flap. One of the chauffeurs finally admitted that he had taken some of the association's stationery and left it in a room he used to rent on East 52nd Street. This now proved to be rented by a tenant who called himself A. H. Fish, and his handwriting in the boarding house register was identical with that of the letter writer. King kept watch on the room for three weeks before Albert Fish – the mild little old man – returned. He agreed unhesitatingly to go to headquarters for questioning, but at the street door, suddenly lunged at King with a razor in each hand. King disarmed and handcuffed him. Back at police headquarters, Fish made no attempt to deny the murder of Grace Budd. He had gone to her home, he explained, with the intention of killing her brother Edward, but when Grace had sat on his knee during dinner, had decided that he wanted to eat her.

He took the police to the cottage in Westchester, where they unearthed the bones of Grace Budd. Later, under intensive questioning, he admitted to killing about four hundred children since 1910. (The figure has never been confirmed, and a judge involved in the case placed the true figure at sixteen.)

Soon after his arrest, Fish was visited by a psychiatrist named Fredrick Wertham, who would appear for the defence. 'He looked', wrote Wertham, 'like a meek and innocuous little old man, gentle and benevolent, friendly and polite. If you wanted someone to entrust your children to, he would be the one you would choose.' When Fish realized that Wertham really wanted to understand him, he became completely open and forthcoming.

Fish was a strange paradox of a man. His face lit up when he talked of his 12-year-old grandchild, and he was obviously sincere when he said: 'I love children and was always soft-hearted.' He was also deeply religious, and read his Bible continuously. The answer to the paradox, Wertham soon concluded, was that Fish was insane. He genuinely believed that God told him to murder children.

Albert Hamilton Fish had been born in Washington, DC., in 1870; his father, a riverboat captain, was 75 at the time. Various members of the family had mental problems and one suffered from religious mania. One brother was feeble-minded and another an alcoholic. The father had died when Fish was five years old, and he was placed in an orphanage, from which he regularly ran away. On leaving school he was apprenticed to a house painter, and this remained his profession for the rest of his life. Access to other people's homes also gave him access to children. He was 28 when he first married, but his wife eloped with the lodger. Later, there were three more marriages, all bigamous.

Fish talked with complete frankness about his sex life – he had always enjoyed writing obscene letters, and no doubt confessing to Wertham gave him the same kind of pleasure. Wertham wrote:

> Fish's sexual life was of unparalleled perversity . . . I found no published case that would even nearly compare with his . . . There was no known perversion that he did not practise and practise frequently.
>
> Sado-masochism directed against children, particularly boys, took the lead in his sexual regressive development. 'I have always had a desire to inflict pain on others and to have others inflict pain on me. I always seemed to enjoy anything that hurt. The desire to inflict pain, that is all that is uppermost.' Experiences with excreta of every imaginable kind were practised by him, actively and passively. He took bits of cotton wool, saturated them with alcohol, inserted them in his rectum and set fire to them. He also did this to his child victims. Finally, and clearly also on a sexual basis, he developed a craving going back to one of the arch-crimes of humanity – cannibalism.
>
> I elicited from him a long history of how he preyed on children. In many instances – I stated under oath later 'at least a hundred' – he seduced them or bribed them with small sums of money or forced them and attacked them. He often worked in public buildings and had an excuse for spending times in cellars and basements and even garrets. He would put on his painters' overalls over his nude body, and that permitted him to undress in a moment . . .
>
> Most, if not all, of his victims came from the poorer classes. He told me that he selected coloured children especially, because the authorities didn't pay much attention when they were hurt or missing. For example, he once paid a small coloured girl five dollars regularly to bring him little coloured boys. Frequently after a particularly brutal episode he would change his address completely . . . Altogether he roamed over twenty-three states, from New York to Montana. 'And I have had children in every state.' He also made a habit of writing letters to women, trying to persuade them to join him in whipping boys.
>
> Fish told me that for years he had been sticking needles into his body in the region near his genitals, in the area between the rectum and the scrotum. He told me of doing it to other people too, especially to children. At first, he said, he had only stuck these needles in and pulled them out again. They were needles of assorted sizes, some of them big sail needles. Then he had stuck others in so far that he was unable to get them out, and

they stayed there. 'They're in there now,' he said. 'I put them up under the spine . . . I did put one in the scrotum too; but I couldn't stand the pain.'

I checked this strange story on a series of X-rays of his pelvic and abdominal region. They showed plainly twenty-nine needles inside his body. One X-ray of the pelvic region showed twenty-seven. They were easily recognisable as needles . . . Some of them must have been years in his body, for they were eroded to an extent that would have taken at least seven years. Some of the needles were fragmented by this erosion so that only bits of steel remained in the tissue.'

In his middle fifties, says Wertham, Fish began to develop psychosis with delusions and hallucinations. (He was 58 when he murdered Grace Budd.)

At times he identified himself with God and felt that he should sacrifice his own son. He tried to stick needles under his finger-nails but could not stand the pain. He made the poignant remark: 'If only pain were not so painful!'

He had visions of Christ and his angels . . . He heard them saying words like 'stripes', 'rewardeth' and 'delighteth'. And he connected these words with verses from the Bible and elaborated them delusionally with his sadistic wishes. 'Stripes means to lash them, you know.'

He felt driven to torment and kill children. Sometimes he would gag them, tie them up and beat them, although he preferred not to gag them, circumstances permitting, for he liked to hear their cries. He felt that he was ordered by God to castrate little boys . . . 'I am not insane. I am just queer.' After murdering Grace Budd he had cooked parts of the body with carrots and onions and strips of bacon, and ate them over a period of nine days. During all this time he was in a state of sexual excitement.

His state of mind while he described these things in minute detail was a peculiar mixture. He spoke in a matter-of-fact way, like a housewife describing her favourite methods of cooking. You had to remind yourself that this was a little girl that he was talking about. But at times his tone of voice and facial expression indicated a kind of satisfaction and ecstatic thrill. However you define the medical and legal borders of sanity, this certainly is beyond that border.

It became apparent that Fish was a wanted killer who had become known as 'the Brooklyn Vampire', who committed four child murders in 1933 and 1934, luring little girls to a basement, flogging them, then garrotting them with a rope. In 1932, a 16-year-old girl had been killed and mutilated near Massapequa, Long Island, where Fish was painting a house. Other murders almost certainly committed by Fish were those of 7-year-old Francis X. McDonnell on Staten Island in 1924, 4-year-old Billy Gaffney in Brooklyn in 1927, and 11-year-old Yetta Abramowitz, who was strangled and mutilated in the Bronx in 1927. (Billy Gaffney's mother subsequently had a series of nervous breakdowns from grief.) Detective Will King, who investigated these murders, was not allowed to introduce them as evidence, since the D.A. was anxious to prove that Fish was sane, and too many murders might throw doubt on this.

To Fish's delight, he was sentenced to death – he remarked with unconscious humour that being electrocuted would be 'the supreme thrill of my life'. When he was on Death Row, the prison chaplain had to ask him not to 'holler and howl' so loud as he masturbated during services. In the execution chamber on 16 January 1936 he mumbled 'I don't know why I'm here' just before the switch was thrown.

Wertham records that he tried hard to get Fish's sentence commuted. 'To execute a sick man is like burning witches,' he told the prison governor. He went on to make this important observation – even more relevant today than it was in 1936: 'Science is prediction. The science of psychiatry is advanced enough that with proper examination such a man as Fish can be detected and confined before the perpetration of these outrages, instead of inflicting extreme penalties afterwards. The authorities had this man, but the records show that they paid no attention.' Understandably, the governor was unmoved. Like the D.A, he probably recognized that Fish was legally insane, but felt that it made no difference – that there was no point in burdening society with the keep of such a man. What Wertham had failed to recognize is that the execution of a murderer like Fish actually serves a ritual function. The public wants to see sadistic killers executed, in the same way that children want fairy stories to end with the defeat of the wicked giant. It serves the purpose of exorcising the horror.

What turns a man into a sado-masochist? In the case of Albert Fish, fortunately, we know the answer. In 1875, his father suffered a heart attack in the Pennsylvania Station. Unable to provide for twelve children, Ellen Fish was forced to consign most of them to an orphanage. The 5-year-old boy had no idea why he had been suddenly abandoned; he was deeply miserable, and at first ran away repeatedly. Discipline in the St John's Refuge was rigid and severe; the matron made them pray for hours every day and made them memorize chapters from the Bible. The slightest infringement of discipline was punished by flogging, administered by the matron. Fish discovered that he enjoyed being whipped on his naked bottom. His fellow orphans teased him because punishment always gave him an erection. What they did not know was that watching other boys being whipped also produced sexual excitement in him. Since it was a co-educational institution (although the boys and girls were kept strictly segregated outside class) there was naturally a great deal of sex talk. After a while, the young Fish was initiated into masturbation and other sex games. By the time his mother took him away from the orphanage two years later – she had obtained a government job – sado-masochism had been firmly 'imprinted' in the 7-year-old boy. He told Wertham of an occasion when he and some friends had soaked a horse's tail in kerosene and set it on fire.

He was a sickly and introverted child, and a fall from a cherry tree produced concussion; thereafter he suffered severe headaches, dizzy spells and a severe stutter. (It has been pointed out that a large number of serial killers have suffered head injuries in childhood.) He continued to wet the bed for many years, and his companions taunted him about it. Fish's reaction to the jeers was to retreat into a world of daydreams. At about this time he insisted on being called Albert (the name of a dead younger brother) rather than Hamilton because his schoolmates called him Ham and Eggs. He began to suffer from convulsive fits.

The daydreams were often of being beaten or watching others being beaten. When his elder brother Walter came home from the Navy and showed Albert books with pictures of naked men and women, and told him stories of cannibalism which he claimed to have witnessed, more sado-masochistic traits were 'imprinted'. His favourite reading was Poe's story 'The Pit and the Pendulum', with its details of mental torture, and this led him on to study everything he could find about the Spanish Inquisition. He became a devotee of true murder cases, and began carrying newspaper clippings in his pockets until they disintegrated. (He was carrying an account of the Hanover 'butcher' Fritz Haarmann when he was arrested.) Yet at the same time he continued to be a devoted student of the Bible, and to dream of becoming a clergyman. Having become habituated to sexual and religious fantasy from an early age, he saw no contradiction between them.

When he was 12, Fish began a homosexual relationship with a telegraph boy who excited him by describing what he had seen in brothels. This youth also introduced to Fish peculiar practices such as drinking urine and tasting excreta. By his late teens, Fish was tormented with a violent and permanent sexual appetite that never left him alone. (But this is less unusual than it sounds; the majority of teenagers could tell a similar story.) When he moved to New York at the age of 20, he quickly became a male prostitute, and spent much of his weekends at public baths where he could watch boys. It was at this time that he began raping small boys. By now the pattern was set, and even a marriage – arranged by his mother – failed to change it. A period in Sing Sing – for embezzlement – virtually ended the marriage, and he returned to homosexuality. After his wife's desertion, he began to show signs of mental disturbance; he heard voices, and on one occasion wrapped himself up in a carpet and explained that he was following the instructions of St John. Then began his period of wandering around the United States and working as a painter and decorator; during this time, he told Wertham, he raped more than a hundred children, mostly boys under six.

When he was 28, a male lover took him to see the waxworks gallery in a museum; there he was fascinated by a medical display showing the bisection of a penis. He returned to see it many times, and 'imprinting' occurred again, leading to a new obsession with castration. During a relationship with a mentally defective homosexual, Fish tied him up and tried to castrate him. The rush of blood frightened him and he fled. Now he began adding castration to his rapes, on one occasion severing a child's penis with a pair of scissors. He began going to brothels where he could be spanked and whipped. He committed his first murder – of a male homosexual – in Wilmington in 1910. In 1919 he mutilated and tortured to death a mentally retarded boy. From now on, murder also became a part of his pattern of perversion.

Here, then, we are able to study in unusual detail the development of a sado-masochistic obsession. It is impossible to doubt that it began in the St John's Refuge in 1875, when he was first whipped by the matron of the Episcopal Sisterhood. It is possible to say with some degree of confidence that if Fish had not been sent to an orphanage at the age of 5, he would never have developed into one of the most remarkable examples of 'polymorphous perversion' in the history of sexual abnormality.

Then why did his fellow-orphans never achieve the same dubious notoriety? Presumably because they lacked his intensely introverted temperament, the tendency to brood and daydream about sex and pain. In short, they lacked the ability to retreat so totally into a world of fantasy. It is difficult to avoid the conclusion that what turned Fish into a dangerous pervert was precisely the same tendency to morbid brooding and fantasy that turned Edgar Allan Poe into a writer of genius.

How far does this enable us to understand the serial killer? It enables us, at least, to grasp that there is a link between his abnormality and what we recognize as normality. Fish was turned into a serial killer by a kind of 'hothouse' conditioning that led him to spend most of his childhood brooding about sex. We must bear in mind that he was born in 1870, at a time when sex crime was almost non-existent. By the time of the Jack the Ripper murders, Fish was 18 – old enough, in theory, to have committed them himself. But he was still living in a world of Victorian morality and Victorian behaviour, where 'dirty books' were still banned – most of the 'obscenity' prosecutions of that period now strike us as incomprehensible – and prostitution regarded with deep disapproval. Fish became a fully-fledged pervert by accident, starting with the accident of being sent to an orphanage at the age of 5. If Fish had been alive today, he would have had no difficulty finding material to feed his fantasies, from hard porn magazines to 'snuff videos'. In most large American cities he would have found streets lined with male and female 'hookers' willing to cater to every perversion. It becomes possible to see why, some twenty-five years after the relaxation of the laws governing pornography, serial crime suddenly began to develop into an epidemic.

Earle Nelson and Albert Fish were undoubtedly psychopaths; in our own time, they would probably have been found guilty but insane. Carl Panzram is an entirely different matter; he belongs to a breed of killer that we shall not encounter again for another three decades: the highly intelligent, highly articulate 'resentment killer'.

When Carl Panzram was locked into his cell in the Washington District Jail on 16 August 1928, no one even guessed that he was one of the world's most brutal mass murderers. It is just possible that no one ever *would* have known – except for a fortunate coincidence. That same week, a young guard named Henry Lesser also arrived in the jail.

Washington DC is a hot city in August – the temperature often soars into the 90s – and the first thing Lesser noticed was the stench of human sweat and disinfectant. The prison was basically a long box, with tier upon tier of barred doors facing each other down either side. The sun entered through tall, dirty windows covered in bars. As Lesser climbed the iron stairs, he noticed the silhouette of a man framed against the afternoon sunlight – a big man with massive shoulders and a round, almost hairless head. There was something about the prisoner that made an immediate impression – Lesser declared later: 'There was a kind of stillness about him.' He noticed the name outside the cell door: 'C. Panzram'. And as he started to walk away, an odd feeling made him turn round. The man was watching him, his huge hands gripping the bars of the door. Lesser asked him when his case came up in court.

'November eleventh.' The face was so hard, the eyes so flat and stony, that Lesser assumed he must be a gangster.

'What's your racket?' he asked.

Panzram gave an odd smile. 'I reform people.'

The two other prisoners in the cell gave a snort of laughter.

Lesser checked on why the big man was in jail. To his surprise it was not violence or extortion – merely burgling the home of a dentist. A fence had been caught selling a radio, and had admitted that Panzram had asked him to dispose of it. The police went along to a room in a cheap rooming house, and found a 'bearlike man with a limp, a heavy black moustache and agate-hard eyes'. They handcuffed him and asked his occupation; Panzram replied indifferently that he was a thief, then suddenly grinned. When the policeman asked why he was smiling, Panzram said: 'Because a charge of stealing a radio is a joke.'

'What do you mean?'

Panzram said evenly: 'I've killed too many people to worry about a charge like that.'

The police assumed this was boasting, and the District Attorney took the same view when they told him about it. Panzram, he said, was a 'chiseler', a man who tried to waste time by getting extradition to another state – claiming to have committed crimes that could never be proved against him. Panzram had a long prison record, but it was mostly for burglary and vagrancy.

Henry Lesser soon became well liked among the prisoners. A young Jew from a poor background, he was more liberal and humane than the other guards. Panzram seemed perfectly willing to engage in conversation, although he never initiated it. A few days later Lesser asked him what he meant by 'reforming people'. Panzram said without expression:

'The only way to reform people is to kill them.'

Lesser hurried away. What he had just heard disturbed him profoundly. Yet there was something about Panzram that aroused a curious feeling of response.

The prison governor, William L. Peak, would have found that attitude incomprehensible. He was a tough man who regarded the prisoners as dangerous subhuman creatures who had broken the laws of society, and had to take their punishment. Sympathizing with them would be as pointless as rewarding naughty children. Panzram made no secret of the fact that he hated Peak, and would welcome a chance to get his hands round his throat.

Later that day, the guards were ordered to do a 'shakedown' of Panzram's tier, searching for weapons or illegal substances. Two guards entered Panzram's cell, one of them holding a short iron rod with which he tapped the window bars, while the other one watched the prisoners. One of the bars gave a dull sound instead of a clear, metallic ring. The guards looked at one another and left immediately. Ten minutes later, they were back with handcuffs, which they clicked on to Panzram. They knew better than to bother with his cellmates; only Panzram's immense hands would have had the strength to gradually loosen the bar in its cement setting.

Panzram was taken down to the basement of the jail. The iron beams of the ceiling were supported by thick pillars. Panzram's hands were passed around one of these pillars, and then re-handcuffed. Then a rope was passed through the chain of the cuffs and thrown over a beam; Panzram was heaved up until only his toes touched the floor. The angle of his arms around the pillar almost dislocated his shoulders, and the pain was agonizing. For the next twelve hours he was left in this position, the prison doctor periodically checking with a stethoscope to make sure his heart was holding out.

The next morning, Lesser saw him lying on the floor of the isolation cell, the skin of his wrists in ribbons, and his arms covered with bruises where the guards had beaten him with saps. He only muttered when Lesser asked if he was all right. But when one of the other guards looked into the cell, Panzram stirred himself enough to call him a son of a bitch. Soon after, four guards entered the cell; when Panzram resisted, he was knocked unconscious with a blackjack. When he woke up, he was once again standing on his toes in the basement, his arms chained around the pillar. All night he cursed and shrieked defiance at the guards; blows seemed to make no difference. One of the 'trusties' – a convict trusted by the guards – told Lesser that, in his agony, Panzram had roared that he had killed dozens of people and would kill more if he got the chance.

The next day, when Panzram was back in his own cell, Lesser handed the trusty a dollar to give to Panzram. He knew that a dollar meant extra food and cigarettes.

When the trusty passed on the dollar, Panzram obviously thought it was a joke. When the trusty assured him that it was no joke, Panzram's eyes filled with tears.

Later, when Lesser passed his cell, Panzram limped to the bars and thanked him. 'That's the first time a screw has ever done me a favour.' He told Lesser that reporters had been asking to see him since word of his 'confessions' had leaked out, but he had refused to see them.

'But if you'll get me a pencil and paper, I'll write you the story of my life.'

This was strictly against the rules; prisoners were only allowed to write a limited number of censored letters. But Lesser decided to break the rules. The next morning, he smuggled the pencil and paper through the bars, and Panzram hid them under his mattress. That evening, after midnight, Lesser slipped up to Panzram's cell and was handed a batch of manuscript. They had time for a short conversation, and for the first time, Lesser realized that Panzram had a powerful if uncultivated mind. He was startled, for example, when the prisoner told him that he had read the German philosopher Schopenhauer, and he agreed entirely that human life was a trap and a delusion.

Panzram's autobiography began: 'This is a true statement of my actions, including the times and places and my reasons for doing these things, written by me of my own free will at the District Jail, Washington D.C., November 4, 1928.'

As he began reading the account of Panzram's childhood, Lesser had no idea that 'these things' would include twenty brutal and violent murders.

Just over a week later, Panzram limped into court. With his record of previous convictions, it was likely that the burglary charge would earn him a five-year sentence. In such circumstances, most prisoners would have done their best to seem harmless and repentant. But Panzram seemed to be in the grip of a demon. Having told the judge that he would represent himself, he sat in the witness chair and faced the jury, staring at them with his cold, baleful eyes.

'You people got me here charged with housebreaking and larceny. I'm guilty . . . What I didn't steal I smashed. If the owner had come in I would have knocked his brains out.'

This man was obviously a raging psychopath. The jurors looked pale and shaken. Panzram went on evenly:

'While you were trying me here, I was trying all of you too. I've found you guilty. Some of you I've executed. If I live I'll execute some more of you. I hate the whole human race . . . I believe the whole human race should be exterminated. I'll do my best to do it every chance I get. Now, I've done my duty, you do yours.'

Not surprisingly, the jury took less than a minute to find him guilty. The judge sentenced him to twenty-five years in Leavenworth, one of America's toughest jails.

Lesser was shocked when he heard of the sentence. But, unlike the other occupants of the Washington Jail, he knew exactly why Panzram had done it. He had been reading Panzram's autobiography, and it revealed a man whose bitterness was so deep that he would have cheerfully destroyed the world. Lesser's own childhood, while poverty-stricken, had been full of family warmth and affection. Now he read with horror and fascination the story of a man who had never received any kind of love, and therefore never learned to give it.

Carl Panzram had been a tramp and a jailbird since he was

14. He had been born one year before the worst depression in American history so far. His father was a poor German immigrant, an ex-soldier who had hoped to make his fortune in America. Instead, he was forced to work as a farm labourer until he scraped together the money to buy a small farm in Minnesota. A man with a violent temper and a brooding disposition, John Panzram saw his investment wasting away through drought and hard times. Carl, their fourth child, was born on 28 June 1891. By now his overworked wife was suffering from high blood pressure and dizzy spells. One day, John Panzram walked out and the family never saw him again.

Carl was a difficult child. He longed for attention, but no one had any time to give it to him. So he behaved badly to gain attention, and was only spanked and then ignored. His first appearance in court was at the age of 8, on a charge of being drunk. At school he had further beatings with a strap – on his hands, because at this stage he was sickly and often ill. One day he decided to run away out west to be a cowboy; he broke into the home of a rich neighbour and stole some cake and apples, and a revolver. But before he had travelled more than a few miles he was caught. At the age of 11 he was sent to his first reform school. 'Right there and then I began to learn about man's inhumanity to man.' He was often tied naked to a wooden block, and salty water allowed to dry on his back. The strap with which he was beaten had holes punched in it, so the skin came up through them as it struck the flesh, causing small blisters; when these soon burst, the salt caused agony.

Panzram was a strongminded boy. 'I began to hate those who abused me. Then I began to think I would have my revenge as often as I could injure someone else. Anyone at all would do. If I couldn't injure those who had injured me, then I would injure someone else.'

Back home after two years, he was sent to a Lutheran school whose preacher-teacher detested him on sight and often beat him. One day Panzram stole a revolver, and when the preacher began to hit him, pulled it out and pulled the trigger. It misfired. Before he could be sent back to reform school, he jumped into an empty car on a freight train and went west.

Back in detention for robbery, he escaped with another youth, and they teamed up. 'He showed me how to work the stick-up racket and how to rob the poor box in churches. I in turn taught him how to set fire to a church after we robbed it.' They enjoyed destruction for its own sake – even boring holes in the floor of wagons full of wheat so the grain would run away along the tracks, and emptying sand into the oil boxes of the freight cars so they would seize up.

A brief period in the army ended in court martial for insubordination, and a three-year sentence in a military jail. The sentence was signed by the Secretary of War Howard Taft; thirteen years later, Panzram burgled Taft's home and stole $3,000. He never forgave or forgot.

Panzram served his three years, together with an extra month for trying to escape. But he succeeded in burning down the prison workshop. 'Another hundred thousand dollars to my credit.' He wrote later: 'I was discharged from that prison in 1910. I was the spirit of meanness personified.' During the next five years his only honest employment was as a strikebreaker – which ended when he was beaten unconscious by strikers. There were also several spells in prison for burglary. But the episode that had turned him into an enemy of society had happened in 1915, when he was 23. In San Francisco, he had been arrested for burgling the home of a bank president. The District Attorney offered him a deal; if he would confess where he had hidden the loot, they would 'go easy' on him and give him a minimum sentence. The law broke its word; Panzram was sentenced to seven years.

In an insane rage, Panzram succeeded in breaking out of his cell, plugging all the locks so no guards could get in, then set about wrecking the jail. He tore radiators and pipes off the walls, piled up everything that would burn, and set fire to it. The guards finally broke in and 'knocked his block off'. Then Panzram was shackled and sent off to the Oregon State Penitentiary, one of the most inhumane in America.

He swore that he would not complete his sentence; the warden, a brutal man named Minto, swore that he would. One of Panzram's first acts was to hurl his chamberpot in a guard's face; he was beaten, then handcuffed to the door of a dark cell known as 'the Hole' for thirty days. A few weeks later he was flogged and thrown in again when he was caught trying to hack a hole in the prison roof. When released, he was made to wear a uniform of red and black stripes, recently designed for dangerous troublemakers. The 'punishment' misfired; prisoners wearing the 'hornet suit' were regarded by other convicts as heroes.

When Warden Minto was shot to death in a hunt for an escaped convict, his brother – who was equally brutal – took over the job. He set out to make Panzram's life difficult; Panzram set out to make Minto's life difficult. He broke into the storeroom and stole bottles of lemon extract – which contained alcohol – and got a crowd of prisoners drunk; they started a riot, while Panzram, who remained sober, sat back and grinned. Next Panzram burned down the prison workshops – but was caught and thrown back into the Hole. Then he was confined in a specially built isolation block called the Bullpen.

Panzram won this round. He roared and cursed all night, beating his slop bucket on the door. The other prisoners joined in. Tension was already high because the warden had cut wages from a dollar to twenty-five cents a day. The warden decided it would be wiser to release Panzram, and assigned him to a job in the kitchen. Panzram went berserk with an axe, causing everyone to flee, and had smashed all the locks in an empty block of cells before he was clubbed unconscious.

Tension mounted until guards refused to go into the yard alone. When two convicts escaped, Minto ordered that Panzram and another suspected plotter should be 'firehosed' – a punishment outlawed by the state. The two prisoners were 'water-hammered' until they were battered and bruised all over. But the news reached the state governor, who sent for Minto and ordered him to resign.

The new warden, a man named Murphy, believed that prisoners would respond to kindness. When told that Panzram had been caught sawing the bars of his cell, he asked how many times Panzram had been thrown into the Hole; the guard said eight. 'Then it doesn't seem to be working, does it?' said Murphy, and ordered that Panzram should have extra rations and given books to read. When, a few weeks later, Panzram was again caught with a hacksaw that someone had dropped into his cell, the warden sent for him. Murphy told Panzram that he had heard he was the wickedest man in the jail. Panzram said he quite agreed. And then Murphy gave Panzram the greatest shock of his life. He told him that he could walk out of the prison and go anywhere he liked – provided he gave his word of honour to return by supper time. Panzram gave his word – without the slightest intention of keeping it – and when supper time came, found that some curious inner compulsion made him go back.

Gradually, Murphy increased his freedom and that of the other prisoners. He revived the honours system, and Panzram became virtually a 'trusty'. But one night when he was 'on leave' in the local hospital, Panzram got drunk with a pretty nurse and stayed out too late. He decided to abscond. It took a week to catch him, and then he made a determined attempt to kill the deputies who cornered him. Murphy's critics had a field day and the honours system was undermined. Panzram was given an extra ten years and thrown back into solitary confinement. But soon after that, he succeeded in escaping. At least he had won his bet with the deceased Warden Minto.

The experience of Murphy seems to have been a turning-point in Panzram's life. So far he had hated the world, but not himself. His betrayal of Murphy's trust seems to have undermined his certainty that his hatred and violence were justified. It was after his escape, in May 1918, that he began his career of murder.

In New York Panzram obtained seaman's papers and sailed for South America. He and another sailor planned to hijack a small schooner and murder everybody on board; but the sailor got drunk and tried to carry out the plan alone. In fact, he killed six men, but was caught. Panzram sailed for Europe, where he spent some time in Barlinnie Jail in Glasgow – as usual, for theft . . .

Back in New York he burgled the home of Howard Taft, the man who had confirmed his earlier sentence. He bought himself a yacht with the $3,000 in cash that he found.

'Then I figured it would be a good plan to hire a few sailors to work for me, get them out to my yacht, get them drunk, commit sodomy on them, rob them and then kill them. This I done . . .'

He explained how he would hire two sailors, take them to his yacht and wine and dine them, then blow out their brains in the middle of the night with a revolver he had stolen. Then he would drop their weighted bodies into the sea from a rowboat. 'They are there yet, ten of 'em.'

He hired two more sailors and sailed down the coast, robbing other yachts. It had been his intention to murder his latest two helpers, but the yacht went on to rocks and sank. Instead of killing them, Panzram paid them off.

A second attempt to become rich through burglary ended in a six-month jail sentence. Once again, Panzram signed on as a sailor, and this time went to the Belgian Congo. A job with an oil company came to an end when he sodomized the boy who waited at table – Panzram observes ironically that the youth did not appreciate the benefits of civilization. Shortly after, Panzram picked up another black boy, raped him, then battered in his skull.

'Then I went to town, bought a ticket on the Belgian steamer to Lobito Bay down the coast. There I hired a canoe and six niggers and went out hunting in the bay and backwaters. I was looking for crocodiles. I found them, plenty. They were all hungry. I fed them. I shot all six of of those niggers and dumped 'em in.' (Panzram explains that he shot them in the back.) 'The crocks done the rest. I stole their canoe and went back to town, tied the canoe to the dock, and that night someone stole the canoe from me.'

Back in America in 1920, Panzram returned to burglary and stick-ups. He also raped and murdered another boy. After taking a job as a caretaker at a yacht club in New Haven, he stole a yacht and sailed it down the coast. A man who offered to buy it tried to hold him up at gunpoint, but Panzram was ready for him; he shot him to death and dumped his body overboard.

The police soon caught up with him, but this time a good lawyer succeeded in getting him acquitted, in exchange for the yacht. When the lawyer tried to register the yacht, it was promptly reclaimed by its owner. By that time, Panzram was back in New Haven, where he committed his last rape murder, bringing the total up to twenty.

He now signed on as a sailor to go to China, but was fired the same day for getting drunk and fighting. The next day he was caught as he was burgling the express office in Larchmont, NY. Once again, the prosecution offered a deal; if he would plead guilty, he would receive a light sentence. History repeated itself; he received the maximum sentence: five years.

This time he was sent to America's toughest prison: Dannemora, NY. Enraged again by sheer brutality, he attempted to escape, but fell thirty feet on to concrete and broke both ankles. There was no attempt to set them; he was simply left alone for months until they healed. 'I was so full of hate that there was no room in me for such feelings as love, pity, kindness or honor or decency. I hated everybody I saw.' One day he jumped from a high gallery, fracturing a leg; he walked for the rest of his life with a limp. He spent his days dreaming of revenge, planning how to destroy a passenger train by setting a bomb in a tunnel, or poisoning a whole city's water supply.

Within a short time of being released from Dannemora, Panzram burgled a house in Washington and stole a radio. And it was in Washington District Jail that he wrote his story of murder and vandalism for Henry Lesser . . .

On 30 January 1929, Carl Panzram and thirty-one other prisoners were chained together and placed on a train for Leavenworth Penitentiary, Kansas. Henry Lesser was sent along as one of the escorts; they hoped that his presence would calm the 'dingbat', as Panzram was known. It was a strange experience for Lesser – to look at this man 'under his care', and to know that he had committed more than a dozen sex murders, and that no one but he and Panzram knew the whole truth.

Panzram was in a bad mood. He made a grab for Warden Peak's personal 'trusty', but only had time to spit on him before he was manhandled back into line. But he was heard to mutter that he intended to 'get' Peak – who was travelling with them – and hoped to wreck the train. Peak had somehow found out that Panzram hoped to pull the emergency cord when the train was at top speed, to try to derail it; accordingly, the emergency cord had been disconnected.

Harris Berman, the doctor who had tested Panzram's heart while he was beng flogged, sat up all night watching the 'dingbat'. He had heard that Panzram was planning to break loose, and would try to kill Peak – or possibly himself. Panzram eyed the doctor with contempt, and made jeering accusations of sodomy with his assistant. He shouted the same accusations at Warden Peak whenever he showed his face.

When Lesser saw Panzram staring at two small boys who were peering in through the window at a station, he shuddered as he imagined what might be going through Panzram's mind.

When the train finally pulled up in the grey stone walls of Leavenworth, the ground was covered with dirty snow. The Leavenworth rule book contained no fewer than ninety rules – including total silence during meals; breaking any single one of them entailed harsh punishment.

While Lesser and his fellow guards were taken on a tour of the five-storey cell blocks – all jammed to capacity – Warden Peak paid a call on Warden T. B. White, and warned him that the most dangerous man in the new batch was Carl Panzram. He advised

White to keep him in solitary. But White, a lanky Texan, had his own ideas of reform – or perhaps he felt that Panzram was only one of dozens of dangerous prisoners. He decided to ignore the warning, and assigned Panzram to the laundry. Warden Peak and his contingent of guards returned to Washington.

When Deputy Warden Zerbst gave Panzram the regulation lecture on what was expected of him, Panzram only shrugged, then said levelly: 'I'll kill the first man that bothers me.'

Like so many before him, Zerbst thought this was bluff.

The laundry was one of the worst assignments in the prison: damp, badly ventilated and either too hot or too cold. The man in charge, Robert Warnke, was a short, plump civilian who was a member of the local Ku Klux Klan. He had been warned that Panzram was dangerous, but seems to have felt no misgivings as he directed him to work on a machine with a skinny burglar named Marty Rako.

Years later, in a tape-recorded interview, Rako described his impressions of Panzram. The big prisoner was a loner, seldom speaking to others. But he read throughout his spare time, including volumes of Schopenhauer and Nietzsche. And when he took a dislike to his dirty and illiterate cellmate, he ordered him to apply for a 'transfer'. (One of the few privileges the prisoners were allowed was to move out of a cell if they disliked their cellmate.)

Panzram received regular letters from Henry Lesser, although many of these failed to get through – the authorities were naturally obstructive concerning anything that gave prisoners pleasure. Lesser told Panzram that he had shown the autobiography to the famous literary critic H. L. Mencken, and Mencken had been impressed by the keenness of Panzram's mind. But he thought the confessions were too horrific to publish. Mencken had told Lesser: 'This is one of the most amazing documents I have ever read.'

Panzram was flattered, but he had other things on his mind. He hated the laundry, and its plump foreman. But he had thought of a way out. If a prisoner was punished – by being thrown in the Hole – he was seldom sent back to his previous work; most supervisors had no desire to work with a man they had punished.

Accordingly, Panzram made no real attempt to hide the fact that he was breaking the rules by laundering extra hankerchiefs.

Many prisoners were wealthy men who were serving sentences for fraud; these were willing to pay for good food and for special services. When Warnke found out, he had Panzram demoted – which meant loss of wages – and sent to the Hole.

So far, Panzram's scheme was working. But when he came out of the Hole, he learned that the second part had misfired. He was being sent back to the laundry. Possibly Warnke felt he would lose face by allowing Panzram to be transferred, since Panzram was known to hate him. Or possibly he simply saw through Panzram's scheme and decided to frustrate it. He also turned down Panzram's direct request for a transfer.

The weather was becoming stifling, and new batches of prisoners made the jail intolerably overcrowded. There were so many that there were no fewer than nine sittings in the dining hall. The main meal of the day consisted of boiled rice with tomato sauce.

Thursday, 20 June 1929 looked like being another blazingly hot day as foreman Warnke walked into the laundry, and prepared to check on the prisoners. He walked down the aisle towards a disassembled washing machine that stood near some open packing cases, strolling past a heavy steel pillar that held up the ceiling – not unlike the one Panzram had been chained to in the Washington Jail – and stood surveying the washing machine. Then he turned, and realized that Carl Panzram had been standing behind the steel pillar, and that he was holding a crowbar that had been used to open the packing cases. Warnke had no time to notice anything else as the crowbar was brought down on his head, shattering the bone. Panzram screamed with rage and satisfaction as he went on pounding the skull of the fallen man's head to a pulp. Then, when he was sure Warnke was dead, he turned on the other prisoners and guards; they fled in all directions as he flourished the bloodstained crowbar.

Like some great limping ape, Panzram shambled down the street outside, and into the office of the Deputy Warden. Fortunately for Zerbst, he was late that morning. Panzram opened the door of the mailroom and limped in, swinging the bar; yelling clerks scattered in all directions. A convict who came in with a message was chased down the street. Then Panzram made his way back to the locked gate of the isolation unit. 'Let me in.'

'Not with that in your hand,' said the startled guard.

Panzram threw away the crowbar, and the guard unlocked the steel door. Now Panzram's rage was all dissipated, he looked relaxed and almost serene as he walked into the nearest cell.

When Warden Peak heard the news in Washington, he lost no time in summoning the press and saying 'I told you so.' Lesser was shocked and depressed – as much by the death of a fellow prison employee as by Panzram's predicament.

Panzram himself was startled when no one tried to beat him to death, or even drag him off to the Hole. Instead, he was placed in a large, airy cell, next door to a prisoner named Robert Stroud (who would become known as 'the Bird Man of Alcatraz'), and although he was kept locked in without exercise, he was allowed to read all day long. He told Lesser: 'If, in the beginning I had been treated as I am now, then there wouldn't have been quite so many people in this world that have been robbed, raped and killed . . .'

In reply, Lesser suggested that he himself should try and raise support from influential people – like Mencken – to get Panzram a reprieve. Panzram replied: 'Wake up, kid . . . The real truth of the matter is that I haven't the least desire to reform . . . It took me 36 years to be like I am now; then how do you figure that I could, if I wanted to, change from black to white in the twinkling of an eye?'

Lesser declined to take no for an answer, and persuaded a famous psychiatrist, Karl Menninger, to go and see Panzram. Forty years later, Menninger recalled how he had interviewed Panzram – under guard – in the anteroom of a federal court. When he told Panzram that he did not believe he would harm someone who had never done him any harm, Panzram's reply was to hurl himself at Menninger as far as his chains would allow him, and to shout: 'Take these off me and I'll kill you before their eyes.' Then Panzram went on to describe with gruesome satisfaction all his murders and rapes.

In spite of the fact that a Sanity Commission decided that Panzram was insane, on 15 April 1930 the jury in a federal courtroom in Topeka, Kansas, found him guilty, and the judge sentenced him to death. Panzram was pleased with the verdict, and interrupted his defence attorney to say that he had no wish to appeal.

One problem for the state was that executions in Kansas were illegal. Panzram's sentence caused indignation in anti-capital-punishment groups. One such group was permitted to appear outside his cell to ask him to sign a petition for clemency. They were startled to be met with shrieks of rage and obscenity. Subsequently Panzram wrote a long and brilliantly lucid letter to a penal reform group explaining precisely why he had no desire to escape the death sentence. He even wrote to President Herbert Hoover telling him not to interfere and reprieve him. He managed to make an unsuccessful attempt at suicide, eating a plate of beans that he had concealed until they had gone black and poisonous, and somehow slashing a six-inch wound in his leg. His magnificent constitution saw him through.

Shortly before six on the morning of 5 September 1930, Panzram was led from his cell, singing a pornographic song of his own composition. Seeing two men in clerical garb among the spectators in the corridor, he roared an obscenity about 'Bible-backed cocksuckers', and told the warden to get them out. When this had been done, he said: 'Let's get going. What are we hanging around for?'

On the scaffold, the hangman, who was from Ohio and therefore known as a 'Hoosier', asked him if there was anything he wanted. 'Yes, hurry it up, you Hoosier bastard! I could hang a dozen men while you're fooling around.'

Moments later, the trap fell, breaking his neck.

Panzram remains one of the most fascinating cases in criminal history because he pursued hatred and revenge with a kind of ruthless logic. He possessed an extremely strong will – the kind of will that makes great statesmen and soldiers and reformers. It was a characteristic he shared with Michelangelo, Luther, Beethoven and Lenin. But when Panzram met with opposition, and he was sure he was in the right, he charged like a mad bull. It made no difference if he ran into a brick wall; he almost enjoyed battering his head against brick walls. Attempts to beat him into submission only made him twice as determined – and twice as violent and dangerous.

Riding the freight trains at the age of 14, he had another lesson in inhumanity when he invited four burly tramps into the comfortable box car he had found. Ignoring his struggles, they held him down and raped him. The same thing happened again in a small town in the mid-west when he approached a crowd of loafers sitting around a fire and tried to beg food. They got him drunk on whiskey, and he only realized what had happened when he recovered consciousness. The lesson Panzram learned from this was simple: Might makes Right.

Panzram was a highly sexed youth, but even the cheapest whores were too expensive for a teenage tramp. Instead, he developed a taste for sodomy. On one occasion when a brakeman caught him hiding in a freight car, Panzram pulled out a revolver and sodomized him at gunpoint, then forced two other hoboes to do the same. It was his crude and simple method of taking revenge on the world.

Sexual frustration also turned Panzram into a rapist – but not of women. After catching gonorrhoea from a prostitute, he decided that women were not for him. He picked up boys whenever he could, and when he robbed men, he often tied them to a tree to commit rape. If someone had accused Panzram of being homosexual, he would have been astonished. It was merely a sexual outlet – and an outlet for his aggression. By committing anal rape, he was somehow repaying what had been done to him; he called it the Law of Compensation.

Although he never actually says so, it is clear that he had acquired another curious perversion – pyromania, a tendency to experience sexual excitement from causing fires. He arrived in Houston, Texas, during the great fire of February 1912. 'I . . . walked through the town, enjoying the sights of all the burning buildings, and listening to the tales of woe, the moans and sighs of those whose homes and property were burning. I enjoyed it all . . .'

His hatred of society – and of respectable people – dominated his life. Like the Marquis de Sade, he was convinced that society is built on corruption, and on the strong exploiting the weak. It gave him immense satisfaction to record the sins of those in authority – for example, of the warden of Deer Lodge Prison, Montana, who was also the mayor. 'He wound up his career by blowing out his own brains because he was due for a bit of his own cells for charges of stealing the state funds and a host of other crimes.'

What baffles the reader of Panzram's autobiography is why he never used his intelligence to avoid punishment. It is understandable why he tried to burn down the San Francisco jail when the authorities broke their word and sentenced him to seven years. But it is impossible to understand why the first thing he did at the Oregon jail was to throw a full chamberpot in a guard's face, earning himself thirty days of torment.

The answer has to be that Panzram never acquired any kind of self-discipline. And it may have been this recognition that led to the virtually suicidal activities of his final years. This becomes very clear in a story told by Lesser. He had been told to test the bars of Panzram's cell with a steel rod. As he left the cell, Panzram said in a strangled voice: 'Don't ever do that again. Turning your back on me like that.'

Lesser protested: 'I knew you wouldn't harm me.'

'Yes, you're the one man in the world I don't want to kill. But I'm so erratic I'm liable to do anything.'

It was as if Panzram had trained a part of himself – a kind of savage dog – to leap at people's throats. But the dog was now out of control . . .

Perhaps the cruellest thing that ever happened to Panzram was Warden Murphy's offer to allow him to walk out of the jail if he promised to return. It was a proof that the murderous logic on which he had based his life was founded on a fallacy. To hate 'Society' is to hate an abstraction. Society is a mass of individuals. And when he finally betrayed Murphy's trust, Panzram suddenly began to hate himself as well as other people. The subsequent murders were an attempt to kill something inside himself. But when Lesser sent him the dollar, and Panzram's eyes filled with tears, he knew that it was still alive. Suddenly, he experienced an overpowering need to cleanse himself through confession . . .

In the 1930s, America again had a series of murders as mysterious as those of the New Orleans Axeman; the killer was known as 'the Mad Butcher of Kingsbury Run' or 'the Cleveland Torso Killer', and the crimes are still unsolved.

On a warm September afternoon in 1935, two boys on their way home from school walked along a dusty, sooty gully called Kingsbury Run, in the heart of Cleveland, Ohio. On a weed-covered slope known as Jackass Hill, one challenged the other to a race, and they hurtled sixty feet down the slope to the bottom. Sixteen-year-old James Wagner was the winner, and as he halted, panting, he noticed something white in the bushes a few yards away. A closer look revealed that it was a naked body, and that it was headless.

The police who arrived soon after found the body of a young white male clad only in black socks; the genitals had also been removed. It lay on its back, with the legs stretched out and the arms placed neatly by the sides, as if laid out for a funeral. Thirty feet away, the policemen found another body, lying in the same position; it was of an older man, and had also been decapitated and emasculated.

Hair sticking out of the ground revealed one of the heads a few yards away, and the second was found nearby. The genitals were also found lying nearby, as if thrown away by the killer.

One curious feature of the case was that there was no blood on the ground or on the bodies, which were quite clean. It looked as if they had been killed and beheaded elsewhere, then carefully washed when they had ceased to bleed.

Medical examination made the case more baffling than ever. The older corpse was badly decomposed, and the skin discoloured; the pathologists discovered that this was due to some chemical substance, as if the killer had tried to preserve the body. The older victim had been dead about two weeks; the younger man had only been dead three days. His fingerprints enabled the police to identify him as 28-year-old Edward Andrassy, who had a minor police record for carrying concealed weapons. He lived near Kingsbury Run and had a reputation as a drunken brawler.

But the most chilling discovery was that Andrassy had been killed by decapitation. Rope marks on his wrists revealed that he had been tied and had struggled violently. The killer had apparently cut off his head with a knife. The skill with which the operation had been performed suggested a butcher – or possibly a surgeon.

It proved impossible to identify the older man. But the identification of Andrassy led the police to hope that it should not be too difficult to trace his killer. He had spent his nights gambling and drinking in a slum part of town and was known as a pimp. But further investigation also revealed that he had male lovers. Lead after lead looked marvellously promising. The husband of a married woman with whom he had had an affair had sworn to kill him. But the man was able to prove his innocence. So were various shady characters who might have borne a grudge. Lengthy police investigation led to a dead end – as it did in another ten cases of the killer who became known as 'the Mad Butcher of Kingsbury Run'.

Four months later, on a raw January Sunday, the howling of a dog finally led a black woman resident of East Twentieth Street – not far from Kingsbury Run – to go and investigate. She found the chained animal trying to get at a basket near a factory wall. Minutes later, she told a neighbour that the basket contained 'hams'. But the neighbour soon recognized the 'hams' as parts of a human arm. A burlap bag proved to contain the lower half of a female torso. The head was missing, as were the left arm and lower parts of both legs. But fingerprints again enabled the police to trace the victim, who had a record for soliciting. She proved to be a 41-year-old prostitute named Florence Polillo, a squat, double-chinned woman who was well known in the bars of the neighbourhood.

Again, there were plenty of leads, and again, all of them petered out. Two weeks later, the left arm and lower legs were found in a vacant lot. The head was never recovered.

The murder of Flo Polillo raised an unwelcome question. The first two murders had convinced the police that they were looking for a homosexual sadist; this latest crime made it look as if this killer was quite simply a sadist – like Peter Kürten, the Düsseldorf killer, executed in 1931; he had killed men, women and children indifferently, and he was not remotely homosexual. And now the pathologist recalled that, a year before that first double murder, the torso of an unknown woman had been found on the edge of Lake Erie. It began to look as if the Mad Butcher was quite simply a sadist.

At least the Cleveland public felt they had one thing in their favour. Since the double killing, the famous Elliot Ness had been appointed Cleveland's Director of Public Safety. Ness and his 'Untouchables' had cleared up Chicago's Prohibition rackets, then, in 1934, Ness had moved to Cleveland to fight its gangsters. With Ness in charge, the Head Hunter of Kingsbury Run – another press soubriquet – would find himself becoming the hunted.

But it was soon clear to Ness that hunting a sadistic pervert is nothing like hunting professional gangsters. The killer struck at random, and unless he was careless enough to leave behind a clue – like a fingerprint – then the only hope of catching him was in the act. And Ness soon became convinced that the Mad Butcher took great pleasure in feeling that he was several steps ahead of the police.

The Head Hunter waited until the summer before killing again, then lived up to his name by leaving the head of a young man, wrapped in a pair of trousers, under a bridge in Kingsbury Run; again, two boys found it on 22 June 1936. The body was found a quarter of mile away, and it was obvious from the blood that he had died where he lay. And medical evidence showed that he had died from decapitation. It was not clear how the killer had prevented him from struggling while he did it. The victim was about 25, and heavily tattooed. His fingerprints were not in police files. Three weeks later, a young female hiker discovered another decapitated body in a gully; the head lay nearby. The decomposition made it clear that this man had been killed before the previously discovered victim.

The last 'butchery' of 1936 was of another man of about 30, found in Kingsbury Run; the body had been cut in two, and emasculated. A hat found nearby led to a partial identification: a housewife recalled giving it to a young tramp. Not far away there was a 'hobo camp' where down-and-outs slept; this was obviously where the Butcher had found his latest victim.

The fact that Cleveland had been the scene of a Republican Convention, and was now the site of a 'Great Expo', led to even more frantic police activity and much press criticism. The murders were reported all over the world, and in Nazi Germany and Fascist Italy were cited as proof of the decadence of the New World.

As month after month went by with no further grisly discoveries, Clevelanders hoped they had heard the last of the Mad Butcher. But in February 1937, that hope was dashed when the killer left the body of a young woman in a chopped-up pile on the shores of Lake Erie. She was never identified. The eighth victim, a young negress, *was* identified from her teeth as Mrs Rose Wallace, 40; only the skeleton remained, and it looked as if she might have been killed in the previous year.

Victim no. 9 was male and had been dismembered; when he was fished out of the river, the head was missing, and was never found. This time the killer had gone even further in his mutilations – like Jack the Ripper. It was impossible to identify the victim. Two men seen in a boat were thought to be the Butcher with an accomplice, but this suggestion that there might be two Butchers led nowhere.

The Butcher now seems to have taken a rest until nine months later. Then the lower part of a leg was pulled out of the river. Three weeks later, two burlap bags in the river proved to contain more body fragments, which enabled the pathologist to announce that the victim was female, a brunette of about 25. She was never identified.

The killer was to strike twice more. More than a year after the last discovery, in August 1938, the dismembered torso of a woman was found on a dump on the lakefront, and a search of the area revealed the bones of a second victim, a male. A quilt in which the remains of this twelfth victim were wrapped was identified as having been given to a junk man. Neither body could be identified.

One thing was now obvious: the Butcher was selecting his victims from vagrants and down-and-outs. Ness decided to take the only kind of action that seemed left to him: two days after the last find, police raided the 'shantytown' near Kingsbury Run, arrested hundreds of vagrants, and burned it down. Whether or not by coincidence, the murders now ceased.

The suspects? Two of the most efficient of the manhunters, Detectives Merylo and Zalewski, had spent a great deal of time searching for the killer's 'laboratory'. At one point they thought they had found it – but, like all leads, this one faded away.

Next, the investigators discovered that Flo Polillo and Rose Wallace – victim no. 8 – had frequented the same saloon, and that Andrassy – no. 2 – had been a 'regular' there too. They also learned of a middle-aged man called Frank who carried knives and threatened people with them when drunk. When they learned that this man – Frank Dolezal – had also been living with Flo Polillo, they felt they had finally identified the killer. Dolezal was arrested, and police discovered a brown substance like dried blood in the cracks of his bathroom floor. Knives with dried bloodstains on them provided further incriminating evidence. Under intensive questioning, Dolezal – a bleary-eyed, unkempt man – confessed to the murder of Flo Polillo. Newspapers announced the capture of the Butcher. Then things began to go wrong. The 'dried blood' in the bathroom proved not to be blood after all. Dolezal's 'confession' proved to be full of errors about the corpse and method of disposal. And when, in August 1939, Dolezal hanged himself in jail, the autopsy revealed that he had two cracked ribs, and suggested that his confession had been obtained by force.

Yet Ness himself claimed that he knew the solution to the murders. He reasoned that the killer was a man who had a house of his own in which to dismember the bodies, and a car in which to transport them. So he was not a down-and-out. The skill of the mutilations suggested medical training. The fact that some of the victims had been strong men suggested that the Butcher had to be big and powerful – a conclusion supported by a size 12 footprint near one of the bodies.

Ness set three of his top agents, Virginia Allen, Barney Davis and Jim Manski, to make enquiries among the upper levels of Cleveland society. Virginia was a sophisticated girl with contacts among Cleveland socialites. And it was she who learned about a man who sounded like the ideal suspect. Ness was to call him 'Gaylord Sundheim' – a big man from a well-to-do family, who had a history of psychiatric problems. He had also studied medicine. When the three 'Untouchables' called on him, he leered sarcastically at Virginia and closed the door in their faces. Ness invited him – pressingly – to lunch, and he came under protest. When Ness finally told him he suspected him of being the Butcher – hoping that shock tactics might trigger a confession – Sundheim sneered: 'Prove it.'

Soon after this, Sundheim had himself committed to a mental institution. Ness knew *he* was now 'untouchable', for even if Ness could prove his guilt, he could plead insanity.

During the next two years Ness recieved a series of jeering postcards, some signed 'Your paranoid nemesis.' They ceased abruptly when 'Sundheim' died in the mental institution.

Was 'Sundheim' the Butcher? Probably. But not certainly. In Pittsburgh in 1940, three decapitated bodies were found in old boxcars (i.e. railway coaches). Members of Ness's team went to investigate, but no clue to the treble murder was ever discovered. But then, the Mad Butcher was also blamed for the horrific Black Dahlia killing in Hollywood in 1947, in which model Elizabeth Short was tortured before the killer cut her body in half at the waist, although no serial killer has ever been known to leave an eight-year gap between murders. The Torso case remains unsolved.

6

The 1940s

The decade of the 1940s has many sex murders – more than the previous decade – yet almost no mass murders like those of the 1920s and 1930s. Perhaps the mass slaughter of the Second World War kept potential serial killers otherwise occupied. One of the few exceptions is the German Paul Ogorzov – the 'S-Bahn rapist' – who, in fact, began his career of violence shortly before the war.

His first victim, a gym teacher named Frieda Lausche, was travelling on the S-Bahn (short for Schnell-Bahn, or fast railway) on the evening of 20 September 1940, when the man sitting opposite her in the dimly lit carriage suddenly flung open the door and hurled her out. Because she was supple and in good training, she succeeded in falling safely, and hurried to the police. They were frankly incredulous. Why should a man simply fling a woman from a moving train, with no attempt at either assault or robbery? And why was she not scratched and bruised? They agreed to look into the case, then quietly forgot about it.

Three weeks later they had to revise their opinion. On 11 October 1940, a secretary named Ingeborg Goetz was travelling on the elevated railway between Rummelsberg and Karlshorst around midnight when a man in the carriage struck her on the head with some sort of club, then slashed her stomach with a knife. After this he opened the door and threw her out. She recovered in hospital, but was unable to describe her attacker, except to say he wore a peaked cap and some kind of uniform with brass buttons.

Now the police were inclined to wonder if the attacker might have been responsible for a murder that had happened a week before the attack on Ingeborg Goetz: a war widow named Gerda Dietrich had been found stabbed to death in her cottage near the S-Bahn, in the suburb of Sommerland. It had been assumed she was the victim of a burglar, but wounds in the stomach – similar to those of Frau Goetz – suggested the madman who hurled women from trains.

Three weeks later, on 3 December, the corpse of a girl was found near the S-Bahn station at Rummelsberg; she was identified as 22-year-old Matilda Hollesch, and she had been clubbed to death with a blow on the back of the head, and then raped. A few hours after this attack, another woman was found by the S-Bahn track nearby; she had been struck violently on the head and hurled from the train. This victim, 20-year old postal clerk Irmgard Frank, had not been raped.

The following day, a passenger found the murder weapon down the back of a seat: a two-foot piece of lead-covered cable, stained with blood and human hairs. Forensic tests established that it had been used to kill both women.

Nearly three weeks later, at 7 o'clock in the morning on 22 December, the killer bludgeoned and hurled from the train a housewife named Maria Bahr, again killing her.

Now Detective Wilhelm Ludtke, one of Berlin's leading investigators, decided to try placing decoys on the trains – armed policewomen or volunteers. He also decided that 'official guides' would escort young women who had to travel home late at night. But only two weeks later, on 3 January 1941, a man who had claimed to be an official guide pushed a cinema usher out of the train; fortunately, she was only scratched and bruised. But forty-eight hours later, a 23-year-old telephone operator named Sonia Marke died when she was hurled from a train.

The skill shown by the S-Bahn rapist in avoiding traps suggested either a policeman or a railway employee: the description of survivors suggested the latter. But soon after the last murder one of the women 'decoys' almost succeeded in arresting the killer. Alone in a carriage with an S-Bahn employee, she became suspicious of his sudden movements and his evident desire to make her nervous, and announced that she was a policewoman and that he was under arrest. The man leapt from the train as it pulled into a platform and disappeared.

On 11 February another woman, Martha Zernowski, was

killed as she was clubbed and hurled from a train. On 20 February Lisa Novak, a 30-year-old factory worker, was raped, clubbed and hurled to her death from the train.

This time an arrest was made – a known sex offender named Richard Bauer, whose footprint was found in the girl's blood. He insisted that he had merely stumbled over her in the dark, but was kept in custody as a suspect.

Another possible suspect – among many – was a 28-year-old railway worker named Paul Ogorzov, a married man with two children. The Rummelsberg stationmaster admitted that he was friendly with Ogorzov, and often told him what measures the police were planning. But Ogorzov was at work at the time of many of the murders, and workmates vouched for him; he was dropped as a suspect:

The attacks now ceased until 3 July 1941, when a woman named Olga Opell was found dead beside the tracks. Since Bauer was in prison, he was automatically exonerated and released.

But investigators now learned that Paul Ogorzov had slipped away from his job as a telegraph operator at about the time of the murder of Olga Opell – he had been seen climbing over a fence. Under interrogation, Ogorzov admitted this, and explained that he had a girlfriend who lived nearby. This proved to be true; moreover, the girl declared that Ogorzov had been with her at the time Olga Opell was attacked. But when traces of blood were found on Ogorzov's tunic, the questioning was renewed. He explained that one of his children had cut his finger. But Ludtke now took a long look at the map showing where attacks had taken place, and observed that most of them were along the route between the Rummelsberg station and Ogorzov's home. This seemed too much of a coincidence, so he began pressing Ogorzov about reports from women that a man had shone his torch in their eyes. Ogorzov finally admitted that he had done this on two occasions. Pressed to name precisely where this had happened, Ogorzov became confused, then mentioned a location where, in fact, a rape had occurred.

The victims who had escaped were brought in to confront Ogorzov; one positively identified him, and mentioned that he had worn a coat with a very wide collar; when police found such a coat in Ogorzov's home, he admitted to attempted assault on four women. Asked to pinpoint the places, he mentioned Sommerland, where Gerda Dietrich had been stabbed to death in her cottage. His state of confusion was now so great that he admitted that Gerda Dietrich had been one of the women he had beaten with his fists. This left Ludtke in no doubt that there had been so many victims that he was mixing them up.

Finally, shock tactics worked where long questioning had failed; when Ludtke showed him the smashed skulls of several victims, the harassed Ogorzov suddenly broke down, and admitted that he was the S-Bahn killer. He also admitted that he had been guilty of a number of sexual attacks on women since 1939, mostly in the course of attempts to pick them up.

The incident that had turned him into a killer had occurred a few weeks before he threw the first victim – the gym teacher – from the moving train. He had accosted a woman near the Rummelsberg station, and she had screamed, bringing her menfolk from a nearby house. They beat up Ogorzov so badly that he had to spend a week in bed. He emerged vengeful and ruthless. Women would pay for this affront to his dignity . . .

And so the first two victims were hurled from the train, an act that he confessed gave him sadistic pleasure – his voice became hoarse as he described the sensation of opening the door and throwing them out into the darkness. But he quickly progressed to rape and murder, killing most victims with a tremendous blow from the lead-covered cable.

Perhaps because Ogorzov was a member of the Nazi Party, and the authorities wished to avoid embarrassment, his trial (on 21 July 1941) was rushed through in one day, and he was beheaded the following day.

The same embarrassment seems to have led the Nazis to hush up the crimes of another serial killer, Bruno Lüdke.

Lüdke was born in 1909; he was definitely mentally defective, in the same way as Earle Nelson. He began his murders at the age of 18. During the war he found it easy to kill. He was arrested for a sexual assault and sterilized by order of Himmler's SS. He was a petty thief (like Kürten) and a sadist who enjoyed torturing animals and (on one occasion) running down a woman with his horse-drawn delivery van. (He worked as a laundry roundsman.)

On 29 January 1943, a 51-year-old woman, Frieda Rösner, was found strangled on the outskirts of a wood near Berlin where she had been collecting fuel. Kriminal Kommissar Franz, in charge of the case, examined all the known criminals in Köpenick, the nearby village. These included Lüdke, who lived at 32 Grüne Trift. When he was asked if he had known the murdered woman, Lüdke admitted that he had, and that he had last seen her in the woods. Asked if he had killed her, he sprang at his interrogator and had to be overpowered; he then admitted he was the murderer, and added that under Paragraph 51 (concerning mental defectives) he could not be indicted for the crime. Lüdke went on to confess to killing eighty-five women throughout Germany since 1928. His normal method was strangulation or stabbing with a knife, and although he stole their belongings, rape was the chief motive. Franz investigated the murders and after a year, reported that it seemed to be true that Lüdke was responsible for all the crimes he confessed to. But it is also true that local police chiefs blamed all their unsolved murders on Lüdke, the ideal scapegoat.

Lüdke believed that he could never be indicted because he was insane. In fact, the embarrassment of various police forces who had arrested innocent men for Lüdke's crimes led to the case being hushed up and treated as a State secret. Lüdke was sent to a hospital in Vienna where he was a guinea-pig for various experiments, and one of the injections killed him on 8 April 1944.

In London during the days of the blitz, another sadistic killer was responsible for a brief reign of terror that was comparable to that of Jack the Ripper.

In the early hours of 9 February 1942, a 40-year-old schoolmistress, Miss Evelyn Hamilton, was found strangled in an air-raid shelter in Montagu Place, Marylebone. Her handbag was missing; she had not been sexually assaulted. On 10 February, Mrs Evelyn Oatley, known as Nita Ward, a 35-year-old ex-revue actress, was found dead in her Wardour Street flat. She was found naked on the bed; her throat had been cut and the lower part of her body mutilated with a tin-opener. Fingerprints were found on the tin-opener and a mirror.

On 11 February, a Tuesday, another woman was murdered, although the police did not find out about it until three days later. She was Mrs Margaret Lowe, aged 43; she lived alone in a flat in

Gosfield Street in the West End. She had been strangled with a silk stocking, and mutilated with a razor blade in the same way as Mrs Oatley. She was discovered on Friday by her 14-year-old evacuee daughter who came to pay a visit.

Some hours after Mrs Lowe's body was found, the fourth victim was also discovered. She was Mrs Doris Jouannet, whose husband was the night manager of a Paddington Hotel. When he returned home on Friday evening he noticed that the milk had not been taken in. Mrs Jouannet had been strangled with a stocking and mutilated with a razor blade. It soon transpired that Mrs Jouannet had been in the habit of picking up soldiers in Leicester Square pubs while her husband was on night duty; he had last seen her alive at ten o'clock on the previous evening.

Shortly after Mrs Jouannet's body was discovered, a young airman tried to accost a Mrs Heywood in a pub near Piccadilly. She refused, and he followed her out into the blacked-out street, saying 'You must at least kiss me good night.' He dragged her into a doorway and throttled her into unconsciousness. A passer-by heard the scuffle, and investigated; the man ran away, leaving behind his gas-mask. This had his service number stencilled on it.

The young airman immediately picked up another woman and drove with her in a taxi to her flat in Southwark Street, Paddington. She was Mrs Mulcahy, known as Kathleen King. In her room, the light failed, and the airman seized her by the throat. Her terror of the 'ripper' who had already killed four women made her fight violently and scream. The airman fled, leaving behind his belt.

From the gas-mask case, the attacker was identified as Gordon Frederick Cummins, a 28-year-old RAF cadet, married and living in North London. He was arrested within twelve hours of the attack on Kathleen King, on returning to his billet in St John's Wood.

Cummins had a curious record. Although he came from a good family and was well educated, he had been dismissed from a series of jobs as unreliable and dishonest. He had married in 1936 the private secretary of a theatrical producer. One of his companions declared he was a 'phoney', that he spoke with a fake Oxford accent and claimed he had a right to use 'honourable' before his name because he was the illegitimate son of a member of the House of Lords. He was known as 'the Duke' to his companions.

His fingerprints corresponded with those on the mirror and tin-opener; also, like the killer, he was left-handed. It appeared later that another prostitute had had a narrow escape from death; Cummins had accompanied her home on the night he killed Mrs Oatley, but she had mentioned that she had no money, and Cummins, who killed for cash, left her alone.

He was sentenced to death at the Old Bailey, and executed on 25 June 1942, during an air raid. Sir Bernard Spilsbury, who had performed the post-mortem on Mrs Oatley, also performed one on Cummins.

Like Cummins, Neville Heath would have undoubtedly gone on to commit more murders if he had not been caught – or, in fact, virtually given himself up. Born in 1917, Heath was one of those men who seem to be born to be petty crooks. By the age of 20 he had been dismissed from the RAF for bouncing cheques and stealing a car. After that, posing as 'Lord Dudley', he bounced more cheques and received probation; still under 21 he was sent to Borstal for three years for stealing jewellery from a family he was staying with – he was engaged to the daughter. (Heath was immensely attractive to women – one brother officer called him the male equivalent of the *femme fatale*.) At the outbreak of the war he was allowed to join the army, but was soon in trouble in Cairo for somehow getting the paymaster to give him two salaries, and was again cashiered. On his way back to England on a troopship, he seduced a mother and her 17-year-old daughter, and terrified the daughter by hitting her as he made love, inflicting some unpleasant bruises. He decided to remain in South Africa, and swindled a bank in Durban by producing an apparently genuine letter on Air Ministry notepaper authorizing a bank to pay him money. When Durban began to see through him he moved to Johannesburg and swindled hotels with plausible stories about money that was on its way from England. Then, incredibly, he was admitted into the South African Air Force, and even when they learned that he was a con-man, they allowed him to remain. By this time he had married a girl from a wealthy family, and for a year at least, the marriage was happy. Then, in 1944, he was seconded to the RAF again, and at Finmere, Oxfordshire, succeeded in getting engaged to nine girls at the same time. (The reason, almost certainly, is that 'respectable' girls would only go to bed with a man when he had promised marriage.)

When the body of a WAAF was found not far from the station, with bruises and injuries to her genitals, Heath was suspected, but never charged. Back in South Africa, he was involved in a car accident that left a young nurse burned to death – Heath claimed he had been thrown out of the car by the crash. His wife divorced him. Arrested again for dud cheques and posing as a lieutenant-colonel, he was cashiered from the South African Air Force and deported to England.

In February 1946 the police were called to the Strand Palace Hotel in London, where Heath had been caught – naked – whipping a nearly unconscious girl. Because she refused to lodge a complaint he was released. Soon after this he was fined ten pounds for posing as an Air Force officer. Not long after, he was again caught flogging a naked girl, who was tied to a bed in a hotel bedroom; again the woman refused to charge him.

Finally, on 21 June 1946, Heath was carried away as he flogged a 32-year-old artist named Margery Gardner, and this time no one interupted them – perhaps because he made sure that her face was rammed into the pillow. She suffocated to death – but not before Heath had flogged her with a riding whip, bitten her nipples until they were almost detached, and rammed a poker into her vagina. The body was discovered the next morning by a chambermaid. By that time Heath was already on his way to the Ocean Hotel at Worthing, from which he telephoned the girl who had spent the previous Saturday night with him in the same hotel where he had killed Margery Gardner – the Pembridge Court in Notting Hill. On a visit to the girl's parents, he learned that the police wanted to question him about the murder, whereupon he wrote them a letter claiming that he had lent his room key to Margery Gardner and a male friend, and found her body when he visited the room early the next morning.

A week later, on 3 July, he was staying in the Tollard Royal Hotel in Bournemouth, posing as Group Captain Rupert Brooke. There he met a pretty ex-Wren named Doreen Marshall. He persuaded her to have dinner with him, and to allow him to walk her back to her own hotel, the Norfolk. Witnesses who saw them together could see that she was nervous and tense. Five days later, Doreen Marshall's body was found in a wooded dell called Branksome Dene Chine, beaten, mutilated and stabbed to death. The major injury was a Jack-the-Ripper-type slash from the inside of the thigh to the breasts. By then, Heath had already volunteered his help to the local police, and they had recognized him as the man wanted by Scotland Yard. A cloakroom ticket in Heath's pocket led them to a briefcase that contained the riding whip with which Margery Gardner had been lashed.

Heath was tried for the murder of Margery Gardner – an odd decision, since her death was probably accidental – and executed at Pentonville on 16 October 1946. If, as seems likely, he was also guilty of the two earlier murders, then he certainly qualifies for a place in this book as a serial killer.

Even Germany – with its astonishing record of serial murder, from Grossmann to Ogorzov – became relatively quiescent in the 1940s. Apart from Lüdke, there is only Rudolf Pleil, a sex murderer who committed suicide in his cell in 1958. Pleil was a habitual criminal, a burglar among other things, who began by attacking women in order to rob them. (He always robbed his female victims as well as raping them.) Since 1945 he reckoned to have killed fifty women. He was a small, fat man with a friendly face (although he had a receding forehead which produced an ape-like effect).

Pleil, like Kürten, enjoyed murder, and referred to himself boastfully as 'der beste Totmacher' (the best death-maker). Full details of his crimes are unfortunately not available at the time of writing. Like Kürten, he used many weapons for his murders – stones, knives, hatchets and hammers to kill and mutilate his victims. When in prison he often wrote to the authorities, offering to reveal the whereabouts of another murder; in this way he would get an 'airing' to the town where he had buried one of his victims. On one occasion, he wrote to the mayor of a town offering his services as hangman, and telling him that if he wanted to study his qualifications, he should look in the well at the end of the town; a strangled body was discovered in this well. Pleil was a vain man who took pleasure in the horror he aroused and described himself as 'quite a lad'. He is quoted as saying: 'Every man has his passion. Some prefer whist. I prefer killing people.'

America has no cases of mass murder that date from the war years. But in June 1946, an 18-year-old Chicago student named William Heirens was caught as he tried to burgle an apartment building, and was grilled by the police until he confessed to three murders: those of Josephine Ross, a widow who was stabbed in the throat on 3 June 1945; Frances Brown, who was shot and then stabbed in her apartment; and Suzanne Degnan, a 6-year-old girl who was removed from her bed on 7 January 1946 and dismembered. Heirens claimed that the murders were actually committed by an alter ego called George, and explained that he had started burgling apartments to steal women's panties. He was sentenced to life imprisonment. In recent years, Heirens' defenders – like Dolores Kennedy (author of *William Heirens: His Day in Court*) – have argued that the confession was forced out of him by threats of the electric chair; Heirens himself continues to insist that he is totally innocent of everything but burglary. He also claims that the famous inscription written in lipstick about the body of Frances Brown – 'For heaven's sake catch me before I kill more I cannot control myself' – was written by a reporter. In an anthology called *Murder in the 1940s*, I have printed Heirens' own account of the case, which makes some telling points in favour of his innocence. *If* he is innocent, of course, this would be one of the most disturbing miscarriages of justice in legal history. But even if not, it could be argued that a man who has served more than forty-five years in jail has more than paid for crimes committed as a teenager, and deserves to be paroled. (In fact, Heirens has had his application for parole rejected several times.)

The crimes of Marcel Petiot, a French doctor who, under the pretence of helping Jews to escape from occupied France, murdered them in a gas chamber and stole their posessions, belong to the realm of mass murder for profit rather than serial killing. So do the murders committed by Raymond Fernandez and Martha Beck, the 'Lonely Hearts' killers. Fernandez answered 'lonely hearts' advertisements, seduced the women, then absconded with their savings. A woman he married in 1947 died on their honeymoon in Spain under mysterious circumstances, almost certainly poisoned by her husband. When Fernandez met Martha Beck, he was hoping to swindle her; in fact, she fell frantically in love with him, and all his efforts to escape were a failure. Together – with Martha posing as his sister – they plotted the death of Fernandez's latest bride, Myrtle Young, who died of a brain haemorrhage after a massive dose of barbiruratés. The next bride, Janet Fay, was murdered by Martha with a hammer after a quarrel, and was buried in a cellar in Queens, New York. Fernandez then married a widow with a 2-year-old daughter, Delphine Dowling. Delphine was despatched with her former husband's service revolver, and her daughter Rainelle was drowned in a washtub. Suspicious neighbours alerted the police, who soon uncovered the two bodies in the basement. The two killers, labelled 'America's most hated murderers', were electrocuted in March 1951.

The main interest of the case in this context is that Fernandez had been a normal, law-abiding citizen until he received a heavy blow on the head from a falling hatch on board a ship, and that it was after this that he turned into a 'sex maniac', an insatiable seducer of lonely women who kept many affairs going at the same time – in one case he even seduced a seriously deformed woman. When we recollect that Earle Nelson and Albert Fish had suffered similar accidents (and that the same is true of the 1970s serial killer Henry Lee Lucas), it raises the interesting question of whether such a blow could stimulate sex hormones to a degree that would turn such a person into a 'sex maniac?' (Ken McElroy, the town bully of Skidmore, Missouri, who was murdered by angry fellow citizens in 1981, also received a severe head injury when he was 18, and turned into a thief and rapist.) It is a question that is worth bearing in mind in the investigation of serial killers.

Another American murderer who deserves a brief mention in this survey is Howard Unruh, as the first of the 'crazy gunmen' – men who go berserk and kill at random. Unruh was an ex-GI who returned to his home in Camden, New Jersey, after the war. He enrolled at the university, and spent all his spare time studying the Bible. Over the years he became increasingly paranoid, developing a particular hatred of various neighbours who had treated him with what he considered to be a lack of respect. He began to collect high powered weapons. When, on 5 September 1949, some prankster removed a gate he had installed in his garden fence, his control snapped, and he left the house with two loaded pistols. In the next twelve minutes he shot to death thirteen people – Unruh was a crack shot – then barricaded himself in his bedroom until the police persuaded him to surrender. He was found to be insane and committed to an asylum.

Unruh was not a serial killer – in the perfectly obvious sense that all his murders were committed at the same time; he was what FBI agent Robert Ressler calls a 'spree killer'. But the resentment, the smouldering hatred of 'society', is typical of the serial killer, and during the next four decades, the 'crazy gunman' syndrome would become almost as familiar as the closely related problems of the political terrorist and the serial killer.

7

The 1950s

When I began to assemble an anthology of famous murder cases of the 1950s, I noticed that I had approximately twice as many to choose from as in the earlier volumes on the 1930s and 1940s. One reason, I knew, was partly that the murder rate began to climb steadily after the war, as it does after most wars. But a glance down the list revealed something more disturbing: that an increasing number of people began to experience the *compulsion* to kill – from Christie, who turned his house into a kind of private morgue, and Werner Boost, who liked to murder courting couples, to Heinrich Pommerencke, who admitted that he became a wild animal when he killed. All these were, of course, sex crimes, and in retrospect they can be seen as a prelude to the epidemic of 'serial murder' that becomes apparent in the 1970s.

Another interesting change can be seen if we compare killers like Christie and Glatman with killers like Manuel, Boost and Rees. Christie and Glatman seem to belong to an 'older' type of killer, the conventional little man with a violent sexual appetite that drives him to rape in much the same furtive spirit as a poacher stealing game. In Manuel, Boost and Rees we encounter a type of criminal who will become increasingly familiar in the following decades: the rebel against society who seems to feel that he has a *right* to kill. It is significant that the 'Moors murderer' Ian Brady cited Nietzsche, Sade and Dostoevsky among his intellectual mentors. Christie had no intellectual mentors – although a number of witnesses described his desire to be known as a doctor and a man of learning. It is also possible to infer from the trial evidence that he possessed at least one characteristic of the successful doctor – a soothing bedside manner that lulled his victims into a state of trust.

The climax of what has been called 'the greatest murder mystery of all time' developed on the afternoon of 24 March 1953 at a tiny, shabby house in London's Notting Hill area. A Jamaican tenant named Beresford Brown was preparing to redecorate the ground-floor kitchen, and was looking for a place where he could put up a shelf. When he tapped the wall in the corner it sounded hollow, and he realized that he was looking at a cupboard that had been covered over with wallpaper. He peeled back a strip of wallpaper from the corner and discovered a hole in the door; he switched on a torch and peeped through. And what he saw was unmistakably the back of a naked woman, who seemed to be bending forward with her head between her knees, as if being sick. It explained the offensive smell in the kitchen, not unlike that of a dead rat.

The police were there within minutes; so was the pathologist Dr Francis Camps. The cupboard door was opened, and the seated body was seen to be supported by a piece of blanket which was knotted to her brassiere. The other end of the blanket was part of the covering of a tall object leaning against the wall. A closer look revealed this was another body. And beyond it, against the back of the cupboard – which had obviously been a coal cellar – there was yet another object that looked ominously like an upright body.

The first corpse proved to be that of a rather pretty young woman, with a mark around her throat indicating that she had been strangled to death; a 'stalactite' of mould was growing out of her nose. Medical examination showed she had been dead about a month. Bubbling from her vagina was a large quantity of sperm – about 5 cc – suggesting that her killer had either had a tremendous orgasm, or had raped her more than once. The second body also proved to be of a young woman, wearing only a cardigan and vest; she too had been raped and strangled. The body had been placed in the cupboard upside down. Medical examination showed that she had been in the cupboard about two months. Body three was again of a young woman, upside down and wrapped in a blanket. And, as in the case of body two, a piece of cloth had been placed between the legs in the form of a diaper. She was wearing only a pink silk slip and bra, with two vests. She was six months pregnant, and had been in the cupboard from two to three months.

These were not the only remains found at No. 10 Rillington Place. Beneath the floor boards in the front room there was another naked body wrapped in a blanket. This proved to be a middle-aged woman, who had been dead for between three and four months. Between her legs there was also a piece of silk in the position of a diaper. A search of the garden revealed that a bone propping up a fence was a human femur. Digging revealed bones belonging to two more female bodies.

There was no problem about identifying the killer. He was John Reginald Halliday Christie, who had lived in the ground-floor flat for the past fifteen years, and had had the exclusive use of the garden. Christie was described as a tall, thin, bespectacled man with a bald head. The corpse under the floorboards was that of his 54-year-old wife Ethel. Christie had left the flat four days earlier, sub-letting it to a couple named Reilly (from whom he took rent of £8). That same evening the Jamaican landlord, Charles Brown, had arrived and found the Reillys in occupation; he had ordered them to leave the following morning – since Christie had no right to sub-let the flat.

Now the hunt was on for Christie; police naturally feared he might commit more sex murders. One week later, on 31 March 1953, a police constable near Putney Bridge thought he recognized a man staring gloomily into the water and asked him if he was Christie; the man admitted it quietly, and accompanied PC Ledger to the station. He seemed relieved it was over.

The finding of the bodies brought to mind another tragedy that had occurred in the same house five years earlier. On 2 December 1949, the police had found the bodies of 20-year-old Beryl Evans and her one-year-old daughter Geraldine in the wash-house outside the back door. The husband, an illiterate labourer named Timothy Evans, had been charged with both murders and hanged. Now everyone was asking the question: was Christie the killer of Beryl and Geraldine Evans? Christie himself answered part of this question a few weeks later when he confessed to strangling Beryl Evans with a stocking; he claimed she had asked him to help her commit suicide. But Christie strongly denied murdering the baby Geraldine.

Reg Christie (as he was known) was born in Yorkshire in April 1898, the son of a carpet designer who bullied and ill-treated his family. He was a weak child who was regarded as a 'cissy' by his schoolfellows. He was often ill, and frequently in trouble with the police for minor offences – he was the unlucky type who always seemed to get caught. At the age of 15 he became a clerk to the Halifax police, but was sacked for pilfering. And when he lost a job in his father's carpet factory for petty theft, his father threw him out of the house. He served in the First World War and, according to his own statement, was gassed. In 1920 he got a job as a clerk in a wool mill, and began courting a neighbour, Ethel Waddington, a plain, homely girl of a passive disposition; they married in 1920.

But Christie continued to be a petty criminal. In 1921 he was a postman, and people complained that letters and postal-orders failed to arrive. Investigation revealed that Christie had been stealing them, and he was sentenced to three months in jail. In 1923 he was put on probation for obtaining money by false pretences. In 1924 he was sentenced to nine months for theft. This was too much for Ethel, and she left him. He moved to London and settled down with another woman whom he met on a coach going to Margate. But Christie's dislike of work led to quarrels, and after one of these he hit her with a cricket bat, almost shattering her skull. For this he was sentenced to six months for malicious wounding. And in 1933 he received another three months for stealing the car of a priest who had befriended him. He wrote to Ethel in Sheffield, asking her to come and visit him in prison. When he came out, they again moved in together. Their new home was the small, shabby house at the end of a cul-de-sac called Rillington Place. The rent was twelve shillings and nine pence a week.

In September 1939 Christie became a war reserve policeman, and he became unpopular in the area for his bullying and officious behaviour – he loved to run in people for minor blackout infringements. During this period, Ethel often went to visit her family in Sheffield, and in 1943 Christie began to have an affair with a young woman from the Harrow Road police station. Her husband, a soldier, heard about it and went and caught them together at Rillington Place. He beat Christie up, and later divorced his wife, citing Christie as co-respondent.

It may have been this humiliation that led to Christie's first murder. Some time soon after the divorce scandal, Christie picked up a young Austrian prostitute named Ruth Fuerst – she had been stranded in England by the war – and took her back to Rillington Place. Ethel was in Sheffield. As they had sex, he strangled her with a piece of rope. The fact that he used rope suggests that the murder was premeditated; he probably decided to kill her while she undressed. But why? The answer was supplied to me by Dr Francis Camps, the pathologist on the case, when I met him in 1959. Camps told me that one of the odd things about the case that never came out in court was that he found dried sperm in the seams of Christie's shoes. For Camps, this showed clearly that Christie had masturbated as he stood over a corpse. And this, in turn, indicates that Christie had to *see* the corpse to achieve maximum stimulation. In short, he was a necrophile. In fact, he admitted later that the most overwhelming emotional experience of his life was to see the corpse of his grandfather when he was 8 years old.

Christie was almost certainly lying when he said he had normal intercourse with Ruth Fuerst. In his teens, Christie was the laughing stock of the local youths because he was reputed to be impotent; after a humiliating experience with a local girl, he became known as 'Reggie No-Dick' and 'Can't do-it Christie'. With shy, passive women (like Ethel) he could achieve intercourse, although he claims that they had been married for two years before they had sex. The same is probably true of the soldier's wife with whom he had an affair. But with most women he was impotent unless they were unconscious or dead. So when Ruth Fuerst came back to his flat, he probably prepared a piece of 'strangling rope' (with a knot at either end) and placed it under the pillow, intending to kill her and make sexual use of the corpse until Ethel came back. In fact, he was interrupted. A telegram arrived shortly after the murder, announcing her return. He had to conceal the body hastily under the floor boards, and bury it in the garden at the first opportunity. Now he had killed a woman, the aching sense of inferiority – brought to a head by the beating from the angry soldier – was assuaged.

In December 1943 temptation came his way again. Now no longer a policeman, he worked for a firm called Ultra Radio, and met a plump, attractive little woman called Muriel Eady. She told him she suffered from catarrh, and Christie had an idea. He told her he had a cure for catarrh, and invited her back to

Rillington Place while Ethel was away. The cure, he said, was to lean over a bowl of steaming Friar's Balsam, with a cloth over the head to keep in the steam. Christie ran a rubber pipe from the gas tap, and inserted it under the cloth. Muriel Eady passed out peacefully. Trembling with excitement, Christie moved her on to the bed, removed her clothes, and raped her. Looking at the body, he later described how he experienced a sense of exquisite peace. 'I had no regrets.' Muriel Eady also found her way into the garden.

Six years passed before he killed again, and it is possible the murder was unpremeditated. Timothy and Beryl Evans had moved into the upstairs flat, but they quarrelled a great deal; one of the quarrels was about a blonde girl who had moved in with them; the girl had to leave. In one of his confessions, Christie claimed that he strangled Mrs Evans at her own request, because she wanted to die. There may be an element of truth in this. But what Christie failed to mention is that Beryl Evans had again discovered herself to be pregnant, and wanted an abortion. Christie, who loved to swagger, had told Timothy Evans that he had once studied to be a doctor. And Evans asked Christie if he could perform an abortion.

What happened next is a matter for conjecture; but the view of Ludovic Kennedy, in his book *Ten Rillington Place*, is well argued. Christie went into the room, where Beryl Evans was waiting for him; she removed her knickers and lay down with her legs apart. Christie inserted a finger, or perhaps a spoon, then was overcome with sexual desire, and tried to climb on her. Beryl struggled; Christie strangled her, and then raped her. When Timothy Evans came home, Christie told him that his wife had died as a result of the abortion, and that he, Evans, would almost certainly be blamed.

Evans, a man of subnormal intelligence, panicked. He allowed Christie to do his thinking for him. And what Christie apparently advised was that the baby should be looked after by some people in Acton, and Evans should vanish. Evans *did* vanish – to Merthyr Vale, in Wales, and spent ten days with an aunt and uncle; then he decided to go back to London, to give himself up to the police. They came and found the bodies in the wash-house, and Evans was charged with murder.

And here we encounter the first mystery of the case. Evans then made a full confession to murdering his wife and baby by strangulation. This was, admittedly, his second confession – in the first he had stated that Beryl had died as a result of an abortion performed by Christie. But he repeated his confession to murdering his wife and child the following day. So although he withdrew this second confession a fortnight later, the police had no reason to believe his assertion that the real killer was Christie. At the trial, Christie appeared as a witness for the prosecution, and Evans was hanged on 9 March 1950.

Ethel Christie had a strong suspicion, amounting to a certainty, that her husband was somehow involved in the murders – she had noticed his extreme nervousness at the time. She confided her belief to a neighbour, and when Christie came in and caught them discussing the case, he flew into a rage. This could explain why, on 14 December 1952, he strangled her in bed. It could also have been that he experienced a compulsion to commit more sex crimes, and Ethel stood in the way. Christie told her family in Sheffield that she was unable to write because she had rheumatism in her fingers.

In mid-January 1953 Christie picked up a prostitute called Kathleen Maloney in a pub in Paddington, and invited her back to his flat. As she sat in a deck-chair in the kitchen, he placed the gas pipe under the chair; she was too drunk to notice. When she was unconscious, he raped her and put her in the cupboard.

The next victim, Rita Nelson, was six months pregnant; Christie may have lured her back with the offer of an abortion. She also ended in the cupboard – the second body.

About a month later, Christie met a girl called Hectorina Maclennan, who told him she was looking for a flat. She and her boyfriend actually spent three nights in Christie's flat, now devoid of furniture (Christie had sold it). On 5 March Hectorina made the mistake of going back to the flat alone. She grew nervous when she saw Christie toying with a gas-pipe and tried to leave; Christie killed her and raped her. When her boyfriend came to inquire about her, she was in the cupboard, and Christie claimed not to have seen her. As Christie gave him tea, the boyfriend noticed 'a very nasty smell', but had no suspicion he was sitting within feet of Hectorina's corpse.

This was Christie's last murder. Two weeks later, he left Rillington Place, and wandered around aimlessly, sleeping in cheap lodgings and spending the days in cafés until he was arrested. He confessed to all the murders of women, usually insisting that it was *they* who made the advances. He was executed on 15 July 1953.

The major mystery remains – was Timothy Evans innocent? Long after his death, he was officially absolved of all responsibility and guilt; yet that leaves some major questions unanswered. For example, why did he confess to the murders?

Ludovic Kennedy, in *Ten Rillington Place* takes the view that Evans was innocent of both murders. He confessed, says Kennedy, out of misery and confusion. But this is almost impossible. Evans had had ten days in Wales to think things over. There is no earthly reason why he should have confessed to strangling Beryl (after a quarrel) and then Geraldine. (Kennedy argues that he was too fond of both).

In *The Two Stranglers of Rillington Place*, Rupert Furneaux takes the opposite view. He points out that Beryl and Timothy Evans often quarrelled violently, and that nothing was more likely than that Evans would kill Beryl in a rage. He argues closely and convincingly, and is, on the whole, more plausible than Kennedy. And he believes that it was Christie who murdered the baby.

But this still leaves a major mystery: why, in that case, did Evans also confess to murdering Geraldine?

The answer is surely supplied by a curious piece of evidence from another murderer, Donald Hume, who was in prison at the same time as Evans, on a charge of murdering a man named Stanley Setty and throwing pieces of his body out of an aeroplane. Evans asked Hume's advice, and when Hume asked 'Did you kill your wife?' Evans replied: 'No, Christie murdered her.' Here he could well have been lying, for by now his defence was that Christie had killed her in the course of an abortion. But when Hume asked if he killed the baby, Evans made the surprising statement that Christie had strangled Geraldine while he, Evans, watched. He said that the baby's crying had got on his nerves.

This rings true. Evans was in a frantic state, and he could well have stood by while Christie killed Geraldine. In doing so, he had become, in effect, her killer, so his confession to murdering her was not far short of the truth. Guilt probably increased his sense of being her murderer. And this, I would argue, is almost certainly the answer to the riddle. There *were* two stranglers of Rillington Place. And baby Geraldine was, in a sense, killed by both of them.

* * *

The question of whether Peter Manuel should be classed as a serial killer is a difficult one. John Bingham's book *The Huntng Down of Peter Manuel* (1973) begins: 'Peter Thomas Anthony Manuel was found guilty of murdering seven people. He certainly killed nine. In addition to the murders, he raped one woman, assaulted others, and was a housebreaker of some renown, being in all a versatile criminal.' And a few pages later: 'Manuel did kill for pleasure. He liked killing. The act of killing thrilled him.' This certainly sounds like a precise definition of a serial killer.

Manuel seems to have been one of those habitual crooks who find it impossible to stay out of trouble. Unfortunately, little is known of his childhood, and the circumstances that turned him into a criminal. Born in Manhattan in 1927, he returned to England with his British parents at the age of 5. His parents were good Catholics. The family lived in Motherwell, Scotland, then moved to Coventry. There, at the age of 12, Manuel made his first appearance in court for burgling the shop of a cycle dealer, and received twelve months' probation. When he appeared before the same court five weeks later for housebreaking he was sent to an approved school. He escaped eleven times, and was usually returned after being caught housebreaking – on one occasion he attacked the householder with a hammer. In 1942 he robbed and indecently assaulted the wife of a school employee, and was eventually caught hiding in the school chapel. This time he was sent to Borstal. After being released two years later, he rejoined his family, who had returned to Scotland. His father worked as a foreman in the local gasworks, and was on the District Council. Soon afterwards Manuel was acquitted on yet another charge of housebreaking.

Manuel's problem was that, as a criminal, he was not particularly competent. Worse still, he was unlucky. Soon after midnight on 16 February 1946, he broke into a bungalow in Sandyhills, near Glasgow. A local constable called Muncie was called to the scene, and spent most of the night searching the house, in case the burglar was still concealed there. He was not, so Muncie went home for breakfast. Soon, he was called back to an empty bungalow very close to the one he had already investigated – a neighbour had reported seeing an intruder. In fact, Peter Manuel was hiding in the loft, but Muncie failed to find him, and left after a search. Later that morning, Muncie remembered that he had left behind a teacup with fingerprints on it, and drove back to the bungalow with a colleague. While the colleague was collecting the keys from a neighbour, a well-dressed youth – Manuel was 19 – walked towards Muncie's car from the direction of the bungalow; Muncie stopped him and asked his identity. The youth said he was Peter Manuel, then admitted that he had come from the garden of the bungalow, where he had been 'watching'. At the police station, he was found to have in his possession a gold watch that Muncie had last seen in the bungalow. Manuel was placed under arrest and charged with burglary.

Unfortunately, he was allowed out on bail. And within two weeks, he had committed three sexual attacks. The first two were unsuccessful; a woman with a 3-year-old child fought and screamed so hard that he ran away, and a nurse was saved by the appearance of a motorcyclist. Muncie had already recognized the description of the attacker as that of the burglar, but Manuel was nowhere to be found. The third victim, a married woman, was attacked from behind on a lonely road after dark. She had only just been released from hospital, and was in no condition to resist. Manuel dragged to a railway embankment, beat her into submission, then raped her.

The next day Muncie caught up with him. In an identity parade, the first two victims immediately identified Manuel as the attacker. The third victim had not seen his face; but fragments of red sandstone – from the railway embankment – in Manuel's clothes left no doubt that he was the rapist. He received an eight-year sentence.

Back in Glasgow in 1953, he worked for the Gas Board and British Rail, and even became engaged for eleven months to a bus conductress. There was a curious episode during the engagement that throws light on Manuel's complex psychology. The girl received a letter alleging that Manuel's real father had been electrocuted in America, and that Manuel himself had been in the Secret Service. Manuel shrugged it off as a calumny; in fact, he had written it himself. It was typical of his desire to 'be' someone, to appear as more interesting and exciting than he actually was. In fact, the girl cancelled the marriage because Manuel refused to go to confession. (Both were Catholics.)

During this period, Manuel tried hard to make trouble for Muncie by alleging perjury in the rape case; he also offered information about two murders, claiming to know the identity of the killer. The police dismissed the claims. In December 1954,

Manuel also tried to gain American citizenship, and tried to support the claim by offering information about various crimes he claimed to know about, and information about national security. The Americans decided he was a liar and fantasizer, and sent him away. Muncie, who interviewed him again about these claims, decided that he had an overpowering craving for attention.

On 30 July 1955 – the day he was supposed to have been married – Manuel made another bungled attempt at rape. The girl, Mary McLaughlin, was forced into a field at knifepoint, but her screams were heard, and people began searching nearby fields with torches. Manuel forced her to the ground and placed a knife at her throat, threatening to kill her and cut off her head. He also put his hand inside her underwear. When the searchers had gone away, the girl tried talking him out of rape, asking if he was in trouble, and Manuel told her that he had been due to get married that day, but that the girl, a bus conductress, had broken it off the previous evening. Then, after smoking cigarettes and talking for more than an hour, they made their way back across the fields. Manuel had thrown away the knife with which he threatened her. When he asked her if she meant to report him to the police, she told him that she intended to forget the whole thing.

In fact, after telling her mother and sister what had happened, she went to the police. Muncie recognized the description as being similar to Manuel, and soon Manuel was under arrest. At first he alleged an alibi, which was quickly disproved. But in court, he elected to defend himself, and soon revealed that he was a highly articulate young man. He told the jury that he and Mary McLaughlin had been courting, but had quarrelled. They had met by accident on the day of the alleged assault, and she had gone with him voluntarily . . .

He told the story so plausibly that the jury – who knew nothing of his criminal record – decided that he deserved the benefit of the doubt, and brought in a Scottish verdict of 'not proven'. Subsequently, Manuel's father saw Mary McLaughlin at a bus stop and spat at her.

Manuel's next attack on a woman proved fatal. Ten weeks later, on 4 January 1956, a man taking a walk in a copse near the East Kilbride golf course saw a girl lying face down, her head battered in. She proved to be 19-year-old Anne Knielands, who had set out the previous evening to meet a boyfriend. But her young man was celebrating Hogmanay, and had forgotten about their date.

She had been attacked from behind, and had run away across a field, losing both shoes and scrambling over barbed wire that had lacerated her. Finally, she had been overtaken, and struck on the back of the head with a piece of angle iron so violently that the skull was shattered into fifteen pieces. Yet although her knickers – and one stocking – were missing, she had not been raped.

Not far from the site of the murder, men from the Gas Board were working at a building site, and among the workers was Peter Manuel. The man who had found the girl's body learned that Manuel had a criminal record that included sex attacks, and informed the police. Manuel was questioned, and explained that the scratches on his face had been acquired in a brawl. He had been at home on the evening when Anne Knielands had been killed. His father supported his alibi, although he knew some of his son's statements were false. The police had to accept his word.

In March, police received a tip that Manuel and another man intended to rob a colliery at Blantyre, near Manuel's home. They pounced as the men were breaking in; one was arrested, but the other – Manuel – ran away. However, he left behind a fragment of clothing on a barbed wire fence, and was finally charged with the attempted break-in. His trial date was set for 2 October, seven months away. Meanwhile, he was released on bail.

Six months later, in September 1956, there were three burglaries in Lanarkshire. The first, on 12 September, was in an empty house in Bothwell. The burglar had scattered soup on the floor, walked on the bedcover in dirty boots, and slashed the mattress and quilt. He had drunk the juice from a tin of pears and left the pears on the carpet. A stopwatch, an electric razor and some tools were missing, but other valuable items were untouched.

The second burglary took place in High Burnside, not far from East Kilbride, on 15 September. Again, soup was scattered on the carpet, as well as spaghetti; there were dirty footmarks on the bed. But all that had been stolen were four pairs of nylon stockings and two gold rings.

Two days later, the daily help arrived at 5 Fennsbank Avenue, High Burnside, the home of baker William Watt, and found a glass panel broken in the front door. In the house, three women lay dead, shot in the head at close range: Mrs Marion Watt, her sister Margaret Brown and her 16-year-old daughter Vivienne. All were wearing nightclothes, although Margaret Brown's pyjama bottoms had been torn, and Vivienne's had been removed. A brassiere, apparently torn from her body, lay on the floor of Vivienne's bedroom. The girl had a bruise on her chin where she had obviously been struck but there was no sign of rape or sexual assault. A cigarette had been stubbed out on the carpet.

William Watt had been away on a fishing trip when the women were murdered, but ten days later he was arrested and charged with the murders – the policeman who had arrested him had felt that he did not behave like a man whose family has just been slaughtered, and a check of his alibi convinced the police that he *could* have returned home during the night and committed the crimes.

Yet the police also had reason to suspect Manuel. Further along Fennsbank Avenue, at number 18, another burglary was discovered. The burglar had again poured tomato soup on the carpet and stubbed out a cigarette. A pair of nylon stockings was found on a chair in the lounge.

They had another reason. An informant told the police that Manuel had boasted that he intended to 'do a Jew's house' on the evening of the murders, and to use a revolver. He told the informant that he had tested the revolver by shooting a cow up the nostril.

By chance, Muncie – now a chief inspector – had noticed a dead cow in a field, and learned from the vet that it had blood in its nostril. Unfortunately, it already lay in a vat at the knacker's yard. In an attempt to find the bullet, Muncie and a squad of policemen spent four days searching through piles of stinking offal; unfortunately, they were unable to find anything.

Manuel was questioned – his father blustered that he was going to complain about police harassment to his local MP – and Manuel simply refused to account for his movements on the evening of the murders. Soon after, he was sentenced to eighteen months for the colliery burglary. He was placed in Barlinnie Jail, alongside William Watt . . .

Now Manuel behaved in the strangely irrational manner that seems typical of a certain type of serial killer – unless, that is, he was suddenly struck by remorse, or a flash of human decency. He sent for Watt's lawyer and told him that he, Manuel, knew that Watt was innocent, and that he knew the name of the man who had actually committed the murders. To prove this, he described the position of certain articles of furniture in the Watts' house, claiming that the murderer hold told him – and that he had also asked him to dispose of the gun. The lawyer checked the furniture and found that Manuel's statement was accurate. But there was still no proof that Manuel was the murderer. Finally, after sixty-seven days in jail, Watt was released.

Almost a year later, in November 1957, Manuel was also released. His first action was to arrange a meeting with William Watt, and tell him that the murders had been committed by a man called Tallis. His description of the inside of the house was so accurate that Watt accused him of having been inside it. Manuel denied this. There was nothing Watt could do about his suspicion that he had spoken to the killer of his wife, daughter and sister-in-law.

On 8 December, a few days after this talk with William Watt, Manuel went to Newcastle upon Tyne, and hired the taxi of a driver named Sidney Dunn. Near Edmundbyers, he shot Dunn in the back of the head, then cut his throat; then he smashed the windows and headlamps of the taxi, and dragged the body on to the moorland grass. He left the driver's wallet untouched. The precise motive – apart from the pleasure of killing – remains a mystery.

Twenty days after the Newcastle murder, Manuel killed another girl. On the evening of 28 December 1957, Isabelle Cooke set out from her home in Mount Vernon to go to a dance. She failed to reach the dance or return home. A woman who lived nearby heard a woman cry out.

The police were still searching for the body on New Year's Eve when Manuel massacred another family. Peter Smart, a successful civil engineer of 45, lived with his wife and 10-year-old son in a house he had built himself at Sheepburn Road, Uddingston. His relatives had been expecting him to drop in for Hogmanay celebrations, but when he failed to arrive, simply assumed that he had found something else to do. When he failed to arrive at work on 6 January, and the police reported finding his car abandoned in a Gorbals street, two of his colleagues went to the house in Sheepburn Road; when there was no reply to their knocks, they called the police. The three Smarts were found dead in their bed; all had been shot at close range in the head.

Two local residents named McMunn shivered when they heard the news. On 4 January, a burglar had peered round their bedroom door, but had fled when Mr McMunn asked his wife: 'Where's the gun?' and she replied 'Here it is.' The burglar had gained admittance by breaking a window.

Peter Manuel was an immediate and obvious suspect. And suspicion of his involvement increased when Joe Brennan, a friend of Manuel's who was now in the police force, reported that Manuel had been broke on New Year's Eve and spending freely on New Year's Day. And now, at last, the police had the break they had been hoping for. Peter Smart had been to the local bank on New Year's Day and had drawn out £35. The money, as it happened, was in new notes, in consecutive numerical order. The customer who had drawn out cash immediately after Peter Smart was interviewed, and still had some of his notes, also numbered consecutively. From this, the police could deduce the numbers of the notes drawn out by Peter Smart. They then went around hotels and pubs where Manuel had spent money on New Year's Day, and were able to trace notes he had spent; they were from the lot drawn out by Peter Smart.

Early on 13 January 1958, the police swooped on the house of Manuel's father. He was as aggressive and unhelpful as ever, threatening again to complain to his MP. Peter Manuel was roused from sleep, and became angry. 'You haven't found anything yet – you can't take me.' The word 'yet' convinced the police that they were on the right track.

In the house they found a camera and a pair of gloves lined with lambswool. On Christmas Day, there had been a burglary at the home of the Revd. Alexander Houston, in Mount Vernon, in which a camera and gloves lined with lambswool had been stolen. When the minister identified them as his property, the police at last had something with which they could charge Peter Manuel. For good measure, his father was also charged.

Peter Manuel's reaction was as unexpected and irrational as ever. He asked to see the police superintendent, and told him that the money had been given him by a man called Samuel McKay, in payment for showing McKay around the Sheepburn Road area, with a view to spying out suitable houses for burglary.

When told of this accusation, McKay – who was not normally

the kind of man who would help the police – became indignant, and offered them a useful piece of information: that just before Christmas, Manuel had been in possession of a Biretta pistol.

And now, two days after his arrest, the totally unexpected happened, and Manuel decided to confess. He asked to see the inspector in charge of the murder team, and told him that he could help him clear up some unsolved crimes. Then, in front of members of the team, he wrote a statement declaring that he would give information about the murders of Anne Knielands, Isabelle Cooke, the Watt family and the Smarts, if they would release his father. Then he confessed – verbally – to breaking into the Smarts' house and killing all three. His parents were sent for, and Manuel repeated his confession to them. After that, Manuel took the police to the spot where he had buried Isabelle Cooke. In the grave – in a field not far from where she had last been seen – the girl's almost naked body was uncovered.

Later, Manuel was able to lead the police to the place beside the River Clyde where he had thrown the Beretta; this was recovered by a diver. The pistol was wrapped in a pair of Mrs Smart's gloves.

The trial, which opened on 12 May 1958, should have been an anticlimax, since Manuel had confessed, and the police had overwhelming evidence against him. But Manuel still had a few surprises. He dismissed his defence counsel and undertook his own defence – no doubt recalling the previous occasion when this tactic had succeeded in producing a verdict of 'not proven'. His basic assertion was that his 'confessions' had been forced from him, in that his father was also in custody, charged with burglary. He also charged that William Watt had murdered his own family, and had confessed this to him. But when he examined his own mother, she admitted that when she and her husband had been called to the police station, her son had said 'I don't know what makes me do these things.' Manuel tried hard to get her to retract this, without success. The jury, understandably, felt that if Manuel's own mother was willing to acknowledge that he had confessed, then there could be little doubt of it.

They took two hours and twenty-one minutes to find Manuel guilty on all counts except the Anne Knielands murder, on which the judge had instructed them that the evidence was insufficient. Manuel was sentenced to death.

In Barlinnie Jail, Manuel had to be kept apart from other

prisoners – rapists and child killers are always unpopular. Precautions were even taken to make sure he could not be poisoned. When his appeal was rejected, Manuel suddenly stopped speaking, and gave up smoking; for three weeks he was silent. Two days before his execution, when he heard that the Home Secretary had rejected an appeal for clemency, he suddenly became his old self again, talking in the odd, compulsive way that had already caused him so many problems. On 11 July 1958, he made his confession to a priest, ate breakfast with a large tot of whisky, then went quietly to meet the hangman.

From the point of view of this book, the main interest of the Manuel case lies in the fact that Manuel was one of the earliest 'self-esteem killers'. Fellow prisoners knew him as a braggart who wanted to be respected as a master criminal. His most urgent desire was to be 'known', to be famous or notorious. Yet unlike other boastful killers – for example, Richard Speck, the murderer of the eight Chicago nurses (whom we shall encounter in the next chapter) – he was a man of considerable intelligence, and psychiatrists noted that he could be articulate and well-mannered. But he continued to refuse to acknowledge the murders, claiming that the police had 'framed' him. He explained his burglaries by saying with disarming candour that he was a dishonest person who happened to have been born that way.

But how do we explain the fact that, except in one case, his female victims were never raped? John Bingham has suggested that the reason is that Manuel would reach orgasm before he arrived at this point. After the Mary McLaughlan assault, semen stains were found in his trousers, and this could explain why, after groping around inside her underwear, he suddenly calmed down and smoked a cigarette. Vincent Verzeni and Peter Kürten often achieved orgasm in the act of throttling victims; when this was over, they became harmless.

Manuel may also have been an underwear fetishist. Anne Knieland's knickers, and her missing stocking, were never found. In one of his burglaries, Manuel left a pair of nylon stockings on a chair; he may have used them to cover his hands and prevent fingerprints, but also because they sexually excited him. The torn pyjama trousers in the case of Margaret Brown, the removal of Vivienne Watts's pyjama trousers, and the fact that most of Isabelle Cooke's clothes had been removed, point unmistakably to a sexual motive. Yet the bus conductress to whom Manuel was engaged said that he never made sexual advances. This seems to suggest that Manuel was interested in sex only when it was associated with the 'forbidden'. What excited him was tearing off a girl's underwear or pyjamas; while doing this the excitement may have been so great that he achieved a climax.

Another curious detail is that neighbours of the Smarts noticed that the curtains were sometimes drawn and sometimes undrawn in the days following New Year's Day. This suggests that Manuel returned to the house day after day. John Bingham's theory is that his murders sprang out of an association of violence with sexuality, and even that this may have had something to do with the phases of the moon. Whether or not this is true, it seems clear that Manuel was one of those for whom criminality itself is somehow sexual. But he lacked insight into his own condition; he was undoubtedly speaking the truth when he told his parents: 'I don't know what makes me do these things.'

One thing seems very clear – and explains the amount of space devoted to this curiously untypical case. In spite of his intelligence, Manuel was driven by a totally irrational resentment. Like Panzram, he wanted to 'get his own back' on society. This could well have been the result of his period in Borstals – we have already seen that this was one of the major factors that led 'Brides in the Bath' Smith to become a criminal, and in the next chapter we shall see that this is also the key to the 'Moors murders'. Manuel followed the search for Isabelle Cooke with gloating satisfaction, and even dropped hints to his policeman friend Joe Brannan that he knew something about it. It didn't worry him that he knew Brannan was a policeman, and that he had probably been told to report on him. It made the game more interesting. As he and Brannan sat on top of a bus, looking at police searching a high railway viaduct, Manuel said: 'Wouldn't it be a fine sight to see one of those bastards hanging by the neck from the viaduct? Preferably one with stripes on his arm . . .' He was obviously *glad* to have a policeman there as an audience; at last he was being allowed to give them 'a piece of his mind', just as if he was standing on stage under a spotlight with an audience of coppers . . . A comment like this enables us to understand Manuel's mentality in a single flash. He was saying: 'If I can't be a part of society – with the pre-eminence I deserve – then I'm going to do my best to screw things up, until the bastards feel sorry they *didn't* pay me more attention . . .'

This is an attitude we shall see again and again in later serial killers. Lacenaire was perhaps the first notable criminal to embody this irrational resentment, and he would have regarded Manuel as a worthy – if somewhat unimaginative – successor, lacking the foresight and cunning that make a truly great criminal.

Lacenaire might well have entertained a higher opinion of the criminal who might be regarded as the German counterpart of Peter Manuel: Werner Boost, who was arguably Germany's most dangerous serial killer since Peter Kürten. And, unlike Manuel, he certainly could not be accused of lack of planning: he spent hours in libraries reading the lives of notorious criminals, studying their methods and making notes on how to avoid their mistakes.

For the Düsseldorf police, the story began on the cold, snowy night of 7 January 1953. Shortly before midnight, a fair-haired young man who was bleeding from a head wound staggered into the police station and said that his friend had just been murdered. The 'friend', it seemed, was a distinguished lawyer named Dr Lothar Servé. The officer on duty immediately telephoned Kriminal Hauptcommissar Mattias Eynck, chief of the North Rhineland murder squad, who hurried down to the station. The young man had identified himself as Adolf Hullecremer, a 19-year-old student, and explained that he and Dr Servé had been sitting in the car 'discussing business', and looking at the lights on the river, when both doors of the car had been jerked open by two men in hankerchief masks. One of the men began to swear, then shot Servé in the head. As Hullecremer begged for his life, the second man whispered that if he wished to stay alive, he should 'sham dead'. He then hit Hullecremer on the head with a pistol. As he lost consciousness, Hullecremer heard him say: 'He won't wake again.' When the men had gone, he made off as fast as he could . . .

After Hullecremer's head had been bandaged, he said he felt well enough to take the police and the doctor back to the car. It was parked in a grove of trees on the edge of the river, its engine still running. Across the rear seat lay the body of a man of about 50, bleeding from a wound in the temple. The doctor pronounced him dead.

The motive was clearly robbery – the dead man's wallet was missing. Eynck concluded that the robbers were 'stick-up men' who had chosen this spot because it was known as a 'lovers' lane'. The fact that the two had been in the rear seat when attacked suggested a homosexual relationship.

Forensic examination revealed no fingerprints on the car, and falling snow had obliterated any footprints or other tyre tracks. The murder enquiry had reached an impasse when, a few weeks later, a tramp found a .32 calibre pistol – of Belgian make – in the woods, and forensic tests showed it to be the murder weapon. Photographs of its bullets were sent to all police stations, and the Magdeburg police – in East Germany – contacted Eynck to say that the same gun had been used in a murder a few years earlier in a small town called Hadersleben. Two East Germans attempting to flee to the West had been shot with the same weapon. This seemed to suggest that the murderer was himself an East German refugee who had moved to Düsseldorf. But there the trail went cold – thousands of East Germans had fled the communist regime to the large cities of West Germany since the war.

Almost three years later, in October 1955, Eynck found himself wondering whether the double killers had struck again. A young couple had vanished after an evening date. The man was 26-year-old Friedhelm Behre, a baker, and his fiancée was 23-year-old Thea Kurmann. They had spent the evening of 31 October in a 'bohemian' restaurant called the Cafe Czikos, in the old quarter of Düsseldorf, and had driven off soon after midnight in Behre's blue Ford. The next day, worried relatives reported them missing. But there was no sign of the couple or of the blue car. Four weeks later, a contractor standing by a half-dredged gravel pit near Düsseldorf was throwing stones at a metal object when he realized that it was the top of a blue car. He called some of his men, and they heaved it ashore. In the back seat lay two decomposing corpses. They proved to be those of the missing couple, the girl still dressed in her red satin evening dress, which had been torn and pulled up.

The medical report revealed that Friedhelm Behre had been shot through the head at close range, The girl had been garrotted, possibly by a man's tie, after being raped. It looked as if the killer had wrenched open the rear door as the couple were petting, shot the man, then dragged the girl out. After rape, her body was thrown into the back seat, and the car driven to the gravel pit, where it was pushed into the water.

To Eynck, this sounded ominously like the Servé murder.

Again, there were no fingerprints – suggesting that the killer had worn gloves. The bullet had disappeared. It had gone right through the victim's skull, but it should have been somewhere in the car. Its absence suggested that the murderer had removed it to prevent the identification of the gun.

The murder caused panic among Düsseldorf's young lovers, and over the Christmas period the usual lay-bys were deserted. Meanwhile, Chief Inspector Botte, in charge of the investigation, quickly found that he had run out of clues.

Three months later, on the morning of 8 February 1956, a businessman named Julius Dreyfuss reported that his Mercedes car was missing – together with its chauffeur, a young man named Peter Falkenberg. The chauffeur had failed to arrive to pick up his employer. It seemed possible that Falkenberg had driven away to sell the expensive car. But an hour or so later, a woman reported that a black car was parked in front of her house with its headlights on. It proved to be the missing Mercedes. And there was a great deal of blood inside – in both the front and the rear seats.

At about the same time, a woman had reported that her daughter, 23-year-old Hildegard Wassing, had failed to return home after a date. A few days before, Hildegard and a friend had met a young man named Peter at a dance; he had told them he was a chauffeur. Hildegard had agreed to go out with him the following Tuesday, 7 February, and her brother had noticed that he was driving a black Mercedes. To Eynck, it sounded as if Peter Falkenberg and Hildegard Wassing had fallen victim to the 'car murderer'.

The next morning, a gardener was cycling to work near the small village of Lank-Ilvereich, near Düsseldorf, when he saw the remains of a burning haystack some distance from the path. He strolled over to look – and then rushed for the nearest telephone as he saw the remains of two corpses among the burnt hay.

Eynck arrived soon after, and noticed the smell of petrol. Both bodies were badly charred, but rain had prevented the fire from totally incinerating them. Forensic examination revealed that the man – identified from dental charts as Peter Falkenberg – had been shot through the head. Hildegard Wassing had been raped and then strangled – the rope was still sunk in the burnt flesh.

Thousands of Düsseldorf residents were questioned, but once again, there were no obvious leads. The car killer was evidently a man who took great care to leave no clues. Then a detective named Bohm came upon a possible suspect. In the small town of Buderich, not far from the burnt haystack, he was told of a young man named Erich von der Leyen, who had once attacked some children with a manure fork, and was regarded as a 'loner' by his neighbours. He was originally from East Germany, and now lived in lodgings in a place called Veert. Von der Leyen worked as a travelling salesman for agricultural machinery, so his log-book should have shown precisely where he was when the couple were murdered. But the entry for 7 February had been made later, and the travelling times for drives seemed implausible. Moreover, there were red spots on the front seat-covers. These were sent for forensic examination, and were reported to be human bloodstains. Erich von der Leyen was placed under arrest. Stains on his trousers also proved to be blood.

Von der Leyen insisted that he had no idea where the stains came from – the only way he could account for them was to recall that his girlfriend's dachshund had been in his car when it was on heat. That sounded unlikely. The police asked another forensic expert to examine the bloodstains on the trousers, and see if he could determine their age. Under the microscope, he saw epithelial cells – evidence that it *was* menstrual blood. The stains on the car seat were re-tested, and the laboratory admitted with embarrassment that these were also of menstrual blood – and, moreover, from a dog. The police had to release von der Leyen, and to apologize for the intense interrogations he had endured.

Soon after this, on the evening of 6 June 1956, a forest ranger named Erich Spath was walking through woods near Meererbusch, not far from the burnt haystack site, when he saw a man lurking in the undergrowth, and peering from behind a tree at a car in which a courting couple were petting. The man was so absorbed that he did not hear the ranger. Then Spath saw him draw a revolver from his pocket, and creep towards the car.

Spath placed his rifle to his shoulder and crept up behind the young man. 'Drop it!' The man turned round, then threw away his gun and ran. Spath chased him and soon caught up with him, crouching in a hollow.

Half an hour later, the car with the courting couple – and also containing the ranger and his captive – pulled up in front of Düsseldorf's main police station. The suspect – who was dark and good-looking – had accompanied them without protest and without apparent concern, as if his conscience was clear. And when they stood in the office of Kriminal Hauptkommissar Mattias Eynck, Spath understood why. The young man – who gave his name as Werner Boost – explained that he had merely been doing a little target practice in the woods, and had thought *he* was being attacked. He obviously felt that no one could disprove his story and that therefore the police would be unable to hold him.

'Is your gun licensed?' asked Eynck.

'Well . . . no. It's a war trophy . . .'

'In that case, I am charging you with possessing an illegal weapon.'

The gun was found in the undergrowth where Boost had thrown it. Nearby was a motorcycle, which proved to have been stolen. Boost was also charged with its theft. A magistrate promptly sentenced him to six months in jail, which gave Eynck the time he needed to investigate the suspect.

At first the trail seemed to be leading nowhere. The pistol had not been used in any known crime; Boost was, as he said, an electrical engineer who worked in a factory, and who was regarded as a highly intelligent and efficient worker; he had been married for six years, had two children, and was a good husband and provider. His wife, Hanna, told Eynck that he spent most of his evenings at home, working in his own laboratory or reading – he was an obsessive reader. Occasionally, she admitted, he became restless and went out until the early hours of the morning.

She led Eynck down to the basement laboratory. There he discovered various ingredients for explosives, as well as some deadly poisons. He also found a quantity of morphine.

Back in the flat, Eynck noticed a letter postmarked Hadersleben. He recalled that the Belgian pistol, which had been found within a few hundred yards of Boost's flat, had been used in a double murder in Hadersleben, near Magdeburg. 'Do you know someone in Hadersleben?' he asked. Hanna Boost told him that it was her home town, and that she had married her husband there.

'How did you both escape from East Germany?'

'Werner knew a safe route through the woods.'

But she insisted that, as far as she knew, her husband had never owned a gun.

Now, at last, the case was beginning to look more promising. Back in his office, Eynck looked through the latest batch of information about Boost. This had come from a town called Helmstedt, which had been taken over by the Russians in 1945. And at about this period, there had been a great many murders – about fifty in all – of people trying to escape from the Russian to the British zone. Werner Boost had been in Helmstedt at the time. Then he had moved to Hadersleben, and the murders had ceased. But the two would-be émigrés had been shot in Hadersleben while trying to escape . . .

There was another interesting item – a notebook which had been found in the saddle of Boost's stolen motorcycle. And it contained an entry: 'Sunday, June 3. Lorbach in need of another shot. Must attend to it.'

Eynck sent for Boost and questioned him about the item. Boost said smoothly:

'Franz Lorbach is a friend of mine, and we go shooting together. On that day, he just couldn't hit the bull's eye, so I made a note to give him another shot.'

Eynck did not believe a word of it. He asked Boost about his days in Helmstedt, and whether he had ever helped refugees to escape. Boost admitted that he had, and said he was proud of it. 'And did you ever shoot them?' Boost looked horrified. 'Of course not!'

Eynck now sent out one of his detectives to try to locate Franz Lorbach. This was not difficult. Lorbach proved to be a man of 23 with dark curly hair, whose good-looking face lacked the strength of Werner Boost's. He was a locksmith, and insisted that he only had the most casual acquaintance with Boost. Eynck knew that he was lying. He also noticed Lorbach's dilated pupils, and surmised that he was a drug addict, and that Boost was his supplier. He was certain that, when his craving became strong enough, Lorbach would talk. He held him in custody for questioning.

Meanwhile, Boost and Lorbach were placed in a police line-up, wearing hankerchief masks over the lower half of their faces. Adolf Hullecremer, the student who had been with Dr Servé when he was shot, was able to identify Boost as Servé's assailant. He said he recognized the eyes. But he failed to identify Lorbach.

After a day or two in custody, Lorbach began to show symptoms of withdrawal from drugs. And one day, as Eynck was questioning Boost again – and getting nowhere – he received a phone call saying that Lorbach wanted to talk to him.

Lorbach was pale, his eyes were watery, and his nose twitched like a rabbit's.

'I want to tell you the truth. Werner Boost is a monster. It *was* he who killed Dr Servé, and I was his accomplice . . .

Lorbach admitted that it was a love of poaching that had drawn the two of them together in 1952. They often went shooting in the woods. But Boost seemed to have a maniacal hatred of courting couples. 'These sex horrors are the curse of Germany.' So they would often creep up on couples who were making love in cars and rob them. Then, he said, Boost had an idea for rendering them unconscious. He had concocted some mixture which he forced them to drink. Then he and Lorbach would rape the unconscious girls. 'Some of them were very lovely. I feel ashamed – my wife is going to have a baby. But it was Boost who made me do it. I had to do it. He kept me supplied with morphine, which he obtained from the chemist who sold him chemicals.'

He insisted that he had taken part only in the attack on Servé and Hullecremer. Boost had been indignant to see two men in a car together, and had ordered him to kill the young man. But Lorbach had not the stomach for it. Instead, he had whispered to him to pretend to be dead. Lorbach's failure to shoot Hullecremer enraged Boost – he made Lorbach kneel in the snow, and said: 'I ought to kill you too . . .'

Lorbach led the police to a place at the edge of the forest, where Boost kept his loot concealed. In a buried chest, they found watches, rings and jewellery. There were also bottles of poison, some knives and a roll of cord which proved to be identical to that which had been used to strangle Hildegard Wassing.

Lorbach also disclosed that Boost had ordered Lorbach to kill his wife, Hanna Boost, if he was arrested. There was a phial of cyanide hidden behind a pipe in his flat, and Lorbach was to slip it into her drink, so that she could not incriminate her husband. Eynck found the phial exactly where Lorbach had said it was.

Lorbach also confirmed that he and Boost had been involved in an earlier attempt at crime, a year before the murder of Dr Servé. The two men had placed a heavy plank studded with long nails across the road, to force motorists to stop. But the first car to come along had contained four men – too many for them to tackle

– and it had driven on to the verge and around the plank. Two more cars also contained too many passengers. Then a security van came, and a man with a gun removed the plank. After that, police arrived – evidently alerted by one of the cars – and Boost and Lorbach had to flee. In fact, as long ago as 1953, Eynck had suspected that Dr Servé's murderer was responsible for this earlier attempt.

Lorbach also detailed Boost's plans to rob a post office by knocking everyone unconscious with poison gas, and to kidnap and murder a child of a rich industrialist for ransom.

Werner Boost had been born on 6 May 1928 in an industrial area of Hadersleben, the son of an unmarried mother who was only 17; he never knew the identity of his father. He had been placed in a government-run home, and been in trouble with the law from an early age. Leaving school in 1942, at the age of 14, he had worked in a series of menial jobs. He was released from a juvenile institution just before the war ended, and conscripted into the army. Taken prisoner by the British, he was set free within two months.

Unable to find work as an electrician, he had engaged in black marketeering and any other illegal activity that would pay. This is the period when, it is believed, he began smuggling would-be escapees across the border into West Germany, murdering them en route and stealing all they had. Since they would be carrying all their wealth with them, it would have been a profitable occupation,

Back in Hadersleben, in 1950, Boost married, and seems to have been an affectionate husband and father (the couple had two daughters). But there is evidence that he murdered the pair who were shot with the Belgian pistol, perhaps to finance an escape to West Germany. There he chose Lorbach as a partner in crime, and embarked or a career of robbery and murder.

On 11 December 1956, Boost was charged with the murders of Dr Servé, Friedhelm Behre, Thea Kurmann, Peter Falkenberg and Hildegard Wassing. But when Lorbach, the main prosecution witness, suffered a nervous breakdown due to drug problems, the trial had to be postponed. Meanwhile, Boost was extradited to Magdeburg for questioning about the murder of the couple at Hadersleben. But he stonewalled his questioners as he had tried to stonewall the Düsseldorf police, and was finally returned to Eynck's jurisdiction with no additional charges against him.

Boost's trial began in the courthouse at Düsseldorf on 3 November 1961, before Judge Hans Naecke, two associate magistrates, Dr Warda and Dr Schmidt, and a six-man jury. Boost maintained his total innocence, and his lawyer, Dr Koehler, lost no time in pointing out that the testimony of a drug addict like Franz Lorbach was hardly reliable. Lorbach himself was a poor witness, who mumbled and became confused. But he was able to tell one story that strengthened the case against Boost. Lorbach confessed that Boost had blackmailed him – by threatening withdrawal of his drug supply – into taking part in another attack on a couple. They had held up two lovers in the woods. Boost had tried to kill the man, but the gun had misfired. The girl had run away screaming, and Boost had ordered Lorbach to catch her. Lorbach had done so – but then whispered to her to lie low for a while. When he returned, Boost had knocked the man unconscious – but Lorbach had warned him there was a car coming, and they had roared away on Boost's motorbike.

Eynck told the court that he had traced this couple, and that they had confirmed the story in every detail. They were not married – at least not to one another – which is why they had failed to report the incident. But Eynck was able to offer their deposition in evidence.

Boost's lawyer counter-attacked by pointing out that there had recently been a murder of a couple in a car near Cologne, and that Boost was obviously not guilty of this crime.

After a month of listening to this and similar evidence, the six jurors decided that the evidence that Boost had murdered the two couples was insufficient. But they found him guilty of murdering Dr Servé. He was sentenced to life imprisonment, and Lorbach to three years as his accomplice – much of which he had already served. Boost's sentence was exactly the same as if he had been found guilty on all charges.

The psychiatric examination had uncovered some of the causes of his criminality. Fatherless, brought up under harsh and loveless conditions, Boost – like Panzram and Manuel – reacted by making a conscious decision to become an 'enemy of society'. An account of Boost by George Vedder Jones contains the lines: 'He developed an almost fanatical jealousy towards men who had been rich and successful through opportunities that had been denied him in his youth,' and 'His bitter hatred of mankind – originating in his warped childhood and manifested by his fantastic plans for mayhem and violence – seemed to supply motivation for the five Lovers' Lane murders.'

But it must also be recognized that Boost was primarily a *sex* criminal – a man of immense sex drive whose 'hatred of society' simply provided a rationalization for rape–murder. In this sense, there was an element of self-deception, of unconscious dishonesty, in Boost's hypocritical attitude about lovers petting in cars – 'These sex horrors are the curse of Germany' – when he himself then went on to rape the women.

It should finally be noted that in spite of his ruthlessness, Boost was a victim of self-pity, convinced he had never been given a chance. Like so many criminals, it would never have entered his head to consider placing some of the blame on himself. Here again we have a basic key to the mind of most serial killers.

Boost's contemporary Heinrich Pommerencke was an altogether more straightforward killer – an uncomplicated example of a man driven by such an urgent craving for sex that it overrode all other considerations. This emerged clearly in an exchange that took place when the prosecutor Franz Schorp asked Pommerencke if he felt no remorse after his murders. Pommerencke shook his head. 'All I felt was the physical desire to possess these women.' 'Do you know what people call a man who can commit such crimes and feel no remorse?' Pommerencke answered softly: 'A monster.'

On the morning of 5 June 1959 a pretty blonde girl was found dead by the railway line south of Freiburg. It was immediately obvious to police commissioner Gut, of the Freiburg murder squad, that this was a sex crime; her red dress was torn down the front, and she lay in the typical rape position, her underwear in the bushes beside her. Her body was covered with scratches and bruises, and there were cinders embedded in her flesh.

As it happened, Gut already knew her identity, because he had been involved in the search for her. She was 21-year-old Dagmar Klimek, a trainee teacher from Heidelberg. Three days earlier, she had boarded the Riviera Express with a group of twenty-nine other young women, en route for a package holiday in the Italian lakes. At about 11.30 at night, she had said goodnight to her friends and made her way to the toilet in the next coach – she had paused to ask the tour director where it was. Then she had vanished. A few minutes later, someone had pulled the communication cord and jumped from the train.

Commissioner Gut could have no doubt what had happened. A man had been waiting on the small open platform at the end of coach 405 – this was established by the fact that someone had removed the light bulbs from this particular platform – and had hurled her from the train as she passed him. Then he had pulled the communication cord and run back to find her. The girl had still been alive, but probably unconscious, as the man dragged her into the bushes, and raped her. Then he had stabbed her in the chest, killing her instantly. The body was so well concealed that it was not found until three days later.

Only two witnesses had seen the killer. One was a salesman who had boarded the train at Freiburg, climbing on at the platform of coach 405. He had noticed the tall, slim young man with blond hair because he looked somehow furtive. The man had been wearing a shabby grey suit.

The other witness had been dozing in the same carriage when the train braked to a halt. He had seen a man jump from the train and run out of sight behind bushes; he described him as tall and gaunt, and wearing a loose-fitting grey suit that made him look like a scarecrow.

A check into Dagmar Klimek's background indicated that she had no male admirer who might have killed her. The killer was clearly a sex maniac who had chosen her at random because she walked past him on her way back from the toilet.

On the supposition that the killer must have been bloodstained, the police checked cleaning establishments from Frankfurt to Freiburg, looking for the grey suit; they met with no success. Careful interrogation of dozens of known sex offenders also produced no result. Every railway ticket clerk south of Frankfurt was asked if he recalled a tall skinny man in the grey suit; no one did.

Could this killer have struck before? When Gut looked through the record of unsolved sex crimes in Baden-Württemberg, he found three that sounded as if they might have been committed by the same man. Towards the end of February 1959, a Karlsruhe waitress named Elke Braun had been walking home when a man had seized her from behind and thrown her on the ground. He was brandishing a knife and ripping at her clothes when a passing taxi driver heard her screams. The man – who was tall and blond – ran off as the taxi driver approached. The girl said her attacker had 'the face of a baby', with soft skin.

But his expression as he attacked her left her in no doubt that he intended to kill her.

The following morning, the body of a 34-year-old cleaning woman named Hilde Konther was found in bushes near her home. She had been beaten and raped, then strangled. It looked as if the waitress's attacker had been lying in wait for her as she returned home from work in the early hours of the morning.

The other crime that sounded as if it had been committed by the same man had taken place a month later, on 26 March 1959. In the nearby town of Hornberg, a beautician named Karin Walde had also failed to return home from work. The next morning, her parents found her naked body in bushes close to her home. She had been battered to death with a heavy stone and raped.

One more sex crime had an ominously similar ring. On 30 May an 18-year-old girl had been attacked in her bedroom in Zingen, another small town on the Karlsruhe railway line. Someone had climbed in through the window while she was asleep, beaten her insensible before she could resist, then raped her. It had been a moonlit night, and she had seen him clearly – a tall man with piercing eyes and a 'baby face'. He had escaped by the way he came in.

Three days after the body of Dagmar Klimek was found, another girl disappeared. Rita Walterspacher was an 18-year-old office worker who travelled by train from her home in Rastatt, south of Karlsruhe, to her job in Baden Baden, a mere ten kilometres to the south. On 8 June 1959, she telephoned her parents to say she would be a little late arriving home; she expected to be back by seven. When she had failed to return by the next morning, her parents enquired at the local railway station – to be told by the stationmaster that he had seen their daughter alight from the 6.06 train.

Rita's way home lay south along a wooded road. The police organized a search party, and there was an appeal on local radio for anyone who might have seen her. Soon after this, a woman from a neighbouring town drove to the Rastatt police station. She had been on a slightly later train the evening before, she explained, and at about 6.15, just before they reached Rastatt, she saw a girl running along the road beside the track, pursued by a man. She was screaming, but the woman thought they were simply two lovers having fun. The man – who was tall, with blond hair – grabbed the girl and dragged her into the woods. The woman thought no more about it until she heard the appeal on the radio.

When she added that the man was wearing a grey suit, the detective realized that this was almost certainly the rapist of the Riviera Express. A larger search party was organized, and spread out through the woods near the spot where the woman had seen the incident. The girl's body was found a few hours later by a farmer's dog, hidden under a pile of fir branches, not far from the railway line. From her position, it was clear that she had been raped there, then covered over. The cause of death was strangulation.

When Commissioner Gut saw the body he had no doubt that this was the man he was looking for. This was clearly a sex maniac in the most precise meaning of the term. When he was trying to rape a girl, he went into a frenzy, beating her violently and tearing at her clothes until they were in tatters. The fact that he might have been seen from the passing train did not deter him. Until the rape was accomplished, he became a wild animal incapable of any other thought.

Two rape–murders within a week suggested that the killer was reaching a peak in a cycle of violence that is typical of sex criminals, and that he had to be caught quickly. But the area over which he had committed his crimes was enormous, ranging from Karlsruhe in the north to Hornberg, a hundred kilometres south.

On the off-chance that the killer lived in the Rastatt area, the police instituted door-to-door enquiries, looking for anyone who might resemble the Riviera rapist – who had by now acquired himself a press nickname: the Monster of the Black Forest. Many suspects who matched the description were brought in for questioning, but all were able to prove their innocence. Again there was an extensive search for a bloodstained suit at local cleaners, but it was as unsuccessful as before. As the days went by, Gut experienced an increasing frustration, realizing that all he could do was to wait for the next attack to occur, and hope that this time the 'Monster' left some clue.

Fortunately, the Riviera rapist was caught before he could kill again.

On the morning of 19 June, a tailor named Johann Kohler opened his shop at eight o'clock. Soon after this, his first customer arrived – a young man named Heinrich Pommerencke, who had worked as a waiter in Hornsberg's Hotel Baren. Kohler was glad to see him, for the youth had ordered some clothes two months earlier – a sports jacket and trousers – and had paid a deposit. But he had failed to collect them.

Pommerencke had a soft, almost girlish face, with pink, smooth skin. Although tall, he looked much younger than his twenty-two years. He was wearing a baggy grey suit.

Pommerencke apologized for the delay in collecting the clothes, explaining that he now worked in a hotel in Frankfurt, and had been unable to get to Hornberg. He asked the tailor how much he owed, and paid from a wad of notes.

'Would you mind if I changed my clothes here? I can't stand this old suit a moment longer.'

Kohler indicated the changing cubicle, and Pommerencke vanished inside, leaving a bulging briefcase on a chair in the shop. He emerged a few minutes later, and surveyed himself with satisfaction in the mirror.

'Now all I need is a haircut. Could I leave you to wrap up my old suit while I go?'

When Kohler had packed the suit, he moved the heavy briefcase on to the floor. As he did so, the defective catch burst open, and Kohler was startled to find himself looking at a rifle whose barrel and butt had both been shortened with a hacksaw.

At that moment, his wife came into the shop. The tailor showed her the weapon.

'I can't understand what such a quiet young man is doing with a gun like this. He doesn't look as if he'd say boo to a goose.'

Frau Kohler shook her head. 'A weapon like that could have only one purpose – robbery. You ought to report it to the police.'

Within minutes, an inspector named Posedowski had arrived from the local station on his bicycle. He viewed the sawn-off rifle with distaste, then looked through the briefcase. It contained some soiled clothing, money, pornographic books, a bottle of pink liquid labelled 'love cocktail', a box of bullets and a ticket stub from Karlsruhe to Zingen.

The suit itself was unpacked, and Posedowski saw why its owner was anxious to change it. There were many spots where cleaning fluid had been used to remove some dark stain, and these showed as unsightly blotches.

Like every other policeman in Baden-Württemberg, Posedowski

knew about the Monster of the Black Forest and his grey suit. And although this pink-cheeked young man hardly sounded like a multiple killer, his reasons for carrying a sawn-off rifle obviously demanded investigation.

Heinrich Pommerencke looked mildly surprised to find a policeman waiting for him, but raised no objection when asked to accompany him to the local police station. He seemed so unconcerned that Posedowski relaxed his vigilance, and was taken by surprise when the young man took to his heels. Posedowski blew his whistle and pursued him on his bicycle. Fortunately, they had almost arrived at the station, and another policeman soon joined the chase. They eventually cornered Pommerencke in the grounds of a carnival on the edge of town. Posedowski snapped handcuffs on him, and the two policemen marched him back to the station.

When Commissioner Heinrich Koch saw the sawn-off rifle, he reacted with satisfaction.

'I've just been notified of a burglary at Durlach station last night. A track worker walked in on the robber, who threatened him with a sawn-off rifle, then ran away.' The thief had stolen some money from a cashbox.

The rest of the contents of the briefcase also intrigued the commissioner. The 'love cocktail' – presumably a mild aphrodisiac – and the pornography certainly suggested a man with sex on his mind. The stub of the rail ticket from Karlsruhe to Zingen reminded Koch of the rape of the 18-year-old girl in her bedroom by a man with a 'baby face'.

The grey suit was sent to Freiburg for forensic analysis; the blood serum test would reveal whether spots that still showed under the cleaning fluid were human blood.

Koch then interviewed the youthful suspect, and accused him without further ado of being the Durlach burgler. He noticed that, far from looking worried, Pommerencke seemed relieved. He admitted that he had purchased the rifle in a pawnshop, and had used it in the burglary the night before. He also admitted to three other recent burglaries – of a textile mill, an ammunition factory and a cafeteria in Rastatt. These admissions gave Koch the grounds he needed to charge his suspect, and Pommerencke was taken to the cells.

The investigation into Pommerencke's background was continued by the police in Frankfurt. In his room in the hotel they found papers that established that he had lived in various West German cities, including Karlsruhe, and that he had served a prison sentence for burglary. He had apparently worked as a housepainter and handyman, as well as a waiter. Those who worked with him in Hornberg and Frankfurt said that he was a 'loner' who spent much of his time at the cinema or in his room. He was known as a good worker who neither smoke nor drank.

Four days after his arrest, Pommerencke was taken to Freiburg, where the two commissioners who had been in charge of the case – Gut and Zismann – were waiting to interview him. They had also prepared a surprise for him. He was given a grey suit, and placed in an identity parade. The girl who had been raped in her bedroom in Zingen instantly identified him as her attacker.

Pommerencke indignantly denied it. 'I may be a burglar but I've never attacked a girl.'

But there were still four witnesses to view the police line-up. They were the two men who had seen the rapist on the Riviera Express, the woman who had seen Rita Walterspacher being attacked near Rastatt, and the waitress who had been saved by the taxi driver in Karlsruhe. All of them picked out Pommerencke.

Zismann told his suspect that they now had powerful circumstantial evidence to link him with Karlsruhe – where Hilde Konther had died – with Hornberg, where Karin Walde had died, and with Rastatt and the Riviera Express. Faced with this evidence, Pommerencke sullenly admitted that he had been the man who had attacked the girl in Zwingen and the waitress in Karlsruhe. But he strongly denied the rape–murders.

When the results of the test on the grey suit came from the forensic lab, Zismann was also able to tell Pommerencke that they now had evidence to link him to Hilde Konther, Dagmar Klimek and Karin Walde – the blood on the suit corresponded to their blood groups. And hairs on the suit had been identified as being from the head of Rita Walterspacher.

It was fortunate that Pommerencke was ignorant of forensic science, or he would have known that – at that time – neither blood nor hairs could be identified as coming from a particular person. Blood could only be 'grouped' – and in fact, the stains had been too faint for grouping. The lab had only been able to establish that they were of human origin. Moreover, there had been no hairs on the suit.

But Pommerencke was taken in by the bluff. His defiance suddenly collapsed. With averted eyes, he asked for a pencil to write his confession.

What this document made clear was that Pommerencke had been attacking and raping women for years – he had no idea of how many rapes he had committed. He had also committed scores of burglaries.

Heinrich Pommerencke had been born in Bentwisch, near Rostock in East Germany, in 1937. He was the child of a broken marriage, and described himself as an extremely lonely litle boy. But he seems to have inherited an extremely powerful sexual urge, which troubled him from an early age. 'When I was a boy I never had a friend in the world. After a while I got the urge to assault females. I had a girlfriend once but we split up, and I went back to my old ways. Other men always had girlfriends with them. I wanted girlfriends too, but I never succeeded.'

Pommerencke claimed – almost certainly untruthfully – that he had seduced his first girl at the age of 10. At the age of 15 he began to hang around the local dance hall in Bentwisch and made a few clumsy attempts to attack girls. Because of one of these attempts at rape, he fled from Bentwisch in 1953, when he was 16 and went to Switzerland. There he served a prison sentence for burglary, and was deported. He drifted around West Germany, living in Hamburg, Heidelberg, Düsseldorf, Karlsruhe, Hornberg and Frankfurt.

Living alone in rented rooms, reading pornography and indulging in sexual daydreams, Pommerencke's fantasies had reached an intensity that sooner or later had to be translated into action. He was not of high intelligence, and tended to be inarticulate – which meant that he completely lacked the arts of a seducer. 'Whatever I did [when with girls] was always wrong. I was never a good dancer, and girls avoided me because of that. When I was alone with them, I didn't know what to say.' This social inadequacy, combined with an overpoweringly strong sexual urge, meant that rape was virtually his only way of obtaining the sexual favours he craved. And it was finally in Hamburg, according to his confession, that he gave way to the compulsion and committed seven rapes between 1955 and 1957. It was after this that he was jailed for burglary.

But his first murder had been committed in Karlsruhe soon after he moved there in 1959. There he had been to see Cecil B. de Mille's film called *The Ten Commandments* with Charlton Heston. In the scene with the half-naked women dancing around the Golden Calf, he had suddenly decided that many women are evil, and deserve to die. When he left the cinema he bought a knife, then walked around until he saw the waitress Elke Braun. But as he was attacking her, the taxi driver had interrupted, and he had been forced to flee. But the compulsion was now overpowering, and he had attacked the cleaning woman a few hours later, battering her unconscious when she resisted, then strangling her. But Pommerencke admitted that it was after killing his second victim, beautician Karin Walde, in Hornberg, that this violent method of obtaining satisfaction became a fixed obsession that drove him to seek further victims.

Pommerencke's trial opened in Freiburg on 3 October 1960, before Judge Friedrich Kaufmann. The defence evidence consisted mainly of character testimony from many people who said that the prisoner was extremely shy, and blushed when he talked to women. His mother came from Switzerland to testify that her son certainly did not hate women; he adored them. Girls who had been out with him testified that he was too nervous even to attempt to kiss them.

His factual account of his various murders chilled the spectators. He described how, after throwing Dagmar Klimek from the train, he had had to walk back for half an hour along the tracks before he found her. He had dragged her into the bushes and torn off her clothes in a frenzy, then, after raping her, had stabbed her to death. Then he had walked to the nearest village, washed in the public fountain, and hitched a lift back to Frankfurt from a passing motorist.

He admitted that he had felt no remorse after the murders, because he had been so overwhelmed by a desire to possess women. But now, he conceded, he saw that 'everything I did was cruel and bestial. From the bottom of my heart I would like to undo all this.'

After a five-week trial, Heinrich Pommerencke was sentenced to eight terms of life imprisonment, plus a further 156 years, a sentence to be served with hard labour. It meant that he would spend the rest of his life in jail.

On the other side of the Atlantic, at the time when Heinrich Pommerencke was nerving himself to commit his first sex attack, another mild little man was collecting pornographic photographs and fantasizing about rape. But his tastes were less straightforward than Pommerencke's; being of a timid disposition, Harvey Glatman dreamed only of violating girls who were tied hand and foot.

On the evening of 1 August 1957, Robert Dull, a young pressman on the *Los Angeles Times*, called at a Hollywood apartment block to see his estranged wife, and was not surprised to hear that she was not at home. Judy was an exceptionally beautiful girl, greatly in demand as a photographic model, and it was this that had led to the break-up of their marriage – Robert Dull objected to her posing in the nude.

Judy's flatmate, Lynn Lykles, explained that she had gone off with a photographer called Johnny Glynn at about two that afternoon.

'Do you know where she went?'

'No, but he left a telephone number.'

'Would you ask her to call me at work when she comes in?'

But two hours later, there was still no sign of Judy. By that time, two photographers had called in to complain that she had failed to keep appointments. At 9 p.m., a young contractor telephoned to say that Judy had failed to show up for a dinner date, at which she was supposed to meet a lawyer to discuss her marital problems. Lynn gave him Johnny Glynn's telephone number. A few minutes later, he called back.

'That number was a machine shop in Pico. They'd never heard of a photographer called Johnny Glynn.'

Now they were both seriously worried. There had been a number of attacks on girls in Hollywood recently, and only two evenings before, Judy had complained that a strange man had followed her home.

The contractor hurried off to look in a number of Sunset Strip cafes that Judy frequented; meanwhile, Lynn rang Robert Dull, who hurried over immediately. They telephoned Judy's parents, relatives and friends without success, then went to report her disappearance at the West Hollywood police station. And when a routine check of hospitals failed to locate her, the sheriff put out a call to radio cars cruising Sunset

Strip, asking them to watch out for a pretty 19-year-old blonde. He asked:

'Who is this Johnny Glynn?'

Lynn decribed how, two evenings before, a little rabbit-like man with jug-handle ears had knocked on the door of their apartment, asking to see Lynn. It so happened that the only person at home was Betty Carver, a recent arrival from Florida; like Lynn and Judy, she was a photographic model. And, since Betty had a friend with her, she allowed the little man into the apartment. He identified himself as Johnny Glynn, a magazine photographer, and said he had obtained Lynn's name from an agency. Would it, he asked, be possible to see her portfolio? But when Betty returned with it, he pointed to the photograph of Judy on the wall. 'Now she's the type I'm really looking for. Could I see her portfolio as well?' As he leafed slowly through it, Betty could see that he was fascinated. When he had finished, he asked for Judy's personal telephone number.

Two mornings later, the three girls were eating breakfast when Johnny Glynn telephoned. He had a rush assignment, he explained, and wanted Judy to pose for him that afternoon. Judy was reluctant; she had a busy schedule, and Betty's description of Johnny Glynn aroused her suspicions. But when he mentioned that his own studio was being used, and that he would have to use Judy's apartment, her doubts evaporated, and she agreed to see him at two that afternoon.

He arrived looking as scruffy and unprepossessing as on his previous visit; moreover, he was without his photographic equipment. This, he explained, was because a friend had agreed to lend him his own studio. When Judy mentioned her hourly fee, he agreed immediately. And a few minutes later, they left the apartment, with the photographer carrying Judy's case. Lynn Lykles had felt uneasy as she watched them leave.

At mid-morning the following day, a bulletin was issued listing Judy Van Horn Dull as a missing person, possibly kidnapped; she was described as 19 years old, five feet four inches tall, with golden hair and a suntanned complexion. Johnny Glynn was described as about 29 years old, of slim build, five feet nine inches tall, with horn-rimmed glasses, and dressed in a rumpled blue suit.

Sergeant David Ostroff, who was handed the assignment, checked on all the Hollywood photographers and modelling agencies he could find; none of them had heard of Johnny Glynn, or knew anyone who answered his description.

The disappearance of the beautiful model made newspaper headlines, and Ostroff was kept busy for weeks following up tips. It soon became clear that the modelling business was not Hollywood's safest occupation. Several young models came forward to decribe how they had been rash enough to accept jobs from unknown 'photographers' who had then forced their attentions on them, sometimes at knife- or gunpoint. A number of men were questioned, but none of them had the distinctive appearance of Johnny Glynn. Ostroff recalled the disappearance of a beautiful young actress named Jean Spangler eight years before, in October 1949, but although they studied her file, it failed to throw any light on Judy's disappearance.

Even Judy's husband Robert seemed a possible suspect; he and Judy had not been on the best of terms since he had seized their fourteen-month old daughter Suzanne while Judy was at work. But a little investigation cleared him of suspicion; he was known to be still in love with his wife, and hoping for a reconciliation. None of Judy's friends could offer any clue to the mystery. After following up dozens of futile leads, Sergeant Ostroff concluded that Johnny Glynn was a false name, and that the rabbit-like man was probably some kind of sex pervert. It seemed likely that Judy Dull was dead.

Or was it possible that Judy had gone into hiding before the court case that would decide the custody of her daughter? At the hearing – on 9 August 1957 – there was an unusual number of reporters and photographers. Judy was known to be deeply attached to her daughter – so attached that she was even considering giving up modelling to devote more time to her. When there was no sign of her in court, her husband told the press that he was certain she had been murdered.

Five months after her disappearance, on 29 December 1957, a ranch worker walking in the desert near US Highway 60, between Indio and Thousand Palms – 130 miles east of Los Angeles – wondered what was causing his dog to bark. It was standing above a human skull that lay in a cotton field. He summoned the police, and they discovered a half-buried skeleton not far from the skull. The mouldering brown dress and underwear revealed that it was a woman. Remains of hair sticking to the skull indicated that she was a blonde. It was impossible to determine the cause of death.

Could this be Judy Dull? She had been last seen wearing a brown dress. And the skeleton was the same height as Judy – five feet four. But a forensic expert concluded that the dead woman was in her mid-thirties, and when Judy's husband failed to identify the pearl ring found on the finger, Ostroff concluded that this was not the woman he was looking for.

As it happened, he was mistaken . . .

On Sunday 9 March 1958, the Los Angeles police heard about another disappearance. The woman's name was Shirley Ann Loy Bridgeford, a 24-year-old divorcee with two children. The night before she had gone out with a stranger on a blind date, and had not been seen since.

From Shirley's mother, the San Fernando Valley police learned that Shirley had been lonely and bored. And since a man she had been hoping to marry had suddenly lost interest in her, she had also been depressed, convinced that she was now 'on the shelf'. A friend had suggested that Shirley should join a Lonely Hearts Club, and she had seized on the idea with the enthusiasm of the desperate. For a fee of $10, she had become a member of a dating club in Los Angeles. Her first date had arrived early on Saturday evening – an unprepossessing, bespectacled man with jug-handle ears and an appearance that suggested he had no interest in clothes. He had introduced himself as George Williams, a plumber who lived in Pasadena. Shirley had introduced him to the family – her mother, grandmother, brother and sister, and he had looked awkward and embarrassed. A few minutes later they had left – he said he was taking her to a square dance. No one had bothered to look to see what kind of car he was driving.

The obvious lead was the Lonely Hearts Club. Its organizer was able to provide the police with George Williams's address, but it turned out – as they expected – to be false. Another girl – a Hollywood secretary – who had actually spent an evening with 'George Williams' told them that he had been a 'perfect gentleman', and that they had spent the evening quietly in her apartment. She was unable to offer any leads.

To Sergeant Ostroff, it sounded as if George Williams and Johnny Glynn might be the same person. But this was no help to the investigation, since it was impossible to find any trace of either. The only thing that was clear was that 'George Williams' had almost certainly joined the club with the intention of abducting a girl. The Hollywood secretary had described him as clean shaven, yet Shirley's family said he wore a moustache. Since he had dated Shirley only two days after the secretary, that meant it had to be a false one. Since only a man with some misdemeanour in mind would go out on a blind date with a false moustache, the likeliest conclusion was that Shirley Bridgeford was now dead. Another was that unless the abductor was caught, he would strike again.

When another model vanished in late July, Lieutenant Marvin Jones of the Los Angeles police suspected that this is exactly what had happened. The landlord of a small apartment block on West Pico Boulevard, in the Wilshire district of Los Angeles, reported that one of his tenants was missing. She was 24-year-old Ruth Rita Mercado, who – using the alias Angela Rojas – worked as a stripper and a nude model. Her landlord had passed her door on the evening of 23 July and heard her inside talking to her collie dog. There was a 'Do Not Disturb' sign on the door. When, four days later, he observed the mail piling up in her mailbox, he used his pass key to enter the apartment. It was empty, with no sign of a struggle; but the collie pup was in the bathroom, exhausted from lack of food. Her parakeets were in a similar condition – fortunately they had been found in time. It seemed obvious that Ruth had not left them voluntarily. She had cared for her pets as though they were babies.

Oddly enough, the landlord wrote to Ruth's mother in Plattsburg, New York, instead of going to the Los Angeles police, and Lieutenant Jones learned of the model's disappearance from the New York police. He sent Sergeant Paul A. Light to investigate. Light felt he had found a promising lead when he learned that Ruth had left her previous apartment on South Kenmore Avenue because she had been receiving obscene phone calls, and had one evening found an obscene note pushed under her door. And when, with some help from the local police, he tracked down the author of the note, he felt that he might have found his man. His hopes collapsed into disappointment. The man had been harassing the girl because he objected to having a model as a neighbour, and he was able to prove that he had nothing to do with her disappearance.

When Lieutenant Jones checked the files of other disappearances, he observed the similarity to the case of Judy Dull. And it was clear that Ruth Mercardo's way of life involved even more risk than Judy's. As well as being a stripper, she advertised her services as a nude model in newspapers, and even provided photographic equipment for amateurs. And since she lived alone, she had less protection than Judy in her shared apartment. Her boyfriend – a piano player – was at present in Bermuda, so could be eliminated as a suspect. And so, eventually, were several other photographers who had worked with both Judy Dull and Ruth Mercado. And this time there was not even a description of the abductor. As he surveyed the total absence of clues, Lieutentant Jones surmised that he would turn out to have jug-handle ears and a dishevelled appearance.

Three months after Ruth Mercado's disappearance, late on the evening of Monday 27 October 1958, Officer Thomas F. Mulligan of the California Highway Patrol turned his motorcycle into a dark avenue near the small town of Tustin, 35 miles south-east of Los Angeles, and was startled when his headlight illuminated a couple who were struggling at the side of the road. At that moment, the couple separated, and as he braked to a halt and shouted to ask what was happening, he saw that the woman was holding a gun, which she was pointing at a man. The woman was small and plump, and her clothing was in a state of disarray. The Highway Patrolman raised his revolver and ordered them to stand still and hold up their hands. Both did so immediately. The woman, who was almost hysterical, shouted: 'He's a killer. He was going to rape me.' The man made no attempt to deny this, or to escape as Mulligan radioed Tustin for assistance. A few minutes later, the Tustin police arrived.

Meanwhile, the girl – who identified herself as Lorraine Vigil – told Mulligan what had happened. A model named Diane, who also ran a modelling agency, had telephoned her two hours ago to ask if she wanted to do a modelling job. Lorraine was a secretary who was determined to break into the modelling business, and she accepted immediately. But before the client arrived, Diane rang her back to tell her to be on her guard. Although she knew the man – Frank Johnson – and had done some modelling for him before, she felt uneasy about him. That was why she herself had refused to accept the job unless she was allowed to take a chaperone along. And Johnson had refused . . .

Frank Johnson arrived at her Wilshire apartment soon afterwards, and Lorraine saw why Diane was uneasy. He was a shifty little man with jug-handle ears and an untidy appearance – he looked as if he slept in his clothes. He didn't even come to her door, but blew his horn outside. When she went out, she asked for money in advance, and he handed her $15. Then they drove off in the direction of downtown Los Angeles. But instead of heading for Diane's agency in Sunset Strip, he turned south-east. When Lorraine objected, he explained that he was going to take her to his own studio in Anaheim.

In fact, he drove straight through Anaheim. And in the dark road near Tustin, he pulled up and told her he had a flat tyre. Then he pulled out a small automatic, ordered her to keep quiet, and produced a length of rope. Lorraine pleaded not to be tied up, offering to do whatever he wanted. But as a car came past, she tried to open the door. He grabbed her and pulled her back, then threatened her again, and tried to tie her up. She began to struggle, and he became increasingly angry and abusive. As he pointed the gun at her, she grabbed it and tried to pull it away. It went off, and she felt the bullet burn her thigh. But the man seemed as shocked as she was by the sound of the shot. As he stared at the smoking gun in bewilderment, she leapt across him, forced open his door, and fell out on to the road with the man underneath her. Clinging tightly to his gun, she tried to pull it out of his hand; when he tried to point it at her, she bit him as hard as she could. He gave a cry of pain, and released the gun. Lorraine pointed it at him and tried to pull the trigger. It was at that moment that they were illuminated by the patrolman's headlight.

Taken to the Santa Ana police station, the man gave his name as Harvey Murray Glatman, aged 30, a TV repairman. He proved to have nearly a thousand dollars on him, which led the police to suspect him of being a holdup man. He made no attempt to deny his attempt to assault Lorraine Vigil, but said it had been a sudden impulse, and he was sorry. He also admitted that he had a police record and had been in prison. He had come to Los Angeles, he said, in the previous year. But when the police asked him what he had been doing since then, he was evasive, and they felt he was concealing something.

A bulletin describing the arrest was sent to police throughout the area, asking if the suspect could be linked to any other crimes. When it landed on the desk of Lieutenant Marvin Jones, he immediately noted that the suspect, as well as his intended victim, lived in his area. Moreover, Glatman lived a few blocks from Ruth Mercado in San Pico Boulevard.

When the police called at the white shingle bungalow at 1011 South Norton Avenue, they noted its run-down appearance, the tar-paper on the roof and the bars on the windows. Inside, they found the walls covered with nude pinups, in some of which the girls were bound and gagged. There were also a number of lengths of rope. It seemed that Harvey Glatman was interested in bondage.

The following day, Glatman was asked if he would take a lie detector test, and he agreed. Two sergeants from Wilshire went to Santa Ana to watch. They walked in while Glatman was being questioned – wired up to the lie detector – and when they were introduced as two detectives investigating the disappearance of two girls, the polygraph recorded no sudden alarm. But when he was asked about 'Angela' – Ruth Mercado – the stylus gave a nervous leap. A few minutes later, Glatman was confessing to killing Ruth. 'I killed a couple of other girls too.'

And now, at last, the police heard the full story of the disappearance of three women.

Harvey Murray Glatman was born in Denver, Colorado, in 1928; he was a 'mother's boy' who was also an excellent student. (A later test showed that his IQ was 130.) When he was 12 years old, his parents came home one day to observe that he had red marks around his neck. Under pressure, Harvey admitted that he had been in the attic, tied a rope round his neck, and tightened the noose until he experienced sexual satisfaction. (Many masochists accidentally hang themselves when obtaining release in this way.) The family doctor was consulted, but advised them not to worry – Harvey would outgrow it. Meanwhile, the best way to avoid more self-strangulation was exercise . . .

Girls at school found the scrawny, jug-eared boy unattractive; he made his bid for attention by snatching their purses, running away, then flinging them back at them. Mrs Glatman is quoted as saying tolerantly: 'It was just his approach.'

When he was 17, Glatman tired of frustration and sexual fantasy; one night in Boulder, Colorado, he pointed a toy gun at a teenage girl and ordered her to undress. She screamed and he lost his nerve and ran. Picked up by the police, he was released on bail – and broke bond to make his way to New York. There he satisfied his aggressive urges against women, robbing them at gunpoint; he became known as the 'Phantom Bandit'. He also graduated to burglary, but was soon caught, and sentenced to five years in Sing Sing. Once inside, he proved a docile prisoner, seemed to respond to psychiatric treatment, and was released in 1951. He moved back to Colorado, and worked at TV repairs. In 1957, he moved to Los Angeles, where his doting mother, who took a lenient view of his 'mistakes', found the money to set him up in a TV repair business.

Glatman's problem was simple: a powerful inferiority complex made him incapable of the normal courtship procedures. In order to maintain a state of sexual excitement, he had to have the girl completely at his mercy – preferably bound and gagged. The result was that at 28 he was still a virgin, whose sex life was confined to lurid daydreams of bondage.

He may have thought of the idea of becoming a photographer after seeing picture of bound girls on the covers of true detective magazines. He soon learned that even an amateur photographer could pay to photograph unclothed girls in public studios. But his glimpses of female nudity only made his celibacy more agonizing. Which is why, on 29 July 1957, he called at the apartment of Lynn Lykles to try and persuade her to pose for him. But when he saw the photograph of Judy Dull on the wall, he realized that she was the girl he had always wanted. Two days later, his dream was fulfilled; Judy was in his old black Dodge, being driven to his 'studio' – no doubt he had removed the pinups and bondage photos from the wall for the occasion.

Judy was wearing a dress; Glatman told her to remove it and put on a pleated skirt and cardigan. When he produced a length of rope, Judy reacted with alarm. He soothed her by explaining that he was taking photographs for the cover of a true detective magazine, and she had to be bound and gagged. And when she was seated in an armchair, her knees tied together, he hands behind her, a gag in her mouth, Glatman pushed up her skirt to reveal the white underskirt. Then, having taken some pictures, he unbuttoned the cardigan, pulled down her bra, and unzipped the skirt at the waist. Then, unable to contain himself any longer, he lifted her on to the floor – she was only five feet four inches tall, and very light – and removed everything but her panties. When he began to fondle her, Judy struggled and tried to scream; Glatman felt his excitement evaporating. He rushed out of the room and returned with an automatic pistol. He placed this against her head and told her that if she resisted, she would be killed – he was an ex-convict, and would not hesitate to shoot. When she nodded her acquiescence, he removed the gag.

He found the sight of a bound girl so satisfying that he decided to prolong the pleasure; he left her tied on the floor while he had something to eat. Now anxious to pacify him, Judy promised to do whatever he wanted, and not to report him to the police. She explained that she was due to appear in court in ten days' time, hoping to obtain the custody of her daughter, and that if she went to the police, it would only confirm her husband's contention that she was unfit to be a mother.

Glatman responded with apparent concern. When Judy's nose began to bleed, he stanched the blood with a pillowcase. Then he made her sit on the settee for more bondage photographs. Finally, he did what he had been waiting to do; he removed his own clothes and raped her twice.

After that, he switched on the television, and the two of them sat naked and watched it, while she allowed him to fondle her. Now it was all over, he was not sure what to do next. Could he believe her when she said she would not report him to the police? If he did, and she broke her word, he would be in jail for the rest of his life . . .

Finally, he explained what he had decided to do. He would take her to some remote spot, then release her. After that, he would leave town. Judy tried to persuade him to let her take a taxi back home, but he refused. She apparently believed his threat to shoot her, for she made no attempt to escape when he forced her to climb into his car. They drove out on the San Bernardino freeway, then into the desert. There he made her pose for more 'cheesecake' photographs on a blanket, which he took with a flash. Finally, he made her lie on her stomach, and looped the rope around her neck; then he bent her legs back and tied it around her ankles. At this point, Judy must have realized she was going to die, and began to struggle. It was too late; Glatman pulled on the rope until she lay still.

Glatman was not a violent man; now she was dead he felt sorry. He apologized to her body before dragging it further into the desert, and burying it in a shallow grave. A fetishist to the end, he took her shoes for souvenirs.

For weeks, Glatman lived in fear of being caught. Would Judy's flatmates provide the police with enough clues to track him down? Would they visit some of the agencies and studios he had used. But as the weeks went by, he began to feel calmer. After Christmas, the craving for another woman became too strong to resist. This time he joined the Lonely Hearts club, and arranged a date. The first girl he visited was the Hollywood secretary. But she was simply not his type – a talker. She offered him tea and biscuits and they conversed. It was impossible for Glatman to feel master of the situation. So he took his leave, and rang the club for another date. They gave him the name of Shirley Ann Bridgeford.

As soon as he saw Shirley Ann, he knew she found him a disappointment; for a moment he was afraid she would find some excuse not to go out. But once they were in the car she seemed to reconcile herself to the evening ahead; she even raised no objection when he explained that he was not fond of square dancing, and suggested they go for a drive instead. This time they drove past Long Beach and down south towards San Diego. But when he stopped the car on a side road in the Anza desert, and put his arm round her, she balked. Wasn't it about time to go home? Glatman's anger surged, but he controlled it; they were still too close to a main road to risk force. He pretended to agree, and said they would find a drive-in for a meal.

As he drove with one hand on the wheel, he tried to fondle her, and his resentment was fuelled by her resistance. Finally, on a dark mountain road inland, he stopped the car and produced his automatic. Then he ordered her into the back seat, and told her to undress. When she resisted, he tore off her clothes, then raped her. After that, he drove on into the desert, and stopped where a track came to an end. He removed his photographic gear, spread out the blanket on which he had killed Judy Dull, and ordered Shirley – now once again wearing her dress – to sit on it while he took some photographs. And when he had enough souvenirs, he made her lie on her stomach, looped the rope around her neck, and garrotted her. This time he was too lazy to dig a grave; he covered her body over with brushwood; before leaving, he removed her red panties as a keepsake.

He had allowed almost seven months to elapse between his first and second murders. Now, as with most sex criminals, the urge became more insistent. And when he saw a newspaper advertisement in which the model offered to be photographed nude, it seemed too good an opportunity to miss. He called on Angela Rojas on the evening of 22 July 1958, and was not particularly surprised when she shook her head ands explained that she felt ill. He was used to rejection. The following evening he went back, and found the apartment in darkness. He whiled away an hour in a bar, then returned; this time, the light was on. When she showed no sign of being willing to admit him, he pulled out the gun and ordered her inside. Like Judy Dull, Ruth Mercado was small, and he liked this. He ordered her into the bedroom, made her undress, then tied her up and raped her. After that he took souvenir photographs. Before they left the apartment he had raped her several times more.

When she mentioned that she was expecting her boyfriend soon – a lie – he told her he wanted to take her for a picnic. He seemed so convincing that she believed him, and even offered to provide two bottles of brandy. They drove off down towards San Diego, beyond Escondido, and in the early hours of the morning they were thirty or so miles from the spot where he had killed Shirley Ann Bridgeford.

This time Glatman had decided to take his time. In this lonely spot they were unlikely to be interrupted. He and Ruth Mercado spent the whole of the following day out in the desert; they slept, ate, drank, took photographs and made love. Ruth had decided that she had nothing to lose by trying to please him, and Glatman found himself increasingly unwilling to kill her. She was the kind of girl he would enjoy living with. Yet he again had to recognize the impossibility of allowing her to stay alive. More than twenty-four hours after kidnapping her, as she lay face downward in nothing but her panties, Glatman garrotted her in the same manner as the other two. He again took the panties as a memento, as well as all her identification. Like Shirley Ann Bridgeford, she was left unburied.

That was the conclusion of Harvey Glatman's two-hour confession. By the light of the full moon, the detectives drove down to the Anza desert, and with Glatman's help, located the bones of Shirley Ann Bridgeford and Ruth Mercado. Back in prison, Glatman was questioned about more unsolved sex killings in Los Angeles, but his openness convinced police that he knew nothing about them. Meanwhile, police searching his apartment again found a locked toolbox that contained the bound photographs of his victims, two pairs of panties and one pair of shoes.

In court in San Diego in November, 1958, Harvey Glatman

pleaded guilty to the murders of Shirley Ann Bridgeford and Ruth Mercado. His lawyer had proposed a plea of guilty but insane, but Glatman opposed it, saying he would prefer to die rather than spend a life behind bars. Superior Court Judge John A. Hewicker duly obliged, and on 18 September 1959, Harvey Glatman died in the gas chamber at San Quentin.

One of the most sensational cases of the late 1950s was that of the necrophile Ed Gein. Strictly speaking, Gein does not qualify as a serial killer; yet it is impossible to doubt that, in the psychological sense, he belongs in the same gallery as Pommerencke and Glatman.

On the freezing afternoon of 8 December 1954, a customer who dropped into Mary Hogan's tavern in Plainfield, Wisconsin, found the place deserted, and a large bloodstain on the floor. A spent .32 cartridge lay near it. Bloodstains ran out of the back door and into the parking lot, where they halted beside tyre tracks that looked like those of a pickup truck. It looked as if Mary Hogan had been shot and then taken away.

Police were unable to find any clues to the disappearance. But a few weeks later, when a sawmill owner named Elmo Ueeck spoke of the disappearance to a little handyman called Ed Gein, Gein replied with a simplicity reminiscent of Stan Laurel: 'She isn't missing. She's at the farm right now.' And Ueeck who, like most of the residents of Plainfield, regarded Gein as little brighter than Stan Laurel, could not even work up the interest to ask him what he meant.

Three years passed. On the evening of 16 November 1957, Frank Worden returned from a day's hunting to find his mother's hardware store locked up, although the lights were on. A local garage attendant told him that he had seen Mrs Worden's delivery truck driving away at about 9.30 that morning. With sudden foreboding, Frank Worden rushed home and collected the spare key to the store. Inside, as he expected, there was no sign of his mother. But the cash register was missing, and there was a patch of blood on the floor.

'He's done something to her,' said Worden.

'Who?' asked sheriff Art Schley.

'Ed Gein. My mother said he'd been hanging around and behaving oddly recently . . .'

The sheriff lost no time in driving to Gein's farm, six miles west of Plainfield. It was deserted. But he knew that one of Gein's few friends was his cousin Bob Hill. As Schley arrived at Hill's house, he saw Gein's pickup truck about to drive away; Gein was at the wheel, with Bob Hill and his sister Darlene. The sheriff halted them, and asked Gein to get in the squad car for questioning. Gein's replies sounded typically inconsequential and inconsistent, but when he remarked that someone was trying to frame him for Mrs Worden's death, Sheriff Schley decided to take him into custody. No one had mentioned Mrs Worden.

The doors of Ed Gein's farmhouse were locked, but the door of a woodshed – or 'summer kitchen' – at the rear opened when Schley pushed it with his foot. Since the farm had no electricity, the sheriff had to use a torch. What it showed him was the naked corpse of a woman hanging upside down from a crossbeam, the legs spread wide apart, and a long slit running from the genitals almost to the throat. But the throat, like the head, was missing. The genitals and the anus were also missing. Bernice Worden had been disembowelled like a deer.

When a portable electric generator had been installed, the investigators were able to explore the farmhouse. It looked as if it had not been tidied or cleaned for years, and there were piles of rubbish everywhere, as well as dozens of horror comics and magazines. More ominously, there were also human skulls, two of which adorned Gein's bedposts. The seat of a chair proved to be made of human skin. So did a lampshade, a wastepaper basket and even a drum. They also found a shirt made of human skin, and a number of shrunken heads, one of which proved to be Mary Hogan's. The head of Bernice Worden was in a sack, while her entrails and heart were neatly wrapped nearby.

Who were the other corpses (ten of them) – or rather, whose body parts? Gein cleared this up after confessing to the shooting of Mrs Worden; he had dug them up in the local graveyard. Asked if he had had sexual relations with them, Gein shook his head vigorously. 'No, they smelt too bad.'

Slowly, his story emerged. His mother, Augusta Gein, had been crankily religious. Every time it rained heavily, she would read him the story of Noah from the Bible and prophesy the end of the world. She was convinced that the modern world was so full of sin that God would destroy it at any minute – women wearing lipstick and short skirts . . . Ed Gein was the younger of two brothers, and he became a mother's boy. His father died in 1940, and his brother Henry two years later. Henry had also been a bachelor – their mother's upbringing had made both men very nervous of women – and he died in 1944, the same year in which Augusta Gein also suffered a stroke. Her son nursed her until she died in the following year. Ed was then 38, a small, thin man with a pleasant smile, well liked by everyone. Admittedly, there was an odd story about him. His nearest neighbours, the Bankses, had invited him to their house in 1942 when a female relative was in the house; she was wearing shorts, and Gein clearly found it hard to keep his eyes off her legs. That night, a man broke into the woman's house and seized her small son by the throat, asking him where his mother had gone. The man fled before he found out, but the boy thought he recognized Gein. Ever since then, the Bankses had had reservations about their quiet, pleasant neighbour.

What happened seems fairly clear. Gein was a sexually normal man – his mother's undivided attention had not turned him into a homosexual – but he was frightened of women, and not very attractive to them. He had a woman friend, with whom he went out for twenty years, but she finally decided against marrying him. She said his conversation was all about murder. Alone in the farmhouse, he thought endlessly about sex, until one day he saw a newspaper report of a woman who had been buried that day. In the middle of the night, he set off with his pick-up truck and a spade. He dug up the woman, unscrewed the coffin, and put her into the truck; then replaced the coffin and carefully remade the grave. Then he took the corpse home, feeling happier than ever before. At last he had a woman alone and all to himself. He was probably so enthusiastic that he didn't know how to start. But he had plenty of time . . . He explained: 'It gave me a lot of satisfaction.'

Gein's graveyard excursions were not very frequent. Over ten years there were only nine. He suffered from remorse, and decided every time never to do it again. The craving was so strong that it went beyond the desire to perform normal acts of love. He ate parts of the bodies, and made waistcoats of the skin, which he wore next to his flesh. His gravedigging expeditions – and murders – were always at the time of the full moon.

Gein understood himself well enough to realize that his mother was the root of all the trouble. Consciously, he loved her, unconsciously, hated her: hence his choice of elderly women as the only two victims he actually murdered.

At Christmas, 1957, it was decided that Gein was insane, and he was committed to Waupan State Hospital for life. No doubt some of the people of Plainfield for whom he acted as a baby-sitter think about their narrow escape; but there is no evidence that Gein was violently inclined towards young women or children. Gein died of cancer on 26 July 1984, at the age of 78.

Another case of the late 1950s deserves to be mentioned at this point, because although it cannot be classified as serial murder, it is among the best known cases of 'spree killing' in American criminal history. 'Spree killing' describes a murder rampage – a group of murders that occur over a short period of time, in which the killer seems to decide that he may as well be hanged for a sheep as for a lamb, and goes on killing until he is stopped – usually by arrest or a policeman's bullet.

Nineteen-year-old Charles Starkweather, of Lincoln, Nebraska, was an admirer of film star James Dean. His girlfriend, Caril Ann Fugate, was five years his junior. In January 1958, Starkweather had an argument with Caril's mother – who believed her daughter to be pregnant – and shot her dead. He went on to kill her stepfather and two-year-old sister. After two days alone in the house with Caril, he fled when police began to try to gain entrance.

In a brief murder rampage, Starkweather killed seven more people: a farmer named August Meyer, a young couple, Robert Jensen and Carol King (the latter was raped), a businessman, C. Lauer Ward, his wife Clara and their maid, and a shoe salesman, Merle Collison, who was murdered as he napped at the wheel of his car beside the road. Another motorist, ordered to release the handbrake on Collison's car, grappled with Starkweather, and Starkweather fled in the car, pursued by police who had come upon the struggle. He surrendered when they shot out his rear window. Starkweather was electrocuted in June 1959, declaring that his last wish was to have Caril (who had turned against him) sitting on his knee. Caril Fugate was sentenced to life imprisonment by a jury that declined to believe that she had merely been a terrified captive, but was paroled in 1981.

A film, *Badlands* (1974), represented Starkweather exactly as he wanted to be remembered – as a courageous 'rebel without a cause'. In fact, his random killings required no courage, and as he surrendered, Starkweather was close to panic, complaining loudly that he had been cut by flying glass.

The 1950s ended with a case of serial murder that could be regarded as a portent of the future. Melvin Rees was a self-esteem killer, a man who felt he had every right to defy society in the name of his own moral standards.

On 26 June 1957 an army sergeant was driving home for a weekend with a girlfriend, Margaret Harold. They had stopped in a lonely spot near Annapolis, Maryland, when a green Chrysler pulled in front of them. A tall, thin-faced man got out, and identified himself as the caretaker of the property. He asked for a cigarette, then for a lift. Suddenly he pulled out a gun and climbed into the back seat. He demanded money, and wound his fingers into Margaret Harold's hair, pulling her head back. 'Don't give it to him,' she said angrily. There was a shot, and she slumped forward. The sergeant pushed open the door and ran as hard as he could. A mile along the road he found a farmhouse and asked to use the phone. When the police arrived some time later, Margaret Harold was still across the front seat, without her dress. The killer had violated the corpse.

The police searched the area, and found a cinder-block building nearby, with a broken basement window. Inside, the walls were covered with pornographic photographs, and police morgue shots of women who had been murdered. One photograph stood out from the others as normal – it had been clipped out of a college yearbook. The girl in it was finally identified as a 1955 graduate of Maryland University, Wanda Tipson; but she had no recollection of dating any male who corresponded to the sergeant's description of the murderer.

On 11 January 1959 Carrol Jackson was out driving with his wife Mildred and their two daughters, Susan, aged 5 and Janet, eighteen months. Carrol Jackson was a non-smoker and teetotaller who had met his wife at a Baptist church; she was president of the women's missionary society. As he drove along a road near Apple Grove, Eastern Virginia, an old blue Chevrolet began to overtake, flashing his lights. When Jackson pulled over, the Chevrolet pulled in front and stopped. Jackson screeched to a halt, and was about to lose his temper when a man jumped out of the other car and waved a gun in his face. The tall, thin-faced man with long, ape-like arms and a beetling brow forced the Jackson family to get out of their car and into the boot of his Chevrolet. Then he drove off. Later that afternoon, Mildred Jackson's aunt drove along the same road and recognized her niece's husband's car, abandoned.

The search for the Jacksons revealed nothing. Then another couple came forward to say that they had been forced off the road earlier that afternoon by an old blue Chevrolet. A man had walked back towards their car, but they had quickly reversed and driven away.

Two months later, on 4 March, two men whose car had bogged down on a muddy back road near Fredericksburg picked up armfuls of brush to gain traction, and found themselves looking at the body of a man. It proved to be Carrol Jackson, his hands bound in front of him with a necktie. He had been shot in the skull. Underneath him was the body of his eighteen-month-old daughter, who had simply been tossed into the ditch, and died of suffocation under her father's body. There was no sign of Mildred or Susan Jackson.

On 21 March, boys hunting squirrels close to the spot where Margaret Harold had been murdered noticed freshly dug earth; they brushed some of it aside and saw the blonde hair of a little girl. Police uncovered the bodies of Mildred and Susan Jackson. Mildred had a stocking tied around her neck, but it was loose. Susan had been beaten to death with a blunt instrument. There was evidence that both had been raped. Police theorized that the stocking around Mildred Jackson's neck had been used as a tourniquet to force her to commit some sexual act that disgusted her.

The grave was within a few hundred yards of the cinder-block structure in which the obscene photographs had been found two years earlier. And a quarter of a mile away, the police found a broken-down shack with relatively fresh tyre-marks nearby. Inside, police found a red button from Mildred Jackson's dress.

Again, the investigation came to a halt. But two months later, the police received an anonymous letter that accused a jazz musician called Melvin Davis Rees of the murders of Margaret Harold and of the Jackson family. The man, who said he was a salesman, said that he and Rees had been in a town not far from the spot where Margaret Harold had been murdered, and that Rees had been hopped up on Benzedrine. The writer said he had later asked Rees point-blank if he had killed the Jackson family; Rees had not denied it, but only evaded the question. Police searched for Rees – whose job as a jazz musician kept him travelling – without success. Then, early in 1960, the writer of the letter, who identified himself as Glenn L. Moser, went to the police, to say that he had received a letter from Rees, who was working as a piano salesman in a music shop in West Memphis, Arkansas. An FBI agent went into the store and told Rees he was under arrest. Later that day, the sergeant identified Rees in a line-up as the man who had murdered Margaret Harold.

Detectives hastened to the home of Rees' parents in Hyattsville, armed with a search warrant; in an attic they found a saxophone case containing a .38 revolver, and various notes describing sadistic acts – including the murder of the Jacksons.

'Caught on a lonely road . . . Drove to a select area and killed husband and baby. Now the mother and daughter were all mine . . .' He went on to describe a perverted sex act, probably forcing fellatio on her. 'Now I was her master,' he says with relish. He then described killing her slowly in a way that made it clear that his sexual hang-up was sadism.

Maryland police now discovered links between Rees and four other sex-murders of teenagers: two schoolgirls, Marie Shomette and Ann Ryan, had been intercepted in College Park, near the University of Maryland, and shot and raped; the bodies of Mary Fellers and Shelby Venable had been found in Maryland rivers.

Rees was tried in 1961, and executed for the murder of the Jackson family.

People who had worked with Rees (who played the piano, guitar, saxophone and clarinet) found it hard to believe that he was guilty of the crimes, and described him as mild-mannered and intelligent. The girl whose photograph had been found in the hut had, in fact, known him very well, and had given him up because he was married; it just never struck her that the killer of Margaret Harold could be the jazz musician.

Peter Hurkos, the psychic, was called into the case after the disappearance of the Jackson family, and his description of the killer was remarkably accurate – over six feet tall, left-handed, tattooed on the arm, with a walk like a duck and ape-like arms.

At the scene of Margaret Harold's murder, Hurkos walked to a bush and plucked off the dead woman's torn skirt which had been there unnoticed since the murder. Hurkos added that the man had committed nine murders. This concurred with the figure the police themselves finally arrived at.

Rees had told Glenn Moser: 'You can't say it's wrong to kill – only individual standards make it right or wrong' – the argument that Sade had advanced but never attempted to put into practice. We may also note Moser's comment: 'I asked him point blank if he had killed these people. He evaded the question. He didn't deny it.' H. H. Holmes would have cast his eyes up to heaven and said: 'My dear fellow, what an appalling suggestion.' Rees's self-esteem would not permit him to lie about it, even if – as happened – it cost him his life.

8

The 1960s

On Good Friday, 27 March 1959, a married woman named Hazel Woodard – a resident of a small town called Laurel, in Sarasota County, Florida – was watching television, when a shot came through the screen door and struck her between the eyes. She died the next day in hospital. The bullet that had killed her had been fired by a .22 pistol.

Sheriff Ross Boyer interviewed virtually everybody in the town, and everyone seemed to agree that Hazel Woodard, a retired schoolteacher, had no enemies. Then, looking at the TV guide, Boyer noticed an odd coincidence: at the time Hazel Woodard had been shot, a programme called 'The Sniper' had just been shown on television.

One of the residents they interviewed was a man named Norman Smith, who lived in a caravan half a mile from the Woodard home, and who made a living from sea shells. Smith denied owning a gun, and said he had been with a friend all evening. Asked if he had watched 'The Sniper' he shook his head. 'Afraid I missed it.'

Further investigations produced a promising lead. Two residents mentioned a Peeping Tom who peered through bedroom windows – in fact, one of them had fired a shot to scare him off. And a third man was finally able to tell them the Peeping Tom's identity – Norman Smith. The sheriff immediately checked with the friend with whom Smith claimed to have spent the evening. This man agreed that he had – but said he had left soon after they had finished watching 'The Sniper'.

When he also told the police that Smith owned a .22 pistol,

they returned to the caravan and took Smith in for questioning. Smith denied the shooting, and agreed to a lie detector test; it showed that he was lying. Soon after this, Smith cracked and confessed to shooting Mrs Woodard. He had been watching 'The Sniper', and after his friend had left, had simply taken the gun and gone out to find someone to shoot . . .

When I came across this case, it struck me as so odd that I mentioned it in the preface to the *Encyclopedia of Murder* that I was then compiling, classifying it as a 'crime of boredom'. I pointed out that, in that sense, it resembled the 1924 case of the two Chicago students, Richard Loeb and Nathan Leopold, who had become fascinated by Nietzsche's gospel of the Superman, and killed 14-year-old Bobby Franks to show that they had no respect for man-made laws. I had argued that the 'crime of boredom' is a result of a moral vacuum that springs out of a sense of being free, *but of having nothing to do with our freedom*. Dostoevsky had explored the problem in *The Devils*, where the anti-hero Stavrogin complains that he had never found anything to do with his strength, and has consequently committed a whole series of meaningless acts, some of them criminal, merely to escape a sense of futility and meaninglessness.

It was also in 1959 that a pretty blonde named Penny Bjorkland, of Daly City, California, accepted a lift from a gardener named August Norry and shot him to death. Trapped by the evidence of the bullet, she explained that she wanted to see if she could kill a man 'and not worry about it afterwards'.

Now in fact, it is obvious that no crime is really 'motiveless'. Penny Bjorkland's shooting may have been motivated by childhood abuse. Norman Smith's random sniping may have been a form of sexual aggression, like that of a later New York serial killer, David Berkowitz, known as 'Son of Sam'. And the murder committed by Leopold and Loeb was clearly an act of *ego-assertion*. They felt that they were immensely superior to their fellow students, but it was necessary to *do* something to prove it to themselves.

I saw in this type of 'motiveless crime' an ominous portent for the future. And this feeling crystallized when I read of a mass murder that took place in Mesa, Arizona, on 13 November 1966, when an 18-year-old student named Robert Benjamin Smith walked into a hairdressing parlour called the Rose-Mar College of Beauty, ordered four young women and a 3-year-old girl to lie face downward on the floor, then shot them all in the back of the head. Asked why he did it, Smith said: 'I wanted to get known, to get myself a name.' He added: 'I knew I had to kill a lot of people to get my name in the newspapers all over the world.'

Such a motive seems absurd and incomprehensible – until we recall the Greek Herostratus, who in 356 BC burnt down the temple of Artemis at Ephesus 'to make his name immortal'. In 1938 Sartre wrote a story called 'Herostratus' about a man who decided to shoot half a dozen people at random for the same reason (the first of the 'crazy gunmen').

Now, as most contemporary psychologists acknowledge, the hunger for self-esteem is one of the most basic human urges. The first to develop this notion as a basis for psychotherapy was Freud's disciple (later his opponent) Alfred Adler, who argued that man has turned his physical inferiority to animals to his advantage by developing his *brain*. And in the same way, physically weak individuals compensate for their inferiority to stronger ones by developing their intelligence. This becomes their source of 'superiority' and self-esteem. Adler suggested that the 'inferiority complex' is the most basic cause of neurosis.

The American psychologist Abraham Maslow found himself torn between the Freudian explanation of neurosis (sexual repression) and the Adlerian (inferiority) until it struck him that *both* play a fundamental role. Maslow reconciled them by creating his theory of the 'hierarchy of needs.'

What Maslow suggested, briefly, is this. If human beings are at the bottom of the social scale, their chief desire is just to stay alive – to have the basic means of subsistence. A man who has been half-starved since birth feels that if only he could have three good meals a day, he would be ecstatically happy. But if this level of need is satisfied, the next emerges: for security, a roof over one's head (every tramp daydreams of retiring to a cottage with roses round the door). If *this* level is satisfied, the next emerges – the sexual level: not just the need for sex, but for love, for companionship. And if this level is satisfied, the next need emerges: to be *recognized* and respected: in other words, the need for self-esteem. And if this level is satisfied, a final level sometimes (though not always) emerges: what Maslow called 'self-actualization' – creativity: not necessarily writing novels or symphonies, but the need to do something well merely for the sake of doing it well. Even stamp collecting counts as self-actualization.

Cases like that of Robert Smith made me aware that a new level of crime was beginning to emerge as a successor to 'the age of sex crime': what might be called the crime of self-esteem. This was followed by the insight that in the past two centuries, society itself has passed through the levels of Maslow's hierarchy of needs. In the days of the *Newgate Calendar* (1774), that immense compilation of criminal cases, sex crime was virtually unknown; criminals were too busy merely staying alive to bother about rape. When rape did occur it was often treated with remarkable leniency: in the *Encyclopedia*, I cite a nineteenth-century record that mentions a man being sentenced to death for stealing a loaf of bread, and a man who received two weeks in jail for raping a servant girl.

In the Victorian age, with its higher level of prosperity, Maslow's second level emerges: crime committed for domestic security. Belle Gunness epitomizes it perfectly: what she wanted was not just cash, but the ideal home and the social security that goes with it.

The third level of need, the sexual level. begins to emerge in the second half of the nineteenth century, and is symbolized by Jack the Ripper. The age of sex crime had begun.

And now, in the late 1950s and early 1960s, we see the emergence of the next level: self-esteem. This is the ultimate motivation of Peter Manuel, Werner Boost, Melvin Rees.

But at this point, a serious objection occurs. These three men were, after all, sex criminals. Yet we only have to compare them with 'sex maniacs' like Earle Nelson, Harvey Glatman or Heinrich Pommerencke – or even Ed Gein – to see that there is a major difference. The typical rapist killer is suffering from a kind of sexual starvation, and he 'steals' sex as a starving man might steal food. He recognizes it as wrong, but the compulsion is overwhelming. The self-esteem killer denies that what he is doing is wrong. Like some bomb-throwing revolutionary, he feels that society is somehow to blame – or God, or the laws of nature. It is true that he is a sex criminal, but sex is no longer the basic driving force. What such men are really interested in is power, self-esteem. Sartre catches it perfectly in a scene in 'Herostratus' in which the hero goes to a prostitute and simply makes her remove her clothes and walk about the room, while he sits in an armchair, fully clothed, holding a revolver in his lap. He explains elsewhere in the story that he never indulges in sexual intercourse; he feels this would be a kind of surrender to a woman who is his inferior.

Here, suddenly, we can grasp the reason for the sadism involved in so many modern sex crimes. The sex is inextricably entangled with the craving for self-esteem, for personal 'superiority'. And as soon as we see this, we can also see that this throws a new light on the fantasies of the Marquis de Sade. Sade had a keen sense of his own intellectual superiority, yet it was being continually challenged by those in authority. Sade's novels are *authoritarian* daydreams rather than sexual daydreams. This is why he devotes as much time to intellectual argument as to sexual fantasy. We may see Sade as an 'in-betweener', someone who is in between two levels of Maslow's hierarchy, sex and self-esteem.

Maslow's hierarchy also suggests why so many burglars urinate and defecate in the course of robbery. As a crime, burglary belongs to the lower levels of Maslow's hierarchy – the need for subsistence and security. But the sexual level is also beginning to emerge, and it is sexual excitement that prompts the urge to 'do something dirty' as well as merely stealing property. Lowering the trousers is essentially a sexual act. And here again, the crime involves *two* adjacent levels of Maslow's hierarchy, and the criminal may be seen as an 'in-betweener'.

Maslow's 'hierarchy' is about *human evolution*. And this in turn explains why human beings are capable of so much more violence and cruelty than animals: in man, this evolutionary urge is far more acute and painful.

And what of Maslow's next level, self-actualization? We can also see the increasing emergence of this level in the latter part of the twentieth century: for example, in the increasing interest in the 'expansion of consciousness', in yoga, in 'occultism', in the 'psychedelic revolution' and virtual reality. Now it can be found in any town or village anywhere – even the small Cornish village where I live has a yoga group.

Now, self-actualizers do not commit crimes – at least, not murder. For example, there is no known example of a writer or artist committing a premeditated murder. (A few have killed men in duels, or – like the composer Gesualdo, who caught his wife in bed with a lover – in a fit of jealousy; but never a coldly calculated killing.) Shaw underlined the point by observing that we judge an artist by his highest moments, a criminal by his lowest. Once a man has decided that he is an artist – one of the 'unacknowledged legislators of the world' – then he has achieved a level of self-esteem at which crime is no longer a valid option. There is a sense in which he feels 'above' society as Sartre's Herostratus feels 'above' sex with prostitutes.

There is, nevertheless, a point at which sex, self-esteem and self-actualization mingle rather uncomfortably. The level of self-actualization is, for example, the religious level, and there are many examples of religious prophets and 'messiahs' who are still entangled in the need for sex and self-esteem. The usual assumption is that such men are simply confidence tricksters who prey on the gullible, like Sinclair Lewis's Elmer Gantry. But this is not necessarily true. Many possess a genuine urge to self-transcendence, but still mixed with sex and self-esteem urges. Edward Wilson, who preferred to be called Brother Twelve, possessed remarkable religious gifts, which emerge clearly in his writings.[1] But as soon as he became a successful prophet, he engaged in seduction and became a kind of power-maniac, who finally absconded with the money collected from his disciples. The Revd. Jim Jones, who ordered nine hundred disciples to commit mass suicide in Guyana in 1978, also seems to have started out with genuine religious inspiration. So did Jeffrey Lundgren, a breakaway Mormon who started a religious community in Kirtland, Ohio, in the 1980s. Lundgren invented a ceremony called Intercession, in which female disciples had to dance naked in front of him, while he masturbated into their panties, explaining that his shedding of semen was analogous to Christ's shedding of his blood for the redemption of sin. Lundgren eventually ordered his followers to murder a family of five disciples, whom he accused of backsliding, and was sentenced to death in 1990.[2]

A certain scepticism is inevitable in considering such cases; it is easier to dismiss such 'messiahs' as confidence men. Yet unless we can grasp that genuine 'self-actualization' needs can

[1] See *Brother Twelve*, by John Oliphant (McClelland and Stewart, Toronto, 1991).

[2] *The Kirtland Massacre*, by Cynthia Statter Sasse and Peggy Murphy (Willder, Donald I. Fine Inc., New York, 1991).

be entangled with sex and self-esteem needs, we fail to grasp an important aspect of what has been happening since the 1960s. When the Charles Manson 'family' came to trial in 1970, the general public was thoroughly confused by Manson's attempt to turn the trial into an indictment of bourgeois society. Manson explained: 'You made my children what they are.' Asked if she thought the killing of eight people was unimportant, Susan Atkins countered by asking if the killing of thousands of people with napalm was important. It looked like thoroughly muddled logic. Yet it is only necessary to read some of the interviews Manson has given in prison, or watch them on videotape, to recognize that Manson still believes that his 'philosophy' was really about self-actualization, and that the murders were intended as a kind of violent protest against a society that denied him self-actualization. Again, on 9 October 1970, an ecology enthusiast named John Linley Frazier murdered eye surgeon Victor Ohta and his family, leaving behind a note that declaimed against those who 'misuse the natural environment', and concluding: 'Materialism must die or mankind will stop.'

It is also worth bearing in mind that Frazier, like the Manson family – and most of the hippies in the 1960s – spent a great deal of his time on 'acid trips'. And one of the effects of psychedelic drugs is to produce visions of 'transcendence' which authorities like Aldous Huxley, Timothy Leary and Arthur Koestler agree to be valid, rather than some kind of drug-induced delusion. On the other hand, drugs are clearly a short cut to 'expanded states of awareness', which explains why such states are usually unstable.

This also explains why criminals like Manson and Frazier are so puzzling and difficult to place: because they are 'in-betweeners', existing uneasily between the levels of self-esteem and self-actualization.

It seems likely that this is also the key to one of the most sensational murder cases of the decade: the 'Moors murders' – a case that, as journalist Fred Harrison commented, 'has tormented the psyche of a nation'. On 19 April 1966, Ian Brady, 28, and Myra Hindley, 23, appeared in court in Chester, accused of three murders: two of children, Lesley Ann Downey and John Kilbride, one of a teenage boy, Edward Evans. They were also believed to have killed Pauline Reade, 16, and Keith Bennett, 12, but the bodies had not been found.

What produced the sense of shock was that a young girl – and apparently one who loved animals and children – should have participated in the sex murder of children. Commentators on the case seemed divided between those who thought Brady a hypnotic Svengali, and those who thought they were probably both equally bad. In his introduction to *The Trial of Ian Brady and Myra Hindley*, Jonathan Goodman makes it clear that he simply regards Brady as a monster. More insight is provided by Jean Ritchie in *Myra Hindley: Inside the Mind of a Murderess* (1988), who seems to have based part of her account on interviews with Brady's foster parents.

Ian Brady – christened Ian Duncan Stewart – was born on 2 January 1938 in Glasgow; his mother, 28-year-old Margaret Stewart, worked as a waitress in hotel tea-rooms; his father was a Glasgow journalist, who died three months before Ian's birth. Margaret Stewart did her best to support the child, farming him out to babysitters when she had to work in the evening, but finally advertised for a full-time 'childminder'. Mary and John Sloan took him into 'their warm and friendly home', where his mother, who now called herself Peggy, came to visit him every Sunday, bringing him clothes and presents. So it hardly seems that Ian Brady can be classified with Carl Panzram as someone who was subjected to childhood neglect and brutality.

Jean Ritchie has one highly significant story to tell: how, at the age of 9, he was taken on a picnic to the shores of Loch Lomond.

> For Ian it was a day of discovery. He discovered in himself a deep affinity with the wild, rugged and empty scenery around the lake. He was moved by the grandeur of the hills, awed by the vastness of the sky. When it was time to go home, the family found him halfway up one of the hills, standing still absorbing something – who knows what? – from the strange, open, inspiring scenery around him. It was an unusual Ian who came down the hill, one who babbled happily about his day out to his foster sisters . . .

This story sounds as if it came from the Sloan family, and it is supported by other comments from those who knew him: for example, Lord Longford, who visited him in prison. The latter is also on record as saying that Brady knew his Tolstoy and Dostoevsky better than anyone he had known. Others have spoken of his interest in Nietzsche. This hardly sounds like the sadistic psychopath described by Goodman.

What most writers on the case seem agreed upon is that Brady was – as Jean Ritchie puts it – 'a loner, an outsider'. He was also a highly dominant child at school, a born leader, who seems to have embarked on burglary at an early age (9 has been quoted) – not, as in the case of Panzram, out of envy of contemporaries from wealthier backgrounds, but simply out of devilment.

When he was 10, the family were moved from the Gorbals to a new council estate at Pollock, with – as Jean Ritchie says – 'indoor bathroom and lavatory, a garden and nearby fields'. At the age of 11 he started attending Shawlands Academy, a school for above-average pupils, but seems to have taken a certain pleasure in misbehaving, perhaps in reaction against richer schoolmates.

At the age of 13 he came before a juvenile court for burglary, but was bound over; nine months later, he was again bound over for the same thing. At 16 he appeared again before a Glasgow court with nine charges against him. This time he was put on probation on condition that he joined his mother in Manchester. Margaret Stewart had moved there when her son was 12, and had married a meat porter named Patrick Brady, whose name Ian was to take.

His stepfather found him a job in the fruit market. He was still a loner, spending hours in his room reading. But in November 1955, he was again in court, this time on a charge of aiding and abetting. A lorry driver had asked him to load some stolen lead onto his lorry. The scrap dealer gave him away to the police, and he in turn implicated Brady. In court, Brady pleaded guilty, expecting a fine for such a trivial offence – after all, everybody in the market was 'on the fiddle'. But because he was on probation, the judge decided that severity was called for. To his bewilderment – and rage – Brady was remanded to Strangeways jail to await his sentence.

There he spent three months among professional criminals, and deliberately cultivated fences, cracksmen, even killers. He had made up his mind that society was going to get what it deserved. This reaction – reminiscent of Joseph Smith, Carl Panzram, Peter Manuel and Werner Boost – is typical of the high-dominance male faced with what he considers outrageous injustice. The two-year Borstal sentence that followed only confirmed the decision – particularly when, in an open Borstal at Hatfield, he found himself in further trouble. He had been selling home-distilled liquor and running a book on horses and dogs. One day, after getting drunk and having a fight with a warder, he was transferred to an altogether tougher Borstal housed in Hull prison. This, says Jean Ritchie, 'was where he prepared himself to become a big-time criminal'. The aim was to become wealthy as quickly as possible, so he could enjoy the freedom he dreamed about. This was why he studied book-keeping in prison – to learn to handle money.

Three months in Strangeways and two years in Borstal had turned a youth with a minor criminal record and a tendency to bookishness into an antisocial rebel. Even taking into account the fact that he had been on probation, the ineptitude of the law seems incredible.

He was released at the end of two years, but remained on probation for another three. When he was released, he returned home to Manchester, as he had to under the terms of the probation. But Fred Harrison, the journalist who interviewed Brady in prison, and who wrote a book on the case,[1] has an interesting passage that makes it clear that Brady soon became actively involved in crime. He speaks of a Borstal friend named Deare, who delivered a stolen Jaguar to Manchester – not to Brady but to another man. The car was to be used in a 'job'. The other man, says Harrison, made the mistake of not getting rid of the Jaguar after the 'job', and was arrested. He gave Deare's name to the police. Deare subsequently vanished, and Harrison suggests that Brady was responsible. Now in fact, Gilbert Deare was still around at the time of Brady's arrest for the Moors murders, and died some time later in a drowning accident. On this topic, Harrison is inaccurate. But the significance of the passage is that it makes clear that Brady was involved in crimes that required a getaway car soon after he returned to Manchester, and that he had at least two accomplices. What is also clear is that Brady spent a great deal of time 'casing' banks and building societies, watching the transportation of money.

But apart from one brush with the law for being drunk and

[1] *Brady and Hindley: Genesis of the Moors Murders* (Ashgrove Press, Bath 1986).

disorderly, Brady managed to stay out of trouble. His probation officer obliged him to take a labouring job in a brewery, which he understandably detested. In 1959, at the age of 21, he succeeded in changing this for something less disagreeable; the book-keeping training led to a job as a stock clerk with Millwards Ltd, a small chemical firm. He was a careful and neat worker, although inclined to be unpunctual, and to slip out of the office to place bets with a local bookmaker. But he remained a loner, spending the lunch hour alone in the office, reading books which included *Mein Kampf* and other volumes on Nazism.

What seems clear, then, is that Ian Brady was turned into a criminal by a sense of injustice. Whether this attitude was justified is beside the point; given his background, and the two years in Borstal, it was inevitable. Although a loner as a child, he was by no means an outcast among his contemporaries, who regarded him as a daredevil. His brushes with the law had been infrequent, and he was treated leniently until the lead episode. In the Manchester fruit market he was 'on the fiddle' – like everyone else – but was basically prepared to settle down. The decision to remand him to Strangeways was the true origin of the Moors murders.

Among writers on the case there has been a fairly concerted effort to represent Brady as a mindless devotee of violent comics and book with titles like *The Kiss of the Whip*. This is clearly inaccurate, since his reading included *Crime and Punishment* and *Thus Spake Zarathustra*, as well as Sade's *Justine* (the early 'non-pornographic' version of 1787). Fred Harrison records that Brady discovered *Crime and Punishment* in the Manchester public library in 1958, around the time of his twentieth birthday. Its hero, Raskolnikov, justifies his murder of an old woman by explaining that he asked himself what Napoleon would have done in his place – if, instead of having the opportunity to prove himself at Toulon at the age of 25, he had been a poor student in St Petersburg, who had to make his own opportunities?

This seems, in many ways, to be the key to Brady's personality. Since childhood he had never doubted that he was a 'somebody'. Nietzsche talks about 'how one becomes what one is'. But *how* could he find a way of becoming 'somebody?' Beethoven never had any doubt that he was a composer, Nietzsche that he was a philosopher, Dostoevsky that he was a writer, Einstein that he was a scientist. All of them had difficult early struggles – Einstein even worked as a clerk in a patent office – but they had a sense of purpose, of what Sartre calls a 'project'. What was Brady's 'project?' To some extent it had been determined by those early forays into burglary to obtain pocket money. He wanted the opportunity to live as he wanted, to go where he wanted, at any time he felt inclined. That seemed to point to a career in crime. His aim was to make a large sum of money from robbery, then probably to retire abroad.

The second major influence was Hitler's *Mein Kampf*. Anyone who wonders how an antisemitic tirade could have exercised such an immense influence on a whole generation should push aside preconceptions and try reading it, as I did in my late teens. Its keynote is reasonableness, and it reminds us that when Albert Speer first went to hear Hitler speak, expecting a ranting maniac, he was amazed to discover a man who talked quietly and rationally, almost pedantically. Hitler begins by speaking of his father, the son of a poor cottager, who set out from his home village at the age of 13, with a satchel on his back and three gulden in his pocket, to launch himself into the strange, unknown world of Vienna. He became a civil servant, then retired at 56 and became a farmer.

Hitler goes on to speak of himself.

> It was at this time I began to have ideals of my own. I spent a good deal of time playing about in the open, on the long road from school, and mixing with some of the roughest of the boys, which caused my mother many anxious moments. All this tended to make me the opposite of a stay-at-home. I gave no serious thought to a profession; but I was certainly out of sympathy with the kind of career my father had followed. I think that an inborn talent for speaking now began to develop . . . I had become a juvenile ringleader who learned well and easily at school, but who was rather difficult to manage.

Every word must have struck Brady as a reflection of himself.

Hitler's father was determined that he should become a civil servant; Hitler was equally determined that he would not. The conflict began when Hitler was 11, and became more bitter when, at the age of 12, he decided to become an artist.

Then, in his early teens, his father and his mother died in quick succession. He was left in poverty. And so, like his father, he was forced to go to Vienna to seek his fortune.

By this point the reader is hooked. Hitler's description of his sufferings and poverty in Vienna are simple and undramatized. And when he goes on to speak of a corrupt society, rotten with injustice and poverty, it seems that he is speaking common sense. Suddenly, it is possible to see how Hitler exercised such an immense influence on his audiences; they felt he was simply articulating what they had always felt. He goes on to conjure up a family of seven living in a dark basement, where every minor disagreement turns into a quarrel. Sometimes the father assaults the mother in a fit of drunken rage. All religious and political and humanistic values seem an illusion. The truth is simply the brutal struggle to survive. A child brought up in such an environment is totally anti-authoritarian. When he leaves school he is cynical and resentful. And he soon ends up in a reformatory, which completes his education in self-contempt and criminality . . .

Hitler goes on to describe how, working in the building trade, he first came up against trade unionism and Marxism. When told he had to join the union, he refused. As he got to know his fellow workers better, he knew he could never 'join' them; they struck him as too stupid. Finally, when they threatened to throw him from the scaffolding, he left. By that time he had come to despise socialism, which seemed to him the glorification of the mediocre.

According to Hitler, it took him a long time to recognize the connection between socialism and the Jews. At first he was simply disgusted by the antisemitic press. Then he began to recognize the part played by Jews in socialism, particularly Marxism. It was Marxism that aroused his most furious disgust, with its dislike of entrepreneurs and – by implication – of individual enterprise. Dostoevsky had expressed the same disgust with socialism in *The Possessed* (a book that Brady read five times). Hitler ends his second chapter by stating ominously that 'should the Jew, with the aid of his Marxist creed, triumph over the people of this world, his crown will be the funeral wreath of humanity . . .'

It becomes possible to see why Hitler's doctrine achieved such enormous influence. Since the collapse of communism in Russia, most people can acknowledge that they share his sentiments about Marxism. What Hitler was proposing to put in its place was a purified German nationalism based upon the greatness of the German cultural heritage – Goethe, Beethoven, Nietzsche, Wagner . . . The result is a highly potent brew which, when distilled into films like Leni Riefenstahl's *Triumph of the Will*, seems to offer a simple and seductive solutions to all the problems of the modern world.

There was another element in Brady that Fred Harrison was the first to bring out: a curious black romanticism associated with death. Harrison describes how Brady became an atheist at the age of 12, when he prayed that his pet dog would not die, and his prayers remained unanswered. Two years later, cycling to a job interview, he felt giddy and halted in the doorway of a newsagent's shop. There he saw 'a green, warm radiation, not unattractive to the young man who tried to steady himself. The features were unformed but still recognizable. Ian knew that he was looking at The Face of Death . . . he instantly knew that his salvation was irrevocably bound to its demands. "I'll do it a favour, and . . . it will do me favours." The bond with death was fused by the green radiation.'

For two years Brady worked quietly at Millwards, reading, learning German and playing records – including Hitler speeches – and almost certainly continued to keep in touch with ex-Borstal friends and plan 'jobs'. Then, on Monday 16 January 1961, an 18-year-old shorthand typist named Myra Hindley came to work at Millwards, and Ian Brady dictated her first letter. She was four and a half years younger than Brady, a completely normal working-class girl, not bad-looking, with a blonde hair-do and bright lipstick, interested in boys and dancing. She had been born a Catholic, brought up a Protestant, and returned to Catholicism when she was 16. When she was 4, the birth of a sister made the home too cramped, and she went to live with her grandmother nearby. This was not particularly traumatic since she could spend as much time as she liked at her home around the corner.

At school she received good marks and wrote poetry and excellent English essays. She played the mouth organ and was known as a high-spirited tomboy.

She had been engaged but had broken it off, finding the boy 'immature'. This was one of the problems for working-class girls at that time, whose notions of male attractiveness were formed by cinema and television – hard-bitten heroes with strong jaws, or charismatic rebels like James Dean and Elvis

Presley. By contrast, the youths they met at dance halls seemed commonplace and boring.

Ian Brady was certainly not that. He had slightly sulky good looks reminiscent of Elvis Presley, and a dry and forceful manner. His self-possession was intriguing. So was his total lack of interest in her. Myra's infatuation blossomed, and she confided it to her red diary. 'Ian looked at me today.' 'Wonder if Ian is courting. Still feel the same.' 'Haven't spoken to him yet.' Then: 'Spoken to him. He smiles as though embarrassed.' On 1 August: 'Ian's taking sly looks at me at work.' But by November: 'I've given up with Ian. He goes out of his way to annoy me . . .' Then, on 22 December 1961: 'Out with Ian!' They went to see the film *King of Kings*, the life story of Jesus. Just over a week later, on the divan bed in her gran's front room, Ian Brady and Myra Hindley became lovers. 'I hope Ian and I love each other all our lives and get married and are happy ever after.'

Many books on the Moors murder case imply that Brady's attitude towards her was cold and manipulative. In fact, it seems to have been exceptionally close. Myra was overawed and fascinated by her lover. She declared later: 'Within months he had convinced me there was no God at all: he could have told me the earth was flat, the moon was made of green cheese and the sun rose in the west, I would have believed him.' Brady is on record as saying that the relationship was so close that they were virtually telepathic. They spent every Saturday night together, went on for visits to the moors on Ian's motorbike, taking bottles of German wine, read the same books, and went to see his favourite films, such as *Compulsion*, based on the Leopold and Loeb murder case.

Now he had a female partner, but the central problem remained: how to escape the boring rut of working-class existence, and find a more fulfilling way of life. According to Fred Harrison, it was early in 1963 – after they had been lovers for a year – that Brady suggested that the two of them should collaborate on robbing a bank or a store. But this raises some obvious questions. Brady already had at least two criminal contacts; it is unlikely that he took a year to tell Myra about them, and about his plans for a payroll robbery. It seems far more likely that she knew about these plans from the beginning. At all events, it is clear from her later admissions to Detective

Chief Superintendent Topping that he had no trouble persuading her to participate.

For a payroll robbery it would be necessary to possess a car. Myra began to take driving lessons, and passed her test at the first attempt. Also at about this time, Brady took up photography, and bought a camera with a timing device. He took photographs of Myra in black crotchless panties; she photographed him holding his erect penis; then, using a timing device, they photographed themselves having sexual intercourse. The intention, apparently, was to make money selling the pictures.

In April 1963, he wrote to her that he would be surveying an 'investment establishment' (i.e. bank or building society) in the Stockport Road. In June 1963, Brady moved into the house of Myra's gran, and Myra acquired a car, a second hand minivan. It was then, according to Harrison, that he began to talk to her about committing a murder.

In a letter to the press in January 1990, Brady wrote that the murders were 'the product of an existentialist philosophy, in tandem with the spiritualism of Death itself'. What seems clear is that crime had become a form of dark romanticism, and that this philosophy was based on Nietzsche, Dostoevsky and Sade.

The first 'Moors murder', that of Pauline Reade, happened on 12 July 1963, a month after Brady had moved in with Myra. The only account we have of the murder is from the confession Myra Hindley made to Topping in January 1987. According to Myra, she picked up Pauline Reade – who was 16 – in the minivan, and asked her to help her come and look for an expensive glove which she had lost at a picnic on Saddleworth Moor. She offered her a pile of gramophone records in exchange. When they had been on the moor about an hour, Brady arrived on his motorbike, and was introduced as Myra's boyfriend. Brady and Pauline then went off to look for the glove, while Myra waited in the car. Later Brady returned to the car, and took her to Pauline's body. Her throat had been cut and her clothes were in disarray, indicating rape. They then buried the body with the spade that Myra had brought in the back of the van.

In his open letter of 1990, Brady claimed that Myra had been involved in the actual killing, and had also made some kind of sexual assault on Pauline Reade. On the whole, his account sounds the more plausible. Myra's account of the murders invariably has her elsewhere at the time, and Topping admits that Myra told the truth only in so far as it suited her.

It seems clear that Brady was now totally in the grip of the criminal-outsider syndrome. The plans for the payroll robbery – or robberies – were well advanced. And so were plans for more murders. The one thing we know for certain about sex crime is that it is addictive. The satisfaction in all sex derives from the 'forbidden', but the forbiddenness is diluted by the need for mutual consent; rape – possessing a woman without her consent – is like undiluted corn liquor. Few rape killers have succeeded in stopping of their own accord. But it is also important to grasp that the murders were only a part of Brady's 'agenda'.

In October 1963, three months after the murder of Pauline Reade, Ian Brady made the acquaintance of 16-year-old David Smith, the husband of Myra's sister Maureen (who was now also working at Millwards). Smith was a big youth who had been a member of a street gang and had been in trouble with the law. Soon David and Maureen took a trip to Lake District with Ian and Myra, where they sailed on Windermere. While not homosexual, Smith experienced an emotional attraction to males; soon he was almost as completely under Brady's spell as Myra was.

On Saturday 23 November, Ian Brady and Myra Hindley drove to the small market town of Ashton-under-Lyne. A 12-year-old boy named John Kilbride had spent Saturday afternoon at the cinema, then went to earn a few pence doing odd jobs for stallholders at the market. It began to get dark and a fog came down from the Pennines. At that moment, a friendly lady approached him and asked him if he wanted a lift. It seemed safe enough, so he climbed in. It was the last time he was seen alive. Later, Brady was to take a photograph of Myra kneeling on his grave on the moor.

On 16 June 1964, 12-year-old Keith Bennett set out to spend the night at his grandmother's house in the Longsight district. When his mother called to collect him the following morning, he had failed to arrive. Like John Kilbride, Keith Bennett had accepted a lift from a kind lady. His body has never been found.

Meanwhile, David Smith's admiration for his mentor was steadily increasing. Brady took him up to Saddleworth Moor and they engaged in pistol practice – Myra had obtained two pistols by the expedient of joining the Cheadle Rifle Club. Myra was not entirely happy about this intimacy; her attitude to Smith had an undertone of hostility; in fact, both of them were getting sick of the Smiths. She was glad when her gran was rehoused in Wardle Brook Avenue, in the suburb of Hattersley, in September 1964, and she and Ian moved into the little house at the end of a terrace. Nevertheless, Ian continued to consolidate his influence over David. If he was going to rob banks, a partner would be needed. Soon David Smith was recording in a notebook sentences like: 'God is a disease, a plague, a weight round a man's neck' and 'Rape is not a crime, it is a state of mind. God is a disease which eats away a man's instincts, murder is a hobby and a supreme pleasure.' Soon he and Brady were 'casing' banks and drawing up elaborate plans.

One day Brady asked him: 'Is there anyone you hate and want out of the way?'

Smith mentioned several names, including an old rival named Tony Latham. After some discussion, they settled on Tony Latham as the murder victim. But first, Brady explained, he would need a photograph. This was no problem. Smith had a polaroid camera, and he knew the pub where Latham drank. The next evening, Ian and Myra drove him to the pub, then drove away. Unfortunately, Smith had forgotten to insert the film, and when he went into the toilet to develop the photograph, found the camera empty.

When he went out to Wardle Brook Avenue to confess his failure, Brady seemed to take it casually enough. In reality he did not believe Smith was telling the truth and was alarmed. Now, suddenly, David Smith was a potential risk. If he had participated in the murder of Tony Latham, he would have been bound to Ian and Myra. Now Brady began to think seriously about removing him. Oddly enough, it was Myra who dissuaded him. 'It would hurt Mo' (Maureen).

On 26 December 1964, there was another murder. Like the others, this was planned in advance. Myra had arranged for her grandmother to stay the night with an uncle at Dukinfield. At about six o'clock that evening, she picked up 10-year-old Lesley Ann Downey at a fair in Hulme Hall Lane. In her 'confession' to Topping, Myra gave her own version of what happened. They took Lesley back to the house in Wardle Brook Avenue, and switched on a tape recorder. Myra claims that she was in the kitchen when she heard the child screaming. Brady was squeezing her neck and ordering her to take off her coat. Lesley was then made to undress, and to assume various pornographic poses, while Brady filmed her. On the tape, Myra can be heard ordering her to 'put it in, put it in tighter', presumably referring to the gag that appears in the photographs. Lesley screams and asks to be allowed to go home. At this point, Myra claims she was ordered to go and run a bath; she stayed in the bathroom until the water became cold. When she returned, Lesley had been strangled, and there was blood on her thighs. The following day they took the body to the moors and buried it.

In his open letter to the press, Brady denies that Myra played no active part in the murder. 'She insisted upon killing Lesley Ann Downey with her own hands, using a two foot length of silk cord, which she later used to enjoy toying with in public, in the secret knowledge of what it had been used for.'

Brady had killed approximately once every six months since July 1963: Pauline Reade, John Kilbride, Keith Bennett, Lesley Ann Downey. For some reason, July 1965 went by – as far as we know – without a further murder. But in September, Brady decided to kill out of sequence. The aim seems to have been to cement David Smith's membership of the 'gang' (which fairly certainly involved other people beside himself and Myra). According to Smith, during a drinking session on 25 September Brady asked Smith: 'Have you ever killed anybody? I have – three or four. The bodies are buried up on the moors.'

Two weeks later, on 6 October, Smith turned up at Wardle Brook Avenue – he was now living close by, in a council flat in Hattersley – hoping to borrow some money, but they were all broke. Brady had already suggested that they should rob an electricity board showroom, and the robbery had been planned for two days later. Smith's urgent need for money to pay the rent suggested that now was the time to 'cement' him beyond all possibility of withdrawal. (It seems unlikely that this robbery would involve only three of them – after all, Smith was totally inexperienced.)

Towards midnight, Myra called at her sister's flat with a message for their mother, then asked David Smith to walk her home. As he stood waiting in the kitchen – expecting to be offered a drink – there was a scream from the sitting room, and Myra called 'Dave, help him!' As Smith ran in, Ian Brady was hacking at the head of a youth who was lying on the floor. In spite of blow after blow, the youth continued to twist and scream. Finally, when he lay still, Brady pressed a cushion over the face and tied a cord around the throat to stop the gurgling noises. Brady handed Smith the hatchet. 'Feel the weight of that.' Smith's fingers left bloodstained prints on the handle.

Gran called down to ask what the noise was about, and Myra shouted that she had dropped a tape recorder on her foot.

When the room had been cleaned up, the body was carried upstairs between them – Brady commented: 'Eddie's a dead weight.' The victim was 17-year-old Edward Evans, who had been picked up in a pub that evening.

They all drank tea, while Myra reminisced about a policeman who had stopped to talk to her while Brady was burying a body. After this, Smith agreed to return with an old pram the next day, and help in the disposal of Edward Evans.

When he arrived home Smith was violently sick. And when he told Maureen what had happened, it was she who decided to go to the police.

At eight o'clock the next morning, a man dressed as a baker's roundsman knocked on the door of 16 Wardle Brook Avenue. Myra answered the door, still rubbing the sleep out of her eyes. The man identified himself as a police officer, and said he had reason to believe there was a body in the house. Brady was on the divan bed in the living room, writing a note to explain why he was not going to work that day. Upstairs, the police demanded to see into a locked room. When Myra said the key was at work, a policeman offered to go and fetch it. At this, Brady said: 'You'd better tell him. There was a row here last night. It's in there.' Under the window in the bedroom there was a plastic wrapped bundle. Two loaded revolvers were found in the same room.

David Smith told the police that Brady had stored two suitcases in the left luggage at Manchester Central Station, and these were recovered. (The cloakroom ticket was later found where Brady had described it – in the spine of a prayer book.) These proved to contain pornographic photographs – including nine of Lesley Ann Downey – the tape of Lesley Ann pleading to be allowed to leave, various books on sex and torture, and wigs, coshes and notes on robbing banks. Other photographs led them to dig on the moors, where the bodies of Lesley Ann Downey and John Kilbride were recovered.

On 6 May 1966, Ian Brady and Myra Hindley were both sentenced to life imprisonment. There had been no confession – this was to come many years later, Brady to the journalist Fred Harrison, and then Myra to Topping. At the time, Brady maintained that Lesley had been brought to the house by two men, who had taken her away after taking the photographs. It was not until July 1987 that Brady returned to the moor, under police escort, and tried – without success – to help locate the body of Keith Bennett. Pauline Reade had already been located, with the help of Myra's confession.

It is easy to understand why the Moors murders have 'tormented the psyche of a nation' for more than a quarter of a century. Like the Jack the Ripper murders, they seem to embody some of our worst nightmares about human cruelty. Brady has often been described as 'Britain's most hated murderer'. But our business is not to dwell on the horror, but to try to understand how it came about.

After she attended the trial, Pamela Hansford Johnson wrote a book about it called *On Iniquity*. Her argument was that Brady and Hindley seemed totally 'affectless', totally without feeling. This view sounds plausible enough until we recall that both killers had an enormous affection for animals, and that when she learned that her dog had died in police custody, Myra burst out: 'They're just a lot of bloody murderers.' She was equally upset by the death of her sister Maureen's baby. And Brady's affection for his mother and stepmother – as well as for Myra – indicates that he possessed the same human feelings as the rest of us. Harrison reveals that after the arrest, he did his best to dissociate Myra from the crimes.

In fact, from the criminological view, the main interest of the Moors case is that it reveals so clearly the basic psychological patterns of a certain type of antisocial behaviour.

One of the fundamental problems of human beings, particularly in adolescence, is to discover 'who they are'. The certainties of childhood are behind them; they face an adult world in which they have to play an active part. But unless they happen to be lucky enough to have clear 'role models', or to have acquired some basic enthusiasm (like art or science) in childhood or early teens, their identity remains a kind of blank, like a gap on a census form, waiting for someone to fill in a name.

In the case of a dominant male, the question is particularly acute. Biological studies have established that approximately one in twenty of any animal group is 'dominant' – that is, 5 per cent. The dominant 5 per cent are, on the whole, natural leaders. They crave a means of expressing their dominance. Those of purely physical dominance may establish a place in life by sheer force of personality. In childhood, Brady seems to have established this kind of dominance over his contemporaries. But in his teens, it ceased to be so simple. Fred Harrison comments: 'Ian Brady knew that he was special. He did not *feel* the same way as ordinary people . . .' The word 'outsider' turns up with monotonous regularity. An American serial killer, Douglas Clark, expressed it in another way: 'I march to a different drummer.'

Although Brady's background was less stressful than that of Panzram, it is clear that the two years in Borstal produced much the same effect as Panzram's early periods of imprisonment: a feeling that 'authority' was the enemy, and that the insult would not be forgotten or forgiven.

The years of his late teens, when he read Dostoevsky, Nietzsche, Sade, and *Mein Kampf*, were a period of intellectual ferment in which he seems to have begun to perceive the outline of his 'real identity'. The influence of *Mein Kampf* can hardly be underestimated. Even its title – my struggle – helps to explain the profound influence it still exercises among youthful right-wingers who would indignantly reject the label of 'Nazi thugs'. To these enthusiasts, it is a kind of archetypal Hollywood success story, the autobiography of an 'outsider' with all the cards stacked against him, who somehow succeeded in imposing his own vision on the world. And certainly, it is as impossible to deny Hitler's intelligence as to deny Brady's. Moreover, with his admiration of Goethe, Beethoven, Nietzsche, Wagner, it is also impossible to deny that he must be described as an 'idealist'.

The fly in the ointment is, of course, the racism. Any normally intelligent person knows that it is impossible to generalize about any racial group. Yet Hitler's 'conspiracy' theory about Zionism and Marxism looks plausible because there is undoubtedly an element of truth in it. Swallow that particular gnat, and you are ready to swallow the camel of antisemitism and black inferiority.

And then suddenly everything looks marvellously simple. It is merely necessary to embrace nationalism and racial purity to have a marvellously clear vision of a utopian society in which 'outsiders' are not suppressed and ignored.

This kind of oversimplification is not confined to 'fascists'. Bernard Shaw tells how, as a poverty-stricken young man, he attended a lecture by the socialist Henry George and bought a copy of his book *Progress and Poverty*. It had upon him exactly the same effect as *Mein Kampf* on Ian Brady.

> Thus a bee, desperately striving to reach a flower bed through a window pane, concludes that he is the victim of evil spirits or that he is mad, his end being exhaustion, despair and death. Yet if he only knew, there is nothing wrong with him; all he has to do is to go out as he came in, through the open window or door . . . Your born Communist begins like the bee on the pane. He worries himself and everybody else until he dies of peevishness, or is led by some propagandist pamphlet . . . to investigate the structure of our society. Immediately everything becomes clear to him. Property is theft; respectability founded on property is blasphemy; marriage founded on property is prostitution; it is easier for a camel to go through the eye of a needle than for a rich man to enter the kingdom of heaven. He now knows where he is, and where this society that has so intimidated him is.

Shaw swallowed socialism; Brady swallowed Nazism. As it happened, Shaw's socialism did not lead him to acts of violence because, as a born writer, he was an instinctive self-actualizer. But many members of Red Brigades and People's Liberation Armies use socialism as a justification for acts of violence, even murder – all in the name of the future utopia.

With *Mein Kampf*, Brady had a creed, but not an identity. It was the relationship with Myra that seems to have caused this to crystallize. The German jurist Rosenstock-Huessy said: 'Even a man who believes in nothing needs a girl to believe in him.' Quite apart from the sexual drive – which is usually overpowering in those of high dominance – the admiration of a member of the opposite sex is like a mirror in which a man can see his own face.

But the 'mirror' also represents a call to action, a demand that the dominant male should *assert* his identity. So far he may have been content to regard 'society' from a distance, the aloof outsider, happy to nurse his own sense of superiority, and to daydream of the world at his feet. But when a girl accepts his dominance, it becomes urgently necessary to *do* something to justify her admiration. The ideal would be something that brings instant wealth and fame.

Now, unlike Shaw, Brady he had no means of achieving this. Under different circumstances, he might have turned his latent rebelliousness to account in the manner of Sade and Jean Genet – in literature of defiance. Unfortunately, although highly articulate (and the winner of essay prizes at school) Brady had never seen himself as a writer. Neither had he ever developed any early enthusiasm – for science, for art, for acting – that might have offered an outlet for his frustrated energies. But the two years in Borstal had offered him a kind of identity: as a criminal. As he read Nietzsche and *Mein Kampf*, he conceived himself as a kind of samurai, one who stands out from society because of his self-discipline and will-power.

With Myra, a normal girl of medium dominance who regarded him as a superior being, the need for a 'project' became urgent. It had to be crime, but not petty crime: something more like the Great Train Robbery. And meanwhile, while he looked around for the right opportunity, the philosophy of crime had to be put into effect on a smaller scale.

The murder of Pauline Reade was clearly a watershed. He obviously regarded it as an act of self-creation, Nietzsche's 'how one becomes what one is'. It involved not only dominance and self-assertion, but also risk and danger – almost like Russian roulette. After the murder, there could be no doubt who he was: he was the man who had the courage to set himself apart from society, to do what others did not dare to do, to take a risk that might bring him to the gallows. (At that time there was still capital punishment in England.) Like Raskolnikov's murder, it was a 'definitive act', an act as meaningful as a monk's vows of renunciation or a general's attempt at a *coup d'état*. Now, in a sense, there could be no going back. The face that looks out of the police photograph seems to express that attitude: the eyes staring straight into the camera, the mouth firm but slightly contemptuous.

Yet in just over two years, an unexpected problem arose. Harrison records it in Brady's own words: 'I felt old at 26. Everything was ashes. I felt there was nothing of interest – nothing to hook myself onto. I had experienced everything.' Lord Byron had similarly declared that his early initiation into sex – by a maidservant at the age of 9 – was responsible for his later tendency to satiety and melancholy: 'having anticipated life'.

But the problem is simpler than that. Everyone is familiar with it. Experience is 'interesting' only in so far as we put a certain effort, a certain *attention*, into it. If I really want to enjoy an experience, the best way is to think about it in advance, to build up anticipation, so that when it actually happens, I give it my full and complete attention. If I approach my experience in a casual way, taking it for granted, it soon palls. If we do not wish to be subject to this law of diminishing returns, we have to put as much into experience as we get out of it. This explains the apparently irrational behaviour of saints and ascetics, starving themselves and sleeping on bare boards. A man who is starving finds a crust and a glass of water as delicious as the most expensive meal, because discomfort has *stretched* his attention. This stretching of attention is like stretching a spring, or pulling back a rifle bolt: it charges the mind with vital energy. And if he could learn this trick of 'stretching' his attention, he could enjoy everything with the same intensity, even at the age of 90. Conversely, a youth of 16 can experience boredom and satiety by habitually relaxing the attention, taking experience for granted.

Sex is a particularly interesting case in point. Because the appetite is so powerful, we assume that it is analogous to the appetite for food, which is basically physical. In fact, as we have seen, it is almost entirely 'mental', based on a sense of 'forbiddenness'. A man who badly wants a girl can work up an 'appetite' so powerful that she seems like a goddess, an embodiment of the eternal feminine, and the very thought of possessing her produces a foretaste of ecstasy. But because sex contains such a large mental component, it can collapse into boredom if the element of 'preparedness', of focused attention, is neglected.

Sex crime is particularly subject to this law of diminishing returns. Just as the starving man imagines that three good meals a day would leave him totally satisfied, just as the tramp imagines that a country cottage would make him blissfully happy, so a sex-starved man imagines that a certain sexual abundance would bring total fulfilment. All three are mistaken, because as soon as one level of need is fulfilled, another opens up.

In Brady's case, the problem was complicated by the need to

crystallize a sense of identity and purpose – Maslow's self-esteem level. He was intelligent, determined, strong-willed – but was not sure what to *do* with these qualities – a situation that must have reminded him of one of his favourite fictional characters, Dostoevsky's Stavrogin in *The Possessed*. At the age of 23, Brady urgently needed a 'project'. And the only project he had been trained in was crime.

Matters were further complicated by his almost Wordsworthian mysticism about nature. (He has stated that *The Prelude* is one of his favourite poems.) Harrison describes how, when he wanted to talk about the murders, Brady only wanted to tell him about a childhood trip to Oban and Tobermory, which he had found enchanting. He also records that David Smith had difficulty in sharing Brady's sense of beauty in miles of black peat moors. Such an obsession obviously belongs to Maslow's self-actualizing level. And what distinguishes the self-actualizer – or 'outsider' – is a tormented need for self-expression.

In short, Ian Brady was a powder-keg waiting to explode. All that was needed was a match. Myra Hindley provided the match; the moment he met her, *some* kind of violence became inevitable.

The reason for this lies in the psychology of what has been called *folie à deux*. In most murders involving two killers – other cases are Leopold and Loeb and Fernandez and Beck – there is almost invariably a leader and a follower, one of high dominance, one of medium dominance.

Maslow was also one of the first to grasp the immense significance of patterns of dominance behaviour. It all sprang from his observation of monkeys in the Bronx zoo in the mid-1930s. He was at this time puzzling about the relative merits of Freud and Adler: Freud with his view that all neurosis is sexual in origin, Adler with his belief that man's life is a fight against the feeling of inferiority, and that his mainspring is his 'will-to-power'. In the Bronx zoo, he was struck by the dominance behaviour of the monkeys and by the non-stop sex. He was puzzled that sexual behaviour seemed so indiscriminate: males mounted females or other males; females mounted other females and even males. There was also a distinct 'pecking order', the more dominant monkeys bullying the less dominant. There seemed to be as much evidence for Freud's theory as for Adler's. Then, one day, a revelation burst upon Maslow. Monkey sex *looked* indiscriminate because the more dominant monkeys mounted the less dominant ones, whether male or female. Maslow concluded, therefore, that Adler was right and Freud was wrong – about this matter at least.

Since dominance behaviour seemed to be the key to monkey psychology, Maslow wondered how far this applied to human beings. He decided to study dominance behaviour in human beings and, since he was a young and heterosexual male, decided that he would prefer to study women rather than men. Besides, he felt that women were usually more honest when it came to talking about their private lives. In 1936, he began a series of interviews with college women; his aim was to find out whether sex and dominance are related. He quickly concluded that they were.

The women tended to fall into three distinct groups: high-dominance, medium-dominance and low-dominance, the high-dominance group being the smallest of the three. High-dominance women tended to be promiscuous and to enjoy sex for its own sake – in a manner we tend to regard as distinctly masculine. They were more likely to masturbate, sleep with different men, and have lesbian experiences. Medium-dominance women were basically romantics; they might have a strong sex drive, but their sexual experience was usually limited. They were looking for 'Mr Right', the kind of man who would bring them flowers and take them out for dinner in restaurants with soft lights and sweet music. Low-dominance women seemed actively to dislike sex, or to think of it as an unfortunate necessity for producing children. One low-dominance woman with a high sex drive refused to permit her husband sexual intercourse because she disliked children. Low-dominance women tended to be prudes who were shocked at nudity and regarded the male sexual organ as disgusting. (High-dominance women thought it beautiful.)

Their choice of males was dictated by the dominance group. High-dominance women liked high-dominance males, the kind who would grab them and hurl them on a bed. They seemed to like their lovers to be athletic, rough and unsentimental. Medium-dominance women liked kindly, home-loving males, the kind who smoke a pipe and look calm and reflective. They would prefer a romantic male, but were prepared to settle for a hard worker of reliable habits. Low-dominance women were distrustful of all males, although they usually wanted children and recognized that a man had to be pressed into service for this purpose. They preferred the kind of gentle, shy man who would admire them from a distance for years without daring to speak.

But Maslow's most interesting observation was that *all* the women, in all dominance groups, preferred a male who was slightly more dominant than themselves. One very high-dominance woman spent years looking for a man of superior dominance – meanwhile having many affairs; and once she found him, married him and lived happily ever after. However, she enjoyed picking fights with him, provoking him to violence that ended in virtual rape; and this sexual experience she found the most satisfying of all. Clearly, even this man was not *quite* dominant enough, and she was provoking him to an artificially high level of dominance.

The rule seemed to be that, for a permanent relationship, a man and woman needed to be in the same dominance group. Medium-dominance women were nervous of high-dominance males, and low-dominance women were terrified of medium-dominance males. As to the males, they might well show a sexual interest in a woman of a lower dominance group, but it would not survive the act of seduction. A medium-dominance woman might be superficially attracted by a high-dominance male; but on closer acquaintance she would find him brutal and unromantic. A high-dominance male might find a medium-dominance female 'beddable', but closer acquaintance would reveal her as rather uninteresting, like an unseasoned meal. To achieve a personal relationship, the two would need to be in the same dominance group. Maslow even devised psychological tests to discover whether the 'dominance gap' between a man and a woman was of the right size to form the basis of a permanent relationship.

It was some time after writing a book about Maslow (*New Pathways in Psychology*, published in 1972) that it dawned on me that this matter of the 'dominance gap' threw an interesting light on many cases of partnership in crime. The first case of the sort to arouse my curiosity was that of Albert T. Patrick, a scoundrelly New York lawyer who, in 1900, persuaded a manservant named Charles Jones to kill his employer with chloroform. Jones had been picked out of the gutter by his employer, a rich old man named William Rice, and had every reason to be grateful to him. Yet he quickly came under Patrick's spell and took part in the plot to murder and defraud. The plot misfired; both were arrested. The police placed them in adjoining cells. Patrick handed Jones a knife saying 'You cut your throat first and I'll follow . . .' Jones was so completely under Patrick's domination that he did not even pause to wonder how Patrick would get the knife back. A gurgling noise alerted the police, who were able to foil the attempted suicide. Patrick was sentenced to death but was eventually pardoned and released.

How did Patrick achieve such domination? There was no sexual link between them, and he was not blackmailing Jones. But what becomes very clear from detailed accounts of the case is that Patrick was a man of extremely high dominance, while Jones was quite definitely of medium dominance. It was Patrick's combination of charm and dominance that exerted such a spell.

It struck me that in many cases of duo-murder (partnership in murder), one of the partners is usually high-dominance and the other medium – as already noted, Loeb and Leopold even referred to themselves as 'master and slave'. It is true that the Lonely Hearts murders – Fernandez and Beck – are slightly less simple: Fernandez *was* the dominant one of the pair, with his belief that he could hypnotize women and seduce them by magic; yet it was Martha who dragged him into murder. And in the Moors case, Myra's chin alone reveals that she was a woman of fairly high dominance, so Brady's claim that she took an active role in the murders sounds plausible. Yet it is still perfectly obvious that Brady was the dominant one, and that Myra was putty in his hands.

The simple truth seems to be that in most cases of *folie à deux*, neither partner would be capable of murder if it were not for the stimulus of the other. Some strange chemical reaction seems to occur, like a mixture of nitric acid and glycerine that makes nitroglycerine.

One of the most interesting examples of the syndrome was the Thurneman case, which occurred in Sweden in the 1930s. Dr Sigvard Thurneman was a psychiatrist – and a hypnotist – who saw himself as a kind of Professor Moriarty. Between 1930 and 1936, a series of robberies and murders occurred in the area of Sala, near Stockholm. A man named Eriksson was found shot in a frozen lake. A wealthy mining official named Kjellberg was found, together with his housekeeper, in his burnt home, shot in the head, and a safe full of wages had been forced. A woman named Blomqvist was found in her burnt home, her jewellery missing. But when, in June 1936, a quarryman carrying the payroll was murdered, an elderly man heard the shot, and saw an American car driving away.

Newspaper publicity led the thieves to panic and abandon the car by the roadside; it then became clear that its number plates had been altered by a professional. This man was tracked down in a routine investigation of garages, and implicated his employer, a man named Hedstrom. Hedstrom denied it, but as soon as the police left, rang a number in Stockholm – Dr Sigvard Thurneman. The police had tapped his phone, and went to call on Thurneman – a young man in his late twenties with a receding chin and a high forehead, not unlike the pictures of Moriarty. He flatly denied knowing anything about the crimes.

It was Hedstrom who decided to confess, when one of the murder guns was found in his garage. He and Thurneman had met at the University of Uppsala, where Thurneman had been fascinated by hypnosis and occultism. Thurneman had also spent a great deal of time planning 'perfect crimes'. The first victim, Eriksson, had become one of Thurneman's patients, and had been regularly hypnotized for nervous problems. He had agreed to take part in a robbery, but had changed his mind at the last moment; this is why he had been killed. A number of crimes – including the murders and several robberies – had then been committed by Hedstrom and other patients of Thurneman.

Faced with Hedstrom's confession, Thurneman decided to tell everything. He even wrote an autobiography in prison, telling the whole incredible story of his domination of the gang by hypnosis. It might be used by Adlerian psychologists as a classic demonstration of the way that physical inferiority – Thurneman was a sickly and undersized child – can lead to over-compensation. Thurneman had studied yoga, then occultism, and finally become a cult leader. He seduced underage girls under hypnosis then disposed of them in the white slave trade. A bisexual, he caused one of his male lovers to commit suicide by hypnotic suggestion. He induced a deep trance in another gang member and injected a fatal dose of poison.

His aim was to become a millionaire and retire to South America, and at the time of his arrest he was planning to rob a Stockholm bank by blowing it open with a huge quantity of dynamite.

Thurneman and four accomplices were sentenced to life imprisonment, but Thurneman soon became unmistakably insane, and was transferred to a criminal lunatic asylum.

Here we have a very clear parallel with the Brady case – in some ways, Thurneman was what Brady might have hoped to become, if his career had not been cut short by David Smith's decision to go to the police.

A curiously similar case took place in Copenhagen in 1951, when a man named Palle Hardrup killed two bank officials in the course of an unsuccessful hold-up. The police were tipped off that the real killer was a man named Bjorn Nielsen, who had absolute and total control of Hardrup, whom he had met in prison. Faced with Nielsen in the police interrogation room, Hardrup seemed to go into a trance, in which he insisted that Nielsen had nothing to do with the crime. But a policeman noticed that Nielsen was holding up two crossed fingers. Hardrup's wife also stated that Nielsen had gained total ascendancy over her husband, and that he had done this through hypnosis. She told how Nielsen had stripped her and flogged her with a leather belt, while her normally admiring husband looked on.

In police custody, Hardrup periodically improved – until he received a letter from Nielsen signed with an X, at which he would revert to his trance-like insistence that he alone was guilty. A police psychiatrist was able to establish that Hardrup had been hypnotically conditioned to go into a trance when he saw an X.

Finally, kept away from Nielsen – and Xs – Hardrup suddenly demanded paper, and wrote a confession describing how Nielsen had become his 'master' through hypnosis, and now, under Nielsen's orders, he had committed an earlier robbery and handed Nielsen the complete proceeds – £5,000. The police were able to establish that this had been paid into Nielsen's bank the day after the robbery.

In court, with Nielsen's blazing eyes fixed upon him, Hardrup withdrew his confession, but the jury – who had noted this change of demeanour – decided that Nielsen was the real culprit, and sentenced him to life imprisonment. Hardrup was placed in a psychiatric hospital.

In these two cases involving hypnosis, we seem to be in the presence of the archetypal criminal daydream: to be able to commit crime by proxy, and to have complete control of the human robot who is the instrument of the super-criminal. The assumption that underlies the daydream is expressed by Harry Lime, in Graham Greene's *The Third Man*, in the scene on the Big Wheel in Vienna. When the hero reproaches him with selling adulterated life-saving drugs that actually cause death, Lime points to the people 'moving like black flies' on the ground, and asks: 'Would you really feel any pity if one of those dots stopped moving for ever? If I said you can have twenty thousand pounds for every dot that stops, would you really tell me to keep my money?' Sade's argument is basically identical: human beings are fundamentally selfish. We cannot feel love – or even interest – towards people we have never met. So why pretend that all men are brothers? Why not accept the truth: that we all care for 'number one', and only care for others in so far as it suits us?

There is an obvious element of truth in this, or someone as intelligent as Sade – or Brady – would not have been taken in by it. But it misses the essential point. Self-actualization is basically about the *control of consciousness*. It brings a curious sense of power over oneself, and an awareness of the immense *meaningfulness* of the external world. Such moments bring the recognition that our usual notions about consciousness are based on a misconception: upon the notion that consciousness proceeds automatically, like a television picture, and that the 'you' that watches it is essentially *passive*. Moments of intensity – and even the sexual orgasm must be included – make us aware that we are 'in control': that we can alter the brightness, the colour, even the speed at which it moves. We are affected by great music, great poetry, great art, because the artist has somehow learned the trick of inducing these moods of intensity and control. It is as if he has changed a black-and-white picture on television into colour.

Now, as Sade noted, there are other ways of achieving this sense of control. One of them is sex. Another is manipulating other people. Even eating and drinking can bring this sensation of heightened control. (It is significant that when Sade was confined to the lunatic asylum, he overate until he became enormous.) When human beings have discovered some method of inducing the feeling, they tend to repeat it over and over again, like a laboratory rat pushing at the lever that releases its food. This is obviously the key to sex crime – it involves a feeling of power, followed by a feeling of peace. This is the reason that politicians cling so obsessively to power. This is the reason that actors love to feel their power over an audience. This is the reason that juvenile delinquents steal cars and drive at ninety miles an hour. All these are simply attempts to achieve that sense of power and control that is achieved far more fully in the moment of self-actualization. And the moment of self-actualization makes all the short-cuts seem irrelevant – in fact, absurd and unnecessary.

The problem is that, as a method of self-actualization, crime is counterproductive. Self-actualization brings a sense of fullness, of relaxation, of harmony, in which past brutalities and stupidities are seen simply as shameful mistakes that demand an apology. Therefore, the basic law of moral common sense is never to do anything that will block your evolution, just as it is physical common sense not to ruin your health for the sake of some temporary pleasure. Sex killers like Rees, Brady and – as we shall see – Bundy have reached a conscious decision that their personal evolution demands certain 'forbidden' pleasures. They also believe, like Ibsen's Norah in *A Doll's House*, that personal evolution is so important that all rival demands can be ignored with a good conscience. From the psychological point of view, what is interesting about this decision is that it bears a generic resemblance to the decision often taken by men of genius in their youth – that self-development involves ignoring the demands of family and society, and pursuing the path of the 'loner'. Such loners usually justify themselves by pointing to other loners who have finally 'succeeded' by ignoring the demands of society (Nietzsche's 'herd') – from saints and yogis to drunken painters and self-destructive poets. What they fail to grasp is the law of compensation by which violence towards others is oddly counterproductive. In practice, as we can see in case after case of serial murder, it amounts to violence towards oneself. This is the real objection to crime: not a religious or moral objection, but a psychological one: it is a process of self-destruction.

One of the most sensational unsolved cases of the 1960s might serve as an illustration of this peculiar mechanism.

Between February 1964 and January 1965, the bodies of six women – mostly prostitutes – were found in areas not far from the Thames. The first of the bodies, that of a 30-year-old prostitute named Hanna Tailford, was found in the water near Hammersmith bridge. She was naked except for her stockings, and her panties had been stuffed into her mouth. Her jaw was bruised, but this could have resulted from a fall. On 18 April, the naked body of Irene Lockwood, a 26-year-old prostitute, was found at Duke's Meadows, near Barnes Bridge, not far from the place where Hanna Tailford had been found. She had been strangled, and, like Hanna Tailford, she had been pregnant. A 54-year-old Kensington caretaker, Kenneth Archibald, confessed to her murder, and he seemed to know a great deal about the girl; but at his trial, it was established that his confession was false, and he was acquitted. There was another reason for believing in his innocence; while he was still in custody, another naked girl was found in an alleyway at Osterley Park, Brentford. This was only three weeks after the discovery of Irene Lockwood's body. The dead girl – the only one among the victims who could be described as pretty – was identified as a 22-year-old prostitute and striptease artist, Helen Barthelemy. There were a number of curious features in the case. A line around her waist showed that her panties had been removed after death, and there was no evidence of normal sexual assault. But four of her front teeth were missing. Oddly enough, the teeth had not been knocked out by a blow, but deliberately forced out; a piece of one of them was found lodged in her throat. Medical investigation also revealed the presence of male sperm in her throat. Here, then, was the cause of death; she had been choked by a penis, probably in the course of performing an act of fellatio. The missing teeth suggested that the killer had repeated the assault after death. It was established that she had disappeared some days before her body was found.

Where, then, had her body been kept? Flakes of paint found on her skin suggested the answer, for it was the type of paint used in spraying cars. Clearly, the body had been kept somewhere near a car spraying plant, but in some place where it was not likely to be discovered by the workers.

The 'nude murders' became a public sensation, for it now seemed likely that they were the work of one man. Enormous numbers of police were deployed in the search for the spray-shop, and in an attempt to keep a closer watch on the areas in which the three victims had been picked up – around Notting Hill and Shepherds Bush. Perhaps for this reason, the killer decided to take no risks for several months.

The body of the fourth victim – Mary Fleming, aged 30 – found on 14 July, confirmed that the same man was probably responsible for all four murders. Her false teeth were missing; there was sperm in her throat; and her skin showed traces of the same spray paint. She had vanished three days earlier.

Her body was found, in a half-crouching position, near a garage in Acton, and the van was actually seen leaving the scene of the crime. A motorist driving past Berrymede Road, a cul-de-sac, at 5.30 in the morning, had to brake violently to avoid a van that shot out in front of him. He was so angry that he contacted the police to report the incident. If he had made a note of the van number, the nude case would have been solved. A squad car that arrived a few minutes later found the body of Mary Fleming in the forecourt of a garage in the cul-de-sac.

The near-miss probably alarmed the killer, for no more murders occurred that summer. Then, on 25 November 1964, another naked body was found under some debris on a car park at Hornton Street, Kensington. She was identified as Margaret McGowan, 21, a Scot. Under the name Frances Brown, she had been called as a witness in the trial of Stephen Ward, and Ludovic Kennedy described her (in his book on the trial) as a small, bird-like woman with a pale face and fringe. Margaret McGowan had disappeared more than a month before her body was found, and there were signs of decomposition. Again, there were traces of paint, and a missing front tooth indicated that she had died in the same way as the previous two victims.

The last of the stripper's victims was a prostitute named Bridie O'Hara, 28. She was found on 16 February 1965, in some undergrowth on the Heron Trading Estate, in Acton.

She had last been seen on 11 January in the Shepherds Bush Hotel. The body was partly mummified, which indicated that it had been kept in a cool place. As usual, teeth were missing, and sperm was found in the throat. Fingermarks on the back of her neck revealed that, like the other victims, she had died in a kneeling position, bent over the killer's lap.

Detective Chief Superintendent John du Rose was recalled from his holiday to take charge of the investigation in the Shepherds Bush area. The Heron Trading Estate provided the lead they had been waiting for. Investigation of a paint spray shop revealed that this was definitely the source of the paint found on the bodies – chemical analysis proved it. The proximity of a disused warehouse solved the question of where the bodies had lain before they were dumped. The powerful spray guns caused the paint to carry, with diminishing intensity, for several hundred yards. Analysis of paint on the bodies enabled experts to establish the spot where the women must have been concealed: it was underneath a transformer in the warehouse.

Yet even with this discovery, the case was far from solved. Thousands of men worked on the Heron Trading Estate. (Oddly enough Christie had been employed there.) Mass questioning seemed to bring the police no closer to their suspect. Du Rose decided to throw an immense twenty-mile cordon around the area, to keep a careful check on all cars passing through at night. Drivers who were observed more than once were noted; if they were seen more than twice, they were interviewed. Du Rose conducted what he called 'a war of nerves' against the killer, dropping hints in the press or on television that indicated the police were getting closer. They knew he drove a van; they knew he must have right of access to the trading estate by night. The size of the victims – who were all short women – suggested that the killer was under middle height. As the months passed, and no further murders took place, du Rose assumed that he was winning the war of nerves. The killer had ceased to operate. He checked on all men who had been jailed since mid-February, all men with prison records who had been hospitalized, all men who had died or committed suicide. In his book *Murder Was My Business*, du Rose claims that a list of twenty suspects had been reduced to three when one of the three committed suicide. He left a note saying that he could not bear the strain any longer.

The man was a security guard who drove a van, and had access to the estate. At the time when the women were murdered, his rounds included the spray shop. He worked by night, from 10 p.m. to 6 a.m. He was unmarried.

Another serial killer of the 1960s provides an interesting – and virtually unique – illustration of the same mechanism.

Between June 1962 and January 1964 the city of Boston, Massachusetts was terrorized by a series of murders that achieved worldwide publicity. The unknown killer, who strangled and sexually abused his victims, became known as the Boston Strangler. The first six victims were elderly women, whose ages ranged from 55 to 85.

On 4 June 1962 55-year-old Anna Slesers was found in her apartment in the Back Bay area of Boston. She had been knocked unconscious with a blunt instrument – later determined to be a lead weight – and then strangled. The body, clad only in an open housecoat, was lying on its back with the legs apart. No semen was found in the vagina, but she had evidently been sexually assaulted with some hard object such as a soda bottle. The apartment had been ransacked.

Two weeks later on 30 June, 68-year-old Nina Nichols failed to call back a friend after a telephone conversation had been interrupted by a ring at the doorbell. The friend asked the janitor to check her apartment. Nina Nichols was lying on the bedroom floor, strangled with a stocking, her legs open in a rape position. Her killer had also bitten her. Medical examination revealed that she had been sexually assaulted with a wine bottle after death. There was semen on her thighs, but not in the vagina.

Two days later, on Monday 2 July, neighbours of a 65-year-old retired nurse named Helen Blake, who lived in Lynn, north of Boston, became anxious at not having seen her for two days, and sent for the police. Helen Blake was lying face downwards on her bed, a stocking knotted around her throat. Again, there was dried semen on her thighs but not in the vagina. Mrs Blake had apparently been killed on the previous Saturday, the same day as Nina Nichols.

On 21 August Mrs Ida Irga, 75, was found dead in her apartment. Death was due to manual strangulation, after which a pillow case had been tied round her neck. She had been sexually assaulted with some hard object, and bitten. It was estimated that she had been dead for two days.

The last of the elderly victims was 67-year-old Jane Sullivan, another nurse. She was found in a kneeling position in the bathtub, her face in six inches of water. She was a powerful Irishwoman, and had evidently put up a tremendous fight – her assailant must have been very strong to overpower her. Two stockings were knotted around her neck. She had been killed on the day after Ida Irga, but the body was not found for more than a week; consequently it was impossible to determine whether she had been raped, but she had been sexually assaulted with a broom handle.

Boston was in a state of hysteria, but as weeks went by without further stranglings, it slowly subsided. A hot summer was succeeded by a very cold winter. In the early evening of 5 December 1962 two girls rang the doorbell of the apartment they shared with a 20-year-old black girl, Sophie Clark, and were surprised when she failed to answer. They let themselves in, and found Sophie lying on the floor; she was naked and in the rape position. She had been strangled with nylon stockings knotted round her neck. Medical examination established that she had been raped, and a semen stain on the carpet beside the body indicated that her killer had later masturbated over her. This was the first case in which rape was unquestionably established, and it led to the speculation that her killer was a second Boston Strangler, one who preferred young girls.

Three weeks later, on the last day of 1962, a businessman stopped his car outside the apartment of his secretary at 515 Park Drive and blew his horn. When she failed to come down, he assumed that she had already left, but when he found that she was not at the office, he rang the superintendant of her apartment building to ask him to check on her apartment. Patricia Bissette, 23, was lying in bed, covered with the bedclothes. She had been strangled with stockings, and medical examination established that she had been raped.

On 18 February 1963 a German girl named Gertrude Gruen survived an attack by the Strangler. A powerfully built man with a beaky nose, about five feet eight inches tall, knocked on her door and told her he had been sent to do work in her apartment. She was suffering from a virus, and only allowed him in after some argument. The man removed his coat and told her that she was pretty enough to be a model. Then he told her she had dust on the back of her dressing gown; she turned, and he hooked a powerful arm round her neck. She fought frantically, and sank her teeth into his hand until they bit to the bone. The man pushed her away, and as she began to scream, he ran out of the apartment.

The police were excited when the girl reported the attack – and then frustrated when they discovered that the shock had wiped all traces of the Strangler's face from her memory.

A month later, on 9 March 1963, the Strangler killed another elderly victim. Sixty-nine-year-old Mrs Mary Brown lived in Lawrence, an industrial town twenty-five miles from Boston. The fact that her breasts had been exposed and a fork stuck in one of them should have suggested that she had been murdered by the 'Phantom' (as the press had now labelled the killer). However, because her skull had been beaten to a pulp with a piece of brass piping, she was not recognized as a Strangler victim – it was assumed that she had disturbed a burglar. In fact, she had been manually throttled.

The next victim was also nontypical. On 9 May 1963 a friend of 23-year-old graduate student Beverly Sams was puzzled when she failed to answer the telephone, and borrowed a key from the building supervisor. Beverly had been stabbed in the throat, and a stocking knotted around her neck. She was naked, and her legs spreadeagled and tied to the bed supports. Medical examination revealed that she had been raped.

Four months later, on 8, September friends of 58-year-old divorcee, Evelyn Corbin, wondered why she failed to keep a lunch appointment and let themselves into her flat. Evelyn Corbin was lying almost naked on the bed, nylon stockings knotted around her throat and her panties rammed into her mouth. There was semen in her vagina and in her mouth.

On 23 November 1963, the day President Kennedy was assassinated, the Strangler killed his next victim in Lawrence. She was Joanne Graff, a Sunday school teacher. She had been strangled with stockings and raped.

The final victim was strangled on 4 January 1964. She was 19-year-old Mary Sullivan, who was found by room-mates when they came back from work. She was sitting on the bed, her buttocks on the pillow, her back against the headboard. Her knees had been parted, and a broom handle inserted into her vagina. Semen was running from the corner of her mouth. A card saying 'Happy New Year' had been propped against her foot. The killer had placed her body in a position where it would be seen as soon as anyone opened the door.

The murders ceased; but a rapist who became known as The Green Man – because he wore green clothes – began operating over a wide area that included Massachusetts, Connecticut, New Hampshire and Rhode Island. On one occasion he raped four women in a single day. He gained entrance to the apartment – sometimes forcing the lock with a strip of plastic – and often threatened the victim with a knife. When she was stripped, he would caress her with his hands and mouth; then, if he judged she wanted him to, he 'raped' her. (He was later to insist that the 'Green Man' had never raped an unwilling woman.) He was never physically violent, and had even been known to apologize before he left.

On the morning of 27 October 1964 a young married woman was dozing in bed after her husband had gone to work when a man entered the bedroom. He was dressed in green trousers, a green shirt, and wore green sunglasses, and he insisted that he was a detective. After seizing her by the throat he threatened her with a knife. He tore off her nightclothes, stuffed a pair of panties into her mouth, and tied her wrists and ankles to the bedposts. Then he kissed and bit her from head to foot, finally ejaculating on her stomach. His sexual appetite was obviously enormous; he continued to abuse her sexually for a great deal longer before he seemed satisfied. Then, after apologizing, he left. The girl called the police immediately, and went on to describe her assailant in such detail that a police artist was able to make a sketch of his face. As one of the detectives was studying it, he commented: 'This looks like the Measuring Man.' The 'Measuring Man' had been a harmless crank named Albert DeSalvo, who had been arrested in 1960 for talking his way into girls' apartments claiming to represent a modelling agency. If the girl indicated that she might be interested in modelling, he would take her measurements with a tape measure. After that he would thank her politely and leave. The aspiring model would never hear from him again, and it was this that made some of them so indignant that they reported him. The police were baffled, since there seemed to be no obvious motive – although some girls admitted that they had allowed him to raise their skirts to measure from the hip to the knee. On a few occasions, he had allowed himself an intimate caress; but if the girl protested, he immediately apologized. One girl, as he crouched with his hand on her panties, had said: 'I'd better get these clothes off or you won't get the right measurements,' and stripped. On this occasion, as on a number of others, the 'Measuring Man' had ended up in bed with the girl.

On 17 March 1960 a police patrol that had been set up to trap the 'Measuring Man' saw a man acting suspiciously in a backyard in Cambridge, Mass., and arrested him. Girls identified him as the 'Measuring Man', and he finally admitted it – claiming that he did it as a kind of lark, in order to make himself feel superior to college-educated girls. In May 1961 DeSalvo was sentenced to serve two years in the Middlesex County House of Correction. He served eleven months before being released. He had told a probation officer that he thought there was something wrong with him – that he seemed to be wildly oversexed, so that he needed intercourse six or more times a day. No one suggested that he needed to see a psychiatrist.

Albert DeSalvo had clearly graduated from caressing girls as he measured them to rape. He was arrested on 5 November 1964 and identified by some of his victims. On 4 February 1965 he was committed to the Bridgewater State Hospital, a mental institution in Massachusetts.

Bridgewater had – and still has – many sexual psychopaths in residence, and many spoke freely about their exploits, particularly in the group therapy sessions. Albert DeSalvo was not reticent about his own sexual prowess, which was apparently considerable. He described how, in the summer of 1948, when he was 17, he had worked as a dishwasher in a Cape Cod motel, and spent much time swimming and sunbathing on the beach. There were many college girls there, and they found the powerfully built youth attractive. Word of DeSalvo's amazing sexual prowess soon spread. 'They would even come up to the motel sometimes looking for me and some nights we would spend the whole night doing it down on the beach, stopping for a while, then doing it again . . .'

Possibly because he encountered a certain scepticism – he had a reputation as a boaster – DeSalvo began hinting that he had done far more serious things than raping a few women. Only one of his ward-mates took him seriously: a murderer called George Nassar. At first, Nassar also thought DeSalvo was merely boasting – particularly when he confided that he was the Boston Strangler. What finally convinced him was DeSalvo's detailed knowledge of the crimes. 'He knows more about them stranglings than the cops.'

Nassar knew there was a large reward for the Boston Strangler, and he spoke to his attorney, F. Lee Bailey, who had achieved fame when he obtained freedom for Dr Sam Sheppard, accused of murdering his wife. Bailey was also sceptical – there are endless fake confessions to almost every widely publicized murder – but when he went to see DeSalvo on 4 March 1965, he soon realized that this sounded authentic. DeSalvo was not a man of high intelligence – although bright and articulate – and it seemed unlikely that he could have read and memorized newspaper accounts of the murders. He even mentioned a murder that no one knew about – an old lady of 80 or so who had died of a heart attack as he grabbed her. In fact, DeSalvo's account enabled the police to identify her as 85 year-old Mary Mullens who had been found dead in her Boston apartment two weeks after the murder of Anna Slesers, the first Strangler victim. DeSalvo's descriptions of other murder scenes made it clear that he knew details that had never been published. Most important of all, he knew exactly what the Strangler had done to various victims. This information had been deliberately suppressed, giving rise to all kind of wild rumours of torture and perversion. DeSalvo knew, for example, precisely what position Mary Sullivan – the last victim – had been left in, and that she had a broom handle inserted into her vagina; and he was able to describe in precise detail the rooms of most of the victims.

There were some odd complications. Several witnesses who had seen a man entering apartment buildings where stranglings had taken place failed to identify DeSalvo as the man. And two women who had seen the Strangler – including Gertrude Gruen, the German girl who had fought him off – not only failed to identify DeSalvo, but identified George Nassar as the strangler. Yet DeSalvo's incredibly detailed knowledge of the crimes finally convinced most of those involved with the case that he alone was the Boston Strangler.

In the long run, all this proved irrelevant. Albert DeSalvo stood trial for the Green Man rapes, and in 1967 was sentenced to permanent detention in the Walpole State Prison, where he could receive psychiatric treatment. On 26 November 1973 DeSalvo was found dead in his cell, stabbed through the heart.

No motive was ever established, and whoever was responsible was never caught.

In January 1964, while the Boston Strangler was still at large, the assistant attorney-general of Massachusetts, John S. Bottomly, decided to set up a committee of psychiatrists to attempt to establish some kind of 'psychological profile' of the killer. One of the psychiatrists who served on that committee was Dr James A. Brussel, the man who had been so successful in describing New York's 'Mad Bomber'. When he attended his first meeting, Brussel discovered that there was a sharp division of opinion within the committee. One group believed that there were two stranglers, one of whom killed old women, and the other young girls; the other group thought there was only one strangler.

It was at his second meeting of the committee – in April 1965 – that Brussel was hit by a sudden 'hunch' as he listened to a psychiatrist pointing out that in some cases, semen was found in the vagina, while in others it was found on the breasts, thighs, or even on the carpet. When it came to his turn to speak, Brussel outlined the theory that had suddenly come to him 'in a flash'.

'I think we're dealing with one man. The apparent differences in M.O., I believe, result from changes that have been going on in this man. Over the two-year period during which he has been committing these murders, he had gone through a series of upheavals . . .'

The first five victims, said Brussel, were elderly women, and there was no semen in the vaginas. They had been manipulated in other ways – 'a type of sexual molestation that might be expected of a small boy, not a man'. A boy gets over his sexual obsession with his mother, and transfers his interest to girls of his own age. 'The Strangler . . . achieved this transfer – achieved emotional puberty – in a matter of months.' Now he wanted to achieve orgasm inside younger women. And with the final victim, Mary Sullivan, the semen was in her mouth and over her breasts; a broom had been inserted in the vagina. The Strangler was making a gesture of triumph and of defiance: 'I throw my sex in your face.'

This man, said Brussel, was a physically powerful individual, probably in his late twenties or early thirties, the time the paranoid reaction reaches its peak. He hazarded a guess that the

Strangler's nationality was Italian or Spanish, since garrotting is a method used by bandits in both countries.

Brussel's final 'guesses' were startlingly to the point. He believed that the Strangler had stopped killing because he had worked it out of his system. He had, in effect, grown up. And he would finally be caught because he would be unable to resist talking about his crimes and his new-found maturity.

The rest of the committee was polite but sceptical. But one year later, Brussel was proved correct when DeSalvo began admitting to George Nassar that he was the Boston Strangler.

In 1966, Brussel went to Boston to interview DeSalvo. He had been half-expecting a misshapen monster, and was surprised to be greeted by a good-looking, polite young man with a magnificent head of dark hair. (Brussel had even foretold that the Strangler would have well-tended hair, since he was obsessed by the impression he made on women.) Brussel found him charming, and soon realized how DeSalvo had talked his way into so many apartments; he seemed a thoroughly nice young man. Then what had turned him into a murderer? As usual, it proved to be the family and childhood background. DeSalvo's father was the worst kind of brute. He beat his wife and children mercilessly – on one occasion he broke his wife's fingers one by one. He beat one son with a hosepipe so badly – for knocking over a box of fruit – that the boy was not allowed on the beach all summer because he was covered in black and yellow bruises. He often brought a prostitute home and had sex with her in front of the children. Their mother was also less than satisfactory. She was indifferent and self-preoccupied, and had no time for the children. As a child Albert had been a 'loner', his only real friend a dog that lived in a junkyard. He developed sadistic compulsions at an early age. He and a playmate called Billy used to place a dog and cat in two compartments of an orange crate and starve them for days, then pull out the partition, and watch as the cat scratched out the dog's eyes. But, like so many psychopaths (Albert Fish and Gary Heidnik, for example) he could display considerable charm and make himself liked.

The real key to DeSalvo was sex. From an early age he was insatiable, 'walking around with a rail on most of the time, ready to take on any broad or fag come along, or to watch some broad and masturbate . . . thinking about sex a lot, more than anything, and needing it so much all the time. If only somebody could've seen it then and told me it was not normal, even sick . . .' DeSalvo is here exaggerating; a large proportion of healthy young males go around in much the same state. DeSalvo's environment offered a great deal of sexual stimulus. He participated in sex games with his brothers and sisters when he was 5 or 6 years old. At the age of 8 he performed oral sex on a girl at school, and was soon persuading girls to do the same for him. Albert DeSalvo was turned into a sexual psychopath by the same kind of 'hothouse environment' that had nurtured Albert Fish. Combined with the lack of moral restraint that resulted from his family background, his tremendous sex urge soon led him to rape – his own estimation was that he had raped or assaulted almost two thousand women. During the course of the Green Man attacks, he raped four women in a single day, and even then tried to pick up a fifth. This was something that Brussel had failed to recognize. The Strangler had not been 'searching for his potency' – he had always been potent. During his teens, a woman neighbour had asked him if it was true that he had a permanent erection, and when he modestly admitted it, invited him into her apartment. 'She went down on her knees and blowed me and I come almost right off and she said: "Oh, now you went and come and what am I going to have to get screwed with?", and I said: "Don't worry, I'll have a hard on again in a few minutes".' When he left her, she was exhausted, but he was still unsatisfied. It was not potency DeSalvo was searching for, but emotional stability.

Yet Brussel was undoubtedly correct about the main thing: that DeSalvo's murders were part of an attempt to grow up. The murders of elderly women were acts of revenge against the mother who had rejected him; but the murder of the young black girl Sophie Clark signalled a change. When he knocked on her door DeSalvo had no idea that she would be so young – he was looking for elderly women, like his mother. Her white dress and black stockings excited him. He talked his way into her apartment by claiming to be a workman sent to carry out repairs – the method he invariably used – then, when she turned her back, hooked his arm round her neck and squeezed until she was unconscious. After that he raped her, then strangled her. The experience taught him that he preferred young girls to older women, and caused the change in his method.

Yet from the beginning, DeSalvo suffered from the same

problem as so many sex killers: self-division. A month before he killed Anna Slesers – the first victim – DeSalvo talked his way into the apartment of an attractive Swedish girl, claiming that he had been sent to repair the ceiling. 'She was laughing and she was very nice. An attractive, kind woman.' In the bathroom she turned her back on him, and DeSalvo hooked his powerful forearm round her neck. As he began to squeeze, he saw her face in the bathroom mirror, 'the look of awful fear and pain.' 'And I see myself, the look on my own face . . . and I can't do it. I take my arm away.' The girl asked him what he was going to do, and he admitted that he was going to rape her and possibly kill her. 'I tell you now that I was ashamed – I began to cry.' He fell on his knees in front of her and said: 'Oh God, what was I doing? I am a good Catholic man with a wife and children. I don't know what to do . . . Please call the police.' The girl told him to go home. 'She was a kind person and she was trying to be good to me. But how much better it would have been if she had called the police right then and there.' The episode is an interesting confirmation of a theory advanced by Brussel to his fellow committee members: that the Strangler only attacked women who turned their backs on him, because it seemed a form of 'rejection'.

After killing Sophie Clark, he came very close to sparing his next victim, Patricia Bissette. 'She was very nice to me, she treated me like a man – I thought of doing it to her and I talked myself out of it.' She offered him coffee, and when he offered to go out and get some doughnuts, told him she had food there. 'Then it was as good as over. I didn't want it to happen but then I knew that it would.' After he had throttled her into unconsciousness and was raping her, 'I want to say that all the time I was doing this, I was thinking about how nice she had been to me and it was making me feel bad. She had treated me right, and I was doing this thing to her . . .'

At other times, Mr Hyde took over – as in his next murder, that of Mary Brown in Lawrence. This murder was not, at the time, recognized as one of the Strangler's crimes, because its ferocity seemed untypical. DeSalvo described how he had knocked on the door and explained to the grey-haired lady who answered that he had come to paint the kitchen. She let him in without question. In his pocket, DeSalvo had a piece of brass pipe that he had found in the hallway. 'As she walked to the kitchen, her back was to me. I hit her right on the back of the head with the pipe . . . this was terrible, and I don't like talking about it. She went down and I ripped her things open, showing her busts . . . she was unconscious and bleeding . . . I don't know why but then I hit her again on the head with the pipe. I kept on hitting and hitting her with the pipe . . . this is like out of this world . . . this is unbelievable . . . oh, it was terrible . . . because her head felt like it was all gone . . . terrible . . . then I took this fork and stuck it into her right bust.' As in so many other cases, DeSalvo was unable to say why he did it. (Similarly, he had been unable to explain why he rifled the apartments after committing the murders: he was not looking for anything specific and apparently took nothing.) What he failed to recognize was that, like so many other serial killers, he had been taken over – literally possessed – by a sadistic compulsion, the sheer joy of destruction. Yet even as he did it, he continued to feel 'This is terrible.'

DeSalvo never suceeded in overcoming his feeling of guilt. He intimidated the tenth victim, 23-year-old Beverly Sams, with a knife; she made him promise not to rape her, because she was afraid of pregnancy. When he had her lying on the bed, DeSalvo decided to gag her. 'Then I thought that I wouldn't want a broad like that, with her stupid ideas to see me, so I tied a blindfold over her eyes.' When she recovered consciousness and discovered that he was raping her, she called him an animal. This enraged him enough to make him stab her. When he could kill like this – giving rein to his resentment – he experienced no guilt.

The last victim, Mary Sullivan, tried to reason with him, to talk him out of rape. Her words struck home. 'I recall thinking at the time, yes, she is right, I don't have to do these things any more now . . . I heard what this girl is saying and it stayed with me.' At the time he was angry, and hit her several times. As he tied her up and prepared to rape her, he realized 'I would never be able to do it again'. After raping her, he strangled her manually, while she struggled to get up. 'This is what I don't like to talk about. This is killing me even to talk about.' After death, her face looked 'surprised and even disappointed with the way I had treated her'. Then DeSalvo propped her up against the head of the bed, straddled her chest, and masturbated so that the sperm would strike her face. 'She is sitting there with the stuff on her nose and mouth and chin. I am not in control of myself. I know that something awful has been done, that the whole world of human beings are shocked and will be even more shocked.' He went into the kitchen and fetched a broom, then inserted it into her vagina, 'not so far as to hurt her . . . you say it is funny that I worry about hurting her when she is already dead, but that is the truth . . . I do not want to hurt her'. And, after leaving the apartment; 'as far as I was concerned it wasn't me. I can't explain it to you any other way.' When Brussel later pressed him to explain why Mary Sullivan was his final victim, he admitted that she had reminded him of his daughter: Dr Jekyll was back in control.

That he would now remain in control was demonstrated in a sensational manner. In February 1967, a month after being sentenced to life imprisonment, DeSalvo and two more inmates escaped from the Bridgewater mental institution. The city of Boston was plunged into panic. Interviewed by the press, Brussel was unconcerned. He pointed out that DeSalvo had left a note behind, apologizing for taking unauthorized leave, and explaining that he was only doing so to draw attention to the fact that he was receiving no psychiatric treatment. He promised that he would harm nobody. Brussel stated that he was sure DeSalvo would honour his promise. In fact, DeSalvo gave himself up after only thirty-six hours. His protest failed in its purpose – he was transferred to the virtually escape-proof Walpole Prison, but still failed to receive any psychiatric treatment.

At least Brussel had proved his point. The Boston Strangler had raped and murdered his way to a kind of maturity.

While the Boston Strangler was still at large, an unusual case of serial sex murder was taking place behind the Iron Curtain.

In July 1964, the communist regime in Poland was getting prepared to celebrate the twentieth anniversary of the liberation of Warsaw by Russian troops; a great parade was due to take place in Warsaw on the 22nd. On 4 July the editor of *Przeglad Polityczny*, the Polish equivalent of *Pravda*, received an anonymous letter in spidery red handwriting: 'There is no happiness without tears, no life without death. Beware! I am going to make you cry.' Marian Starzynski thought the anonymous writer had him in mind, and requested police protection. But on the day of the big parade, a 17-year-old blonde, Danka Maciejowitz, failed to arrive home from a parade organized by the School of Choreography and Folklore in Olsztyn, one hundred and sixty miles north of Warsaw. The next day, a gardener in the Olsztyn Park of Polish Heroes discovered the girl's body in some shrubbery. She had been stripped naked and raped, and the lower part of her body was covered with Jack-the-Ripper-type mutilations. And the following day, the 24th, another red-ink letter was delivered to *Kulisy*, a Warsaw newspaper: 'I picked a juicy flower in Olsztyn and I shall do it again somewhere else, for there is no holiday without a funeral.' Analysis of the ink showed that it had been made by dissolving red art paint in turpentine.

On 16 January 1965, the Warsaw newspaper *Zycie Warsawy* published the picture of a pretty 16-year-old girl, Aniuta Kaliniak, who had been chosen to lead a parade of students in another celebration rally the following day. She left her home in Praga, an eastern suburb of Warsaw, and crossed the river Vistula to reach the parade. Later, she thumbed a lift from a lorry driver, who dropped her close to her home at a crossroads. (The fact that a 16-year-old girl would thumb a lift like this indicates that the level of sex crime in Poland must be a great deal lower than in England or the US.) The day after the parade, her body was found in a basement in a leather factory opposite her home. The killer had removed a grating to get in. The crime had obviously been carefully planned. He had waited in the shadows of the wall, and cut off her cry with a wire noose dropped over her head. In the basement, he had raped her, and left a six-inch spike sticking in her sexual organs (an echo of the Boston Strangler). While the search went on another red-ink letter advised the police where to look for her body.

Olsztyn and Warsaw are one hundred and sixty miles apart; this modern Ripper differed from his predecessor in not sticking to the same area. Moreover, he was a man with a strong dramatic sense: the selection of national holidays for his crimes, the letters philosophizing about life and death.

The Red Spider – as he had come to be known, from his spidery writing – chose All Saints' Day, 1 November, for his next murder, and Poznan, two hundred kilometres west of Warsaw, as the site. A young, blonde hotel receptionist, Janka Popielski, was on her way to look for a lift to a nearby village, where she meant to meet her boyfriend. Since it was her holiday, the freight terminal was almost deserted. Her killer pressed a chloroform-soaked bandage over her nose and mouth. Then he removed her skirt, stockings and panties, and raped her behind a packing shed. After this, he killed her with a screwdriver. The mutilations were so thorough and revolting that the authorities suppressed all details. The Red Spider differed from many sex killers in apparently being totally uninterested in the upper half of his victims. Janka was stuffed into a packing case, where she was discovered an hour later. The police swooped on all trains and buses leaving Poznan, looking for a man with bloodstained clothes; but they failed to find one. The next day, the Poznan newspaper *Courier Zachodni* received one of the now-notorious letters in red ink, containing a quotation from Stefan Zeromsky's national epic *Popioly* (1928): 'Only tears of sorrow can wash out the stain of shame; only pangs of suffering can blot out the fires of lust.'

May Day, 1966, was both a communist and a national holiday. Marysia Galazka, 17, went out to look for her cat in the quiet suburb of Zoliborz, in northern Warsaw. When she did not return, her father went out to look for her. He found her lying in the typical rape position, with her entrails forming an abstract pattern over her thighs, in a tool shed behind the house. Medical evidence revealed that the killer had raped her before disembowelling her.

Major Ciznek, of the Warsaw Homicide Squad, was in charge of the case, and he made a series of deductions. The first was that the Red Spider was unlikely to confine himself to his well-publicized murders on national holidays. Such killers seek victims when their sexual desire is at maximum tension, not according to some preconceived timetable. Ciznek examined evidence of some fourteen other murders that had taken place since the first one in April 1964, one each in Lublin, Radom, Kielce, Lodz, Bialystock, Lomza, two in Bydgoszcz, five in the Poznan district. All places were easily reached by railway; the *modus operandi* was always the same. Every major district of Poland within four hundred kilometres of Warsaw was covered. Ciznek stuck pins in a map and examined the result. It looked as if Warsaw might be the home of the killer, since the murders took place all round it. But one thing was noticeable. The murders extended much farther south than north, and there were also more of them to the south. It rather looked as if the killer had gone to Bialystock, Lomza and Olsztyn as a token gesture of extending his boundaries. Assuming, then, that the killer lived somewhere south of Warsaw, where would this be most likely to be? There were five murders in the Poznan district, to the west of Warsaw. Poznan is, of course, easily reached from Warsaw. But where in the south could it be reached from just as easily? Cracow was an obvious choice. So was Katowice, twenty miles or so from Cracow. This town was also at the centre of a network of railway lines.

On Christmas Eve, 1966, Cracow was suddenly ruled out as a possibility. Three service men getting on a train between Cracow and Warsaw looked into a reserved compartment and found the half naked and mutilated corpse of a girl on the floor. The leather miniskirt had been slashed to pieces; so had her abdomen and thighs. The servicemen notified the guard, and a message was quickly sent to Warsaw, who instructed the train-driver to go straight through to Warsaw, non-stop, in case the killer managed to escape at one of the intervening stations. A careful check of passengers at Warsaw revealed no one stained with blood or in any way suspicious. But the police were able to locate the latest letter from the killer, dropped into the post slot of the mail van on top of all the others. It merely said: 'I have done it again,' and was addressed to *Zycie Warsawy*. It looked as if the Red Spider had got off the train in Cracow, after killing the girl, and dropped the letter into the slot.

The girl was identified as Janina Kozielska, of Cracow. And the police recalled something else: another girl named Kozielska had been murdered in Warsaw in 1964. This proved to be Janina's sister Aniela. For Ciznek, this ruled out Cracow as the possible home of the killer. For he would be likely to avoid his home territory. Moreover, there surely had to be some connection between the murders of the two sisters . . . The compartment on the Cracow–Warsaw train had been booked over the telephone by a man who said his name was Stanislav Kozielski, and that his wife would pick up the tickets. Janina had paid 1,422 zloty for them – about twenty-five pounds. Janina had come to the train alone and been shown to her compartment by the ticket inspector. She said that her husband would be joining her shortly. The inspector had also checked a man's ticket a few moments later, but could not recall the man. It was fairly clear, then, that the Red Spider knew the girl well enough to persuade her to travel with him as his wife, and had probably paid for the ticket. He had murdered her in ten minutes or so, and then hurried off the train.

Ciznek questioned the dead girl's family. They could not suggest who might have killed their daughter, but they mentioned that she sometimes worked as a model – as her sister had. She worked at the School of Plastic Arts and at a club called The Art Lovers Club.

Ciznek recollected that the red ink was made of artist's paint dissolved in turpentine and water; this looked like a lead.

The Art Lovers Club proved to have one hundred and eighteen members. For an Iron Curtain country, its principles were remarkably liberal; many of its members painted abstract, tachiste and pop-art pictures. Most of them were respectable professional men – doctors, dentists, officials, newspapermen. And one of them came from Katowice. His name was Lucian Staniak, and he was a 26-year-old translator who worked for the official Polish publishing house. Staniak's business caused him to travel a great deal – in fact, he had bought an *ulgowy bilet*, a train ticket that enabled him to travel anywhere in Poland.

Ciznek asked if he could see Staniak's locker. It confirmed his increasing hope that he had found the killer. It was full of knives – used for painting, the club manager explained. Staniak daubed the paint on with a knife blade. He liked to use red paint. And one of his paintings, called 'The Circle of Life', showed a flower being eaten by a cow, the cow being eaten by a wolf, the wolf being shot by a hunter, the hunter being killed by a car driven by a woman, and the woman lying with her stomach ripped open in a field, with flowers sprouting from her body.

Ciznek now knew he had his man, and he telephoned the Katowice police. They went to Staniak's address at 117 Aleje Wyzwolenia, but found no one at home. In fact, Staniak was out committing another murder – his last. It was a mere month after the train murder – 31 January 1967 – but he was impatient at the total lack of publicity given to the previous murder. So he took Bozhena Raczkiewicz, an 18-year-old student from the Lodz Institute of Cinematographic Arts, to a shelter built at the railway station for the use of stranded overnight travellers, and there stunned her with a vodka bottle. In accordance with his method when in a hurry, he cut off her skirt and panties with his knife. He had killed her in a few minutes between six o'clock and six twenty-five.

The neck of the broken bottle had a clear fingerprint on it.

Staniak was picked up at dawn the next day; he had spent the night getting drunk. His fingerprints matched those on the bottle. He was a good-looking young man of twenty-six. And when he realized that there was no chance of escape, he confessed fully to twenty murders. He told the police that his parents and his sister had been crossing an icy road when they were hit by a skidding car, being driven too fast by the young wife of a Polish Air Force pilot. The girl had been acquitted of careless driving. Staniak had seen the picture of his first victim in a newspaper, and thought she looked like the wife of the pilot; this was his motive in killing her. He had decided against killing the wife of the pilot because it would be traced back to him.

Sentenced to death for six of the murders – the six described here – Staniak was later reprieved and sent to the Katowice asylum for the criminally insane.

Staniak, like Brady, is an example of the relatively new phenomenon of the 'high IQ killer'. It is true that Landru, Kürten and Rees were men of some intelligence; but where murder was concerned, the intelligence was overruled. Like Earle Nelson and Fritz Haarmann, they were simply driven by a compulsion to violate. By comparison, Rees, Brady and Staniak represent a new level of motivation in serial killers. The desire to violate is less than compulsive, but they use their intelligence to justify it, asking themselves – in an almost philosophical spirit – 'Why not?'

The same pseudo-Sadeian logic lay behind a series of murders that created panic on the campuses of Michigan in the late 1960s.

At nine o'clock on a warm Sunday evening, a man relaxed on his front porch in Ypsilanti, Michigan, enjoying the first cool breeze of the day. He recognized the attractive, slightly-built brunette who was strolling towards him as Mary Fleszar, the niece of one of his workmates; she was a college student who lived in an apartment on the next corner. As she walked past him, a car slowed down, and a young man leaned out of the window and spoke to her – it sounded as if he was asking if she wanted a lift. Mary shook her head and walked on. The car turned at the next corner. A few moments later, to the man's surprise, the car reappeared from the same direction, shot past the girl, and pulled into a private driveway, blocking her path. Once again the driver seemed to be trying to persuade her to get in, but the girl again shook her head, and walked around the rear of the car. The driver backed out and drove off down the street. As the man watched anxiously, ready to intervene, he saw that Mary was within yards of the front door of her apartment block; she was obviously safe now . . .

Twenty-four hours later – 19 July 1967 – Mary's flatmate rang the girl's home. Mary had apparently gone out for a breath of air the previous evening, only ten minutes after returning home, and had not been back since.

At first the police were unconcerned, pointing out that most 19-year-old college students were old enough to look after themselves, and often took off for the night without telling anyone. Mary's parents protested that she was a quiet, studious girl, and that she had walked out in the clothes she stood up in.

The day after the police had issued a missing person report, a detective tracked down the neighbour who had seen Mary accosted by the young man. He was able to say that the car was an old model, that it looked like a Chevrolet, and that it was blueish grey.

From then on, investigations led nowhere. The Fleszars came to accept that their daughter was dead – no other theory made sense. Fortunately, they were a deeply religious family, and their faith enabled them to accept their loss as the will of God.

Four weeks after Mary's disappearance, on 7 August 1967, two teenage boys were trying to repair a tractor in a field near Superior Township, two miles north of Ypsilanti. When they heard a car door slam, they looked at one another with mischievous smiles, and crept off into the brush towards the broken-down farmhouse at the edge of the field. Because it afforded shelter from the main road, the spot had become a lovers' lane. But before the boys reached the area favoured by courting couples, they heard a car start up and drive away. In the clearing near the old farmhouse, they found fresh tyre tracks. They also observed a nauseating smell. A few yards further on they discovered its source – a fly-infested mass of rotten meat that looked like a dead animal. A closer look revealed that, although the extremities of the limbs were missing, it had an oddly human appearance.

The local police who hurried to the scene – and who at first assumed the boys had found a dead deer – soon recognized it as a human body. The Ypsilanti pathologist, Dr H. A. Scovill, was able to tell them that it was of a female, and that she had been baking in the hot sun for many weeks. A careful search of the area failed to discover the victim's clothing. But fifty yards away, in dense weeds, a policeman found a female sandal. Later the same afternoon, the Fleszars identified it as their daughter's.

The autopsy on the remains revealed that the girl had been stabbed in the chest and abdomen about thirty times – obviously by someone in a frenzy.

Two days later, a blue-grey Chevrolet pulled up in front of the Moore Funeral Home, where Mary's remains were awaiting burial, and a powerfully built, good-looking young man got out. In the reception, he explained that he was a friend of the Fleszar family, and would like to take a photograph as a keepsake for the parents. When told that was impossible, he shrugged and left. But the girl behind the desk noticed that he was not carrying a camera . . .

When, almost a year later, at the beginning of another hot July, a student at Eastern Michigan University telephoned to report that her flatmate was missing, the Ypsilanti police had a sense of *déjà vu*. The circumstances were oddly similar to those of the disappearance of Mary Fleszar. Joan Schell, a 20-year-old art student, had returned to her apartment on the evening of Sunday 2 July – a mere three blocks from Mary's apartment – and decided to go out again. She wanted to get into nearby Ann Arbor, to spend the night at the flat of a girlfriend. In fact, her boyfriend had telephoned to say he had arrived in town unexpectedly and was waiting there for her. Her room-mate accompanied her to catch the 10.30 bus from in front of the university. Three quarters of an hour later, it was clear that she had missed it. At that point, a two-tone red car had pulled up, and a young man climbed out and called 'Want a ride?' He looked about 20, and was wearing an East Michigan University sweatshirt. And since there were also two other young men in the car, Joan decided it was safe enough. Seconds later, Joan was in the back seat. But as the door closed, she called that she would telephone as soon as she reached her friend's flat in Ann

Arbor. And when, two and a half hours later, she failed to call, the flatmate decided to ring the police.

Five days later, two workmen at a construction site in Ann Arbor were taking a breather from digging storm drains when one of them wrinkled up his nose. 'Can you smell something?' He began looking in the high weeds. A moment later he called: 'It's a dead girl.'

The sex of the corpse was obvious since her blue miniskirt and white underslip had been tugged up around her neck. The torso was covered with a mass of wounds. The pathologist who was called to the scene reported that she had been stabbed to death, and had been dead for some time, perhaps a week. What intrigued the police was the evidence that the body had lain in its present location for less than twenty-four hours. This was revealed by the fact that parts of the body that had been exposed to the sun were nevertheless still fresh and undecayed, while the underside was tough and leathery. The pathologist also noted signs that the victim had been raped.

Joan Schell's body was identified through the clothing she was wearing. A few days later, the missing boyfriend – with whom she had intended to spend the night – was located and questioned. But he had a perfect alibi. He had been waiting at the flat of Joan's girlfriend in Ann Arbor during the crucial hours following her abduction.

But enquiries among the university students revealed a possible clue. At least two of them believed they had seen Joan late on the night she vanished, walking with a young man. And although neither of them was prepared to be positive, both thought it was an Eastern Michigan University student named John Norman Collins.

The detectives lost no time in interviewing Collins. He proved to be a well-built, handsome youth of 21 with short dark hair, who was was majoring in education. But he flatly denied being with Joan Schell. He had spent the weekend at home in the Detroit suburb of Center Line, and had not returned to his room near the campus until early Monday morning. He did not even know Joan Schell, although she lived just across the street. The detectives decided that John Collins was either innocent or a superb liar. Besides, there was the problem of the car containing *three* men. And since the identifications of him had not been positive, he was allowed to go.

As in the case of Mary Fleszar, the investigation soon ran out of leads. It was ten months later, on 21 March 1969, that a 13-year-old schoolboy returned home at 7.15 in the morning to tell his mother that he had found a gift-wrapped present in a shipping bag near the cemetery. A note on the package said: 'I love you, Jane.' Together, mother and son returned to the spot where he had found it. Outside the cemetery, near the gate, she saw something covered with a yellow raincoat. It was a girl's body, lying on its back. Although the skirt had been pulled up above the waist, and the pantyhose rolled down, it was fully clothed. A few hours earlier, the Ypsilanti police had received a missing person report on 23-year-old Jane Mixer, a law student at the University of Michigan. A check with a photograph in the Yearbook revealed that this was the victim.

Jane had been due home that weekend, a semester recess. She had telephoned her parents in Muskegan, a few hours away, to say that she had succeeded in finding someone to give her a lift, but had never arrived. Jane had been shot in the back of the head and then strangled. A sanitary pad that was still in place indicated why there had been no sexual attack.

Four days later, on Tuesday 25 March 1969, a construction worker in Ann Arbor, working close to the spot where Joan Schell's body had been found, tripped over an arm that was sticking out of a batch of weeds. It was the body of a young girl, lying in a rape position; a branch had been jammed into the vagina, and the head and body showed signs of a brutal beating. She was identified as 16-year-old Maralynn Skelton, and investigation revealed that she was a known drug user – and dealer – whose relations with her family were strained. She had vanished on Friday – the day Jane Mixer's body had been found – when hitch-hiking, on her way to see her boyfriend. It seemed likely that she had been picked up by her killer. The newspapers had no doubt whatever that the killer was the man they were now calling 'the Ypsilanti Co-ed Slayer'.

Other than that, there were no clues – no witnesses, no leads. The police were encountering total frustration. So far they had not even succeeded in finding the exact spot where any of the victims had been killed.

In that respect, at least, their luck was about to change.

Two victims in four days suggested that the Ypsilanti killer was being driven by an increasing obsession, and that unless he was caught soon, the time between the murders would grow shorter.

That fear was confirmed when, three weeks later, early on the morning of 16 April 1969, the body of another young girl was found. She was a teenager, and she was wearing only a white blouse and a white bra, pushed up around her neck. She had been strangled with black electrical flex, and her full breasts had been slashed again and again. It looked like the sadistic frenzy the police had come to associate with the Ypsilanti co-ed slayer. An early morning motorist had seen the body lying at the side of a country road near Ypsilanti, in a patch of weeds.

The girl proved to be the youngest victim yet: 13-year-old Dawn Basom, a junior high-school student. She had gone out to see friends early on the previous evening, and had failed to return home.

The police launched a thorough search of the area, and soon found both her shoes, at different locations near the body. The local sheriff, Douglas Harvey, decided to keep the discovery of the body secret, and to stake out the area in case the killer returned. But at the news conference he gave a few hours later, an embarrassed young reporter admitted that it was already too late: he had learned of the discovery from a policeman, and had promptly telephoned it to his office.

Yet the fact that the body had been found so soon after Dawn's disappearance filled Sheriff Harvey with a sense of getting close to the killer. He ordered the search for her clothes to be extended over a wider area. And a few hours later, a deputy looking through rubble at a deserted farmhouse not far from Dawn Basom's home found a bright orange sweater – the one Dawn had been wearing when she left home. The place was full of empty beer bottles and used condoms – it was obviously a site used by lovers. And in the basement, police discovered Dawn's blouse, and a length of the same black electrical flex that had been used to strangle her.

They had found where Dawn had been murdered, but there were no clues to her killer: no tyre marks, footprints or anything else that might provide a lead. But a week later, when the investigation was already marking time, another clue was found in the farmhouse: a cheap gold-plated ear-ring that was identified as belonging to Dawn. It had undoubtedly not been there a few days earlier. The only conclusion was that the co-ed killer was deliberately taunting the police with their failure to catch him. Two weeks later, on 16 May, the barn at the farm site caught fire. A reporter looking over the smoking ruins the next day found five purple lilac blossoms lying nearby; they were fresh, as if newly cut. Five blossoms, five murders.

The co-ed slayer obviously had a liking for deserted farms. On the afternoon of Monday 9 June 1969, three teenage boys taking a short cut through a disused farmyard saw a body lying beside the path. It was a girl, and her torn clothes were scattered around her. The pathologist hazarded a guess that she was in her early twenties, and that she had been dead for less than a day. She had been shot in the head and stabbed repeatedly before her throat had been cut. The sheer frenzy of the attack was the signature of the co-ed slayer.

Because of the remoteness of the spot, Sheriff Harvey again decided to order a news blackout. And once again he was frustrated: one of the teenagers who had found the body had phoned the news to a local radio station that had a standing offer of $25 for news items.

The girl was identified as Alice Elizabeth Kalom, a student from Kalamazoo who was taking a design course in Ann Arbor. She had last been seen at a party for a local rock musician in the early hours of the previous Sunday morning, and left to walk home. The co-ed slayer had obviously offered her a lift.

Four murders in three months caused panic in the local community; reward money of $42,000 was offered for information. The police were heavily criticized; yet they knew that they had done everything possible to catch the killer. So far, two news leaks had frustrated their best hope of catching him. Sheriff Harvey was determined that it wouldn't happen again.

On 23 July 1969, the campus police at Eastern Michigan University received a phone call telling them that an 18-year-old student named Karen Sue Beineman had failed to appear at dinner or in her room after curfew. By this time, the Ypsilanti police were ready to act instantly in the case of a missing girl. Karen's room-mates told them that she had last been seen around midday, on her way to a downtown wig shop.

Joan Goshe, the proprietress of the wig shop, had an interesting story to tell. The girl had come in to pick up a small headpiece that had been made for her. As she paid $20 for it, she made the comment that she had done two foolish things in her life: bought a wig, and accepted a lift on a motorcycle from a complete stranger – the young man who was now waiting outside. Joan Goshe had commented that accepting lifts from strangers was not safe these days. But she had to admit that the young man *looked* decent enough – good-looking, with short dark hair. He was wearing a horizontal-striped sweater. A few minutes later, Karen had roared off on the back of his motorcycle. An assistant in the Chocolate House next door was able to identify it as a Triumph.

Another girl student who was interviewed described how a good-looking young man in a horizontal-striped sweater had reecently tried hard to persuade her to go for a ride on his motorbike, but had only shrugged good-humouredly when she declined.

Four days later, a doctor and his wife out for an afternoon walk found Karen Sue Beineman's body in a wooded gully not far from their suburban home. The naked corpse lay on its belly as if rolled over the edge. As soon as Sheriff Harvey received the call, he gave orders for a news blackout. Like most of the other victims, Karen had been strangled and brutally beaten. Medical examination revealed that she had been raped and that her panties had been stuffed into her vagina. One curious fact noted by the medical examiner was that there were human hair-clippings stuck to the panties.

That night, the gully was surrounded by police officers, and in the place of Karen Sue Beineman lay a store mannequin.

Towards midnight, a storm broke, and the watchers did their best to keep out of sight while bitten by gnats and soaked by the rain. Shortly after midnight, one of the policemen thought he saw a man running out of the gully; the heavy rain had prevented him from seeing him earlier. He tried to contact colleagues on his walkie-talkie, but the rain had made it inoperative. By the time he had made his way to other watchers on the main road, the man was already far away. They heard an engine start up, and a car drive away. The police followed, but they were too late. What had happened, they realized, was that the killer had made his way back to the 'body', found it was a mannequin, and left at top speed. To the frustrated police, the luck of the co-ed slayer seemed inexhaustible.

In fact, it had already run out. Descriptions of the young man on the motorbike had led a young campus policeman,

Larry Mathewson, to note their similarity to one of his former Fraternity fellows, John Norman Collins, the student who had already been interviewed in connection with the death of Joan Schell. He succeeded in borrowing a photograph of Collins from a fellow student, and showed it to Joan Goshe, the wig-shop owner. Both Joan Goshe and her assistant identified it as the young man who had been waiting for Karen Sue Beineman on his motorcycle.

The Sunday evening after the stake-out, two young policemen called on John Norman Collins at the pleasant, wooden frame house at 619 Emmet Street that he shared with his friend Arnold Davis. They were enthusiastic but inexperienced, and one of them tried to shock Collins into an admission by telling him that he had been the last person seen with Karen Sue Beineman. Collins said there must be some mistake. When the police asked if he was willing to take a lie-detector test, he flushed and said: 'I guess so.'

When he got back to his room after the interview, Collins told Davis indignantly that the police had accused him of being the co-ed slayer. But Davis was later to describe how, the following evening, Collins emerged from his bedroom with a box covered in a blanket. As he opened the door for Collins, Davis glimpsed its contents: women's shoes and clothing, and a woman's bag. Collins returned later without the box.

On the evening of Tuesday 29 July 1969, Police Corporal David Leik returned from a twelve-day holiday with his wife Sandra, and three young sons. The following morning, Mrs Leik carried a basket of washing down to the machine in the basement, and was mildly annoyed to notice patches of black paint on the concrete floor. Her husband denied all knowledge of it, and was puzzled to realize that the paint had the dull finish of spray paint. There had been a can of black spray paint in the basement, but it had gone.

His wife pointed out that some washing powder and a bottle of ammonia were also missing. Only one person could have taken them: her nephew, who had kept an eye on the house and fed the dog in their absence. But why should he spray black paint on the floor?

They were still puzzling about it when the telephone rang. It was the police post down on Michigan Avenue, and the sergeant asked if David Leik would mind coming over immediately. Half an hour later, Leik was talking to Sergeant Chris Walters, who lost no time in explaining why he needed to see him so urgently:

'That nephew of yours, John Collins. He's the prime suspect in these co-ed murders.'

Leik was incredulous; Collins was like a younger brother. But when Walters had outlined the strength of the evidence, and mentioned that Collins had backed down from taking a lie-detector test, the shaken Leik had to acknowledge that there was very powerful evidence that his nephew could be the co-ed slayer.

He decided against telling his wife; although only ten years Collins's senior, Sandra seemed to regard him as a son. But late that night, Leik tiptoed down to the basement and scraped off some of the black paint with a knife. Underneath, there was a stain that looked ominously like blood.

Early the next morning, while his wife and children were still asleep, Leik hurried to the police post to report his find; he returned to find his wife on the telephone to Collins. 'John wants to know if you've found anything about that black paint yet.' 'Not yet,' said Leik. Then, when she had hung up, he tried to tell her, as gently as possible, that her sister's youngest son was almost certainly the co-ed killer. Sandra was shattered by the news, and cried uncontrollably for a long time.

The lab men arrived two hours later. After erecting floodlights, they scraped fragments of the brown stain on to paper, and tested it with benzidine solution. If it had been blood, the benzidine should have turned blue-green; in fact, it remained transparent.

One forensic expert remarked: 'It *looks* like a varnish stain.'

Leik clapped a hand to his forehead. 'Oh my God! Of course! I used varnish on some window shutters . . . I'm sorry.'

'Don't be sorry. What I'd like to know is why someone covered up varnish stains with spray paint.'

As the lab men went on studying the floor, one of them peered into the space next to the washing machine. What he saw was hair – tiny clippings of human hair. Leik explained that his wife cut the children's hair in the basement. He looked stunned when the lab man explained that tiny clippings of hair had been found inside the panties that the killer had stuffed into Karen Sue Beineman's vagina.

A closer examination of the floor revealed tiny brown spots that looked like – and proved to be – bloodstains. They also proved to be of human origin.

That afternoon, David Leik and Police Captain Walter Stevens called on John Collins. Collins looked shaken when told he was the prime suspect, and when Stevens told him that the stains on the basement floor had been varnish, he burst into tears. They expected a confession; but Collins pulled himself together, and continued to deny knowing anything about Karen Sue Beineman. Later the same day, after laboratory examination had revealed that the bloodstains were of the same type as Karen's, John Norman Collins was placed under arrest.

A search of Collins's rooms failed to reveal anything incriminating; the detectives cursed when his room-mate Arnold Davis told them of the box that Collins had disposed of on the previous Monday evening. It had almost certainly contained evidence to tie Collins to the earlier murders. Examination of the basement furnace revealed nothing but ashes. What it meant was that the only evidence against Collins were the hairs and human bloodstains found in Leik's basement. If these failed to convince a jury – and juries are notoriously unwilling to convict on purely circumstantial evidence – John Collins might still go free. And if Collins had not made the absurd mistake of spraying varnish stains with black paint, the evidence in Leik's basement would never have been discovered.

Collins's friend Arnold Davis provided some interesting insights into the suspected killer. Collins was apparently a habitual thief; this explained how he was able to afford to run four motorcycles – he stole spare parts, even to wheels and engines – in fact, one of the motorcycles was stolen. And more recently, Collins had been committing burglaries with another former room-mate, Andrew Manuel – not because he needed the money (he was an indefatigable odd-job man), but simply for fun.

The police wanted to talk to Andrew Manuel for another reason. When Collins's arrest had been broadcast on national news networks, it had mentioned that he had just returned from a trip to California. On 30 June that year, near Salinas, a pretty 17-year-old girl, Roxie Ann Phillips, had vanished after telling a friend that she had a date with a man called 'John' from Michigan; John and his friend were staying in a camper-trailer. In fact, the trailer had been left behind in Salinas – in the backyard of Andrew Manuel's grandfather. The strangled and battered body of Roxie Ann Philips had been discovered in a ravine on 13 July. The trailer-hire company were still trying to recover their property.

Manuel was finally located in Phoenix, Arizona, and charged with burglary and stealing the trailer. He denied knowing anything about any of the murders, although he admitted hastily leaving Ypsilanti when he heard that the police had been asking questions about Collins. Eventually, he was sentenced to five years' probation.

On 22 June 1970, the trial of John Norman Collins opened in the Washtenaw County Building in Ann Arbor before Judge John Conlin. The prosecution, led by William F. Delhey, had finally decided that he would be charged only with the murder of Karen Sue Beineman – it had been impossible to collect enough evidence to risk other charges. The defence, led by Joseph Louisell, an immensely successful lawyer from nearby Detroit, spent two weeks challenging jurors who might be prejudiced, so the actual trial opened on 20 July.

It was uphill work for the defence. The wig-shop owner and the assistant from the Chocolate House testified that it had been Collins they saw waiting outside on his motorcycle for Karen Sue Beineman; Neil Fink, for the defence, questioned them about their eyesight. Room-mate Arnold Davis was led to testify that the police had questioned him for sixty hours – the implication being that he had been harassed into testifying against Collins. Corporal David Leik (now a sergeant) was pressed about whether there was any actual evidence that Collins had been in their house while he was away, and had to admit that there was not.

But the heart of the case, as everyone realized, lay in the hair evidence. Walter Holz, a graduate chemist from the Department of Health's Criminalistics Section, testified that the hairs in the girl's panties were identical with those found on the Leiks' basement floor; the defence argued that a comparison of sixty-one hairs from the panties and fifty-nine from the floor was inadequate. Similar objections were made to the evidence of other experts on hair. In due course, the defence called its own experts to object that precise identification of hairs was impossible. Louisell also suggested that the hairs in the panties might have been picked up in a girls' dormitory if a brown-haired girl had clipped her bangs, and – when the judge sustained an objection – that they might have been picked up in the wig shop (although Louisell failed to explain how they had found their way under the girl's clothes).

On 13 August 1970, Prosecutor Delhey concluded a brisk summary of the evidence with the remark that common sense dictated a verdict of guilty. Louisell rested his defence on the uncertainty of the hair evidence. But when having lunch with the judge and the prosecutor, he admitted that he expected a guilty verdict. He was correct. On Wednesday 19 August 1970, the jury brought in a unanimous verdict of guilty. Two days later, John Collins was sentenced to life imprisonment – meaning a minimum of twenty years. He heard the sentence with the same impassivity he had shown throughout the trial.

What motivated a personable young student – known as a good athlete, an excellent student and an 'all-American boy' – to kill eight or more young women? The answer is that we do not know. His family background had been unstable. His father left his mother for another woman soon after John Collins' birth in 1947; her second marriage lasted only a year; her third husband turned out to be an alcoholic who beat her and the the children – she divorced him when Collins was 9. In his early years at college it suddenly became clear that he was less than honest – he was suspected of taking $40 from the entertainment fund, and of numerous petty thefts. One of his professors suspected him of some 'pretty ambitious cheating'. So, like so many men who graduate to murder – Landru, Petiot, Smith, Heath – he had a deeply ingrained crooked streak. We can only assume that, as a higly sexed young man, this crooked streak led him to 'steal' sex as he had earlier stolen money and motorcycles, and that – as in the case of Ian Brady – he knew how to overrule his conscience with intellectual justifications.

By comparison, the case of another American serial killer of the late 1960s seems like a flashback to the era of Albert Fish and Earle Nelson. Although a brilliant mechanic and something of a genius with electronic equipment, Jerome Henry Brudos was anything but intellectual; his murders were as simple and compulsive as a schoolboy stealing jam tarts.

It was on 10 May 1969 that the police in Portland, Oregon knew for certain that there was a sex killer at large. A fisherman standing on the Bundy Bridge, which crossed the Long Tom River, saw something that looked like a parcel floating in the water; when he climbed down for a closer view, he realized that it was a bloated corpse, still clad in a coat. The police officers who were despatched from the Benton County sheriff's office soon confirmed that it was the body of a girl, and that it had been weighted down with a car transmission unit that weighed as much as she did.

The forensic pathologist, Dr William Brady, estimated that the body had been in the water about two weeks. Cause of death was strangulation with a ligature. Because the body had been immersed for so long, it was impossible to determine whether she had been raped. There was one curious feature that the doctor found hard to explain. A few inches below each armpit there was a needle puncture, surrounded by an area of burn.

It was not difficult to identify the girl. She was 22-year-old Linda Dawn Salee, who had vanished just over two weeks ago, on 23 April, after leaving her office job in Portland. Her car had been found in the underground parking garage. She had failed to arrive at the swimming pool, where she was due to meet her boyfriend, who was a lifeguard. Linda had been one of many girls who had vanished in Oregon during the past two years.

Police divers spent the next two days searching the river for clues. It was on the morning of Monday 12 May that one of them located another body, fifty feet from the spot where Linda Salee had been found. This one was also weighted down with a car part – this time a cylinder head. And since the pathologist estimated that the body had been in the water for around two months, this suggested that it was 19-year-old Karen Sprinker, a university student from the Oregon State University in Corvallis, who had vanished on 27 March. Her parents soon verified the identification. Karen had been due to meet her mother for lunch in a department store in Salem, Oregon, but had failed to arrive. Her car was found in the parking garage, still locked.

Again, there were some curious – and grisly – features. The body was fully clothed, but the cotton bra had been replaced by a waist-length black bra that was too big. Both breasts had been removed, and in their place were two screwed-up pieces of brown paper. Like Linda Salee, Karen had been strangled with a ligature.

Linda and Karen were only two of a dozen girls who had vanished in Oregon in the past two years. Before the Long Tom river discovery, only one of them had been found: a skeleton lying on the banks of a creek had been identified as that of 16-year-old Stephanie Vilcko, who had vanished from her Portland home in July 1968. But two other cases bore an ominous resemblance to those of Linda and Karen. Linda Slawson, a 19-year-old encyclopedia saleswoman, had failed to return to her Portland home on 26 January 1968. And 23-year-old Susan Jan Whitney had vanished en route from Eugene, Oregon, to McMinnville, south of Portland, on 26 November 1968. Her car was found parked by the highway, incapacitated by a mechanical defect.

The policeman who had been investigating the disappearance of Karen Sprinker was Detective Jim Stovall. Now her body had been found, but he still had no clues to her killer, except that he was probably an electrician – both bodies had been tied with electrical wire – and a car mechanic, an inference based on the car parts used to weight the bodies.

Stovall decided to begin at the Corvallis campus, eighty miles south of Portland, where Karen had been a student. Stovall and his colleague Jim Daugherty took over a room on campus and spent days talking to every girl student in the university. The only possible leads that materialized were several mentions of a stranger who had made a habit of telephoning the hall of residence, asking for various girls by their first names. When a girl answered, he would talk at some length about himself, claiming to be a Vietnam veteran, and giving other details – such as that he was 'psychic'. He usually asked for a date, but seemed unoffended when refused. It was when one of the girls mentioned that she had agreed to meet the 'Vietnam veteran' that Stovall's interest suddenly increased.

The man had seemed interested when she mentioned that she was taking a psychology course, and told her that he had been a patient at the Walter Reed Hospital, where he had learned about some interesting new techniques. When he suggested coming to the dorm for a coffee, the girl agreed.

The man's appearance had been a disappointment. He was overweight, freckled, and looked as if he was in his thirties. He had a round, unprepossessing face and the narrow eyes gave him an oddly cunning look, like a schoolboy who is planning to steal the jam tarts. But he seemed pleasant enough, and they sat in the lounge and talked at some length. Nevertheless, she had the feeling that he was a little 'odd'. This suddenly came into focus when he placed a hand on her shoulder and remarked: 'Be sad.' 'Why?' 'Think of those two girls whose bodies were found in the river . . .' And when he left, he asked her to go for a drive, and when she declined, made the curious comment: 'How do you know I wouldn't take you to the river and strangle you?'

Stovall and Daugherty began to feel excited when the girl told them that the 'Vietnam veteran' had mentioned that he might call again.

'If he does, would you agree to let him come here? Then call us immediately?'

The girl was reluctant, but agreed when the police told her that they would be there before the man arrived. She merely had to make some excuse to delay him for an hour.

A week later, on Sunday 25 May, the Corvallis Police Department received the call they had been hoping for. The girl told them that the 'Vietnam veteran' had telephoned a few minutes ago, asking if he could come over. The girl had told him she wanted to wash her hair, and asked him to make it in about an hour.

When the overweight, freckle-faced man in a tee shirt walked into the lounge of Callaghan Hall, two plain-clothes policeman walked up to him and produced their badges. The man seemed unalarmed; he gave his name as Jerry Brudos, and said that he lived in Salem; the only sign of embarrassment was when he admitted that he had a wife and two children. He was now in Corvallis, he explained, because he was working nearby – as an electrician.

Brudos had committed no offence for which he might be arrested, or even taken in for questioning. But when they escorted him outside to his green Comet station wagon, the policemen made a note of its licence number.

A preliminary check on Brudos showed that he was what he claimed to be – an electrician working in Corvallis. But when Stovall looked into his record, he realized that he had a leading suspect. Jerome Henry Brudos, 30 years of age, had a record of violence towards women, and had been in the State Mental

Hospital. Moreover, at the time of the disappearance of Linda Slawson, Brudos had lived in Portland, in the area where she was trying to sell encyclopedias.

The first thing to do was to check him out. Stovall called on Brudos at his home in Center Street, Salem, and talked to him in his garage. Stovall's colleague, Detective Jerry Frazier, also went along, and noted the lengths of rope lying around the room, and the hook in the ceiling. He also noticed that one of the ropes was knotted, and the knot was identical to one that had been used to bind the corpses in the river.

This, Stovall decided, had to be their man. Everything fitted. He worked as an electrician and car repairman. He had been working at Lebanon, Oregon, close to the place where Jan Whitney's car had been found. And he had been living close to the place from which Karen Sprinker had disappeared in Salem.

There was another piece of evidence that pointed to Brudos. On 22 April, a 15-year-old schoolgirl had been grabbed by an overweight, freckled man holding a gun, as she hurried to school along the railroad tracks; she had screamed and succeeded in running away. She immediately picked out the photograph of Jerry Brudos from a batch shown to her by the detectives.

Except for this identification, there was no definite evidence against Brudos. This is why Stovall was reluctant to move against him. But five days after Brudos had been questioned in Corvallis, Stovall realized he could no longer take the risk of leaving him at large. As he was on his way to arrest Brudos for the attempted abduction of the schoolgirl on the railway tracks, he received a radio message saying that Brudos and his family had left Corvallis, and were driving towards Portland. Shortly after this, Brudos's station wagon was stopped by a police patrol car. At first it looked as if Brudos was not inside; but he proved to be lying in the back, hidden under a blanket.

Back at the Salem police station, Brudos was asked to change into overalls. When he removed his clothes, he was found to be wearing ladies' underwear.

When Stovall first questioned Brudos, he failed to secure any admissions. It was the same for the next three days. Stovall did not ask outright if Brudos had murdered the girls; he confined himself to general questions, hoping to pick more clues. But at the fifth interview, Brudos suddenly began to talk about his interest in female shoes and underwear. Then he described how he had followed a girl in attractive shoes, broken into her home through a window, and made off with the shoes. Soon after this, he described how he had stolen the black bra – found on Karen Sprinker's body – from a clothesline. Now, at last, he had virtually admitted the killing. Then, little by little, the rest came out – the curious history of a psychopath who suffered from the curious sexual abnormality for which the psychologist Alfred Binet coined the word fetishism.

In Jerry Brudos's case, it first showed itself when he was five years old, when he found a pair of women's patent leather shoes on a rubbish dump, and put them on at home. His mother was furious and ordered him to return them immediately; instead he hid them and wore them in secret. When his mother found them, he was beaten and the shoes were burned. In first grade at school, he was fascinated by the high-heeled shoes that his teacher kept as spares; one day he stole them and hid them in the schoolyard; they were found and handed back to the teacher. When he later confessed, and she asked him why he did it, he rushed out of the room. The truth was that he could not have told her.

When he was 16 – in 1955 – he stole the underwear of a girl who lived next door. Then he approached the girl and told her he was working for the police as an undercover agent, and could help her to recover the stolen articles. She allowed herself to be lured into his bedroom on an evening when his family was away. Suddenly, a masked man jumped on her, threatened her with a knife, and made her remove all her clothes. Then, to her relief, he merely took photographs of her with a flashlight camera. At the end of the session, the masked man walked out of the bedroom, and a few minutes later, Jerry Brudos rushed in, claiming that the masked intruder had locked him in the barn. The girl knew he was lying, but there was nothing she could do about it.

In April 1956, Brudos invited a 17-year-old girl for a ride in his car. On a deserted highway, he dragged her from the car, beat her up and ordered her to strip. A passing couple heard her screams, and Brudos actually agreed to accompany them back to their home, where they called the police. His story that the girl had been attacked by 'some weirdo' was soon disproved, and he was arrested. The girl next door now came forward, and told her story of the photographic session.

Psychiatrists who examined the young Brudos decided that he was not mentally ill and – in spite of the beating he had administered – had no violent tendencies. Back in his home, police found a large box of women's underwear and shoes. They sent him to the Oregon State Hospital for observation, and he was released after nine months.

A period in the army followed, but he was discharged because of his bizarre delusions – he was convinced that a beautiful Korean girl sneaked into his bed every night to seduce him.

Back in Salem, he attacked a young girl one night and stole her shoes. He did it again in Portland. Then, just as it looked as if nothing could stop him from turning into a rapist, he met a gentle 17-year-old girl who was anxious to get away from home, and who agreed to marry him. She was sometimes a little puzzled by his odd demands – making her dress up in silk underwear and high-heeled shoes and pose for photographs – but assumed that most men were like this.

While his wife was in hospital having a baby, Brudos followed a girl who was wearing pretty shoes. When he broke into her room that night, she woke up, and he choked her unconscious. Then, unable to resist, he raped her. He left her apartment carrying her shoes.

Now he was like a time bomb, waiting for another opportunity to explode. It happened when an encyclopedia saleswoman knocked on his door one winter evening . . .

Linda Slawson – a slight, plain girl with short-cropped hair – had seen Brudos in his yard in Portland, and asked if he was interested in buying encyclopedias. He had invited her into his garage, explaining that his wife had visitors. And when she bent down to take an encyclopedia from her case, he had knocked her unconscious with a heavy piece of wood. Then he knelt beside her and strangled her to death. Brudos's mother was upstairs, together with his two children; he sent them out to get supper at a hamburger joint, then hurried back to his garage.

To his delight, the dead girl was wearing pretty underwear. Brudos opened the box of panties and bras he had stolen from clotheslines, and spent the next hour or so dressing and undressing the body like an oversize doll. Oddly enough, he felt no desire to rape her. That night, when his family was asleep, he loaded the body into his station wagon, drove it out to the Willamette River, and tossed it off the bridge, weighted down with part of a car engine. He kept only one part of her – a foot – in the freezer in his garage; he wanted it to try shoes on . . .

That November, he found his second victim. On his way home from work in Lebanon, he stopped beside a car that had broken down on the freeway. The driver was student Jan Whitney, and she had two passengers – two male hippies to whom she had given a lift. Brudos explained that he was a car mechanic, but that unfortunately he did not have his tools with him. He would be glad to go home and get them . . . The three climbed into his station wagon, and were driven to Salem. There the two hippies got out. Back in his garage, Brudos left the girl while he went to check that his wife was not at home – she was going out to visit friends for the evening. Then he moved into the seat behind the unsuspecting girl, looped a leather strap round her neck, and strangled her. After that he placed her in the rear seat of his car and performed an act of anal sex. He spent the next hour or so 'playing dolls', dressing and undressing the body, taking photographs, and also committing rape. Finally, he suspended her by the wrists from a hook in the ceiling.

This time Brudos was determined not to dispose of the body the same day; he was enjoying his plaything. For the next two days he hurried down to his garage after work – it was locked, so his family could not wander in – and played dolls again. He even removed one of her breasts, with the intention of making a paperweight, but finally abandoned the idea because the hardener failed to set satisfactorily.

A few days later, his necrophiliac obsession nearly brought about his downfall. He took his family to Portland for Thanksgiving – 28 November – leaving the girl hanging in his garage. When he got back, he saw to his alarm that a corner of his garage had been demolished. A car driver had gone out of control and knocked a hole in the wall. The police had come to investigate, but were unable to get into the garage. A policeman who had peered through the hole in the wall had failed to see the body in the dark garage. Brudos lost no time in moving Jan Whitney into the pumphouse before he called the police and allowed them to inspect his garage. That same night he threw her into the Willamette River, weighed down with scrap iron.

After this close shave, Brudos made no more attempts at abduction until the following March. He drove to the Meier and Frank department store in Salem on Saturday the 27th, and was 'turned on' by a girl in high-heeled shoes and a miniskirt. He parked and hurried into the store looking for her, but she was nowhere to be seen. But walking back towards his car he saw a pretty girl with long dark hair about to get into her car. He grabbed her by the shoulder, pointed a pistol at her, and said: 'Come with me and I promise not to hurt you.' Instead of screaming – which would probably have saved her life – Karen Sprinker begged him not to shoot, and accompanied him to his car. Brudos drove her back to his garage, then ordered her out at gunpoint. She told him she would do whatever he liked. Brudos asked her if she was a virgin; she said yes, and added that she was having her period. (This part of the confession confirmed Stovall's belief that he had the right man; Karen's mother had told him that the girl was menstruating.) Brudos made her lie on the floor and raped her. Afterwards, the girl said she had to go to the toilet; Brudos took her into the house and allowed her to use the family bathroom. (His wife was away again.) Then he took her back to the garage and made her pose for pictures – some in her white cotton panties and bra, some in the more 'glamorous' stolen underwear and patent leather high-heeled shoes. Finally he tied her hands behind her, placed a rope round her neck, and pulled on it. He asked the girl if it was too tight, and she said it was. Then Brudos pulled her clear of the ground, and watched her suffocate. 'She kicked a little and died.' Brudos then violated the corpse. Later still he repeated the violation, cut off her breasts, and disposed of her remains in the Long Tom River that same evening, weighted down with a cylinder head.

Linda Salee, a pretty, athletic little girl (only five feet one inch tall) was also walking to her car – her arms loaded with packages – when Brudos approached her, showed her a police badge, and told her he was arresting her for shoplifting. She believed him, and protested that she had sales slips to prove that she had paid for the parcels. Brudos told her he was 'taking her in', and drove her back to his garage.

Like Karen Sprinker, Linda Salee behaved with a docility that undoubtedly cost her life. Brudos drove into the garage and closed the doors. Then he told her to follow him, and started across the yard to the house. At this point, Brudos's wife came out on the porch, and Brudos turned and signalled the girl to stand still. A single scream now – or a run for the gate – would have saved her life. Darcie Brudos failed to see her, and her husband took the girl back into the garage and tied her up. Then, incredibly, he went into the house for dinner. By the time Brudos returned

– his wife had now gone out – the girl had freed herself, but had not picked up the garage telephone and called the police. 'She was just waiting for me, I guess,' said Brudos.

Now, too late, she decided to put up a fight. But she was no match for the overweight killer. When he had subdued her, Brudos put the leather strap around her neck and tightened it. The girl asked: 'Why are you doing this to me?' Then she went limp. Brudos was in the act of raping her as she died.

Now, to 'punish' her, Brudos suspended her by the neck from the hook in the ceiling. He had decided to try an experiment. He stuck two hypodermic syringes into her ribs on either side – these were the two puncture marks that puzzled the pathologist – and attached them to electric wires. When he switched on the current, he was hoping she would dance. 'Instead it just burned her.'

Brudos kept her for another day, and violated the body just once more. This time he experienced no temptation to cut off the breasts; he did not like the pink nipples. ('They should be brown.') Instead he decided to make plastic moulds of the breasts; but the epoxy fibre glass somehow failed to work. On the second night, Brudos drove the body away in his station wagon, and dumped it in the Long Tom River, weighted down with a car overdrive unit.

Brudos made these confessions with a certain pedantic precision, as if explaining how to dismantle a gear box; it never seemed to strike him that Detective Jim Stovall might be horrified or sickened. In fact, Stovall went out of his way not to react; he had no wish to interrupt the flow of confession.

Brudos was charged with the murder of Karen Sprinker. The following day, a search warrant was issued, and the detectives entered the empty house – Darcie Brudos had moved away, together with her children. In the attic, police found his collection of shoes, girdles, bras and panties – dozens of them. On the living room shelf there was a replica of a female breast – at least, it looked like a replica until they looked more closely, and saw that it was real, and that it had been made solid with epoxy. In the basement, they found a tool box that contained photographs of the missing girls – some suspended from the hook in the ceiling, others posing for Brudos's camera in underwear. The police were to learn that Brudos had telephoned his wife from prison, and asked her to destroy the contents of the tool box; for once in her life, she had decided to disobey him.

One picture found under the workbench incriminated Brudos beyond all possible doubt. He had photographed the hanging girl reflected in a mirror lying below her on the floor, and had inadvertently caught his own reflection too.

Because Brudos pleaded guilty to four counts of murder, he was sentenced without trial to life imprisonment. When a neighbour alleged that she had seen Darcie Brudos helping her husband to force a woman wrapped in a blanket into her home, Darcie was charged with taking part in the murder of Karen Sprinker. But the jury found her not guilty. By the time she was acquitted, her husband had already started to serve his term of life imprisonment in the Oregon State Penitentiary.

His first year in prison was a difficult one. Sex criminals are detested by other prisoners, and are often kept segregated for their own good. Brudos was not segregated; but he was ignored. No one would talk to him or eat with him. He lost a great deal of weight. When someone managed to give him a hard blow on the side of the head with a bucket of water, he was taken to the prison hospital; but there proved to be no grounds for the suspicion that his eardrum was perforated.

In later years, Brudos's life improved. He proved to have a natural gift for electronics, and was soon virtually running the prison's computer system. The prison authorities have also allowed him, to some small extent, to pursue his lifelong interest in women's shoes and undergarments. His cell has stacks of mail order catalogues full of glossy photographs. Once again, Jerome Henry Brudos is living in his own private world. But now, fortunately, there are no real women who can be forced into helping him act out his fantasies.

Two of the most widely publicized murder cases of the 1960s qualify as mass murders – or 'spree killings' – rather than serial killings, but both deserve a brief mention at this point.

On 13 July 1966, 24-year-old Richard Speck knocked on a door in a nurses' hostel in Jeffrey Manor, Chicago, and pointed a gun at the Filipino nurse who opened it. He ordered her into another bedroom where three nurses were sleeping, and bound and gagged them. Speck smelt strongly of alcohol, but he kept assuring the women that he had no intention of hurting them. Five more nurses came in late, and were also bound and gagged.

Then, one by one, he took the nurses into the next room. The Filipino, Corazon Amurao, struggled to free herself and tried to persuade the others to attack the man, but no one was prepared to act. Corazon Amurao rolled under a bunk, and lay there, hoping the man would not look for her. Fortunately, he seemed to lose count. When he finally left at 5 a.m., she looked into the next room, and saw that the other eight nurses were dead. She screamed for help from the balcony. Police who entered the hostel soon after found that seven of the girls had been stabbed to death, the eighth strangled. Only one, Gloria Davy, had also been raped and sodomized.

Corazon Amurao described the killer as pockmarked, with a tattoo 'Born to raise hell' on his arm. He was quickly identified through a nearby seamen's hiring hall, where he had applied for a berth, and his name and description published in newspapers. Two days later, a doctor attending a patient who had been admitted with slashed wrists recognised the 'Born to raise hell' tattoo, and sent for the police.

In court, spectators who had expected to see a monster were astonished to find that the multiple killer looked like a down-at-heel nobody. Psychiatrists learned that Speck had been a delinquent all his life. A man of low self-esteem, he could be modest and agreeable when sober, but became boastful and violent when drunk. A nurse who had dated him said that he seemed to be seething with hatred and resentment. At 20 he had married a 15-year-old girl, whom he had come to hate. He had raped a 65-year-old woman during a burglary, and was believed to be responsible for the murder of a barmaid. He was also in the area of Indiana Harbour when three girls wearing swimsuits vanished one day – their bodies were never found.

Sentenced to a total of six hundred years in jail, Richard Speck died of a heart attack on 5 December 1991, a day before his fiftieth birthday.

Charles Manson, who was sentenced to death in April 1971, may or may not have actually killed anyone, but his followers – known as 'the Family' – killed at least nine people, possibly more. (Their prosecutor, Vincent Bugliosi, estimates thirty-five.)

When Charles Manson was released from jail in 1967 – at the age of 32 – he had spent most of his life in prisons or reformatories. When he came to San Francisco, and found himself among flower children and hippies, all smoking pot and preaching sexual abandon, he felt he had arrived in heaven. Manson, who played the guitar and advocated a rambling philosophy of freedom not unlike that of Aleister Crowley ('Do what thou wilt shall be the whole of the law'), was soon regarded as a kind of guru among the young people of the Haight-Ashbury district, many of whom were runaways. In the following year, surrounded by a crowd of disciples – mostly female – Manson moved into a ranch owned by an old man named George Spahn, who allowed them to live rent free in exchange for stable work and sexual favours from the girls.

One respectable college graduate named Charles Watson fell under Manson's spell and joined the 'family.' He later described to FBI agent Robert Ressler how Manson preached a philosophy of total abandonment of the ego – 'cease to exist' – which was reinforced by sessions with psychedelic drugs and sexual promiscuity. When they were stoned on LSD, Manson would paint word pictures of murder and torture. He dreamed of some tremendous social revolution – 'Helter skelter' – in which the pigs (bourgeoisie) would be finally suppressed, and blacks would be exterminated. To some extent, these vengeful dreams were the outcome of his own constantly dashed hopes of achieving fame as a pop musician.

One of the male disciples, Bobby Beausoleil, murdered a drug dealer named Gary Hinman – after Manson had sliced off Hinman's ear. Watson, who now thought of himself as Manson's rival – or at least, chief lieutenant – decided that it was time to assert his own authority, and realize Manson's dreams of slaughter. He agrees that Manson did not specifically *tell* him to go out and kill, but is certain that Manson wanted it. Watson led a band of three female disciples to the house of film actress Sharon Tate on 8 August 1969 – her husband Roman Polanski was in Europe, and she had three guests to dinner – an ex-lover and a Polish writer and his mistress. Entering the drive of the house, they shot and killed a teenage boy who was just leaving, then went into the house, bound the four occupants, then shot and stabbed them all to death – Sharon Tate, who was pregnant, was stabbed in the stomach. After the murders, Manson is believed to have gone to the house, to make sure everyone was dead.

That evening, there were two more victims – supermarket owner Leno LaBianca and his wife Rosemary. Manson entered the house first and tied them at gunpoint, then invited in Watson and two female disciples, who stabbed the LaBiancas to death, and wrote 'Death to pigs' on the walls in their blood. (The intention was to try to convince the world that the murders were the work of Black Panthers, and to try to start a massace of blacks by whites.)

Two months later, after the 'family' had moved to a deserted ranch in Death Valley, most of them were arrested on suspicion of burning a bulldozer belonging to park rangers. In prison, Susan Atkins, who had been one of the three who killed Sharon Tate, could not resist dropping hints about the murders to fellow prisoners, who in turn told the police.

The trial was one of the longest and most expensive in Los Angeles history (until the Hillside Stranglers a decade later), and ended with seven of the 'family' – including Manson and Watson – being sentenced to death or life imprisonment.

Unlike the Moors murders in England, the Manson case aroused a great deal of support for the accused, particularly among the beatnik and hippie population of the west coast. The feeling seemed to be that Manson was a genuine rebel against bourgeois society, and that his plea that this society had 'made his children what they were' had some justification. In fact, it is hard to see how Manson was any more justified than Brady. Both were inspired by a kind of mysticism of death and violence – a mysticism that had its roots in the ego. And, in spite of a genuine element of self-actualization, both must be classified as self-esteem killers.

9

The 1970s

The 1970s was the era in which the general public suddenly became conscious of the problem of the serial killer. This was due mainly to six cases, five American, one British. In four out of five of the American cases, the murders reached double figures. It seemed that violence in the late twentieth century was spiralling out of control – and that, moreover, the killers were becoming increasing sadistic. At least the Boston Strangler and Jerry Brudos had simply murdered and raped their victims; Dean Corll and the Hillside Stranglers also tortured theirs. All this caused a shock impact not unlike that of the Jack the Ripper murders on the Victorians.

Dean Corll, a homosexual who was still attached to his teddy bear, was the first serial killer to create this feeling that human depravity had reached new depths.

Shortly after 8 a.m. on 8 August 1973, the telephone operator in the Pasadena Police Department received a call from someone with a boyish voice and a broad Texas accent. 'Y'all better come on here now. Ah jes' killed a man.' He gave the address as 2020 Lamar Drive.

Within a minute, two squad cars were on their way. Lamar Drive was in a middle-class suburb of Pasadena – a south-eastern suburb of Houston – and 2020 Lamar was a small frame bungalow with an overgrown lawn. Three teenagers were sitting on the stoop by the front door: two boys and a girl. The girl, who was small and shapely, was dressed in clothes that looked even more tattered than the usual teenage outfit. All three were red-eyed, as if they had been crying. A skinny, pimply youth with an incipient blonde moustache identified himself as the one who had made the phone call. He pointed at the front door: 'He's in there.'

Lying against the wall in the corridor was the naked body of a well-built man, his face caked with blood that had flowed from a bullet wound. There were more bullet holes in his back and shoulder. The bullet in the head had failed to penetrate fully, and the end was sticking out of his skull. He was very obviously dead.

The three teenagers had identified themselves as Elmer Wayne Henley, 17, Timothy Kerley, 16, and Rhonda Williams, 15. Henley, the youth who had made the call, also acknowledged that he had shot his friend, whose name was Dean Arnold Corll. The teenagers were driven off to the Pasadena police headquarters. Meanwhile, an ambulance was summoned to take the corpse to the morgue, and detectives began to search the house.

It was obvious that Corll had moved in recently – the place was only half furnished. The bedroom outside which the corpse was lying contained only a single bed and a small table. It smelt strongly of acrylic paint – the type used in 'glue-sniffing'. The oddest thing about the room was the transparent plastic sheeting that covered the whole carpet. And lying beside the bed was an eight-foot length of plywood with handcuffs attached to two of its corners, and nylon ropes to the other two. A long hunting knife in its scabbard lay nearby. A black box proved to contain a seventeen-inch dildo – an imitation male sexual organ – and a tube of vaseline. It did not require the powers of a Sherlock Holmes to deduce that these objects were connected with some bizarre sexual ritual in which the victims were unwilling.

The new Ford van parked in the drive produced the same impression. There were navy blue curtains that could be drawn to seal off the whole of the rear portion, a piece of carpeting on the floor, and rings and hooks attached to the walls. There was also a considerable length of nylon rope. In a large box – covered with a piece of carpet – there were strands of human hair. Another similar box in a shed had air-holes drilled in its sides.

Back at the police station, Elmer Wayne Henley was explaining how he came to shoot his friend Dean Corll. He was nervous, and chain-smoked as he made his statement.

He had met Corll, he said, when he had lived in a run-down area of Houston called the Heights. Corll, who was sixteen years his senior, had recently moved into a house that had belonged to his father; it was in Pasadena. On the previous night, he and Timothy Kerley had gone to a glue-sniffing party at Corll's house. But in the early hours of the morning, the two boys had made some excuse to go out and collect Rhonda Williams, who had just decided to run away from home. Rhonda had been in a state of tension and misery ever since her boyfriend had vanished a year ago.

Corll had been furious when the boys arrived back at the house with Rhonda. 'You weren't supposed to bring a girl,' he yelled, 'You spoilt everything.' But after a while he seemed to control himself and regain his good humour, and the four of them settled down to glue-sniffing in the living room. Acrylic paint was sprayed into a paper bag, which was then passed around so they could all breathe in the fumes. Within an hour, they were all stretched out unconscious on the floor.

When Wayne Henley woke up, daylight was filtering through the drawn curtains, and Corll was snapping handcuffs on his wrists; his ankles were tied together. The other two were already handcuffed and bound. As they all began to recover their senses and struggle against their bonds, Corll revealed that his good humour of a few hours ago had been deceptive. He was seething with resentment and fury. He waved the knife at them and told them he was going to kill them all. 'But first I'm gonna have my fun.' Then he dragged Henley into the kitchen and rammed a revolver in his belly.

Henley decided that his only chance of escape was to 'sweet talk' Corll, persuading him that he would be willing to join in the murder of the other two. It took some time, but finally Corll calmed down and removed the handcuffs. Henley would rape Rhonda while he raped Timothy Kerley. Corll went and picked up Kerley, carrying him to the bedroom like some huge spider. Then he came back and carried off Rhonda. He turned on the portable radio to its top volume to drown any screams or protests.

When Henley went into the bedroom, Corll was naked, and was handcuffing Kerley, who was also naked, to the plywood board. Kerley, like Rhonda, was gagged. Corll handed Henley the knife and ordered him to cut off Rhonda's clothes. Rhonda was still dazed from the glue-sniffing, and was only half-aware of what was happening. But Kerley understood, and struggled violently as Corll tried to sexually assault him.

Knowing he was under observation, Henley pretended to rape Rhonda; in fact, he was incapable. But as Kerley thrashed and struggled violently, trying to throw off the heavy man, Henley shouted above the music: 'Why don't you let me take her outa here? She don't want to see that.' Corll ignored him. Henley jumped to his feet and grabbed the .22 pistol from the night table. 'Back off, Dean! Stop it!' Corll lurched to his feet. 'Go on Wayne, kill me. Why don't you?' As he lurched towards Henley, the boy fired; the bullet struck Corll in the head, and he staggered past, while Henley fired another shot into his shoulder. As Corll fell through the door and hit the wall of the corridor, Henley emptied the rest of the bullets into his back. Corll slumped down slowly to the floor, resting finally with his cheek and shoulder against the wall.

Henley quickly found the handcuff key and released the two teenagers – Rhonda was still unable to take in what had happened. But when she saw Corll lying in a pool of blood, she began to scream. Henley calmed her, and the three of them dressed – Rhonda making do with her slashed clothes. They discussed what to do next – whether to simply leave the corpse and go away. But it would be found sooner or later, and if neighbours had seen them entering or leaving the house, they would be in serious trouble. So Henley looked up the number of the Pasadena police department and rang them. As the tension relaxed, all three of them found they were unable to stop sobbing.

It took Henley an hour and a half to make his statement. Meanwhile, Kerley was able to confirm the story. But Kerley also mentioned something that intrigued the detectives. 'While we were waiting for the police, Wayne told me that if I wasn't his friend, he could have got fifteen hundred dollars for me.'

Questioned about the plywood board and the dildo, Henley told the police that Corll liked little boys, and had been paying him to procure them for him. But why, in that case, had Henley decided to kill him? 'He made one mistake', said Henley, 'He told me that I wouldn't be the first one he'd killed. He said he'd already killed a lot of boys and buried them in the boat shed.'

The words made the detectives glance at one another. So

far, they had been assuming that this was a simple case of glue-sniffing and sexual perversion, and that Corll's threats to kill the teenagers had been intended to frighten them. Henley's words raised a far more unpleasant suspicion. For nearly three years now, boys had been disappearing in the Heights area of Houston. Some were assumed to be runaways, but in the case of many of them, the parents had ruled it out as impossible – as, for example, in the case of a 9-year-old boy. Now the police had learned that Corll had lived in the Heights area until he moved to Pasadena, and one of his homes had been directly opposite that of the missing 9-year-old . . .

'Where is this boat shed?'

Henley said he wasn't sure; he had been there only once. But it was somewhere in south-west Houston. And now he was able to recollect three of the names that Corll had mentioned: Marty Jones, someone called Cobble, and someone called Hilligiest.

Even now, none of the detectives really believed they were dealing with mass murder. It was more likely that Henley was still under the influence of the 'glue'. But it had to be checked.

Detective Sergeant Dave Mullican asked Henley: 'Can you remember how to get to this boat shed?'

'I think so. It's near Hiram Clark Road.'

The first stop was the Houston police headquarters. There Henley was shown pictures of two boys who had been missing since 27 July, thirteen days ago. Henley identified them as Charles Cobble, 17, and Marty Jones, 18. The teenagers had shared a room, and both had good school records. Neither had any reason to run away.

The Pasadena detectives – accompanied by two of their Houston colleagues – now headed south to Hiram Clark Road. Another group of detectives were ordered to collect spades and ropes, and to meet them there. It was already late afternoon when the two cars arrived at the rendezvous, and Henley now took over the navigating. This was an area of open fields with cattle grazing in them. Finally, they pulled up beside a barbed wire fence on Silver Bell Street, and Henley pointed out the corrugated iron shed standing well back from the road.

Southwest Boat Storage was virtually a car park for boats, with twenty roofed 'stalls'. The police cars drove into the compound, and Henley directed them to stall number eleven. 'That's Dean's.'

The double doors were padlocked, and the lady who lived in a large house next to the compound – a Mrs Mayme Meynier – told them she had no key: the renters provided their own padlock. When they explained that Dean Corll was dead, she gave them permission to break in.

There was no boat inside: only a half-dismantled car, a bicycle and a large iron drum. The place was like an oven. There were also some cardboard boxes, water containers, and – ominously – two sacks of lime. The earthen floor was covered by two long strips of old carpet. A large plastic bag proved to contain a mixed lot of male clothing, including a pair of red shoes.

Wayne Henley stood at the door, looking inside. Then he walked back towards the cars, sat down on the ground, and buried his head between his knees.

The first task was to move everything out of the shed. While this was being done, a detective noted the registration numbers on the car and the bicycle and radioed them to headquarters. The answer came back quickly: the car had been stolen from a used car lot, and the bicycle belonged to a 13-year-old boy named James Dreymala who had vanished less than a week ago.

Now the place had been emptied, the two strips of carpet were also rolled out. Mullican pointed to a swelling in the floor near the left wall, and told two 'trusties' – convicts from the local jail who had been brought along to help – to start digging.

Even with the doors open, the heat was still stifling. Both men were soon perspiring heavily. Six inches down in the sandy earth, they uncovered a white substance.

'That's lime,' said Mullican, 'Keep digging.'

Suddenly, the shed was filled with a sickening stench; the detectives held their noses. The next carefully excavated shovelful revealed a face looking up at them. The younger trusty dropped his spade and rushed outside, making retching noises. A policeman took up the spade and went on clearing the earth. Minutes later, the policemen found themselves looking down at a large plastic bag that contained the body of a boy. He looked about 12 or 13, and was naked. When the bag had been carefully lifted from the ground, it was obvious that the body inside had been recently buried. One of the detectives radioed headquarters to send forensic experts.

Outside, the press was starting to arrive. One radio reporter had allowed Wayne Henley to use his car telephone to call up his mother. They heard him say: 'Mama, I killed Dean.' Over his own microphone the reporter heard Mrs Henley said: 'Oh Wayne, you *didn't*!' From what followed, it was clear that Henley's mother wanted to rush out to the site; a detective shook his head.

Moments later, as Henley hung up, the body was carried out from the boat shed in its plastic sheeting. The boy was clearly shaken. 'It was all my fault.' 'Why?' asked a detective casually. 'Because I introduced him to them boys.' And the teenager went on to explain that, during the past two years, he had procured many boys for Dean Corll.

By the time the radio reporter went on the air at six o'clock, a second body had just been discovered. As it began to grow dark, a fire engine with a floodlight and two air-extractors arrived. Soon after that, two more bodies were uncovered. One had been shot in the head, the other strangled with a Venetian blind cord that was still knotted tight around the throat. As the news of the finds was broadcast, crowds of spectators arrived to stare over the barbed wire fence. The air extractors blasted the smell of decaying corpses at them. One reporter had already minted a striking phrase: 'There are wall to wall bodies in there.'

Mrs Meynier, the owner of the site, was being questioned about her former tenant. She described him as 'the nicest person you'd ever meet', a 'gentleman' with a charming smile and dimples. He had never been behind with his $5 a week rent. But recently, she had been baffled when he told her he wanted to rent another stall. Why should he need more space? Surely he already had plenty?

Asked how long Corll had rented the stall, she replied: 'Since 1971.' The detective turned away muttering: 'My God!'

Henley, meanwhile, was also telling reporters how nice Corll could be. His mother liked 'ol' Dean' and did not object to their friendship. But as the fourth body was carried out, he became nervous; it was obvious that he was suffering from a glue-sniffing hangover. At ten o'clock he was driven back to the police station. Two hours later, the body count had risen to eight, and the diggers were exhausted. They decided to call it a day.

Back in the Heights, many families with missing teenage sons were now watching their television screens for the printed messages that gave the latest news, and trying to convince themselves that *their* child could not be among those in the boat shed. But for those whose children had known Dean Corll, that was a slender hope. Now the parents found themselves wondering why they had failed to suspect Corll of being a sexual pervert. He and his mother had run a candy factory in the Heights, and Corll was popular with the children because he gave them candy. He also gave them lifts in his white Dodge van.

By midnight, a planeload of reporters from other parts of the country arrived in Houston. And from all over the world, reporters were converging on the corrugated iron boat shed. Dean Corll had been dead for only sixteen hours, but his name had already reached every part of the globe. If the number of his suspected victims was confirmed – and the detectives had a list of forty-two youngsters who had vanished since 1970 – he would be America's worst mass murderer to date. Even H. H. Holmes had only confessed to twenty-eight.

Two hours after the lights went out at Southwest Boat Storage on Silver Bell Street, a car containing five people drew up at the barbed wire fence. They identified themselves to the police on guard as the Hilligiest family. Thirteen-year-old David Hilligiest had disappeared more than two years earlier, on 30 May 1971. He had set out for the local swimming pool early that afternoon, and failed to arrive there. On that same day, another local boy, George Malley Winkle, 16, had vanished. The Hilligiests had spent eleven hundred dollars on a private detective, but had failed to find the slightest trace of their son. Now, after telephoning police headquarters, they had learned that Wayne Henley had mentioned David Hilligiest as one of the victims buried in the boat stall. They begged the police guard to allow them to go to the boat stall. The police explained sympathetically that that was impossible; the lights were out and the place was now locked up. They had better go home, get some sleep, and prepare for their ordeal of the next day.

At ten the next morning, after a visit from his mother and a light breakfast, Henley was again sitting opposite Mullican in the Pasadena interrogation room. The rings under his eyes made it obvious that he had slept badly.

'Tell me about the boys you procured.'

Henley explained that he had met Corll two years earlier, and that Corll had then offered him $200 each for any boys he could 'bring along'. For a year he did nothing; then, when he badly needed money, decided to take up the offer. Corll had not actually paid him the full $200 for the first boy he had procured. And he had not paid subsequently.

Now Henley made his most significant admission so far: that he had been present when Corll had killed some of the boys. This suddenly changed the whole situation. The police had been assuming that they were dealing with an insatiable homosexual rapist and a youth he had persuaded to help him find boys. Now it began to look as if Wayne Henley had been an active partner in the murders.

They were interrupted by the telephone. It was the Houston police headquarters. A man named Alton Brooks had turned up at the police station with his 18-year-old son David, explaining that David had known Corll and wanted to talk about it. And David Brooks was now giving a statement that implicated Henley in the murders.

When Mullican hung up, he told teenager on the other side of the desk: 'That was Lieutenant Porter at Houston Homicide. He says he has a boy named David Brooks in there, and Brooks is making a statement about you and Dean Corll.'

Oddly enough, Henley looked relieved.

'That's good. Now I can tell you the whole story.'

Mullican's next question was: 'Did you kill any of the boys yourself?'

Henley answered without hesistation: 'Yes, sir.'

Mullican did his best to show no emotion during the statement that followed. But it was difficult to look impassive. What Henley was describing how he had lured some of his own best friends into Corll's lair, witnessed their torture and rape, and then participated in their murders.

It seemed that David Brooks had been Corll's original accomplice, as well as his lover. He had been procuring victims for Corll long before Henley came along. In fact, Henley was intended to be just another victim when he was taken along to meet Corll in 1971. But Corll soon realized that Henley would be more useful as an accomplice. He had lot of friends, and would do anything for money. In fact, said Henley, he was pretty sure that Corll still planned to kill him sooner or later, because he had his eye on Henley's 14-year-old brother Ronnie, and knew he would have to kill Wayne before he could get his hands on Ronnie . . .

The method of obtaining victims was usually much the same.

Corll would drive around with Henley until they saw a likely victim, and Corll would offer him a lift. Since there was already a teenager in the car, the boy would suspect nothing. That was how Dean had picked up that 13-year-old blond kid a few days ago. Dean was parked in front of a grocery store when the kid came past on his bike. Dean called him over and told him he had found some Coke bottles in his van, and the kid could go and collect the deposit on them. The boy (it was 13-year-old James Dreymala) took the bottles and came back a few minutes later with the money. Then Dean remembered that he had a lot more Coke bottles back in his garage, and if the kid would like to come along, he could have them. So James Dreymala allowed Dean to put his bike in the back of the van, and went back to Dean's house on Lamar Street. The boy said he had to ring his father to ask if he could stay out, but the father refused. After the call, Dean 'had his fun', then strangled the boy, taking the body out to the boatshed to join the others . . .

At about this time, Mullican heard the latest report from the boat shed. Four more victims had been found in the past two hours, bringing the total up to twelve. And beside one of them his genitals had been found in a plastic bag. Part of Dean's 'fun' was castrating his victims.

Henley's new confession went on for two more hours. It was rambling and often incoherent, but Mullican gathered that Henley had been present at the murder of at least nine boys. He admitted shooting one of them himself. The bullet had gone up his nose, and the boy had looked up and said: 'Wayne, why did you shoot me?' Henley pointed the gun at the boy's head and pulled the trigger again; this time the boy died.

Had Corll buried any bodies in other places beside the boat-shed? Mullican wanted to know. Oh sure, said Henley, there were some on the shores of Lake Sam Rayburn, and more on High Island Beach, east of Galveston . . .

It was now past noon, but it seemed a good idea to bring Wayne Henley and David Brooks face to face. Then get Henley to show them where the bodies were buried at Lake Sam Rayburn.

When they arrived at the Houston police station, Lieutenant Breck Porter took Mullican aside. David Brooks was doing plenty of 'confessing', but it was all about Wayne Henley and Dean Corll. According to Brooks he had been merely an innocent bystander.

David Brooks proved to be a tall, round-faced, long-haired youth who wore granny glasses; apparently he had recently married. He looked startled to see Wayne Henley – no one had warned him Henley was on his way. Henley stared across at his former friend. 'David, I told 'em everything. You better do the same.'

Brooks looked defensive. 'I don't know what you're talking about.'

'Yes you do. And if you don't tell everything, I'm gonna change my confession and say you was responsible for all of it.'

David Brooks said he wanted to talk to his father, and was taken out of the room. Later that day, he was told he was under arrest for being implicated in the murders. He was subdued and tearful as he was led away.

Henley, on the other hand, seemed to have been infused with a new life since his confession. On the way out to Lake Sam Rayburn – a hundred and twenty miles away, in the Angelina National Park – he talked non-stop, and made a number of damaging admissions. 'I choked one of them boys until he turned blue, but Dean still had to come and finish him off.' When a deputy asked how a decent boy like him could get involved in murder, he made the odd reply: 'If you had a daddy that shot at you, you might do some things too.'

An hour later he was leading them into the woods on the shores of Lake Sam Rayburn. He was already implicating David Brooks, although not by name. 'We picked them up and Dean raped and killed them.' Asked by a reporter if there had been any torture, He replied cryptically: 'It wasn't what you would really call torture.' But he declined to elaborate. Then, refusing to allow reporters and photographers to accompany them, he led the police to the sites of four more bodies. One of them had been buried underneath a board; it emerged later that when Henley and Corll had returned to bury another body, they had found a hand sticking out of the ground, so had re-buried it with the board on top.

Before darkness made further digging impossible, two bodies had been unearthed. The latest news from the boat shed in south Houston was that the digging was now finished, and seventeen bodies – or parts of bodies – had been found. The ones that had not been buried in plastic bags had decayed, so that little but bones remained. The body count so far was nineteen.

The following morning, it rose to twenty-one, with the uncovering of the other two bodies at Lake Sam Rayburn. By mid-morning, the convoy of police and reporters was on its way south to High Island, where Henley insisted there were eight more bodies buried.

The search of the High Island beach turned into a kind of circus. Three helicopters had arrived with camera crews, and the reporters almost outnumbered the crowds of morbidly fascinated spectators. Henley was in good spirits, offering to race the overweight sheriff up the beach – an offer which, in view of the 90 degree heat, the sheriff politely declined. David Brooks, who had been brought down from Houston, was much more subdued; he sat there much of the time, his arms around his knees, refusing to speak to reporters.

Only two more bodies were found that afternoon, bringing the total up to twenty-three. Later, four more would be unearthed on the beach. The other two mentioned by Henley were never discovered. But even a total of twenty-seven made Dean Corll America's worst mass murderer so far.

While Wayne Henley was helping the police at Lake Sam Rayburn, David Brooks was offering the first complete picture of Corll's career of homicidal perversion in the Houston interrogation room. He still insisted that he had never taken an active part in the killings, but his questioners suspected that this was because he had sworn to his father that he was innocent of murder. Henley, who seems to have been the more truthful of the two, stated that Brooks *had* taken an active part in several murders. The picture that emerged left little doubt that this was true.

Meanwhile, reporters were learning all they could about the background of America's worst mass murderer. For the most part, it proved to be surprisingly innocuous.

Dean Arnold Corll was born on Christmas Day 1939, in Waynesdale, Indiana, the first child of Arnold and Mary Corll, who were in their early twenties. But the parents were temperamentally unsuited; both were strong characters, and their quarrels could be violent. Mary Corll adored her eldest son; Arnold Corll – a factory worker who became an electrician – was a disciplinarian who found children tiresome. When Dean was six, the couple divorced, and Arnold Corll was drafted into the Army Air Force. Mrs Corll bought a house trailer and drove to join her husband at his base in Tennessee, but the quarrels continued and they separated again. An elderly farm couple agreed to look after the boys – Dean had a younger brother, Stanley – while Mary Corll went out to work.

From the beginning, Dean was an oversensitive loner. Because his feelings were hurt at a birthday party when he was six, he always refused to go to other people's houses. While Stanley played with other children Dean stayed at home.

The Corlls made yet another attempt at reconciliation after the war, and in 1950 drove the trailer to Houston. But the marriage still failed to work out, and they parted again.

At this point, it was discovered that Dean had a congenital heart ailment, and he was ordered to avoid sport. In fact it was hardly necessary; he was not the sporting type.

Life for Mrs Corll was hard; she worked while the boys went to one school after another. In 1953 she married a travelling clock salesman named Jake West, by whom she had a daughter. They moved to Vidor, Texas, a small town where, as one commentator put it, 'the big event is for the kids to pour kerosene on the cat and set it afire'. Since he spent so much time without his parents, Dean became intensely protective of his siblings – a kind of surrogate mother.

Now a teenager, Dean took up skin-diving, but had to quit when he fainted one day, and the doctor diagnosed a recurrence of the heart problem. But he was allowed to continue playing the trombone in the school band. He was always quiet, always polite, and never complained or 'fussed'.

One day, a pecan-nut salesman observed Mrs West's efficiency at baking pies and asked her why she didn't take up candy making. She liked the idea, and was soon running a candy business in their garage, with Jake West as travelling salesman and Dean as the errand boy and 'gofer' ('go fer this, go fer that . . .') He was often overworked, but remained cheerful and uncomplaining. After his graduation from high school at the age of 20, Dean went back to Indiana to be with Jake West's widowed mother, while the family returned to Houston. There the candy business continued to be underfunded. Two years later, when Dean moved back to Houston, he took a job with the Houston Lighting and Power Company, and made candy at nights. Women who worked there were overawed at his industry.

In 1964, Dean Corll was drafted into the army. This seems to have been a watershed in his life, for it was the time when he first realized he was homosexual. No details are available, but it seems obvious that some homosexual affair made him realize what he had so far failed to suspect. Released from the army after eleven months – pleading that his family needed him to work in the candy business – he returned to Houston to find his mother's second marriage in the process of dissolution. Mr and Mrs West had become business rivals rather than partners, and when Jake West threw her out of the shop one day, Mary West went off and started one of her own. Dean didn't mind; he had never liked his stepfather.

Now living in an apartment of his own, Dean began making friends with the children of the neighbourhood – notably the boys – giving away free candy. Yet when a boy who worked for the company made some kind of sexual advance, Dean was angry and upset, and pleased when his mother dismissed him. Nevertheless, a fellow-worker noticed that another teenage employee always made sure that he was never left alone with Corll.

Dean's mother remained intensely protective, treating him as if he was still a teenager. But he was once again seeing something of his father, for whom he had great admiration.

Meanwhile, Mary West now repeated her error and married yet again – this time a merchant seaman. She found him stupid and coarse, and soon began to suspect he was a psychotic. They divorced – and then re-married. He became neurotically jealous of his wife, and they separated again. But his continual attempts to force his way into the candy factory destroyed her enthusiasm for the place. When a psychic told her to move to Dallas, she took his advice, and divorced the merchant seaman yet again. And Dean, now left alone in Houston, suddenly felt that he was free to do as he liked.

Corll's Mr Hyde aspect had at first manifested itself simply as a powerful attraction to boys, with whom he enjoyed playing the part of an elder brother. One boy said: 'He acted real nice to me. He never tried to mess with me or nothin'.' But the desire was there, and Mr Hyde began to break out when he realized that some boys would permit oral sex in exchange for money. Fourteen-year-old David Brooks was one of these. In fact, he was delighted to have an 'elder brother', and became totally emotionally dependent on Corll – so dependent that he made no attempt to denounce him when he learned that he was a killer.

This emotional dependence of David Brooks undoubtedly played a major part in the tragedy that followed. His love for Corll meant that he was willing to subjugate his will to Corll's. And Corll, in turn, was encouraged to give way to his Mr Hyde personality. It was a case of *folie à deux*.

Brooks was a lonely schoolboy when he met Dean Corll in the Heights in 1969. The two had something in common: their parents had broken up, and they were on their own. Corll's mother had wound up the candy factory she ran with her son's help, and gone off to live in Dallas. Corll had found himself a $5 an hour job with the Houston Lighting and Power Company, and moved his few possessions into a shed. Corll had propositioned Brooks, and the teenager had agreed to allowing Corll to have oral sex for a payment of $5. But their relationship was not purely commercial. Corll was able to give Brooks something he needed badly – affection. Brooks, in turn, worshipped Corll: 'Dean was a real good dude', 'a brilliant and generous man'. And when he returned to Houston in 1970 – escaping from his disintegrating family – Brooks began to see a great deal of Corll: during the next three years they often shared rooms for brief periods. By that time, it seems probable that Corll had already committed his first murder. A 21-year-old student from the University of Texas in Austin, Jeffrey Alan Konen, had hitch-hiked to his home in Houston on 25 September 1970. He had last been seen at six o'clock in the evening, looking for another lift. It seems probable that it was Corll who picked him up, and invited him back to his apartment at 3300 Yorktown. Konen's body was one of the last of those found – on High Island beach – and was so decomposed that it was impossible to determine cause of death. But the fact that the body had been bound hand and foot suggested that Corll had killed Jeffrey Konen in order to to commit sodomy.

What made Corll's murderous mission so easy was the teenage drug culture of the Heights. In the claustrophobic, run-down environment, all the kids were bored and discontented; they felt they were stuck there for life. The mere suggestion of a party was enough to make their eyes light up. They all smoked pot – when they could afford it. They also popped pills – Seconal, Nembutal, phenobarbital, Quaaludes, even aspirin, washed down with beer or Coca Cola. But because it was cheap, acrylic paint was the easiest way of obtaining a quick 'high'. Although one boy collapsed and died when he tried to play football after a long glue-sniffing session, it made no difference to the others; he was merely 'unlucky'. Moreover, the possession of 'glue' was perfectly legal; and in an environment where a teenager was likely to be searched for drugs at any hour of the day, this went a long way towards making acrylics the most popular form of escape.

The fact that most of the kids were permanently broke conferred another tremendous advantage on a predatory homosexual like Corll. Allowing a 'queer' to perform oral sex was an easy and quick way of obtaining a few dollars. There can be no doubt that many of Corll's victims had been back to his room several times before his demand for a more painful form of sex caused them to baulk, and led to their deaths. The fact that there *were* a fairly high number of runaways from the Heights meant that occasional disappearances caused little stir.

The central key to the Houston murders is Corll's craving for sexual violation. At some point, oral sex ceased to satisfy him. Brooks admitted: 'He killed them because he wanted sex, and they didn't want to.' Even Brooks himself seems to have withheld anal sex. He describes how, after he had introduced Corll to Wayne Henley, the latter knocked him unconscious as he entered Corll's apartment; Corll then tied him to the bed and sodomized him. This would obviously have been pointless if anal sex had been a normal part of their relationship. Yet in spite of the rape, Brooks continued to worship Corll, and to participate in the murders and disposal of the bodies.

It also seems clear that Corll was in love with Henley. But Henley remained independent. Far more avaricious than Brooks, he became Corll's accomplice for cash. In spite of Henley's denial, there can be no doubt that Corll paid him large sums of money as a procurer. One friend of Henley's later described how Henley had suggested that they should go to Australia together as homesteaders – Henley declared that he would provide the $1,700 each they would need. 'Where would you get it?' asked his friend. 'I already have it.' Henley's later assertion that Corll never paid him is almost certainly an attempt to conceal the appalling truth: that he sold his friends to Corll for $200 each.

By the end of 1970, Corll was firmly in the grip of 'Mr Hyde'. Brooks later tried to justify the murders: 'Most of the boys weren't good boys. This . . . probably sounds terrible, but most of 'em wasn't no great loss. They was in trouble all the time, dope fiends and one thing or another.' This is almost certainly a repetition of somethng Corll said to Brooks – perhaps on many occasions.

Not long after the murder of Jeffrey Konen, David Brooks walked into Corll's Yorktown apartment unannounced, and found Corll naked. In another room there were two naked boys strapped to a plywood board. Corll demanded indignantly what Brooks was doing there, and ordered him to leave. Later, he told Brooks that he had killed both boys, and offered him a car as the price of his silence. In fact, he gave Brooks a new Corvette. The identity of these two victims has never been established, but they were probably among the bodies found on the High Island beach.

Having accepted the Corvette, Brooks was now an accomplice. He would go 'cruising' with Corll and offering lifts to teenage boys. One unknown youth was picked up some time in November 1970, and taken back to Corll's apartment. Corll raped and murdered the boy while Brooks looked on. No further details of this murder – or victim – are known.

Corll's appetite for murder was growing. Many of the boys he used to befriend in the days of the candy factory, and who had always been welcome visitors in his room, now noticed that he was becoming bad tempered and secretive, and they stopped calling round. Many of these boys later insisted that Corll had simply been 'nice' to them, without any attempt to make sexual advances. Many others, like David Brooks, had undoubtedly accepted money for oral sex.

On 15 December 1970, Brooks persuaded two boys back to an apartment that Corll had rented on Columbia Street. They were 14-year-old James Eugene Glass, and his friend Danny Michael Yates, 15. Both had been to church with James Glass's father, and had agreed to meet him later. Glass had already been back to Corll's apartment on a previous occasion, and had taken a great liking to Corll. This time, both boys ended on the plywood board, after which they were strangled. By this time, Corll had decided that he needed somewhere closer than High Island or Lake Sam Rayburn (where his family owned a holiday cabin), so he rented the boat shed on Silver Bell Street. The two boys were buried there.

Corll had apparently enjoyed the double murder so much that he was eager to try it again. Six weeks later, two brothers, 14-year-old Donald Edward Waldrop, and 13-year-old Jerry Lynn Waldrop, were lured to a newly rented apartment at 3200 Mangum Road. (Corll changed apartments frequently, almost certainly to prevent curious neighbours from gossiping about his activities.) The father of the Waldrop boys was a construction worker who worked next door to Corll's new apartment. The boys were also strangled and buried in the boat shed. Brooks admitted: 'I believe I was present when they were buried.' This was typical of his general evasiveness.

On 29 May 1971, David Hilligiest, 13, disappeared on his way to the swimming pool; his friend, 16-year-old George Malley Winkle, also vanished on the same day. Malley was on probation for stealing a bicycle. That same evening, just before midnight, the telephone rang; it was Malley, contacting his mother to tell her that he was in Freeport – a surfing resort sixty miles to the south – with some kids. They would be on their way home shortly. That night, Mrs Winkle slept badly, with a foreboding that her son was in trouble. When he failed to return, she asked young people in the neighbourhood if they had seen him, and learned that he had climbed into a white van, together with David Hilligiest.

The frantic parents spent weeks following up every possible lead. They had posters printed, offering a thousand dollars' reward, and friendly truckers distributed them all over southern Texas. So did a lifelong friend of David Hilligiest's – Elmer Wayne Henley, another child of a broken home. He tried to comfort the Hilligiests by telling them that he was sure nothing had happened to David. A psychic who was consulted by the Hilligiests disagreed: he plunged them into despair by telling them their son was dead.

Ruben Watson, 17, another child of a broken home, went off to the cinema on the afternoon of 17 August 1971, with a few dollars borrowed from his grandmother; he later rang his mother at work to say he would meet her out at 7.30. He never arrived, and she never saw him again. Brooks later admitted being present when Ruben was murdered.

By this time, Wayne Henley had entered the picture. He had

become friendly with David Brooks, and Brooks had introduced him to Dean Corll. Henley was intended as a victim, but Corll seems to have decided that he would be more useful as a pimp. The fact that Henley was skinny and pimply may also have played a part in Corll's decision to let him live. The Hilligiests' son Greg – aged 11 – came home one day to say that he had been playing an exciting game called poker with Wayne Henley, David Brooks, and an older friend of Henley's who made candy. Dorothy Hilligiest knew the man who made candy – in the previous year, she had gone looking for David, and found him at the candy factory with Malley Winkle and the round-faced man who owned the place. Mrs Hilligiest had bought a box of candy from him before she took David away . . .

Another friend of Henley's was 14-year-old Rhonda Williams, a shapely girl who was as anxious to escape the Heights as most of its other teenagers. Since she had been sexually assaulted as a child, her attitude to sex was inhibited and circumspect. Like so many Heights teenagers, she was part of a one-parent family – her mother had collapsed and died of a heart attack as she was hanging out the washing. Rhonda craved affection and security, and she seemed to have found it when she met 19-year-old Frank Aguirre. He was slightly cross-eyed, but serious-minded, and was already saving money – from his job in a restaurant – to get married to Rhonda. But on 24 February 1972, Frank Aguirre failed to return home from his work, and was never seen again. He left his pay cheque uncollected. Rhonda was shattered and went into nervous depression for a year; she was only just beginning to recover on that evening of August 1973 when she informed Wayne Henley that she had decided to run away from home, and Henley took her over to Dean Corll's house in Pasadena to stay the night . . .

On 21 May 1972, 16-year-old Johnny Delome vanished. The body was found at High Island fourteen months later; he had been shot as well as strangled. Johnny Delome must have been the youth that Henley shot up the nose, and then in the head. He was killed at the same time as Billy Baulch, 17, who was also buried at High Island. Six months later, Billy's 15-year-old brother Michael would become another victim of Dean Corll. In the meantime, he had killed another two boys, Wally Jay Simoneaux, 14, and Richard Hembree, 13, on 3 October 1972. Their bodies were found together in the boat shed.

Another victim of 1972 was 18-year-old Mark Scott, whose body was was one of those that were never identified; Brooks stated that he was also one of Corll's victims.

And so the murders went on into 1973: Billy Lawrence, 15, on 11 June; Homer Garcia, 15, on 7 July; Charles Cobble, 17, on 25 July, who vanished with his friend Marty Jones, 18, on the same day. The final victim was 13-year-old James Dreymala, lured to Corll's Pasadena house to collect Coke bottles, and buried in the boat shed. There were undoubtedly other victims in 1973, possibly as many as nine. Brooks said that Corll's youngest victim was a 9-year-old boy.

On Monday 13 August, five days after the death of Dean Corll, a Grand Jury began to hear evidence against Henley and Brooks. The first witnesses were Rhonda Williams and Tim Kerley, the two who had almost become Corll's latest victims. It was clear that Kerley had been invited to Corll's house by Henley in order to be raped and murdered – this is what Henley meant when he told Kerley that he could have got fifteen hundred dollars for him. He was exaggerating, but was otherwise telling the truth. And when Corll had snarled: 'You've spoilt everything,' he meant that the arrival of Rhonda Williams now made it impossible to murder Kerley. At that moment, it seems, he thought of a solution: to kill all three teenagers.

Rhonda Williams, it emerged, had decided to run away with Henley, whom she now regarded as her boyfriend. In fact, Corll knew all about the arrangement and had no objection – he himself was planning to move to Colorado, where his mother was living, and to take Henley and Rhonda Williams with him. The fact that he also planned to take an old flame of his pre-homosexual days called Betty Hawkins, as well as her two children, suggests that Corll had decided to give up killing teenagers. But Rhonda had arranged to run away on 17 August, nine days later; and when she arrived at Corll's house in the early hours of 8 August, he felt that his fun had been spoiled.

After listening to the evidence of various teenagers, the jury indicted Henley and Brooks on murder charges. Henley was charged with taking part in the killing of Billy Lawrence, Charles Cobble, Marty Jones, Johnny Delome, Frank Aguirre and Homer Garcia; Brooks for his part in the murders of James Glass, Ruben Watson, Billy Lawrence and Johnny Delome. Efforts by the lawyers to get bail were turned down.

Houston was stunned by the events of the past week, and criticism of the police department was bitter and uninhibited. The main complaint of the parents of missing teenagers was that they had been unable to get the police to take the slightest interest; they were told that their children were runaways. The Police Chief Herman Short counterattacked clumsily by publicly stating that there had been no connection between the missing teenagers – implying that there would have been little for the police to investigate. The statements of Henley and Brooks – indicating that most of the victims knew one another – flatly contradicted this assertion. Short went on to say that the murders indicated that parents should pay closer attention to the comings and goings of their teenagers, a remark that drew outraged comments from parents like Dorothy Hilligiest, whose children had simply vanished on their way to or from some normal and innocent activity. Short went on angrily to attack the Soviet newspaper *Izvestia*, which had referred to the 'murderous bureaucracy' of the Houston police department, pointing out that the Soviet government had a reputation for making dissenters disappear. All this failed to impress the public or the politicians, and Short resigned three months later after the municipal elections.

There was also criticism of the attitude of the police towards the search for more bodies. One of Corll's ex-employees, Ruby Jenkins, had mentioned the interesting fact that, during the last years of the candy factory's existence, Corll was often seen handling a shovel and digging holes. He dug under the floor of his private room in the factory – known jokingly as the 'pouting room', because he often retired there to sulk – then cemented over the excavation. He also dug holes near the rear wall of the factory, and on a space that later became a parking lot. He always did this by night. His explanation was that he was burying spoiled candy because it drew bees and bred weevils. No one at the time questioned this curious explanation, or asked him what was wrong with placing the spoiled candy in a plastic bag and dropping it in the trash can. 'He had this big roll of plastic sheet, four or five foot wide, and he had sacks of cement and some other stuff back in his pouting room.' Clearly, this was something that required investigating. But when the police came along to look at the spots indicated by Ruby Jenkins, they dug only half-heartedly in a few places, and soon gave up. 'Lady, this is old cement. There couldn't be any bodies there.'

After the finding of bodies 26 and 27 – on High Island beach, tied together – the search for more bodies was dropped, even though Henley insisted that two more were buried there. Another curious feature of this final discovery was that there were two extra bones – an arm bone and a pelvis – in the grave, plainly indicating a twenty-eighth victim.

Lieutenant Porter received two calls about bodies on the same morning. A Mr and Mrs Abernathy had been camping on Galveston Island – about fifty miles down the coast from High Island – when they saw two men carrying a long bundle over the dunes. Another man had been camping on east Galveston beach when he saw a white car and another car parked near a hole in the beach; a long plastic bundle the size of a body lay beside the hole. There were three men beside the hole. The man identified two from photographs as Dean Corll and Wayne Henley. The third man had long blond hair – like David Brooks. As the campers sat looking at this curious scene in their own car, Henley advanced on them with a menacing expression, and they drove off.

These two events took place in March and June, 1973. In fact, the first 1973 victim identified (from the Lake Sam Rayburn burial site) was Billy Lawrence, who vanished on 11 June. It seems unlikely that a man who had been killing as regularly as Corll should allow a seven-month period to elapse between victims (the last known victim of 1972 is Michael Baulch, Billy Baulch's younger brother). The unidentified victims found in the boat shed had obviously been buried much earlier, probably in 1971.

The Galveston authorities flatly declined to allow the Houston police to follow up this lead, refusing to permit digging on their beach.

Meanwhile, the police switchboard in Houston continued to handle hundreds of enquiries about missing teenagers – one mother, whose son had been working with a circus, and had vanished in Houston, was certain that he was one of Corll's victims. In most of these cases, the police were forced to state that they were unable to help.

When Brooks and Henley appeared for their arraignment, there was a heavy guard of armed police – dozens of threatening phone calls had been received from all over Texas. Henley's defence lawyer, Charles Melder, indicated that his defence would be one of insanity. Brooks's attorney, Ted Musick, indicated that he would follow the same line. At the same time, the District Attorney announced that each of the accused would be tried on one charge only: Henley for the murder of Charles Cobble, and Brooks for that of Billy Lawrence.

Since Corll was already dead, and the two accused had already confessed, the trial itself was something of an anticlimax. Its venue was changed, on the insistence of the lawyers, and it opened at San Antonio, Texas, in July 1974, before Judge Preston Dial. Predictably, the jury rejected the insanity defence, and Henley was convicted on nine counts (not including the shooting of Dean Corll), drawing a total sentence of 594 years. Brooks was convicted on only one count, and received life imprisonment. Henley appealed in 1979, and was convicted for a second time.

It is easy to understand the sense of shock produced by the Corll murders – analogous to that felt in England after the Moors murder case. The impression produced by the evidence is that Corll was a sadistic monster, the kind we would expect to encounter in a horror film, possessed by evil spirits. But our study of other serial killers – like Haarmann and Kürten – makes it clear that nothing is ever as simple as that. The evidence shows that Corll was basically a spoilt brat who always wanted his own way, and that he remained emotionally a child – this aspect of his personality is caught in the notorious photograph that shows him holding a teddy bear.

In fact, like so many serial killers, Corll drifted into it by slow steps – as a man becomes a drug addict or an alcoholic. He wanted young boys; he bought their sexual favours. Then he began raping and killing them. It was a gentle progression down a slope, like walking slowly into a pond . . .

This is also true of another case that received even more publicity than the Corll murders. Ted Bundy is a textbook case of the 'high IQ killer'.

On 31 January 1974, a student at the University of Washington, in Seattle, Lynda Ann Healy, vanished from her room; the bedsheets were bloodstained, suggesting that she had been struck violently on the head. During the following March, April and May, three more girl students vanished; in June, two more. In July, two girls vanished on the same day. It happened at a popular picnic spot, Lake Sammanish; a number of people saw a good-looking young man, with his arm in a sling, accost a girl named Janice Ott and ask her to help him lift a boat on to the roof of his car; she walked away with him and did not return. Later, a girl named Denise Naslund was accosted by the same young man; she also vanished. He had been heard to introduce himself as 'Ted'.

In October 1974 the killings shifted to Salt Lake City; three girls disappeared in one month. In November, the police had their first break in the case: a girl named Carol DaRonch was accosted in a shopping centre by a young man who identified himself as a detective, and told her that there had been an attempt to break into her car; she agreed to accompany him to headquarters to view a suspect. In the car he snapped a handcuff on her wrist and pointed a gun at her head; she fought and screamed, and managed to jump from the car. That evening, a girl student vanished on her way to meet her brother. A handcuff key was found near the place from which she had been taken.

Meanwhile, the Seattle police had fixed on a young man named Ted Bundy as a main suspect. For the past six years, he had been involved in a close relationship with a divorcee named Meg Anders, but she had called off the marriage when she realized he was a habitual thief. After the Lake Sammanish disappearances, she had seen a photofit drawing of the wanted 'Ted' in the *Seattle Times* and thought it looked like Bundy; moreover, 'Ted' drove a Volkswagen like Bundy's. She had seen crutches and plaster of Paris in Bundy's room, and the coincidence seemed too great; with immense misgivings, she telephoned the police. They told her that they had already checked on Bundy; but at the suggestion of the Seattle police, Carol DaRonch was shown Bundy's photograph. She tentatively identified it as resembling the man who had tried to abduct her, but was obviously far from sure. (Bundy had been wearing a beard at the time.)

In January, March, April, July and August 1975, more girls vanished in Colorado. (Their bodies – or skeletons – were found later in remote spots.) On 16 August 1975, Bundy was arrested for the first time. As a police car was driving along a dark street in Salt Lake City, a parked Volkswagen launched into motion; the policeman followed, and it accelerated. He caught up with the car at a service station, and found in the car a pantyhose mask, a crow-bar, an icepick and various other tools; there was also a pair of handcuffs.

Bundy, 29 years old, seemed an unlikely burglar. He was a graduate of the University of Washington, and was in Utah to study law; he had worked as a political campaigner, and for the Crime Commission in Seattle. In his room there was nothing suspicious – except maps and brochures of Colorado, from which five girls had vanished that year. But strands of hair were found in the car, and they proved to be identical with those of Melissa Smith, daughter of the Midvale police chief, who had vanished in the previous October. Carol DaRonch had meanwhile identified Bundy in a police line-up as the fake policeman, and bloodspots on her clothes – where she had scratched her assailant – were of Bundy's group. Credit card receipts showed that Bundy had been close to various places from which girls had vanished in Colorado.

In theory, this should have been the end of the case – and if it had been, it would have been regarded as a typical triumph of scientific detection, beginning with the photofit drawing and concluding with the hair and blood evidence. The evidence was, admittedly, circumstantial, but taken all together, it formed a powerful case. The central objection to it became apparent as soon as Bundy walked into court. He looked so obviously decent and clean-cut that most people felt there must be some mistake. He was polite, well-spoken, articulate, charming, the kind of man who could have found himself a girlfriend for each night of the week. Why *should* such a man be a sex killer? In spite of which, the impression he made was of brilliance and plausibility rather than innocence. For example, he insisted that he had driven away from the police car because he was smoking marijuana, and that he had thrown the joint out of the window.

The case seemed to be balanced on a knife-edge – until the judge pronounced a sentence of guilty of kidnapping. Bundy sobbed and pleaded not to be sent to prison; but the judge sentenced him to a period between one and fifteen years.

The Colorado authorities now charged him with the murder

of a girl called Caryn Campbell, who had been abducted from a ski resort where Bundy had been seen by a witness. After a morning courtroom session in Aspen, Bundy succeeded in wandering into the library during the lunch recess, and jumping out of the window. He was recaptured eight days later, tired and hungry, and driving a stolen car.

Legal arguments dragged on for another six months – what evidence was admissible and what was not. And on 30 December 1977, Bundy escaped again, using a hacksaw blade to cut through an imperfectly welded steel plate above the light fixture in his cell. He made his way to Chicago, then south to Florida; there, near the Florida State University in Tallahassee, he took a room. A few days later, a man broke into a nearby sorority house and attacked four girls with a club, knocking them unconscious; one was strangled with her pantyhose and raped; another died on her way to hospital. One of the strangled girl's nipples had been almost bitten off, and she had a bite mark on her left buttock. An hour and a half later, a student woke up in another sorority house when she heard bangs next door, and a girl whimpering. She dialled the number of the room, and as the telephone rang, someone could be heard running out. Cheryl Thomas was found lying in bed, her skull fractured but still alive.

Three weeks later, on 6 February 1978, Bundy – who was calling himself Chris Hagen – stole a white Dodge van and left Tallahassee; he stayed in the Holiday Inn, using a stolen credit card. The following day a 12-year-old girl named Kimberly Leach walked out of her classroom in Lake City, Florida, and vanished. Bundy returned to Tallahassee to take a girl out for an expensive meal – paid for with a stolen credit card – then absconded via the fire escape, owing large arrears of rent. At 4 a.m. on 15 February, a police patrolman noticed an orange Volkswagen driving suspiciously slowly, and radioed for a check on its number; it proved to be stolen from Tallahassee. After a struggle and a chase, during which he tried to kill the policeman, Bundy was captured yet again. When the police learned his real name, and that he had just left a town in which five girls had been attacked, they suddenly understood the importance of their capture. Bundy seemed glad to be in custody, and began to unburden himself. He explained that 'his problem' had begun when he had seen a girl on a bicycle in Seattle, and 'had to have her'. He had followed her, but she escaped. 'Sometimes', he admitted, 'I feel like a vampire.'

On 7 April, a party of searchers along the Suwanee river found the body of Kimberly Leach in an abandoned hut; she had been strangled and sexually violated. Three weeks later, surrounded by hefty guards, Bundy allowed impressions of his teeth to be taken, for comparison with the marks on the buttocks of the dead student, Lisa Levy.

Bundy's lawyers persuaded him to enter into 'plea bargaining': in exchange for a guarantee of life imprisonment – rather than a death sentence – he would confess to the murders of Lisa Levy, Margaret Bowman and Kimberley Leach. But Bundy changed his mind at the last moment and decided to sack his lawyers.

Bundy's trial began on 25 June 1979, and the evidence against him was damning; a witness who had seen him leaving the sorority house after the attacks; a pantyhouse mask found in the room of Cheryl Thomas, which resembled the one found in Bundy's car; but above all, the fact that Bundy's teeth matched the marks on Lisa Levy's buttocks. The highly compromising taped interview with the Pensacola police was judged inadmissible in court because his lawyer had not been present. Bundy again dismissed his defence and took it over himself; the general impression was that he was trying to be too clever. The jury took only six hours to find him guilty on all counts. Judge Ed Cowart pronounced sentence of death by electrocution, but evidently felt some sympathy for the good-looking young defendant. 'It's a tragedy for this court to see such a total waste of humanity. You're a bright young man. You'd have made a good lawyer . . . But you went the wrong way, partner. Take care of yourself . . .'

Bundy was taken to Raiford prison, Florida, where he was placed on Death Row. On 2 July 1986, when he was due to die a few hours before serial killer Gerald Stano, both were granted a stay of execution.

The Bundy case illustrates the immense problems faced by investigators of serial murders. When Meg Anders – Bundy's mistress – telephoned the police after the double murder near Lake Sammanish, Bundy's name had already been suggested by three people. But he was only one of 3,500 suspects. Later Bundy was added to the list of 100 'best suspects' which investigators constructed on grounds of age, occupation and past record. Two hundred thousand items were fed into computers, including the names of 41,000 Volkswagen owners, 5,000 men with a record of mental illness, every student who had taken classes with the dead girls, and all transfers from other colleges they had attended. All this was programmed into thirty-seven categories, each using a different criterion to isolate the suspect. Asked to name anyone who came up on any three of these programs, the computer produced 16,000 names. When the number was raised to four, it was reduced to 600. Only when it was raised to twenty-five was it reduced to ten suspects, with Bundy seventh on the list. The police were still investigating number six when Bundy was detained in Salt Lake City with burgling tools in his car. Only after that did Bundy become suspect number one. And by that time, he had already committed a minimum of seventeen murders. (There seems to be some doubt about the total, estimates varying between twenty and forty; Bundy himself told the Pensacola investigators that it ran into double figures.) Detective Robert Keppel, who worked on the case, is certain that Bundy would have been revealed as suspect number one even if he had not been arrested. But in 1982, Keppel and his team were presented with another mass killer in the Seattle area, the so-called Green River Killer, whose victims were mostly prostitutes picked up on the 'strip' in Seattle. Seven years later, in 1989, he had killed at least forty-nine women, and the computer had still failed to identify an obvious suspect number one.

The Bundy case is doubly baffling because he seems to contradict the basic assertions of every major criminologist from Lombroso to Yochelson. Bundy is not an obvious born criminal, with degenerate physical characteristics; there is (as far as is known) no history of insanity in his family; he was not a social derelict or a failure. In her book *The Stranger Beside Me*, his friend Ann Rule describes him as 'a man of unusual accomplishment'. How could the most subtle 'psychological profiling' target such a man as a serial killer?

The answer to the riddle emerged fairly late in the day, four years after Bundy had been sentenced to death. Before his conviction, Bundy had indicated his willingness to co-operate on a book about himself, and two journalists, Stephen G. Michaud and Hugh Aynesworth, went to interview him in prison. They discovered that Bundy had no wish to discuss guilt, except to deny it, and he actively discouraged them from investigating the case against him. He wanted them to produce a gossipy book focusing squarely on himself, like bestselling biographies of celebrities such as Frank Sinatra. Michaud and Aynesworth would have been happy to write a book demonstrating his innocence, but as they looked into the case, they found it impossible to accept this; instead, they concluded that he had killed at least twenty-one girls. When they began to probe, Bundy revealed the characteristics that Yochelson and Samenow had found to be so typical of criminals: hedging, lying, pleas of faulty memory, and self-justification: 'Intellectually, Ted seemed profoundly dissociative, a compartmentalizer, and thus a superb rationalizer.' Emotionally, he struck them as a severe case of arrested development: 'he might as well have been a 12-year-old, and a precocious and bratty one at that. So extreme was his childishness that his pleas of innocence were of a character very similar to that of the little boy who'll deny wrongdoing in the face of overwhelming evidence to the contrary.' So Michaud had the ingenious idea of suggesting that Bundy should 'speculate on the nature of a person capable of doing what Ted had been accused (and convicted) of doing'. Bundy embraced this idea with enthusiasm, and talked for hours into a tape recorder. Soon Michaud became aware that there were, in effect, two 'Teds' – the analytical human being, and an entity inside him that Michaud came to call the 'hunchback'. (We have encountered this 'other person' – Mr Hyde – syndrome in many killers, from William Heirens and Peter Sutcliffe to the Boston Strangler.)

After generalizing for some time about violence in modern society, the disintegration of the home, and so on, Bundy got down to specifics, and began to discuss his own development.

He had been an illegitimate child, born to a respectable young girl in Philadelphia. She moved to Seattle to escape the stigma, and married a cook in the Veterans' Hospital. Ted was an oversensitive and self-conscious child who had all the usual daydreams of fame and wealth. And at an early stage he became a thief and something of a habitual liar – as many imaginative children do. But he seems to have been deeply upset by the discovery of his illegitimacy.

Bundy was not, in fact, a brilliant student. Although he struck his fellow students as witty and cultivated, his grades were usually Bs. In his late teens he became heavily infatuated with a fellow student, Stephanie Brooks, who was beautiful, sophisticated, and came of a wealthy family. Oddly enough, she responded and they became 'engaged'. To impress her he went to Stanford University to study Chinese; but he felt lonely away from home, and his grades were poor. 'I found myself thinking about standards of success that I just didn't seem to be living up to.' Stephanie wearied of his immaturity, and threw him over – the severest blow so far. He became intensely moody. 'Dogged by feelings of worthlessness and failure', he took a job as a busboy in a hotel dining-room. And at this point, he began the drift that eventually turned him into a serial killer. He became friendly with a drug addict. One night, they entered a cliffside house that had been partly destroyed by a landslide, and stole whatever they could find. 'It was really thrilling.' He began shoplifting and stealing 'for thrills', once walking openly into someone's greenhouse, taking an eight-foot tree in a pot, and putting it in his car with the top sticking out of the sunroof.

He also became a full-time volunteer worker for Art Fletcher, the black Republican candidate for Lieutenant-Governor. He enjoyed the sense of being a 'somebody' and mixing with interesting people. But Fletcher lost, and Bundy became a salesman in a department store. He met Meg Anders in a college beer joint, and they became lovers – she had a gentle, easy-going nature, which brought out Bundy's protective side. But she was shocked by his kleptomania.

In fact, the criminal side – the 'hunchback' – was now developing fast. He acquired a taste for violent pornography – easy to buy openly in American shops. Once, walking round the university district, he saw a girl undressing in a lighted room. This was the turning point in his life. He began to devote hours to walking aroud, hoping to see more girls undressing. He was back at university, studying psychology, but his night prowling prevented him from making full use of his undoubted intellectual capacities. He obtained his degree in due course – this may tell us more about American university standards than about Bundy's abilities – and tried to find a law school that would take him. He failed all the aptitude tests and was repeatedly turned down. A year later, he was finally accepted – he worked for the Crime Commission for a month, as an assistant, and for the Office of Justice Planning. His self-confidence increased by leaps and bounds. When he flew to San Francisco to see Stephanie Brooks, the girl who had jilted him, she was deeply impressed, and willing to renew their affair. He was still having an affair with Meg Anders, and entered on this new career as a Don Juan with his usual enthusiasm. He and Stephanie spent Christmas together and became 'engaged'. Then he dumped her as she had dumped him.

By this time, he had committed his first murder. For years, he had been a pornography addict and a Peeping Tom. ('He approached it almost like a project, throwing himself into it, literally, for years.') Then the 'hunchback' had started to demand 'more active kinds of gratification'. He tried disabling women's cars, but the girls always had help on hand. He felt the need to indulge in this kind of behaviour after drinking had reduced his inhibitions. One evening, he stalked a girl from a bar, found a heavy piece of wood, and managed to get ahead of her and lie in wait. Before she reached the place, where he was hiding, she stopped at her front door and went in. But the experience was like 'making a hole in a dam'. A few evenings later, as a woman was fumbling for her keys at her front door, he struck her on the head with a piece of wood. She collapsed, screaming, and he ran away. He was filled with remorse, and swore he would never do such a thing again. But six months later, he followed a woman home and peeped in as she undressed. He began to do this again and again. One day, when he knew the door was unlocked, he sneaked in, entered her bedroom, and jumped on her. She screamed and he ran away. Once again, there was a period of self-disgust and revulsion.

This was in the autumn of 1973. On 4 January 1974, he found a door that admitted him to the basement room of 18-year-old Sharon Clarke. Now, for the first time, he employed the technique he later used repeatedly, attacking her with a crow-bar until she was unconscious. Then he thrust a bar torn from the bed inside her, causing internal injuries. But he left her alive.

On the morning of 1 February 1974, he found an unlocked front door in a students' rooming-house and went in. He entered a bedroom at random; 21-year-old Lynda Healy was asleep in bed. He battered her unconscious, then carried the body out to his car. He drove to Taylor Mountain, 20 miles east of Seattle, made her remove her pyjamas, and raped her. When Bundy was later 'speculating' about this crime for Stephen Michaud's benefit, the interviewer asked: 'Was there any conversation?' Bundy replied: 'There'd be some. Since this girl in front of him represented not a person, but again the image of something desirable, the last thing we would expect him to want to do would be to personalize this person.'

So Lynda Healy was bludgeoned to death; Bundy always insisted that he took no pleasure in violence, but that his chief desire was 'possession' of another person.

Now the 'hunchback' was in full control, and there were five more victims over the next five months. Three of the girls were taken to the same spot on Taylor Mountain and there raped and murdered – Bundy acknowledged that his sexual gratification would sometimes take hours. The four bodies were found together in the following year. On the day he abducted the two girls from Lake Sammanish, Bundy 'speculated' that he had taken the first, Janice Ott, to a nearby house and raped her, then returned to abduct the second girl, Denise Naslund, who was taken back to the same house and raped in view of the other girl; both were then killed, and taken to a remote spot four miles north-east of the park, where the bodies were dumped.

By the time he had reached this point in his 'confession', Bundy had no further secrets to reveal; everything was obvious. Rape had become a compulsion that dominated his life. When he moved to Salt Lake City and entered the law school there – he was a failure from the beginning as a law student – he must have known that if he began to rape and kill young girls there, he would be establishing himself as suspect number one. This made no difference; he had to continue. Even the unsuccessful kidnapping of Carol DaRonch, and the knowledge that someone could now identify him, made no difference. He merely switched his activities to Colorado. Following his arrest, conviction and escape, he moved to Florida, and the compulsive attacks continued, although by now he must have known that another series of murders in a town to which he had recently moved must reduce his habitual plea of 'coincidence' to an absurdity. It seems obvious that by this time he had lost the power of choice. In his last weeks of freedom, Bundy showed all the signs of weariness and self-disgust that had driven Carl Panzram to contrive his own execution.

Time finally ran out for Bundy on 24 January 1989. Long before this, he had recognized that his fatal mistake was to decline to enter into plea bargaining at his trial; the result was a death sentence instead of life imprisonment. In January 1989, his final appeal was turned down and the date of execution fixed. Bundy then made a last-minute attempt to save his life by offering to bargain murder confessions for a reprieve – against the advice of his attorney James Coleman, who warned him that this attempt to 'trade over the victims' bodies' would only create hostility that would militate against further stays of execution. In fact, Bundy went on to confess to eight Washington murders, and then to a dozen others. Detective Bob Keppel, who had led the investigation in Seattle, commented: 'The game-playing stuff cost him his life.' Instead of making a full confession, Bundy doled out information bit by bit. 'The whole thing was orchestrated,' said Keppel, 'We were held hostage for three days.' And finally, when it was clear that there was no chance of further delay, Bundy confessed to the Chi Omega Sorority killings, admitting that he had been peeping through the window at girls undressing until he was carried away by desire and entered the building. He also mentioned pornography as being one of the factors that led him to murder. Newspaper columnists showed an inclination to doubt this, but Bundy's earlier confessions to Michaud leave no doubt that he was telling the truth.

At 7 a.m., Bundy was led into the execution chamber at Starke State prison, Florida; behind Plexiglass, an invited audience of forty-eight people sat waiting. As two warders attached his hands to the arms of the electric chair, Bundy recognized his attorney among the crowd; he smiled and nodded. Then straps were placed around his chest and over his mouth; the metal cap with electrodes was fastened on to his head with screws and the face was covered with a black hood. At 7.07 a.m. the executioner threw the switch; Bundy's body went stiff and rose fractionally from the chair. One minute later, as the power was switched off, the body slammed back into the chair. A doctor felt his pulse and pronounced him dead. Outside the prison, a mob carrying 'Fry Bundy!' banners cheered as the execution was announced.

* * *

The Bundy case makes it clear that, in one respect at least, the science of criminology needs updating.

It seems to be the general consensus among criminologists that the criminal is a social inadequate, and that the few exceptions only underscore the rule. Faced with difficulties that require courage and patience, he is inclined to run away. He lacks self-esteem; he tends to see himself as a loser, a failure. Crime is a 'short cut' to achieve something he believes he cannot achieve through his own merit. But everyone who reads this description must be aware that, to some extent, it fits himself. Being undermined by self-doubt is part of the human condition. Which of us, faced with problems, has not at some time chosen a judicious retreat?

The Bundy case underlines the point. Even as a schoolboy he was witty and amusing, and in his early twenties he developed a poise and confidence that were the envy of other males. Michaud quotes a fellow office worker: 'Frankly, he represented what it was that all young males ever wanted to be . . . I think half the people in the office were jealous of him . . . If there was any flaw in him it was that he was almost too *per*fect.'

In their classic book *The Criminal Personality* (1976), Samuel Yochelson and Stanton E. Samenow argue that criminality is closely connected with inadequacy, laziness and self-pity; it is another name for defeat-proneness. By the time he was in his mid-twenties, Bundy had tasted enough success to stand outside this definition. Then what went wrong?

Ann Rule's book contains the vital clue. She comments that Bundy became violently upset if he telephoned Meg Anders from Salt Lake City – where his legal studies were foundering – and got no reply. 'Strangely, while he was being continuously unfaithful himself, he expected – demanded – that she be totally loyal to him.'

In 1954, the science fiction writer A. E. Van Vogt had encountered this same curious anomaly when he was studying male authoritarian behaviour for a novel called *The Violent Man*. He was intrigued by the number of divorce cases in which habitually unfaithful husbands had expected total fidelity from their wives; such a husband might flaunt his own infidelities, while erupting into murderous violence if his wife so much as smiled at another man. Such men obviously regarded women with deep hostility, as if they expected to be deceived or betrayed – this is why they chose to marry gentle and unaggressive women. Their 'conquests' were another form of aggression, the aim being to prove that they were masterful seducers who could have any woman they liked. Their whole unstable structure of self-esteem was founded upon this notion that women found them irresistible; so it was essential for the wife to behave like a slave in a harem. This also explained another characteristic of such men: that they could not bear to be contradicted or shown to be in the wrong; this also threatened their image of themselves as a kind of god or superman. If confronted with proof of their own fallibility, they would explode into violence rather than acknowledge that they had made a mistake. For this reason, Van Vogt labelled this type 'the Right Man' or 'the Violent Man'. To his colleagues at work he might appear perfectly normal and balanced; but his family knew him as a kind of paranoid dictator.

Only one thing could undermine this structure of self-delusion. If his wife walked out on him, she had demonstrated beyond all doubt that she rejected him; his tower of self-delusion was undermined, and often the result was mental breakdown, or even suicide.

Expressed in this way, it seems clear that the Right Man syndrome is a form of mild insanity. Yet it is alarmingly common; most of us know a Right Man, and some have the misfortune to have a Right Man for a husband or father. The syndrome obviously arises from the sheer competitiveness of the world we are born into. Every normal male has an urge to be a 'winner', yet he finds himself surrounded by people who seem better qualified for success. One common response is boasting to those who look as if they can be taken in – particularly women. Another is what the late Stephen Potter called 'One-upmanship', the attempt to make the other person feel inferior by a kind of cheating – for example, by pretending to know far more than you actually know. Another is to bully people over whom one happens to have authority. Many 'Right Men' are so successful in all these departments that they achieve a remarkably high level of self-esteem on remarkably slender talents. Once achieved, this self-esteem is like an addictive drug and any threat of withdrawal seems terrifying. Hence the violence with which he reacts to anything that challenges it.

It is obvious that the Right Man syndrome is a compensatory mechanism for profound self-doubt, and that its essence lies in convincing others of something he feels to be untrue; in other words, it is a form of confidence-trickery. It is, that is to say, a typically criminal form of 'shortcut', like cheating in an exam, or stealing something instead of saving up to buy it.

Now the basic characteristic of the criminal, and also of the Right Man, is a certain lack of self-control. Van Vogt writes that the Right Man 'makes the decision to be out of control' – that is, makes the decision to *lose* control at a certain point, exploding into violence rather than calling upon a more mature level of his personality. But he is adept at making excuses that place the blame for this lack of self-control on other people for provoking him. One British sex killer, Patrick Byrne, explained that he decided to terrorize women 'to get my own back on them for causing my nervous tension through sex'.

But the lack of self-control brings its own problems. Every time it happens he is, in effect, lowering his own bursting point. Carl Panzram told Henry Lesser never to turn his back on him: 'You're the one man I don't want to kill. But I'm so erratic I'm liable to do anything.' He is like a man who has trained an Alsatian dog to leap at people's throats, and finally realizes that the dog is stronger than he is. A 22-year-old sex killer named Stephen Judy begged the judge in Indianapolis to sentence him to death. He had been committing rapes and sex crimes since he was 12, and was on trial for killing a young mother and her three children. Aware that he would never be able to stop committing sex crimes, he told the jury: 'You'd better put me to death. Because next time it might be one of you or your daughter.' They agreed, and Judy was executed in 1981. Just before his death he told his stepmother that he had killed more women than he could remember, leaving a trail of bodies across the United States.

It should now be possible to see that the Right Man syndrome is the key to the serial killer, and that Bundy is a textbook case. From the beginning, he was obsessed by success: 'I found myself thinking about standards of success that I just didn't seem to be living up to.' The affair with Stephanie Brooks made it seem that success was within his grasp; he went to Stanford to study

Chinese. But he lacked the application and self-confidence and she threw him over. This was the turning point; his brother commented: 'Stephanie screwed him up . . . I'd never seen him like this before. He'd always been in charge of his emotions.' It was after this rejection that Bundy became a kleptomaniac. This may seem a strange response to the end of a love affair. But stealing is a way of making a gesture of defiance at society. And this is what Bundy's thieving amounted to – as when he stole an eight-foot tree from a greenhouse and drove off with it sticking out of the roof of his car. It was essentially a symbolic gesture.

Seven years later, Bundy took his revenge on Stephanie Brooks. When she rang him to ask why he had not contacted her since their weekend together, he said coldly: 'I have no idea what you're talking about,' and hung up on her. 'At length', says Ann Rule, 'she concluded that Ted's high-power courtship in the latter part of 1973 had been deliberately planned, that he had waited all these years to be in a position where he could make her fall in love with him, just so he could drop her, reject her as she had rejected him.' Stephanie Brooks wrote to a friend: 'I escaped by the skin of my teeth. When I think of his cold and calculating manner, I shudder.' The Right Man had escaped his feeling of vulnerability; he had established his dominance. Oddly enough, he committed his first violent sexual attack immediately after the weekend with Stephanie. He had proved that he was the conqueror; now, in this mood of exultation, he broke into the bedroom of a female student, battered her unconscious, and thrust an iron bar into her vagina. Three weeks later he committed his first murder. It was also completely typical of the Right Man that, when eventually caught, he should continue to deny his guilt, even in the face of overwhelming evidence.

But the remarks of Yochelson and Samenow about inadequacy certainly apply to the case of David Berkowitz, known as 'Son of Sam.'

On the night of 29 July 1976 two young girls sat talking in the front seats of a car on Buhre Avenue, New York City; they were Donna Lauria, a medical technician, and Jody Valenti, a student nurse. Donna's parents, on their way back from a night out, passed them at about 1 a.m., and said goodnight. A few moments after they reached their apartment, they heard the sound of shots and screams. A man had walked up to the Oldsmobile, pulled a gun out of a brown paper bag, and fired five shots. Donna was killed, Jody wounded in the thigh.

Total lack of motive for the shooting convinced police they were dealing with a man who killed for pleasure, without knowing his victims.

Four months later, on 26 November, two young girls were sitting talking on the stoop in front of a house in the Floral Park section of Queens, New York; it was half an hour past midnight when a man walked towards them, started to ask if they could direct him, then, before he finished the sentence, pulled out a gun and began shooting. Donna DeMasi and Joanne Lomino were both wounded. A bullet lodged in Joanne's spine, paralyzing her. Bullets dug out of a front door and a mail box revealed that the two youn women had been shot by the same .44 that had killed Donna Lauria and wounded Jody Valenti.

Although the police were unaware of it at this time, the same gun had already wounded yet another victim. Over a month earlier, on 23 October 1976, Carl Denaro and his girlfriend Rosemary Keenan were sitting in his sports car in front of a tavern in Flushing when there were several loud bangs; then a bullet tore through the rear windscreen, and Denaro fell forward. He was rushed to hospital, and in three weeks, had begun to recover, although his middle finger was permanently damaged. The .44 bullet was found on the floor of the car.

On 30 January 1977 a young couple were kissing goodnight in a car in the Ridgewood area of New York; there was a deafening explosion, the windscreen shattered, and Christine Freund slumped into the arms of her boyfriend John Diel. She died a few hours later in hospital.

On 8 March 1977 Virginia Voskerichian, an Armenian student was on her way home, and only a few hundred yards from her mother's house in Forest Hills, when a gunman walked up to her, and shot her in the face at a few yards range; the bullet went into her mouth, shattering her front teeth. She died immediately. Christine Freund had been shot only three hundred yards away.

By now police recognized that the bullets that had killed three and wounded four had all come from the same gun. And this indicated a homicidal psychopath who would probably go on until he was caught. The problem was that the police had no clues to his identity, no idea of where to begin searching. Unless he was caught during an attempted murder, the chance of arresting him seemed minimal. Mayor Beame of New York gave a press conference in which he announced: 'We have a savage killer on the loose.' He was able to say that the man was white, about five feet ten inches tall, well groomed, with hair combed straight back.

On the morning of 17 April 1977 there were two more deaths. Alexander Esau and Valentina Suriani were sitting in a parked car in the Bronx when the killer shot both of them. Valentina died instantly; Esau died later in hospital, three bullets in his head. Only a few blocks away, Donna Lauria and Jody Valenti had been shot.

In the middle of the street, a policeman found an envelope. It contained a letter addressed to Captain Joseph Borrelli, and it was from the killer. 'I am deeply hurt by your calling me a weman-hater. I am not. But I am a monster. I am the Son of Sam. I am a little brat . . .' It claimed that his father, Sam, was a brute who beat his family when he got drunk, and who ordered him to go out and kill. 'I love to hunt. Prowling the streets looking for fair game – tasty meat. The wemen of Queens are prettyist of all . . .' It was reminiscent of the letters that Jack the Ripper and so many other 'thrill killers' have written to the police, revealing an urge to 'be' somebody, to make an impact on society. A further rambling, incoherent note, signed 'Son of Sam', was sent to a New York columnist, James Breslin.

The next attack, on 26 June 1977, was like so many of the others: a young couple sitting in their car in the early hours of Sunday morning, saying goodnight after a date. They were Salvatore Lupo and Judy Placido, and the car was in front of a house on 211 Street, Bayside, Queens. The windscreen shattered, as four shots were fired. The assailant ran away. Fortunately, his aim had been bad; both these victims were only wounded, and recovered.

It was now a year since Son of Sam had killed Donna Lauria; on the anniversary of her death, Queens and the Bronx were swarming with police. But Son of Sam had decided that these areas were dangerous, and that his next shootings would be as far away as possible. On 31 July Robert Violante and

Stacy Moskowitz were sitting in a parking lot close to the Brooklyn shore; it was 1.30 on Sunday morning. The windscreen exploded as four shots were fired. Both were hit in the head. Stacy Moskowitz died hours later in hospital; Robert Violante recovered, but was blinded.

But this shooting brought the break in the case. A woman out walking her dog had noticed two policemen putting a ticket on a car parked near a fire hydrant on Bay 16th Street. Minutes later, a man ran up to the car, leapt in and drove off. Only four parking tickets had been issued in the Coney Island area that Sunday morning, and only one of those was for parking near a hydrant. The carbon of the ticket contained the car's registration number. And the vehicle licensing department was able to identify its owner as David Berkowitz, aged 24, of Pine Street, Yonkers.

On the Wednesday after the last killing, detectives found the Ford Galaxie parked in front of an apartment building in Pine Street. They peered in through its window, and saw the butt of a gun, and a note written in the same block capitals as the other Son of Sam letters. The car was staked out. When David Berkowitz approached it at 10.15 that evening, Deputy Inspector Tim Dowd, who had led the hunt, said, 'Hello, David.' Berkowitz looked at him in surprise, then said, 'Inspector Dowd! You finally got me.'

After the terror he had aroused, Son of Sam was something of an anticlimax, a pudgy little man with a beaming smile, and a tendency to look like a slightly moronic child who has been caught stealing sweets. He was a paranoid schizophrenic, a man who lived alone in a room lit by a naked bulb, sleeping on a bare mattress. The floor was covered with empty milk cartons and bottles. On the walls he had scrawled messages like 'In this hole lives the wicked king', 'Kill for my Master', 'I turn children into killers'. His father, who had run a hardware store in the Bronx, had retired to Florida after being robbed. Nat Berkowitz was not Son of Sam's real father. David Berkowitz, born 1 June 1953, was a bastard, and his mother offered him for adoption. He had felt rejected from the beginning.

He reacted to his poor self-image by boasting and lying – particularly about his sexual prowess. In fact, he was shy of women, and almost certainly a virgin when captured. He told the police that demons began telling him to kill in 1974 – although one psychiatrist who interviewed him is convinced that this is untrue, and that Berkowitz's stories of 'voices' was an attempt to establish a defence of insanity. Living alone in apartments that he allowed to become pig-sties, kept awake at night by the sound of trucks or barking dogs, he slipped into paranoia, telling his father in a letter that people hated him, and spat at him as he walked down the street. 'The girls call me ugly, and they bother me the most.' On Christmas Eve 1975, he began his attempt at revenge on women by taking a knife and attacking two of them. The first one screamed so loudly he ran away. The second, a 15-year-old schoolgirl, was badly cut, and had one lung punctured, but recovered. Seven months later, Berkowitz went out with a gun and committed his first murder.

The name Sam seems to have been taken from a neighbour called Sam Carr, whose black Labrador sometimes kept Berkowitz awake. He wrote Carr anonymous letters, and on 27 April 1977 shot the dog – which recovered. He also wrote anonymous letters to people he believed to be persecuting him. He had been reported to the police on a number of occasions as a 'nut', but no one suspected that he might be Son of Sam.

Berkowitz was judged sane, and was arraigned on 23 August 1977. He pleaded guilty, saving New York the cost of a trial. He was sentenced to 365 years in prison.

The aftermath is worth describing. His Yonkers apartment block became a place of pilgrimage for sensation-seekers. They stole doorknobs, cut out pieces of carpet, even chipped pieces of paint from Berkowitz's door. In the middle of the night, people shouted 'David, come out' from the street. Berkowitz's apartment remained empty, and a quarter of the building's tenants moved out, even though the landlord changed its number from 25 to 42 Pine Street to try to mislead the souvenir hunters.

Worth mentioning as an interesting parallel to the Son of Sam murders is the Zodiac case, which took place in San Francisco in the 1960s. Between December 1968 and October 1969, an unknown killer committed five 'random' murders, and seriously wounded two more victims. On 20 December 1968 a man approached a car in a 'lovers' lane' near Vallejo, California and shot to death two teenagers. On 5 July 1969 he opened fire on another couple in a car near Vallejo, killing the woman and wounding the man. Letters sent to two San Francisco newspapers were signed 'Zodiac', and claimed credit for the murders. Lines in code – decoded by a cipher expert – boasted that hunting humans was the most exciting of all sports.

On 27 September 1969, a plump, bespectacled man wearing a hood held two people at gunpoint in a picnic area beside Lake Berryessa and stabbed them both repeatedly, killing the woman. 'Zodiac' reported his latest murder to the police by telephone. Two weeks later, on 11 October, he shot to death a taxi driver in San Francisco, and sent a letter boasting of the crime to the San Francisco *Chronicle*, together with a bloody fragment of the driver's shirt. This was 'Zodiac's' last known murder, although he continued to write letters threatening more killings. On 22 October 1969, a man claiming to be Zodiac took part in a Bay Area phone-in TV programme – in which he identified himself as 'Sam'. The call was, in fact, traced to the Napa State Hospital, and the caller proved to be a mental patient there. It is interesting to speculate if David Berkowitz read about the programme – which received nationwide publicity – and was influenced by it in choosing his *nom de guerre*.

Perhaps the most basic characteristic of the serial killer is one that he shares with most other criminals: a tendency to an irrational self-pity that can produce an explosion of violence. In that sense, Paul John Knowles may be regarded not merely as the archetypal serial killer but as the archetypal criminal.

Knowles, who was born in 1946, had spent an average of six months of every year in jail since he was 19, mostly for car thefts and burglaries. In Raiford Penitentiary in 1972, he began to study astrology, and started corresponding with a divorcee named Angela Covic, whom he had contacted through an astrology magazine. She flew down to Florida, was impressed by the gaunt good looks of the tall red-headed convict, and agreed to marry him. She hired a lawyer to work on his parole, and he was released on 14 May 1972. Knowles hastened to San Francisco to claim his bride, but she had had second thoughts; a psychic had told her that she was mixed up with a very dangerous man. Knowles stayed at her mother's apartment, but after four days Angela Covic told him she had decided to return to her husband, and gave him his air ticket back to Florida. Knowles exploded with rage and self-pity; he later claimed that he went out on to the streets of San Francisco and killed three people.

This was never verified, but it is consistent with the behaviour of the Right Man.

Back in his home town of Jacksonville, Florida on 26 July 1974, Knowles got into a fight in a bar and was locked up for the night. He escaped, broke into the home of a 65-year-old teacher, Alice Curtis, and stole her money and her car. But he rammed a gag too far down her throat and she suffocated. A few days later, as he parked the stolen car, he noticed two children looking at him as if they recognized him – their mother was, in fact, a friend of his family. He forced them into the car and drove away. The bodies of 7-year-old Mylette Anderson and her 11-year-old sister Lillian were later found in a swamp.

What followed was a totally unmotivated murder rampage, as if Knowles had simply decided to kill as many people as he could before he was caught. The following day, 2 August, in Atlantic Beach, Florida, he broke into the home of Marjorie Howie, 49, and strangled her with a stocking; he stole her television set. A few days later he strangled and raped a teenage runaway who hitched a lift with him. On 23 August he strangled Kathie Pierce in Musella, Georgia, while her 3-year-old son looked on; Knowles left the child unharmed. On 23 September, near Lima, Ohio, he had several drinks with an accounts executive named William Bates, and later strangled him, driving off in the dead man's white Impala. After driving to California, Seattle and Utah (using Bates's credit cards) he forced his way into a caravan in Ely, Nevada, on 18 September 1974, and shot to death an elderly couple, Emmett and Lois Johnson. On 21 September he strangled and raped 42-year-old Mrs Charlynn Hicks, who had stopped to admire the view beside the road near Sequin, Texas. On 23 September, in Birmingham, Alabama, he met an attractive woman named Ann Dawson, who owned a beauty shop, and they travelled around together for the next six days, living on her money; she was murdered on 29 September. For the next sixteen days he drove around without apparently committing any further murders; but on 16 October he rang the doorbell of a house in Marlborough, Connecticut; it was answered by 16-year-old Dawn White, who was expecting a friend. Knowles forced her up to the bedroom and raped her; when her mother, Karen White, returned home, he raped her too, then strangled them both with silk stockings, leaving with a tape recorder and Dawn White's collection of rock records.

Two days later, he knocked on the door of 53-year-old Doris Hovey in Woodford, Virginia, and told her he needed a gun and would not harm her; she gave him a rifle belonging to her husband, and he shot her through the head and left, leaving the rifle beside her body.

In Key West, Florida, he picked up two hitch-hikers, intending to kill them, but was stopped by a policeman for pulling up on a kerb; when the policeman asked to see his documents, he expected to be arrested; but the officer failed to check that Knowles was the owner of the car, and let him drive away.

On 2 November, Knowles picked up two hitch-hikers, Edward Hilliard and Debbie Griffin; Hilliard's body was later discovered in woods near Macon, Georgia; the girl's body was never found.

On 6 November, in a gay bar in Macon, he met a man named Carswell Carr and went home with him. Later that evening, Carr's 15-year-old daughter Mandy heard shouting and went downstairs, to find Knowles standing over the body of her father, who was tied up. It emerged later that Carr had died of a heart attack; Knowles had been torturing him by stabbing him all over with a pair of scissors. He then raped Mandy Carr – or attempted it (no sperm was found in the vagina) – and strangled her with a stocking. The bodies were found when Carr's wife, a night nurse, returned home.

The next day, in a Holiday Inn in downtown Atlanta, Knowles saw an attractive redhead in the bar – a British journalist named Sandy Fawkes; she went for a meal with him and they ended in her bedroom. But he proved impotent, in spite of all her efforts. He had introduced himself to her as Daryl Golden, son of a New Mexico restaurant owner, and the two of them got on well enough for her to accept his offer to drive her to Miami. On the way there, he hinted that he was on the run for some serious crime – or crimes – and told her that he had a premonition that he was going to be killed some time soon. He also told her that he had tape-recorded his confession, and left it with his lawyer in Miami, Sheldon Yavitz. In another motel, he finally succeeded in entering her, after first practising cunnilingus and masturbating himself into a state of excitement. But even so, he failed to achieve orgasm – she concluded that he was incapable of it.

Long before they separated – after a mere six days together

– she was anxious to get rid of him. She had sensed the underlying violence, self-pity, lack of discipline. He pressed hard for another night together; she firmly refused, insisting that it would only make the parting more sad. He waited outside her Miami motel half the night, while she deliberately stayed away; finally, he gave up and left.

The following day, she was asked to go the the police station, and there for the first time realized what kind of a man she had been travelling with. On the morning after their separation, 'Daryl Golden' had driven to the house of some journalists to whom he had been introduced four days earlier, and offered to drive Susan Mackenzie to the hairdresser. Instead, he took the wrong turn, and told her that he wanted to have sex with her, and would not hurt her if she complied. When he stopped the car and pointed a gun at her, she succeeded in jumping out and waved frantically at a passing car. Knowles drove off. Later, alerted to the attempted rape, a squad car tried to stop Knowles, but he pointed a shotgun at the policeman and drove off.

Knowles knew that he had to get rid of the stolen car. In West Palm Beach, he forced his way into a house, and took a girl named Barbara Tucker hostage, driving off in her Volkswagen, leaving her sister (in a wheelchair) and 6-year-old child unharmed. He held Barbara Tucker captive in a motel in Fort Pierce for a night and day, then finally left her tied up and drove off in her car.

Next day, Patrolman Charles F. Campbell flagged down the Volkswagen – now with altered licence plates – and found himself looking down the barrel of a shotgun. He was taken captive and driven off, handcuffed, in his own patrol car. But the brakes were poor, and, using the police siren, he forced another car – driven by businessman John Meyer – off the road, then drove off in Meyer's car, with Meyer and the patrolman in the back. In Pulaski County, Georgia, Knowles took them into a wood, handcuffed them to a tree, and shot both in the back of the head.

Soon after, he saw a police roadblock ahead, and drove on through it, losing control and crashing into a tree. He ran into the woods, and a vast manhunt now began, involving two hundred police, tracker dogs and helicopters. Knowles was arrested by a courageous civilian, who saw him from a house, and he gave himself up quietly.

The day after his appearance in court, as he was being transferred to a maximum security prison, Knowles unpicked his handcuffs and made a grab for the sheriff's gun; FBI agent Ron Angel shot him dead. Knowles had been responsible for at least eighteen murders, possibly as many as twenty-four.

Sandy Fawkes had seen Knowles in court, and was overwhelmed by a sense of his 'evil power'. But she had no doubt that he now had what he had always wanted: he was famous at last.

> And enjoying his notoriety. The papers were filled with pictures of his appearance at Midgeville and accounts of his behaviour. The streets had been lined with people. Sightseers had hung over the sides of balconies to catch a glimpse of Knowles, manacled and in leg irons, dressed in a brilliant orange jumpsuit. He had loved it: the local co-eds four-deep on the sidewalks, the courtroom packed with reporters, friends, Mandy's school chums and relatives of the Carr family. It was an event, he was the centre of it and he smiled at everyone. No wonder he had laughed like a hyena at his capture; he was having his hour of glory, not in the hereafter as he had predicted, but in the here-and-now. The daily stories of the women in his life had turned him into a Casanova killer, a folk villain, Dillinger and Jesse James rolled into one. He was already being referred to as the most heinous killer in history.

So at last Knowles had achieved the aim of most serial killers: 'to become known'. He was quoted in a local newspaper as saying that he was 'the only successful member of his family'.

In the second half of the 1970s, another case of serial murder by a homosexual aroused uneasy memories of Dean Corll.

Between 1976 and his arrest in December 1978, John Wayne Gacy, a Chicago building contractor, killed thirty-two boys in the course of sexual attacks. Gacy's childhood – he was born in 1932 – was in many ways similar to Corll's, with a harsh father and a protective mother. He was a lifelong petty thief. Like Corll, he also suffered from a heart condition. In childhood, he had been struck on the head by a swing, which caused a bloodclot on the brain, undetected for several years. He married a girl whose parents owned a fried-chicken business in Waterloo, Iowa, and – again like Corll – became a successful businessman.

(Maslow would point out that this indicates that both belong to the 'dominant five per cent'.) He was also known as a liar and a boaster. His marriage came to an end when Gacy was imprisoned for sexually molesting a teenager (although Gacy always claimed he had been framed). Out of jail, he married a second time and set up in business as a building contractor. He was successful (although notoriously mean), and was soon regarded as a pillar of the local community – he was even photographed shaking hands with First Lady Rosalynn Carter, the wife of President Jimmy Carter. His own wife found his violent temper a strain, and they divorced.

In 1975, while he was still married, one of his teenage employees vanished; it was after this that his wife noticed an unpleasant smell in the house. After their separation in the following year, Gacy made a habit of picking up teenage homosexuals, or luring teenagers to his house 'on business', handcuffing them, and then committing sodomy. They were finally strangled, and the bodies disposed of, usually in the crawl space under the house.

In March 1978, a 27-year-old named Jeffrey Rignall accepted an invitation to smoke pot in Gacy's Oldsmobile. Gacy clapped a chloroform-soaked rag over his face, and when Rignall woke up he was being sodomized in Gacy's home. Gacy raped him repeatedly and flogged him with a whip; finally, he chloroformed him again and left him in a park. In hospital, Rignall discovered that he had sustained permanent liver damage from the chloroform. Since the police were unable to help, he set about trying to track down the rapist himself, sitting near freeway entrances looking for black Oldsmobiles. Eventually he saw Gacy, followed him, and noted down his number. Although Gacy was arrested, the evidence against him seemed poor.

On 11 December 1978 Gacy invited a 15-year-old boy, Robert Piest, to his house to talk about a summer job. When the youth failed to return, police tracked down the building contractor who had offered him the job, and questioned him at his home in Des Plaines. Alerted by the odour, they investigated the crawl space and found fifteen bodies and parts of others. When Gacy had run out of space, he had started dumping bodies in the river.

Gacy's story was that he was a 'dissociated' personality, and that the murders were committed by an evil part of himself called

Jack. In court, one youth described how Gacy had pulled him up, posing as a police officer, then handcuffed him at gunpoint. Back in Gacy's home, he was sodomized, after which Gacy made an attempt to drown him in the bath; but Gacy changed his mind and raped him again. Then, after holding his head under water until he became unconscious, Gacy urinated on him, then played Russian roulette with a gun which turned out to contain only a blank. Finally, Gacy released him, warning him that the police would not believe his story. Gacy proved to be right. The jury who tried him believed a psychiatrist who told them that Gacy was suffering from a narcissistic personality disorder that did not amount to insanity, and on 13 March 1980 John Wayne Gacy was sentenced to death.

But the case that, in retrospect, seems most typical of the late 1970s – in the way that Manson seems typical of the late 1960s – is that of the Hillside Stranglers, Kenneth Bianchi and Angelo Buono.

In fact, the first book on the case was called simply *The Hillside Strangler*,[1] because at that time the role of Bianchi's cousin was not fully grasped. Since then, it has become clear that this is one of these cases in which the interaction of two criminal personalities produces an explosive combination.

The crimes attributed to the Hillside Strangler took place in Los Angeles between October 1977 and February 1978. But it was another crime, which took place a year later, and almost a thousand miles to the north, that finally led the police to the killers.

The small town of Bellingham, in Washington State, looks out on one of the most beautiful views in the American northwest: the pine-covered slopes of San Juan and Vancouver Islands, and the Strait of Juan de Fuca. With a population of only forty thousand, violent crime is a rarity. Which is why, when police chief Terry Mangan was told on a Friday morning that two girls were missing his first thought was that they had decided to go off on a long weekend. Their names were Karen Mandic and Diane Wilder, and both were students at Western Washington University. Karen's boyfriend was insistent that she would never go away without telling him. And when Police Chief Mangan learned that Karen had left her pet cat unfed, he

[1] Published by Doubleday, New York, 1981.

had a sudden intuition that he was dealing with a double murder.

On the previous evening – 11 January 1979 – Karen had told her boyfriend that she and Diane were going on a 'house-sitting' job. It was at the home of a couple who were travelling in Europe. Apparently its security alarm system had failed, and Karen merely had to sit there for two hours while the alarm was taken away and repaired; moreover she would be paid $100 for the inconvenience.

The man who had offered her this job was a security supervisor named Kenneth Bianchi. Mangan's first step was to check with Bianchi's boss Mark Lawrence, who owned the Coastal Security agency. Lawrence declared positively that it was impossible that Ken Bianchi had anything to do with the disappearance of the two girls. He was a young man of excellent reputation, and a conscientious worker. He lived with a local girl named Kelli Boyd; they had a baby son, and Bianchi was known to be a devoted father and breadwinner. In any case, he had no authority to offer Karen a 'house-sitting' job. There had to be some kind of mistake . . .

This was soon confirmed by Bianchi himself. He told his boss that he had never heard of Karen Mandic, and had certainly offered no one a house-sitting job. He had spent Thursday evening at a Sheriff's Reserve meeting.

But by now, the police had learned some strange facts about the house-sitting job. Karen had told her boyfriend that the man who had offered it had sworn her to secrecy. He had also telephoned the woman who lived next door to the house, and who went in once a day to water the plants, to warn her not to go near it during the course of the evening. He explained that the security alarm was being repaired, and armed guards would be on patrol. It began to look as if someone had lured the missing students to the empty house.

Police were immediately despatched to the empty house in the expensive Bayside area. A locksmith opened the front door, and the detectives entered cautiously. They were half-expecting to find two corpses, but everything seemed to be in order. The house was neat, and there was no sign of a struggle. But on the kitchen floor, the searchers found a single wet footprint. It was that of a man, and since it was still wet, must have been made within the last twelve hours or so.

At noon that day, the local radio began broadcasting descriptions of Karen's car – a green Mercury Bobcat – and asking the public to report any sightings. At 4.30 that afternoon, the description was heard by a woman who had just come home from work. She had seen such a car when she left home that morning, parked in a nearby cul-de-sac. She immediately rang the police.

As Detective Bill Geddes approached the car, he already knew what he was going to find. A glance through the rear window confirmed his fear. The corpses of the two girls lay huddled together, as if they had been thrown into the vehicle. Both were fully clothed. Examination by the police doctor would reveal that both had been violently strangled and then subjected to some form of sexual assault.

Bianchi was obviously the chief suspect; he had to be arrested immediately. But at this point no one knew where he was; he was out somewhere driving his security truck. His boss, Mark Lawrence, agreed to set a trap. He contacted Bianchi by radio and asked him to go to a guard shack on the south side of town to receive instructions. Half an hour later, the police car arrived. The detectives approached cautiously; they had been warned that Bianchi was armed. But the good-looking young man who was waiting for them merely looked surprised to see them, and surrendered without protest. He seemed so totally free of guilt that Detective Terry Wright, who made the arrest, began to suspect that this was all a mistake. Either Ken Bianchi was innocent, or he was a superb actor.

Back at the police station, Bianchi denied knowing Karen Mandic. If someone calling himself Kenneth Bianchi had offered her a job, then it must be some impostor who had been using his name. The interrogators were inclined to believe him. They were even more convinced when Kelli Boyd, his common-law wife, arrived at the station. She was obviously horrified at the very idea that Ken Bianchi might be a murderer. He was a gentle lover and adoring father, totally incapable of violence. When the police asked permission to search their home, both gave it without hesitation.

The search revealed that, whether Bianchi was a murderer or not, he was certainly a thief. Hidden in the basement, the police found several expensive telephones and a new chain saw in its box; all these items had been reported stolen from places where

Bianchi had worked as a security guard. Bianchi was charged with grand theft, and taken to the county jail.

A search of Bianchi's security truck revealed more evidence – the keys of the Bayside house, and a woman's scarf. Diane Wilder's friends reported that she had a passion for scarves.

But the most convincing evidence came from examination of the bodies. Both girls had been strangled by some kind of ligature applied from behind, and its angle also made it clear that the murderer had been standing above them at the time, as if walking downstairs. On the stairs leading to the basement of the Bayside home, detectives found a single pubic hair. Two more pubic hairs fell from Diane Wilder's body when it was lifted on to a sterile sheet. Semen stains were found on the underwear of both girls. Examination of Bianchi's underwear also revealed semen stains. Diane had been menstruating at the time of her death, and there was also menstrual blood on Bianchi's underpants. Carpet fibres found on the clothing of both girls, and on the soles of their shoes, matched the fibres in the empty house. For all his protestations of innocence, Bianchi had to be guilty.

Now, at last, it became possible tentatively to reconstruct the crime. Ken Bianchi had telephoned Karen Mandic and offered her the house-sitting job – he had made her acquaintance when he was a security guard in the department store where she worked. (This made it clear that he was lying when he said he had never heard of her.) He had sworn her to silence 'for security reasons'. But Karen had told her boyfriend where she was going. She had also telephoned a friend who was a security guard at the university and told him about the job. Her friend had been suspicious about the size of the remuneration, but he knew that the Bayside area contained many wealthy homes, full of valuables. If this was one of them, it *could* be worth it.

At seven o'clock that evening, Karen and Diane had driven to the Bayside house. Bianchi was already waiting for them in his security truck – local residents had noticed it. Karen parked her car in the drive, outside the front door. Bianchi had asked her to accompany him inside to turn on the lights, while Diane waited in the Mercury. When he reappeared a few minutes later, Diane had no suspicion that her friend was now lying dead in the basement. Like Karen, she walked down the stairs with Bianchi behind her, and the ligature was dropped over her neck and pulled tight with tremendous force. As far as could be determined, the killer had not raped either girl – or had been satisfied with only brief penetration, ejaculating on the underwear. Then he had carried both bodies out to Karen's car, and dumped them in the back. He drove to the cul-de-sac, carefully wiped the car clean of fingerprints, and walked back to the Bayside house where his own truck was parked, disposing of the ligature on the way. The baffling thing about the crime was that it seemed so oddly pointless.

Still, the case against Bianchi looked conclusive, even though he continued to insist – with the greatest apparent sincerity – that he had no memory of the murders. His bail was posted at $150,000. And now he was safely in jail, the police began checking on his background. He had been living in Glendale, a town (or suburb) eight miles north of downtown Los Angeles, before his move to Bellingham in the previous May. An investigating detective rang the Los Angeles County Sheriff's Department to see if they knew anything about Kenneth Bianchi. The call was taken by Detective Sergeant Frank Salerno, of the Homicide Division. And when Salerno was told that a former Glendale resident named Kenneth Bianchi had been booked on suspicion of a double sex murder, he was seized by immense excitement.

For the past fourteen months, Salerno had been looking for a sex killer who had committed a dozen similar murders in Los Angeles. The newspapers had christened him the Hillside Strangler. The last murder had taken place shortly before Bianchi left Los Angeles for Bellingham.

The first corpse had been found sprawled on a hillside near Forest Lawn cemetery, south of the Ventura freeway. The girl was tall and black, and had been stripped naked. It seemed clear that her body had been removed from a car and tossed down the slope.

It was the morning of 17 October 1977. The girl's body temperature indicated that she had been killed some time the previous evening. The first problem was to identify her, and this proved unexpectedly easy. Her prints were on file, and revealed her to be a prostitute named Yolanda Washington, who operated around Hollywood Boulevard. The autopsy showed that sexual relations had taken place and had involved two men. One of these was a 'non-secretor', a man whose blood group cannot be determined from his bodily fluids. But the men could simply have been 'johns', and had nothing to do with her murder. Cause of death was strangulation with a piece of cloth, and it had taken place when she was lying down, with the murderer above her, possibly on the floor of a car.

The crime aroused little interest in the media; murders of prostitutes are too common to rate wide coverage.

The same was true of a second victim, discovered on the morning of 1 November. She lay close to the kerb in Alta Terrace Drive in La Crescenta, a town not far from Glendale, and it looked again as if she had been dumped from a car. As in the case of Yolanda Washington the body was naked, and death was due to strangulation with a ligature. She was little more than a child – 15 at the most. Marks on her wrists and ankles, and in the area of her mouth, indicated that she had been bound with adhesive tape. Fibres on her eyelids also revealed that she had been blindfolded.

The autopsy disclosed a possible connection with the murder of Yolanda Washington. The girl had been subjected to anal and vaginal intercourse by two men, one of them a non-secretor. The position of the body also indicated that she had been carried by two men, one holding her under the armpits and the other by the knees. All this was an advance on the Yolanda Washington case. Now at least the police knew they were looking for two killers.

This time, unfortunately, her prints were not on file. Sergeant Frank Salerno, investigating her death, had no definite starting point. A hunch led him to ask questions in the area of Hollywood Boulevard, and to display the police artist's sketch of the dead girl to its floating population of drug addicts and prostitutes. Several of the 'street people' had told him that she resembled a girl called Judy Miller, who had not been seen recently. It took Salerno another week to track down her parents. They lived in a cheap motel room, and one of their two remaining children slept in a cardboard box. With the curious lack of response of people who have received too many blows, they identified the morgue photographs as their daughter Judy, who had run away from home a month ago. Salerno already knew that she had made a living from prostitution – but in a half-hearted, amateurish way. She had given it away free to a casual boyfriend only an hour before she was last seen alive.

By the time Salerno located Judy's parents, there had already been another nude murder. On 6 November, a jogger near the Chevy Chase Country Club in Glendale saw the body lying near the golf course. She had been strangled with a ligature and subjected to a sexual assault that had caused vaginal bleeding. This time identification was easy. Soon after a news broadcast describing the discovery of the body, a man telephoned the police to say that his daughter had been missing for two days. She was a 20-year-old dancer named Lissa Kastin, and she had recently been working as a waitress. The man's description made it likely that she was the unknown victim, and an hour later, Lissa Kastin's father identified her face on a television monitor screen.

Glendale was outside Salerno's jurisdiction, but he went to view the body nevertheless. The ligature marks around the neck, and lines around the wrists and ankles, suggested that the stranglers had been at work again. As Frank Salerno looked down at the body – the third in three weeks – it passed through his mind that this was beginning to look like an epidemic.

Even Salerno was unprepared for what actually happened in the last three weeks of November 1977 – seven more strangled corpses, six of them naked. Eighteen-year-old Jill Barcomb, discovered on 10 November, was a prostitute; her body was found at Franklin Cyn Drive and Mulholland. Kathleen Robinson, 17, differed from the other victims in being clothed when her body was found at Pico and Ocean Boulevards on 17 November, so it was possible that she was not another victim of the sex killer.

But the day that shocked the media into awareness of the 'Hillside Strangler' was Sunday 20 November, when three nude corpses were found, two of them schoolgirls. These were Dollie Cepeda, 12, and Sonja Johnson, 14, and their bodies were discovered on a rubbish dump in an obscure street called Landa, near Stadium Way. The 9-year-old boy who found them thought they were discarded mannequins from a department store. Both girls had been missing since the previous Sunday evening, and the autopsy revealed that both had been raped and sodomized. Earlier that same day, another nude body had been discovered on a street corner in the hills that separate Glendale from Eagle Rock. The following morning, a missing person report helped to identify her as Kristina Weckler, a 20-year old art student who lived in an apartment building in Glendale.

The next body was found on 23 November, in some bushes off the Golden State freeway. She was identified as a 28-year-old scientology student named Jane King, who had been missing since 9 November. And the last victim of that November of spree killing was found in some bushes in Cliff Drive, Glendale on the 29th. Her parents identified her later in the day as Lauren Wagner, an 18-year-old student who had failed to return home the previous night. Lesions on her palms looked like burn marks, and suggested that she had been tortured before death.

Ten sex murders in six weeks was something of a record, even for Los Angeles, where there are several murders a day. The press reacted with a hysteria that was reminiscent of the coverage of the Son of Sam murders in New York earlier the same year. In fact, the 'Hillside Strangler' featured in television reports all over the world. (The police took care not to advertise their certainty that they were looking for two men, for the less the killers knew about the progress of the investigation, the better.) Women became afraid to go out alone at night, and shops that sold tear gas and Mace quickly ran out of supplies. By the time Lauren Wagner's body was discovered, Los Angeles was in a state of panic. The reaction of the police department was to create a combined task force from members of the Los Angeles Police, the Glendale Police and the Los Angeles Sheriff's Office, for which Salerno worked.

In spite of the frustrating lack of clues, the investigation was making some progress. On the evening of the disappearance of the two schoolgirls, a boy had seen them go up to a car and speak to someone on the passenger side. Clearly, then, there had been a passenger. The girls had apparently been nervous of speaking to strangers, but one of them was known to admire policemen. It was therefore possible that the killers had posed as policemen. Under hypnosis, the boy was able to say that the car was a large two-colour sedan.

There was also a promising lead in the Lauren Wagner case. Her father had looked out of the window on the morning of 29 November and noticed her car across the street. Closer examination showed that the door was open and the interior light still on. In the house in front of which the car was parked, a woman named Beulah Stofer described how she had seen Lauren abducted. As Lauren's car had pulled up, another car

– a big dark sedan with a white top – had halted alongside, and two men had got out. There was an argument, then Lauren had entered the other car and been driven away. Mrs Stofer had heard her say: 'You won't get away with this.' She was even able to describe the men: the older one had bushy hair and was 'Latin-looking', while the other, who was taller and younger, had acne scars on his neck. Beulah Stofer had been alerted to the incident when her dog had barked.

When a detective talked to Mrs Stofer later, that day, she was in a state of near-collapse. The telephone had just rung, and a rough male voice with an East Coast accent asked her if she was the lady with the dog. When she said she was, the voice had told her that she had better keep quiet about what she saw last night, or she was as good as dead. It was a clear indication that the stranglers knew her evidence could be of central importance to the investigation.

If the police had grasped the significance of this phone call, they might have terminated the career of the Hillside Strangler within days. The only way a man could have obtained a telephone number without knowing the name of the subscriber was through some friend at the telephone exchange. A check on the girls with access to such information would almost certainly have revealed the Strangler's identity. But in the general confusion of the investigation, this was overlooked, and the Strangler was free to strike again.

This happened two weeks later, on 14 December. The victim was a 17-year-old prostitute named Kimberly Diane Martin, and her naked body was found sprawled on a vacant lot on Alvorado Street, within sight of City Hall. This time there were more clues, for she had been sent by a call girl agency – appropriately named the Climax – to the Tamarind Apartment building in Hollywood. A man had called the agency, asking for a blonde in black underwear, for whom he would pay $150 in cash. The agency asked for the caller's telephone number and queried what sounded like a public telephone. The caller assured them he was at home (although a later check on the number revealed it to be that of the public library). The girl was despatched to the Tamarind Apartments, and disappeared. The police interviewed everyone in the apartment building, and one tenant – a personable young man named Kenneth Bianchi – admitted that he had heard screams. And at the Hollywood public library, a woman described how a bushy-haired man had followed her around and glared at her ferociously. But there the investigation ran into its usual blank wall.

In mid-February, the police ignored what could have been another promising lead. A middle-aged schoolteacher described how she had seen two men trying to drag a girl into their car on Riverside Drive in Birbank; she had jumped out of her car and told the men to let the girl alone. One of them – a bushy-haired man – had snarled: 'God will get you for this'; then they had driven off. The police decided that the woman was a crank and that her story was not worth investigating.

For the remaining weeks of 1977, there were no more murders, and the Los Angeles police hoped fervently that the Stranglers had moved elsewhere. On 17 February 1978, that hope was dashed when someone reported an orange Datsun halfway down a cliff below a lay-by on the Angeles Crest Highway north of Glendale. The trunk proved to contain another naked body. The girl was identified as Cindy Hudspeth, 20, a part-time waitress at the Robin Hood Inn, and ligature marks on the wrists left Frank Salerno in no doubt that she was another victim of the stranglers. The medical evidence indicated that two men had raped and sodomized her repeatedly,

Then, at last, the murders ceased.

That is why, when Sergeant Frank Salerno heard that Kenneth Bianchi had been arrested for a double sex killing, he lost no time in getting to Bellingham. And within hours of arriving, he was certain that he had found at least one of the Hillside Stranglers. A large cache of jewellery had been found in Bianchi's apartment, and at least two items matched jewellery taken from the victims.

Bianchi was apparently continuing to behave like an innocent man, and was being highly co-operative. He had told the police that his only close friend in Los Angeles was his cousin Angelo Buono, an automobile upholsterer who owned a house in Glendale. Salerno was excited. A German detective had flown from Berlin solely to tell the Strangler task force that he believed the stranglers were two brothers who were probably Italian. At the time no one had paid much attention. Now it sounded as if he might be very close.

A check on Angelo Buono – by an undercover agent – made it seem highly likely that he was the other strangler. He had bushy hair, and was 45 years old – seventeen years older than his cousin Ken. Like Bianchi, Buono had been born in Rochester, New York, and Beulah Stofer, the woman who had received the threatening phone call, had thought the man had a New York accent. And when Bianchi's face appeared in the Los Angeles newspapers, the schoolteacher who had interrupted the abduction of the girl in Birbank came forward again and told her story to Homicide Sergeant Bob Grogan of the Strangler task force. Her description of the two men certainly sounded like Bianchi and Buono.

More interesting information about Buono came from a wealthy Hollywood lawyer. In August 1976, he had telephoned a call girl agency – the Foxy Ladies – and asked for a woman to be sent over to his Bel-Air home. The 15-year-old girl who arrived at his home looked so miserable that the lawyer asked her how she came to be working as a prostitute when she obviously hated it. The answer, it seemed, was that a girl named Sabra had lured her from her home in Phoenix – where she was unhappy – to work for a man named Angelo Buono. Buono and his cousin Ken had terrorized the girl and told her that she would be killed if she tried to run away. Buono had subjected her to sodomy so frequently that she had to wear a tampon in her rectum. He also made a habit of forcing his penis down her throat until she vomited.

The lawyer was horrified, and promptly bought the girl an air ticket back to Phoenix. Buono had then made threatening phone calls – until the lawyer had sent a well-muscled bouncer to see him. The bouncer had found Buono working in a car, and when he addressed him, Buono ignored him. The bouncer had reached in through the window and dragged Buono out by his shirtfront, demanding: 'Do I have your attention, Mr Buono?' After that, the lawyer heard no more from Buono or his Foxy Ladies agency.

The lawyer was able to give Grogan the Phoenix address of Becky Spears, as well as that of the other call girl, Sabra Hannan, who had now returned to Arizona. They were brought to Los Angeles, and verified that Buono and Bianchi had offered them jobs as 'models', then forced them to work as prostitutes, beating them and threatening them with death.

As the detectives delved into his background, it became clear that Buono was a highly unsavoury character. He had been married four times and fathered eight children; all the wives had left him because of his brutality. He was proud of his sexual stamina – he was virtually insatiable – and liked to refer to himself as the Italian Stallion. He had several girlfriends, some in their early teens, and had habituated them all to fellatio and sodomy.

Grogan and Salerno were feeling pleased with themselves. There seemed little doubt that Buono and Bianchi were the Hillside Stranglers – in that order. Buono was the dominant one; Bianchi, for all his charm, was something of a weakling and a drifter. Even his girlfriend, Kelli Boyd, was sick of his lack of maturity – she had left him in Los Angeles to rejoin her family in Bellingham, but Bianchi had followed her there.

The police also thought they were beginning to understand how Buono and Bianchi had developed into serial killers. Their activities as pimps had made them accustomed to dominating and beating women. (Becky and Sabra had not been their only call girls; there were several more.) For a man who prided himself on his macho image, the episode with the bouncer must have been a keen humiliation for Angelo Buono – the kind of thing that could fester. And there had been another irritating setback. From an experienced professional prostitute, they had purchased a list of men who liked to have girls sent over to their homes. The list had been duly delivered, but turned out to be of men who wanted to visit a prostitute in her room. Buono had been enraged at the trick that had been played on him. He had no idea where to find the prostitute who had sold him the useless list. But he *did* know where to find one of her friends, an expensively dressed black prostitute who had been with her when the list was delivered. The name of the friend was Yolanda Washington, the first victim of the Stranglers . . .

It began to look as if the case was virtually tied up. Bianchi would undoubtedly be found guilty of the Bellingham murders. In Washington State, that would probably mean the death sentence. With that hanging over him, he would be eager to return to Los Angeles, where he could expect a life sentence. It would therefore be in his interest to confess to the Hillside murders, and to implicate his cousin. At present, evidence against Angelo Buono was slim; but with Bianchi's co-operation, it could be made impregnable. Buono had now been interviewed two or three times, and his attitude had an undertone of mockery; he seemed to be enjoying the thought that the police had no real evidence against him All that, Salerno reflected with satisfaction, would change when his cousin returned to Los Angeles . . .

And then, with bewildering suddenness, the whole case threatened to collapse. What had happened was that Kenneth Bianchi had managed to get himself declared insane. Or, at all events, the next best thing: a 'multiple personality'. In layman's parlance, that means a Jekyll and Hyde character whose Jekyll is totally unaware of the existence of his evil alter ego.

Ever since his arrest, Bianchi had been insisting that he remembered absolutely nothing of the evening on which he killed Karen Mandic and Diane Wilder. The police, understandably, thought that was a feeble and not very inventive attempt to wriggle out of responsibility. But Bianchi's lawyer, Dean Brett, was impressed by his apparent sincerity, his protestations of horror at the thought of killing two women, and his hints that he was contemplating suicide. He called in a psychiatric social worker, John Johnston, who was equally impressed by Bianchi's charm, gentleness and intelligence. If his protestations of amnesia were genuine, then there was only one possible conclusion: he was a multiple personality.

The general public had become aware of the riddle of multiple personality as a result of the 1957 movie *The Three Faces of Eve*, based on the book by two psychiatrists. But doctors had known about the illness since the early nineteenth century. It seems to be caused by severe psychological traumas in childhood, experiences so bad (like sexual abuse or extreme cruelty) that the personality literally blots them out and hides them away in some remote corner of the mind. In later life, some violent shock can reactivate the trauma, and the 'everyday self' blanks out, and a new personality takes over – for hours or sometimes days or months.

Whether Bianchi knew about multiple personalities at this stage is a matter for debate – the police were certainly unaware that he was an avid student of psychology, who hoped one day to become a professional psychoanalyst. What *is* clear is that Johnston's suggestion came to him as a revelation. So did a showing of the feature film *Sybil* – another study of multiple personality – on the prison television. From this, Bianchi learned that 'multiples' often suffer from blinding headaches and weird dreams. He also learned that psychiatrists try to gain access to the 'other self' through hypnosis. So when Professor John G. Watkins, a psychologist from the University of Montana, suggested hypnosis, Bianchi professed himself eager to co-operate. And within a few minutes of being placed in a trance, he was speaking in a strange, low voice and introducing himself as someone called Steve. 'Steve' came over as a highly unpleasant character with a sneering laugh. He told Dr Watkins that he hated 'Ken', and that he had done his best to 'fix him'. Then, with a little more prompting, he went on to describe how Ken had walked in one evening when his cousin Angelo Buono was murdering a girl. At which point, Steve admitted, he had taken over Ken's personality, and made him into his cousin's willing accomplice.

Frank Salerno and his colleague Pete Finnigan were sitting quietly in a corner of the room, listening to all this. In his notebook Frank Salerno wrote down a single word: 'Bullshit'. But he knew that the investigation was in trouble. If Bianchi could convince a judge that he was a multiple personality, he would escape with a few years in a mental hospital. And since the testimony of a mental patient would be inadmissible in court, Angelo Buono would be beyond the reach of the law.

Back in Los Angeles, the investigation was looking slightly more promising. The boyfriend of Judy Miller – the second victim of the Stranglers – had identified a photograph of Angelo Buono as the 'john' who had enticed Judy into his car on the evening she disappeared. And Beulah Stofer, the woman who had seen Lauren Wagner pushed into a car by two men, identified them from photographs as Buono and Bianchi. That would certainly help the case against Buono. But without Bianchi's testimony, it would still be a weak case.

The picture of Buono that had been built up through various interviews made it clear that he was brutal, violent and dangerous. He had hated his mother, and always referred to her as 'that cunt'; later in life, it became his general term for all women. From the time he left school he had been in trouble with the police, and had spent his seventeenth birthday in a reform school. His hero was Caryl Chessman, the 'Red Light bandit', who liked to hold up women at gunpoint and make them perform oral sex. At the age of 20 Buono had married a 17-year-old girl who was pregnant, but left her within weeks.

After a short period in jail for theft, he married again, and quickly fathered four more sons. But he was always coarse and violent: one day when his wife declined to have sex, he threw her down and sodomized her in front of the children. She left him and filed for divorce. So did his third wife. The fourth one left him without bothering about divorce. After that, Angelo lived alone in his house at 703 Colorado Street, Glendale. A friend who had once shared an apartment with him described him as being obsessed by young girls. The friend had entered the room one day and found Angelo peering down at a girls' playground through a pair of binoculars and playing with himself. Angelo had boasted that he had seduced his 14-year-old stepdaughter. And one of Angelo's sons had confided that his father had seduced him too. Clearly, Angelo Buono was a man who spent his days thinking and dreaming about sex.

Back in the Whatcomb County Jail in Washington, Ken's sinister alter ego 'Steve' was also telling stories of Buono's insatiable sexual appetite, and of his habit of killing girls after he had raped and sodomized them. These stories tended to contain certain anomalies – almost as if Steve wished to minimize his own part in the murders and throw most of the blame on Angelo – and the same applied to his later confessions to the police; but the general picture that emerged was clear enough. The first victim was the prostitute Yolanda Washington, who had been killed for revenge but raped by both men. They had found the experience so pleasant that two weeks later they had picked up 15-year-old Judy Miller, then, – pretending that they were policemen and she was under arrest – taken her back to Buono's house, where both had raped her. The rape and kidnapping had been unnecessary, since she would have been glad to submit to sex for a payment of a few dollars. Then, with Bianchi kneeling on her legs, they had strangled her and suffocated her at the same time, placing a plastic supermarket bag over her head.

The next victim was the out-of-work dancer Lissa Kastin. They stopped her in her car and identified themselves as policemen, showing a police badge. Then they told her they were taking her to the station for questioning. Back in Buono's house, she was kept handcuffed while they cut off her clothes with scissors. But when they found she had hairy legs, both men felt repelled. Bianchi raped her with a root-beer bottle, then strangled her, while Buono sat on her legs shouting 'Die, cunt, die.' Bianchi was in no hurry to kill her; he enjoyed tightening the cord until she lost consciousness, then loosening it to revive her; it gave him pleasure to feel that he had the absolute power of life and death. But they agreed afterwards that she had been a disappointment, a 'dog'. They dumped her near the Chevy Chase golf course.

Four days later, on 9 November, they were out hunting again. Bianchi saw an attractive girl waiting alone at a bus stop and began a conversation; she told him she was a Scientology student, and Bianchi asked her to tell him all about it. In the midst of the conversation, Buono drove up, pretending he hadn't seen Bianchi for months, and offered him a lift home. Jane King made the mistake of agreeing to let them drive her home. Back in Buono's house, they were delighted to find that her pubis was shaven. She resisted Buono's rape, and struggled so hard as Bianchi sodomized her that they decided she needed a lesson. She was hog-tied, and a plastic bag placed over her head while Bianchi sodomized her; when Bianchi climaxed she was dead. They were surprised to read later in the newspaper that she was 28; she seemed younger.

The shaven pubis had excited them both; now Buono dreamed of raping a virgin. Only four days after their last killing, they saw two schoolgirls, Dollie Cepeda and Sonja Johnson, boarding a bus in Eagle Rock Plaza. The idea of raping two girls at once appealed to them. They followed the bus, and when the girls disembarked near their home, beckoned them over to the car. Bianchi identified himself as a policeman and told them that a dangerous burglar was loose in the neighbourhood. The schoolgirls were vulnerable; they had just stolen a hundred dollars worth of costume jewellery from a department store, and were not disposed to argue with the police. Back in Buono's house, both had been subjected to violation, then Sonja was murdered in the bedroom. When they came to get Dollie, she asked: 'Where's Sonja?' and Buono told her: 'You'll be seeing her soon.' Their corpses were dumped on a rubbish tip that Buono knew from his courting days. The police had reasoned, correctly, that whoever had dumped the bodies must have known the area intimately.

The next victim was a girl Bianchi had known when he lived in an apartment building on East Garfield, in Hollywood. Kristina

Weckler was an art student, and she had spurned Bianchi when he had made advances. Now they knocked on her door, and Bianchi said: 'Hi, remember me?' He told her that he was now a member of the police reserve, and that someone had crashed into Kristina's VW, parked outside the building. She went down with them to see, and was bundled into Buono's car and taken to his house. After the rape, they decided to try a new method of murder: injecting her with a cleaning fluid. It produced convulsions, but not death. At Buono's suggestion, they placed a bag over her head and piped coal gas into it, strangling her at the same time.

The Thanksgiving killing spree was almost over. On Monday 28 November 1977, they saw a red-headed girl climbing into her car, and followed it. And when Lauren Wagner pulled up in front of her parents' home, Bianchi flourished his police badge and told her they were arresting her. While she protested – and a dog barked loudly in nearby house – they bundled her into their car and drove her away. When she realized that their purpose was rape, she pretended to be co-operative, mentioning that she had spent the evening in bed with her boyfriend and was ready for more. While being raped, she behaved as if she enjoyed it. Nevetheless, she was strangled, after an unsuccessful attempt to electrocute her had only produced burns on her palms.

The realization that they had been seen by a neighbour made them decide to be more cautious. But three weeks later, both were dreaming of another rape. Kimberly Martin, a call girl, was summoned to the Tamarind Apartments, and taken back to Buono's. After raping her, both agreed she was no good in bed. Her body was dumped or a vacant lot.

The final Hillside killing was almost an accident. On 16 February, Bianchi arrived at Buono's house to find an orange Datsun parked outside. A girl named Cindy Hudspeth had called to ask Buono to make new mats for her car. The opportunity was too good to miss. The girl was spreadeagled naked on the bed, her wrists and ankles tied to the legs, then they raped her for two hours. After that they strangled her. The Datsun was pushed off a cliff with her body in the trunk.

Bianchi had been twice questioned by the police in routine enquiries – he was one of thousands. But Buono was becoming nervous and irritable. He was getting sick of his cousin's lack of maturity, his naïvety and his carelessness. So when Bianchi told him that his girlfriend had left him and moved back to Bellingham, Buono strongly advised him to go and join her. At first Bianchi was unwilling – his admiration of his cousin amounted almost to worship. But Buono finally prevailed. On 21 May 1978, Kenneth Bianchi drove to Bellingham and rejoined Kelli Boyd and their newborn son. He obtained a job as a security guard, and was soon promoted to supervisor. But the small town bored him. He longed to prove to his cousin that he had the makings of a master criminal. And in the first week of January 1979, the craving for rape and murder became an intolerable itch. His mind went back to an attractive student called Karen Mandic, whom he had known when he worked in a department store.

A week later he was under arrest, and the Hillside stranglings were finally over.

The news that Kenneth Bianchi had accused his cousin of being his accomplice made Buono unpopular in the neighbourhood, and he received several threatening letters.

But it began to look more and more likely that neither Bianchi nor Buono would ever appear in a Los Angeles courtroom. In the Whatcomb County Jail, Bianchi had not only convinced Professor Watkins that he was a multiple personality, but had aroused equal interest and enthusiasm in another expert on the subject: Dr Ralph B. Allison, author of a remarkable work on multiple personality called *Minds in Many Pieces*. Allison's obvious sympathy made 'Steve' even more confiding, and led him to make what would later prove to be a crucial mistake. At Allison's request he revealed his last name: Walker – although at the time, this interesting and important fragment of information went unnoticed. And in the May issue of *Time* magazine, America learned that Bianchi had been pronounced a multiple personality by two of America's most eminent psychiatrists. Ken was innocent; it was Steve who had killed a dozen or so girls.

At this point, the prosecution decided it was time to bring in their own expert. Dr Martin T. Orne, of the University of Pennsylvania Hospital, was known as an authority on hypnosis. The sessions with 'Steve' had been videotaped, and Orne was able to study them. They failed to answer the question that troubled him most: whether Bianchi was hypnotized or only pretending to be. But he *did* notice that the character of 'Steve' seemed to develop during the course of the sessions. Steve was always coarse and foul-mouthed – his favourite term for the psychiatrists was 'motherfuckers' – but he seemed to slip deeper into his role as the sessions progressed. To Dr Orne, that suggested an actor rather than a true alter ego.

When the professor came to interview him, Bianchi was his usual co-operative self. Under hypnotic suggestion, he quickly slipped into a trance. Orne now decided to try a crucial experiment. Good hypnotic subjects can be made to hallucinate the presence of another person. Orne told Bianchi that his defence lawyer, Dean Brett, was sitting in an empty chair. And Bianchi immediately did something that Orne had never seen before in a similar situation: leapt to his feet and shook the hand of the imaginary lawyer. At that moment, Orne was certain that Bianchi was only feigning hypnosis. Genuinely hypnotized subjects are content to talk to their hallucinations; they never try to touch them.

Now Dr Orne tried another interesting experiment. In the course of conversation, he casually dropped the information that most multiple personalities have more than one alter ego. And at the next session, Bianchi immediately produced another 'personality', a frightened child named Billy. Asked if he knew Steve, Billy whispered miserably: 'He's a bad egg.' Now Orne knew beyond all doubt that Bianchi was malingering.

But it was Frank Salerno and his partner Pete Finnigan who made the discovery that finally exploded Bianchi's claim to be a muliple personality. Listening to the Allison tape, they heard 'Steve' declare that his last name was Walker. Suddenly, both recalled that they had seen the name Steve Walker somewhere in Bianchi's papers. A careful search revealed a letter to the registrar at California State University signed 'Thomas Steven Walker' – in Bianchi's handwriting – which requested a diploma without the name filled in. A little sleuthing revealed that the real Steve Walker *was* a graduate in psychology from California State University at Northridge, and he had answered an advertisement for a job by sending some of his academic papers. The advertisement had actually been placed by Bianchi, who had then used Walker's name – and his papers – to obtain himself a fake diploma in psychology.

The defence psychiatrists declined to be convinced that

Bianchi was shamming and should stand trial. (Dr Allison was later to admit that he was mistaken; he had meanwhile become a prison psychiatrist, and professed himself shocked to discover that criminals were habitual liars.) Dr Martin Orne and his colleague Dr Saul Faerstein – who had also interviewed Bianchi, at the request of the prosecution – were insistent that Bianchi was a malingerer, and it was their opinion that carried the day at the sanity hearing on 19 October 1979. At that hearing, Bianchi pleaded guilty to the two Bellingham murders and to five murders in Los Angeles, sobbing and professing deep remorse. Under Washington law, the judge then sentenced him to life imprisonment without the formality of a trial. But there were still five more murder charges to answer in Los Angeles. And when the Los Angeles County DA's office offered Bianchi a deal – plead guilty and testify against his cousin, and he would get life with the possibility of parole – he quickly accepted. In interviews with Frank Salerno and Peter Finnigan, he described all the murders with a precision of detail that left no doubt that it was Ken, not Steve, who had committed them.

On 22 October 1979, Angelo Buono was finally arrested and charged with the Hillside stranglings. He was placed in the county jail, where Bianchi already occupied another cell. But Bianchi was already reneging on his plea-bargaining agreement, explaining that he had made it only to save his life, and that he was genuinely innocent. The reason for his change of heart was simple. The DA's office had made the incredible decision to drop the other five Los Angeles murder charges, for which Bianchi could have been sentenced to death. So now he had nothing to lose by refusing to be co-operative.

As far as Salerno and Grogan were concerned, it did not make a great deal of difference. The jewellery found in Bianchi's house linked him to some of the victims, while a wisp of fluff on the eyelid of Judy Miller, the second victim, was demonstrated by forensic scientists to be identical to a foamy polyester material found in Buono's house. Strand by strand, the case against the Hillside stranglers was becoming powerful enough virtually to ensure Buono's conviction.

For Bianchi, the case was by no means over. One of the characteristics of the psychopath is that he just never gives up. And in June 1980, Bianchi glimpsed an incredible chance of proving his innocence. He received a letter signed 'Veronica

Lynn Compton, pen name Ver Lyn', asking for his co-operation on a play she was writing. The plot, she explained, was about a female mass murderer who injects male semen into the sex organs of her victims, thus making the police think that the killer is a male.

Bianchi was interested. He became even more interested when Veronica Compton came to visit him, and he realized that this glamorous brunette was obsessed by him. They fantasized about how nice it would be to go on a killing spree together, and Virginia suggested that they should cut off the private parts of the victims and keep them in embalming fluid. Soon after that they were exchanging love letters. Finally, Bianchi confided to her his brilliant scheme for getting out of jail. All she had to do was to go to Bellingham, and transform her play into reality: strangle a woman and inject semen into her vagina through a syringe. And Bianchi would then be able to point out that the Bellingham murderer was obviously still at large, and that he must therefore be innocent. But where would she get the semen? Simple, said Bianchi, he would provide it. And he did so by masturbating into the finger of a rubber glove, which he then smuggled to her in the spine of a book.

Veronica flew to Bellingham, and registered at a motel called the Shangri-la. In a nearby bar she made the acquaintance of a young woman named Kim Breed, and had several drinks with her. When she asked her to drive her back to her motel, her new friend agreed. At the Shangri-la, Veronica invited her into her room for a drink. Once inside, she excused herself to go to the toilet, armed herself with a piece of cord, then tiptoed out and sneaked up behind her unsuspecting victim, who was seated on the bed. Fortunately, Kim Breed was something of an athlete. She struggled frantically, and succeeded in throwing Veronica over her head and on to the floor. Then she fled. When she returned to the motel with a male friend, Veronica had also fled. But the police had no difficulty in tracing her through her airline reservation. She was arrested and, in due course, the 'copycat' slayer, as the newspapers labelled her, was sentenced to life. As soon as he learned of her failure, Bianchi lost interest in her, thereby fuelling deep resentment.

The case of Angelo Buono was due to come to court in September 1981. But pre-trial hearings, before Judge Ronald M. George, began long before that. The first matter on which

Judge George had to make up his mind was a motion by the defence to allow bail to the accused. George turned it down. The next motion was to sever the ten murder charges from the non-murder charges such as pimping, rape and sodomy; this would ensure that the jury should know as little as possible about Buono's background. Because it might provide grounds for an appeal, the judge decided to grant this motion.

The next development staggered everybody, including the judge. In July, the assistant District Attorney, Roger Kelly, proposed that all ten murder counts against Buono should be dropped. The reason, he explained, was that Bianchi's testimony was so dubious and self-contradictory that it was virtually useless. Buono should be tried at a later date on the non-murder charges, and meanwhile be allowed free on a fifty-thousand-dollar bail . . . Grogan and Salerno could hardly believe their ears. It meant that even if Buono was convicted on the other charges, he would serve only about five years in jail.

The judge agreed to deliver his ruling on 21 July 1981. During the week preceding that date, morale among the police was at rock bottom; no one doubted that the judge would agree to drop the charges – after all, if the DA's office was so unsure of a conviction, they must know what they were talking about.

On the day of the ruling, Buono looked cheerful and his junior counsel, Katherine Mader, was beaming with confidence. But as the judge reviewed the evidence, it became clear that their confidence was misplaced. Whether Bianchi was reliable or not, said the judge, the evidence of various witnesses, and the Judy Miller fibre evidence, made it clear that there was a strong case against Buono. Therefore, concluded Judge George, he was denying the District Attorney's motion. And if, he added, the DA showed any lack of enthusiasm in prosecuting Buono, he would refer the case to the Attorney-General.

Buono, who had expected to walk free from the courtroom, had to cancel his plans for a celebratory dinner with his lawyers.

At this point the DA's office decided to withdraw from the case. Thereupon, the Attorney-General appointed two of his deputies, Roger Boren and Michael Nash, to prosecute Buono.

The trial, which lasted from November 1981 to November

1983, was the longest murder trial in American history. The prosecution called 251 witnesses and introduced over a thousand exhibits. But although the transcript was eventually to occupy hundreds of volumes, the trial itself held few surprises. It took until June 1982 to get to Bianchi's evidence – he was the two hundredth witness to testify – and he at first showed himself typically vague and ambiguous. But when the judge dropped a hint that he was violating his original plea-bargaining agreement, and that he would have to serve out his time in Washington's Walla Walla – a notoriously tough jail – he became altogether less vague. Bianchi spent five months on the stand, and the results were damning to his cousin.

The defence team raised many objections, and pursued a tactic of trying to discredit witnesses and evidence. On the submission that testimony obtained under hypnosis should be inadmissible, the judge ruled that Bianchi had been faking both hypnosis and multiple personality. More serious was a motion by the defence to dismiss the whole case because one of the prosecution witnesses – Judy Miller's boyfriend – had been in a mental home. This was also overruled: it was the defence's fault, the judge said, for failing to spot the material in the files. Finally, the defence called Veronica Compton, the 'copycat slayer', to try to prove that she and Bianchi had planned to 'frame' Angelo Buono. Veronica, still seething with resentment, gave her evidence with histrionic relish. But when she admitted that she had once planned to open a mortuary so she and her lover could have sex with the corpses, it was clear that the jury found it hard to treat her as a reliable witness.

In the final submissions in October 1983, Buono's defence lawyer Gerald Chaleff argued that Bianchi had committed the murders alone, and that his cousin was an innocent man. The judge had to rebuke him for implying that the whole case against his client was a conspiracy. The jury retired on 21 October 1983, and when they had spent a week in their deliberations, the defence began to feel gloomy and the prosecution correspondingly optimistic. It emerged later that one juror, who was resentful about not being chosen as foreman, had been consistently obstructive. But finally, on 31 October (Hallowe'en), the jury announced that it had found Angelo Buono guilty of the murder of Lauren Wagner. During the following week they also found him guilty of murdering

Dolores Cepeda, Sonja Johnson, Kristina Weckler, Jane King, Lissa Kastin and Cindy Hudspeth. But – possibly influenced by the fact that Bianchi had already escaped the death penalty – they decided that Buono should not receive a death sentence. On 4 January 1984, the judge ordered that, since he had done everything in his power to sabotage the case against his cousin, Kenneth Bianchi should be returned to serve his sentence in Washington. He then sentenced Angelo Buono to life imprisonment without possibility of parole, regetting that he could not sentence him to death. In his final remarks he told the defendants:

'I am sure, Mr Buono and Mr Bianchi, that you will both probably only get your thrills reliving over and over again the torturing and murdering of your victims, being incapable, as I believe you to be, of feeling any remorse.'

Asked later whether such acts as Buono and Bianchi had committed did not prove them insane, he commented: 'Why should we call someone insane simply because he or she chooses not to conform to our standards of civilized behaviour?'

Perhaps more than any other case in this book, this one raises the question: what motivates people to do such things? This is not intended as an expression of moral indignation, which has no place in criminology, but as a question in practical psychology.

To grasp its significance, we need to look back over some of the ground we have covered in discussing the rise of pornography. There is a sense in which sex is not a 'personal' relationship, particularly for the male (on whom we are focusing). A healthy male responds 'automatically' to certain sights, such as a female undressing, just as a male stickleback will attack a piece of red cardboard because its aggression is aroused by another male's red underside. An inexperienced teenager may spend much of his time in a state of sexual arousal which is as impersonal as a dog's response to a bitch in heat. On the other hand, when a husband sees his wife removing her clothes on their honeymoon, his response is a mixture of 'impersonal' desire and 'personal' tenderness. And, since the purpose of sex is ultimately the raising of children, this is obviously closer to what sex is supposed to be. We all feel instinctively that sex without any 'personal' dimension is rather crude and shameful, in that that it leaves some basic human craving unsatisfied.

All human beings experience this desire for human contact and warmth, and this clearly applied to Buono and Bianchi, both of whom had close sexual relationships – albeit Buono preferred underage girls. How, then, could they continue to kidnap, rape and murder girl after girl, without any sense of compunction? Did they never feel sorry for some exhausted, violated victim as she was pleading for her life? If not, then how did they feel when they returned to their 'normal' human relations – as Bianchi did with his common-law wife and child?

To say that they 'divided their minds' is no answer. We can easily see that a man who began to develop a sadistic pleasure in beating dogs or children would find it difficult to return to being an affectionate master or father.

In this case, we observe – yet again – that rape becomes an addiction. The murder of Yolanda Washington removed their inhibitions about rape/murder, and from then on, the craving returned periodically. It was basically a desire to treat the woman *purely* as a sexual stimulant, with no personal relationship. Moreover, this also developed into a desire to torture the woman as well as rape her. It is as if treating women as 'sexual throwaways' caused the development of some element that *may* be latent in all males, but about which 'normal' males feel a deep inhibition.

What *is* it that can turn normal males into ruthless sexual predators? A sex-starved adolescent might suppose that it is simply the act of undressing a girl and penetrating her body, which strikes him as infinitely exciting. But a married couple know this is not true. 'Normal' sex tends to stay normal, and not to develop into violence and rape.

Roy Hazelwood came close to an answer when he said that sex crime is not about sex but about power. We have seen that this statement needs to be qualified. *Some* sex crime springs purely out of sexual frustration, and is therefore 'about sex'. But in the majority of modern serial killers, it is true that sex crime is about power.

But why should that be addictive? In spite of the anarchist dictum that power corrupts, a man who achieves power in everyday life, say as colonel of a regiment or supervisor of an office, does not automatically want to become Commander in Chief or head of the corporation. He may have reached a level at which he feels comfortable. Then why is the kind of power involved in sex crime so addictive?

The answer clearly lies in the sense of revelation associated with sex – the sense of breaking through barriers, of overcoming obstacles, of asserting masculinity: in a word, the surge of *freedom*. The sex criminal would argue that the average man can never 'drink his fill' of sex; he is only allowed to satisfy his desire within certain socially recognized limits. Sex murderer Leonard Lake – whom we shall encounter in the next chapter – expressed this attitude when he wrote: 'The perfect woman is totally controlled . . . There is no sexual problem with a submissive woman. There are no frustrations – only pleasure and contentment.' In drinking his fill of freedom, the sex killer imagines that he will experience total pleasure and contentment, and end with all his problems solved. A particularly articulate serial killer might argue that he regards rape as an instrument of spiritual evolution, just as a saint regards prayer, or a yogi meditation.

All this leads to the most interesting question of all: why, in fact, is there no case on record of a sex killer achieving 'higher consciousness' through sex? Why, in fact, do so many of them – like Ian Brady and Ted Bundy – end with a curious sense of futility, of having 'done it all'? After all, no saint or yogi or artist or philosopher ends with a sense of having 'done it all'.

The answer lies partly in the fact that man is essentially a social being, and that sex is an activity involving another person. (Even masturbation involves the image of another person.) Sade does his best to argue that the individual has no obligation to society, and can take his satisfaction as straightforwardly as a tiger eating its dinner. But if Sade really meant what he said, he would not bother to present it as an argument, for an argument is presented *to* other people, and involves the tacit assumption that they have the same rights that you have. No tiger argues with its dinner.

But there is another paradox. The 'freedom feeling' involves a sense of expansion, of happiness and benevolence. In sex between lovers, this feeling finds its natural object in the other person. In violation, the act itself contradicts the sensation it arouses. Freedom is about the transcendence of the personality, the 'godlike' sensation in which the personality seems to dissolve, to give way to immense vistas of 'possibility'. By contrast, crime involves entrapment in the personality, a sense of doing something that you prefer other people not to know about. The two sensations are in total opposition, pulling in opposite directions. The sex killer may dream about total fulfilment and higher consciousness, but when he has finished with his victim, he has to think about hiding the body, getting away without being seen, leaving no clues. The prison door has slammed again. Worse still, he feels trapped in a pattern of violence which has become his master. He is like a man who has become enslaved by a blackmailer.

In the 1970s, California became virtually the serial-killer centre of the world. In addition to the Hillside Stranglers, there was John Linley Frazier, Herb Mullin, Ed Kemper and Richard Chase. With the possible exception of Kemper, it could be argued that all four were mentally disturbed to the point of psychosis, and therefore belong in a textbook of psychiatry rather than the present volume. Significantly, California at this time was pursuing a policy of turning out mental patients into the community.

When, in October 1970, Victor Ohta and his family were found murdered in their California home, a note on the doctor's Rolls-Royce read: 'Today World War III will begin, as brought to you by the people of the free universe . . . I and my comrades from this day forth will fight until death or freedom against anyone who does not support natural life on this planet. Materialism must die or mankind will stop.' The killer, the 24-year-old drop-out John Linley Frazier, had told witnesses that the Ohta family was 'too materialistic' and deserved to die. In fact, Frazier was reacting with the self-centred narcissism of the children described by Becker. ('You gave him more juice.' 'Here's some more then.' 'Now *she's* got more juice than me . . .') He felt he had a long way to go to achieve 'security', while Ohta had a swimming pool and a Rolls-Royce parked in the drive.

The irony is that Ohta himself would serve equally well as an example of Becker's 'urge to heroism'. He was the son of Japanese immigrants who had been interned in 1941; but Ohta had finally been allowed to join the American army; his elder brother was killed in the fighting in Europe. Ohta had worked as a railway track-layer and a cab driver to get through medical school, and his success as an eye surgeon came late in life. Ohta achieved his sense of 'belongingness' through community work; he was one of the founders of the Dominican Hospital in Santa Cruz – a non-profit-making hospital – and often gave free treatment to patients who could not afford his fees. Frazier was completely unaware of all this. But it would probably have made no difference anyway. He was completely wrapped up in his own little world of narcissism.

In April 1973, 25-year-old Ed Kemper – six foot nine inches tall – crept into his mother's bedroom and killed her with a hammer; the following day he killed her friend Sara Hallett. Then he drove to Pueblo, Colorado, and rang the Santa Cruz police department to confess. In custody, Kemper confessed to six horrific sex murders, all with a strong necrophiliac element. In 1963, at the age of 14, Kemper had murdered his grandfather and grandmother, with whom he was living, and spent five years in mental hospitals. In 1972, he picked up two female hitchhikers, threatened them with a gun, and murdered them both; he later dissected the bodies, cutting off the heads. Kemper's usual method was to take the bodies back to his mother's house – she worked in a hospital – and rape and dissect them there; he particularly enjoyed having sex with a headless body. The bodies were later dumped over cliffs or left in remote mountain areas. Kemper was sentenced to life imprisonment.

Another psychopathic mass killer, Herb Mullin, was operating in California at the same time as Kemper. As a teenager, Mullin had been voted by his class 'most likely to succeed', but by the time he was 21 – in 1969 – he was showing signs of mental abnormality. In October 1972, driving along a mountain highway, Mullin passed an old tramp, and stopped to ask the man to take a look at the engine; as the man bent over, Mullin killed him with a baseball bat, leaving the corpse by the roadside. Two weeks later he picked up a pretty college student, stabbed her with a hunting knife, and tore out her intestines. In November 1972 he went into a church and stabbed the priest to death. On 25 January 1973, he committed five murders in one night, killing a friend and his wife, then murdering a woman and her two children who lived in a nearby log cabin. In the Santa Cruz State Park he killed four teenage boys in a tent with a revolver. On 13 February 1973, he was driving to his parents' home when a voice in his head told him to stop and kill an old man who was working in his front garden. A neighbour heard the shot, and rang the police, who picked up Mullin within a few blocks. At his trial, Mullin explained that he was convinced that murders averted natural disasters – such as another San Francisco earthquake. But he was found to be sane and sentenced to life imprisonment.

Richard Chase – who earned himself the soubriquet 'the Dracula Killer' – was first arrested in August 1977, near Pyramid Lake, Nevada, when police found a raw liver – apparently human – in a plastic bucket in his car. Nearby, Chase – aged 27 – was sitting on a rock, half naked and covered in blood. But when tests revealed that the liver was from a cow, Chase was released. If the police had decided to question his sanity, several lives would have been spared.

Four months later, on 29 December 1977, a Sacramento engineer named Ambrose Griffin was shot as he walked between his car and his house – apparently by a random sniper. He died some days later in hospital. The following day, a man sitting in a car fired a handgun at a boy on a bicycle, fortunately missing him. The bullet was found and proved to be fired from the gun that had killed Ambrose Griffin.

On 23 January, an intruder walked into the house of newly married Teresa Wallin, 22, in the Watt Avenue area of Sacramento, and shot her three times, then mutilated the body with a knife. There was no sign of rape, but evidence that the killer had drained some of her blood into a yoghurt cup and drunk it.

Around that time, many people in the area reported seeing a dirty, dishevelled man in an orange jacket, who sometimes knocked on doors and made incomprehensible demands.

Four days later, 38-year-old Evelyn Miroth, the mother of two small sons, was found shot and mutilated on her bed, and a boyfriend, Danny Meredith, was found shot dead in the next room. One of her children, 6-year-old Jason, had also been shot. A 22-month-old baby, David Ferreira, whom the victim had been baby-sitting, was missing. Evelyn Miroth's other two sons were away from home at the time. The post mortem showed that she had been sodomized. Again, there was evidence that the killer had drunk some of her blood.

The following day, a woman named Nancy Holden contacted the police, and told them about an encounter she had had with a man named Richard Chase, on the day of the Wallin murder. Chase, who had been at school with her, had accosted her in a store and tried to persuade her to give him a lift. Worried by his wild appearance, she had made some excuse.

The police checked on Chase and discovered that he had a record of mental illness. When they called at his apartment to interview him, Chase tried to run away; he was finally handcuffed before he could draw a gun.

The body of David Ferreira was found – decapitated – in a box near a church.

On 2 January 1979, Richard Chase was tried on six counts of murder. It became clear from the evidence that one of his peculiarities was to dabble his fingers in the intestines of his victims – hence the nickname 'the Dracula Killer'. Chase was sentenced to death, but on 26 December 1980, he committed suicide with an overdose of his anti-depression pills, which he had been saving up for weeks.

Oddly enough, it was in England that the most widely publicized case of serial murder of the 1970s occurred. As the years passed without any clue to his identity, 'the Yorkshire Ripper' achieved the same notoriety as Jack the Ripper in the late nineteenth century. Typically, much of this evaporated with the arrest of the murderer.

On an evening in late August 1969, a prostitute walking down St Paul's Road, in the red-light area of Bradford, Yorkshire, was struck violently on the head by a brick in a sock. She followed her assailant, and noted the number of the van in which he drove away. The police soon traced the owner of the van, who told them that he had been in the red-light area with a friend, who had vanished down St Paul's Road late at night. The police went to see the friend, whose name was Peter Sutcliffe. He was a shy, rather inarticulate young man, who insisted that he had only struck the woman with the flat of his hand. Since he had no criminal record, he was let off with a caution. The attack was the first crime of the man who would become known as the Yorkshire Ripper.

This attack was not quite 'motiveless'. Two months earlier, Sutcliffe had become intensely jealous of his girlfriend, Sonia, who was seeing another man and – he believed – being unfaithful to him. To 'get even', he picked up a prostitute – the first time he had ever done such a thing – but the encounter was not a success. The woman took his £10, then got her pimp to chase him away. Three weeks later, he saw the woman in a pub, and demanded his money back; instead, she jeered at him and made him a laughing-stock. Sutcliffe was a shy, sensitive man, and the experience filled him with rage and embarrassment. It festered until he became a sadistic killer of women – innocent housewives and schoolgirls as well as prostitutes.

Five years later, on 4 July 1975, Sutcliffe walked up behind a pretty divorcee named Anna Rogulskyj, and struck her three times on the head with the ball end of a ball-pein hammer. Then, as she collapsed, he raised her blouse and made several slashes with a knife. He was about to plunge it into her stomach when a man's voice called out to ask what was happening. Sutcliffe fled. Anna Rogulskyj recovered after a brain operation. Six weeks later, on 15 August 1975, he crept behind a 46-year-old office cleaner named Olive Smelt, and struck her to the ground with the hammer. Then he raised her clothes and made some slashes on her buttocks with a hacksaw blade before going to rejoin a friend who was waiting for him in a car. When the friend asked him what he had been doing, he explained in a mumble that he had been 'talking to that woman'. Olive Smelt also recovered after an operation to remove bone splinters from her brain.

On 29 October 1975, Sutcliffe picked up a 28-year-old prostitute named Wilma McCann, and went with her to a playing field near her home. But he found it impossible to achieve an erection at short notice. When the woman told him he was 'fuckin' useless', he asked her to wait a moment, got the hammer from the toolbox of his car, and struck her on the head. Then he tugged down her white slacks and stabbed her nine times in the abdomen and five in the chest.

Wilma McCann was the first of thirteen murder victims over the course of five years. Some of the victims were 'amateur prostitutes', mothers of single-parent families trying to earn money. Some, like 16-year-old Jayne MacDonald, were schoolgirls who happened to be returning home late at night. Some were working women, like 47-year-old Marguerite Walls, a Department of Health official who had been working overtime. Although Sutcliffe was later to insist that he was interested only in killing prostitutes, his craving to kill and mutilate extended to all women.

By the late 1970s, the murder hunt for the Yorkshire Ripper (as the press christened him) was the biggest in British criminal history. Thousands of people were interviewed – including Peter Sutcliffe – but all this information was not computerized, and so overwhelmed the investigators. Sutcliffe was interviewed in connection with the murder of a prostitute named Jean Jordan, a 20-year-old Scot, whom he had killed in the Southern Cemetery in Manchester, stripping her naked and stabbing her in a frenzy. After the murder, Sutcliffe looked for her handbag, which contained the £5 note he had given her – a new one he had been paid in his wage packet. In due course, this was found by the police, and all the employees of twenty-five firms in Bradford were interviewed, including Sutcliffe. His wife confirmed his alibi, and the police filed a report saying they had found nothing to arouse their suspicions.

In 1978 and 1979 the police had received three letters signed 'Jack the Ripper', which had led them to mount an extensive investigation in the Wearside area, 100 miles to the north of Bradford. And on 26 June 1979, the police received a recorded tape beginning with the works 'I'm Jack', and taunting them for failing to catch him; the accent was 'Geordie' – again, from the Wearside area. After Sutcliffe's arrest, the letters and the tape were recognized as hoaxes, but at the time, most police officers on the case assumed that the Ripper was from somewhere around Durham.

In December 1980, after the thirteenth murder, the police decided to set up an advisory team consisting of four police officers and a forensic expert, Stuart Kind. There had been seventeen attacks in all – including the ones of Anna Rogulskyj and Olive Smelt, and two more in the autumn of 1979 when the victims survived. The main clues were three sets of tyre tracks at three scenes of crime, three sets of footprints also found near three of the victims, and finally the new £5 note found in Jean Jordan's handbag. It will be recalled that this had been found far from the sites of the earlier Ripper murders, across the Pennines in Manchester, so it seemed highly likely that the 'Ripper' had taken it with him from Bradford – Sutcliffe had received it in his pay packet two days before the murder. But if the Ripper lived in the Bradford area, then the search of Wearside was a waste of time. In that case, the tape was probably also a hoax, for although the 'Geordie' Ripper might live in Bradford, the extensive police investigations had failed to pinpoint such a suspect. This is why, at the beginning of the investigation, the five-man team decided that the tape and letters should be dismissed as irrelevancies.

There was another reason. The team had gone to examine all the murder sites, including that of a Bradford University student, Barbara Leach, who was killed returning to her flat in the early hours of the morning. As they were looking at the site, one of the police officers, Commander Ronald Harvey, had one of these sudden hunches that come from years of experience, and he remarked: 'Chummy lives in Bradford and he did it going home.' What he was suggesting was that the Ripper lived in this area, and that he killed Barbara Leach on his way home, perhaps after an unsuccessful search for a victim.

The comment impressed Stuart Kind, for surely here was an important point: that a murder committed in the early hours of the morning indicated that the killer was not far from home, whereas a murder committed earlier in the evening suggested that he had driven far from home in search of a victim and had to get back. Anna Rogulskyj had been attacked in Keighley, close to Bradford, at 1.10 in the morning. But Olive Smelt, attacked at 11 p.m., had been in Halifax. Josephine Walker had been murdered in Halifax at 11.30 p.m. Helen Rytka had been attacked in Huddersfield – even further from Bradford – at nine in the evening. Vera Millward had been murdered in Manchester at nine in the evening. Admittedly, this pattern did not hold for all the seventeen attacks – Emily Jackson had been murdered in nearby Leeds at seven in the evening – but it held for most of them.

So it looked as if the Ripper was probably a local man living in Bradford or Leeds, where ten out of seventeen attacks took place. Next, the team took a map of the area, and computed the 'centre of gravity' of the attacks. The basic principle was to stick a pin in the seventeen sites, then to take an eighteenth pin, and join it to the other seventeen by lengths of thread, minimizing the amount of thread required. The eighteenth pin proved to be squarely in Bradford. (In fact, the 'pin test' was carried out on the forensic laboratory computer.)

The team suggested that a special squad of detectives should concentrate their energies on Bradford. That would involve re-checking all the men in Bradford who had been interviewed. And since the £5 note was the most vital clue so far, the men who had been interviewed in this connection would have been top of the list. Since the police possessed samples of the tyre tracks of the Ripper's car, it would have been a simple matter to check the tyre tracks of each of these men.

It can be seen that this method should have led infallibly to Peter Sutcliffe, who was by then living with his wife Sonia at 6 Garden Lane, in the Heaton district of Bradford. That it did not do so was due to the simple circumstance that the Yorkshire Ripper was finally arrested within two weeks of the interim report being completed. On 2 January 1981, in the early evening, Peter Sutcliffe drove the 30 or so miles from Bradford to Sheffield, and in the red-light district there, picked up a black prostitute named Olive Reivers, and backed into a drive. She removed her knickers and handed him a condom; he unbuttoned his trousers and struggled uncomfortably across her in the passenger seat. But he was unable to obtain an erection. As he sat beside her again, telling her about his wife's frigidity, they were dazzled by the lights of a police car which pulled up with its nose to the bonnet of Sutcliffe's old Rover. Sutcliffe told Olive Reivers to back up his story that she was his girlfriend, and gave his name as Peter Williams. One of the policemen went to the nearest telephone and checked the car's number plates with the national police computer at Hendon; within two minutes, he had learned that the plates on the Rover actually belonged to a Skoda. Sutcliffe had stolen them from a car scrap-yard and fixed them on with Sellotape, because he knew the police were noting the number plates of cars in red-light areas.

As both policemen escorted Olive Reivers to the police car, Sutcliffe hurried behind a nearby oil storage tank, explaining that he was 'busting for a pee', and there managed to dispose of the ball-pen hammer and knife that had been concealed under his seat. The police then took him to Hammerton Road police station. There he revealed that his name was Sutcliffe, and explained that he was using false number plates because his insurance had lapsed and he was due to appear on a drunken driving charge. He was placed in a cell for the night. And at eight o'clock the next morning – Saturday – he was taken to the Ripper Incident Room at Leeds. Here it was immediately noted that the size of his shoe was the same as that of the footprint found at three of the murder sites. When he volunteered the information that he had been among those questioned about the new £5 note, and had also been questioned routinely as a regular visitor to red-light areas, the investigators suddenly became aware that this man could well be the Ripper. When they learned that his car had also been logged in Manchester, it began to look even more likely. Yet there was still no real evidence against Sutcliffe, and after a long day of questioning, during which he had been pleasantly co-operative, the police recognized this lack of evidence. But five and a half years of fruitless search for the Ripper had made them persistent; they decided to hold him for another night. And, back in Sheffield, the policeman who had arrested him heard that he was still being questioned by the Ripper squad. On an impulse, he went back to the oil storage tank where Sutcliffe had urinated. There he found the hammer and knife on a pile of leaves.

When Sutcliffe was told about the find, he admitted that he was the Yorkshire Ripper, then went on to dictate a statement describing his murders in detail.

'I imagined him to be an ugly hunchback wi' boils all over his face, somebody who couldn't get women and resented 'em for that.' This was the comment of Carl Sutcliffe when he learned that his eldest brother Peter had been changed with being the Yorkshire Ripper. Peter Sutcliffe was not an ugly hunchback; he was strikingly handsome, in a brooding, Elvis Presley sort of way, with black hair and beard and a superb physique. And he had no difficulty getting girls; although a considerate and attentive husband, he seized any opportunity afforded by his wife's absence to sleep with local girls, and found them more than willing to oblige.

Then why did Peter Sutcliffe commit thirteen particularly sadistic murders? A book on the case which appeared within weeks of his conviction – and which claimed to be an 'in-depth study of a mass killer' – shed surprisingly little light on the problem. The portrait of the Ripper that emerged seemed to be entirely in terms of negatives. He was not a brutal or resentful or violent person; on the contrary, he was gentle, meditative, courteous and good-tempered. It was practically impossible to provoke him into anger or self-assertion; and this was not due to an iron self-control, but to a genuine sweetness of disposition. He was the sort of person you would have trusted implicitly as a baby-sitter or an escort for your teenage daughter; what is more, you would have been perfectly right to do so. Under normal circumstances, Peter Sutcliffe would not have harmed a fly.

The mystery, of course, is what peculiar pressures turned this quiet man into a maniac who stole up behind women in the dark, smashed in their skulls with blows from a ball-headed hammer, then pulled up their skirts and blouses and carefully inflicted dozens of wounds with a specially sharpened screw-driver. This is a problem that came to obsess the journalist Gordon Burn, and he sought his answers in the Ripper's home territory – Bingley, near Bradford. The result is a book that will undoubtedly become a classic in the field of investigative criminology.

It was Aldous Huxley, talking about D. H. Lawrence, who commented on the stifling intimacy of working-class family life, an intimacy the middle classes find almost unimaginable. What Huxley could not understand was the curiously *stagnant* mentality created by this kind of environment. When people live that close together, they come to share one another's values, one another's states of mind, just as they would share one another's germs if they all used the same toothbrush. This is why so many people, born into such an environment, end their lives living just around the corner from the place where they were born. They take it utterly for granted that there is no escape. This also explains the oddly resentful attitude towards people who have 'made it'; Gordon Burn mentions the hostility that local people seem to feel about John Braine, who was an assistant librarian in Bingley when he wrote *Room at the Top*.

This is, of course, hard luck on the people who *are* slightly different, but who lack the energy or passion to heave themselves out of the swamp by brute force. Burn's book makes it very clear that this was one of the major factors in the Ripper's inauspicious development.

Peter Sutcliffe was his mother's first child: a shy, scrawny, miserable little boy who spent hours staring blankly into space. He clung – quite literally – to his mother's skirts for years after he had learned to walk. At school he was so withdrawn and passive that after his arrest, most of his schoolteachers could not even remember who he was.

The Sutcliffe home was no background for this kind of child. The father, John Sutcliffe, was a dominant extrovert, a bully who was detested by his family – one daughter admits she had dreams of murdering him. The younger brothers shared some of his characteristics; one of them once floored the local boxing champion by punching him in the testicles. The house was always jammed with people, and John Sutcliffe enjoyed 'feeling up' any young girls who strayed too close. The atmosphere was heavy with sexuality; even Sutcliffe's mother, a quiet doormat of a woman, had a love affair with a local police sergeant; the father retaliated by moving in with the deaf and dumb woman a few doors away. Various kinds of illegality were also taken for granted; Sutcliffe senior was arrested for breaking and entering; the second brother was always in and out of jail; some of Peter's best friends were burglars.

So the pathologically shy boy began to try to develop the characteristics that would make him less of a misfit. He did body-building exercises, learned to walk on his hands, drove at eighty miles an hour in built-up areas, boasted of sleeping with prostitutes. The latter was fantasy; but Sutcliffe *was* morbidly fascinated by the local red-light districts, and liked to cruise around them, just eyeing the prostitutes. All the same, when he finally found himself a girl, it was a Czech emigrée, who was even shyer than he was, and so plain that even Sutcliffe senior never tried to feel her up.

It was this girl – Sonia – who started the train of events that turned Peter Sutcliffe into sadistic killer. She began having an affair with an Italian who owned a sports car; Sutcliffe was plunged into an agony of jealousy. To revenge himself, he went off to the red-light district to find a woman. Even this turned out to be a flop. He was unable to raise an erection, and the girl swindled him out of five pounds. Worse still, when he saw her later in a pub and asked for his money, she jeered at him and told the story at the top of her voice, so he became a laughing stock.

'Life being what it is', said Gauguin, 'one dreams of revenge.'

Sutcliffe was caught in a peculiar emotional whirlpool, dreaming of sex, of violence, of getting his own back. One day, eating fish and chips in a friend's mini-van, he thought he saw the prostitute who had swindled him, and slipped out of the van. He was carrying in his pocket a brick inside a sock for precisely this purpose. He hit the woman on the back of the head, then ran back to the van. She succeeded in taking his number, and the next day he was questioned by the police. He convinced them it had been a straightforward quarrel, and the woman decided not to press charges.

For the next five years he kept out of trouble; to begin with, he was working nights. Sonia had gone to London and had a schizophrenic breakdown, and Sutcliffe nursed her back to health; in 1974 they were married. But hatred of prostitutes continued to obsess him. He would stop the car and ask a woman how much she charged, then persuade her to take less. The bargain concluded, he would shout 'Is that all you're worth?', and drive off. If a woman looked like a prostitute he would ask her roughly if she was on the game. It was totally uncharacteristic of the gentle, courteous Peter; but he was turning into a dual personality.

In July 1975 he approached a woman in the red-light district and, when she turned him down, followed her and hit her with a hammer. Then he raised her clothes and took out a knife. A man saw them and called out; Sutcliffe fled. A month later, he was sitting in a pub with a friend when a 45-year-old office cleaner went past; Sutcliffe said 'I bet you're on the game', and received an abusive answer. Later, he saw her in the street, and slipped out of the car. Again he battered her to the ground with the hammer; again he was disturbed and fled.

Two months later, he picked up a drunken prostitute who was thumbing a lift. They went on to a playing field, where he again failed to raise an erection. Then, as he cursed him, he hit her with the hammer, and stabbed her repeatedly in the breast and stomach.

How does a man acquire a taste for disembowelling women? I suspect the answer may be: all too easily. I read Burns's book on the Ripper on a train journey to London, en route to do a breakfast TV show. On my way back to Paddington, I began to discuss the case with the hire-car driver, Andrew Fowler, who provided me with a hair-raising insight. Fowler told me that he had worked for two years in a slaughterhouse, because it paid so well. He had always been an animal lover, but found that killing cattle could be treated merely as a job. Then, one day, he found that he was beginning to look at horses and dogs with the thought: 'I wonder what it would be like to kill it . . .' He decided that it was time to change his job. Fowler also described to me a slaughterman who was not happy until he was covered from head to foot in blood; once he was in this state, his eyes began to bulge in an odd way . . .

What seems clear is that Sutcliffe's obsession, which began as a hatred of prostitutes, soon became a desire to obtain sexual satisfaction by killing any woman. When he murdered Jean Jordan in Manchester in October 1977, he left the body hidden in bushes. Realizing that the five-pound note he had given her might provide a clue to his identity, he went back a week later to look for her handbag. He stripped her, stabbed her repeatedly, then used a piece of glass to open the body from the knee to the shoulder. The stench made him vomit, but he still went on to try to cut off her head with a hacksaw blade. The worm of death and violence had made its home in his sexual nerve. When he killed 16-year-old Jane MacDonald in the middle of a park, he must have known she was not a prostitute. It made no difference; he had conditioned himself to need this ultimate form of rape, and it was impossible to stop. And when, after thirteen murders, he was caught by a random police check, he had even lost count of the number he had committed – he thought it was eleven.

Perhaps the most important point to emerge from Gordon Burns's book, *Somebody's Husband, Somebody's Son*, is that mass killers like Sutcliffe, Dennis Nilsen, Ian Brady, even Jack the Ripper himself, are not necessarily human monsters, creatures of nightmare, driven by a craving for violence. Sutcliffe was a basically normal person, who slipped into murder as gently and gradually as a child slips into a swimming pool at the shallow end. The morbid craving that drove him to wander round red-light areas, and to spend hours in a waxworks displaying horrible diseases and accidents, can be found in most children, and in far more adults than we would like to believe. Sutcliffe's problem was that he was more shy, more imaginative, more intelligent, than the people around him, and that in his environment, these qualities were worse than useless.

In self-defence, he had to develop opposite qualities. And it was this discordant jumble of primary and secondary qualities, stitched together like a Frankenstein monster, that turned him into the most dangerous man in England. Gordon Burn reveals his insight into the problem when he describes Sutcliffe at his trial as looking like 'a seaside cabinet doll that has known better days'. But that description has one slight inaccuracy: this particular doll had never known better days.

10

The 1980s and 1990s

On 8 September 1888, Mrs Mary Burridge, of 132 Blackfriars Road, South London, bought the Late Final edition of the evening newspaper *The Star*, and when she read the headline about the 'latest horrible murder in Whitechapel', she collapsed and died of 'a fit'. There was much the same profound sense of shock and horror in America in the 1970s as news of the murders of Dean Corll, John Gacy, and the Hillside Stranglers was brought home with nauseating immediacy on the television screen. The general feeling was that the world was going downhill like a toboggan on a ski slope and that nothing could stop it. I recall the impact as being very like that of the revelation of the Nazi death camps in the last days of the Second World War, with the piles of skeletal corpses. But in a sense it was worse; because when Hitler died in the Berlin bunker, the world could at least heave a sigh of relief, and feel that the powers of evil had now been defeated. Corll, Gacy and Bundy revealed that they were as active as ever, and that our welfare society was actually nurturing such monsters.

As already noted, the term 'serial killer' was coined in the late 1970s by FBI agent Robert Ressler, who worked at the new FBI Academy at Quantico, Virginia. The Academy – founded by J. Edgar Hoover – had virtually created a new science called 'psychological profiling'. The study of dozens of murderers had revealed that they left their 'personality fingerprints' behind at the scene of the crime – for example, evidence of panic and confusion usually indicated a young offender. For instance, on 2 September 1977, a 14-year-old schoolgirl named Julie

Wittmeyer disappeared on the way home from school in Platte City, Kansas. Her clothing – minus her panties – was found in a field a few days later, and her naked and mutilated body the next day. The local police decided to try the new Behavioural Science Unit at Quantico. After studying the evidence, the Unit sent back a 'profile' of the offender: that he knew the victim, that he was a sexually frustrated 'loner', probably below average intelligence and of more than average physical development, and that his contemporaries probably regarded him as 'strange'. Police Chief Marion Beeler exclaimed: 'Sure as shootin', that's him' – for the description fitted a youth named Mark Sager. In fact, Sager was found guilty and sentenced to ten years.

Again, in the early 1980s, police in Anchorage, Alaska, were investigating the murder of a number of 'exotic dancers' who worked in bars and strip joints. Most had been buried – naked – in shallow graves, and had been shot in the head. One 17-year-old prostitute escaped from a 'john' who had chained her up and tortured her, and her description sounded like a wealthy and respected businessman named Robert Hansen, who owned a bakery business. But Hansen seemed to have an excellent alibi. The investigators decided to contact the Behavioural Science Unit at Quantico, and offer them the evidence on the crimes without going into detail about their suspect. The resulting 'profile' convinced them that Hansen could indeed be their man. The friends who had given him an alibi were interviewed, and told that it might cost them two years in jail if they were perjuring themselves. They broke and admitted they were. Hansen was arrested, and a search of his home revealed 'trophies' from his victims, and a map dotted with asterisks. This led them to more naked bodies – twenty in all. Hansen then confessed that he drove women out into the woods and asked them for oral sex; if they failed to satisfy him, he made them run naked through the snow, stalking them with a hunting rifle and finally killing them. He was sentenced to life imprisonment.

One interesting point emerges from Hansen's confession. He described how he had killed his first victim when she had asked him for money – he was obsessively mean – and that after murder he was physically sick. Soon afterwards he stabbed to death a prostitute who failed to fellate him satisfactorily. This time he no longer felt sick, but found he was looking back on the murder with pleasure. After that – as with so many serial killers – it became an addiction.

Robert Ressler was consulted in the case of the Sacramento murderer Richard Chase – described in the last chapter. He constructed a 'profile' decribing the killer as thin and undernourished, slovenly and unkempt, with a history of mental illness, and between 25 and 27 years of age. Chase was caught soon after, and proved to fit Ressler's profile with astonishing precision.

When Ressler attended various international seminars on crime in the late 1970s, murders like those of 'Son of Sam' were described as 'Stranger Killings'. At a session at the Bramhill police academy, near London, Ressler heard discussions of crimes that came in 'series' – like rapes, burglaries, arsons and so on. It was after this that Ressler began to refer to 'serial killers' (unaware that crime writer John Brophy had used the term 'serial murderer' in his book *The Meaning of Murder*, in 1966.[1] The label stuck. And by the early 1980s the general public suddenly became aware of its existence when journalists began writing articles about 'serial murder'.

What was being discussed in these early articles was not primarily the type of serial murder committed by Corll and Gacy, in which the killer lured victims into his own home, but the notion of killers who wandered around from place to place, killing casually and at random. It was this that made it all so frightening. One policeman was quoted as saying: 'There may be as many as five hundred of them out there.' This meant ten to every state in America, or about one to every major city. This was the figure accepted by psychiatrist Joel Norris in his book *Serial Killers: The Growing Menace* (1988), although another authority, Elliott Leyton, estimated the number at a hundred.

When writing my own book *The Serial Killers* (with Donald Seaman, 1990), I found myself questioning these figures. It's true that a few serial killers – like Corll and Gacy – had killed thirty people. But even allowing a conservative ten victims per killer, Norris's figure would make about five thousand victims a year – roughly a quarter of the total American murder rate. That seemed impossible. Even Leyton's figure seemed high. So I wrote to FBI agent Gregg McCrary, one of the Quantico

[1] I owe this observation to the criminologist Candice Skrapec.

team who had given us such generous help with our book, and asked for his own estimate. It was less than fifty, accounting for, at most, a few hundred serial murders per year. So the usual estimate *was* well over the top, reflecting the journalist's desire for a bloodcurdling story rather than the true figures.

In the early 1980s the British police were learning the same lessons as their American counterparts. The Yorkshire Ripper case had taught them an important lesson. If suspects, like car number plates, had been fed into a computer, Sutcliffe would probably have been taken in for questioning when he was wearing the boots whose imprint was found beside Jo Whitaker – and three lives would have been saved. A computer would have had no problem storing 150,000 suspects and 22,000 statements. Yet even with the aid of a computer, the task of tracking down a random serial killer like Sutcliffe would have been enormous. It could only display such details as the methods of known sex offenders, and the names of suspects who had been interviewed more than once. In their next major investigation of a serial killer, the Surrey police began with a list of 4,900 sex offenders – which, as it happened, contained the name of the man they were seeking.

The 'Railway Rapist' began to operate in 1982; at this stage, two men were involved in sexual attacks on five women on or near railway stations. By 1984, one of the men had begun to operate alone. He threatened his victims with a knife, tied their hands, and raped them with a great deal of violence. Twenty-seven such attacks occurred in 1984 and 1985. In January 1986, the body of 19-year-old Alison Day was found in the River Lea; she had vanished seventeen days earlier on her way to meet her boyfriend. She had been raped and strangled. In April 1986, 15-year-old Maartje Tamboezer, daughter of a Dutch oil executive, was accosted as she took a short cut through woods near Horsley, and dragged off the footpath; she was also raped and strangled. Her attacker was evidently aware of the most recent advance in forensic detection, 'genetic fingerprinting', by which a suspect can be identified from the distinctive pattern in the DNA of his body cells. The killer had stuffed a burning paper handkerchief into her genitals. A man who had been seen running for a train soon after the murder was believed to be the rapist, and two million train tickets were examined in an attempt to find one with his fingerprints.

A month later, a 29-year-old secretary named Ann Lock disappeared on her way home from work; her body was found ten weeks later. Again, an attempt to destroy sperm traces by burning was found.

It was at this point that the police forces involved in the investigation decided to link computers; the result was the list of 4,900 sex offenders, soon reduced to 1,999. At number 1,594 was a man called John Duffy, charged with raping his ex-wife and attacking her lover with a knife. The computers showed that he had also been arrested on suspicion of loitering near a railway station. (Since the blood group of the Ann Lock strangler had been the same as that of the 'Railway Rapist', police had been keeping a watch on railway stations.) Duffy was called in for questioning, and his similarity to the 'Railway Rapist' noted. (Duffy was small, ginger-haired and pockmarked.) But when the police tried to conduct a second interview, Duffy was in hospital suffering from amnesia, alleging that he had been beaten up by muggers. The hospital authorities declined to allow him to be interviewed. And since he was only one of two thousand suspects, the police did not persist.

Faced with these problems, the investigation team decided that an 'expert' might be able to help. They asked Dr David Canter, a professor of psychology at the University of Surrey, to review all the evidence. Using techniques similar to those used by the Yorkshire Ripper team – studying the locations of the attacks – he concluded that the 'centre of gravity' lay in the North London area, and that the rapist probably lived within three miles of Finchley Road. He also concluded that he had been a semi-skilled worker, and that his relationship with his wife had been a stormy one. When Canter's analysis was matched up against the remaining suspects, the computer immediately threw up the name of John Duffy, who lived in Kilburn. Police kept him under surveillance until they decided that they could no longer take the risk of leaving him at liberty – another schoolgirl had been raped with typical violence since Duffy was committed to hospital – and arrested him. When a fellow martial arts enthusiast admitted that Duffy had persuaded him to beat him up so he could claim loss of memory, the police were certain that he was the man they were seeking. Five of the rape victims picked him out at an identity parade, and string found in the home of his parents proved to be identical with that which had been used to tie Maartje Tamboezer's wrists. When forensic scientists matched fibres from Alison Day's sheepskin coat to fibres found on one of Duffy's sweater, the final link in the chain of evidence was established; although he continued to refuse to admit or deny his guilt, John Duffy was sentenced to life imprisonment.

Dr David Canter has described the techniques he used to pinpoint where the railway rapist lived:

> Many environmental psychology studies have demonstrated that people form particular mental maps of the places they use. Each person creates a unique representation of the place in which he lives, with its own particular distortions. In the case of John Duffy, journalists recognized his preference for committing crimes near railway lines to the extent that they dubbed him the 'railway rapist'. What neither they nor the police appreciated was that this characteristic was likely to be part of his way of thinking about the layout of London, and so was a clue to his own particular mental map. It could therefore be used to see where the psychological focus of this map was and so specify the area in which he lived.[1]

By the time John Duffy was arrested in 1985, the techniques of 'psychological profiling' had already – as we have seen – been in use in America for a decade. And the use of the computer had also been recognized as a vital part of the method. A retired Los Angeles detective named Pierce Brooks had pointed out that many serial killers remained unapprehended because they moved from state to state, and that before the state police realized they had a multiple killer on their hands, he had moved on. The answer obviously lay in linking up the computers of individual states, and feeding the information into a central computer. Brooks's programme was labelled VICAP – the violent criminal apprehension programme – and the FBI Academy at Quantico, Virginia, was chosen as the centre for the new crimefighting team. VICAP proved to be the first major step towards the solution of the problem of the random sex killer.

* * *

[1] *New Society*, 4 March 1988.

In France, unfortunately, the technical resources of the police remained relatively primitive well into the 1980s, which explains why a serial killer who created in Paris the same atmosphere of terror as the Yorkshire Ripper in the north of England was able to remain undetected for so many years.

On 5 October 1984, 91-year-old Germaine Petitot was attacked in her home in the Clichy area by two robbers, and left bound and gagged. She had also been beaten, an unnecessary act of violence that puzzled the police, since she was obviously too old to put up any resistance. Unfortunately, she was too shocked to be able to describe her attackers.

Later the same day, 83-year-old Anna Barbier-Ponthus was inserting her key in her door in the rue Saulnier when she was attacked, pushed inside, and suffocated with a pillow. Her body, gagged and bound, was found soon afterwards. Like the previous victim she had also been beaten. In neither case was there any sign of sexual assault. The motive had been robbery – in this case, to take about £40 from her purse.

Four days later, on 9 October, firemen called to a blaze in the rue Nicolet found the body of Suzanne Foucault, 89, who had been suffocated with a plastic bag. Her watch and some money were missing.

Four weeks passed without further attacks; then, in five days, five more old ladies were murdered. On 3 November 1984, a retired schoolteacher, Iona Seigaresco, 71, was found brutally battered; this time the killers had escaped with 10,000 francs (over £1,000) in bonds. She was found two days later. Alice Benaim, found by her son on 7 November, had been forced to drink caustic soda and strangled. The next day, 80-year-old Marie Choy was found tied up with wire, her skull fractured. The next day again, 75-year-old Maria Mico-Diaz was killed and robbed. Five days later, on 12 November, two bodies were found – those of Jean Laurent, 82, and Paule Victoire, 77; medical evidence showed that these had died about a week earlier.

There had been eight murders in a month, and in every case, the violence had been disproportionate; this was obviously a killer – or killers – who hated old women. The press soon labelled him 'the phantom'. There was a public outcry; riot squads patrolled the XVIIIth *arrondissement*, and all pensioners in the area were asked to attend a meeting at the Town

Hall, where politicians made speeches and tried to sound reassuring.

The meeting seemed effective in frightening the 'phantom', The murders ceased. The police worked as hard as ever, but they had no clues. The fingerprints they had found at the crime scenes matched those of no known offender.

Thirteen months later, the murders began again, although not in the same *arrondissement*. On 20 December 1985, the body of 91-year-old Estelle Donjoux was found in the Observatoire area. On 4 January 1986, Andrée Ladam, 77, was strangled and robbed; on 9 January, Yvonne Couronne, 83, was killed in her home. For their relatives, the only consolation was that the marks of sadistic beatings were absent.

Between 12 and 15 January, three more women – Marjem Jurblum, 81, Françoise Vendôme, 83, and Yvonne Schaible, 77 – were killed, bringing the total up to fourteen. Virginie Labrette, 76, found on 31 January, made fifteen.

There was a five-month break until 14 June 1986, when Ludmiller Liberman, an American widow, was killed in her home in Passy. Then, once more, another long break until late November 1987, when Rachel Cohen, 79, was killed in Entrepot; on the same day, 87-year-old Mme Finalteri was found close by in the rue D'Alsace. But now, at last, the police seemed to have a break; Madame Finalteri was just alive. The killer had suffocated her with a mattress and left her for dead.

While police waited by her bed, Genevieve Germont, 73, was suffocated in a room in nearby rue Cail. Although no one knew it, this was the last murder by the 'phantom'. A few days later, Mme Finalteri was able to give a description of her attacker: a tall half-caste with dyed blond hair and ear-ring. On 1 December 1987, Police Superintendent Francis Jacob saw a young man answering this description in the Entrepot area. He asked to see his identity papers, and the man – who seemed untroubled at being questioned – gave his name as Thierry Paulin, 24. As soon as he was taken in for questioning, Paulin's career as a killer of old women was over; his fingerprints matched those of the 'phantom'. Paulin quickly confessed to twenty murders, and implicated his lover, Jean-Thierry Mathurin.

Paulin had been born in 1963 on the Caribbean island of Martinique, child of a white father, Gaby Paulin, and a West Indian mother, who was only 17 at the time. She soon farmed him out to his white grandmother, but she was too busy running a restaurant to give the child much attention. When he was 9, he returned to his mother's home in the capital, Fort-de-France – she had now remarried – but his stepfather found the child violent and difficult. He was sent to live with his father in Toulouse. But Gaby Paulin found him just as difficult, as well as disappointingly effeminate. When he was 18 Paulin began his military service; home on leave two years later, he threatened an old woman who ran a grocer's shop with a butcher's knife and got away with nearly £200. Arrested soon after, he explained that he had wanted to buy some expensive clothes with the money; he was placed on probation.

After military service he went to Paris and joined the gay community. He worked at the Paradis Latin, which specialized in transvestite revues, and met Jean-Thierry Mathurin, also 21, who came from Guyana; the two became lovers. Paulin's mother came to see the revue and was so shocked at the sight of her son in women's clothes that she left before the end.

After a violent scene in a restaurant with his lover, Paulin lost his job. Short of money, the two men attacked their first victim, Germaine Petitot, following her into her apartment. She survived, and if she had been able to give the police a description of her attackers, the crimes might have ceased there and then. But she was traumatized, and four days later, the 'phantom' murders began.

Paulin's hatred of elderly white women was almost certainly based on dislike of his grandmother, and in the course of the first eight murders, this hatred was given full reign. Then, after the eighth murder in November 1984, Paulin and Mathurin decided that Paris had become too hot to hold them, and moved south to Toulouse, moving in with Paulin's father. But the old antagonism remained, and soon Mathurin moved back to Paris. Paulin, using the money he had acquired from the robberies, set out to try and launch a business as an agency for transvestite revues. He had considerable charm, dressed well, and was a persuasive talker. But by the following November, he was tired of provincial Toulouse, and moved back to Paris and his lover. Now the new series of murders began. Meanwhile, Paulin found himself a job in a theatrical agency called Frulatti, and handled contracts for photographers and models. He became something of a young businessman-about-town, and no one suspected that a large part of his income came from murder. But a huge transvestite party he organized – called 'A Look into Hell' – bankrupted Frulatti.

In August 1986, Paulin was jailed for beating up a cocaine dealer – by now he was himself dealing in drugs – and spent a year behind bars. But the French computer system was too inefficient to identify his fingerprints with that of the 'phantom'. And so he emerged in 1987 to kill more. He celebrated his 24th birthday with an enormous party, sending out printed invitations and providing champagne; it gave him great satisfaction that it took place in a restaurant in Les Halles where he had worked as a waiter during thin times in 1985. Four days later he was arrested.

Paulin's coldness about his victims baffled psychiatrists; he obviously felt no more compunction about slaughtering elderly ladies than a butcher does about killing sheep.

Paulin was charged with eighteen of his twenty murders, but he never came to trial. An X-ray revealed that he was suffering from lesions on the brain (like so many serial killers), and it soon became clear that he was also suffering from Aids. In March 1989 he was rushed to hospital, where he fell into a coma; on the 16th of the following month, he died. At the time of writing, Mathurin is still awaiting trial.

England's equivalent of the Paulin case was solved rather more quickly. In April 1986, it became clear that a killer of old people was operating in South London. (The police even considered the possibility that the 'phantom' had moved across the Channel.) The first victim, 78-year-old Eileen Emms, was an ex-schoolteacher who lived alone in her basement flat in Wandsworth. When she was found dead in bed on 9 April 1986, it was at first assumed that she had died of natural causes; then someone noticed that her television set was missing. Closer examination revealed that she had been strangled and raped. On 9 June, 67-year-old Janet Crockett was strangled in her flat in Overton Road, Stockwell. On 27 June, the killer entered an old people's home in Stockwell and tried to strangle 73-year-old Frederick Prentice. After three unsuccessful attempts to subdue the struggling man, the intruder fled when Prentice pressed the alarm buzzer. But the following night, he returned and strangled two residents at the same home: 94-year-old Zbigniew Stabrawa, and 84-year-old Valentine Gleim, who was also sodomized.

The 'Stockwell Strangler' – as the press now called him – moved to Islington, North London, to kill 82-year-old William Carmen on 8 July 1986, whom he also sodomized. He also stole £500. On 12 July, the strangler killed 75-year-old Trevor Thomas in Clapham. Then he returned to the scene of his second murder, and strangled and sodomized William Downes, 74, in Overton Road, Stockwell. Finally, on 1986, he strangled and raped half-blind and disabled Florence Tisdall, 80, in her flat in Fulham.

The breakthrough came when a palm print found at the scene of the Downes murder was identified in the files as that of 23-year-old Kenneth Erskine, who had a lengthy record of burglaries. He proved to be registered with a Department of Health and Social Security office in Southwark, and was arrested on 28 July when he went to collect his benefit. He proved to have a building society account with £350 in it. Erskine was a half-caste – with a white mother and Antiguan father – who seemed to share with Paulin a pathological hatred of old people. He had a mental age of only 11, and a history of violence, attempting to drown fellow pupils in the school swimming pool and attacking a nurse with a pair of scissors. For the past seven years he had been a drifter who slept rough, lived by petty crime, and took drugs. Erskine – who is believed to have committed at least two more murders – received seven life sentences, and twelve years for the attempted murder of Frederick Prentice.

It was in 1963 that the American public became aware of the 'wandering serial killer', through the arrest of a murderer who seemed to embody everybody's worst nightmares. Over a period of months, a drifter named Henry Lee Lucas confessed to committing over three hundred and sixty murders. Pedro Lopez, the 'Monster of the Andes', had confessed to killing and raping about three hundred and fifty under-age girls in Ecuador and Columbia. And in 1986, while the newspapers were still full of stories about Lucas, another South American killer, Daniel Camargo Barbosa, confessed to killing seventy-two women and girls in Ecuador in the course of that year. But with his 'more than three hundred and sixty', Lucas seemed to be far and away the worst serial killer in American history – in fact, in world history.

The story that was to make world headlines began in the early hours of 15 June 1983, when Joe Don Weaver, the jailer on duty in the Montague County Jail, Texas, was startled by loud shouts coming from one of the cells. Weaver rushed down the hallway.

'What do you want?'

'There's a light in here,' said Henry Lee Lucas in a quavering voice.

'No there's not.' In fact, the cell was in pitch darkness.

'There's a light. And it's talking to me.'

'You're seeing things,' said Weaver, 'Shut up and get some sleep.' He made his way back to the office.

Lucas was a little man – five feet eight inches tall and of slight build – who was in jail for a minor weapons offence; he was also suspected of two murders. Only three nights before, Weaver had found him hanging in his cell, with blood dripping from slashed wrists. After a couple of days in a prison hospital, Lucas had been moved to a special cell in the women's section, where he could be kept under closer observation. But he had looked sick and miserable, and Weaver was not surprised that he was having hallucinations.

Another yell echoed down the hall.

'Jailer! Come here, quick!'

Weaver peered in through the aperture in the food-service door known as the 'bean hole'.

'What the hell is it this time?'

There was a long pause, and then Lucas spoke in a sad, quiet voice.

'Joe Don, I done some pretty bad things.'

Weaver said sternly: 'If it's what I think it is, Henry, you better get on your knees and pray.'

There was another long pause, then Lucas said: 'Joe Don, can I have some paper and a pencil?'

Half an hour later, Lucas handed the letter out through the bean hole. It was addressed to Sheriff Bill F. Conway, and began:

'I have tryed to get help for so long, and no one will believe me. I have killed for the past ten years and no one will believe me. I cannot go own [*sic*] doing this. I allso killed The only Girl I ever loved . . .

Weaver hurried to the telephone. He had no hesitation about waking Sheriff Conway in the middle of the night. This, he knew, was the break Conway had been waiting for.

The unshaven, smelly little vagrant who now waited in his dark cell had been a hard nut to crack. Since the previous September, he had been suspected of killing an 80-year-old widow named Kate Rich, who had vanished from her home; Sheriff Conway had learned that she had been employing an odd-job man called Henry Lee Lucas, together with his common-law wife, 15-year-old Becky Powell. Lucas had left Mrs Rich's employment under a cloud, and gone to live in a local religious commune. Not long after that, Becky had also disappeared.

Sheriff 'Hound Dog' Conway had arrested Lucas in the previous October, and questioned him for days. Lucas was a coffee addict and a chain smoker; but even when deprived of these drugs, he refused to crack. He insisted that he knew nothing about the disappearance of Kate Rich. As to Becky Powell, he claimed that she had run off with a truck driver when they were trying to hitch-hike back to her home in Florida. He had passed several lie-detector tests, and the sheriff had finally been forced to let him go.

A week ago, the situation had changed. The Rev. Reuben Moore, the man who ran the House of Prayer where Lucas lived, had mentioned that Lucas had given his wife a gun for safe keeping. That was against Texas law, for Henry Lee Lucas was an ex-convict, and therefore not entitled to own a gun. The excuse was good enough, and Sheriff Conway had arrested the little tramp again. Once again Conway tried the effect of depriving him of coffee and cigarettes. The first result had been the suicide attempt. But now, it seemed, the technique had worked; Lucas was confessing to the murder of Becky Powell.

A few hours later, Henry Lee Lucas sat in Sheriff Conway's office, a large pot of black coffee and a packet of Lucky Strikes in front of him. He was a strange-looking man, with a glass eye, a thin, haggard face, and a loose, downturned mouth like a shark. When he smiled, he showed a row of rotten, tobacco-stained teeth. In the small office, his body odour was overpowering.

'Henry,' said the sheriff kindly, 'You say in this note you want to tell me about some murders.'

'That's right. The light told me I had to confess my sins.'

'The light?' Conway knew Lucas had smashed the bulb in his cell.

'There was a light in my cell, and it said: "I will forgive you, but you must confess your sins." So that's what I aim to do.'

Lucas *looked* sane enough; after the coffee and cigarettes, he sounded calm and lucid. Conway hid his doubts and said:

'Tell me what you did to Kate Rich.'

'All right. I drove to her house . . .'

'Do you mind if I tape record this?'

'Go ahead. I left the House of Prayer around six in the evening, and drove to her house in Ringgold . . .'

What followed was a chillingly detailed confession – Lucas seemed to have total recall – of the murder of the 80-year-old woman and the violation of her dead body. Lucas described how he had gone to Kate Rich's house and offered to take her to church. She had asked him questions about the disappearance of his 'wife' Becky Powell, and at some point, Lucas had decided to kill her. He had taken the butcher's knife that lay between them on the bench seat of the old car, and suddenly jammed it into her left side. The knife entered her heart and she had collapsed immediately. Then, speaking as calmly as if he was narrating some everyday occurrence, Lucas described how he had dragged her down an embankment, then undressed and raped her. After that, he dragged her to a wide section of drainpipe that ran under the road, and stuffed the body into it. Later, he had returned with two plastic garbage bags, and used them as a kind of makeshift shroud. He buried her clothes nearby. Then he drove back to his room in the House of Prayer, made a huge fire in the stove, and burned the body. The few bones that were left he buried in the compost heap outside.

Sheriff Conway showed no emotion as he listened to this lengthy and detailed recital. By the time it was over, they were both tired. And now he had confessed, Lucas had ceased to look pale and harassed. Whether or not he had been telling the truth about the 'light', he was obviously relieved to be talking frankly.

Later that day, together with another colleague – Texas Ranger Phil Ryan, who had also been working on the case

– they again sat in Conway's office, with the tape recorder running. Conway asked him what had happened to Becky Powell. This time the story was longer, and Lucas's single eye often overflowed with tears. By the time it was over, both Conway and Ryan were trying to hide their feeling of nausea.

Lucas had met Becky Powell in 1978, when she was 11 years old; she was the niece of his friend Ottis Toole, and Lucas was staying at the home of her great aunt in Jacksonville, Florida. Becky's full name was Frieda Lorraine Powell, and she was slightly mentally retarded. Even at 11 she was not a virgin. The family situation was something of a sexual hothouse. Ottis Toole had been seduced by his elder sister Drusilla when he was a child. He grew up bisexual, and liked picking up lovers of both sexes – including Henry Lee Lucas. And he liked watching his pick-ups make love to Becky or her elder sister Sarah.

Ottis had another peculiarity; he liked burning down houses because it stimulated him sexually.

In December 1981, Becky's mother Drusilla committed suicide, and she and her younger brother Frank were placed in juvenile care. Lucas decided to 'rescue' her, and in January 1982, he and Ottis fled with Becky and Frank; they lived on the proceeds of robbery – mostly small grocery stores. Lucas felt heavily protective about Becky, he explained, and she called him 'Daddy'. But one night, as he was saying goodnight to her, and he was making her shriek with laughter by tickling her, they began to kiss. Becky had raised no objection as he undressed her, then himself. After that, the father-daughter relation changed into something more like husband and wife. At 12, Becky looked as if she was 19.

But in the House of Prayer, in 1982, Becky had suddenly become homesick, and begged him to take her back to Florida. Reluctantly, Henry agreed; they set out hitch-hiking. Later, in the warm June night, they settled down with blankets in a field. But when they began arguing about her decision to go home, Becky had lost her temper and struck him in the face. Instantly, like a striking snake, Lucas grabbed a carving knife that lay nearby, and stabbed her through the heart. After that he had violated her body. And then, since the ground was too hard to dig a grave, he cut her into nine pieces with the carving knife, then scattered the pieces in the thick undergrowth. The next day, he hitch-hiked back to the House of Prayer, and told them that Becky had run away with a truck driver. His sorrow was obviously so genuine that everyone sympathized. In fact, Lucas told the law men, he felt as if he had killed a part of himself.

The two policemen felt exhausted, and the night was half over. Ryan asked wearily:

'Is that all?'

Lucas shook his head. 'Not by a long way. I reckon I killed more'n a hundred people.'

Conway and Ryan were experienced policemen, who had heard many confessions. But this one left them shaken and incredulous. If Lucas was telling the truth, he was far and away the worst mass murderer in American criminal history. But was he telling the truth? Or was he merely suffering from hallucinations?

The first step was to check his story about Kate Rich. Lucas had pointed out the spot on a map. Still dazed from lack of sleep, Conway and Ryan drove there in the darkness. They quickly located the wide drainage pipe that ran under the road. Lying close to its entrance was a pair of knickers, of the type that would be worn by an old lady. There was also a length of wood; Lucas had told them he had used a similar piece to shove the body deeper into the culvert. On the other wide of the road, they also found broken lenses from a lady's glasses.

In the House of Prayer, near Stoneburg, they looked into the unutterably filthy room that Lucas had occupied in a converted chicken barn, and in the stove, found fragments of burnt flesh, and some pieces of bone. On the rubbish heap they found more bone fragments.

Later that day, they drove to Denton, a college town north of Dallas, where Lucas said he had killed Becky Powell. This time, Lucas accompanied them. In a field fifty yards off the main highway, in a grove of trees, they found a human skull, a pelvis, and various body parts in an advanced stage of decomposition. Becky's orange suitcase still lay nearby, and articles of female clothing and make-up were strewn around.

So far, it was obvious that Lucas had been telling the truth; he had killed Becky and Kate Rich just as he had described. But what about all the other victims he had mentioned?

Even after killing Becky, Lucas told them, he had murdered another woman. Telling the Rev. Reuben Moore that he was going off to look for Becky, Lucas had drifted to California, then down to New Mexico, then north again to Decatur, Illinois, where he had tried to find work as a labourer. Since he had no identification, he was turned down. A truck gave him a lift to a truck-driver's eatery in Missouri, and there he saw a young woman waiting by the pumps for petrol. He went up to her, pushed a knife into her ribs, and told her he needed a lift, and would not harm her. Without speaking, she allowed him to climb into the driver's seat. All that night he drove south towards Texas, until the woman finally fell into a doze. Lucas had no intention of keeping his promise. He wanted money – and sex. Just before dawn he pulled off the road, and as the woman woke up, plunged the knife into her throat. Then he pushed her out on to the ground, cut off her clothes and violated the body. After that, he dragged it into a grove of trees, took the money from her handbag, and drove the car to Fredericksburg, Texas, where he abandoned it.

Lucas was unable to tell them the woman's name, but his description of the place where he abandoned the car offered a lead. In fact, the Texas Rangers near Fredericksburg were able to confirm the finding of an abandoned station wagon in the previous October. And a little further checking revealed that the police at Magnolia, Texas, had found the naked body of a woman with her throat cut, at about the same time. Again, it was clear that Lucas was telling the truth.

On 17 June 1983, two days after he had started to confess, Henry Lee Lucas appeared in the Montague County Courthouse, accused of murder and of possessing an illegal firearm. A Grand Jury indicted him on both counts.

The following day, in the press room of the Austin Police Department, a bored reporter named Mike Cox was talking casually to a police lieutenant when the lieutenant mentioned that he had heard rumours of a man in north Texas who had been murdering women for sex. Cox did some telephoning, and learned that the man, Henry Lee Lucas, was about to be arraigned in the Montague County Courthouse. It sounded unpromising, but since there was nothing else to do . . .

The following day, Tuesday 21 June 1983, Mike Cox was in the courtroom when the unimpressive little man who looked like an out-of-work roadsweeper was led in between two deputies. The only other reporters in court were from the nearby Wichita Falls television station, who intended to put out an item on their local news. From all appearances, it looked as if the arraigment would take only a matter of minutes.

When Judge Frank Douthitt had heard the indictment concerning Kate Rich, he asked the prisoner if he understood the seriousness of the indictment against him. Lucas replied quietly:

'Yes, sir. I have about a hundred of them.'

It was said so casually that for a moment Cox failed to grasp its significance. Was this man really saying he had killed a hundred people? Yes, apparently he was, for the judge was now asking him if he had ever had a psychiatric examination. The little man replied in the affirmative. 'I tell them my problems and they didn't want to do anything about it . . . I know it ain't normal for a person to go out and kill girls just to have sex with them.'

Moments later, as Lucas was led out of court, Cox rushed over to District Attorney McGaughey. How many murders was Lucas suspected of? The DA was cautious. He had told the police about seven so far. 'But there's still a lot of work to be done. He may be spinning yarns.'

The following morning, the Austin newspapers carried headlines which were a variant on: DRIFTER CONFESSES TO A HUNDRED MURDERS. The wire services immediately picked up the story, and by evening it was on front pages all over the country.

For the past ten years, the American public had been kept in a state of shock at the revelations about mass murderers who had killed an unprecedented number of victims. Cases like that of Ted Bundy made it clear that one of the major problems was simply how to detect a 'wandering' killer, who might not be recognized for what he was because of lack of police co operation between various states. In November 1982, while Henry Lee Lucas was still at large, a meeting of police from all over the country decided to establish a national crime computer, into which details of every homicide would be automatically fed. This became known as the NCAVC, the National Centre for the Analysis of Violent Crime.

And now, just over six months later, the confessions of Henry Lee Lucas made it clear that the NCAVC had been formed not a moment too soon. The 'wandering killer' was obviously a new type of menace. Suddenly, every newspaper in America was talking about serial killers.

Meanwhile, the cause of all this excitement was sitting in his jail cell in Montague County, describing murder after murder to a 'task force' headed by Sheriff Jim Boutwell and Texas Ranger Bob Prince. It soon became clear that a large number of these murders had not been committed on his own, but in company with his lover Ottis Elswood Toole.

Toole, who had a gap in his front teeth and a permanent stubble on his chin, looked even more like a tramp than Lucas. And even before Lucas was arrested in Montague County, Toole was in prison in his home town, Jacksonville. He was charged with setting fires in Springfield, the area where he lived. On 5 August 1983, he was sentenced to fifteen years for arson.

One week later, in a courtroom in Denton County – where he had killed Becky Powell – Lucas staggered everybody by pleading not guilty to Becky's murder. He was, in fact, beginning to play a game that would become wearisomely familiar to the police: withdrawing confessions. It looked as if, now he was in prison, the old Henry Lee Lucas, the Enemy of Society, was reappearing. He could no longer kill at random when he felt the urge, but he could still satisfy his craving for control over victims by playing with his captors like a cat with mice.

It did him no good. On 1 October 1983, in the courtroom where he had been arraigned, Lucas was sentenced to seventy-five years for the murder of Kate Rich. And on 8 November 1983, he was sentenced to life imprisonment for the murder of Becky Powell. Before the courts had finished with him, he would be sentenced to another seventy-five years, four more life sentences, and a further sixty-six years, all for murder. For good measure, he was also sentenced to death.

When Henry Lee Lucas began confessing to murders, it seemed to be a genuine case of religious conversion. Later, when he was moved to the Georgetown Jail in Williamson County, he was allowed regular visits from a Catholic laywoman who called herself Sister Clementine, and they spent hours kneeling in prayer. He was visited by many lawmen from all over the country, hoping that he could clear up unsolved killings. Sometimes – if he felt the policeman failed to treat him with due respect – he refused to utter a word. At other times, he confessed freely. The problem was that he sometimes confessed to two murders on the same day, in areas so wide apart that he could not possibly have committed both. This tendency to lie at random led many journalists to conclude that Lucas's tales of mass murder were mostly invention.

None of the officers who knew him closely believed that for a moment. Too many of his confessions turned out to be accurate.

For example, on 2 August 1983, when he was being arraigned for the murder of a hitch-hiker known simply as 'Orange Socks', Lucas was taken to Austin to be questioned about another murder. On the way there, seated between two deputies, Lucas pointed to a building they passed and asked if it had been a liquor store at one time. The detectives looked at one another. It had, and it had been run by a couple called Harry and Molly Schlesinger, who had been robbed and murdered on 23 October 1989. Lucas admitted that he had been responsible, and described the killings with a wealth of detail that only the killer could have known. He then led the deputies to a field where, on 8 October 1979, the mutilated body of a girl called Sandra Dubbs had been found. He was also able to point out where her car had been left. There could be no possible doubt that Lucas had killed three people in Travis County in two weeks.

When asked if Ottis Toole had committed any murders on his own, Lucas mentioned a man in his fifties who had died in a fire set by Toole in Jacksonville. Toole had poured petrol on the man's mattress and set it alight. Then they had hidden and watched the fire engines; a 65-year-old man was finally carried out, badly burned. He had died a week later. Police assumed he had accidentally set the mattress on fire with a cigarette.

Lucas's description led the police to identify the victim as George Sonenberg, who had been fatally burned in a fire on 4 January 1982. Police drove out to Raiford Penitentiary to interview Toole. He admitted it cheerfully. When asked why he did it, he grinned broadly. 'I love fires. Reckon I started a hundred of them over the past several years.'

There could be no possible doubt about it. Toole and Lucas had committed a number of murders between them. At one point, Lucas insisted that the total was about 360 – he went on to detail 175 committed alone, and 65 by himself and Ottis Toole.

In prison after his original convictions, Lucas seemed a

well satisfied man. Now much plumper, with his rotten teeth replaced or filled, he had ceased to look so sinister. He had a special cell all to himself in Sheriff Boutwell's jail – other prisoners had treated him very roughly during the brief period he had been among them, and he had to be moved for his own safety. But he was now a national celebrity. Magazines and newspapers begged for interviews, television cameras recorded every public appearance. Police officers turned up by the dozen to ask about unsolved murder cases, and were all warned beforehand to treat Lucas with respect, in case he ceased to co-operate. Now, at least, he was receiving the attention he had always craved, and he revelled in it. And some visitors, like the psychiatrist Joel Norris, the journalist Mike Cox – who had filed the original story on Lucas – and the crime writer Max Call, came to interview him in order to learn about his life, and to write books about it. Lucas co-operated fully with Call, who was the first to reach print – as early as 1985 – with a strange work called *Hand of Death*.

Here, for the first time, the American public had an opportunity to satisfy its morbid curiosity about Lucas's rampage of crime. The story that emerged lacked the detail of later studies, but it was horrific enough.

Lucas, Call revealed, had spent most of his life from 1960 to 1975 in jail. After his release he had an unsuccessful marriage – which broke up when his wife realized he was having sex with her two small girls – and lived for a while with his sister Wanda, leaving when she accused him of sexually abusing her young daughter. He seems to have met Ottis Toole in a soup kitchen in Jacksonville, Florida, in 1978. Ottis had a long prison record for car stealing and petty theft, and he invited Lucas back home, where he was soon regarded as a member of the family.

According to Lucas, he had already committed a number of casual murders as he wandered around. These were mostly crimes of opportunity – as when he offered a lift to a girl called Tina Williams, near Oklahoma City, after her car had broken down. He shot her twice and had intercourse with the body. Police later confirmed Lucas's confession.

Even so, the meeting with Toole seems to have been a turning point. Now, according to both of them, they began killing 'for fun'. According to Toole's confession, they saw a teenage couple walking along the road on November 1978, their car having run out of fuel. Lucas forced the girl into the car, while Toole shot the boy in the head and chest. Then, as Toole drove, Lucas raped the girl repeatedly in the back of the car. Finally, Toole began to feel jealous, and when they pulled up, shot the girl six times, and left her body by the road. The police were also able to confirm this case: the youth was called Kevin Key, the girl Rita Salazar. The man in charge of the murder investigation was Sheriff Jim Boutwell, and the case was the first of more than a score of similar murders along the Interstate 35 Highway that kept him busy for the next five years. The victims included teenage hitch-hikers, elderly women abducted from their homes, tramps and men who were killed for robbery. Lucas was later to confess to most of these crimes.

Lucas and Toole began robbing 'convenience stores', forcing the proprietor or store clerk into the back. Lucas described how, on one occasion, they tied up the young girl, but she continued to try to get free. So he shot her through the head, and then Toole had intercourse with her body.

On 31 October 1979, the naked body of a young girl was found in a culvert on the Interstate 35; her clothes were missing, except for a pair of orange socks by the body. After his arrest, Lucas described how he and Toole had picked up 'Orange Socks', who was hitch-hiking, and when she had refused to let Lucas have sex, he strangled her. Lucas eventually received the death sentence for the murder of the unidentified girl.

When Lucas and Toole abducted Becky and Frank Powell in January 1982, they took them with them when they robbed convenience stores; Becky looked so innocent that the proprietor took little notice of the two smelly vagrants who accompanied her – until one of them produced a gun and demanded the money from the till. And, according to Lucas, Becky and Frank often became witnesses to murder – in fact, in one confession he even claimed they had taken part in the killings.

Eventually, Frank and Ottis Toole returned home to Florida, while Becky and Lucas continued 'on the road'. In January 1982, a couple named Smart, who ran an antiques store in Hemet, California, picked them up, and for five months Lucas worked for them. Then the Smarts asked Lucas if he would like to go back to Texas to look after Mrs Smart's mother, Kate Rich. He accepted. But after only a few weeks, the Smarts received a telephone call from another sister in Texas, telling them that the new handyman was spending Mrs Rich's money on large quantities of beer and cigarettes in the local grocery store. Another daughter who went to investigate found Mrs Rich's house filthy, and Lucas and Becky Powell drunk in bed. Lucas was politely fired. But his luck held. Only a few miles away, he was offered a lift by the Rev. Reuben Moore, who had started his own religious community in nearby Stoneburg. Moore also took pity on the young couple, and they moved in to the House of Prayer. There everyone liked Becky, and she seemed happy. She badly needed a home and security. Both she and Henry became 'converts'.

But Becky began to feel homesick, and begged Henry to take her back to Florida. A few days later, pieces of her dismembered body were scattered around a field near Denton. And Lucas's nightmare odyssey of murder was beginning to draw to a close . . .

The American public, which at first followed Lucas's confessions with horrified attention, soon began to lose interest. After all, he was already sentenced. So was Ottis Toole (who would also be later condemned to death for the arson murder of George Sonenburg). And as newspapers ran stories declaring that Lucas had withdrawn his confessions yet again, or that some police officer had proved he was lying, there was a growing feeling that Lucas was not, after all, the worst mass murderer in American history.

It was a couple named Bob and Joyce Lemons who first placed this conviction on a solid foundation. Their daughter, Barbara Sue Williamson, had been murdered in Lubbock, Texas, in August 1975 by an intruder in her home. Lucas confessed to this murder when asked about it by Lubbock lawmen. When the Lemons heard the confession they felt it was a hoax. Lucas said he recalled the house as being white, that he had entered by the screen door, and killed the newly married woman in her bedroom. It was a green house, the screen door had been sealed shut at the time, and Barbara had been killed outside.

The Lemons went and talked to Lucas's relatives, and soon came up with a list of the periods when he had stayed in Florida which contradicted dozens of his 'confessions'. But when they confronted Texas Ranger Bob Prince with these discoveries, he became hostile and ordered them out of his office.

Another investigator was also having doubts. Vic Feazell, District Attorney of Waco, Taxas, was supposed to be prosecuting Lucas for three murders to which he had confessed, and for which there was not a shred of evidence apart from Lucas's own words – no fingerprints, no forensic evidence, no witnesses. Feazell joined forces with the Lemons, and was soon convinced that many of Lucas's confessions were lies. He learned that during one period in 1979, when Lucas had cashed forty-three pay cheques at the local store in Florida – and was therefore presumably resident there – he was on record as confessing to forty-six murders in sixteen states. It was just possible if he rushed around the country by aeroplane, otherwise highly unlikely. (Feazell began to refer to him jokingly as 'Rocket Man'.)

Confronted by Feazell, and shown the evidence that disproved his confessions, Lucas smiled and said: 'I was wonderin' when somebody was goin' to get wise to this.'

When Feazell announced these conclusions to the press, the roof fell in. Within three days he was under investigation by the FBI for corruption, and his house was searched. He was accused of murder, burglary, bribery and racketeering – charges that could have led to a sentence of eighty years in jail. In fact, Feazell defended himself, and was found not guilty on all counts. He sued the Dallas TV station that had repeated the allegations, and was awarded record damages of $58,000,000.

Feazell is convinced that the Texas Ranger Task Force was behind the persecution. Whether true or not, his acquittal and the enormous damages had the effect of discrediting the Task Force – and, of course, Lucas's confessions. Lucas had been convicted of ten murders. Feazell is on record as saying that he may be innocent of all of them.

But if Lucas's own accounts of the murders convinced local police officers that he was guilty – because of the intimate knowledge he showed – then how could he be innocent? According to Feazell (who has become Lucas's attorney), because the Task Force demanded details of the crimes *before* local police forces were allowed to interview him about them, and they allowed Lucas to read the reports. Yet this raises the question of why, in that case, he got the Barbara Sue Williamson murder so wrong.

Equally intriguing is the question of why, if Lucas's confessions to serial murder were all lies, his partner Ottis Toole did not vigorously protest his own innocence to avoid a death sentence. Loyalty to a friend hardly demands accepting a multiple 'murder rap'.

In the resulting confusion, it looks as if Lucas may escape the death sentence – which is clearly what he wants. Yet this in turn raises the further question of whether his new claims of innocence may not be as unreliable as his earlier claims of guilt.

Looking back over the case, from the moment Lucas decided to confess because he saw a 'light' in his cell, it seems virtually impossible to believe that he is totally innocent. At the very least he killed Becky, Kate Rich and 'Orange Socks'.

At the time of writing (1993), it begins to look as if the likeliest scenario was as follows. Lucas's original confessions, whether prompted by hallucinations or by genuine religious conversion, were true: he killed Kate Rich and Becky Powell. It is hard to believe that he made these confessions with his tongue in his cheek. It seems likely that many of his subsequent confessions were also true, including murders committed in partnership with Toole. But as the confessions brought notoriety and comfort – he became aware of the benefits of being a 'star', and began to wonder how he could maintain this status without the inevitable penalty of the electric chair. The answer was to continue confessing to more murders, and to hope that, sooner or later, these confessions would be recognized as lies, and that this would throw doubt on the murders for which he had been convicted. So when Vic Feazell turned up in his cell with proof that at least forty-six murders were inventions, he must have heaved a sigh of relief. 'I was wonderin' when somebody was goin' to get wise to this.'

And what of Boutwell and Prince? Were they dupes, con-men, or simply good policemen who were doing their best? One thing seems obvious: that their present feelings towards Lucas must be highly uncharitable. He brought them celebrity, then derision. Whatever now happens – even if Lucas is executed – their reputations are irreparably damaged. Yet Boutwell knows that Lucas killed Kate Rich, Becky Powell, and probably a number of others. He also knows that, because of Lucas's policy of lying, withdrawing the lie and then repeating it, no one will ever be certain whether Lucas and Toole are America's worst serial killers, or two undistinguished hold-up men. It now seems clear that, whether his claim to be America's most prolific serial killer is true or not, the mild little man with the glass eye has achieved what he always wanted: a place in American history.

Lucas made the world aware of the 'wandering killer', yet in fact, this type of serial murder has remained relatively rare – no doubt because serial killers, like other human beings, prefer the security of a home. So most serial murders have been associated with a specific place – Whitechapel, Hanover, Düsseldorf, Boston. The 'wandering killers' – from Vacher and Earle Nelson to Knowles and Lucas – can be counted on the fingers of both hands. And the cases of serial murder that always create the greatest stir are those in which the murders occur in the same place, and remain unsolved over a period – the classic Jack the Ripper pattern. In this sense, the first 'classic' case of the 1980s was the Atlanta child murders.

By the beginning of July 1980, seven black children in Atlanta had been murdered, and three had vanished without leaving a trace. The series had started a year earlier, when two black teenagers had been found dead near Niskey Lake. In October 1979, two 9-year-old boys vanished; one was found in the crawl-space of an abandoned elementary school. In March 1980, a 12-year-old girl was found tied to a tree and suffocated with her own briefs; she had been raped. But since by now it was assumed that the killer was homosexual (even though there had been no sexual assault), this was not generally counted as one of the 'series'.

The suspicion that white racists were responsible caused civil unrest in Atlanta, but the police were inclined to believe that the killer was a black, since the children had been picked up mostly in black neighbourhoods, where a white would stand out.

By mid-May 1981, the number of victims had risen to twenty-seven, and black groups had formed to demand action and to raise a reward.

The break in the case came on 22 May, when police close to a bridge on the Chattahoochee River heard a splash, and saw a man climb into a station wagon. It proved to be a plump young black named Wayne Williams, 23, who said he was a music promoter. He was allowed to go after being questioned, but when, two days later, the body of 27-year-old Nathaniel Cater was found in the river, attention switched back to Williams. Dog hairs found on the victim's body matched those found in William's station wagon, and a witness testified to seeing Williams leaving a theatre hand in hand with Cater just before his disappearance. Another witness testified to seeing Williams with Jimmy Payne, also found in the river. Forensic examination established that carpet fibres and dog hairs found on ten more victims matched those in the home where Williams lived with his schoolteacher parents. A brilliant young man who studied astronomy and ran his own local radio station, Williams was known to be obsessed by police work. Obsessed also by a desire for quick success, he was also known as a pathological liar.

Although the evidence was circumstantial, Williams was found guilty of the murders of Cater and Payne. Many felt misgivings about the guilty verdict (the black writer James Baldwin regarded the case against Williams as a conspiracy, and saw the rejection of his own book about the case as further evidence of the conspiracy), but the murders stopped after Williams's arrest.

At the time the Henry Lee Lucas case was causing shock waves in America, a British serial killer was causing much the same sensation across the Atlantic. The British have always felt a certain complacency about their murder record, which has remained relatively constant and relatively low for decades. (Per unit of population, the British rate is less than a sixth that of America.) Besides, England is too small for wandering serial killers. But the case of Dennis Nilsen demonstrated that, even in non-violent Britain, it is still appallingly easy to get away with mass murder in a large city.

On the evening of 8 February 1983, a drains maintenance engineer named Michael Cattran was asked to call at 23 Cranley Gardens, in Muswell Hill, north London, to find out why tenants had been unable to flush their toilets since the previous Saturday. Although Muswell Hill is known as a highly respectable area of London – it was once too expensive for anyone but the upper middle classes – No. 23 proved to be a rather shabby house, divided into flats. A tenant showed Cattran the manhole cover that led to the drainage system. When he removed it, he staggered back and came close to vomiting; the smell was unmistakably decaying flesh. And when he had climbed down the rungs into the cistern, Cattran discovered what was blocking the drain: masses of rotting meat, much of it white, like chicken flesh. Convinced this was human flesh, Cattran rang his supervisor, who decided to come and inspect it in the morning. When they arrived the following day, the drain had been cleared. And a female tenant told them she had heard footsteps going up and down the stairs for much of the night. The footsteps seemed to go up to the top flat, which was rented by a 37-year-old civil servant named Dennis Nilsen.

Closer search revealed that the drain was still not quite clear; there was a piece of flesh, six inches square, and some bones that resembled fingers. Detective Chief Inspector Peter Jay, of Hornsey CID, was waiting in the hallway of the house that evening when Dennis Nilsen walked in from his day at the office – a Jobcentre in Kentish Town. He told Nilsen he wanted to talk to him about the drains. Nilsen invited the policeman into his flat, and Jay's face wrinkled as he smelt the odour of decaying flesh. He told Nilsen that they had found human remains in the drain, and asked what had happened to the rest of the body.

'It's in there, in two plastic bags,' said Nilsen, pointing to a wardrobe.

In the police car, the Chief Inspector asked Nilsen whether the remains came from one body or two. Calmly, without emotion, Nilsen said: 'There have been fifteen or sixteen altogether.'

At the police station, Nilsen – a tall man with metal-rimmed glasses – seemed eager to talk. (In fact, he proved to be something of a compulsive talker, and his talk over-flowed into a series of school exercise books in which he later wrote his story for the use of Brian Masters, a young writer who contacted him in prison.) He told police that he had murdered three men in the Cranley Gardens house – into which he moved in the autumn of 1981 – and twelve or thirteen at his previous address, 195 Melrose Avenue, Cricklewood.

The plastic bags from the Muswell Hill flat contained two severed heads, and a skull from which the flesh had been stripped – forensic examination revealed that it had been boiled. The bathroom contained the whole lower half of a torso, from the waist down, intact. The rest was in bags in the wardrobe and in the tea chest. At Melrose Avenue, thirteen days and nights of digging revealed many human bones, as well as a cheque book and pieces of clothing.

The self-confessed mass murderer – he seemed to take a certain pride in being 'Britain's biggest mass murderer' – was a Scot, born at Fraserburgh on 23 November 1945. His mother, born Betty Whyte, married a Norwegian soldier named Olav Nilsen in 1942. It was not a happy marriage; Olav was seldom at home, and was drunk a great deal; they were divorced seven years after their marriage. In 1954, Mrs Nilsen married again and became Betty Scott. Dennis grew up in the house of his grandmother and grandfather, and was immensely attached to his grandfather, Andrew Whyte, who became a father substitute. When Nilsen was seven, his grandfather died and his mother took Dennis in to see the corpse. This seems to have been a traumatic experience; in his prison notes he declares 'My troubles started there.' The death of his grandfather was such a blow that it caused his own emotional death, according to Nilsen. Not long after this, someone killed the two pigeons he kept in an air raid shelter, another severe shock. His mother's remarriage when he was nine had the effect of making him even more of a loner.

In 1961, Nilsen enlisted in the army, and became a cook. It was during this period that he began to get drunk regularly, although he remained a loner, avoiding close relationships. In 1972 he changed the life of a soldier for that of a London policeman, but disliked the relative lack of freedom – compared to the army – and resigned after only eleven months. He became a security guard for a brief period, then a job-interviewer for the Manpower Services Commission.

In November 1975, Nilsen began to share a north London flat – in Melrose Avenue – with a young man named David Gallichan, ten years his junior. Gallichan was later to insist that there was no homosexual relationship, and this is believable. Many heterosexual young men would later accept Nilsen's offer of a bed for the night, and he would make no advances, or accept a simple 'No' without resentment. But in May 1977, Gallichan decided he could bear London no longer, and accepted a job in the country. Nilsen was furious; he felt rejected and deserted. The break-up of the relationship with Gallichan – whom he had always dominated – seems to have triggered the homicidal violence that would claim fifteen lives.

The killings began more than a year later, in December 1978. Around Christmas, Nilsen picked up a young Irish labourer in the Cricklewood Arms, and they went back to his flat to continue drinking. Nilsen wanted him to stay over the New Year but the Irishman had other plans. In a note he later wrote for his biographer Brian Masters, Nilsen gives as his motive for this first killing that he was lonely and wanted to spare himself the pain of separation. In another confession he also implies that he has no memory of the actual killing. Nilsen strangled the unnamed Irishman in his sleep with a tie. Then he undressed the body and carefully washed it, a ritual he observed in all his killings. After that he placed the body under the floorboards where – as incredible as it seems – he kept it until the following August. He eventually burned it on a bonfire at the bottom of the garden, burning some rubber at the same time to cover the smell.

In November 1979, Nilsen attempted to strangle a young Chinaman who had accepted his offer to return to the flat; the Chinaman escaped and reported the attack to the police. But the police believed Nilsen's explanation that the Chinaman was trying to 'rip him off' and decided not to pursue the matter.

The next murder victim was a 23 year-old Canadian called Kenneth James Ockendon, who had completed a technical training course and was taking a holiday before starting his career. He had been staying with an uncle and aunt in Carshalton after touring the Lake District. He was not a homosexual, and it was pure bad luck that he got into conversation with Nilsen in the Princess Louise in High Holborn around 3 December 1979. They went back to Nilsen's flat, ate ham, eggs and chips, and bought £20 worth of alcohol. Ockendon watched television, then listened to rock music on Nilsen's hi-fi system. Then he sat listening to music wearing earphones, watching television at the same time. This may have been what cost him his life; Nilsen liked to talk, and probably felt 'rejected'. 'I thought bloody good guest this . . .' And sometime after midnight, while Ockendon was still wearing the headphones, he strangled him with a flex. Ockendon was so drunk that he put up no struggle. And Nilsen was also so drunk that after the murder, he sat down, put on the headphones, and went on playing music for hours. When he tried to put the body under the floorboards the next day, rigor mortis had set in and it was impossible. He had to wait until the rigor had passed. Later, he dissected the body. Ockendon had large quantities of Canadian money in his moneybelt, but Nilsen tore this up. The rigorous Scottish upbringing would not have allowed him to steal.

Nilsen's accounts of the murders are repetitive, and make them sound mechanical and almost identical. The third victim in May 1980, was a 16-year-old butcher named Martyn Duffey, who was also strangled and placed under the floorboards. Number four was a 16-year-old Scot named Billy Sutherland – again strangled in his sleep with a tie and placed under the floorboards. Number five was an unnamed Mexican or Philipino, killed a few months later. Number six was an Irish building worker. Number seven was an undernourished down-and-out picked up in a doorway. (He was burned on the bonfire all in one piece.) The next five victims, all unnamed, were killed equally casually between late 1980 and late 1981. Nilsen later insisted that all the murders had been without sexual motivation – a plea that led Brian Masters to entitle his book on the case *Killing for Company*. There are moments in Nilsen's confessions when it sounds as if, like so many serial killers, he felt as if he was being taken over by a Mr Hyde personality or possessed by some demonic force.

In October 1981, Nilsen moved into an upstairs flat in Cranley Gardens, Muswell Hill. On 25 November, he took a homosexual student named Paul Nobbs back with him, and they got drunk. The next day, Nobbs went into University College Hospital for a check-up, and was told that bruises on his throat indicated that someone had tried to strangle him. Nilsen apparently changed his mind at the last moment.

The next victim, John Howlett, was less lucky. He woke up as Nilsen tried to strangle him and fought back hard; Nilsen had to bang his head against the headrest of the bed to subdue him. When he realized Howlett was still breathing, Nilsen drowned him in the bath. He hacked up the body in the bath, then boiled chunks in a large pot to make them easier to dispose of. (He also left parts of the body out in plastic bags for the dustbin men to take away.)

In May 1982, another intended victim escaped – a drag-artiste called Carl Stottor. After trying to strangle him, Nilsen placed him in a bath of water, but changed his mind and allowed him to live. When he left the flat, Stottor even agreed to meet Nilsen again – but decided not to keep the appointment. He decided not to go to the police.

The last two victims were both unnamed, one a drunk and one a drug-addict. In both cases, Nilsen claims to be unable to remember the actual killing. Both were dissected, boiled and flushed down the toilet. It was after this second murder – the fifteenth in all – that the tenants complained about blocked drains, and Nilsen was arrested.

The trial began on 24 October 1983, in the same court where Peter Sutcliffe had been tried two years earlier. Nilsen was charged with six murders and two attempted murders, although he had confessed to fifteen murders and seven attempted murders. He gave the impression that he was enjoying his moment of glory. The defence pleaded diminished responsibility, and argued that the charge should be reduced to manslaughter. The jury declined to accept this, and on 4 November 1983, Nilsen was found guilty by a vote of 10 to 2, and sentenced to life imprisonment.

Perhaps the most horrific serial murder case of the 1980s was one that came to light in California in June, 1985.

On Sunday 2 June, a shop assistant at the South City Lumber Store in San Francisco noticed when a young man walked out without paying for a $75 vice. The assistant hurried outside to speak to Police Officer Daniel Wright, and by the time the young man – who looked Asiatic – was putting the vice in the boot of a car, the officer was right behind him. When he realized he was being followed, the young man fled. Wright gave chase, but the skinny youth was too fast for him, and vanished across a main road.

When Wright returned to the car – a Honda Prelude – a bearded, bald-headed man was standing by it. 'It was a mistake,' he explained, 'He thought I'd paid already. But I *have* paid now.' He held out a sales receipt.

That should have ended the incident – except for the fact that the young Asian had fled, ruling out the possibility that it *was* merely an honest mistake. Wright wondered if anything else in the car might be stolen. 'What's in there?', he asked, pointing at a green holdall.

'I don't know. It belongs to him.'

Wright unzipped it and found that it contained a .22 pistol, with a silencer on the barrel. Americans have a right to own handguns, but not with silencers – such attachments being unlikely to have an innocent purpose.

'I'm afraid I'll have to ask you to come down to headquarters to explain this.'

At the police station, the bearded man handed over a driver's licence to establish his identity; it indicated that he was Robin Scott Stapley. He explained that he hardly knew the youth who had run away – he had just been about to hire him to do some work.

'We'll have to do a computer check on the car. But you'll probably have to post bond before you can be released.'

'Stapley' asked if he could have some paper and a pencil, and a glass of water. When the policeman returned with these items, he scribbled a few words on the sheet of paper, tossed a capsule into his mouth and swallowed it down with water. Moments later, he slumped forward on the tabletop.

Assuming it was a heart attack, the police called an ambulance. The hospital rang them later to say that the man had been brain-dead on arrival, but had been placed on a life support system.

The medic added that he was fairly certain the man had not suffered a heart attack; it was more likely that he had swallowed some form of poison. In fact, the poison was soon identified as cyanide. The note 'Stapley' had scribbled had been an apology to his wife for what he was about to do. Four days later, removed from the life support system, the man died without recovering consciousness.

By this time, the police had realized that he was not Robin Stapley. The real Robin Stapley had been reported missing in February. But soon after this there had been a curious incident involving his camper, which had been in collision with a pickup truck. The young Chinaman who had been driving the camper had accepted responsibility and asked the other driver not to report it. But since it was a company vehicle, the driver was obliged to report the accident.

The Honda the two had been driving proved to be registered in the name of Paul Cosner. And Cosner had also been reported missing. He had told his girlfriend that he had sold the car to a 'weird-looking man' who would pay cash, and driven off to deliver it; no one had seen him since.

The Honda was handed over to the forensic experts for examination; they discovered two bullet holes in the front seat, two spent slugs, and some human bloodstains.

If the bearded man was not Robin Stapley, who was he? Some papers found in the Honda bore the name Charles Gunnar, with an address near Wilseyville, in Calaveras County, 150 miles north-east of San Francisco. Inspector Tom Eisenmann was assigned to go and check on Gunnar. In Wilseyville he spoke to Sheriff Claude Ballard, and learned that Ballard already had his suspicions about Gunnar, and about the slightly built Chinese youth, Charles Ng (pronounced Ing) with whom he lived. They had been advertising various things for sale, such as television sets, videos and articles of furniture, and Ballard had suspected they might be stolen. However, checks on serial numbers had come to nothing. What was more ominous was that Gunnar had offered for sale furniture belonging to a young couple, Lonnie Bond and Brenda O'Connor, explaining that they had moved to Los Angeles with their baby and had given him the furniture to pay a debt. No one had heard from them since. And at a nearby camp site at Schaad Lake, another couple had simply vanished, leaving behind their tent and a coffee pot on the stove.

By now, a check on the dead man's fingerprints had revealed that he had a criminal record – for burglary and grand larceny in Mendocino County – and had jumped bail there. His real name was Leonard Lake.

Eisenmann's investigation into Lake's background convinced the detective that this man seemed to be associated with many disappearances. His younger brother Donald had been reported missing in July 1983 after setting out to visit Lake in a 'survivalist commune' in Humboldt County. Charles Gunnar, whose identity Lake had borrowed, had been best man at Lake's wedding, but had also vanished in 1985. Together with Stapley and Costner and the Bond couple and their baby, that made seven unexplained disappearances.

The next step, obviously, was to search the small ranch in Blue Mountain Road, where Lake and Ng had lived. Sheriff Ballard obtained the search warrant, and he and Eisenmann drove out with a team of deputies. The 'ranch' proved to be a two-bedroom bungalow set in three acres of land. It looked ordinary enough from the outside, but the sight of the master bedroom caused the detectives a sense of foreboding. Hooks in the ceiling and walls suggested that it might be some kind of torture chamber, while a box full of chains and shackles could have only one use: to immobilize someone on the bed. A wardrobe proved to contain many women's undergarments and some filmy nightgowns.

There was also some expensive video equipment. This led Eisenbrunn's assistant, Sergeant Irene Brunn, to speculate whether it might be connected with a case she had investigated in San Francisco. A couple called Harvey and Deborah Dubs had vanished from their apartment, together with their 16-month-old baby son, and neighbours had seen a young Chinese man removing the contents of their apartment – including an expensive video. She had the serial numbers in her notebook. Her check confirmed her suspicion: this was the missing equipment.

Deputies came in to report that they had been scouring the hillside at the back of the house, and had found burnt bones that looked ominously human. Ballard and Eisenmann went out to see. Among the bones were teeth that looked human. Ballard also noted a trench that seemed to have been intended for a telephone cable; he ordered the deputies to dig it up.

Close to the trench there was a cinderblock bunker that had been cut into the hillside and covered over with earth. Ballard had heard that 'Gunnar' was a 'survival freak', one who expected a nuclear war to break out, and who was determined to outlive it; this looked like his air raid shelter. He ordered the deputies to break in.

The room on the other side of the door was a storeroom containing food, water, candles and guns. A trap door in the floor led into a kind of cellar, from whose ceiling were suspended more hooks and chains. The walls were covered with pictures of girls posing in their lingerie. What was disturbing about this was that the backdrop of many of these showed a forest scene mural that covered one of the walls; they had obviously been taken in the same room. And the expression on some of the faces suggested that the girls were not enjoying it.

A filing cabinet in the basement proved to be full of videotapes. Eisenmann read the inscription on one of these – 'M. Ladies, Kathy/Brenda' – and slipped it into the recorder.

A moment later, they were looking at a recording of a frightened girl handcuffed to a chair, with a young Chinaman – obviously Charles Ng – holding a knife beside her. A large, balding man with a beard enters the frame and proceeds to remove the girl's handcuffs, then shackles her ankles, and orders her to undress. Her reluctance is obvious, particularly when she comes to her knickers. The bearded man tells her: 'You'll wash for us, clean for us, fuck for us.' After this, she is made to go into the shower with the Chinaman. A later scene showed her strapped naked to a bed, while the bearded man tells her that her boyfriend Mike is dead.

After 'Kathy' the video showed 'Brenda' – identified by Sheriff Ballard as the missing Brenda O'Connor – handcuffed to a chair, while Ng cut off her clothes. She asks after her baby, and Lake tells her that it has been placed with a family in Fresno. She asks: 'Why do you guys do this?', and he tells her: 'We don't like you. Do you want me to put it in writing?' 'Don't cut my bra off.' 'Nothing is yours now.' 'Give my baby back to me. I'll do anything you want.' 'You're going to do anything we want anyway.'

Other videos showed more women being shackled, raped and tortured with a knife. Sergeant Brunn recognized one of these as Deborah Dubs, who had vanished from her San Francisco apartment with her husband and baby. Leonard Lake had spent his last two years making home-made 'snuff movies'. The prefix 'M. Ladies' obviously stood for 'murdered ladies'.

When the deputies digging in the trench outside reported finding two bodies, the shaken police officers became aware that this was could be one of the worst cases of serial murder in California's history – or, indeed, in the history of America.

Lake's accomplice Charles Ng was now one of the most wanted men in America, but had not been seen since his disappearance. Police had discovered that he had fled back to his apartment, travelled out to San Francisco Airport on the Underground, and there bought himself a ticket to Chicago under the name 'Mike Kimoto'. Four days later, a San Francisco gun dealer notified the police that Ng had telephoned him from Chicago. The man had been repairing Ng's automatic pistol, and Ng wanted to know if he could send him the gun by post, addressing it to him at the Chateau Hotel under the name Mike Kimoto. When the gun dealer had explained that it would be illegal to send handguns across state lines, Ng had cursed and threatened him with violence if he went to the police.

By the time Chicago police arrived at the Chateau Hotel, the fugitive had already left. From there on, the trail went dead.

Meanwhile, the team led by Eisenmann and Ballard were continuing to explore Leonard Lake's chamber of horrors. The position of the first two badly decomposed bodies near the top of the trench led to the recognition that there would almost certainly be more lower down. The Coroner Terry Parker was sent for, and Chief Inspector Joseph Lordan in San Francisco notified that additional men would be needed. The next two bodies to be unearthed were black men. Ng, who was known for his hatred of blacks, had once taken two blacks to the ranch as labourers.

Some of the burnt bones dumped on the hillside were in small, neat segments. (Lake had used two fifty-gallon drums as incinerators.) This was explained when the police found a bloodstained power saw, which had obviously been used to cut up the bodies. Coroner Parker supervised the collection of the bones, which were taken away in plastic sacks.

Tracker dogs were brought in to sniff for other bodies. They soon located a grave that proved to contain the remains of a man, woman and baby. These could be either the Dubs family or the Lonnie Bond family – they were too decomposed for immediate recognition. A bulldozer removed the top layer of earth to make digging easier.

As work proceeded in the hundred-degree heat, crowds of reporters lost no opportunity to ask questions. Magazines like *Time* and *Newsweek* had reported the finds, so this latest story of American serial murder soon achieved international notoriety. Earlier cases – like the Dean Corll murders in Texas in the early 1970s, or the John Gacy murders in Chicago in the early 1980s – had caused much the same shock effect. But in this case, even the sensational press seemed oddly subdued in its approach to the story, and gave it less space-inches than might be expected. It was as if the sheer horror of the details was too much even for the most news-hungry editor.

The discovery of the cabinet of snuff videos was followed by one that was in some ways even more disturbing: Lake's detailed diaries covering the same two-year period. The first one, for 1984, began: 'Leonard Lake, a name not seen or used much these days in my second year as a fugitive. Mostly dull day-to-day routine – still with death in my pocket and fantasy my goal.'

The diaries made it clear that his career of murder had started before he moved into the ranch on Blue Mountain Road. He had been a member of many communes, and in one at a place called Mother Lode, in Humboldt County, he had murdered his younger brother Donald. A crude map of northern California, with crosses labelled 'buried treasure', suggested the possibility that these were the sites of more murders; but the map was too inaccurate to guide searchers to the actual locations.

Who was Leonard Lake? Investigation of his background revealed that he had been born in 1946 in San Francisco, and that he had a highly disturbed childhood. Rejected by both parents at an early age, he was raised by his grandmother, a strict disciplinarian. Both his father and mother came from a family of alcoholics. The grandfather, also an alcoholic, was a violent individual who subjected the child to a kind of military discipline. Lake's younger brother Donald, his mother's favourite, was an epileptic who had experienced a serious head injury; he practised sadistic cruelty to animals and tried to rape both his sisters. Lake protected the sisters 'in return for sexual favours'. From an early age he had displayed the sexual obsession that seems to characterize the serial killer. He took nude photographs of his sisters and cousins, and later became a maker of pornographic movies starring his wife.

Lake shared another characteristic of so many serial killers – he lived in a world of fantasy – boasting, for example, of daring exploits in Vietnam when, in fact, he had never seen combat. On the other hand, it seems clear that his experiences in Vietnam caused some fundamental change that made him antisocial and capable of violence. Yet he was skilful in hiding his abnormality, teaching grade school, working as a volunteeer firefighter, and donating time to a company that provided free insulation in old people's homes. He seemed an exemplary citizen. But his outlook was deeply pessimistic, convinced that World War Three would break out at any moment. Like other 'survivalists', he often dressed in combat fatigues, and talked of living off the land. Once out of the marines, his behaviour became increasingly odd. After being forced to flee from the earlier compound because of the burglary charge, he had moved to the ranch near Wilseyville. Marriage to a girl called Cricket Balazs had broken up, but she had continued to act as a fence for stolen credit cards and other items. Lake seems to have loved her – at least he said so in a last note scrawled as he was dying – but he nevertheless held on to the paranoid idea that women were responsible for all his problems.

It was while living in an isolated village called Miranda in the hills of Northern California that Lake thought out the plan he called Operation Miranda: the plan he went on to put into effect in the ranch on Blue Mountain Road. It was to stockpile food, clothing and weapons against the coming nuclear holocaust, and also to kidnap women who would be kept imprisoned and used as sex slaves. 'The perfect woman', he explained in his diary, 'is totally controlled.' (He meant that he, Lake, would have total control over her.) 'A woman who does exactly what she is told to and nothing else. There is no sexual problem with a submissive woman. There are no frustrations – only pleasure and contentment.'

The journal left no doubt about Lake's method for collecting his sex slaves. Leonard Lake had made a habit of luring people to the house, often inviting them – like the Bond family – to dinner. Then the man and the baby were murdered, probably almost immediately. The woman was stripped of her clothes, shackled, and sexually abused until her tormentors grew bored with her. Then she was killed and buried or burned. The thought of the mental torment inflicted on girls like Brenda O'Connor, Deborah Dubs and Kathy Allen sickened everyone on the case.

But one other thing also emerged clearly from these journals, and was noted by the psychiatrist Joel Norris, who published a study of Lake in his book *The Menace of the Serial Killer*: that when Lake killed himself, he was in a state of depression and moral bankuptcy.

> His dreams of success had eluded him, he admitted to himself that his boasts about heroic deeeds in Vietnam were all delusions, and the increasing number of victims he was burying in the trench behind his bunker only added to his unhappiness. By the time he was arrested in San Francisco, Lake had reached the final stage of the serial murderer syndrome: he realized that he had come to a dead end with nothing but his own misery to show for it.

Two weeks after the digging began, the police had unearthed nine bodies and forty pounds of human bones, some burnt, some even boiled. The driving licences of Robin Stapley and of Ng's friend Mike Carroll (the boyfriend of Kathy Allen), and papers relating to Paul Cosner's car, confirmed that they had been among the victims.

When the 'survival bunker' itself was finally dismantled and taken away on trucks, it seemed clear that the site had yielded most of its evidence. This suggested that Lake had murdered and buried twenty-five people there. The identity of many of the victims remained unknown. The only person who might be able to shed some light on it was the missing Charles Ng. It was believed that he had crossed the border into Canada – a man answering to Ng's description had been seen in the men's room at a bus station shaving off his sideboards and trimming his eyebrows.

Then, on Saturday 6 July 1985, nearly five weeks after Ng's flight, a security guard in a department store in Calgary, Alberta, saw a young Chinaman pushing food under his jacket; when he challenged him, the youth drew a pistol; as they grappled, he fired, wounding the guard in the hand. He ran away at top speed, but was intercepted by other guards. The youth obviously had some training in Japanese martial arts, but was eventually overpowered and handcuffed. Identification documents revealed that he was Charles Ng.

FBI agents hurried to Calgary, and were allowed a long interview. Ng admitted that he knew about the murders, but put the blame entirely on Lake. And before the agents could see him again, Ng's lawyers – appointed by the court – advised him against another interview. And after a psychiatric examination, Ng was tried on a charge of armed robbery and sentenced to four and a half years. But efforts by the California Attorney-General John Van de Kamp to make sure he was extradited after his sentence, met with frustration. California, unlike Canada, still had the death penalty, and the extradition treaty stipulates that a man cannot be extradited if he might face the death penalty.

In November 1989, after serving three and a half years of his sentence, Ng was ordered back to California to face the murder charges against him. Amnesty International protested against the extradition on the grounds that it might result in Ng's execution. A government lawyer replied that if Canada became known as a 'safe haven' for killers, other US murderers could flee there. Amnesty Inernational's action caused widespread indignation, and calls for Ng to be sent back immediately. In due course, Ng was returned to California.

At the time of writing, Ng has still not been brought to trial. If and when that happens, the full extent of the horrors that occurred at the Blue Mountain Road ranch may finally emerge in court. But it is hard to see how public disclosure of Lake's depravity can serve any useful purpose.

The case of Leonard Lake and Charles Ng is an example of what we have decribed as *folie à deux* – cases in which crimes would almost certainly not have taken place unless two participants had egged each other on. An earlier case, while it created a sense of shocked incredulity in California, has received far less publicity. Yet it may be seen as the American equivalent of the Moors murder case.

Soon after midnight on Sunday 2 November 1980, a young couple emerged from the Carousel restaurant in Sacramento, California, where they had been attending a dance. As they crossed the car park they were accosted by a pretty blonde whose swollen stomach indicated pregnancy. They stopped politely – then realized she was holding a gun. 'Get in,' she said, pointing to an Oldsmobile van parked a few feet away. The sullen-looking man in the passenger seat was also holding a gun. They decided it would be best to obey and climbed into the back.

Before the blonde could enter the driver's door, a passing student with a freakish sense of humour was ahead of her, slipping into the driver's seat. Andy Beal had invited the young couple back to his room for a late night drink. But a single glance at the face of his friends told him there was something wrong. This was confirmed when the pretty blonde flew at him with a stream of obscenities: 'Get out of my fucking car!', and slapped his face. As he watched the car drive away, with a screech of tyres, Andy Beal had the presence of mind to memorize its numberplate, then write it down. Minutes later, he was telephoning the police to report the abduction of Craig Miller and his fiancée Beth Sowers.

The Oldsmobile proved to be registered to a girl called Charlene Williams, daughter of a wealthy Sacramento businessman. The police found her at her parents' home the following morning. Charlene insisted that she had spent the previous evening alone, and had no idea who had used her car. Soon after the police had left, they heard that Craig Miller's body had been found; he had been shot three times in the back of the head. When they returned to ask Charlene further questions, she had left. So had her 'husband', an ex-convict called Gerald Gallego.

Five days later, the body of Beth Sowers was also found – dumped, like Craig Miller, in a field. She had been raped and shot. It looked as if the motive for the abduction and murder of the young couple had been simply the rape of Beth Sowers.

The manhunt for Gerald Gallego and Charlene Williams ended two weeks later, as Charlene emerged from a Western Union office in Omaha, Nebraska, with $500 her parents had wired her. The Williams had also tipped off the police. By now, the Sacramento police had been doing a great deal of research into the background of Gerald Armand Gallego. It seemed to indicate that he and Charlene made a habit of abduction and murder, and that the motive was Gallego's uncontrollable sexual appetite. On 17 July 1980 a pretty waitress named Virginia Mochel had vanished after leaving the tavern where she worked; her naked body had been found not long before the latest murders. And two years earlier, two teenage girls, Rhonda Scheffler and Kippi Vaught, had vanished from a Sacramento shopping mall. Forty-eight hours later, their bodies were found in a meadow; both had been raped, then knocked out with a tyre iron and shot. In July 1980, the decomposing bodies of two more teenage girls, Stacy Ann Redican and Karen Chipman-Twiggs, were found in Nevada; they had also vanished from a Sacramento shopping centre four months earlier.

When it became clear to Charlene Williams that she and her 'husband' faced the death penalty for the murders of Craig Miller and Beth Sowers, she decided to enter into plea bargaining, and agreed to tell the whole story. They had, she admitted, been responsible for the deaths of the four teenagers abducted from Sacramento shopping malls, and for that of the waitress Virginia Mochel. These, together with Craig Miller and Beth Sowers, made seven. And there were another three, of which the Sacramento police knew nothing. The motive, she explained, was Gerald Gallego's peculiar obsession. He wanted to find 'the perfect sex slave', a girl who would do anything he asked. And she, Charlene, was so besotted with him that she had agreed meekly to help him kidnap the 'slaves'.

Gallego, the police discovered, was already wanted on a different charge in Butte County. In 1978, two weeks after he had killed Rhonda Scheffler and Kippi Vaught, his 14-year-old daughter, Sally Jo, had gone to the police and told them that her father had been committing incest with her since she was 8. And to celebrate his thirty-second birthday, he had spent the afternoon with his daughter and her teenage girlfriend in Charlene's Oldsmobile, commiting rape and sodomy. And Sally Jo, already full of resentment at her father's new ladylove, had decided this was the last straw. Gallego fled to avoid arrest.

Charlene described how she had met Gallego on a blind date in 1977. At 21 she had already been married and divorced twice; most of the men she had been sleeping with since her early teens had been inadequate. This strutting little ex-con – he was only five feet seven tall – had a gruff dominance that enchanted her. According to Charlene, his sexual appetite was immense, and she was expected to help him satisfy it without receiving any pleasure in return. Being something of a masochist, she explained, she accepted this as part of her duty. When he excited himself sexually by confiding in her his violent fantasies of rape and violence, she also accepted this as one of the peculiarities of her macho lover. And when Gallego told her that he dreamed of the 'perfect sex slave', and asked her to help him find one, she felt she had no alternative; he was her master . . .

Gallego was undoubtedly a highly disturbed man, and his life cannot be understood without knowing that his father was also a killer. Gerald Albert Gallego had first been arrested for stealing his stepfather's car; it took seven policemen to get the cuffs on him and he swore revenge. Released from youth custody at the age of 18 in 1946, Gallego senior met an 18-year-old girl who had already been married twice, and married her five hours later; when she gave birth to Gerald Gallego, her husband was doing a stint in San Quentin. He committed his first murder soon after, killing a man in a rage by beating him to death with his fists. But it was in May 1954, when in a town jail on suspicion of murder that Gallego Snr attacked the guard, grabbed his gun, then made him drive out of town before killing him. 'It made me feel real good inside.' Recaptured, he escaped again four months later, with another convicted killer; they overpowered a guard by throwing acid in his eyes, then kicked him to death. Hunted down with bloodhounds, he was executed in the death chamber at San Quentin in March 1955, at the age of 28. His 9-year-old son knew nothing of this – until he was 17 he believed that his father had died in an accident.

But by that time it was obvious that Gerald Armand Gallego was following in his father's footsteps. He had started getting into trouble at the age of 10; at 13 he was found guilty of having sex with a 7-year-old girl, and sentenced to juvenile detention – in the same reformatory where his father had served time.

From now on, his life was dominated by a craving for sex and by hatred of authority. He once told a prison visitor: 'The only thing I want is to kill God.' By the time he was 32 he had been married six times – the sixth wife being Charlene Williams, whom he like to call Ding-a-Ling.

Charlene's father Chuck Williams had started in business as a supermarket butcher, moved to Sacramento as a supermarket manager, and eventually became vice-president of a nationwide supermarket chain. When his wife Mercedes had an accident to her back that made her less mobile, the teenage Charlene took over the job of hostess to her father's business associates.

In her mid-teens, Charlene became a rebel and tried drugs, alcohol and sex. She came close to being expelled from school; but her father was usually able to smooth over her problems. But two marriages quickly collapsed – perhaps because her husbands were unable to live up to her father-image of the dominant male.

In September 1977 she went – unwillingly – on a blind date with a friend; her partner was Gerald Gallego. He had the kind of dominance she admired. But long before they had collaborated on ten murders, Charlene insisted, she had realized her mistake, and longed to escape from the brutal, insensitive little egoist . . .

This, at all events, was Charlene's story. It was flatly contradicted by Gallego, and Eric van Hoffmann, the author of a book on the case called *Venom in the Blood*, agrees with Gallego. According to Hoffmann, Charlene Williams was a bisexual nymphomaniac. Her sex life with Gallego was satisfactory enough until, in 1978, Gallego brought home a 16-year-old go-go dancer, who shared their bed for a night and was sodomized by Gallego. The next day Gallego returned unexpectedly from work to find Charlene and the girl engaged in sex with a dildo. He threw the girl out and beat Charlene; from then on, he lost his appetite for Charlene. But when, on his daughter's fourteenth birthday, Gallego had sex with both her and her girlfriend, it was clear to Charlene (who was present) that he was not impotent. At this point, according to Hoffmann, Charlene suggested the idea of kidnapping and murder. In each case, the victims were forced to have sex with Charlene as well as Gallego. Charlene liked to bite one of the girls – in one case virtually biting off a nipple – as the other brought her to a climax with oral sex. Hoffmann's account suggests that Charlene was the driving force behind the murders. As absurd as it sounds, Gallego emerges at the end of the book as *her* victim.

This certainly makes more sense than the other book on the case, *All His Father's Sins* by Biondi and Hecox, in which Charlene is presented as the pliable victim. And once again we become aware that one of the basic keys to the mind of the serial killer is a kind of 'spoiltness' that leads to a total inability to identify with other human beings. In this case, it seems clear that it was the spoilt rich girl who was trapped in total self-centredness, while the working-class Gallego, for all his faults, was more normal and realistic.

According to Charlene's confession, it was because she was completely enslaved to Gallego that she had approached the two pretty teenagers, Rhonda Scheffler and Kippi Vaught, in the shopping mall and asked them if they would like to smoke some pot. Unsuspectingly, the girls had accompanied her back to the Olsmobile van. Then Gallego had confronted them with a gun, and Charlene had to drive to a remote spot, where the girls were ordered out. They were taken into some pine trees; Gallego was carrying a sleeping bag. Hours later, Gallego returned with the girls, who looked dishevelled and tear-stained. Charlene was told to drive to another remote place; then he took the girls, one by one, and shot them. As they were about to drive away, he noticed that one of them – Kippi Vaught – was still moving; he got out of the van and shot her in the back of the head. The coroner later discovered that the first shot had only grazed her skull. If she had not moved, she would have been alive when the police reached her, and been able to describe her assailant . . .

It was two weeks later that Gallego's daughter told the

police about the long-term incest, and Gallego was on the run.

The next two victims, again teenage girls, were picked up at the annual county fair in Reno on 24 June 1978. Charlene approached Kaye Colley and Brenda Judd, and asked if they would like a job distributing leaflets. In the back of the van, they were confronted by Gallego with a pistol. This time there was a mattress and blankets on the floor. Charlene drove; Gallego ordered the girls to strip – one of them had vomited. Then Gallego raped them both. A long time later, Charlene was ordered to drive on. The girls were taken out one by one and killed with hammer blows to the skull.

Ten months later, on 24 April 1980, Stacy Ann Redican and Karen Chipman-Twiggs were accosted by the pretty blonde girl in the Sunrise Mall in Sacramento; they were totally unsuspicious until confronted by the little man with a gun. This time, in remote Nevada woods, Charlene left the van while Gallego raped the girls and made them perform the various services that might qualify them as 'perfect sex slaves'. Then, as before, he took them off one by one and killed them with a hammer. Not long after that murder, Gallego and Charlene were married. But since Gallego had omitted to get a divorce from a previous wife, it was not legal anyway.

Scarcely a month later, on 6 June 1980, they passed an attractive hippie walking along the road between Port Orford, Oregon, and Gold Beach; her name was Linda Teresa Aguilar, and she was five months pregnant. The man and woman in the van looked safe enough, so she accepted a lift. As Charlene drove, Gallego climbed over into the back with the hippie and ordered her to undress. Then Charlene stopped the van and went for a walk. When she finally returned, Gallego was complaining that the girl had been unable to 'do anything for him'. He took her away and knocked her unconscious with a hammer; an autopsy would later reveal that she was still alive when he buried her in the sand.

The next victim had been the waitress, Virginia Mochel, a pretty blonde girl not unlike Charlene. On 17 July 1980, after the tavern had closed, Gallego accosted the waitress as she climbed into her own car. It was a dangerous thing to do – there were still many customers around, and Gallego had been talking to the girl all evening. Virginia, who had left her two children with a babysitter, begged to be allowed to call and explain that she was delayed. Gallego told her to shut up. They drove back to the apartment Charlene shared with him, and Charlene went inside while Gallego raped Virginia in the van, then strangled her. It was dawn when they finally dumped her on a levee road.

As already noted, Gallego's account, which is accepted by van Hoffmann, has Charlene taking a far more active part in the murders.

Whatever the truth, the rampage was now almost over. After Craig Miller and Beth Sowers had been abducted from outside the Carousel restaurant on 2 November 1980, Charlene drove to a remote field; Miller was made to get out and lie on the ground, then killed with three bullets in the back of the head. Beth Sowers was taken back to the Gallego apartment and raped, while – Charlene declares – she waited in the next room. Then Beth was also taken to a remote place and shot. But this time, Gallego's carelessness – in abducting his latest victims in a parking lot with other customers around – led to his downfall.

At the arraignment proceedings, Gallego leapt to his feet and screamed at reporters: 'Get the hell out of here! We're not funny people! We're not animals.' He fought violently, overturning tables and chairs before he was subdued.

Because of the sheer horror caused by the case, the Gallego trial was moved from Sacramento to Martinez, near San Francisco. It became clear that Gallego was an almost insane egoist. But his attempts to exclude Charlene's testimony – on the grounds that they were married – failed when it was proved that he had still not divorced his second wife. On 21 June 1983, he was sentenced to die by lethal injection in San Quentin. Since that time, he has proved to be a consistently difficult prisoner, whose violence and abusiveness have meant that he has spent most of his time separated from other prisoners. Charlene Williams received sixteen years.

Does not Charlene's involvement contradict the view, suggested elsewhere in this book, that all serial killers are working-class? In fact, as far as I can see, there is no psychological law that dictates that a middle- or upper-class person would be incapable of being a serial killer. The fact that all serial killers have had working-class backgrounds only proves that childhood misery and poverty can produce the kind of resentment that leads to serial murder. But the fifteenth-century child murderer Gilles de Rais was spoilt and wealthy, and there seems to be no reason why a modern Gilles should be an impossibility.

Fortunately, at the time of writing, no such person has emerged. When I came across the case of the New Jersey 'torso killer' Richard Cottingham, I was at first inclined to believe that he was an exception. Cottingham, a computer operator who worked for an insurance company, was arrested in May 1980 after screams from a motel room alerted the manager that something was wrong. Cottingham had been torturing a prostitute for several hours, and fairly certainly intended to kill her, as he had killed half a dozen other women. Cottingham's method was to pick up a woman, take her to a bar and slip a drug into her drink, then take her to a motel and rape and torture her. Some victims were allowed to go; others were strangled and mutilated.

Cottingham was the son of an insurance salesman who was brought up in a suburban home, and had attended high school before he married and became a computer programmer. But Ron Leith's book *The Prostitute Murders* reveals that he was born in the Bronx – which might be regarded as New York's equivalent of London's East End – and spoke with a Bronx accent. He spent the first ten years of his life in the Bronx, before the family moved to New Jersey. His father was absent from home most of the time, and Cottingham – an only child – found it difficult to make friends at school. Nothing is known of the psychological causes of his passion to humiliate and torture women. But it seems clear that Cottingham is another example of the working class serial killer.

Cottingham's most obvious characteristic was a high degree of conceit. Like so many serial killers, he seems to have had no doubt that he was the cleverest person in the courtroom. Ron Leith, who was in court, comments that it was Cottingham himself who cemented the state's case, giving an implausibly intricate alibi, and lecturing the judge on the strange world of prostitution. 'His arrogance seemed limitless.'

This, then, seems to be the common denominator of serial killers – egoism combined with a kind of tunnel vision. But then, we have all known people like that – people who obviously believe that they are the most fascinating person in the world, and who regard it as natural to begin every sentence with 'I'. There must always have been such people. Then why is it that, in our own time, a percentage of them have turned into serial killers?

We have noted already the distinction Robert Ressler made between a serial killer – one who continues killing over a long period, usually at regular intervals – and the 'spree killer', such as Charles Starkweather, Richard Speck or Paul John Knowles, who commits a number of murders in a sudden rampage over a brief period of time. Perhaps the best-known spree killer of the 1980s was Bernard Christopher Wilder, a young and wealthy Australian businessman and racing driver, who lived in luxury in Miami, Florida, from the mid-1970s. In 1980 he was charge with raping two teenage girls after drugging them with a doctored pizza, but was only bound over. Back in Australia he was charged with abducting and raping two 15-year-old girls, but allowed to return to America on bail. In the seven weeks between 26 February 1984 and 12 April 1984, Wilder drove from Florida to Georgia, then Texas, Oklahoma, Kansas, Colorado, Nevada amd California, then returned east to Indiana, New York, Massachusetts and New Hampshire. During this time he abducted eleven women, posing as a magazine photographer looking for models, and raped and killed nine of them. On 20 March 1984, guests in a motel in Bainbridge, south Georgia, broke into a room when they heard a girl screaming, and found a 19-year-old girl who had locked herself in the bathroom. She decribed how she had been picked up in Tallahassee, Florida, by Wilder, who said he wanted her to model for him, and was knocked unconscious as she posed in a public garden. Wilder had then smuggled her into a motel room in a sleeping bag, glued her eyelids with superglue, bound her hands, then raped and tortured her. She had managed to persuade him to allow her to go to the bathroom, then locked herself in and screamed until she was released; Wilder fled.

Most of his other pickups were less fortunate. Only two girls, who were forced to spend a night with him in a motel in Akron, Ohio, escaped with their lives – one of them stabbed several times. In Boston, Wilder put the other on a plane for Los Angeles, handing her five hundred dollars, then abducted another girl whose car had broken down. She succeeded in jumping out of his car at a traffic light. The next day, Friday

13 April, two policemen approached Wilder's car, and as one of them grappled with him, Wilder was fatally shot; the policeman was only wounded.

The nationwide chase after Wilder was one of the major factors that led to the formation of a nationwide crime centre, the National Center for the Analysis of Violent Crime (NCAVC) in Quantico in June, 1984. Here, as we have seen, the crime computer records crimes that take place all over America – which would formerly have been recorded only in the state in which they took place – and searches for similarities that might reveal a travelling criminal. Although difficulties have arisen in recent years – as individual states complain that the NCAVC takes the credit that is often due to them, and sometimes decline to co-operate – the NCAVC has remained the most important advance in crime detection in the late twentieth century.

The importance of these technological advances is emphasized again by the solution of another widely publicized case of the 1980s, that of the man who became known as 'the Night Stalker.'

Throughout 1985 handgun sales in Los Angeles soared. Many suburbanites slept with a loaded pistol by their beds. A series of violent attacks upon citizens in their own homes had shattered the comfortably normality of middle-class life. Formerly safe neighbourhoods seemed to be the killer's favourite targets. The whole city was terrified.

The attacks were unprecedented in many ways. Neither murder nor robbery seemed to be the obvious motive, although both frequently took place. The killer would break into a house, creep into the main bedroom and shoot the male partner through the head with a .22. He would then rape and beat the wife or girlfriend, suppressing resistance with threats of violence to her or her children. Male children were sometimes sodomized, the rape victims sometimes shot. On occasion he would ransack the house looking for valuables while at other times he would leave empty-handed without searching. During the attacks he would force victims to declare their love for Satan. Survivors described a tall, slim Hispanic male with black, greasy hair and severely decayed teeth. The pattern of crimes seemed to be based less upon a need to murder or rape but a desire to terrify and render helpless. More than most serial killers the motive seemed to be exercising power.

The killer also had unusual methods of victim selection. He seemed to be murdering outside his own racial group, preferring Caucasians and specifically Asians. He also seemed to prefer to break into yellow houses.

In the spring and summer of 1985 there were more than twenty attacks, most of which involved both rape and murder. By the end of March the press had picked up the pattern and splashed stories connecting the series of crimes. After several abortive nicknames, such as 'The Walk-In Killer' or 'The Valley Invader', the *Herald Examiner* came up with 'The Night Stalker', a name sensational enough to stick.

Thus all through the hot summer of 1985 Californians slept with their windows closed. One policeman commented to a reporter: 'People are armed and staying up late. Burglars want this guy caught like everyone else. He's making it bad for their business.' The police themselves circulated sketches and stopped anyone who looked remotely like The Night Stalker. One innocent man was stopped five times.

Despite these efforts and thorough forensic analysis of crime scenes there was little progress in the search for the killer's identity.

Things were obviously getting difficult for The Night Stalker as well. The next murder that fitted the pattern occurred in San Francisco, showing perhaps that public awareness in Los Angeles had made it too taxing a location. This shift also gave police a chance to search San Francisco hotels for records of a man of The Night Stalker's description. Sure enough, while checking the downmarket Tenderloin district police learned that a thin Hispanic with bad teeth had been staying at a cheap hotel there periodically over the past year. On the last occasion he had checked out the night of the San Francisco attack. The manager commented that his room 'smelled like a skunk' each time he vacated it and it took three days for the smell to clear.

Though this evidence merely confirmed the police's earlier description, The Night Stalker's next shift of location was to prove more revealing. A young couple in Mission Viejo were attacked in their home. The Night Stalker shot the man through the head while he slept, then raped his partner on the bed next to the body. He then tied her up while he ransacked the house for money and jewellery. Before leaving he raped her a second time and force her to fellate him with a gun pressed against her head. Unfortunately for the killer, however, his victim caught a glimpse of him escaping in a battered orange Toyota and memorized the licence plate. She immediately alerted the police. LAPD files showed that the car had been stolen in Los Angeles' Chinatown district while the owner was eating in a restaurant. An all-points bulletin was put out for the vehicle, and officers were instructed not to try and arrest the driver, merely to observe him. However, the car was not found. In fact, The Night Stalker had dumped the car soon after the attack, and it was located two days later in a car park in Los Angeles' Rampart district. After plain clothes officers had kept the car under surveillance for twenty-four hours, the police moved in and took the car away for forensic testing. A set of fingerprints was successfully lifted.

Searching police fingerprint files for a match manually can take many days and even then it is possible to miss correlations. However, the Los Angeles police had recently installed a fingerprint database computer system, designed by the FBI, and it was through this that they checked the set of fingerprints from the orange Toyota. The system works by storing information about the relative distance between different features of a print, and comparing them with a digitized image of the suspect's fingerprint. The search provided a positive match and a photograph. The Night Stalker was a petty thief and burglar. His name was Ricardo Leyva Ramirez.

The positive identification was described by the forensic division as 'a near miracle'. The computer system had only just been installed, this was one of its first trials. Furthermore, the system only contained the fingerprints of criminals born after 1 January 1960. Richard Ramirez was born in February 1960.

The police circulated the photograph to newspapers, and it was shown on the late evening news. At the time, Ramirez was in Phoenix, buying cocaine with the money he had stolen in Mission Viejo. On the morning that the papers splashed his name and photograph all over their front pages, he was on a bus on the way back to Los Angeles, unaware that he had been identified.

He arrived safely and went into the bus station toilet to finish off the cocaine he had bought. No one seemed to be overly interested in him as he left the station and walked through Los Angeles. Ramirez was a Satanist, and had developed a belief that Satan himself watched over him, preventing his capture.

At 8.15 a.m. Ramirez entered Tito's Liquor Store at 819 Towne Avenue. He selected some Pepsi and a pack of sugared doughnuts; he had a sweet tooth that, coupled with a lack of personal hygiene, had left his mouth with only a few blackened teeth. At the counter other customers looked at him strangely as he produced three dollar bills and awaited his change. Suddenly he noticed the papers' front pages, and his faith in Satan's power must have been shaken. He dodged out of the shop and ran, accompanied by shouts of, 'It is him! Call the cops!' He pounded off down the street at a surprising speed for one so ostensibly unhealthy. Within twelve minutes he had covered two miles. He had headed east. He was in the Hispanic district of Los Angeles.

Ever since the police had confirmed that The Night Stalker was Hispanic there had been a great deal of anger among the Hispanic community of Los Angeles. They felt that racial stereotypes were already against them enough without their being associated with psychopaths. Thus more than most groups, Hispanics wanted The Night Stalker out of action.

Ramirez, by now, was desperate to get a vehicle. He attempted to pull a woman from her car in a supermarket lot until he was chased away by some customers of the barber's shop opposite. He carried on running, though exhausted, into the more residential areas of east Los Angeles. There, he tried to steal a 1966 red Mustang having failed to notice that the owner, Faustino Pinon was lying underneath repairing it. As Ramirez attempted to start the car Pinon grabbed him by the collar and tried to pull him from the driver's seat. Ramirez shouted that he had a gun, but Pinon carried on pulling at him even after the car had started, causing it to career into the gatepost. Ramirez slammed it into reverse and accelerated into the side of Pinon's garage, and the vehicle stalled. Pinon succeeded in wrenching Ramirez out of his car, but in the following struggle Ramirez escaped, leaping the fence and running off across the road. There he tried to wrestle Angelina De La Torres from her Ford Granada. 'Te voy a matar!' (I'm going to kill you!) screamed Ramirez, 'Give me the keys!', but again he was thwarted and he ran away, now pursued by a growing crowd of neighbours. Manuel De La Torres, Angelina's husband, succeeded in smashing Ramirez on the head with a gate bar and he fell, but he managed to struggle up and set off running again before he could be restrained. Incredibly, when Ramirez had developed a lead, he stopped, turned around and stuck his tongue out at his pursuers, then sped off once more. His stamina could not hold indefinitely however, and it was De La Torres who again tackled him and held him down. It is possible that Ramirez would have been lynched there and then had not a patrolman called to the scene arrived: Coincidentally the patrolman was the same age as the killer, and he too was called Ramirez. He reached the scene just as The Night Stalker disappeared under the mob. He drove his patrol car to within a few feet of where Ramirez was restrained, got out and prepared to handcuff the captive.

'Save me. Please. Thank God you're here. It's me, I'm the one you want. Save me before they kill me,' babbled Ramirez. The patrolman handcuffed him and pushed him into the back of the car. The crowd was becoming restless, and the car was kicked as it pulled away. Sixteen-year-old Felipe Castaneda, part of the mob that captured Ramirez remarked, 'He should never, *never* have come to East LA. He might have been a tough guy, but he came to a tough neighbourhood. He was Hispanic. He should have known better.'

'The Night Stalker' was in custody, at first in a police holding cell and then in Los Angeles county jail. While in police care he repeatedly admitted to being 'The Night Stalker' and begged to be killed.

The case against Ramirez was strong. The murder weapon, a .22 semi-automatic pistol, was found in the possession of a woman in Tijuana, who had been given it by a friend of Ramirez. Police also tried to track down some of the jewellery that Ramirez had stolen and fenced, by sending investigators to his birth-place El Paso, a spiralling town on the Texas–Mexico border. Questioning of his family and neighbours revealed that Ramirez' early life had been spent in petty theft and smoking a lot of marijuana. He had never joined any of the rival teenage gangs that fight over territory throughout El Paso, preferring drugs and listening to heavy metal. It had been common knowledge that Ramirez was a Satanist; a boyhood friend, Tom Ramos said he believed that it was Bible-study classes that had turned the killer that way.

The investigators also found a great deal of jewellery, stashed at the house of Ramirez' sister Rosa Flores. The police were also hoping to find a pair of eyes that Ramirez had gouged from one of his victims that had not been found in any previous searches. Unfortunately they were not recovered.

The evidence against Ramirez now seemed unequivocal. In a controversial move, the Mayor of Los Angeles said that whatever went on in court, he was convinced of Ramirez' guilt. This was later to prove a mainstay in a defence argument that Ramirez could not receive a fair trial in Los Angeles.

The appointed chief prosecutor in the case was deputy District Attorney P. Philip Halpin, who had prosecuted the 'Onion Field' cop-killing case twenty years earlier. Halpin hoped to end the trial and have Ramirez in the gas chamber in a relatively short period of time. The prosecutor drew up a set of initial charges and submitted them as quickly as possible. A public defender was appointed to represent Ramirez. However Ramirez' family had engaged an El Paso lawyer, Manuel Barraza, and Ramirez eventually rejected his appointed public defender in favour of the El Paso attorney. Barraza did not even have a licence to practise law in California.

Ramirez accepted, then rejected three more lawyers, finally settling upon two defenders, Dan and Arturo Hernandez. The two were not related, although they often worked together. The judge advised Ramirez that his lawyers did not even meet the minimum requirements for trying a death-penalty case in California, but Ramirez insisted, and more than seven weeks after the initial charges were filed, pleas of 'not guilty' were entered on all counts.

The Hernandez' and Ramirez seemed to be trying to force Halpin into making a mistake out of sheer frustration, and thus to create a mis-trial. After each hearing the Hernandez' made pleas for, and obtained, more time to prepare their case. Meanwhile one prosecution witness had died of natural causes, and Ramirez' appearance was gradually changing. He had had his hair permed, and his rotten teeth replaced. This naturally introduced more uncertainty into the minds of prosecution witnesses as to Ramirez' identity. The racial make-up of the jury was contested by the defence, which caused delays. The defence also argued, with some justification, that Ramirez could not receive a fair trial in Los Angeles, and moved for a change of location. Although the motion was refused it caused yet more delays. It actually took three and a half years for Ramirez' trial finally to get underway.

Halpin's case was, in practical terms, unbeatable. The defence's only real possibility of success was in infinite delay. For the first three weeks of the trial events progressed relatively smoothly. Then Daniel Hernandez announced that the trial would have to be postponed as he was suffering from nervous exhaustion. He had a doctor's report that advised six weeks' rest with psychological counselling. It seemed likely that a mis-trial would be declared. Halpin tried to argue that Arturo Hernandez could maintain the defence, even though he had failed to turn up at the hearings and trial for the first seven months. However this proved unnecessary as the judge made a surprise decision and denied Daniel Hernandez his time off, arguing that he had failed to prove a genuine need.

Halpin, by this stage, was actually providing the Hernandez' with all the information that they required to mount an adequate defence, in order to move things along and prevent mis-trial. For the same reasons the judge eventually appointed a defence co-counsel, Ray Clark. Clark immediately put the defence on a new track: Ramirez was the victim of a mistaken identity. He even developed an acronym for this defence – SODDI or Some Other Dude Did It. When the defence case opened Clark produced testimony from Ramirez' father that he had been in El Paso at the time of one of the murders of which he was accused. He also criticized the prosecution for managing to prove that footprints at one of the crime scenes were made by a size eleven-and-a-half Avia trainer without ever proving that Ramirez actually owned such a shoe. When the jury finally left to deliberate however, it seemed clear that they would find Ramirez guilty.

Things were not quite that easy however. After thirteen days of deliberation juror Robert Lee was dismissed for inattention and replaced by an alternative who had also witnessed the case. Two days later, juror Phyllis Singletary was murdered in a domestic dispute. Her live-in lover had beaten her, then shot her several times. She was also replaced.

At last on 20 September, 1989 after twenty-two days of

deliberation the jury returned a verdict of guilty on all thirteen counts of murder, twelve of those in the first degree. The jury also found Ramirez guilty of thirty other felonies, including burglary, rape, sodomy and attempted murder. Asked by reporters how he felt after the verdict, Ramirez replied, 'Evil.'

There remained only the selection of sentence. At the hearing Clark argued that Ramirez might actually have been possessed by the devil, or that alternatively he had been driven to murder by over-active hormones. He begged the jury to imprison Ramirez for life rather than put him on death row. If the jury agreed, Clark pointed out, 'he will never see Disneyland again', surely punishment enough. After five further days of deliberation, the jury voted for the death penalty. Again, reporters asked Ramirez how he felt about the outcome as he was being taken away, 'Big deal. Death always went with the territory. I'll see you in Disneyland.'

Any attempt to trace the source of Ramirez' violent behaviour runs up against an insurmountable problem. No external traumas or difficulties seem to have brutalized him. He had a poor upbringing, he was part of a racial minority, but these things alone cannot explain such an incredibly sociopathic personality. Ramirez seems to have created himself. He was an intelligent and deeply religious child and early teenager. Having decided at some stage that counter-culture and drug-taking provided a more appealing lifestyle, he developed pride in his separateness. In the El Paso of his early manhood, people would lock their doors, if they saw him coming down the street. He was known as 'Ricky Rabon', Ricky the thief, a nickname he enjoyed as he felt it made him 'someone'. By the time he moved to Los Angeles, he was injecting cocaine and probably committing burglaries to support himself. He let his teeth rot away, eating only childish sugary foods. He refused to wash. He listened to loud heavy metal music.

It has been argued that it was his taste in music that drove him to murder and Satanism, but this would seem to be more part of the mood of censorship sweeping America than a genuine explanation. Anyone who takes the trouble to listen to the music in question, particularly the AC/DC album cited by American newspapers at the time of the murders, will find that there is little in it to incite violence.

Ramirez' obvious attempts to repel others in his personal behaviour, and his heavy drug use, seem more likely sources of violence than early poverty or music. His assumed 'otherness' seems in retrospect sadly underdeveloped, having never progressed beyond a teenager's need to appal staid grown-up society.

This is not to say that Ramirez was unintelligent. His delaying of his trial and his choice of the Hernandez' to continue the delays shows that he had worked out the most effective method of staying alive for the longest period either before or soon after he was captured. His remarks in court upon being sentenced were not particularly original, yet they are clearly expressed:

> 'It's nothing you'd understand but I do have something to say . . . I don't believe in the hypocritical, moralistic dogma of this so-called civilized society. I need not look beyond this room to see all the liars, haters, the killers, the crooks, the paranoid cowards – truly *trematodes* of the Earth, each one in his own legal profession. You maggots make me sick – hypocrites one and all . . . I am beyond your experience. I am beyond good and evil, legions of the night, night breed, repeat not the errors of the Night Prowler [a name from an AC/DC song] and show no mercy. I will be avenged., Lucifer dwells within us all. That's it.

Ramirez remains on Death Row. It is unlikely that he will be executed before the year 2000.

The kind of good fortune that led to the arrest of Ramirez – the single fingerprint that identified the killer – failed to favour the team who spent most of the 1980s trying to trap the sadist who became known as the Green River Killer.

On 12 August 1982, a slaughterman gazing into the slow-flowing Green River, near Seattle, was intrigued by the mass of bubbles surrounding a log – they suggested a decomposing animal. He strolled down a fisherman's track to the riverbank for a closer look. What he saw was a bloated female corpse that had come to rest against a broken tree trunk. The shoulder-length auburn hair floated on the surface.

The police pathologist succeeded in lifting an excellent set of prints from the swollen flesh. These enabled the criminal identification department to name the victim as 23-year-old

Debra Lynn Bonner, known as 'Dub'; she was a stripper with a list of convictions as a prostitute.

The man in charge of the case, Detective Dave Reichert, recalled that a month earlier, another tattooed corpse had been found in the Green River, half a mile downstream, strangled with her own slacks. The girl had been identified as 16-year-old Wendy Coffield. In spite of her age, Wendy had a record as a prostitute – in fact, as a 'trick roll', someone who set up her clients ('johns') for robbery. It was a dangerous game, and Reichert was not surprised that the investigation had failed to turn up a likely suspect. On the whole, he decided, it was unlikely that the two murders were connected.

This view was reinforced by a visit to Dub Bonner's parents in nearby Tacoma. It produced the information that Dub had vanished on 25 July 1982, three weeks earlier, after being bailed from the local jail, together with her drug-dealing pimp. There was, it seemed a possible suspect – another dealer who had threatened Dub Bonner's life unless her pimp paid a drug-debt.

But before he had time to follow this lead, Reichert heard the news that two more bodies had been found in the Green River. The call came just after he had returned from church – it was Sunday, 15 August 1982 – and when Reichert arrived at the scene, they had still not been taken out of the water. Both women were black, both were naked, and they had been weighted down to the river bottom with large rocks. But what made Reichert swear under his breath was that they were only a few hundred yards upstream from the spot where Dub Bonner had been found three days earlier, and that they had almost certainly been there at the time. Reichert had searched up and downstream for clues – but not, apparently, far enough.

Determined not to repeat his error, Reichert tramped along the bank towards the place where Dub Bonner had been found. He was hoping to find the route that the killer had used to transport the bodies. What he found, in fact, was another body. This one lay face downward, and the cause of death was clearly the pair of slacks knotted around her neck. Her upper half was clothed, although her bra had been pulled up to release her breasts. Like the other two, she was black. The out-thrust tongue and the shocked expression on her face showed that death had not come easily.

Reichert's Superior, Major Richard Kraske of the Kings County CID, came to view the bodies, and Reichert described what he had learned about Dub Bonner. This led them to toy with the idea that these women might be victims of a gang war among pimps; then Kraske discounted it. Pimps were unlikely to destroy their means of livelihood. It seemed far more likely that they were dealing with a psychopath – a 'sick trick' – whose perverted needs involved the total domination of his sex-partner, and her final destruction. Reichert recalled gloomily that he had investigated the murder of another prostitute, Leann Wilcox, in March of that same year. Her body had been found miles from the river, but cause of death – strangulation – seemed to fit the pattern.

The medical report on the latest victims deepened his depression. Of the two bodies in the river, one had been immersed for a week, the other for only two or three days. That meant that the killer had returned to the river *since* Dub Bonner had been found. Moreover, the body found on the bank still showed signs of rigor mortis, the stiffening of the muscles which usually disappears within two days. So the killer *had* returned – as many killers do to the sites where they have dumped bodies. He *must* have heard the news of the discovery of Dub Bonner's body, yet he had still returned. And if the police had kept a watch on the riverbank, he would now be in custody . . .

It was the first of a series of mischances that would make this one of the most frustrating criminal cases in Seattle's history. The next – and perhaps the worst – occurred two days later, when a local TV station announced that the riverbank was now under round-the-clock surveillance, and dashed the last hope of catching the killer on a return visit . . .

During the course of the next few days, the three black victims were identified. The first was Marcia Faye Chapman, a 31-year-old prostitute and mother of three children. She was known to work 'the Strip', the motel-studded highway that ran south from Seattle to the airport and on to Tacoma. The method was to stand by the roadside, apparently 'hitching'. If a car pulled up, and the driver indicated his willingness to go to a 'party', he was taken to a cheap motel, or to an area of condemned houses north of the airport, where his needs could be satisfied in the car. With the expansion of the 'Sea-Tac' Airport's traffic in the 1970s, the Strip had also seen a spectacular expansion in prostitution, and the crimes that go with it. Marcia Chapman had been missing since 1 August 1982, when she told her children she was going to the store, and had failed to return.

The second body found in the river was that of 17-year-old Cynthia Hinds, another prostitute who worked the Strip; she had last been seen on 11 August, not far from where Marcia Chapman had disappeared. The third body – the one found on the bank – was that of 16-year-old Opal Mills, a half-caste girl with no record of prostitution, but with a background of quarrels at home and minor brushes with the police. After viewing her daughter's body, Kathy Mills was haunted by the 'silent scream' on her face. She was to campaign for more police activity, and to intensify the frustration that turned this case into a nightmare for investigating officers.

But it was the medical findings on Marcia Chapman and Cynthia Hinds that confirmed the suspicion that the Green River Killer was a 'sick trick'; both women had pointed rocks jammed into their vaginas. There was speculation that they had been dumped in clear water, with their feet weighted by stones, so that the killer could go back and look at their faces magnified by the water. Intact sperm was found in the vaginas of all three victims. Opal Mills's body was scraped and scratched – probably from being dragged over the ground; it looked as if the killer had been interrupted before he could throw her in the river.

In cases involving the murder of prostitutes, investigators are faced with the baffling problem of where to begin. Approximately eighty thousand cars a day drive along the Strip, making eighty thousand possible suspects. Since the contact that led to the murder is made by chance, there is no logical starting point. Vice squad detectives tried questioning prostitutes about 'johns' who had acted suspiciously, and undercover agents hung around bars frequented by pimps, hoping to pick up rumours of 'sick tricks'. They heard many stories of women who had been half-strangled in motel rooms, or who had been driven to remote spots and then raped at gunpoint. Dozens of suspects were questioned, including the drug-dealing pimp who had threatened to kill Dub Bonner; all had to be released.

Meanwhile, more girls were disappearing. Two days after Wendy Coffield's body had been found in the Green River, a 17-year-old prostitute named Giselle Lavvorn vanished on her beat along the Strip. On Saturday 28 August 1982, a prostitute named Kase Lee left her pimp's apartment to 'turn a trick', and vanished. The next day it was Terri Milligan, who took an hour off from soliciting to go for a meal; apparently a car pulled up for her as she walked to the fast-food joint, and, unwilling to reject business, she climbed in.

The following day, 15-year-old Debra Estes – known to the police as Betty Jones – was picked up by a john in a blue and white pickup truck; he drove her to a remote spot, made her undress at gun point, then ordered her to give him a 'blow job'. After that he robbed her of $75 and left her in some woods with her hands tied. This man was pulled in by police who recognized the description of his pickup truck, and identified as the attacker. But a lie-detector test established his innocence of the Green River murders. In fact, while he was still in custody, 18-year-old Mary Meehan, who was eight months pregnant, disappeared, and became victim No. 9.

Ironically, within three weeks of her unpleasant encounter, Debra Estes would become the tenth victim of the real Green River Killer. Six more victims in August, October, November and December would bring his total up to at least sixeen – the largest annual total for any American serial killer up to that time.

Yet, as strange as it sounds, the American public was already beginning to lose interest in the Green River Killer. This was partly because the killer's standard method – strangling or suffocation – failed to produce the same shock effect as the mutilations of Jack the Ripper or the Cleveland Torso Killer. But it was also because this apparently endless disappearance of prostitutes led to a certain attention-fatigue – in March 1983, Alma Smith and Delores Williams; in April, Gail Mathews, Andrea Childers, Sandra Gabbert and Kimi-Kai Pitsor.

Moreover, there was a monotonous similarity about the cases. It was on 17 April that 17-year-old Sandy Gabbert picked up a 'trick' and vanished. Only an hour later, 17-year-old Kimi Kai Pitsor was walking with her pimp when a pockmarked man driving a green pickup truck caught her eye; she climbed in and vanished. Presumably the same man abducted and killed both girls on the same evening. Yet they were not even reported missing to the police for several weeks.

This attention-fatigue could also explain one of the oddest episodes in the case. On 30 April, 18-year-old Marie Malvar and her 'boyfriend' were walking along the Strip when a man in a pickup truck signalled for her to get in. The boyfriend, Bobby Woods, followed in his own car, but lost them; Marie vanished. A few days later, accompanied by Marie's father and brother, Bobby Woods spent hours driving around the area where he had last seen her. In a driveway in a cul-de-sac, he saw a pickup truck that he was certain was the one in which she had last been seen. The police were notified, and called at the house. But when the man who answered the door told them there was no woman in the house, they simply went away. To Bobby Woods it looked as if the police, like the general public, were losing interest in the case: a conclusion that seems to be supported by a subsequent development. On 17 May, Marie Malvar's driving licence was found by a cleaner at the airport. It could well have contained the killer's fingerprints. Yet although the police were notified, nobody bothered to collect the licence, and it was routinely destroyed six months later.

And the disappearances continued: in May, Carol Christensen, Martina Authorlee, Cheryl Wims and Yvonne Antosh; in June, Keli McGinness, Constance Naon, Tammy Lies and Carrie Roice; in July, Kelly Ware and Tina Thompson. Now the killer seemed to have abandoned the river as a dumping ground, preferring remote areas. Sometimes the girl vanished for ever. Sometimes bodies were found that corresponded to none of the known victims.

Photographs of the women often show sullen and defeated faces, and eyes that seem glazed with drugs. Kathy Mills, mother of Opal Mills, paraded with a placard that pointed out that the killer of a policeman's daughter was arrested the next day, while the attitude of the police towards the Green River victims was: 'Too bad.' It was not entirely fair comment, but she had a point. By the end of 1983, the number of the killer's known victims had reached forty, with another seven unaccounted for.

In fact, the police were about to step up the pace of the investigation. In mid-January 1984 they announced the formation of a Green River Task Force that would be devoted entirely to catching the killer. It was led by an experienced detective, Captain Frank Adamson, and its chief consultant was special investigator Bob Keppel, of the Attorney-General's office, the man who had played a major role in tracking down serial killer Ted Bundy. The team included undercover officers who watched prostitutes on the Strip and followed them as they drove off with johns. Dozens of sheepish or angry men were interviewed and asked for identification, and the suspect file continued to swell. And prostitutes who had taken customers to a dead-end road not far from where three skeletons had been discovered continued to be defiant, and to insist that they could look after themselves.

In April 1984, three more skeletons were found near Star Lake, south of Sea-Tac Airport, and another in woods about a mile away. One of these finds presented a new puzzle to the investigators. It was identified as that of Amina Agisheff, who had been missing since 7 July 1982, and was therefore one of the earliest – perhaps the first – of the Green River victims. But Amina did not fit the pattern. She was 35 years old, had two children, worked as waitress, and had no record of prostitution. She had vanished towards midnight as she left her mother to catch a bus. Had she been kidnapped? Or had she been given a lift by someone she knew – someone who turned out to be the Green River killer? It now struck the police as a real possibility that there were two Green River killers, one who dumped his victims in the river, and one who left them on land.

The first step was to investigate Amina Agisheff's background to find a potential killer. The next was to get the crime analysis unit to look back over the past ten years or so, to try to find earlier murders that might be linked to the series. Few mass murderers begin in full spate, so to speak; many have records for lesser sex crimes. The Green River killer might be caught by some earlier crime that had not been recognized as his handiwork . . . But, like so many other promising approaches, these led nowhere.

March 21, 1984, is a highly significant date in the Green River case. On that day, a man working on a sports field north of the airport recognized a bone in his dog's mouth as a human leg bone. A female skeleton was found in nearby bushes. Close by, a police bloodhound found a second skeleton. On that same day, 17-year-old Cindy Ann Smith, a topless dancer and prostitute, vanished, like so many other girls, while hitch-hiking along the Strip. There was one significant difference. As far as we know, Cindy Smith was the last victim of the Green River Killer.

In mid-March of the following year, 1985, the head of the Green River Task Force announced what the general public had guessed for many months: that the murders seemed to have ceased.

But the investigation continued in top gear. By midsummer, Seattle police suspected that the Green River killer had moved south to Portland, Oregon, just over the state border from Washington. Four young prostitutes had vanished; their bodies were found in remote and lonely areas. Then, on 14 July 1985, a young prostitute named Lottie was held at knifepoint by a pudgy customer who bound and blindfolded her, and drove her in his van down the freeway. Desperation gave her the strength to gnaw through her bonds; she tried to grab the knife and the van went into a ditch. Passing drivers seized the abductor. He proved to be Richard Terry Horton, a navy veteran. Triumphant detectives were convinced they had the Green River killer; but Horton's record showed he had been at sea during many of the Green River murders. He was sentenced to two years for kidnapping.

In January 1985, following the discovery of two skeletons near the Mountain View Cemetery, Captain Adamson allowed himself the optimistic prediction that the killer would be caught in 1986. He clearly had a suspect in mind. On 6 February, a trapper named Ernest McLean was arrested. He had a record for burglary, and police survey teams had followed him to many spots where human bones had been found. But McLean insisted that he had been in these places merely to trap animals for their fur. When a lie-detector test indicated his innocence, he was released. In May 1986, the resources of the Green River Task Force were severely cut.

In September 1987, Seattle newspapers asked: 'Is the Green River Killer Back?' Sixteen-year-old Rosie Kurran, a 'mixed-up youngster' who had been given up by her parents as uncontrollable, left home on 26 August, and vanished. Her body was found in a plastic bag in a ditch a week later. In November and December, two more girls, 14-year-old Debbie Gonsales and 24-year-old Dorothea Prestleigh, also vanished. The police declined to put these women on the list of Green River victims. And, to their relief, time seemed to prove them correct.

December 7, 1988, was another crucial date in the Green River case. On that evening, a two-hour TV documentary on the killings was broadcast: *Murder Live: A Chance to End the Nightmare*. The public was asked to ring in with information;

within minutes of the start of the programme, the switchboard was deluged; in two days, a hundred thousand people had called. It looked as if, once again, the investigation was going to be swamped with too many suspects.

One of these tips stood out above the rest. In 1981, a man named William Jay Stevens II, serving a sentence for burglary, had walked out of an open prison, and vanished. It seemed that he had spent much of that time in Spokane, Washington. He had a degree in psychology, had been in the Military Police, and was known to have an obsession about police insignia and uniforms. (It had been suggested many times that the Green River killer may have enticed his victims away by posing as a police officer.)

A check by the Spokane police on Stevens' whereabouts during the period of the Green River murders seemed to confirm that he *could* be the killer. On 9 January 1989, Stevens was arrested at his parents' home in Spokane. Police seized a large number of firearms, a box full of photographs of nude women, several driving licences and credit cards under false names, as well as stolen credit cards. Former friends of Stevens testified that he had frequented the red-light areas of Seattle and shown a deep interest in the Green River case. When stolen items of police equipment were also found, neither the police nor the media had any doubt that Stevens was the Green River Killer. He had even bought a house in Tigard – with stolen money – near which remains of two dead women were found.

The euphoria began to collapse when a study of Stevens' credit cards revealed that he was undoubtedly elsewhere at the time of some of the murders. It was still of course, possible that he might have been guilty of the others. But in October 1989, Captain Bob Evans, the new commander of the Task Force, announced that he had cleared Stevens of involvement in the Green River murders.

Seven and a half years after the murders began, the police had admitted that the expenditure of $12 million, interviews with 15,000 suspects, and the use of a $200,000 computer had left them virtually where they had been at the beginning – when a careless news broadcast had destroyed the main hope of catching the killer in the act.

The anticlimax pleased nobody; but there was at least one consolation: the activities of this sexual predator had turned the Seattle police department into one of the most efficient and up-to-date in the United States.

After Corll, Gacy, Lake and the Green River Killer, it seemed unlikely that any American sex killer would ever again produce quite the same effect of shock on the American psyche. But in 1991, a 31-year-old white male disproved that notion with a series of murders that revived disturbing memories of the Wisconsin necrophile Ed Gein.

On the evening of 22 July, as a police patrol car was cruising along 25th Street, Milwaukee, a cry of 'Help!' made the driver brake to an abrupt halt. A slim black man was running towards them, and a handcuff was dangling from his left wrist. His relief when he saw the police car was almost hysterical, and the tale he babbled out sounded so extraordinary that the officers had difficulty in following it. All they could gather was that a madman had been trying to kill him. The policemen climbed out of car and accompanied the man – who gave his name as Tracy Edwards – to the white low-rise building called Oxford Apartments, a rooming house occupied almost exclusively by blacks.

The tall, good-looking young man who answered the door of room 213 had sandy hair and was white. As he stood aside politely to let them in, he seemed perfectly calm, and looked at Edwards as if he had never seen him before. Both policemen had a feeling that this was a false alarm – until they smelt the unpleasant odour of decay, not unlike bad fish, that pervaded the apartment.

When they asked the man – who gave his name as Jeffrey Dahmer – why he had threatened Tracy Edwards, he looked contrite, and explained that he had just lost his job, and had been drinking. They asked him for the key to the handcuff, and Dahmer suddenly looked nervous and tried to stall. When they insisted, his calm vanished, and he suddenly became hysterical. There was a brief struggle, and another resident heard one of the policemen say: 'The son of a bitch scratched me.' Moments later, Dahmer was face down on the floor in handcuffs, and his rights were being read to him.

The policeman called headquarters on his portable radio, and asked them to run a check on the prisoner; the answer came back quickly: Dahmer had a felony conviction for sexual assault and for enticing a 13-year-old boy.

That supported the story that Edwards – now able to speak calmly – went on to tell them. The 32-year-old Edwards, a recent arrival from Mississippi, had met Dahmer about four hours ago in a shopping mall in Grand Avenue. He had accepted Dahmer's invitation to go back to his apartment for a party.

Edwards did not like the smell of Dahmer's small apartment, nor the male pin-ups on the walls – his own preference was for women. But he was fascinated by a fish tank containing Siamese fighting fish. Dahmer told him he liked to watch them fighting, and that the combat invariably ended with one of them dead. They sat on the settee and drank beer, then rum and coke. Edwards found himself feeling oddly sleepy. But when Dahmer tried to embrace him, Edwards suddenly came awake and and announced that he was going.

Seconds later, a handcuff had snapped around one of his wrists. He began to struggle, and Dahmer's attempt to handcuff the other cuff was unsuccessful. And for the next hour, Edwards sat on Dahmer's bed and watched a video of *The Exorcist*, while Dahmer held a large butcher's knife against his chest.

Finally Dahmer grew tired of the video and told Edwards that he intended to cut his heart out and eat it. But first he was going to strip Edwards and take some photographs . . . As Dahmer stood up to get the camera, the prisoner seized his opportunity; he swung his right fist in a punch that knocked Dahmer sideways; then he kicked him in the stomach and ran for the door. Dahmer caught him up there, and offered to unlock the handcuff; Edwards ignored him, wrenched open the door, and fled for his life . . .

When Edwards had finished telling his story, he was told to wait outside in the hallway, which was crowded with curious neighbours. As they tried to peer into the room, one of them saw a policeman open the door of the refrigerator, and gasp: 'There's a goddam head in here.'

That was the moment Dahmer began to scream – a horrible, unearthly scream like an animal. One of the policemen rushed downstairs for shackles. When the writhing body was secure, the two policemen began their search of the apartment.

Within minutes, they realized that they had discovered a mixture of a slaughterhouse and torture chamber. The freezer compartment of the refrigerator contained meat in plastic bags, one of which looked ominously like a human heart. Another freezer contained three plastic bags, each one with a severed head inside. A filing cabinet contained three skulls – some painted grey – and some bones; a box contained two more skulls, and an album full of more gruesome photographs. Two more skulls were found in a kettle, while another contained some severed hands and a male genital organ. The blue plastic barrel proved to contain three male torsos. An electric saw stained with blood made it clear how Dahmer had dismembered his victims. There was also a large vat of acid.

Journalists and TV crews were soon outside the appartment, and before midday, the people of America had learned that Milwaukee was the scene of the latest outbreak of homosexual serial murder. According to Dahmer, who confessed freely soon after his arrest, he had killed less than Dean Corll or John Gacy – only seventeen. But then, there was a major difference; Dahmer was a cannibal. The plastic bags of meat in the freezer were intended to be eaten. He described how he had fried the biceps of one victim in vegetable oil. The threat to eat Tracy Edwards' heart had been no bluff. Dahmer had little food in the apartment but potato chips, human meat and a jar of mustard.

Back at police headquarters, Dahmer was obviously relieved to be co-operating; he seemed glad that his career of murder was over. The police learned how, as a child, he had been fascinated by dissecting animals. Then, when he was 18 years old, in 1978, he had killed his first male victim, a hitch-hiker, then masturbated over the body. It had been almost ten years before he committed his next murder. But recently, the rate of killing had accelerated – as it often does with serial killers – and there had been no fewer than three murders in the last two weeks. He had attempted to kill Tracy Edwards only three days after his last murder.

Dahmer was also able to help the police towards establishing the identities of the victims – which included twelve blacks, one Laotian, one Hispanic and three whites. Some of their names he remembered; the police had to work out the identities of others from identity cards found in Dahmer's reeking apartment, and from photographs shown to parents of missing youths.

All Dahmer's confessions were sensational; but the story

of one teenage victim was so appalling that it created outrage around the world. Fourteen-year-old Laotian Konerak Sinthasomphone had met Dahmer in front of the same shopping mall where the killer was later to pick up Tracy Edwards; the boy agreed to return to Dahmer's apartment to allow him to take a couple of photographs.

Unknown to Konerak, Dahmer was the man who had enticed and sexually assaulted his elder brother three years earlier. Dahmer had asked the 13-year-old boy back to his apartment in September 1988, and had slipped a powerful sleeping draught into his, then fondled him sexually. Somehow, the boy succeeded in staggering out into the street and back home. The police were notified, and Dahmer was charged with second-degree sexual assault and sentenced to a year in a correction programme, which allowed him to continue to work in a chocolate factory.

Now the younger brother Konerak found himself in the same apartment. He was also given drugged coffee, and then, when he was unconscious, stripped and raped. After that, Dahmer went out to buy some beer – he had been a heavy drinker since schooldays. On his way back to the apartment, Dahmer saw, to his horror, that his naked victim was talking to two black teenage girls, obviously begging for help. Dahmer hurried up and tried to grab the boy; the girls clung on to him. One of them succeeded in ringing the police, and two squad cars arrived within minutes. Three irritable police officers wanted to know what the trouble was about.

When Dahmer told them that the young man was his lover, that they lived together in the nearby apartments, and that they had merely had a quarrel, the policemen were inclined to believe him – he looked sober and Konerak looked drunk. So they left the youth in Dahmer's apartment, to be strangled, violated and dismembered.

Back at District Three station house, the three policemen made their second mistake of the evening – they joked about the homosexual quarrel they had just broken up. But a tape recorder happened to be switched on, and when Dahmer was arrested two months later, and admitted to killing the Laotian boy, the tape was located and played on radio and television.

The public outcry that followed was not due simply to the tragic mistake made by three policemen. It was also because they had apparently preferred to believe Dahmer because he was white, and ignored Konerak because he was coloured – at least, that is how Milwaukees's non-whites saw it. It had also been remarked that when Dahmer had been arrested, TV cameramen had been requested not to take pictures; someone in the crowd had shouted that if he had been black, they would have allowed the cameras down his throat. Again, when Dahmer appeared in court for the first time on 25 July, he was dressed in his own clothes, not in the orange prison uniform; this again was seen as deliberately favouring a white. The Dahmer case caused an unpleasant build-up of racial tension in Milwaukee, and police crossed their fingers that nothing would ignite race riots. Fortunately, nothing did.

The twelve charges read out in court all concerned men who had been murdered since Dahmer had moved into the Oxford Apartments in March 1988. But according to Dahmer, his first murder had taken place thirteen years earlier, at the home in Bath Township, in north-eastern Ohio, where he had grown up and gone to school. At the time, his parents were in the process of a bitter and messy divorce, both alleging cruelty and neglect. Jeffrey had already learned to take refuge in alcohol.

According to Dahmer's confession, he had found himself alone in the family house at 4480 West Bath Road; his father had already left, and his mother and younger brother David were away visiting relatives. He had been left with no money, and very little food in the broken refrigerator. That evening, he explained, he decided to go out and look for some company.

It was not hard to find. A 19-year old white youth, who had spent the day at a rock concert, was hitch-hiking home to attend his father's birthday party. When an ancient Oldsmobile driven by someone who looked about his own age pulled up, the boy climbed in. They went back to Dahmer's house and drank some beer, and talked about their lives. Dahmer found he liked his new friend immensely. But when the boy looked at the clock and said he had to go, Dahmer begged him to stay. The boy refused. So Dahmer picked up a dumbbell, struck him on the head, then strangled him. He then dragged the body to the crawl space under the house, and dismembered it with a carving knife. It sounds an impossible task for an 18-year-old, but Dahmer was not without experience – he had always had a morbid interest in dismembering animals.

He had wrapped up the body parts in plastic bags. But after a few days, the smell began to escape. Dahmer's mother was due back soon, and was sure to notice the stench. He took the plastic bags out to the wood under cover of darkness and managed to dig a shallow grave – the soil was rock-hard. But even with the bags now underground, he still worried – children might notice the grave. So he dug them up again, stripped the flesh from the bones, and smashed up bones with a sledgehammer. He scattered them around the garden, and the property next door. When his mother returned a few days later, there was nothing to reveal that her son was now a killer.

Unfortunately, Dahmer was unable to recall the name of his victim. The Milwaukee police telephoned the police of Bath Township and asked them if they had a missing person case that dated from mid-1978. They had. On 18 June, a youth named Stephen Mark Hicks had left his home in Coventry Township to go to a rock concert. Friends had driven him there, and they agreed to rendezvous with him that evening to take him home. Hicks failed to turn up at the meeting place, and no trace of him was ever found. The family had offered a reward for information, hired a private detactive, and even consulted a psychic.

The Bath Township police had two photographs of Stephen Hicks on file. When shown these, Dahmer said casually: 'Yes, that's him.'

In the crawl space under the house, a blood-detecting chemical called Luminol caused certain spots to glow in the dark; these proved to be human blood. Luminol sprayed on a concrete block caused a bloody handprint to appear. The following day, more bones and three human teeth were found. Dental records eventually revealed that they had belonged to Stephen Hicks.

Dahmer's first murder was the most difficult to confirm. The remaining sixteen were much easier.

For nine years after killing Stephen Hicks, Dahmer kept his homicidal impulses under control. A period of three years in the army had ended with a discharge for drunkenness. After a short stay in Florida, he had moved in with his grandmother Catherine, in West Allis, south of Milwaukee. But he was still drinking heavily, and was in trouble with the police for causing a disturbance in a bar. His family was relieved when he at last found himself a job – in the Ambrosia Chocolate Company in Milwaukee.

Dahmer soon discovered Milwaukee's gay bars, where he became known as a monosyllabic loner. But it was soon observed that he had a more sinister habit. He would sometimes engage a fellow customer in conversation, and offer him a drink. These drinking companions often ended up in a drugged coma. Yet Dahmer's intention was clearly not to commit rape. He seemed to want to try out his drugs as a kind of experiment, to see how much he had to administer, and how fast they worked. But other patrons noticed, and when one of Dahmer's drinking companions ended up unconscious in hospital, the owner of Club Bath Milwaukee told him that he was barred.

On 8 September 1986, two 12-year-old boys reported to the police that Dahmer had exposed himself to them and masturbated. Dahmer alleged that he had merely been urinating. He was sentenced to a year on probation, and told his probation officers, with apparently sincerity: 'I'll never do it again.' (Judges and probation officers were later to note that Dahmer had a highly convincing manner of donning the sackcloth and ashes.) This period ended on 9 September 1987.

A year of good behaviour had done nothing to alleviate Dahmer's psychological problems; on the contrary, they had built up resentment and frustration. Six days after his probation ended, the frustration again exploded into murder. On 15 September, Dahmer was drinking at a gay hang-out called Club 219, and met a 24-year-old man called Stephen Tuomi. They decided to go to bed, and adjourned to the Ambassador Hotel, where they took a room that cost $43.88 for the night. Dahmer claims that he cannot recall much of that night, admitting that they drank themselves into a stupor. When Dahmer woke up, he says Tuomi was dead, with blood coming from his mouth, and strangulation marks on this throat.

Alone in a hotel room with a corpse, and the desk clerk likely to investigate whether the room had been vacated at any moment, Dahmer solved the problem by going out and buying a large suitcase, into which he stuffed the body. Then he got a taxi to take him back to his grandmother's house in West Allis, where he had his own basement flat. There he dismembered it, and stuffed the parts into plastic bags which, like Dennis Nilsen, he put out for garbage collection.

As a result of the murder of Stephen Tuomi, Dahmer seems to have acknowledged that murder was, in fact, what he needed to satisfy his deviant sexual impulse. The fifteen murders that followed leave no possible doubt about it.

These took place between 16 January 1988 and 19 July 1991. The method was usually much the same: Dahmer picked up a male – usually black – and invited him back to his apartment. There the victim was offered a drugged drink, after which he was violated and killed – mostly by strangulation, although Dahmer later began using a knife. The body was dismembered; parts of it were stored for eating, and the rest left out for the garbageman.

In September 1988, Catherine Dahmer had finally decided she could no longer put up with the smells and her grandson's drunkenness. On 25 September Dahmer moved into an apartment at 808 N. 24th Street.

There can be no doubt that Dahmer intended to use his new-found freedom to give full reign to his morbid sexual urges. But an unforeseen hitch occurred. Within twenty-four hours, the four-time murderer was in trouble with the police. On 26 September 1988, he met a 13-year-old Laotian boy named Sinthasomphone, lured him back to his apartment, and drugged him. But the elder brother of later victim Konerak somehow managed to escape, and Dahmer was charged with sexual assault and enticing a child for immoral purposes. He spent a week in prison, then was released on bail. On 30 January 1990, he was found guilty; the sentence would be handed out four months later.

But even the possibility of a long prison sentence could not cure Dahmer of his obsessive need to kill and dismember. When he appeared in court to be sentenced on 23 May 1989, he had already claimed his fifth victim. But Dahmer's lawyer Gerald Boyle argued that the assault on the Laotian boy was a one-off offence, and would never happen again. Dahmer himself revealed considerable skill as an actor in representing himself as contrite and self-condemned. 'I am an alcoholic and a homosexual with sexual problems.' He described his appearance in court as a 'nightmare come true', declared that he was now a changed man, and ended by begging the judge: 'Please don't destroy my life.' Judge William Gardner was touched by the appeal. This clean-cut boy obviously needed help, an was no psychiatric help available in prison. So he sentenced Dahmer to five years on probation, and a year in a House of Correction, where he could continue to work at the chocolate factory during the day.

From the Community Correctional Center in Milwaukee, Dahmer addressed a letter to Judge Gardner, stating: 'I have always believed a man should be willing to assume responsibility for the mistakes he makes in life. The world has enough misery in it without my adding more to it. Sir, I assure you that it will never happen again. That is why, Judge Gardner, I am requesting a sentence modification.'

Dahmer was released from the Correctional Center two months early – on 2 March 1990. Eleven days later, he moved into the Oxford Apartments, and began the murder spree that ended with his arrest eighteen months later. In that time he killed twelve more young men.

Dahmer's career of slaughter almost came to an abrupt end on 8 July 1990; it was on that day that he made the mistake of varying his method. He approached a 15-year-old Hispanic boy outside a gay bar, and offered him $200 to pose for nude photographs. The boy returned to room 213 and removed his clothes. But instead of offering him the usual drugged drink, Dahmer picked up a rubber mallet and hit him on the head. It failed to knock him unconscious, and the boy fought back as Dahmer tried to strangle him. Somehow, the boy succeeded in calming his attacker. And, incredibly, Dahmer allowed him to go, even calling a taxi.

The boy had promised not to notify the police. But when he was taken to hospital for treatment, he broke his promise. For a few moments, Dahmer's future hung in the balance. But when the boy begged them not to allow his foster parents to find out that he was homosexual, the police decided to do nothing about it.

When he saw his probation officer, Donna Chester, the next day, Dahmer looked depressed and unshaven. He said he had money problems and was thinking of suicide. She wanted to know how he could have money problems when he was earning $1,500 a month, and his apartment cost less than $300 a month. He muttered something about hospital bills. And during the whole of the next month, Dahmer continued to complain of depression and stomach pains, and to talk about jumping off a high building. Donna Chester suggested that he ought to find himself another apartment in a less run-down area. She was unaware that Dahmer was an addict who now urgently needed a fix of his favourite drug: murder.

It happened a few weeks later, on 3 September 1990. In front of a bookstore on twenty-seventh, Dahmer picked up a young black dancer named Ernest Miller, who was home from Chicago, where he intended to start training at a dance school in the autumn. They had sex in Apartment 213, then Dahmer offered him a drugged drink, and watched him sink into oblivion. Perhaps because he had not killed for three months, Dahmer's craving for violence and its nauseating aftermath was stronger than usual. Instead of strangling his victim, Dahmer cut his throat. He decided that he wanted to keep the skeleton, so after cutting the flesh from the bones, and dissolving most of it in acid, he bleached the skeleton with acid. He also kept the biceps, which he put in the freezer.

Neighbours were beginning to notice the smell off decaying flesh; some of them knocked on Dahmer's door to ask about it. Dahmer would explain politely that his fridge was broken and that he was waiting to get it fixed.

On 25 March, there occurred an event that psychiatrists believe may be responsible for the final spate of multiple murder. It was on that day that Dahmer's mother Joyce contacted him for the first time in five years. Joyce Dahmer – now Flint – was working as a AIDS cousellor in Freso, California, and it may have been her contact with homosexuals that led her to telephone her son. She spoke openly about his homosexuality – for the first time – and told him she loved him. The call was a good idea – or would have been if she had made it a few years earlier.

But Dahmer was nearing the end of his tether, and even drink could not anaesthetize him for long. Neighbours kept complaining about the smell, and he solved this by buying a 57 gallon drum of concentrated hydrochloric acid, and disposing of some of the body parts that were causing the trouble. All this meant he was frequently late for work, or even absent. On 15 July 1991, the Ambrosia Chocolate Company finally grew tired of his erratic behaviour and fired him.

His reaction was typical. The same day he picked up a 24-year-old black named Oliver Lacy, took him back to his apartment, and gave him a drugged drink. After strangling him, he sodomized the body.

But the murder spree was almost over. Four days later, the head of the final victim joined the others in the freezer. He was 25-year-old Joseph Bradeholt, an out-of-work black who was hoping to move from Minnesota to Milwaukee with his wife and two children. But he accepted Dahmer's offer of money for photographs, and willingly joined in oral sex in Room 213. After that, he was drugged, strangled and dismembered. His body was placed in the barrel of acid, which was swiftly turning into a black, sticky mess.

That Dahmer's luck finally ran out may have been due to the carelessness that leads to the downfall of so many multiple murderers. The last intended victim, Tracy Edwards, was a slightly built man, and should have succumbed to the drug like all the others. For some reason, he failed to do so; it seems most likely that Dahmer failed to administer a large enough dose. Equally puzzling is the fact that, having seen that the drug had failed to work, he allowed Edwards to live, and spent two hours watching a video with him. Was the homicidal impulse finally burning itself out? Dahmer knew that if he failed to kill Tracy Edwards, he would be caught; yet, with a large knife in his hand, he allowed him to escape from the apartment.

It sounds as if he recognized that the time had come to try to throw off the burden of guilt and rejoin the human race.

On 27 January 1992, Wisconsin's worst mass murderer came to trial in Milwaukee before Judge Lawrence Gram, entering a plea of guilty but insane. On 15 February, the jury rejected this plea and found Dahmer guilty of the fifteen murders with which he had been charged. He was sentenced to fifteen terms of life imprisonment.

On 14 April 1992, just two months after Dahmer was sentenced, another trial – this time in Russia – drew the attention of the world's press. The accused was a 48-year-old grandfather named Andrei Chikatilo, and he was charged with the murders of fifty-three women and children.

On 24 December 1978, the mutilated body of 9-year-old Lena Zakotnova was found in the Grushevka River where it flows through the Soviet mining city of Shakhti. It had been tied in a sack and dumped in the water some forty-eight hours before its discovery. She had been sexually assaulted and partially throttled, and her lower torso had been ripped open by multiple knife wounds.

Lena was last seen after leaving school on the afternoon of her death. A woman named Burenkova reported seeing a girl of Lena's description talking to a middle-aged man at a nearby tram stop, and they walked away together.

The Shakhti police soon arrested a suspect. Aleksandr Kravchenko had been in prison for a similar murder in the Crimea. He had been too young to be executed, so served six years of a ten-year sentence. He had been a prime suspect from the beginning of the investigation and when he was caught attempting a burglary the police decided to charge him with the murder.

Unconcerned at the fact that Kravchenko was only twenty-five, not 'middle-aged,' the Shakhti police soon extracted a confession. In the dock Kravchenko insisted that it had been beaten out of him, but this carried little weight with the judge (Soviet trials had no juries; a judge both decided guilt and passed sentence). Kravchenko was found guilty and sentenced to fifteen years in a labour camp.

There was a public outcry at the leniency of the sentence, and the prosecution, as allowed in Soviet law, appealed to increase it to death. A new judge agreed and Kravchenko was executed by a single shot in the back of the head in 1984. By that time the real killer of Lena Zakotnova had murdered at least sixteen other women and children.

Born in the Ukrainian farm village of Yablochnoye on 6 October, 1936, Andrei Romanovich Chikatilo was soon well acquainted with death. Stalin, in his drive to communize the peasantry, had reduced the Ukraine to a chaos of starvation and fear. In his first ten years, Chikatilo witnessed as much state-condoned brutality and killing as any soldier.

When he was 5 years old, Chikatilo's mother told him about the disappearance of one of his cousins, seven years previously, and that she believed he been kidnapped and eaten. The gruesome story made a deep impression on Chikatilo. For years afterwards, he later admitted, he would brood on the story and recreate his cousin's sufferings in his imagination. There can be no doubt that this strongly influenced his sexual development.

Chikatilo's father was called up early in the Second World War and did not return until after the Nazi defeat. But his father's return brought little comfort for the family. Roman Chikatilo had been captured by the Germans and the paranoid Stalin considered returning prisoners of war as virtual traitors to communism. Roman Chikatilo found that he had to tread carefully to avoid the suspicions of the secret police – very little stood between him and a firing squad.

Oddly enough, 10-year-old Andrei Chikatilo agreed with Joseph Stalin and was deeply ashamed of his father. He was a devout communist and his father's survival was a constant source of humiliation. He found relief by escaping into the world of literature.

He was fascinated by a novel called *Molodaya Gvardiya* or *The Young Guard* which concerned the heroic exploits of a group of young Russian partisans fighting the Germans in the vast Soviet forests and eventually dying to a man, proclaiming loyalty to Stalin. A predictably bloody tale, it also contained several scenes in which prisoners were tortured for information. This positive, even heroic depiction of torture in isolated woodland made a deep impression on the child.

At school Chikatilo had few friends and was painfully shy. He was nick-named *Baba* – meaning woman – because he had chubby breasts and lived in terror that his chronic bed-wetting and short-sightedness would be discovered by his classmates. His weak sight was something of an obsession with him and it was not until he was 30 that he eventually obtained a pair of glasses, so keen was he to conceal the defect.

As he grew into his teens, his chubbiness turned to size and strength – his new nick name was 'Andrei Sila' meaning Andrew the Strong. Classmates remembered him as a voracious reader with a prodigious memory. At 16 he became editor of the school newspaper and was appointed as student agitator for political information; a post which required him to read out and explain the articles in *Pravda* and other Party news organs. Even so, his fervour was restricted to politics. He found it almost impossible to communicate socially, especially with the opposite sex.

At 18, he applied for a place in Moscow University to study Law. He was humiliated when he failed the entrance exams and blamed his father's war record. This was typical of Chikatilo; all his life he would blame his failures on others.

Overcoming his shyness with women he attempted several relationships, but they all failed. His major problem was a conviction that he was impotent. Like a lot of teenage boys, he was so scared during his first attempts at sex that he failed to achieve an erection. As the years went on he became convinced that he was incapable of a normal sex life. Addicted to solitary masturbation, he depaired of ever having a happy sex life.

It was during his national service that he first experienced orgasm with a girl, and that was because she suddenly decided that things were going too far and tried to break his hold on her. She had no chance against his abnormal strength and he was surprised at the sexual passion her struggles aroused in him. He held her for only a few moments before releasing her unharmed, but had already ejaculated into his trousers. Thinking about it afterwards he realized that it was her fear and his power over her that had excited him so much. He had started to find sex and violence a stimulating concoction.

In the years following his national service he moved out of the Ukraine, east to Russia, where job prospects and the standard of living were better. He found work as a telephone engineer and a room in Rodionovo-Nesvetayevsky, a small town just north of the large industrial city of Rostov. A short while afterwards his mother, father and sister came to live with him in this comparative luxury. His younger sister, Tatyana, was worried that he was not married at 27 and after several failed matchmaking attempts, introduced him to a 24-year-old girl called Fayina. Chikatilo was as shy as usual, but Fayina found this attractive. Things went well with the courtship and they were married in 1963.

He still thought of himself as impotent and made embarrassed excuses on their wedding night. A week later Fayina persuaded him to try again and, with some coaxing, the marriage was consummated. Even so, Chikatilo showed no enthusiasm for sex. His dammed sexual drives were by then pushing him in other, more unwholesome directions.

In 1971, he passed a correspondence degree course in Russian philology and literature from the Rostov university. With the new qualification, the 35-year-old Chikatilo embarked upon a fresh career as a teacher. He found that he lacked all aptitude for the work. His shyness encouraged the pupils either to ignore his presence or openly to mock him. Other members of staff disliked his odd manner and his tendency to self-pity, so he was virtually shunned by all. Yet he soon found himself enjoying the work as his sexual fantasies began to centre around children.

Over the next seven years Chikatilo committed numerous indecent assaults on his pupils. Apart from voyeurism, these included surreptitious gropings, excessive beatings and, on one occasion, mouthing the genitals of a sleeping boy in a school dormitory. His sexual drive to dominate and control had centred on children as the easiest target and, as time went on, he developed a taste for fantasizing about sadism.

The oddest part of the situation was the inaction of the authorities. Chikatilo was forced to resign from several teaching jobs for his behaviour, but his record remained spotless each time. In the Soviet teaching system the failure of one teacher reflected on his colleagues and superiors as well, so they simply passed him on and pretended that nothing had happened.

In 1978, the Chikatilos and their two children moved to the town of Shakhti. Fayina had heard the rumours of his sexual misdemeanours, but had chosen to ignore them. He behaved quite normally towards their own son and daughter, aged 9 and 11, and she was unable to believe that a man who could barely produce one erection a month could marshal the sexual energy to be a pervert.

Chikatilo now bought an old shack in the slum end of town and began to invite down-and-out young women back with offers of food and vodka. There he would request them to perform sexual acts – notably fellatio – that he would never have requested from his strait-laced wife. He would often be unable to achieve erection, but this seemed to matter less with the kind of derelicts who accepted his invitation. Yet his real interest remained pre-pubescent children, and on 22 December 1978, he persuaded one to follow him to his shack.

Lena Zakotnova had caught his eye as soon as he saw her waiting at the tram stop. He had sidled up to her and started chatting. She soon revealed to the grandfatherly stranger that she desperately needed to go to the toilet and he persuaded her to follow him to his shack.

Once through the door he dropped his kindly facade and started to tear at her clothes. Muffling her screams by choking her with his forearm he blindfolded her with her scarf and tried to rape her. Once again he failed to achieve an erection, but ejaculated anyway. In an ecstasy he pushed his semen into her with his fingers and ruptured her hymen. The sight of the blood caused him to orgasm again and filled him with sexual excitement. Pulling out a pocket knife he stabbed at her repeatedly, tearing open her whole lower torso. When he returned to his senses he felt terrified – he knew he would face the death sentence if caught. Wrapping the corpse in a few sacks he crept outside, crossed the street and a stretch of wasteland and dropped Lena in the fast flowing Grushevka River. The autopsy later showed that she was still alive when she hit the water.

After watching the bundle float away, Chikatilo went home. But in his agitation he forgot to turn off the light in the shack. His neighbours on the slum street had not seen the pair arrive or heard Lena's muffled screams. However, one of them did note that Chikatilo's light had been left on all night and mentioned it to a policeman asking questions from door to door. Chikatilo was called in for questioning.

The police soon guessed that the sullen teacher was using the shack for assignations, but this was not incriminating in itself. What interested them was the fact that some very young girls had been seen entering and leaving with Chikatilo, and a few enquiries at his old schools had revealed his taste for paedophilia.

He was called in for questioning nine times in all. Then the police transferred their attention to Kravchenko. They did not even examine the shack for traces of blood.

Chikatilo continued teaching until 1981, when staff cuts made him redundant. On 3 September 1981, six months after losing his job, he killed again.

He was now working as a supply clerk for a local industrial conglomerate. This involved travelling around, often to the other side of the country, to obtain the necessary parts and supplies to run the Shakhti factory.

It would undoubtedly have been better if Chikatilo had remained a schoolteacher. In a restricted environment his opportunities would have been confined. The new job allowed him to travel, and spend as much time as he liked doing it. Now he was free to hunt as he willed.

He met Larisa Tkachenko at a bus stop outside the Rostov public library. She was a 17-year-old absentee from boarding school who was used to exchanging the odd fling for a nice meal and a drink or two. Her usual dates were young soldiers, but when the middle-aged man asked if she wanted to go to a local recreation area she agreed without much hesitation.

After a short walk they found themselves on a gravel path leading through a deserted stretch of woodland. Away from possible onlookers Chikatilo could not keep his hands off her any longer. He threw her down and started to tear at her trousers. Although she almost certainly expected to have sex with him, this was too frightening for her and she started to fight back. His already overstretched self-control snapped and he bludgeoned her with his heavy fists in an ecstasy of sado-sexual release. To stifle her cries he rammed earth into her mouth then choked her to death. He bit off one of her nipples as he ejaculated over the corpse.

This time he did not come back to earth with a jolt as he had after killing Lena Zakotnova. He ran around the corpse waving her clothes and howling with joy. He later said 'I felt like a partisan', a reference to his childhood favourite *The Young Guard*. After half an hour he calmed down, covered Larisa's corpse with some branches and hid her clothes. She was found the next day, but no clues to the identity of the killer were discovered.

The murder of Lena Zakotnova had made Chikatilo aware of the basic nature of his desires; the murder of Larisa Tkachenko made him aware that he was destined to go on killing.

All serial killers seem to cross this mental Rubicon. The initial horror and guilt gives way to an addiction to hunting that transcends all social and moral boundaries. They never seem to break the habit; once hooked, they continue until they are caught or die.

Ten months later, on 12 June 1982, Chikatilo killed again. Thirteen-year-old Lyuba Biryuk left her home in the little settlement of Zaplavskaya to get some shopping from the nearby village of Donskoi Posyulok. She was last seen alive waiting at a local bus stop, but apparently decided to walk home in the warm sunshine. Chikatilo fell in step with her and started a conversation. Children always found his manner reassuring, but as soon as they came to a secluded stretch of path he attacked and tried to rape her. Failing as usual, he pulled a knife from his pocket and stabbed wildly at her until her struggles and screams ceased. He covered her body, hid her clothes and shopping in the undergrowth and escaped unobserved. She was found two weeks later. In the heat of the southern Russian summer she had decayed to no more than a skeleton.

Chikatilo killed six more times that year: once in July, twice in August, twice in September and once in December. Four of these were girls ranging in age from 10 to 19 but the other two were boys, aged 15 and 9. This bisexual choice of victims would confuse the police investigation later on. Indeed, in the early stages of linking the murders some of the boys were officially classified as girls (despite their male names) because officers could not believe the killer could be attracted to both sexes.

In fact, as any criminal psychologist could have told them, the sex of the victims was almost immaterial. Chikatilo wanted to be in total control of his victims. Boys served his purpose as well as girls. His need to revenge himself on a world he hated and resented pushed him further from the norm, and killing boys was a way of being even more wicked.

Most of these victims were killed in the Rostov region, but two he killed on his business trips to other republics. Even when the majority of his victims had been linked into one investigation, these, and others killed outside the Rostov district, were not connected until Chikatilo himself confessed to them. A police force with more experience of serial crime would have quickly noted a linking pattern in the murders. All the victims were children or teenagers who had somehow been lured to secluded, usually wooded areas. They had been savagely attacked, sexually assaulted and usually butchered with a long bladed knife. Most strikingly, in almost every case, wounds were found around the eyes of the victim.

After killing a 10-year-old girl called Olya Stalmachenok on 11 December 1982, Chikatilo lay low once again. His next murder did not take place until mid-June 1983: a 15-year-old Armenian girl called Laura Sarkisyan. Her body was never found and the murder only came to light when Chikatilo confessed years later.

The next month he met a 13-year-old girl in the Rostov train station. He recognized her as Ira Dunenkova, the little sister of one of his casual girlfriends from teaching days. It was obviously a risk to approach somebody who could – even tenuously – be linked to himself, but from her ragged clothes he quickly realized that she had become one of the innumerable vagrants than haunted every Soviet city, despite their official non-existence. Taking a chance that she might not be missed for some time, if ever, he persuaded her to go for a walk with him in the nearby stretch of heath called Aviators' Park. Reaching a quiet spot he tried to have sex with her and, failing to get an erection, he used a more reliable instrument; a kitchen knife.

Chikatilo killed three more times that summer. On uncertain dates he killed Lyuda Kutsyuba, aged 24 and a woman aged between 18 and 25 whose identity has not been discovered. On 8 August he persuaded 7-year-old Igor Gudkov to follow him to Aviators' Park and then butchered him.

This brought his number of victims to fourteen, of which about half had been discovered by the police. Even for an area with a high – if unofficial – crime rate like Rostov, over half-a-dozen murdered children was enough to catch the attention of the central police authority in Moscow. A team of investigators was sent to assess the situation in September 1983. Their report was highly critical of the inept handling of the murders by the local police and concluded that six victims were definitely the work of one sexual deviant. The report was accepted and its suggestions quickly implemented, but, as was typical of the Soviet system, the public were not warned of the danger.

Shielded by public ignorance, Chikatilo killed three more people before the turn of the year: a 22-year-old woman called Valya Chuchulina and Vera Shevkun, a prostitute aged 19; and finally, on 27 December, a 14-year-old boy called Sergei Markov, his seventeenth victim.

Nineteen-eighty-four was to prove the most terrible year in Chikatilo's murderous career. Between January and September he murdered fifteen women and children.

Shortly after the New Year, he was accused of stealing two rolls of linoleum from his factory and was sacked, but he soon found another supply clerk job in the middle of the teeming city of Rostov.

Chikatilo's method of hunting victims was time-consuming and, fortunately, rarely successful. He would hang around train stations, bus stops, airports and other public places, and would approach potential victims and strike up an innocuous conversation.

If they warmed to him he would offer them the bait. To children he would propose going to his home to watch videos (then and now a rare luxury in Russia). He might also make the same suggestion to young adults, or he might offer to take them, via a little known short-cut, to some place they wanted to go. To vagrants or prostitutes he would simply offer vodka, food or money for sex in the woods.

Living near Rostov it had proved difficult to spend so much time hunting. Now, as he travelled, it was suddenly easier.

On 9 January, he killed 17-year-old Natalya Shalapinina in Aviators' Park. Then on 21 February he killed a 44-year-old tramp called Marta Ryabyenko in almost exactly the same spot. On 24 March Chikatilo killed a 10-year-old girl, Dima Ptashnikov, just outside the town of Novoshakhtinsk. Nearby, police found a footprint in a patch of mud which they were convinced belonged to the murderer. It was little enough, but it was their first solid piece of forensic evidence, and it improved the flagging morale of the investigators.

In May 1984, Chikatilo took his greatest risk ever. Haunting the Rostov train station he bumped into an ex-girlfriend, Tanya Petrosyan, a 32-year-old divorcee whom he had not seen for six years. He invited her for a picnic, but she replied that she had no time then. Common sense dictated that he should have left it at that. If he made a date for a later time she might tell other people about it. Even so, he took her address.

A few days later he arrived at Tanya's house carrying a new doll for her 11-year-old daughter. He was also carrying a knife and a hammer. He later insisted that he had only wanted sex from Tanya, but he now carried his killing tools as a matter of habit. He found himself being introduced to Tanya's elderly mother, and was told that Sveta, the daughter, would have to go with them on the picnic.

They took a train to a nearby stretch of woodland. As Sveta played with her doll a little way off, Chikatilo and Tanya undressed and started to have oral sex. After a while Chikatilo tried to enter Tanya, but failed. It was then that she made the greatest mistake of her life; she jeered at his inability. Seeing red, he grabbed the knife from his pocket and drove it into the side of her head. Then he beat her to a pulp with the hammer.

Hearing her mother's dying screams, Sveta tried to run away, but Chikatilo soon caught her. He knocked her down and then killed her with dozens of blows from the knife and hammer. The attack was so furious that he completely beheaded the little girl. Afterwards he dressed himself and caught the train home.

Tanya's mother was old and mentally subnormal. She waited for three days before contacting the police, and even then could not remember what the stranger had looked like. Once again, his luck had held.

He had now killed twenty-two, and over the next four months this rose to thirty-two. Most were in the Rostov area, but three he killed on business trips; two in Tashkent and one in Moscow. As usual his targets were of both sexes, aged between 11 and 24. He would have doubtless killed more that year, but at last his luck seemed to run out. He was arrested on suspicion of being the Rostov serial killer on 14 September 1984.

Inspector Aleksandr Zanasovski had questioned Chikatilo for acting suspiciously at the Rostov train station two weeks previously. On the evening of 13 September he spotted him again, this time across the square at the Rostov bus station. Again he noted that Chikatilo was trying to strike up conversations with young people with almost manic persistence.

Zanasovski followed Chikatilo until four the next morning. In that time they travelled backwards and forwards on various forms of public transport with no destination ever becoming apparent. Eventually, when Chikatilo appeared to receive oral sex from a young lady on a public bench, the Inspector arrested him. In the briefcase that the suspect had carried all night the police found a jar of vaseline, a length of rope and a kitchen knife with an eight-inch blade.

Yet still Chikatilo's incredible luck held. When the forensic department tested his blood, the case fell apart.

The semen found on and around the victims proved to belong to a 'secreter'; that is, a man who secretes minute amounts of blood into his spittle and semen. The tests had shown the killer to have 'AB' blood – Chikatilo was type 'A'.

Despite this major setback, the investigators found it hard to believe that he was innocent. Under Soviet law they could only hold a suspect for a maximum of ten days without preferring charges, but they needed more time to build a case against him. They checked his previous record, learned about the theft of the two rolls of linoleum and booked him on that.

On 12 December 1984, Chikatilo was found guilty by the people's Court of the crime of Theft of State Property, and sentenced to a year of correctional labour. However, since he had already spent three months in jail, the judge waived the sentence.

On 1 August 1985, Chikatilo went back to killing. The victim was 18-year-old Natalya Pokhlistova, a mentally subnormal transient he met during a business trip to Moscow. They went off to a deserted spot and tried to have sex. When he failed he mutilated her with a knife then strangled her.

Chikatilo killed again that month. On 27 August 1986, he murdered Irina Gulyayeva. Like his last victim, she was an 18-year-old, mentally subnormal vagrant. He met her in Shakhti – the place where he killed for the very first time – and butchered her in the nearby woods. She was his thirty-fourth victim, and the last for a year and nine months.

On 16 May 1987, Chikatilo killed a 13-year-old boy called Oleg Makarenkov in Siberia.

He killed twice more in 1987, both in areas far from Rostov. The thirty-sixth victim was a 12-year-old boy called Ivan Bilovetski, killed in Chikatilo's native Ukraine on 29 July. The thirty-seventh was Yura Tereshonok, aged 16, outside Leningrad on 15 September.

Once again, he ceased killing for the winter months, perhaps because it was harder to get people to accompany him into snowbound woods. Some time in April 1988, he killed an unidentified woman in the Krasny region. Then, on 14 May, he butchered 9-year-old Lyosha Voronko near the Ilovaisk train station in the Ukraine. His last victim that year, bringing the sum total to forty was 15-year-old Zhenya Muratov, on 14 July.

The following year, on 1 March 1989, he killed indoors for the second time. Tatyana Ryzhova, a 15-year-old runaway, was induced to follow Chikatilo to an apartment that belonged to his daughter, Ludmila. The place had been empty since Ludmila had divorced her husband and moved in with her parents. Chikatilo had the job of swapping it for two smaller apartments ('*swapping*' was the typical method of property dealing in the Soviet Union). It was a task he was in no hurry to complete since it provided the perfect place to bring prostitutes.

He gave the girl food and vodka, and tried to have sex with her. Soon she became restless and started to shout. Chikatilo tried to quiet her, but when she started to scream, he silenced her by stabbing her in the mouth. Some of the neighbours heard Tatyana's screams, but did nothing; wife-beating is a common occurrence in Russia.

When Chikatilo had ceased to mutilate Tatyana he realized his danger. Somehow he had to get her body out of the apartment without being seen. He was in a populated area and for all he knew the police might already be on their way.

He solved the problem by cutting off her head and legs and wrapping them in her clothes. Then he mopped the bloody floor and went out to steal a sled to remove the body. Finding one nearby, he set off into the night with Tatyana's remains firmly tied down.

All seemed to be going well until he tried to pull the sled over a rail-crossing and it stuck due to the thin snow cover. To his horror he saw a stranger walking towards him and wondered if he should either run or try to kill the witness. The man pulled level with him and, without a word, helped Chikatilo lift the burdened sled across the tracks, then went on his way. Tatyana's mutilated body was found stuffed into some nearby pipes on 9 March.

Chikatilo killed four more times that year. On 11 May he murdered 8-year-old Sasha Dyakonov in Rostov. Travelling to the Vladimir region to the north-east he killed 10-year-old Lyosha Moiseyev on 11 May. In mid-August he killed Yelena Varga, aged 19, on another business trip, this time to the Rodionovo-Nesvetayevski region. Finally, he murdered Alyosha Khobotov on 28 August.

He met 10-year-old Khobotov outside a video salon (a modern-day Russian equivalent of a movie house) in the town of Shakhti. The boy happily told him that he preferred horror movies above all others. Chikatilo replied that he owned a video machine and a large collection of horror videos. Alyosha jumped at his offer to view them.

Chikatilo led his victim through the local graveyard to a quiet spot where a shovel stood by an open grave. He had dug the trench himself some time earlier in a fit of suicidal depression. Now, in a different mood, he bit out Alyosha's tongue, cut off his genitals and threw him into the pit. Then he filled in the grave.

On 14 January 1990, he murdered 11-year-old Andrei

Kravchenko. As with the last victim, he picked up Andrei outside the Shakhti video salon by offering to show him horror movies. The following 7 March, he persuaded a 10-year-old boy called Yaroslav Makarovto to follow him to a party. He led him into the Rostov Botanical Gardens, then molested and butchered him. His next victim was Lyubov Zuyeva, a 31-year-old mentally handicapped woman whom he met on a train to Shakhti sometime in April. He persuaded her to have sex with him in the woods, then stabbed her.

On 28th July, he persuaded 13-year-old Vitya Petrov, waiting for a late train with his family at Rostov Station, to follow him to the Botanical Gardens. Once out of the sight of others, he stabbed the boy to death. Strangely enough, Chikatilo had tried to pick up Vitya's younger brother, Sasha, only a few hours earlier, but had been scolded away by the boys' mother. Chikatilo's fiftieth victim was 11-year-old Ivan Fomin, killed on a river beach in Novcherkassk on 14 August. The corpse was found three days later.

Chikatilo temporarily now decided to make a journey to Moscow. For some months he had been involved in a petty dispute with some Assyrian builders over garages that had been built next to his son's house, blocking the light. Since his son was away doing his national service, Chikatilo had made strenuous complaints via official channels, but nothing had happened.

Growing increasingly paranoid, Chikatilo decided that some sort of illegal conspiracy was being directed against him, and in Moscow demanded audiences with both President Gorbachev and parliamentary head Anatoly Lukyanov. Needless to say he was granted neither, but stayed on for a few days in the 'tent city' of protesters that had steadily grown outside the Kremlin since the introduction of glasnost. After that he had to return to work, so he packed up his tent and protest sign and went back to Rostov.

On 17 October 1990, he met a mentally handicapped 16-year-old called Vadim Gromov on the Novocherkassk train. He persuaded the young man to get off the train with him at the wooded station of Donleskhoz by offering to take him to a party. Gromov's body was found just over two weeks later, by which time Chikatilo had murdered again. This time the victim was 16-year-old Vitya Tishchenko, who disappeared after buying train tickets from the Shakhti station on the last day of October. He was found, mutilated, three days later.

Oddly enough, the investigators were beginning to feel more optimistic. For most of the inquiry, morale had been abysmal. They had always been undermanned and badly organized, and it had been easy for Chikatilo to play games with them. He would kill in Rostov, and when the police concentrated their manpower in that area, he would kill in Shakhti or Novocherkassk, throwing them into confusion.

Now, the killer was becoming careless. The woman in the Shakhti ticket office reported seeing a tall middle-aged man in dark glasses hanging around when Tishchenko bought the tickets. Her teenage daughter added that she had seen the same man trying to pick up a boy several days before. With this rough description and increased manpower, the investigation at last seemed to have a chance. If only the killer would return to one of his known murder locations they might get him before he murdered again.

This was exactly what Chikatilo did, but, once again, the police missed him. His fifty-third victim was a 22-year-old girl called Sveta Korostik, whom he killed in the woods outside Donleskhoz train station. Trying to double-guess the killer, only one policeman was posted there to check the identities of any suspicious persons alighting on the platform.

Sveta's body was found a week later. But when Sergeant Igor Rybakov, the officer on duty at the station on the day of Sveta's murder, was questioned, an amazing fact emerged. He had interviewed a suspicious-looking man that day and had sent a report in, but, for some reason, it had not been processed.

Rybakov reported that at 4 p.m. on 6 October, he had observed a large, mud-spattered, middle-aged man emerge from the forest and wash his hands in the dribble of water flowing from the platform fire hydrant. The sergeant would probably have ignored him, taking him for one of the many mushroom pickers that frequented the station, but noticed that he was wearing a grey suit, an odd attire for rain-soaked woods. He asked for identification, and was handed a passport that bore the name Andrei Romanovich Chikatilo. The man explained that he had been visiting a friend. The officer studied Chikatilo and noticed that his hand was bandaged and there was a streak of red liquid on his cheek. Nevertheless, he allowed him to board a train and leave.

Chikatilo's name was checked and the investigators learned of the Lena Zakotnova questioning, the paedophilia and the 1984 arrest. But for the fact that his blood group was wrong he would have been a prime suspect. It was at this point that somebody remembered a circular that had been sent around to all Soviet police departments. Japanese scientists had found that in one case in a million, the blood type secreted into the semen and the actual blood type can be different. It was just possible that Chikatilo might be such a person.

Chikatilo was placed under 24-hour surveillance, but the fear that he might commit another murder or commit suicide led the investigators to arrest him on 20 November 1990. He offered no resistance and came quietly. His semen type was tested and proved to be 'AB'; the same as that found on the bodies of the victims.

Now certain they had the right man, the police wanted a confession. After days of relentless questioning, Chikatilo slowly began to admit the truth. He started by confessing to molesting children while he had been a schoolteacher, but eventually described fifty-five sex murders, including that of Lena Zakotnova. The stunned police, who had only linked thirty-six victims to the Rostov murderer, had now to recognize that they had executed an innocent man.

Chikatilo was finally charged with the brutal murder of fifty-three women and children. Shortly before he confessed he said to the interviewing officer, 'Everything I have done makes me tremble . . . I feel only gratitude to the investigating bodies that they captured me.'

Over the next year and a half, Chikatilo was studied by doctors and criminologists. During that time he led officers to undiscovered bodies and, with a shop dummy and a stage knife, acted out how he had killed each victim.

His habits had become fixed over the years. For example, he would usually bite off the victim's tongue and nipples. Wounds on or around the eyes were almost invariable. He would cut or bite off the boys' penises and scrotums and throw them away like so much rubbish. With the girls and women he would cut out the uterus and chew it manically as he stabbed at them. The psychiatrists ruled that this was not technically cannibalism, since he did not swallow human material, but was in fact motivated by the same impulse that makes people give love bites in the height of sexual passion. Chikatilo simply commented, 'I did not want to bite them so much as chew them. They were so beautiful and elastic.'

Chikatilo's wife was stunned when she was told of the reason for his arrest. She had thought he was being persecuted for protesting about the Assyrian garages and, at first, refused to believe that the man she had been married to for twenty-five years was a monster. He had always been a loving, if weak-willed father to their children and doted on their grandchildren. How could he have concealed over a decade of slaughter from her? Yet, when Chikatilo himself admitted the crimes to her face she was forced to accept the terrible truth. She cursed him and left, never to contact him again. For their part, the police believed that she had known nothing of her husband's activities and provided her with a change of identity and a home in another part of the country.

The trial opened on 14 April 1992. The shaven-headed Chikatilo raved and shouted from the cage that held and protected him from the angry public. At one point he even stripped off his clothes and waved his penis at the court shouting, 'Look at this useless thing! What do you think I could do with that?' His extreme behaviour might well have been motivated by the fact that his only hope of escaping execution was a successful insanity plea.

The defence tried to prove that Chikatilo was driven by an insane and undeniable need to kill and was not in control of his actions during the murders. They had little chance of convincing the judge, since Chikatilo clearly planned many of the killings, and had long dormant periods.

An attempt was made on Chikatilo's life during the trial. One day, as the court was being cleared, a young man whose 17-year-old sister had been killed by the defendant took a heavy metal ball from his pocket and hurled it through the bars of the cage. It just missed Chikatilo, smashing into the wall behind his head. The guard commander, seeing that the judge had not witnessed the incident, let the would-be assassin go.

On 14 October 1992, as Chikatilo received individual sentences for fifty-two murders, the court was filled with shrieks that often drowned the judge's voice. But at one point, Judge Akubzhanov showed unexpected agreement with one of Chikatilo's arguments, when he accepted that it was the refusal of the Soviet Union to acknowledge the level of crime that had contributed to Chikatilo's long immunity.

Sixteen months later, on 14 February 1994, Andrei Chikatilo was executed by a single shot in the back of the neck, fired from a small calibre Makarov pistol.

By comparison with Chikatilo's highly publicized homicides and confessions, the case of Arthur Shawcross, the 'Genesee River killer', received very little publicity. The reason may lie in his appearance; unlike Chikatilo – whose staring eyes made him *look* like a monster – Shawcross was a commonplace little man with a large paunch and balding head who looked much older than his forty-four years. Yet, with his penchant for sadism and necrophilia, he was at least as dangerous as either Chikatilo or Dahmer.

The Genesee River flows through the small city of Rochester, in New York State. But it was 15 miles outside Rochester, at a bridge over Salmon Creek, that the body of the first victim, 'Dotsie' Blackburn, a known prostitute, was found on 24 March 1988. She had been strangled, and the killer had bitten a piece out of her genitals. The last time she had been seen alive was a month earlier, in the Rochester red-light district on Lake Avenue.

The second victim, Anna Steffen, vanished in late May. When her body was found, at the edge of the river, it was badly decomposed, but water in the lungs indicated that she had died of drowning.

It was more than a year later, in June 1989, that Dorothy Kneller, a homeless waitress in her late fifties, disappeared. When her body was found it was little more than a skeleton, and the skull was missing. Between then and the end of the year, seven more women vanished from the Rochester area. Only one of these, a retarded girl called June Stotts, was not a prostitute. Her body had been cut open and eviscerated, and her sexual organs wer missing.

The murder caused a panic in the red-light district, and prostitutes began to study potential customers with more care than ever before. Yet the killing continued. Agent Gregg

McCrary, of the FBI team at Quantico, correctly deduced that the killer looked so ordinary and harmless that he was almost invisible. When the local police told him they had arrested a transvestite who was driving a car, he told them: 'No, that's not the man you're looking for.' The killer, it seemed clear, was a driver, but the car would also be nondescript. Since most of the victims were in their late twenties, McCrary deduced that the killer was probably slightly older, in his early thirties. He would probably work in a menial job, and might well be a sportsman – this was deduced from the fact that so many victims had been found in or near the river, which the killer probably knew as a fisherman, and that June Stotts had been eviscerated as a hunter eviscerates game.

Most important, McCrary also suggested that the killer might be the kind of person who liked to return to the body, possibly even to have sex with it. This is why, in January 1990, a police helicopter began to fly over the Genesee River, looking for more victims from the air. At Salmon Creek bridge – where the first victim's body had been found – they spotted a body, almost under the bridge, encased in ice. And on the bridge just above it there was a parked car – a Chevrolet – and a man sitting with his legs out of the passenger door, where he could see the body, apparently masturbating. As the helicopter swooped down, the car drove away down Route 31 – towards the town of Spencerport. The helicopter followed, and saw the car turn into a municipal parking lot. A heavily built man got out and walked across to the Wedgewood Nursing Home on the other side of the street. The police radioed a police patrol car to go and park behind the Chevrolet.

The driver of the patrol car had no difficulty finding the person who had just entered the home. The grey-haired, paunchy man, who seemed completely unperturbed, offered his identity papers, which gave his name as Arthur J. Shawcross, with an address in nearby Rochester. He explained that his girlfriend Clara Neal – the owner of the car – worked in the home as a cook. He seemed to think he was being questioned because – according to his own account – he had been urinating into a bottle on the Salmon Creek Bridge.

Inspector Dennis Blythe found the prisoner co-operative. Shawcross raised no objections when Blythe had him photographed. But when the photograph was taken to a prostitute who had reported a curious encounter with a 'john' who could only obtain an erection when she 'played dead', she immediately picked out Shawcross from a group of other photographs.

A check on police records showed that Shawcross had been arrested for burglary as a teenager, later for arson, and had spent fifteen years in jail for child murder. He had killed – and mutilated – an 11-year-old boy, Jackie Blake, and raped and suffocated an 8-year-old girl, Karen Ann Hill. He had been tried only on the second count, and in 1972 sentenced to twenty-five years. He had been paroled after fifteen, and lived for a while in Binghamton, NY. But when neighbours there had learned of his conviction for child murder, they had virtually 'run him out of town'.

Shawcross was married to a girl named Rose Walley, but he also had a mistress, Clara Neal, whose hired car he was driving.

For the next two days, Shawcross showed himself highly co-operative with the police, but denied knowing anything about the murders. When shown a photograph of the ninth victim, Elizabeth Gibson, and told that he had been seen with her before her disappearance, he was silent. Finally Blythe asked quietly: 'I hope Clara wasn't involved in this?' Shawcross hung his head. 'No, I was the only one involved.'

Shawcross then talked in detail about the murders. He was also to talk about them to psychiatrist – and expert on serial murder – Joel Norris. But although Norris quotes these accounts without comment – in *The Genesee River Killer* – it is very obvious that Shawcross is constantly lying. He explained that he had killed Dotsie Blackburn after she began to give him a 'blow job', and bit his penis until the blood came.

Anna Steffen, the second victim, had been frolicking with Shawcross in the river when he gave her a playful shove and she fell on her side. She began screaming, saying she was pregnant and that she was going to call the police. He held her head under the water until she drowned.

The third victim, Dorothy Keller, was a friend of Shawcross and his wife. They had been spending the morning on an island in the river when – he explained – she threatened to tell his wife Rose that they were lovers. He had hit her with a piece of wood and broken her neck.

Patty Ives, the fourth victim, was removing his wallet from

his back pocket when he caught her. They quarrelled, and he strangled her while having anal intercourse.

The fifth victim, Frances Brown, died accidentally, according to Shawcross. He was 'deep throating her' while he performed cunnilingus, and his penis choked her to death.

June Stotts, the retarded girl, was also a friend of Shawcross and his wife. They went together to a spot beside the river, and she took off her pants and his trousers – after explaining that she was a virgin. After having sex, she began screaming: 'I'm going to tell,' until he silenced her by strangling her. Then he had more sex with the body, and 'cut her wide open in a straight line . . . from her neck to her asshole. Cut out her pussy and ate it. I was one sick person . . .'

Maria Welsh, the seventh victim, also tried to steal his wallet while they were having sex. 'I asked for my money back. She told me to go fuck myself.' So he strangled her.

Darlene Trippi, the eighth victim, declined to return his thirty dollars when he was unable to get an erection, and laughed unsympathetically, so he strangled her.

Elizabeth Gibson also tried to steal his wallet, then scratched his face with her fingernails.

June Cicero, victim number ten, made fun of him when he failed to get an erection, called him a faggot, and threatened to tell the cops (Shawcross did not specify what about). He strangled her, and three days later, returned to the body and cut out the vagina, which he 'ate'.

The eleventh victim was a black prostitute named Felicia Stephens. She put her head in the rear window of his car, and he closed it on her throat, suffocating her. This, he explained, was because black inmates had raped him in jail, and the murder was an act of self-preservation.

Jackie Blake, the first child victim, had also – according to Shawcross – provoked his own murder. The boy, he said, was following him, and when he told him to go home, started cursing and said he would go wherever he wanted to. So Shawcross, in a rage, hit him with his fist. Later, he agreed, he had returned to the corpse and cut off the genitals, which he ate. Medical examination suggested that the boy had been forced to undress and to run some distance beore he had been sexually assaulted and killed.

In the case of the 8-year-old Karen Hill, Shawcross explained that he was 'mad at her for going down to the river alone', He raped her, then, when she began to cry, suffocated her by stuffing grass and leaves into her mouth and up her nose.

What becomes very clear from Norris's book is that Shawcross lacked Chikatilo's honesty in describing his crimes and their motivation. This motivation – which was entirely sexual – sprang out of his low self-esteem. He had a highly dominant mother and a weak father, who allowed her to browbeat him; therefore he lacked a masculine 'role model' – in that sense, Shawcross's situation resembled that of Henry Lee Lucas.

Also – like Lucas – Shawcross suffered a number of head injuries as a child and young adult. Struck on the head with a stone in a local gang fight, he was knocked unconscious and needed several stitches. After that, he began to experience paralysis below the waist. At school he was knocked out on the sports field by a discus, which caused amnesia about the whole incident. As a member of a construction crew he was accidentally struck on the head with a sledgehammer, and was again unconscious for hours. And during infantry training in the army he fell off a ladder and landed on the back of his head, which resulted in concussion.

Dr Dorothy Lewis, a psychiatrist who examined Shawcross, also carried out a study of fourteen juveniles sentenced to death in America, and found that all fourteen had suffered severe head injuries during childhood. Once again – as in so many other cases – we note how often serial killers have suffered brain abnormalities due to head injuries.

Like so many other serial killers, Shawcross was also driven by powerful sexual urges from an early age – he claims he was introduced to oral sex before he was 9 by an aunt who was staying with them, and that he also practised oral sex on his sister, four years his junior. When his mother caught him masturbating – which was more than once – she threatened to cut off his penis with a butcher's knife. At fourteen, when he was leading a fairly active (oral) sex life with his sister, a cousin and a girl at school, he was offered a lift by a man who then raped him, suddenly introducing disturbing traumas into a sex life that had been relatively uninhibited.

According to Shawcross, it was Vietnam that turned him into a serial killer. There, in the jungle, he murdered two Vietnamese girls, raping and disembowelling one and roasting and partly eating the other's severed leg. On another occasion he opened fire on a group of Vietnamese who were sitting around a camp fire, killing (he estimates) twenty-six.

Once back in America, there were more humiliations from his overbearing mother, complex marital problems – and finally, the sex murders of Jackie Blake and Karen Hill. It is clear that Shawcross chose children because his ability to control them brought a sense of power accompanied by sexual potency. And later, when he began murdering prostitutes, he killed them before having sex with the bodies. He also returned to many of them to have sex later. He was considering having sex with the corpse of June Cicero – even though he had cut out her genitals – when the police helicopter saw him on the bridge.

Shawcross's defence was of insanity, but the jury were unconvinced; after a five-week trial they took only a few hours to find him guilty, and he was sentenced to a total of two hundred and fifty years in prison.

Looking back on the case, and on his 'profile' of Shawcross, Gregg McCrary was intrigued to realize that he had been wrong about only one detail. He had estimated Shawcross's age at around 30, when in fact he was in his mid-forties. Then the explanation dawned on him: Shawcross had spent fifteen years in prison. It was exactly as if his life was 'on pause' for that period.

With Dahmer and Shawcross behind bars, America quickly registered another 'first' in serial murder: the first female serial killer. This, of course, has to be immediately qualified by admitting that Anna Zwanziger and Gesina Gottfried were serial poisoners, and that Belle Gunness has a strong claim to be America's first female serial killer. But these three women all had specific motives for getting rid of individual victims: usually profit, sometimes revenge, occasionally a mere passing grudge. If by serial killer we mean someone who experiences a psychopathic need to kill, devoid of apparent motive, then Aileen Wuornos certainly qualifies as America's first female serial killer.

Twelve days before Christmas, 1989, two friends, scrap-metal hunting in the woods outside Ormond Beach, Florida, found a male corpse wrapped in an old carpet. The body had been there for about two weeks and was badly decomposed due to Florida's almost perpetually hot weather. However, the forensics lab managed to identify the victim as Richard Mallory, 51-year-old electrician from the town of Clearwater. The autopsy showed that he had been shot three times in the chest and once in the neck with a .22 calibre handgun.

Because of the proximity of Daytona Beach – a notorious crime black spot – and the overall lack of evidence, the investigating officers made only routine efforts to find the perpetrator. In all likelihood Mallory had been shot in a fight or a mugging, then hidden in the woods to avoid detection. Such crimes took place all the time around Daytona, and the chances of catching the killer were minimal.

The police were soon forced to reappraise the situation. Over the next twelve months, five more victims were discovered in almost identical circumstances. A 43-year-old construction worker, David Spears, was found on 1 June 1990, shot six times with a .22 handgun. Five days later the corpse of rodeo worker Charles Carskaddon, aged 40, was found covered with an electric blanket with nine bullet holes in him. A 50-year-old truck driver called Troy Burress was found on 4 August, killed by two .22 calibre bullets. On 12 September, a 56-year-old child abuse investigator, Charles Humphreys, was found shot six times in the torso and once in the head. Finally, on 19 November, the body of Walter Gino Antonio was found, shot dead by four .22 calibre bullets.

In each case the victim was a middle-aged, heterosexual male. They all appeared to have been killed in or near their cars, just off one of the state highways, and hidden in nearby scrub or woodland. Some were partially stripped, but no evidence of sexual or physical abuse could be found. Used prophylactics found near some of the bodies suggested that they had been involved in a sexual encounter before they were murdered.

In every case, money, valuables and the victim's vehicle had been stolen. The cars were generally found dumped shortly after the murder with the driver's seat pulled well forward, as if to allow a comparatively short person to reach the drive pedals.

When it was found that the same handgun was being used in each of the killings the police were forced to accept that they might have a serial killer on their hands; yet, disturbingly, the murders did not fit any known pattern. Why would a heterosexual serial murderer kill middle-aged men? On the other hand, if the killer was homosexual, why was there no evidence of sexual abuse?

It was the FBI's profiling unit that provided the startling answer: the killer was probably a woman. Predictably, media attention, which had been minimal, grew exponentially when this was revealed.

At least the Florida police started the investigation with a solid lead. Many serial killers steal from their victims, but usually for souvenir purposes only. The Florida Highway Killer was clearly stealing for profit. The money or valuables might be traced when she used or sold them.

As it turned out, the killer made an even more serious blunder. On 4 July 1990, she and her girlfriend skidded off the road in a car she had stolen from Peter Seims, a 65-year-old part-time missionary she had killed in early June, somewhere in southern Georgia. Witnesses told the police that they had seen the two women – one tall and blonde, the other a short, heavy-set brunette – abandon the damaged Pontiac Sunbird after removing the licence plates.

Police took detailed descriptions of the pair, but did not initially connect them with the highway killings. When it became clear that they were looking for a female killer they reviewed the Seims case and, since he was still missing, added him to the list. They also issued artist's impressions of the two women with the request for further information. It seemed the case was taking a new turn; they might have a *pair* of female murderers on their hands.

By December 1990, the police had two names to attach to the artist's sketches, thanks to tips from members of the public. The brunette was possibly one Tyria J. Moore, a 28-year-old occasional hotel maid, and the blonde could be her live-in lover, a 34-year-old prostitute who went under several names, one of them being Lee Wuornos.

Shortly afterwards, a check on a Daytona pawn shop revealed several items that had belonged to Richard Mallory. The pawn ticket that went with the belongings was made out to a Cammie Green, but the statutory thumbprint – that all Florida pawn tickets must carry – proved to be that of Wuornos.

The police arrested her outside the Last Resort bikers' bar on 9 January 1991. Shortly afterwards Tyria Moore was located at her sister's home in Pennsylvania. Strangely enough, the officers who went to pick her up did not arrest her. Instead they took her to a nearby motel. What took place there has yet to be made clear, but it has been alleged that a deal was struck and, possibly, a contract signed.

To understand these claims fully it is necessary to look at the influence of the media on the case, and vice versa. Movies like *The Silence of the Lambs*, *Thelma and Louise* and *Basic Instinct* had recently made serial killers and women outlaws two of the major money-spinners in the US entertainment industries. Even before Wuornos' arrest, up to fifteen movie companies were rumoured to be offering film contracts for the story. An obvious target for such money would be the investigating officers.

By the time of her apprehension the police had ascertained that Tyria Moore could not have been directly involved in at least some of the murders. There were various witnesses who could swear that she was working as a motel maid at the time of these killings. If she was not charged with any criminal offence, the movie contract lawyers could bid for her story without infringing the 'Son of Sam' law. This ruling made it illegal for convicted felons to profit directly from their crimes. Any money from movies, books, press interviews and so forth went to the victims, or their families if the victim were dead.

It has been alleged that in return for immunity from prosecution – and a cut of the profits – Moore signed a contract with officers Binegar, Henry and Munster to sell her story, in conjunction with theirs, to a movie company.

Tyria Moore – who admitted that 'Lee' Wuornos had told her about at least one of the murders – agreed to help the prosecution in return for immunity from the charge of 'accessory after the fact'. She led officers to the creek where Wuornos had thrown the .22 revolver used in the murders and, under police supervision, made eleven bugged phone calls to Lee in prison. In them she claimed that she was still undiscovered by the police and urged Lee to confess. Wuornos, who was plainly still in love with Moore, tried to soothe her and agreed to make a statement.

On 16 January 1991, Wuornos gave a three-hour video-taped confession in Volusia County Jail. In it she admitted to killing Mallory, Spears, Carskaddon, Seims, Burress, Humphreys and Antonio. She also gave details that only a witness to the murders could have known, apparently confirming her testimony.

Defending her actions, she insisted that she had only gone to the woods with them to trade sex for money. Each of the seven men had tried to attack or rape her, she said, forcing her to kill them in self-defence. When asked why she was confessing, she replied that she wanted to clear Tyria Moore's name.

It was decided that Wuornos was to be tried for each murder separately. Her defence counsels contended that it would be prejudicial to the trial if the jury heard evidence connected with the other murders, but at the first trial, for the killing of Richard Mallory, Judge Uriel Blount Jnr ruled otherwise. Florida's Williams Rule allowed evidence of similar offences to be revealed to a jury when the judge considered it important to the case. Of course, this seriously undermined Wuornos's claim that she had fired in self-defence. To believe that even a hard-working street prostitute had to kill seven men in the space of a single year stretched the jury's credulity to breaking-point.

For some reason the defence lawyers declined to call character witnesses for the defendant and, incredibly, did not inform the court that Richard Mallory had previously served a prison sentence for rape. It is possible that this was done deliberately to increase the chances for a claim of mis-trial at any ensuing appeal, but it left Lee Wuornos with hardly a leg to stand on in court. The jury found her guilty and Judge Blount sentenced her to the electric chair.

At a subsequent arraignment for three of the other murders, Wuornos pleaded unconditionally guilty and requested the death sentence without trial on the grounds that she wanted to 'be with Jesus' as soon as possible. It seems likely that this was an all-or-nothing gamble to win the judge's sympathy and receive life imprisonment instead of further death sentences. Wuornos became outraged when the judge complied with her request, shouting that she was being executed for being a rape victim. As she left the courtroom she loudly wished similar experiences on the judge's wife and children.

Lee Wuornos remains on Death Row as of this writing (May 1993). Before the Mallory trial, the 'Son of Sam' ruling remained in force; but, bizarrely enough, the US Supreme Court has recently overturned this law. It is now theoretically possible for a person to become a murderer with the ultimate goal of making money. Lee Wuornos, who has regularly complained that others were making a profit from her suffering, is now allegedly charging $25,000 for interviews and may sign as many movie contracts as she wishes.

Of course, it is arguable that the money will do her little good if she is on her way to the electric chair, but recent revelations concerning the officers who apprehended Tyria Moore may change even that. Following a bugged telephone call, in which he spoke of a movie deal, Major Dan Henry has resigned. The other officers, Sergeant Bruce Munster and Captain Steve Binegar, have been transferred from the Criminal Investigation Division. If it is found that the detectives *had* received money during the investigation, it is possible that all Lee Wuornos' death sentences might be overturned.

In conclusion, there is one important question to be considered: is Aileen Wuornos really a serial killer? If we discount her own defence, that she was a victim of circumstance, we are left with a tantalizing lack of motive for the murders.

Some have argued that she killed simply for financial profit: robbing a client, then shooting him to silence the only witness. To support this view it has been pointed out that she was clearly desperate not to lose her lover, Tyria Moore. On her own part, Moore appears to have been unwilling to work during the period of their relationship, but insisted on living in expensive motels. It seems clear that she knew how Wuornos was getting her money, but never objected to it – even after Lee had told her about the murder of Richard Mallory.

There may indeed be some truth in this theory, but it does not seem enough to explain the murder of seven men, none of whom would have appeared particularly well-off. A more likely theory is that Wuornos killed to revenge herself on men.

She was brought up by her grandparents when her real parents abandoned her as a baby. She has claimed that she was regularly beaten and occasionally sexually abused by her grandfather throughout her childhood. When she was 13, she was driven into the woods and raped by a middle-aged friend of her grandparents. From her early teens on it appears that she made money through prostitution and claims to have been beaten up and raped by clients quite often. She had several affairs and was married to a man fifty years her senior, but they all ended acrimoniously. It was only with Tyria Moore that she seemed to be reasonably happy.

On the available evidence, it seems likely that the first victim,

Richard Mallory, may well have raped Wuornos. Did this push her into serial crime?

Over 1990 she admits to having had hundreds of clients, all but seven of whom she apparently had no trouble with. On the other hand, the similarities between the murder victims and the circumstances of the rape when she was 13 are unmistakable.

Perhaps, like Arthur Shawcross, the 'Genesee River Killer', her trigger was resistance or threat. She may indeed be telling the truth when she insists that the men she killed threatened her and refused to pay after sex. This may have thrown her into a rage in which she – justifiably, in her view – shot them dead.

Whatever the reasons, she has caused a major stir in law enforcement circles. The possibility that she may be the start of a new trend in serial murder has disturbing ramifications. As Robert Ressler – former FBI agent and originator of the term 'serial killer' – said of the case: 'If Wuornos is said to be a serial killer we have to rewrite the rules.'

Since the conviction of Aileen Wuornos, Britain has also convicted its first female serial killer, 23-year-old children's nurse Beverley Allitt. She was arrested in May 1991, after tests on a blood sample from a five-month-old child suggested that someone had injected a large dose of the drug insulin, used in cases of diabetes. And since Paul Crampton was not diabetic, this had brought him very close to death.

Beverley Allitt had been hired as a nurse in mid-February 1991. She was lucky; she had failed many job interviews, and her records – if anyone had bothered to consult them – showed that she suffered from a personality disorder that involved a constant craving for attention. But the small Grantham and Kesteven General Hospital was short-staffed, and no one had replied to their advertisements for nurses. So Beverley Allitt was taken on a six-month contract. In the next fifty-eight days she was responsible for four murders, and attacks on nine other children that left several of them permanently disabled.

On 23 February, seven-week-old Liam Taylor was admitted to Ward 4 with a heavy chest cold. He became suddenly exhausted and listless; thirty six-hours later, his heart stopped, and he died in his parents' arms. A post mortem revealed serious heart damage – of the kind that might be sustained by a middle-aged man who smoked and drank to excess.

After Beverley Allitt's arrest, it was asked: why did this not instantly alert the authorities to the possibility that something suspicious was going on? After all, the death of a baby from something that should only happen to middle-aged men ought to raise urgent questions that are pursued until they are answered. But all this is being wise after the event. No one in that cottage hospital – in a peaceful midland town with a low crime rate – had the least reason to believe that they had a killer in their midst.

Ten days later, 11-year-old Tim Hardwick was admitted after a bout of epilepsy, and died of a massive heart attack. Doctors said that he had died of continual epileptic fits – although, in fact, he had had the last fit four hours before his death. But since the child had been an epileptic, this explanation was accepted.

The next baby to suffer a mysterious collapse was fifteen-month-old Cayley Desmond, whose heart stopped twice. She was transferred to the Queens Medical Centre in Nottingham, where she recovered. No one noticed the black bruise under her armpit where air had been injected into her.

The fourth victim was five-month-old Paul Crampton. Three times in a week his blood sugar sank so low that he fell into a coma. The child became cold, clammy and listless. It was clear that he was suffering from hypoglycemia – caused by low blood sugar – yet there was no obvious reason for this. A sample of Paul's blood was sent off for analysis to the University of Wales. Unfortunately, it was not marked urgent, and the intervention of Easter delayed the analysis further. It was fifteen days before the laboratory discovered that the insulin level in Paul's blood was abnormally high – enough to suggest that someone had injected it . . .

On the day the blood sample was sent off, five-year-old Bradley Gibson was found to have stopped breathing. His parents rushed to the hospital and watched as doctors tried to revive him, using a manual pump to make him breathe. Transferred to the Queens Medical Centre, he recovered. But at home a few days later, he was unable to walk, or to control his bowels or his bladder.

Doctors at the Medical Centre decided that he must have been given the wrong drug by mistake, yet failed to pass on this disquieting information to the Grantham hospital. In fact, the 'wrong drug' was potassium, injected by Beverly Allitt.

The same week, three-month-old Becky Philips, one of a pair of twins, was admitted with breathing problems. After treatment she was allowed home. In the middle of that night she went into a coma. Her parents rushed her to hospital, but it was too late, and she died during attempts at resuscitation. It was diagnosed as a cot death. In fact, it was due to an overdose of insulin.

Concerned about their other twin, Kate, the parents decided to allow her to go into hospital for observation. Tests showed her to be completely normal and healthy. Yet before the day was over, she had had three attacks in which she stopped breathing. After the third, doctors failed in their attempt to start the heart, and her parents were told she was dead. After forty-two minutes, Kate suddenly began breathing again, and recovered. But the attack had caused permanent brain damage which meant that she would always be retarded.

Now, at last, on 12 April 1991, the tests on Paul Crampton's blood – sent fifteen days earlier – revealed that he appeared to have been injected with insulin. The Grantham Hospital was immediately informed. Yet the information only caused bewilderment. How was it possible that such a thing could happen? The only explanation that suggested itself was that some member of the public was getting into the ward, and so one set of doors was locked. It would be another eighteen days before the police were finally informed. And in that time, three more children were attacked, and another one murdered. Christopher King had four attacks of 'breathing difficulty', and his parents were certain he was going to die; but when transferred to the Queens Medical Centre, he unexpectedly recovered. Patrick Elstone – again a twin – came close to death on two occasions, but recovered. Back at home, it was clear that he also had something wrong with his legs which prevented him from keeping up with his twin Anthony. But when two-month-old Christopher Peasgood stopped breathing twice, there was finally a clamour for something to be done. Medical staff requested that video cameras be installed, but were refused.

There would be one more victim, the thirteenth. On Monday 22 April, fifteen-month-old Clare Peck was admitted to Ward 4. Two hours later she was dead. Her blood showed an unusually high level of potassium, but her death was diagnosed as being due to asthma.

Incredibly, it was another eight days before the police were finally called in. The first thing they did was to examine the 'ward notebook' kept by nurses. They immediately noticed that some pages had been cut out – for example, pages relating to Paul Crampton, whose 'insulin attack' had led to suspicion. It took very little time for them to realize that the common factor in all the attacks – twenty-six of them – was the presence of the new nurse Beverley Allitt. When she left the ward, children who had suffered convulsions or breathing difficulties recovered; when she returned, the problems began again.

A search of Beverley Allitt's bedroom revealed some of the missing medical records. Twenty days after the police had been called in, she was arrested. In November 1991 she was finally charged with four murders, eight attacks and ten cases of grievous bodily harm with intent. She had injected insulin and potassium – in one case putting it into the child's drip – and when she had neither available, fell back on suffocation.

At first, parents found it unbelievable. The Philips, who had lost their daughter Becky, then almost lost her sister Kate, were particularly shattered; Beverley Allitt had been holding Becky when she died, and they were convinced that, far from attacking Kate, Beverley Allitt had saved her life. 'Bev' had become a family friend, who often called around after work to take Kate for walks; she was even asked to be her godmother.

Now a study of her medical record quickly revealed that Beverley Allitt should never have been let anywhere near a children's ward. During her two years' nurse's training, she had had no fewer than a hundred and thirty days off with various ailments. She had repeatedly wasted doctors' time with ailments varying from pregnancy to a brain tumour – all false alarms. This disorder is known as Munchausen's Syndrome, in which patients present themselves at hospitals with an endless series of imaginary ailments; it seems to be due to a craving for attention.

None of the doctors who studied her record was able to discover why Beverley Allitt had developed this peculiar illness. Until the age of 13 she had been a perfectly normal child. Then she began to lie, and to behave with cruelty towards friends. (Other cases in this book suggest that such personality change is often the result of a blow on the head, but nothing of the sort seems to be recorded of Beverley Allitt.) Her ex-boyfriend, Steve Biggs, told how he had broken off the affair as a result of her outbursts of violence. 'She'd get mad and kick me in the balls.' When she criticized his driving – on the day she passed her test – and he told her to shut up, she hit him in the face when they were travelling at sixty miles an hour. This was the last straw; but when he told her that he intended to break off the engagement, she grabbed him by the hair and forced him to his knees – he had to be rescued by her sister.

After her arrest, when her destructive urges could no longer be directed at children, they turned inward, and she was often unable to appear in court as a result of anorexia nervosa – the 'slimmer's disease'.

On 28 May 1993, she was found guilty on all counts, and given thirteen life sentences. Mr Justice Latham told her; 'There is no real prospect that a time will ever come when you will be safely released.'

On the day of her sentence, a prison psychiatrist, Dr James Higgins, revealed an interesting sidelight on her motivation. Commenting on her low self-esteem, and her failure to win a place on a nursing course, Higgins quoted her as saying: 'I had to prove I was better than what people thought.'

At first this sounds baffling. Surely murdering helpless children and betraying the trust of their parents proves you are worse, not better, than 'people thought'? But then it becomes clear that she was not speaking about being morally better. She was speaking of feeling superior. 'You may regard me as a nobody, but there's far more to me than you think. In fact, I'm highly dangerous.'

Suddenly we can see that this is one of the basic motivations of the serial killer. Why did Jack the Ripper and Neil Cream write letters to the police? Why did Peter Kürten like to return to the scene of his murders, and listen to the horrified comments of sightseers? Why did John Collins go to a funeral home and ask if he could photograph the corpse of his latest victim? We can see that it is a craving to feel 'different', to feel superior. But is not the act of murder itself enough to convince someone that they are not like other people? Obviously not. We may as well ask why an actor wants to read his reviews, or why a beautiful woman wants to look in a mirror. Human consciousness is feeble; our memory is short. We want to have our sense of 'difference' confirmed by other people.

In other words, you could say that serial murder is the under-achiever's way of of feeling a 'somebody'. And to recognize this is suddenly to understand why there have been so many serial killers since the Second World War. For more than two centuries now, western society has insisted on the equality of man. But when there exists an enormous social gulf between rich and poor, this makes little practical difference. The 'gentleman' seems to be a gentleman by inborn right; the poor man may be his equal before the law, but he doesn't *feel* it. Even if he happens to belong to the 'dominant 5 per cent', he is still inclined to accept a sense of social inferiority.

Two world wars and the 'caring society' have changed all that. As social differences are erased by education – and television – everyone feels that he has some right to a share of the prizes. The pop star may be more responsible for this change in attitude than anyone else; he demonstrates that it is possible to be working-class, an educational dropout, and still become an international icon and a multi-millionaire. (It is significant that Charles Manson wanted to become a pop star, and that the first murders took place in a house that had recently been vacated by a recording agent against whom he had a grudge.)

But on our overcrowded planet, there is still as little 'room at the top' as ever. The result is an ever-increasing number of dominant personalities who feel alienated, frustrated and resentful. A large percentage of these become petty crooks – muggers, burglars, car thieves. A very tiny percentage become serial killers.

Yet even this insight leaves a major question unanswered. In the years since the term 'serial murder' was invented, cases have succeeded one another with such frequency – usually overlapping – that they produce the impression of an epidemic. The increasingly gruesome nature of the crimes lends urgency to the question: what is there about our society that incubates this atavistic urge to *kill*?

At least part of the answer has emerged during the course of this book. Most serial killers have deep emotional problems; seldom overpowering enough to allow us to regard them as insane, but sufficient to make them totally self-absorbed, so that they regard other people as abstractions. This also produces a sensation of meaninglessness – what psychologists call 'lack of affect', inability to feel. Jeffrey Dahmer spoke for most serial killers when he said in a prison interview: 'I couldn't find any meaning in my life when I was out there. I'm sure as hell not going to find it in here.' When the mind is becalmed, negative impulses multiply like algae in a stagnant pond.

Dahmer's biographer Brian Masters has argued that we need to stretch the definition of insanity to cover murderers like Dahmer and Chikatilo. Psychiatrist Dorothy Lewis, who studied Shawcross, is inclined to agree. 'I think it does very bad things to our society if we become a mindless group of people that doesn't care why someone did what he did, and thinks only in terms of punishing the individual or doing away with him.'

John Douglas, head of the Quantico profiling unit, takes a more pragmatic view.

> We have to put ourselves in the shoes of the victims. So what I flash back to is victims who are screaming, begging for their lives. I have tapes here of victims who are being murdered, who are regressing in their behaviour, calling out for their mammies, calling out for their daddies, and begging 'Please God don't kill me.' But they kill them. So when I see the day of execution, and the little vigil outside the penitentiary, I may feel sorry for a second, but then I want to pull out the file jacket of these guys, I want to look at those crime scene photographs, I want to look at that autopsy protocol, and look at those autopsy photographs. I want to see the interviews of the victims and the families. I want to put myself back into that victim. So I have no sympathy at all for these people.

But surely the two points of view are reconcilable? Those who lack Douglas's experience – or lack the imagination to understand what he is saying – may feel sympathy for killers like Dahmer, Chikatilo and Shawcross. But the sympathy is irrelevant. What is needed is real understanding. Dorothy Lewis expressed it as well as anyone when she said: 'If we're going to be a humane society, we have to protect ourselves, but we also have to understand what made these people the way they are, and then work very hard to try to prevent society creating more people like that.'

What this book makes clear is that at the present stage, our understanding is so crude as to be almost non-existent.

Afterword

A woman friend once told me that whenever she was left alone in somebody else's house, she felt an immediate compulsion to go through the drawers. What is interesting is that she was not a juvenile delinquent, but a middle-aged psychiatrist – admittedly, an extremely unconventional one. I recognized immediately that she had handed me a key to one of the fundamental problems of crime – in fact, of human nature itself. Human beings are purposive creatures; they need to be driven by a strong sense of motivation. When they lack motivation, they tend to become bored, then to look around for something they are not supposed to be doing.

Our basic human craving is for what might be called 'the flow experience'. We all recognize what this means on the crudest physical level – for example, the relief of going to the lavatory when the need has become urgent. Even scratching when you itch is an example of the flow experience. So is drinking when you are very thirsty and eating when you are ravenous. All these things release a flow of energy and relief. When our energies are blocked and our purposes frustrated, we experience a sense of stagnation, which can soon turn into a kind of mental constipation, in which our vital energies feel as if they had congealed into a leaden mass.

Human beings *need* the flow experience to change and evolve. Our energies could be compared to a river flowing over a plain. If the flow is too slow, the river begins to meander as it accumulates silt and mud. But a violent storm in the mountains can send down a roaring flood that sweeps away the silt and straightens out the bends, so that once again, the river flows straight and deep. This is why human beings crave the 'flow experience'.

This also offers us the key to sex crime. When Ted Bundy saw a girl undressing behind a lighted window, he experienced a flood of desire that turned him into a highly purposive creature. And since he was above average intelligence, and had a natural sense of his own superiority, this filled him with the conviction that he had discovered the key to his personal evolution. All he had to do was to use his charm to lure girls into a vulnerable position, then treat them as if they were a kind of tailor's dummy, an object designed for his pleasure. And after enough of these 'flash floods', all his self-doubt and immaturity would be swept away; he would be as self-controlled and purposeful as Beethoven, Goethe, Napoleon – in fact, a kind of superman.

Our society is full of constraints, and the most obvious of these constraints is sexual. This remains as true today as in the time of Theodore Durrant, and will no doubt still be as true a century from now. So the highly sexed young man – and most young men *are* highly sexed – finds himself surrounded by desirable creatures whom he is forbidden to touch. If, like Bundy, the desire is strong enough and the constraints weak enough, he may decide to ignore the social taboos and use force to relieve his frustrations. Somewhere at the back of his mind there is the feeling that if he does it often enough, some inner blockage will be swept away and he will outgrow the need that causes him so much discomfort, and be an altogether more full and complete human being. Dostoevsky spent years planning a novel called *Life of a Great Sinner* in which the central character sins his way to salvation. The rapist has something like that in mind.

It is slightly alarming to realize that many perfectly respectable philosophers have been saying the same kind of thing for the past two centuries. William Blake remarked: 'Rather murder an infant in its cradle than nurse unacted desire.' Ibsen caused a scandal with *A Doll's House* when he made the heroine walk out on her husband and children, declaring that the need for self-development – Maslow's self-actualization – was more important than obeying the rules of conventional morality. Undershaft, the armaments manufacturer in Shaw's *Major Barbara*, justifies himself with the statement: 'I moralized and starved until one day I swore I would be a full-fed free man at all costs; that nothing should stop me except a bullet, neither reason nor morals nor the lives of other men. I said "Thou shalt starve ere I starve"; and with that word I became free and great. I was a dangerous man until I had my will: now I am a useful, beneficent, kindly person.' He has, so to speak, sinned his way to salvation. Elsewhere in the play he explains that morality is relative: 'For me there is only one true morality, but it might not fit you, as you do not manufacture aerial battleships . . .'

In *Civilization and Its Discontents*, Freud argues that man has created a civilization that has turned into a prison; it demands that he constantly repress desires that are natural to animals in the wild. Unlike Ibsen and Shaw, he is not arguing that we should cast off conventional morality; his purpose is simply to explain why our society is so riddled with neurosis. But Freud's argument could also be regarded as a justification for seeking the 'flow experience' *at all costs*.

When Blake wrote *The Marriage of Heaven and Hell* there were no criminals capable of adopting his suggestions – he lived in the age of footpads and highwaymen. And when Ibsen wrote in his journal: 'Liberation consists in securing for individuals the right to free themselves, each according to his particular need', there were no sex criminals to quote him as an excuse for rape. It was in the 1880s, when anarchists began to plant bombs on the grounds that all power is corrupt, that it gradually became clear that there is a negative side to individual self-development. Yet even *Major Barbara*, written in 1905, belongs to the 'age of innocence' when criminals were more concerned with burglary and petty theft than heroic rebellion. It would be more than four decades before Melvin Rees would declare 'You can't say it's wrong to kill – only individual standards make it right or wrong', and demonstrate that Undershaft's relativist morality could be used to justify rape and murder.

The struggle for what might be called 'Criminal Liberation' has a long history. A decade before Blake wrote *The Marriage of Heaven and Hell*, Goethe's friend Schiller outraged his contemporaries with a drama called *The Robbers*, whose hero, Karl Moor, declares: 'Law has never produced a man of true grandeur. It is freedom that incubates the colossal and the extreme.' He explains that he is sick of his own age of professors and critics, and prefers the company of the men of action he finds in the pages of Plutarch. When he learns that his father has disinherited him (due to the machinations of his evil brother Franz), he curses the human race and declares that he will become a brigand. From their lair in the forest, his men put the philosophy of freedom into action as they storm cities, rob treasuries and violate nunneries. But even the highly romantic Schiller now found himself faced with an insoluble dilemma. It is true that Karl Moor acts out of noble motives – his hatred of oppression and tyranny – but how is it possible to justify murder and rape? Schiller declines to sidestep the problem by killing off his hero in battle, and ends the play with Karl's decision to hand himself over to the law.

It would be almost two centuries before Ian Brady, incensed at an unfair jail sentence, decided to emulate Karl Moor's example and carry out his own campaign of plunder and rape. But then, Brady had seen *The Third Man* several times when he was 11 and been impressed by Harry Lime's philosophy of moral relativism. Greene was not being serious when he made Lime describe human beings as insects, but when an idea is released into the atmosphere, it is no longer under its creator's control. I have also pointed out the significance of Brady's interest in the character of Stavrogin in Dostoevsky's *Possessed*. Stavrogin is a Byronic rebel who feels he has 'done it all', and can now find nothing to do with his strength – in other words, no longer knows how to induce 'the flow experience'. So he commits all kinds of 'gratuitous acts' – such as seducing a 10-year old girl, then allowing her to kill herself – in an attempt to galvanize himself into positive feeling. He fails, and eventually hangs himself.

Now the point to note is that Schiller and Blake and Ibsen and Shaw were all concerned to 'weigh up' the meaning of human life, to make what might be ponderously called a 'philosophical-existential' judgement on it. And so, in a certain sense, were Melvin Rees, Ian Brady, Ted Bundy, Gerald Gallego and Leonard Lake. Gallego said he was searching for 'the perfect sex slave'. If he were persuaded to attend a philosophical seminar and explain what he meant, he would probably agree that 'the perfect sexual experience' came closer to it. And why should he want the perfect sexual experience? Because all 'positive' experience (i.e. pleasant as against unpleasant) helps to make us the masters of reality rather than its slaves. We have a clear sense, in certain moments, that life yields to a certain kind of effort, and that it is not 'a tale told by an idiot'. Schiller made his own attempt at stating this insight when he said: 'It is freedom that incubates the colossal and the extreme.' He puts it in a poem called 'To a Moralist':

> Why check youth's ardour with thy dull advice,
> And teach that love is labour thrown away?
> Thou shiverest there amid the Winter's ice
> And speakst, contemptuous, of Golden May.[1]

Schiller is certain of one thing: he is a devotee of Golden May, and he hates the winter. Rebellion and revolution seem to be the solution, throwing off the trammels of 'civilization and its discontents'. But Schiller immediately betrays the weak point in his argument when he makes a clear distinction between Karl Moor and his merry men; *they* murder and rape while he reads Rousseau and gazes at the stars. The fact that Karl refuses to join in makes it clear that he recognizes this kind of 'freedom' as morally wrong – that his dream of freedom and the Rights of Man involves actively depriving some people of their freedom and their lives. The same applies to Blake's 'Rather murder an infant in its cradle . . .' (although he obviously intended it as a form of overstatement) and to Undershaft's admission that he decided to ignore reason and morals and the lives of other men in his determination to be a full-fed man. Even Nora's assertion of her right to 'individual self-development' contains the seeds of criminality.

I am not trying to argue in favour of convention, good behaviour and self-sacrifice: only to point out that what looks like an irrefutable argument in favour of human freedom leads us into a quicksand of moral ambiguity. For two centuries now philosophers have been engaged in a muddled argument about human freedom: now the chickens are coming home to roost.

Then what *is* the solution? Since I draw close to the end of this book, I may as well try to state my own view in a few sentences.

T. E. Lawrence once said: 'Happiness is absorption.' Every child has experienced that delicious sensation of curling up in bed and listening to the rain pattering on the windows. Every literate adult has experienced the sensation of becoming so absorbed in a book that he 'doesn't want to put it down'.

[1] Translated by E. P. Arnold-Forster.

We can *focus* the mind in the way that a magnifying glass can focus a beam of sunlight, until we experience a curious sense of inner warmth. It demands the total focus of *attention*. Most of us 'leak' half the time, so never learn to focus our energies. Yet the sheer intensity of these moments of 'focus' makes us aware that the human mind possesses powers that suggest that we are not 'merely human'. In some strange sense, we are gods in disguise.

Experiences we enjoy have the effect of focusing our emotions and energies, and producing a sense of being 'more alive'. But we fail to grasp the fact that the magnifying glass that focuses the energy is *the mind itself*. So we are inclined to go out looking for the experience instead of teaching ourselves to use the magnifying glass. And since the modern world has developed a whole 'substitute experience' industry, from romantic novels to pornographic videos, we are in a far more fortunate position than our ancestors of a mere century ago, who expected life to be fairly dreary and repetitive. Most modern teenagers have had a wider range of experience – imaginative and actual – than most Victorian patriarchs. And when we take into account the loss of inhibition induced by alcohol and drugs, it suddenly becomes clear why an increasing number of young people are willing to risk breaking the law in pursuit of 'experiences they enjoy' and of what they feel to be individual self-development.

In *Crime and Punishment*, Raskolnikov remarks that if he had to stand on a narrow ledge for ever and ever, he would prefer to do that rather than die at once. What would he *do* on the narrow ledge? In practice, probably jump off. Yet we can all *see* why he felt he would prefer *anything* rather than die at once. He has an intuition that *the mind itself* contains the answer, and that if he could learn the trick of 'focusing' its energies, a narrow ledge would afford as much freedom as a ski slope in Switzerland or a beach on the Riviera.

Our everyday consciousness is concerned with 'coping' with problems, and this is the basic source of criminality. If we compare consciousness to a spectrum, then modern man lives almost entirely at the 'red end', preoccupied with purpose, activity, survival. When this need for activity vanishes – as when my psychiatrist friend was left alone in the house – we experience a kind of panic. The blue end of the spectrum seems to threaten us with stagnation. And crime – like alcoholism or drug abuse or any other form of over-indulgence – is a protest against stagnation.

Yet when Raskolnikov says that he would prefer to be confined on a narrow ledge rather than die at once, he has suddenly recognized that he could live just as happily at the blue end of the spectrum – that far from representing stagnation, the 'blue area' represents control, insight, exploration of one's own possibilities. Far from being a kind of blank that threatens us with boredom, exhaustion and nervous breakdown, it seethes with its own inner vitality, like some alchemical crucible that contains the elixir of life.

Regrettably, the human race remains trapped at the red end of the spectrum. It is only in moments of crisis that we glimpse the answer to our problems – the answer Dr Johnson saw so clearly when he remarked that 'the knowledge that he is to be hanged in a fortnight concentrates a man's mind wonderfully'. In the meantime, we find ourselves in the highly dangerous position in which the 'philosophy of freedom' has created one of the worst outbreaks of crime in the history of civilization.

The serial murderer is one of the most interesting – if frightening – symptoms of this melting-pot of moral attitudes. Whether they thought about it or not, Ted Bundy, Gerald Gallego, Leonard Lake believed that enough sex could concentrate the mind into a permanent state of intensity. Of course, it failed to work because what they were seeking – 'the essence of sex' – is an illusion. Sex is a biological urge whose purpose is to persuade us to reproduce the species. To this end, it allures us in exactly the same way that the scent of a flower allures the bee. But if the bee were intelligent, it would realize that most flowers promise far more than they can fulfil; the scent is exquisite, but you cannot eat it or take it home with you. This explains why so many sex killers have ended with a curious sense of moral exhaustion and vacuity, a feeling of having been the victim of a confidence trick.

Dahmer expressed the essence of the problem when he said: 'I couldn't find any meaning for my life when I was out there. I'm sure as hell not going to find it in here.' And in saying this, he makes it clear why it is impossible to draw a clear and sharp dividing line between murderers and the rest of us. We *all* suffer, to some extent, from the 'Dahmer syndrome'. Gurdjieff once explained that what is wrong with human beings is that the gods had implanted in us an organ called 'kundabuffer', which makes us hopelessly confused about illusion and reality, and which prevents us from learning too much about our own stupidity. The only thing – says Gurdjieff – that could awaken us from this illusion of meaninglessness is another organ which would show us *the exact hour of our own death and the death of everyone we see. This* would shock us into a recognition of how we waste our lives.

But every time we study a murder case, with its moronic waste of life, we are momentarily traumatized out of our confusion and stupidity, our tendency to vegetate in a meaningless present. A few days ago I received a letter from a correspondent who remarked that reading Ann West's *For the Love of Lesley*, a book by the mother of Moors murder victim Lesley Ann Downey, had suddenly made him aware of the *reality* of murder, and of what it feels like to be the parent of a child who has disappeared. The book had made the same impact on me. And after re-living the experiences of Lesley's parents, I came back to my own life with a sigh of relief, like awakening from a nightmare. Suddenly I recognized that life without such a burden of misery is full of infinite possibility and potentiality and freedom. Yet we normally live it with a kind of bored casualness, as if fate were to blame for not making the world more interesting. The truth is that if we could use the imagination to grasp the reality of *any* murder, we would suddenly see life as a kind of unending holiday.

This is the ultimate justification of the study of murder: that there is something about its sheer nastiness that can galvanize us out of the 'Dahmer syndrome' that causes human beings to waste their lives.

Index